# ORDNANCE SURVEY

# STREET ATLAS
# South Hampshire

## Contents

| | |
|---|---|
| IV | *Key to maps* |
| VI | *Administrative boundaries* |
| 1 | *Street maps* |
| 219 | *Index explanation and abbreviations* |
| 220 | *Index of towns, villages and rural localities* |
| 221 | *Index of street names* |

PHILIP'S

First edition published 1991
Second edition published 1994
Reprinted 1997 by

Ordnance Survey®       and       George Philip Ltd.
Romsey Road                        an imprint of Reed Books
Maybush                            Michelin House, 81 Fulham Road, London, SW3 6RB
Southampton SO16 4GU               and Auckland, Melbourne, Singapore and Toronto

ISBN 0-540-05855-6 (hardback)
ISBN 0-540-05856-4 (softback)

To the best of the Publishers' knowledge, the information in this atlas was correct at
the time of going to press. No responsibility can be accepted for any errors or their
consequences.

The representation in this atlas of a road, track or path is no evidence of the existence
of a right of way.

**The mapping between pages 1 and 217 (inclusive) in this atlas is derived from
Ordnance Survey® Land-Line® data, and Landranger® mapping.**

Ordnance Survey, Land-Line and Landranger are registered trade marks of
Ordnance Survey, the National Mapping Agency of Great Britain.

Printed and bound in Great Britain by
Bath Press, Bath

# Key to map symbols

|  |  |
|---|---|
| ⊛ | British Rail station |
| ⊖ | London transport station |
| 🚂 | Private railway station |
| ⬤ | Bus or coach station |
| Ⓗ | Heliport |
| ◆ | Police station (may not be open 24 hours) |
| ✚ | Hospital with casualty facilities (may not be open 24 hours) |
| ☐ | Post office |
| + | Place of worship |
| ◼ | Important building |
| P | Parking |
| 174 | Adjoining page indicator |
| ⊗ | No adjoining page |
| ═══ | Motorway or dual carriageway |
| A27(T) | Main or through road (with Department of Transport number) |
| ⊢⊣ | Gate or obstruction to traffic (restrictions may not apply at all times or to all vehicles) |
| - - - - - | Footpath |
| — — — | Bridleway |
| – – – | Path |
| ═══ | Track |

The representation in this atlas of a road, track or path is no evidence of the existence of a right of way

| | | | |
|---|---|---|---|
| Amb Sta | Ambulance station | LC | Level crossing |
| Coll | College | Liby | Library |
| FB | Footbridge | Mus | Museum |
| F Sta | Fire station | Sch | School |
| Hospl | Hospital | TH | Town hall |

| 0 | ¼ | ½ | ¾ | 1 mile |
|---|---|---|---|---|
| 0 | 250m | 500m | 250m | 1 Kilometre |

**The scale of the maps is 3½ inches to 1 mile (1:18103)**

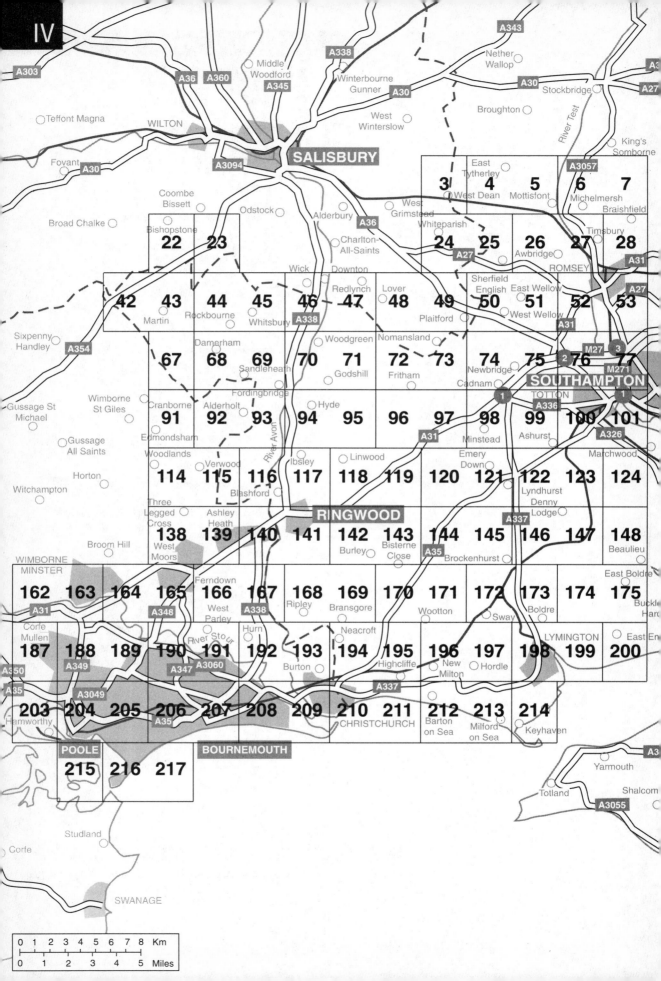

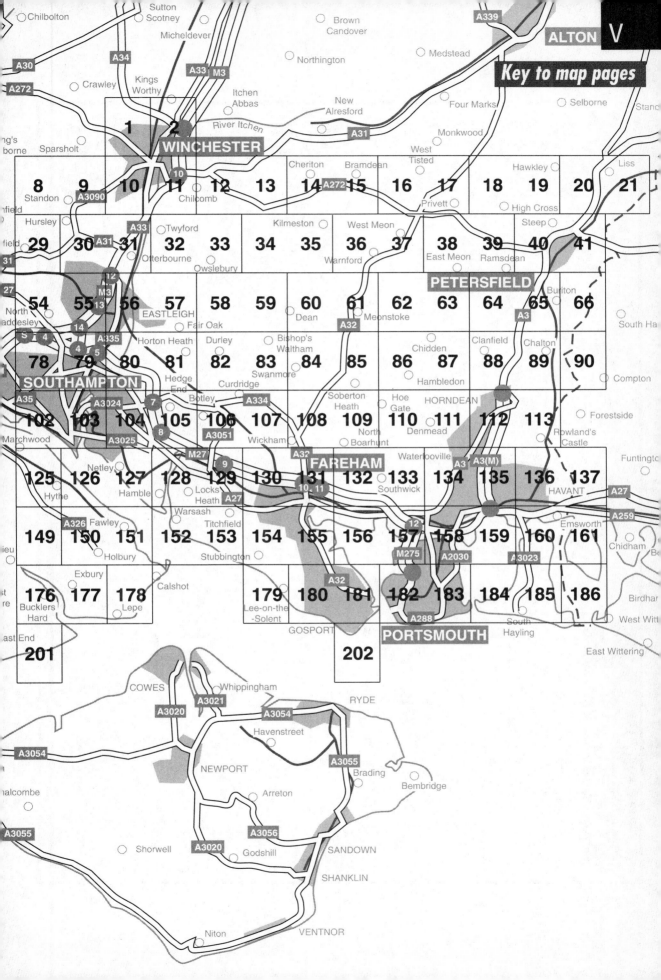

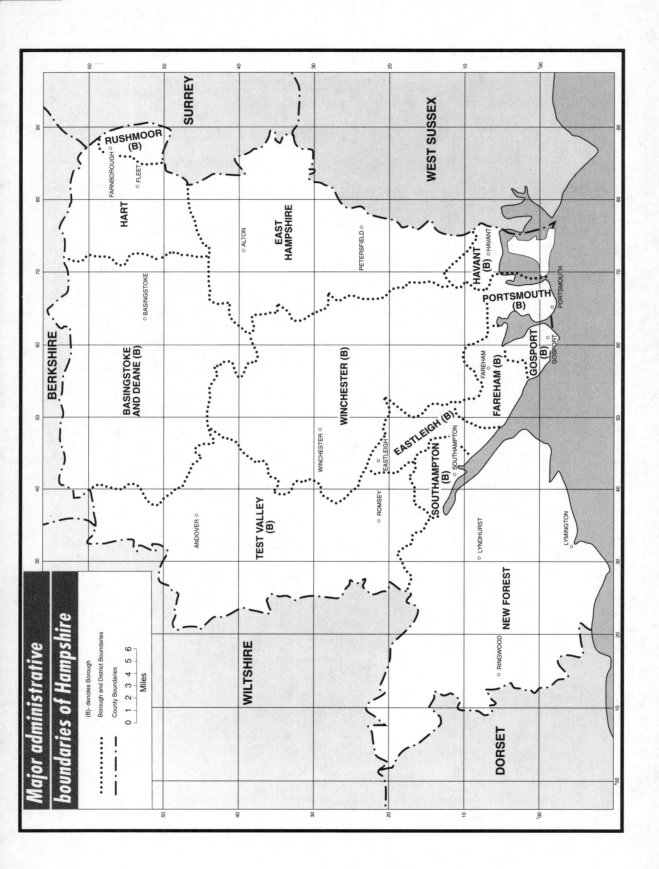

## Major administrative boundaries of Hampshire

(B)- denotes Borough

........... Borough and District Boundaries

—··—··— County Boundaries

0 1 2 3 4 5 6
Miles

SURREY

WEST SUSSEX

RUSHMOOR (B)

FARNBOROUGH ○

○ FLEET

HART

BERKSHIRE

○ ALTON

EAST HAMPSHIRE

PETERSFIELD ○

○ BASINGSTOKE

BASINGSTOKE AND DEANE (B)

WINCHESTER (B)

HAVANT (B)

○ HAVANT

PORTSMOUTH (B)

PORTSMOUTH

FAREHAM (B)

FAREHAM

GOSPORT (B)

GOSPORT ○

○ WINCHESTER

EASTLEIGH (B)

○ EASTLEIGH

SOUTHAMPTON (B)

○ SOUTHAMPTON

ANDOVER ○

TEST VALLEY (B)

○ ROMSEY

○ LYNDHURST

LYMINGTON ○

NEW FOREST

WILTSHIRE

○ RINGWOOD

DORSET

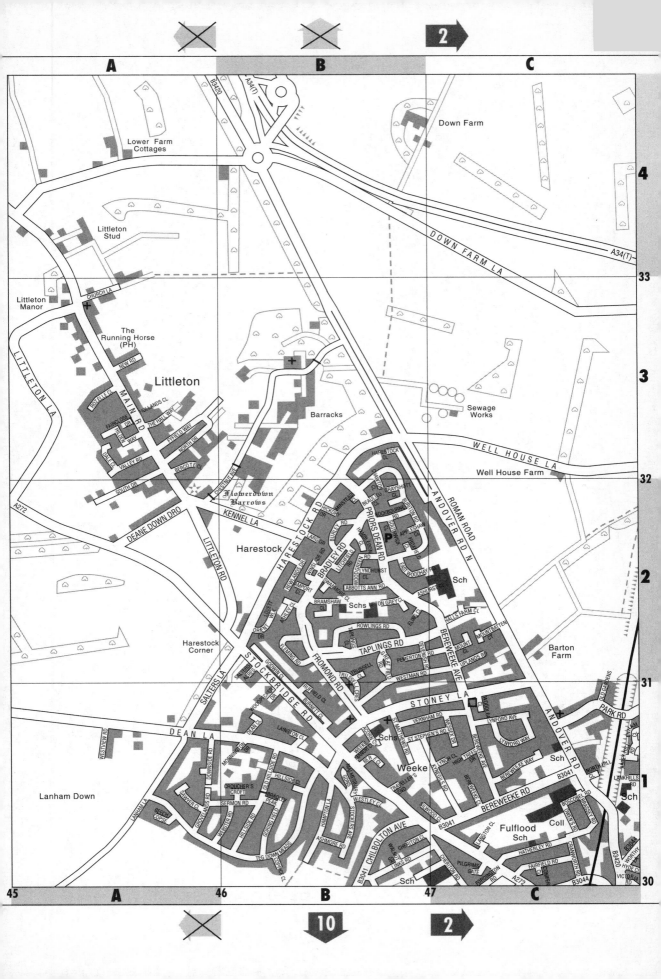

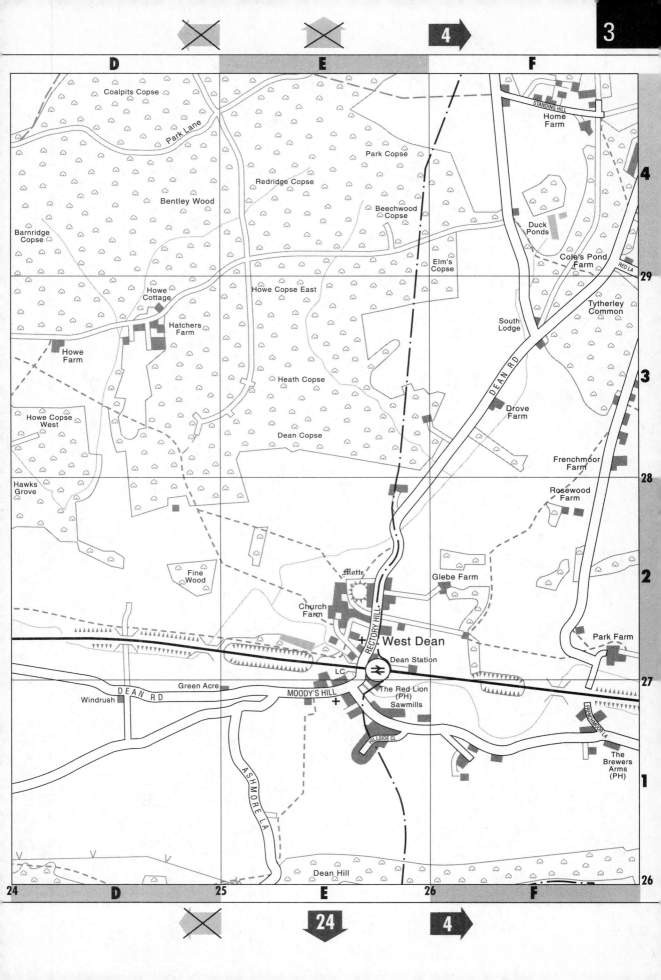

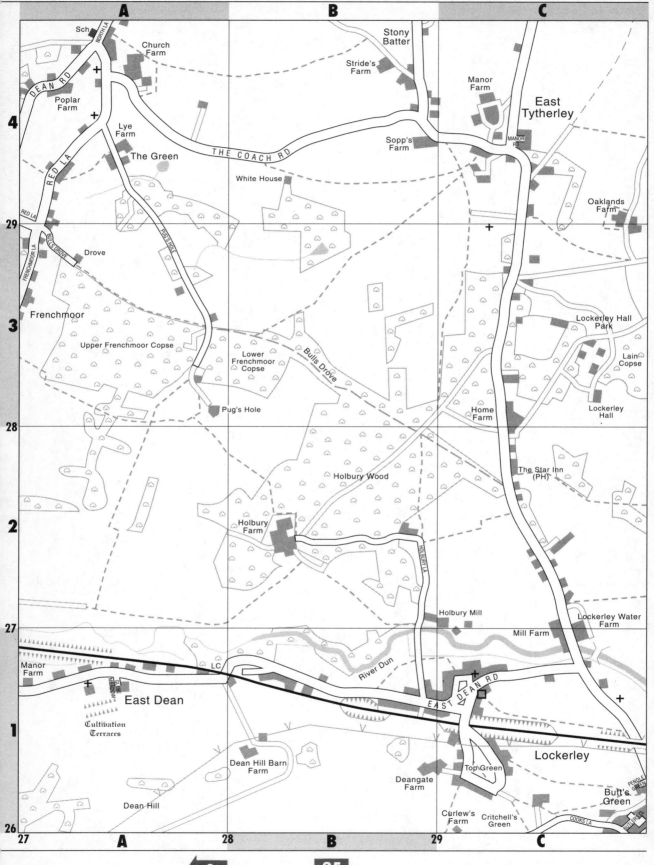

Sch

NORTH LA

Church
Farm

DEAN RD

Poplar
Farm

Lye
Farm

RED LA

The Green

RED LA

FRENCHMOOR LA

BULLS DROVE

Drove

Frenchmoor

Upper Frenchmoor Copse

PUG'S HOLE

Lower
Frenchmoor
Copse

Pug's Hole

Bulls Drove

Stony
Batter

Stride's
Farm

THE COACH RD

White House

Sopp's
Farm

Manor
Farm

East
Tytherley

MANOR
RD

Oaklands
Farm

Lockerley Hall
Park

Lain
Copse

Lockerley
Hall

Home
Farm

The Star Inn
(PH)

Holbury Wood

Holbury
Farm

HOLBURY LA

Holbury Mill

Lockerley Water
Farm

Mill Farm

Manor
Farm

East Dean

LC

River Dun

EAST DEAN RD

Lockerley

Cultivation
Terraces

Dean Hill Barn
Farm

Top Green

Deangate
Farm

Butt's
Green

PENGLE GREEN

Dean Hill

Curlew's
Farm

Critchell's
Green

COOKS LA

BUTTS LA

29

3

28

2

27

1

26

4

29

3

28

2

27

1

26

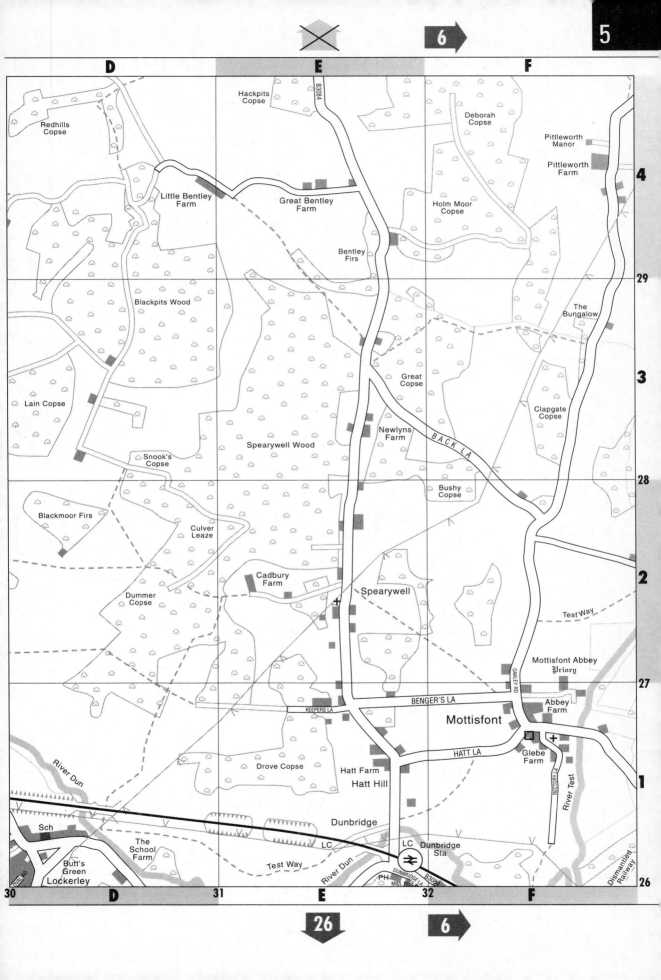

**D**     **E**     **F**

Redhills
Copse

Hackpits
Copse

Deborah
Copse

Pittleworth
Manor

Pittleworth
Farm

Little Bentley
Farm

Great Bentley
Farm

Holm Moor
Copse

**4**

Bentley
Firs

**29**

Blackpits Wood

The
Bungalow

Great
Copse

**3**

Lain Copse

Clapgate
Copse

BACK LA

Newlyns
Farm

Snook's
Copse

Spearywell Wood

**28**

Blackmoor Firs

Bushy
Copse

Culver
Leaze

**2**

Dummer
Copse

Cadbury
Farm

Spearywell

Test Way

Mottisfont Abbey
Priory

**27**

BENGER'S LA

Abbey
Farm

KEEPERS LA

OAKLEY RD

**Mottisfont**

River Dun

Drove Copse

HATT LA

Glebe
Farm

RECTORY LA

River Test

Hatt Farm

**1**

Hatt Hill

Dunbridge

Sch

Test Way

River Dun

LC

LC

Dunbridge
Sta

Dunbridge
Mill Rise La

PH

Butt's
Green
Lockerley

The
School
Farm

B3084

Dismantled
Railway

**26**

**30**    **D**     **31**     **E**     **32**     **F**

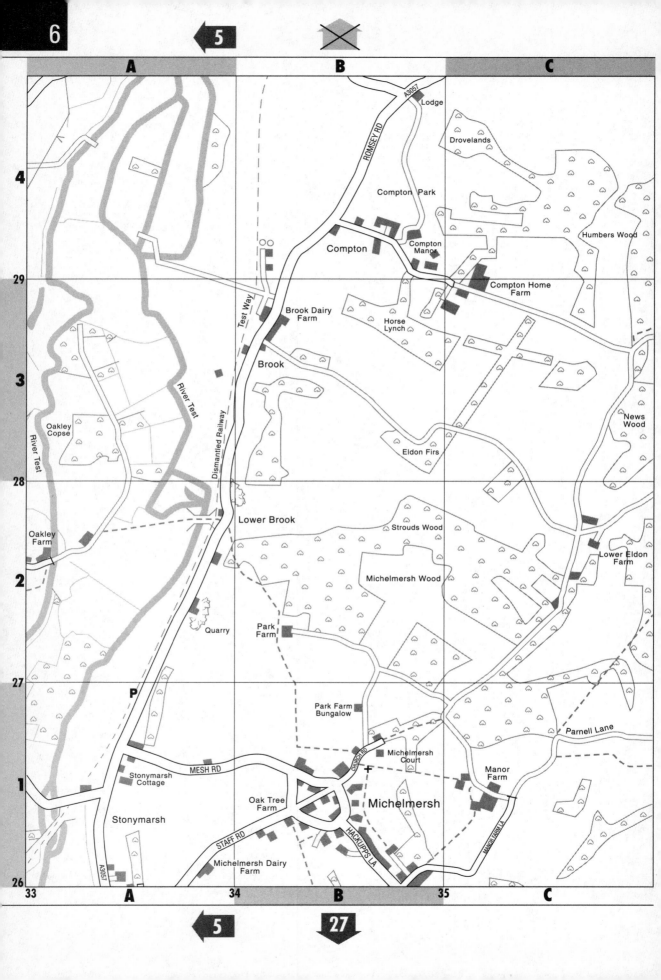

A     B     C

**4**

Lodge

Drovelands

A3057

ROMSEY RD

Compton Park

Humbers Wood

Compton

Compton Manor

**29**

Compton Home Farm

Test Way

Brook Dairy Farm

Horse Lynch

River Test

**3**

Brook

News Wood

Dismantled Railway

Eldon Firs

Oakley Copse

River Test

**28**

Lower Brook

Strouds Wood

Lower Eldon Farm

Oakley Farm

**2**

Michelmersh Wood

Quarry

Park Farm

**27**

P

Park Farm Bungalow

Parnell Lane

MESH RD

Michelmersh Court

Stonymarsh Cottage

Manor Farm

CHURCH RD

**1**

Oak Tree Farm

Michelmersh

Stonymarsh

STAFF RD

HACKUPPS LA

MANOR FARM LA

A3057

Michelmersh Dairy Farm

**26**

33    34    35

A     B     C

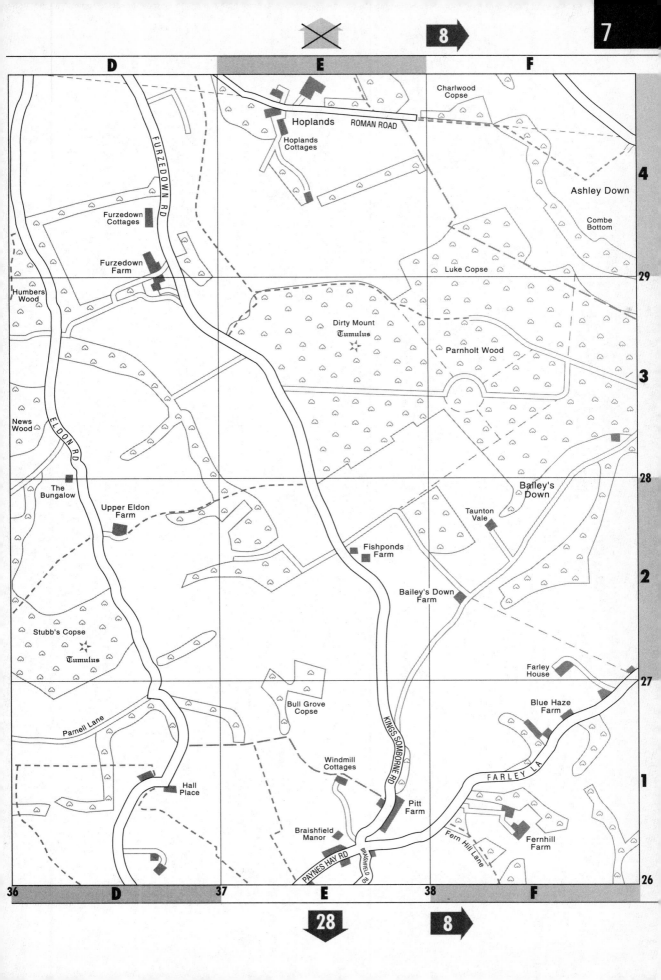

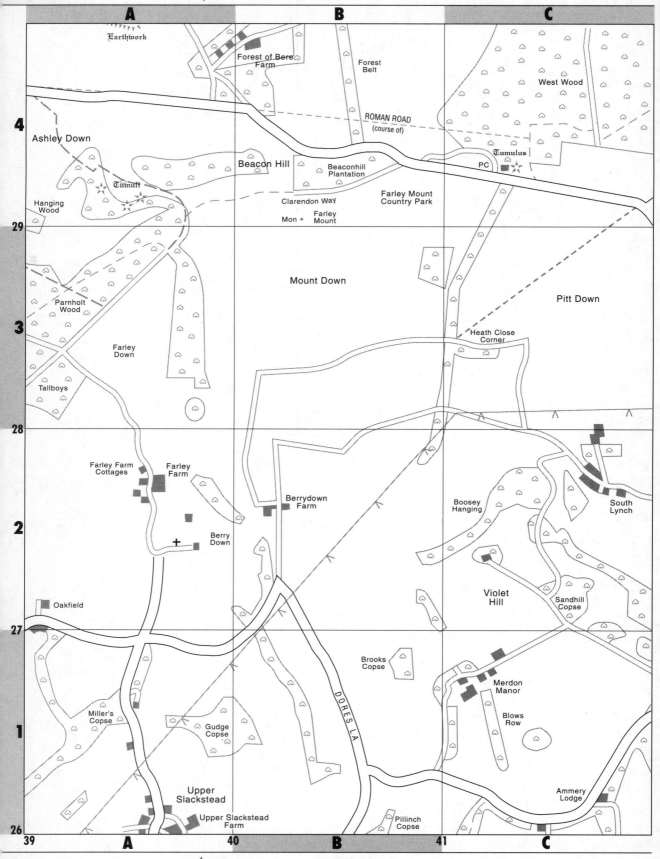

**A**      **B**      **C**

Earthwork

Forest of Bere Farm

Forest Belt

West Wood

ROMAN ROAD
(course of)

**4**

Ashley Down

Beacon Hill

Beaconhill Plantation

Tumulus

PC

Tinnult

Hanging Wood

Farley Mount Country Park

Clarendon Way

Mon • Farley Mount

**29**

Parnholt Wood

Mount Down

Pitt Down

**3**

Farley Down

Heath Close Corner

Tallboys

**28**

Farley Farm Cottages

Farley Farm

Berrydown Farm

Boosey Hanging

South Lynch

**2**

Berry Down

Violet Hill

Sandhill Copse

＋

Oakfield

**27**

Brooks Copse

Merdon Manor

Miller's Copse

Gudge Copse

Blows Row

**1**

D O R E S  L A

Upper Slackstead

Ammery Lodge

**26**

Upper Slackstead Farm

Pillinch Copse

**39**    **A**    **40**    **B**    **41**    **C**

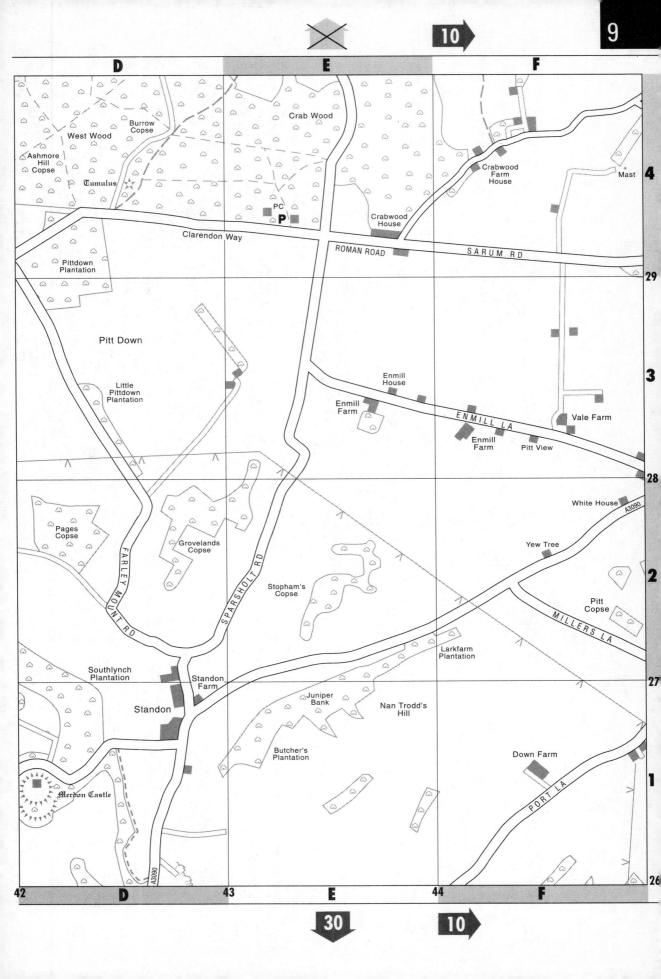

West Wood

Burrow Copse

Ashmore Hill Copse

Tumulus

Crab Wood

PC

P

**4**

Crabwood Farm House

Mast

Crabwood House

Clarendon Way

ROMAN ROAD  SARUM RD

Pittdown Plantation

**29**

Pitt Down

Little Pittdown Plantation

**3**

Enmill House

Enmill Farm

ENMILL LA

Vale Farm

Enmill Farm

Pitt View

**28**

Pages Copse

FARLEY MOUNT RD

Grovelands Copse

SPARSHOLT RD

White House

A3090

Yew Tree

**2**

Pitt Copse

Stopham's Copse

MILLERS LA

Southlynch Plantation

Standon Farm

Larkfarm Plantation

**27**

Standon

Juniper Bank

Nan Trodd's Hill

Down Farm

Butcher's Plantation

**1**

Merdon Castle

PORT LA

A3090

**26**

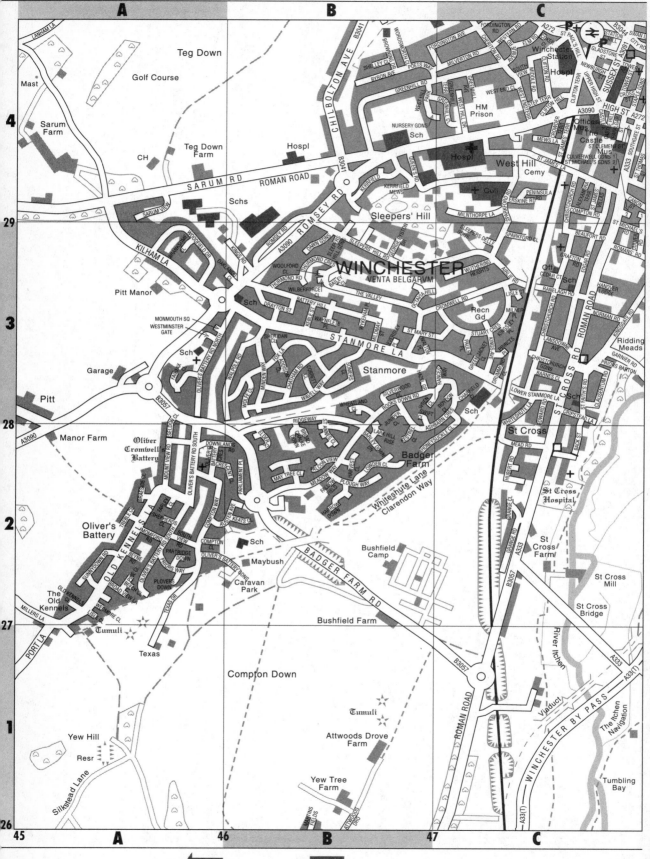

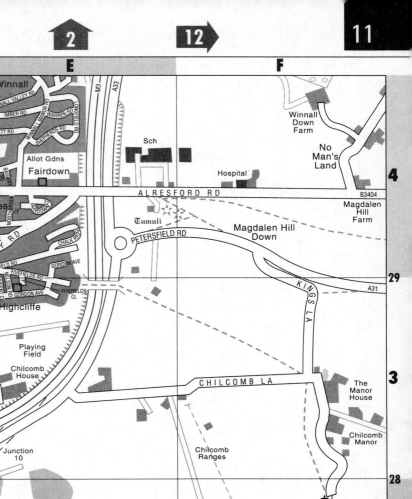
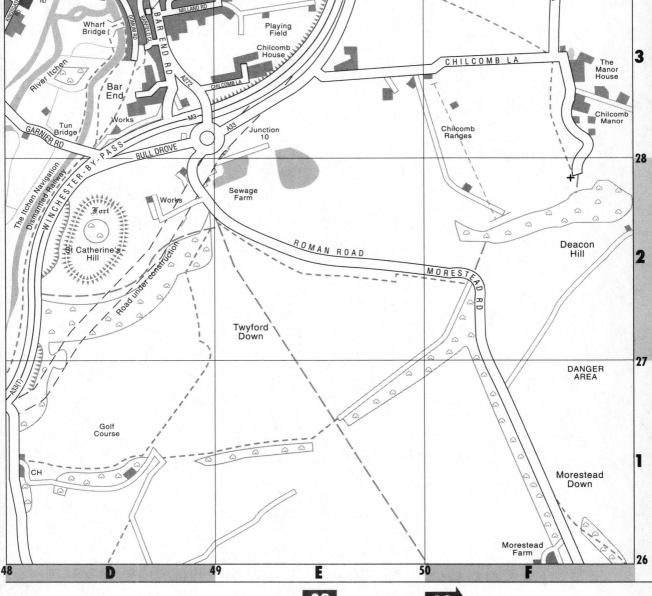

A | B | C

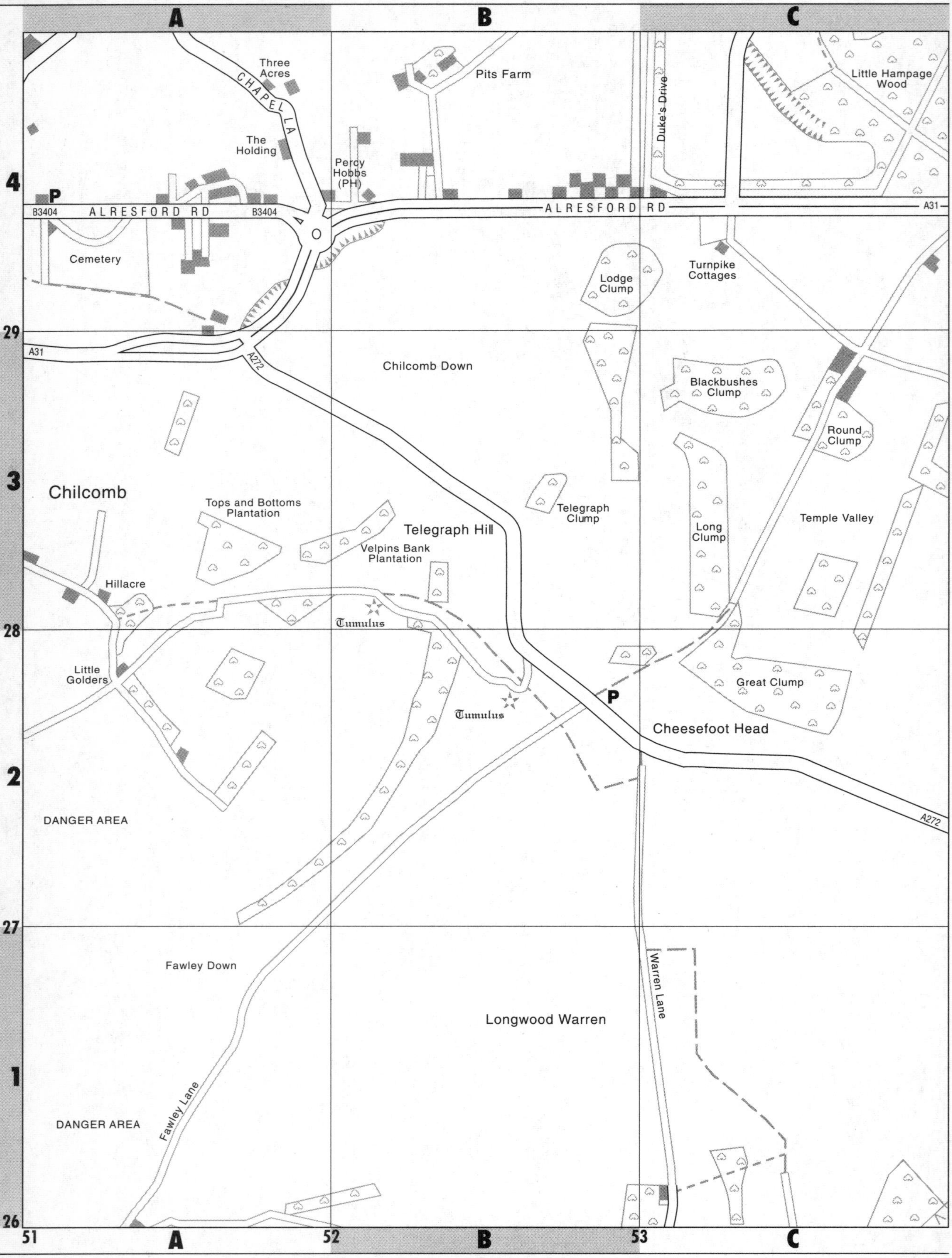

Three Acres

Pits Farm

Little Hampage Wood

CHAPEL LA

Duke's Drive

The Holding

Percy Hobbs (PH)

**4**

P

B3404 ALRESFORD RD B3404

ALRESFORD RD

A31

Cemetery

Lodge Clump

Turnpike Cottages

**29**

A31

A272

Chilcomb Down

Blackbushes Clump

Round Clump

**3**

Chilcomb

Tops and Bottoms Plantation

Telegraph Hill

Telegraph Clump

Long Clump

Temple Valley

Velpins Bank Plantation

Hillacre

Tumulus

**28**

Little Golders

Tumulus

Great Clump

P

Cheesefoot Head

**2**

DANGER AREA

A272

**27**

Fawley Down

Warren Lane

Longwood Warren

**1**

Fawley Lane

DANGER AREA

**26**

51 | A | 52 | B | 53 | C

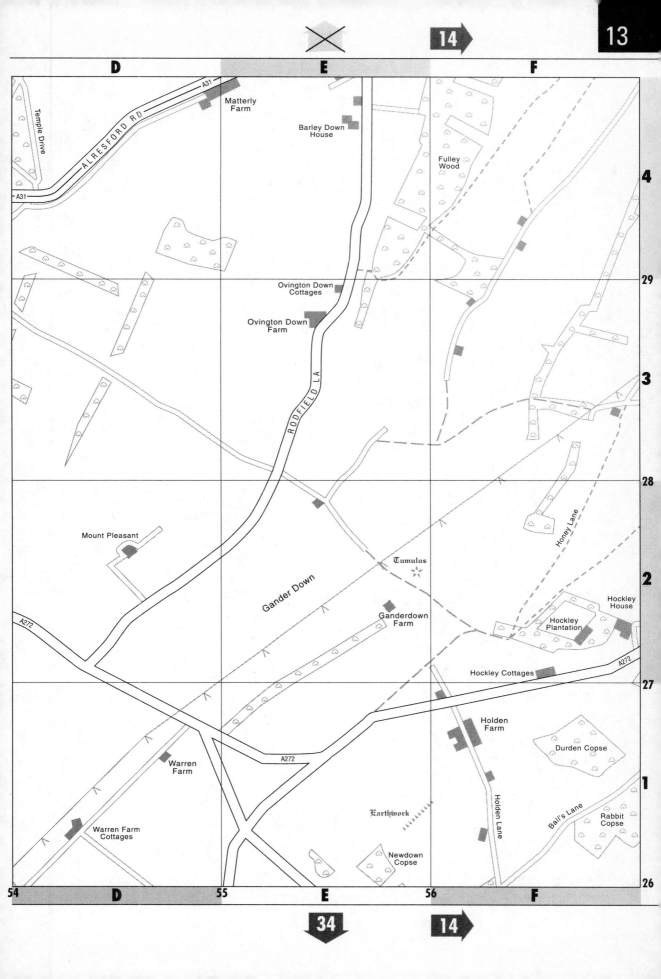

D       E       F

14 ➤

Temple Drive

A31

ALRESFORD RD

A31

Matterly Farm

Barley Down House

Fulley Wood

4

Ovington Down Cottages

29

Ovington Down Farm

RODFIELD LA

3

28

Mount Pleasant

Honey Lane

Gander Down

Tumulus

2

Hockley House

Ganderdown Farm

Hockley Plantation

A272

Hockley Cottages

A272

27

Holden Farm

Durden Copse

Warren Farm

A272

1

Earthwork

Holden Lane

Ball's Lane

Rabbit Copse

Warren Farm Cottages

Newdown Copse

26

54   D    55   E    56   F

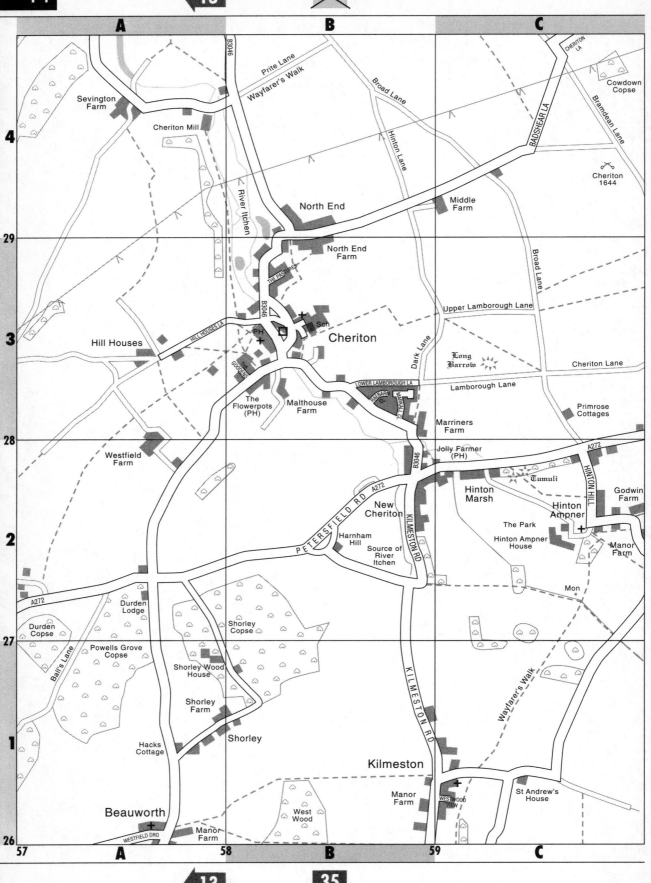

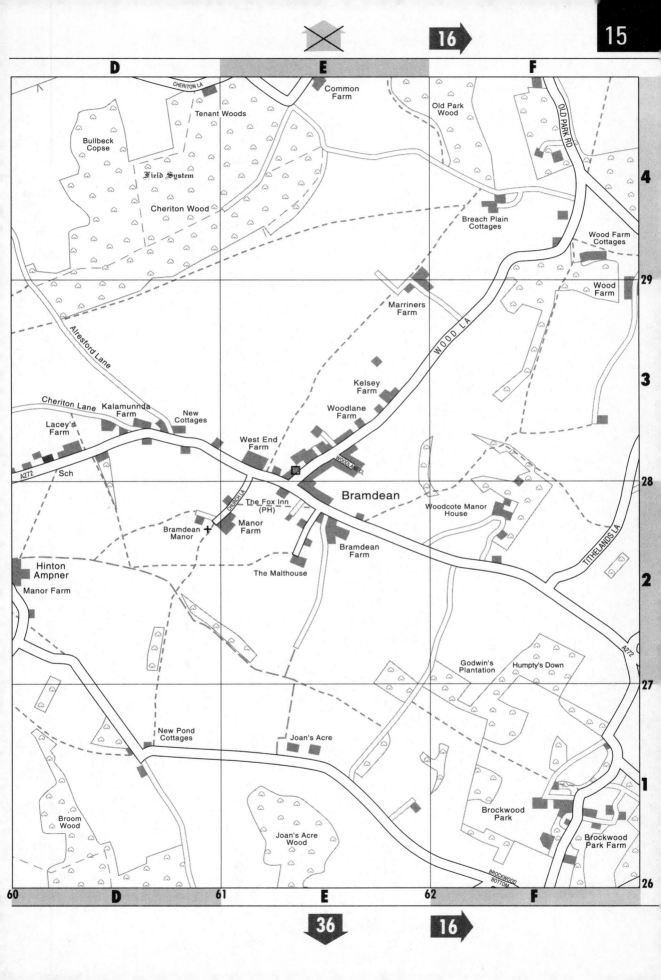

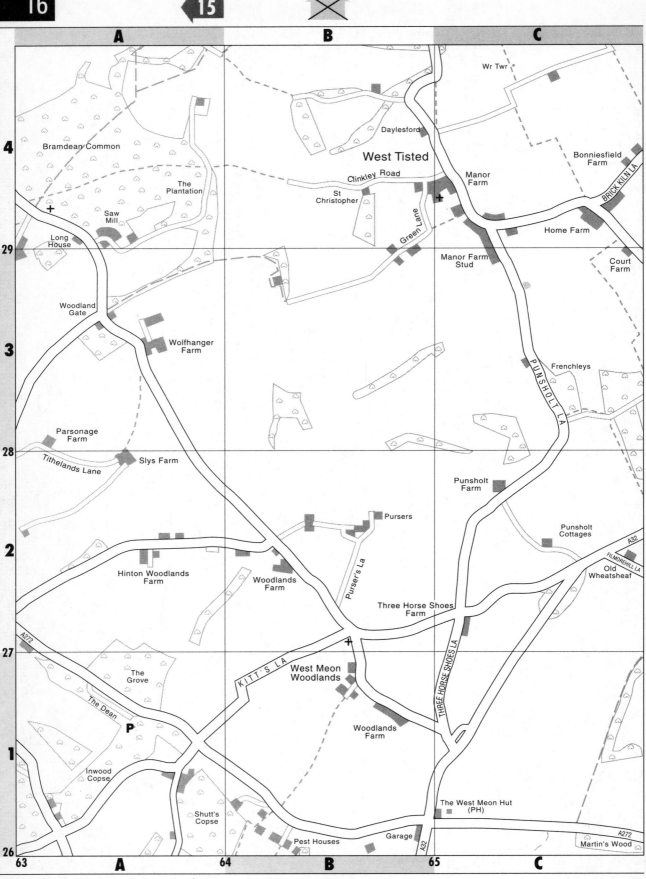

Wr Twr

Bramdean Common

**4**

Daylesford

**West Tisted**

Bonniesfield Farm

Clinkley Road

Manor Farm

BRICK KILN LA

St Christopher

The Plantation

Green Lane

Saw Mill

Home Farm

Long House

**29**

Manor Farm Stud

Court Farm

Woodland Gate

PUNSHOLT LA

Frenchleys

Wolfhanger Farm

**3**

Parsonage Farm

**28**

Tithelands Lane

Slys Farm

Punsholt Farm

Pursers

Punsholt Cottages

**2**

A32

Purser's La

FILMOREHILL LA

Hinton Woodlands Farm

Woodlands Farm

Old Wheatsheaf

Three Horse Shoes Farm

**27**

A272

THREE HORSE SHOES LA

The Grove

KITT'S LA

West Meon Woodlands

The Dean

**P**

**1**

Woodlands Farm

Inwood Copse

The West Meon Hut (PH)

Shutt's Copse

**26**

Pest Houses

Garage

A32

Martin's Wood

A272

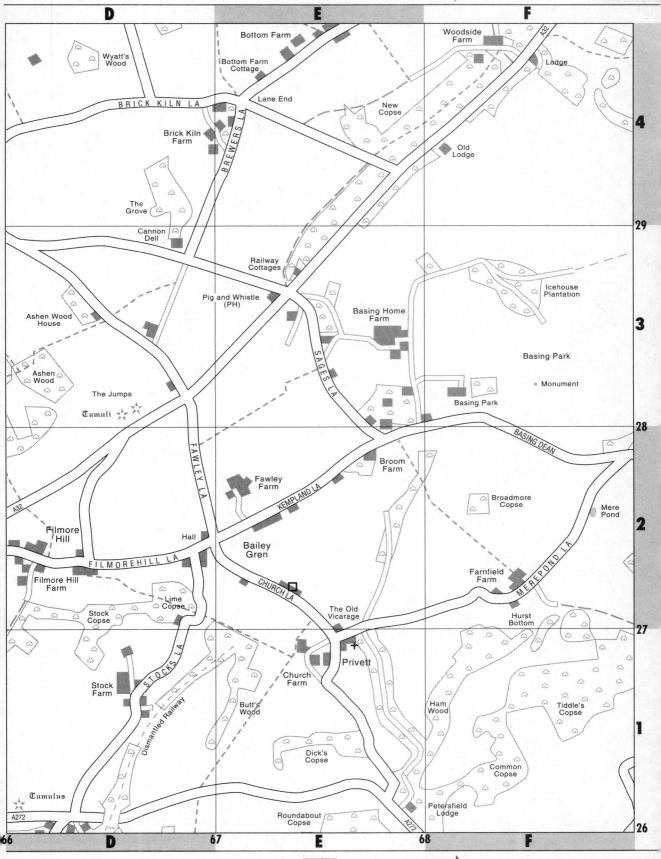

**D**

Wyatt's Wood

BRICK KILN LA

Brick Kiln Farm

The Grove

Cannon Dell

Ashen Wood House

Ashen Wood

The Jumps

Tumuli

Filmore Hill

Hall

FILMOREHILL LA

Filmore Hill Farm

Lime Copse

Stock Copse

Stock Farm

STOCKS LA

Dismantled Railway

Butt's Wood

Tumulus

A272

**E**

Bottom Farm

Bottom Farm Cottage

Lane End

BREWERS LA

Railway Cottages

Pig and Whistle (PH)

New Copse

Basing Home Farm

SAGES LA

FAWLEY LA

Fawley Farm

KEMPLAND LA

Broom Farm

Bailey Gren

CHURCH LA

The Old Vicarage

Church Farm

Privett

Dick's Copse

Roundabout Copse

A272

**F**

Woodside Farm

Lodge

Old Lodge

Icehouse Plantation

Basing Park

Monument

Basing Park

BASING DEAN

Broadmore Copse

Mere Pond

Farnfield Farm

MEREPOND LA

Hurst Bottom

Ham Wood

Tiddle's Copse

Common Copse

Petersfield Lodge

4

29

3

28

2

27

1

26

**D**

**E**

**F**

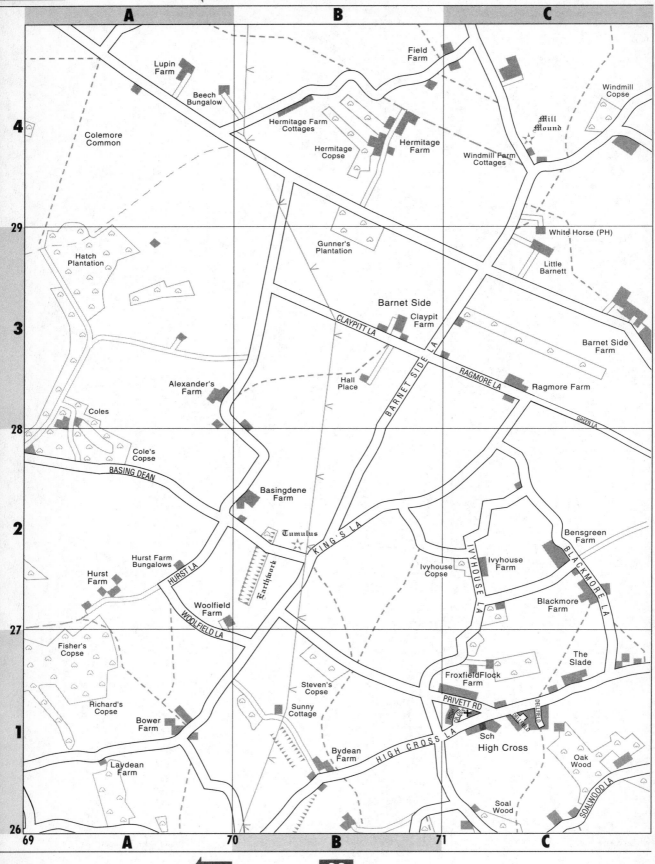

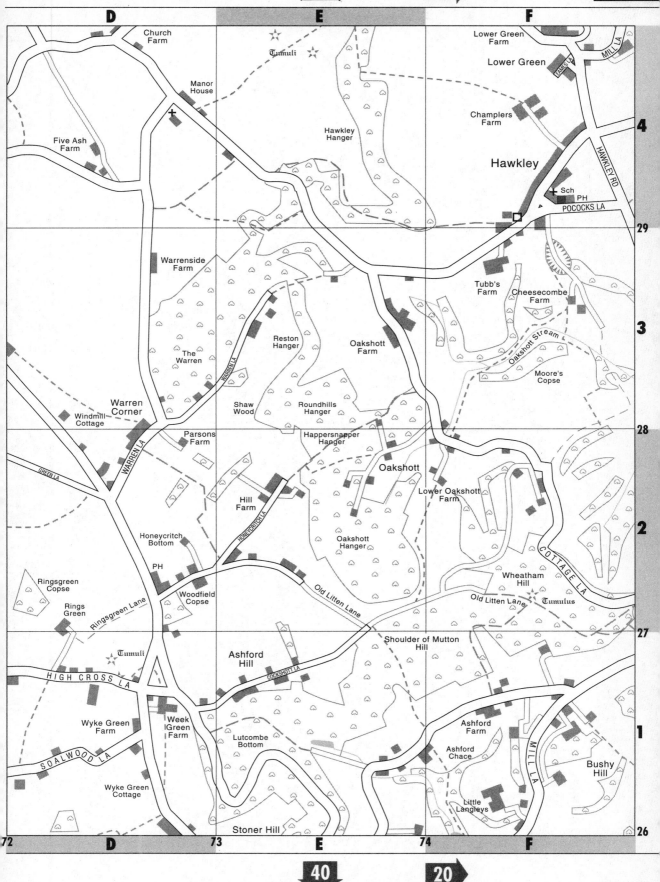

20

Church Farm

Manor House

Five Ash Farm

Tumuli

Hawkley Hanger

Lower Green Farm

Lower Green

Champlers Farm

Hawkley

Sch
PH
POCOCKS LA

Warrenside Farm

The Warren

Reston Hanger

Oakshott Farm

Tubb's Farm

Cheesecombe Farm

Oakshott Stream

Moore's Copse

Warren Corner

Windmill Cottage

Shaw Wood

Roundhills Hanger

Parsons Farm

Happersnapper Hanger

Oakshott

Lower Oakshott Farm

GREEN LA

WARREN LA

Hill Farm

Honeycritch Bottom

PH

Woodfield Copse

HONEYCRITCH LA

Oakshott Hanger

Old Litten Lane

Wheatham Hill

Old Litten Lane

Tumulus

COTTAGE LA

Ringsgreen Copse

Rings Green

Ringsgreen Lane

Shoulder of Mutton Hill

Ashford Hill

COCKSHOTT LA

HIGH CROSS LA

Tumuli

Wyke Green Farm

Week Green Farm

Lutcombe Bottom

Ashford Farm

Ashford Chace

MILL LA

Bushy Hill

SOALWOOD LA

Wyke Green Cottage

Little Langleys

Stoner Hill

HAWKLEY RD

MILL LA

EARLES LA

4

29

3

28

2

27

1

26

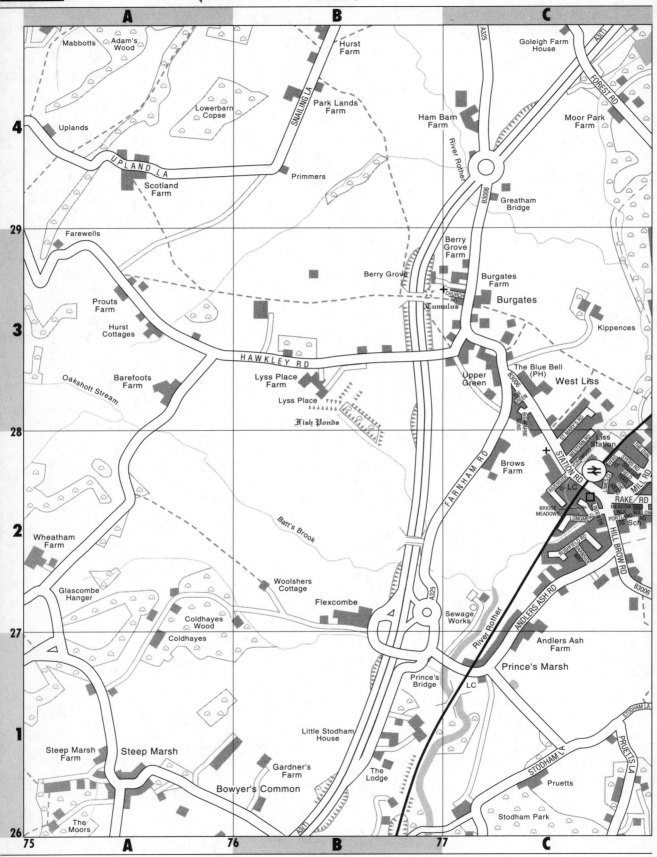

Mabbotts
Adam's Wood
Hurst Farm
Goleigh Farm House

**A**

**B**

**C**

Lowerbarn Copse
Park Lands Farm
A325
FOREST RD
A3127

Uplands
Ham Barn Farm
Moor Park Farm

**4**

UPLAND LA
River Rother

Scotland Farm
Primmers
B3006
Greatham Bridge

**29**

Farewells
Berry Grove Farm
Burgates Farm

Prouts Farm
Berry Grove
CHURCH RD
Burgates
Kippences

**3**

Hurst Cottages
Tumulus
The Blue Bell (PH)
West Liss

Oakshott Stream
Barefoots Farm
HAWKLEY RD
Upper Green
B3006

Lyss Place Farm
GREEN
St MARY'S RD
Liss Station

Lyss Place
ST MARY'S RD

**28**

Fish Ponds
FARNHAM RD
Brows Farm
RIVERSIDE

Batt's Brook
RAKE RD

**2**

Wheatham Farm
MEADOW WLK
WILLOW
Sch

Glascombe Hanger
Woolshers Cottage
BRIDGE MEADOWS
LONGMEAD
RUSHFIELD RD
B3006

Coldhayes Wood
Flexcombe
A325
Sewage Works
ANDLERS ASH RD

**27**

Coldhayes
Prince's Bridge
LC
Andlers Ash Farm
Prince's Marsh

Steep Marsh Farm
Steep Marsh
Little Stodham House
STODHAM LA
PRUETTS LA

**1**

Gardner's Farm
The Lodge
Pruetts

The Moors
Bowyer's Common
Stodham Park

**26**

75
**A**
76
**B**
77
**C**

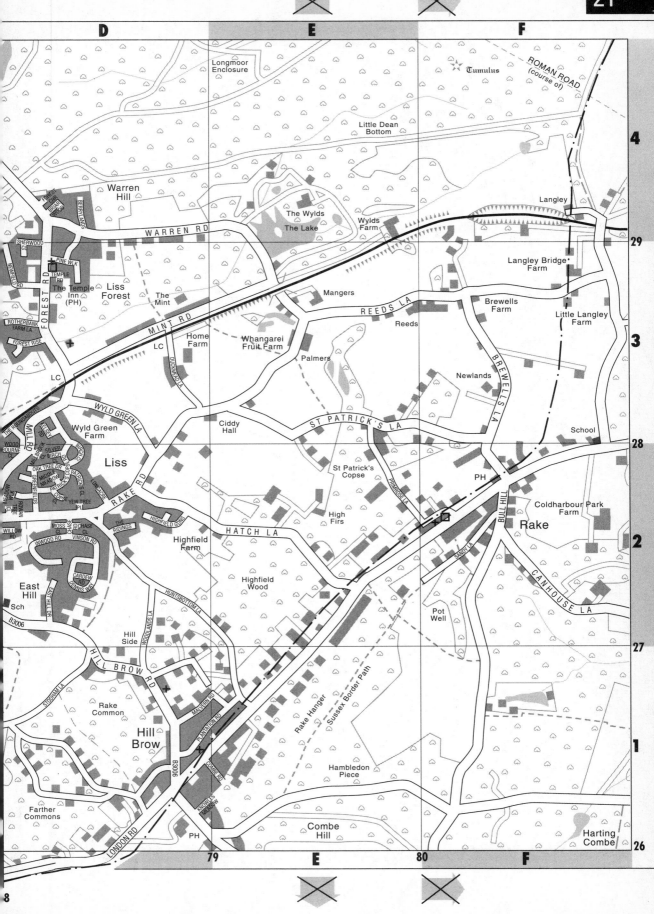

D     E     F

Longmoor
Enclosure

Tumulus

ROMAN ROAD
(course of)

Little Dean
Bottom

**4**

Warren
Hill

Langley

The Wylds

The Lake

Wylds
Farm

WARREN RD

Langley Bridge
Farm

SHERWOOD
CL

PINE WLK

TEMPLE
RD

The Temple
Inn
(PH)

Liss
Forest

The
Mint

Mangers

REEDS LA

Reeds

Brewells
Farm

Little Langley
Farm

**3**

ROTHERBANK
FARM LA

FOREST RISE

MINT RD

LC

Home
Farm

Whangarei
Fruit Farm

Palmers

Newlands

BREWELLS LA

LC

WYLD GREEN LA

Wyld Green
Farm

Ciddy
Hall

ST PATRICK'S LA

School

**28**

MILL RD

Liss

St Patrick's
Copse

PH

RAKE RD

Coldharbour Park
Farm

Rake

HIGHFIELD GDNS

THE RIDINGS

Highfield
Farm

HATCH LA

High
Firs

BULL HILL

SANDY LA

CANHOUSE LA

**2**

East
Hill

Sch

B3006

HUNTSBOTTOM LA

WOODLANDS LA

Highfield
Wood

Pot
Well

Hill
Side

**27**

HILL BROW RD

Rake
Common

Rake Hanger

Sussex Border Path

STODHAM LA

Hill
Brow

MANGER RD

PLANTATION RD

B3006

COMBE RD

Hambledon
Piece

**1**

Farther
Commons

LONDON RD

PH

KNOWLES MEADOW

Combe
Hill

Harting
Combe

**26**

79     E     80     F

8

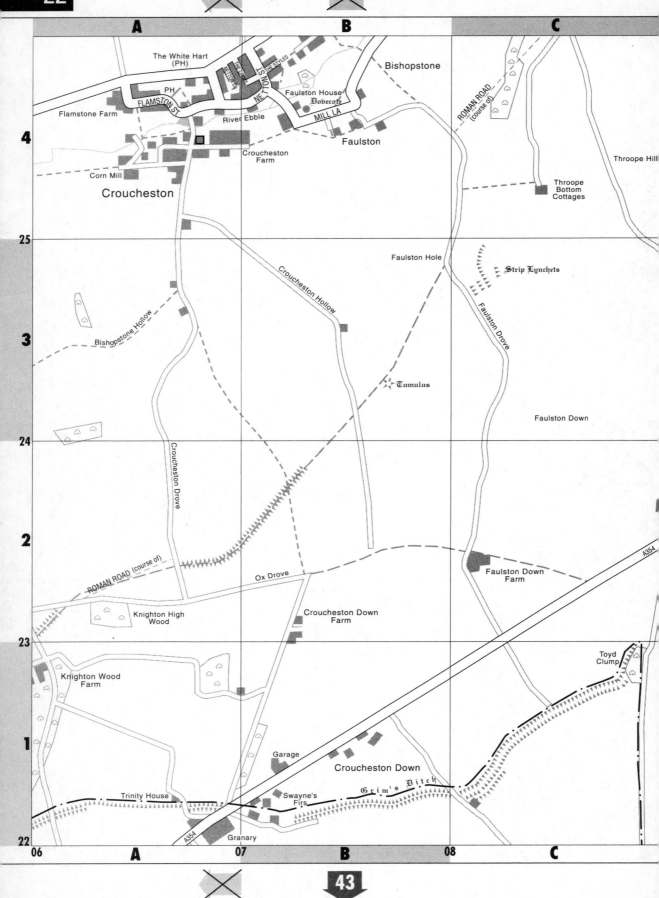

A B C

The White Hart (PH)

Bishopstone

THE STYLES

NEWTON ST

THE STYLES

Faulston House

Dovecote

ROMAN ROAD (course of)

PH

FLAMSTON ST

MILL LA

Flamstone Farm

River Ebble

Faulston

Throope Hill

**4**

Crmoucheston Farm

Throope Bottom Cottages

Corn Mill

**Croucheston**

**25**

Faulston Hole

Strip Lynchets

Croucheston Hollow

Faulston Drove

Bishopstone Hollow

**3**

Tumulus

Faulston Down

**24**

Croucheston Drove

**2**

A354

ROMAN ROAD (course of)

Ox Drove

Faulston Down Farm

Knighton High Wood

Croucheston Down Farm

**23**

Knighton Wood Farm

Toyd Clump

**1**

Garage

Croucheston Down

Grim's Ditch

Trinity House

Swayne's Firs

A354

Granary

**22**

06 A 07 B 08 C

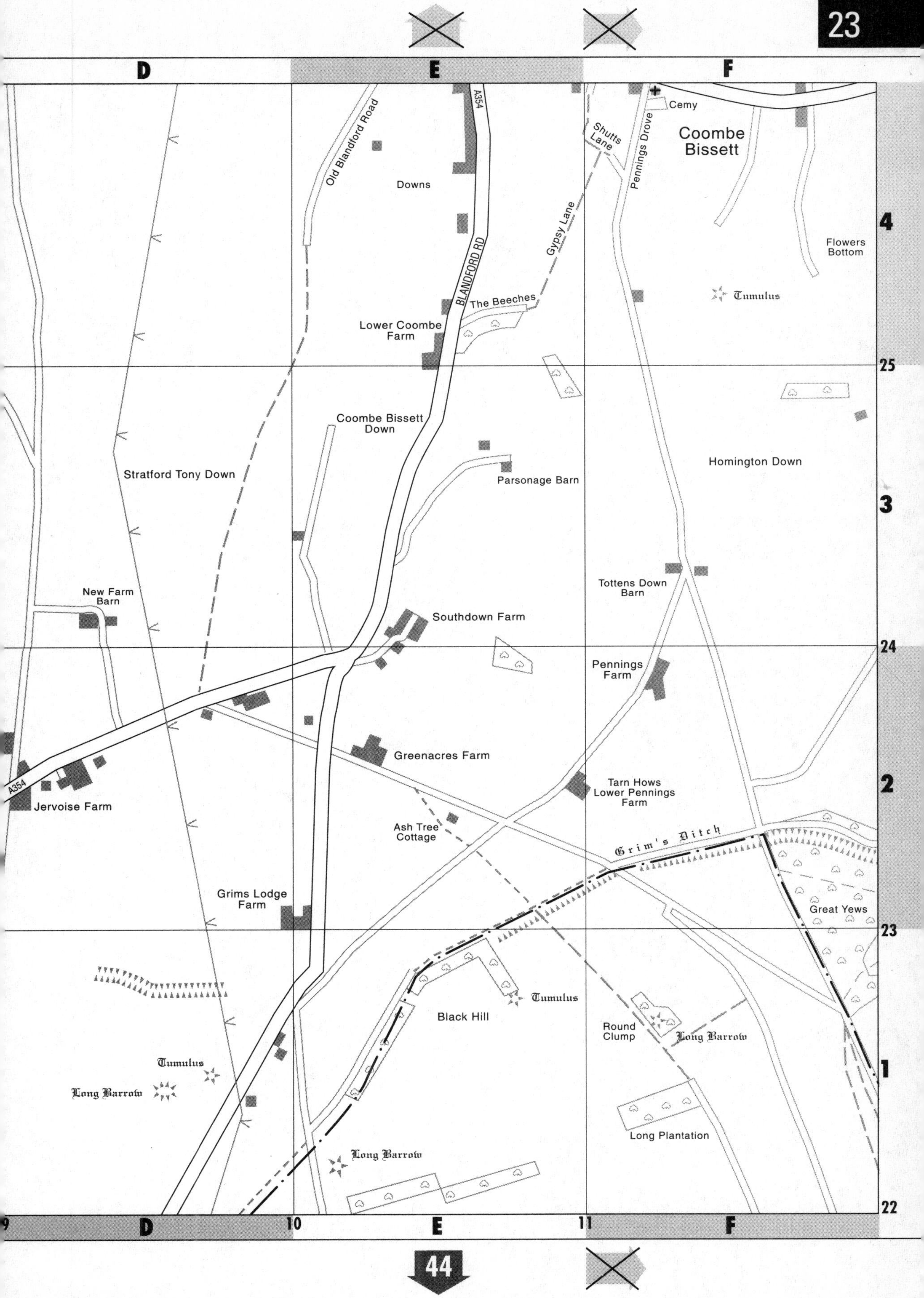

D E F

44

Old Blandford Road

A354

Downs

BLANDFORD RD

Gypsy Lane

Shutts Lane

Pennings Drove

Cemy

**Coombe Bissett**

Flowers Bottom

✳ Tumulus

4

The Beeches

Lower Coombe Farm

25

Coombe Bissett Down

Stratford Tony Down

Parsonage Barn

Homington Down

3

New Farm Barn

Tottens Down Barn

Southdown Farm

24

Pennings Farm

Greenacres Farm

Tarn Hows Lower Pennings Farm

2

Jervoise Farm

A354

Ash Tree Cottage

*Grim's Ditch*

Grims Lodge Farm

Great Yews

23

Tumulus

Black Hill

✳ Tumulus

Round Clump

*Long Barrow*

1

Tumulus

*Long Barrow*

Long Plantation

*Long Barrow*

22

9 D 10 E 11 F

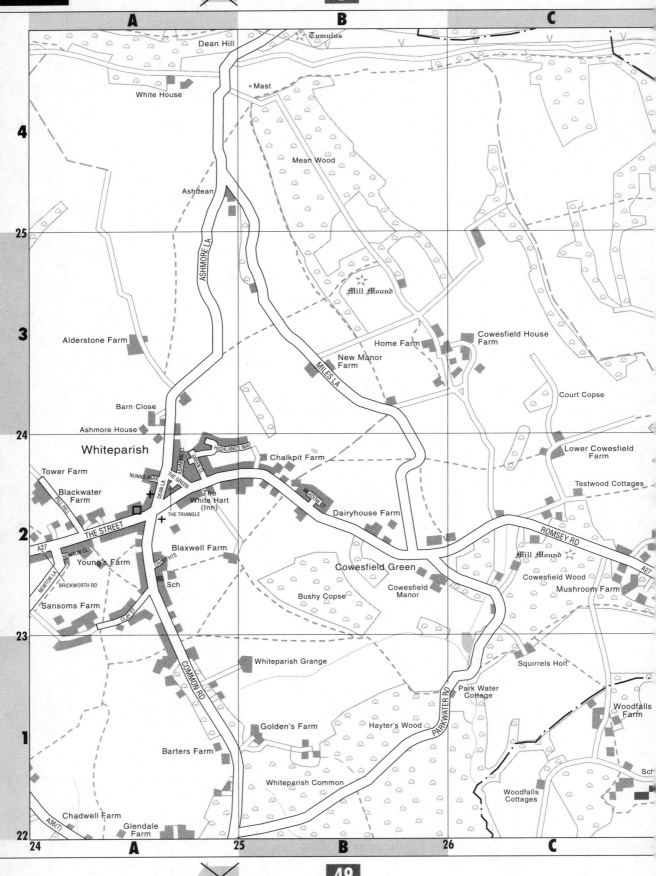

A
B
C

Tumulus

Dean Hill

White House

Mast

Mean Wood

4

Ashdean

ASHMORE LA

25

Mill Mound

3

Alderstone Farm

Home Farm

Cowesfield House Farm

MILES LA

New Manor Farm

Barn Close

Court Copse

Ashmore House

24

Lower Cowesfield Farm

Whiteparish

HIGHLANDS WAY

Chalkpit Farm

THE GREEN

ASHMORE CL

GREEN CL

NUNNS PARK

The White Hart (Inn)

MEADOW CT

Dairyhouse Farm

Testwood Cottages

Tower Farm

DEAN LA

Blackwater Farm

PILL HILL

THE TRIANGLE

ROMSEY RD

Mill Mound

2

A27

NEWTON CL

THE STREET

Blaxwell Farm

CROFTS

Young's Farm

Cowesfield Green

Cowesfield Wood

Mushroom Farm

A27

NEWTON LA

Sch

Cowesfield Manor

BRICKWORTH RD

Bushy Copse

Sansoms Farm

CLAY ST

23

Whiteparish Grange

Squirrels Holt

COMMON RD

Park Water Cottage

Woodfalls Farm

Golden's Farm

Hayter's Wood

PARKWATER RD

1

Barters Farm

Sch

Whiteparish Common

Woodfalls Cottages

Chadwell Farm

A36(T)

Glendale Farm

22

24
A
25
B
26
C

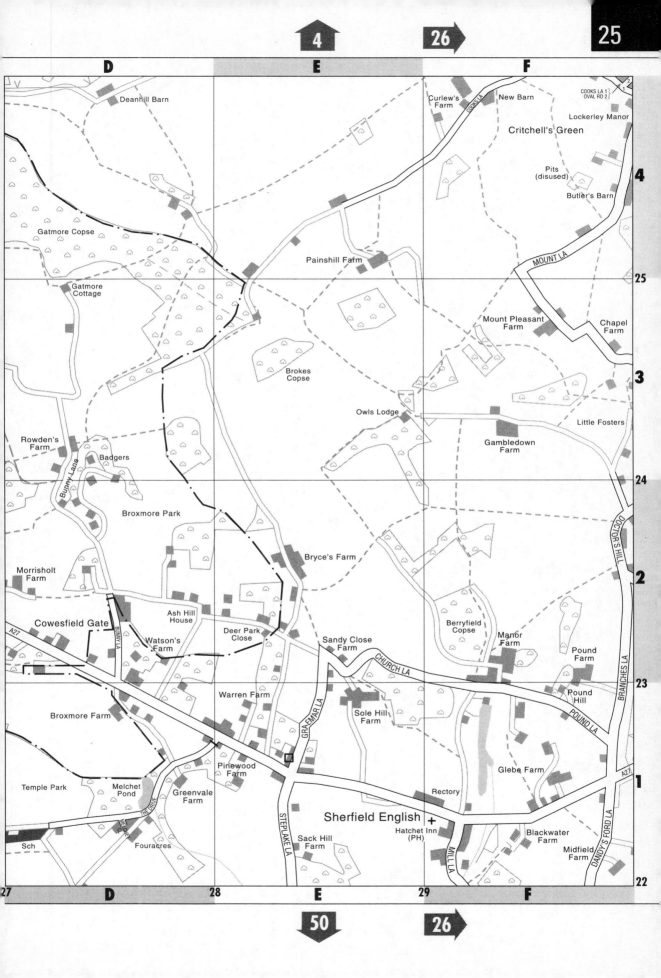

Deanhill Barn

Curlew's Farm

New Barn

COOKS LA 1
OVAL RD 2

COOKS LA

Lockerley Manor

Critchell's Green

Pits
(disused)

4

Butler's Barn

Gatmore Copse

Painshill Farm

MOUNT LA

25

Gatmore Cottage

Mount Pleasant Farm

Chapel Farm

Brokes Copse

3

Owls Lodge

Little Fosters

Rowden's Farm

Gambledown Farm

Badgers

Bunny Lane

24

Broxmore Park

DOCTOR'S HILL

Bryce's Farm

Morrisholt Farm

2

Berryfield Copse

Manor Farm

Cowesfield Gate

A27

Ash Hill House

BUNNY LA

Watson's Farm

Deer Park Close

Sandy Close Farm

CHURCH LA

Pound Farm

BRANCHES LA

23

Warren Farm

GRA EMAR LA

Pound Hill

Broxmore Farm

Sole Hill Farm

Pound Hill

POUND LA

A27

Pinewood Farm

Glebe Farm

1

Temple Park

Melchet Pond

THE DRIVE

MELCHET RD

Greenvale Farm

Rectory

Sherfield English

Hatchet Inn (PH)

Blackwater Farm

DANDY'S FORD LA

Sch

Fouracres

STEPLAKE LA

Sack Hill Farm

MILL LA

Midfield Farm

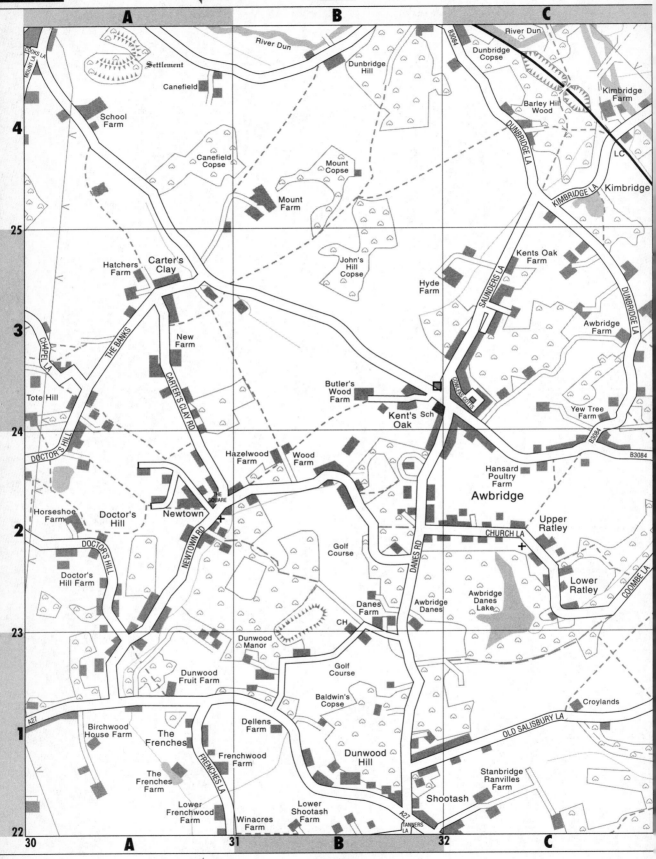

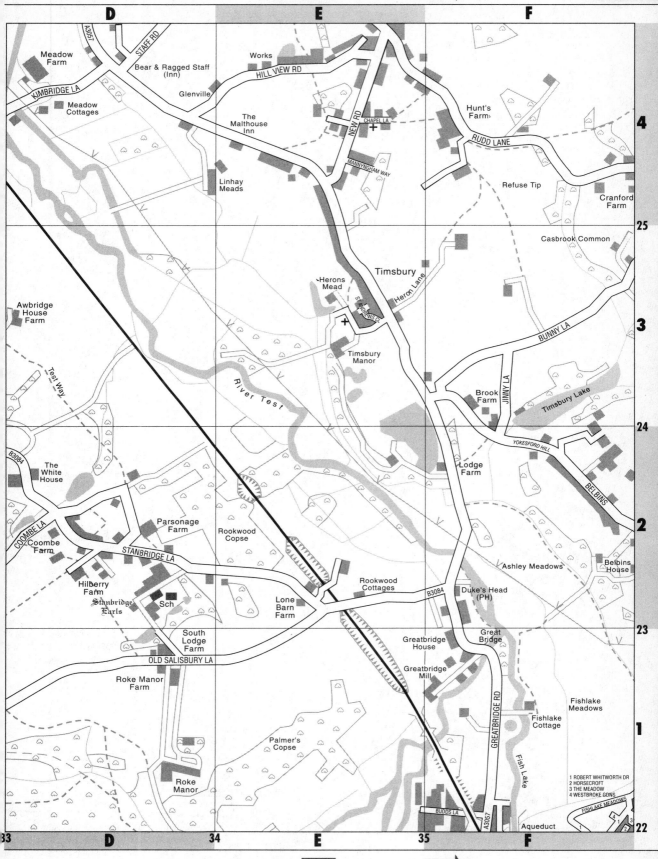

**D**

**E**

**F**

Meadow Farm

A3057

STAFF RD.

Bear & Ragged Staff (Inn)

Works

HILL VIEW RD

Glenville

KIMBRIDGE LA

Meadow Cottages

The Malthouse Inn

NEW RD

CHAPEL LA

Hunt's Farm

RUDD LANE

**4**

Linhay Meads

MANNYNGHAM WAY

Refuse Tip

Cranford Farm

**25**

Casbrook Common

Awbridge House Farm

Herons Mead

Timsbury

Heron Lane

ST. ANDREWS CL.

BUNNY LA

**3**

Test Way

River Test

Timsbury Manor

Brook Farm

JINNY LA

Timsbury Lake

**24**

B3084

The White House

Lodge Farm

YOKESFORD HILL

BELBINS

Coombe La

Parsonage Farm

Rookwood Copse

Ashley Meadows

Belbins House

**2**

Coombe Farm

STANBRIDGE LA

Hilberry Farm

Sch

Lone Barn Farm

Rookwood Cottages

B3084

Duke's Head (PH)

Stanbridge Earls

South Lodge Farm

Great Bridge

**23**

OLD SALISBURY LA

Greatbridge House

Great Bridge

Roke Manor Farm

Greatbridge Mill

GREATBRIDGE RD

Fishlake Meadows

Fishlake Cottage

**1**

Palmer's Copse

Fish Lake

Roke Manor

1 ROBERT WHITWORTH DR
2 HORSECROFT
3 THE MEADOW
4 WESTBROKE GDNS

FISHLAKE MEADOWS

BUDDS LA

A3057

Aqueduct

**22**

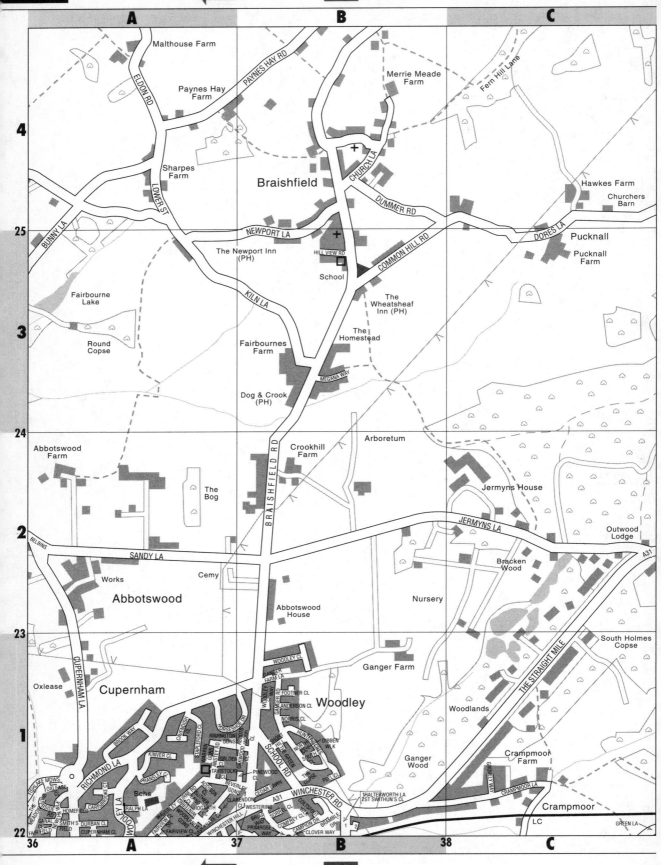

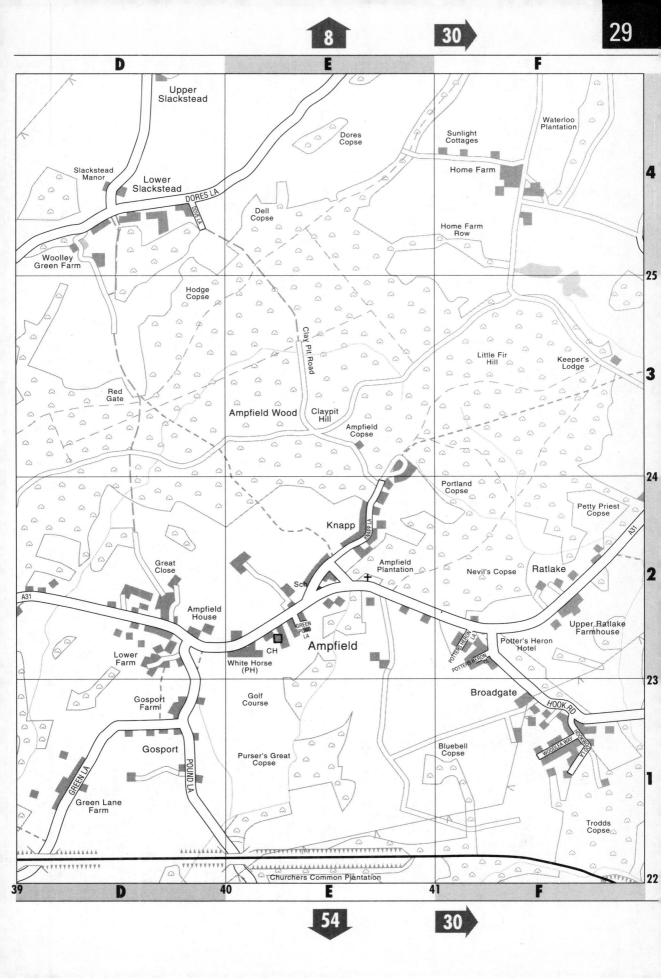

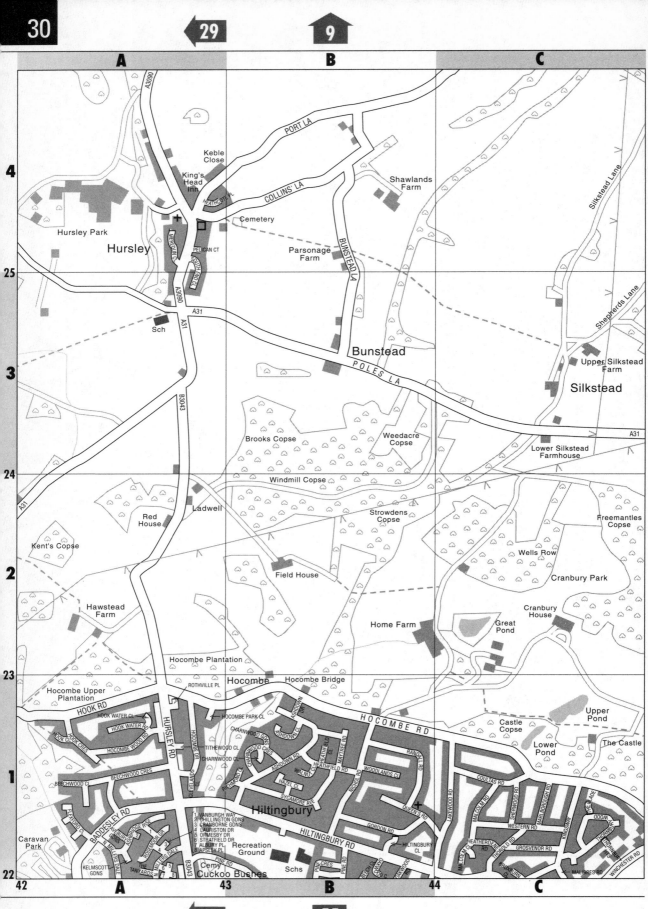

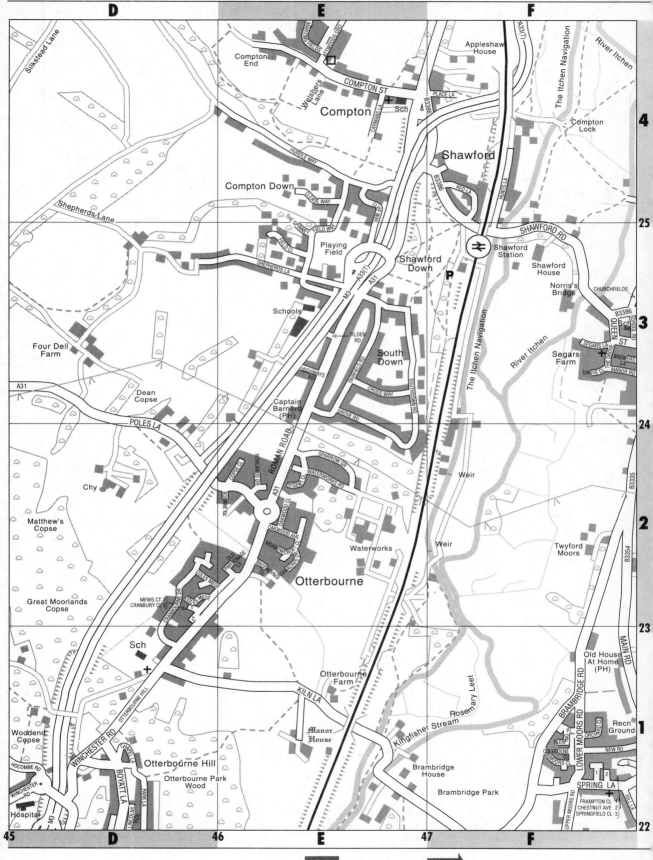

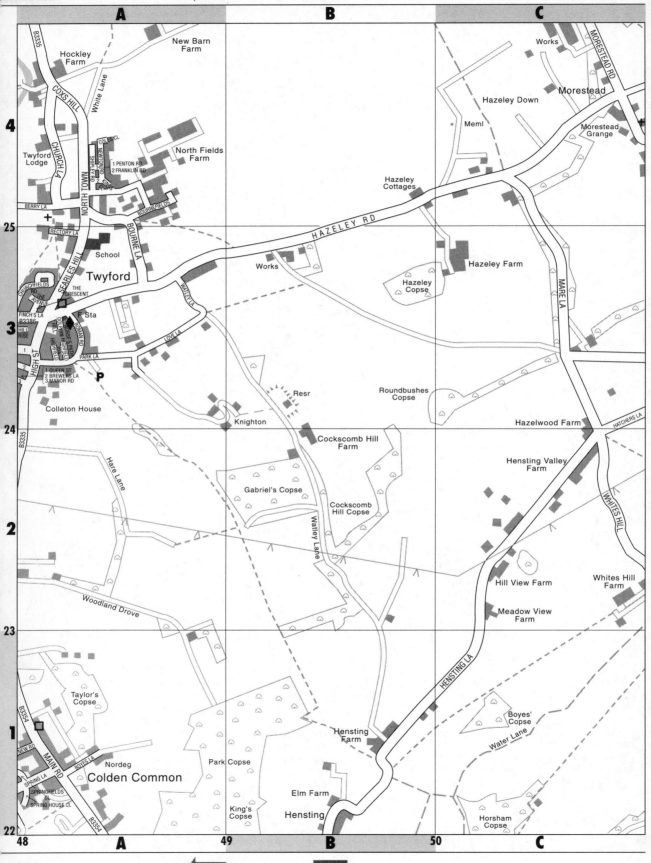

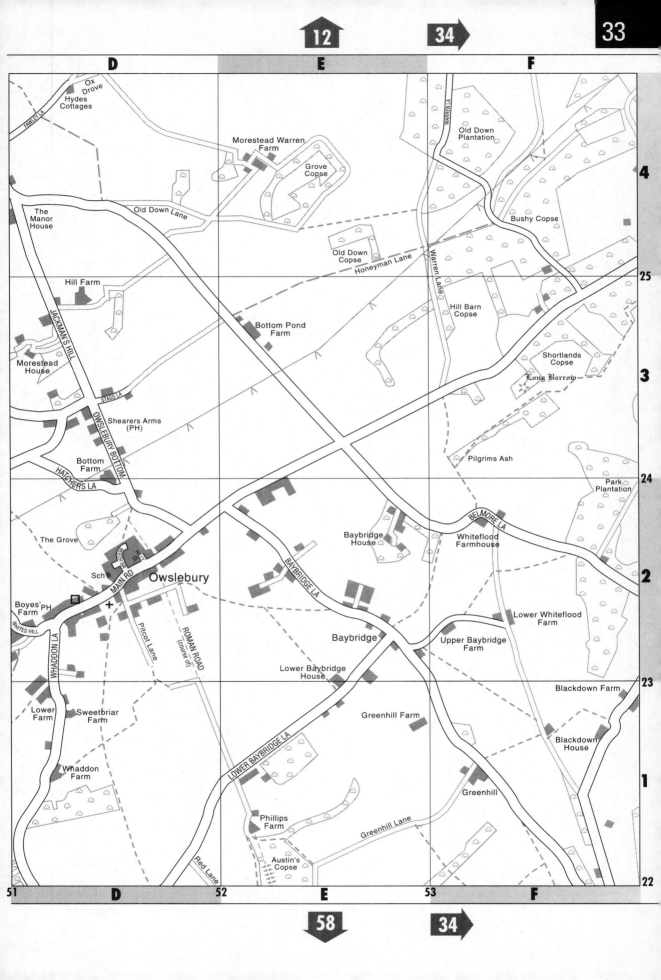

D
E
F

Ox Drove
Hydes Cottages
FAWLEY LA

Morestead Warren Farm
Grove Copse

Old Down Plantation
WARREN LA

Bushy Copse

**4**

The Manor House

Old Down Lane

Old Down Copse
Honeyman Lane

Hill Barn Copse

WARREN LANE

**25**

Hill Farm

Bottom Pond Farm

Shortlands Copse

Long Barrow

**3**

JACKMAN'S HILL

Morestead House

STAGS LA

Shearers Arms (PH)

OWSLEBURY BOTTOM

Bottom Farm

HATCHERS LA

Pilgrims Ash

Park Plantation

**24**

The Grove

Baybridge House

BELMORE LA

Whiteflood Farmhouse

Sch
Owslebury
MAIN RD

BAYBRIDGE LA

Lower Whiteflood Farm

**2**

Boyes' Farm PH

WHITES HILL

WHADDON LA

Picot Lane

ROMAN ROAD (course of)

Baybridge

Lower Baybridge House

Upper Baybridge Farm

Blackdown Farm

**23**

Lower Farm

Sweetbriar Farm

LOWER BAYBRIDGE LA

Greenhill Farm

Blackdown House

Whaddon Farm

Greenhill

**1**

Phillips Farm

Greenhill Lane

Red Lane

Austin's Copse

**22**

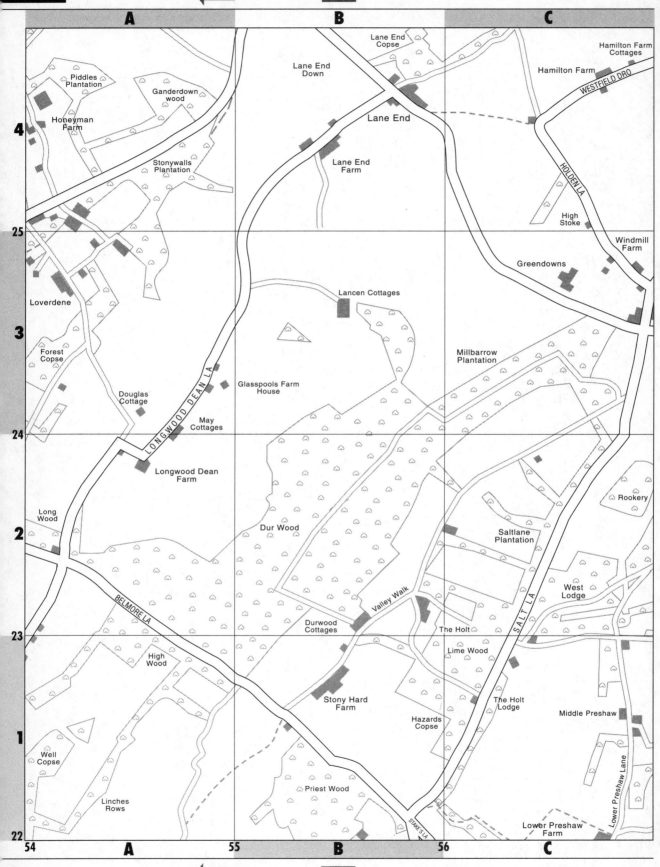

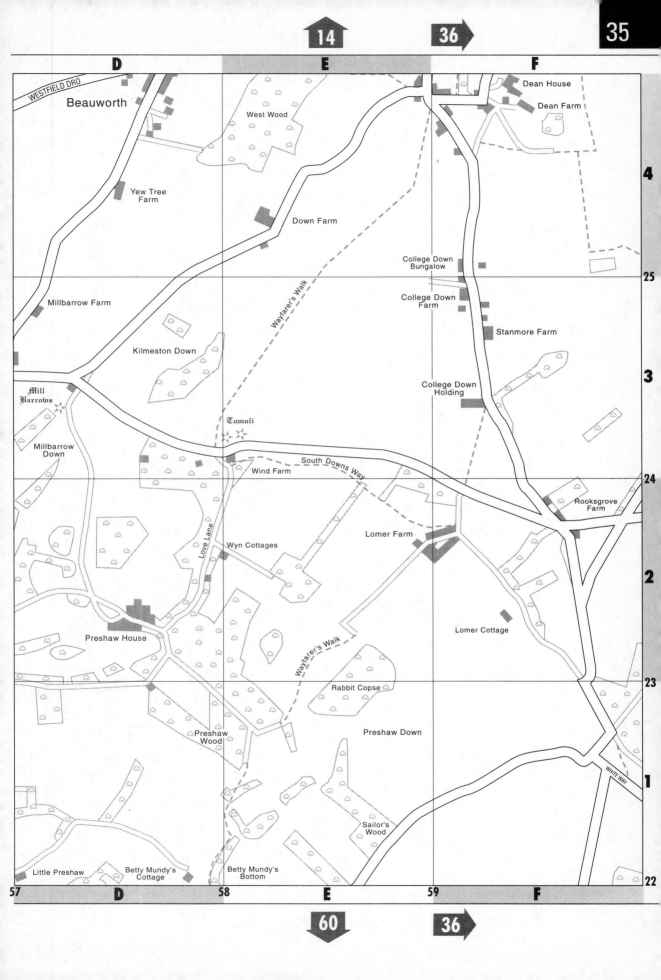

D E F

WESTFIELD DRO

Beauworth

West Wood

Dean House

Dean Farm

4

Yew Tree
Farm

Down Farm

College Down
Bungalow

25

Millbarrow Farm

College Down
Farm

Stanmore Farm

Kilmeston Down

College Down
Holding

3

Mill
Barrows

Tumuli

Millbarrow
Down

South Downs Way

Wind Farm

24

Rooksgrove
Farm

Love Lane

Wyn Cottages

Lomer Farm

2

Preshaw House

Lomer Cottage

Waylarer's Walk

Rabbit Copse

23

Preshaw
Wood

Preshaw Down

WHITE WAY

1

Sailor's
Wood

Little Preshaw

Betty Mundy's
Cottage

Betty Mundy's
Bottom

22

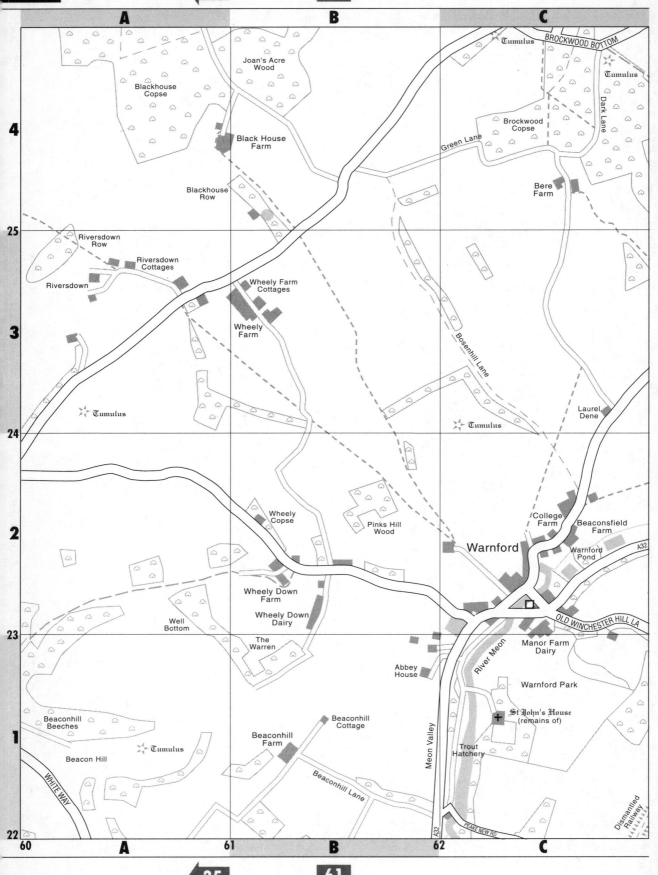

BROCKWOOD BOTTOM

Tumulus

Tumulus

Joan's Acre
Wood

Blackhouse
Copse

Brockwood
Copse

Dark Lane

4

Green Lane

Black House
Farm

Bere
Farm

Blackhouse
Row

25

Riversdown
Row

Riversdown
Cottages

Wheely Farm
Cottages

Riversdown

Wheely
Farm

Bosenhill Lane

3

Laurel
Dene

Tumulus

Tumulus

24

Wheely
Copse

Pinks Hill
Wood

College
Farm

Beaconsfield
Farm

A32

2

Warnford

Warnford
Pond

Wheely Down
Farm

Wheely Down
Dairy

Well
Bottom

Manor Farm
Dairy

OLD WINCHESTER HILL LA

23

The
Warren

Abbey
House

River Meon

Warnford Park

Beaconhill
Beeches

Beaconhill
Cottage

St John's House
(remains of)

Meon Valley

1

Beaconhill
Farm

Beacon Hill

Tumulus

Trout
Hatchery

WHITE WAY

Beaconhill Lane

Dismantled Railway

22

A32

PEAKE NEW RD

**D**      **E**      **F**

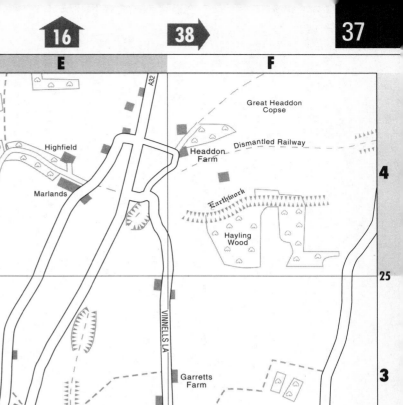

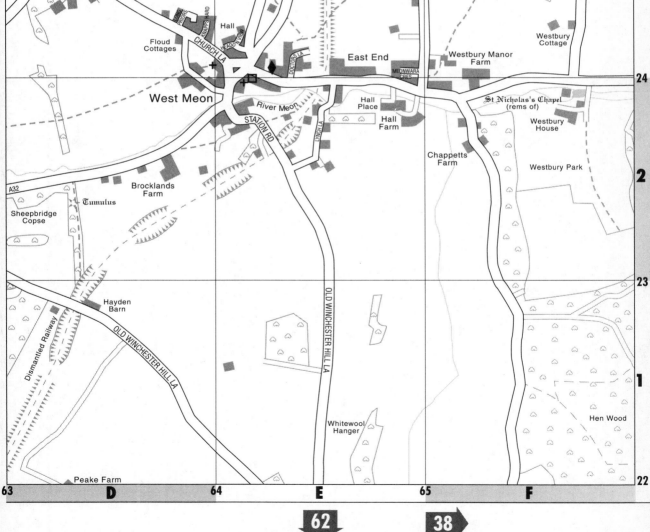

Brick Kiln Farm

Westwood

Sutton Park

Highfield

Marlands

Great Headdon Copse

Dismantled Railway

Headdon Farm

Earthwork

Hayling Wood

4

Marldell Farm

25

Lippen Wood

Court Farm

Lippen Cottages

VINNELLS LA

Garretts Farm

Westbury Cottage

3

Floud Cottages

CHURCH LA

Hall

East End

Westbury Manor Farm

MEONWARA CROSS

24

West Meon

River Meon

STATION RD

LYNCH LA

Hall Place

Hall Farm

St Nicholas's Chapel (rems of)

Westbury House

A32

Tumulus

Brocklands Farm

Chappetts Farm

Westbury Park

2

Sheepbridge Copse

23

Hayden Barn

OLD WINCHESTER HILL LA

OLD WINCHESTER HILL LA

Dismantled Railway

Hen Wood

1

Whitewool Hanger

Peake Farm

22

**63**    **D**      **64**      **E**      **65**      **F**

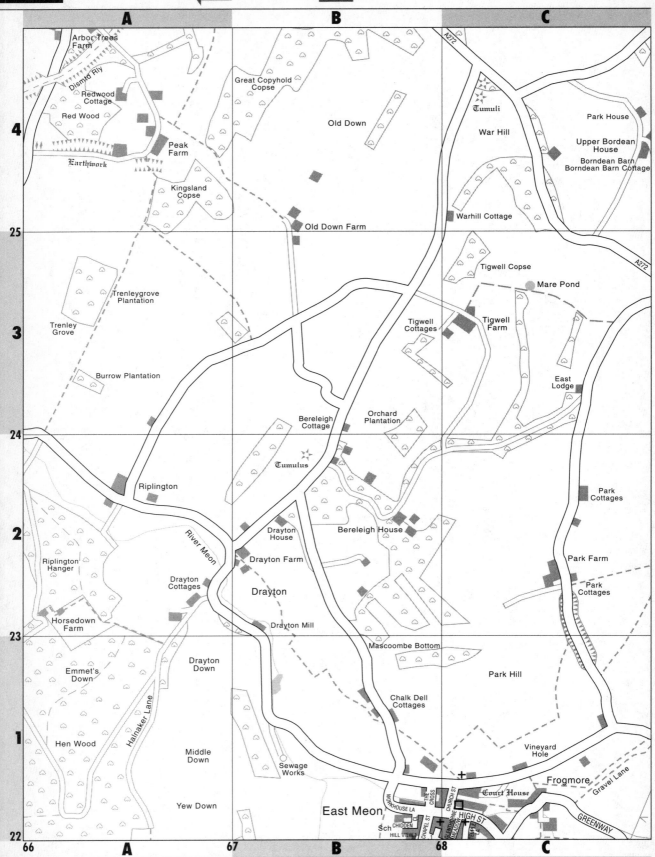

**A**   **B**   **C**

Arbor Trees Farm

Dismtd Rly

Redwood Cottage

Red Wood

Great Copyhold Copse

Old Down

Tumuli

War Hill

Park House

Upper Bordean House

Borndean Barn
Borndean Barn Cottage

**4**

Peak Farm

Earthwork

Kingsland Copse

Warhill Cottage

**25**

Old Down Farm

Tigwell Copse

Mare Pond

Trenleygrove Plantation

Trenley Grove

Tigwell Cottages

Tigwell Farm

**3**

Burrow Plantation

East Lodge

Bereleigh Cottage

Orchard Plantation

**24**

Tumulus

Park Cottages

Riplington

**2**

River Meon

Drayton House

Bereleigh House

Park Farm

Park Cottages

Riplington Hanger

Drayton Farm

Drayton Cottages

Drayton

Horsedown Farm

Drayton Mill

**23**

Mascoombe Bottom

Drayton Down

Park Hill

Emmet's Down

Chalk Dell Cottages

Halnaker Lane

Hen Wood

Middle Down

Sewage Works

Vineyard Hole

Frogmore

Gravel Lane

**1**

THE CROSS
WORKHOUSE LA
CHURCH ST
Court House
HIGH ST
GREENWAY

Yew Down

East Meon

Sch
CHIDDEN
CHAPEL ST
CL
HILL VIEW

**22**

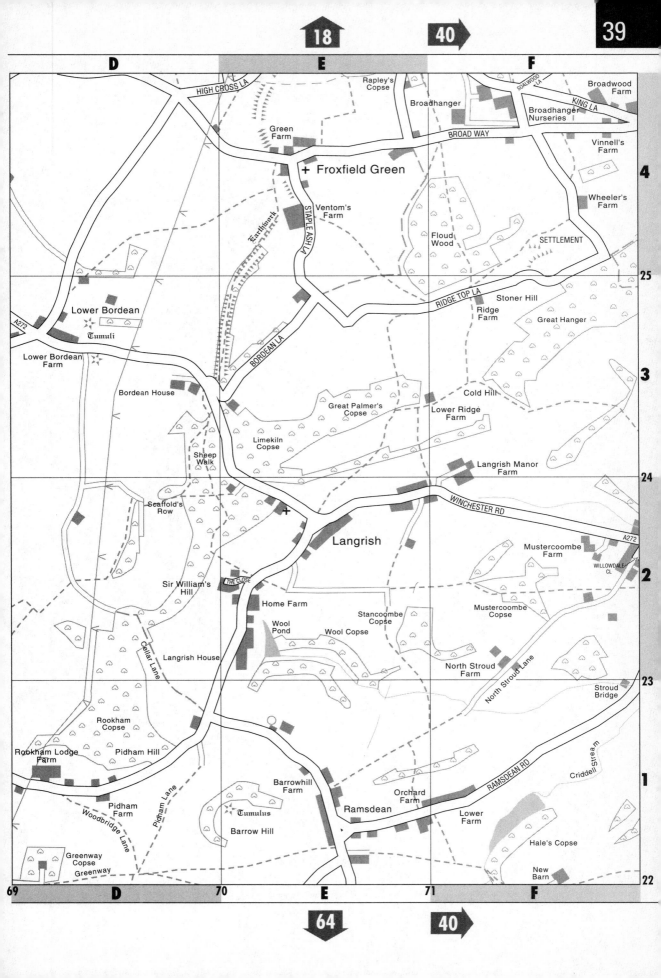

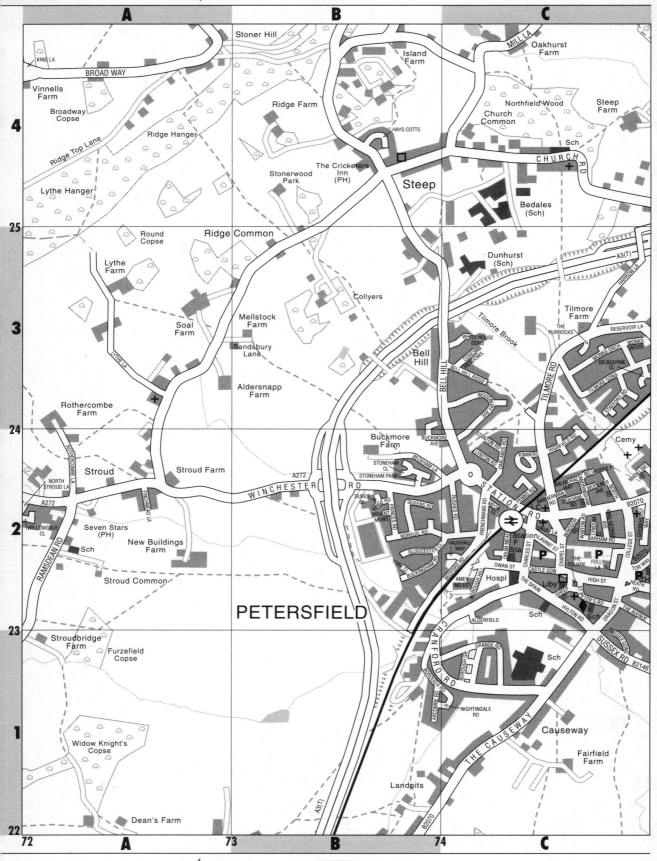

PETERSFIELD

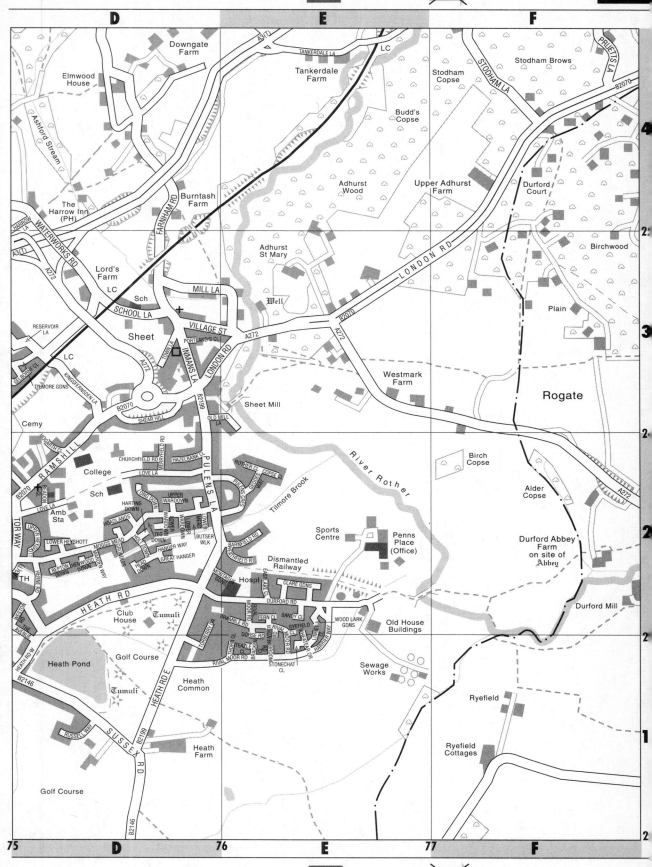

D · E · F

4

2

3

2

2

2

1

2

**Downgate Farm**

**Elmwood House**

Ashford Stream

A3(1)

TANKERDALE LA

LC

**Tankerdale Farm**

**Stodham Copse**

STODHAM LA

**Stodham Brows**

PRUETS LA

B2070

**Budd's Copse**

**Adhurst Wood**

**Upper Adhurst Farm**

**Durford Court**

FARNHAM RD

**Burntash Farm**

The Harrow Inn (PH)

HARROW LA

WATERWORKS RD

A3(1)

A272

**Lord's Farm**

LC

Sch

MILL LA

SCHOOL LA

**Sheet**

RESERVOIR LA

LC

SELBORNE CL

TILMORE GDNS

KINGSFERNSDEN LA

**Cemy**

B2070

SHEAR HILL

TOWN LA

VILLAGE ST

PORTLANDS CL

INMANS LA

LONDON RD

A272

B2199

OLD MILL LA

**Sheet Mill**

**Adhurst St Mary**

Well

LONDON RD

B2070

A272

**Westmark Farm**

**Rogate**

**Birchwood**

**Plain**

River Rother

**Birch Copse**

A272

**Alder Copse**

RAMSHILL

HOGARTH CL

**College**

CHURCHFIELD RD

MERRYFIELD RD

HAZEL BANK RD

LOVE LA

ROTHER CL

COPSE CL

PULENS CRES

B2070

BEACON

LOVE LA

Sch

**Amb Sta**

UPPER HESHOTT

LONG DOWN

UPPER WARDOWN

WARDOWN

LOWER WARDOWN

PULENS LA

GEORGES

REEDS

TILMORE BROOK

HARTING DOWN

HEADLANDS

HANGER WAY

BUTSER WLK

TOR WAY

LOWER HESHOTT

BEPTON DOWN

HENWOOD DOWN

MOGGS MEAD

MADDEN WAY

HERNE RD

TH

TEG DOWN

ROLL DOWN

HEAD DOWN

MERCHISTON

GREAT HANGER

BARNFIELD RD

HEATHFIELD RD

MONTAGUE CL

EASTLAKE CL

**Sports Centre**

**Penns Place (Office)**

**Dismantled Railway**

Hospl

CLARE GDNS

DURFORD RD

**Durford Abbey Farm on site of Abbey**

**Durford Mill**

HEATH RD

**Club House**

**Tumuli**

TORBERRY DR

BRAMBLE RD

FERN CL

SANDY CL

MOOR RD

RYEFIELD CL

RIVAL MOOR RD

ALDER CT

HARDER WAY

**Wood Lark Gdns**

**Old House Buildings**

GORSE RD

TEAZLE CL

BROOM CL

STONECHAT CL

**Sewage Works**

**Ryefield**

**Heath Pond**

B2146

**Golf Course**

**Tumuli**

**Heath Common**

HEATH RD E

HEATH RD W

WESTON RD

THE AVENUE

B2199

SUSSEX RD

RUSSELL WAY

**Heath Farm**

**Golf Course**

**Ryefield Cottages**

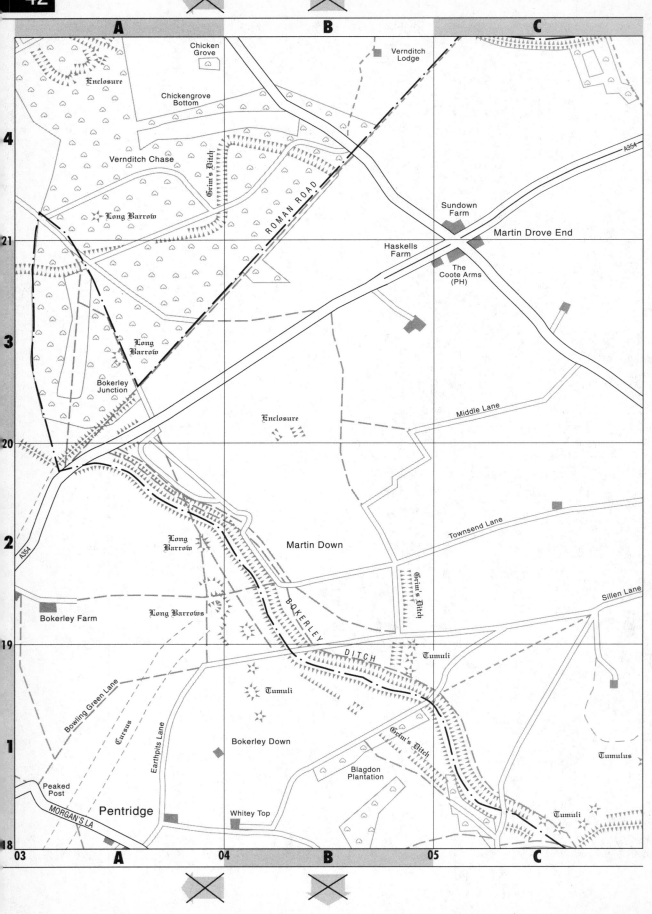

A  B  C

**4**

Chicken Grove

Vernditch Lodge

Enclosure

Chickengrove Bottom

Vernditch Chase

Grim's Ditch

ROMAN ROAD

A354

Sundown Farm

Long Barrow

Martin Drove End

**21**

Haskells Farm

The Coote Arms (PH)

**3**

Long Barrow

Bokerley Junction

Middle Lane

Enclosure

**20**

Townsend Lane

Long Barrow

Martin Down

Sillen Lane

**2**

A354

Grim's Ditch

BOKERLEY

Bokerley Farm

Long Barrows

DITCH

Tumuli

**19**

Grim's Ditch

Tumuli

Bowling Green Lane

Tumuli

Cursus

Earthpits Lane

Bokerley Down

**1**

Tumulus

Blagdon Plantation

Peaked Post

MORGAN'S LA

Pentridge

Whitey Top

Tumuli

**18**

03  A  04  B  05  C

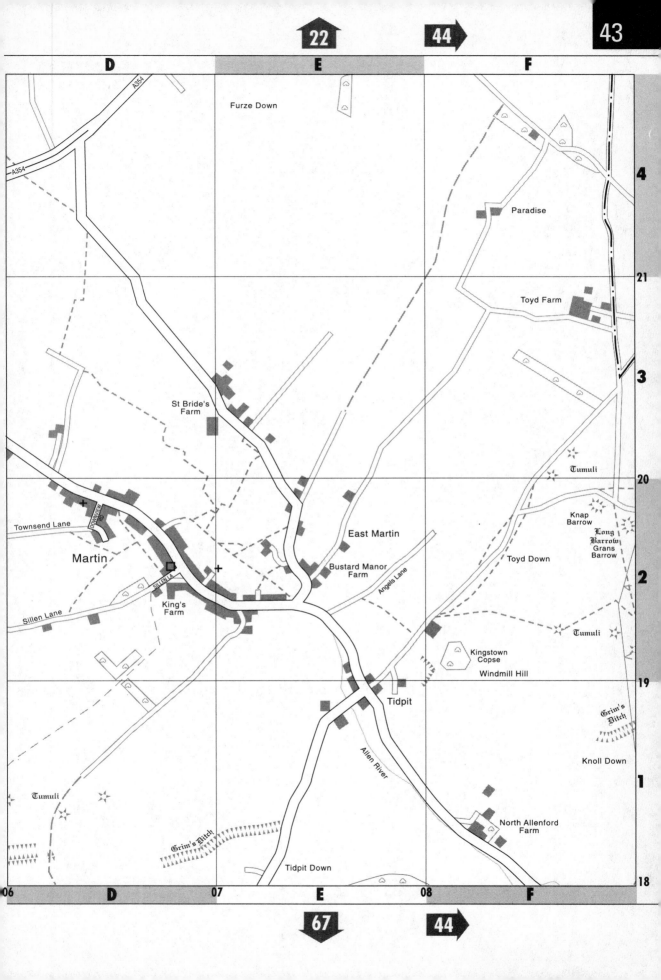

A354

Furze Down

4

Paradise

21

Toyd Farm

St Bride's
Farm

3

Tumuli

20

Townsend Lane

DOWNVIEW

Knap
Barrow

Long
Barrow
Grans
Barrow

Martin

East Martin

Bustard Manor
Farm

Toyd Down

2

SILLEN LA.

King's
Farm

Angels Lane

Sillen Lane

Tumuli

Kingstown
Copse

Windmill Hill

19

Tidpit

Grim's
Ditch

Allen River

Knoll Down

Tumuli

1

North Allenford
Farm

Grim's Ditch

Tidpit Down

18

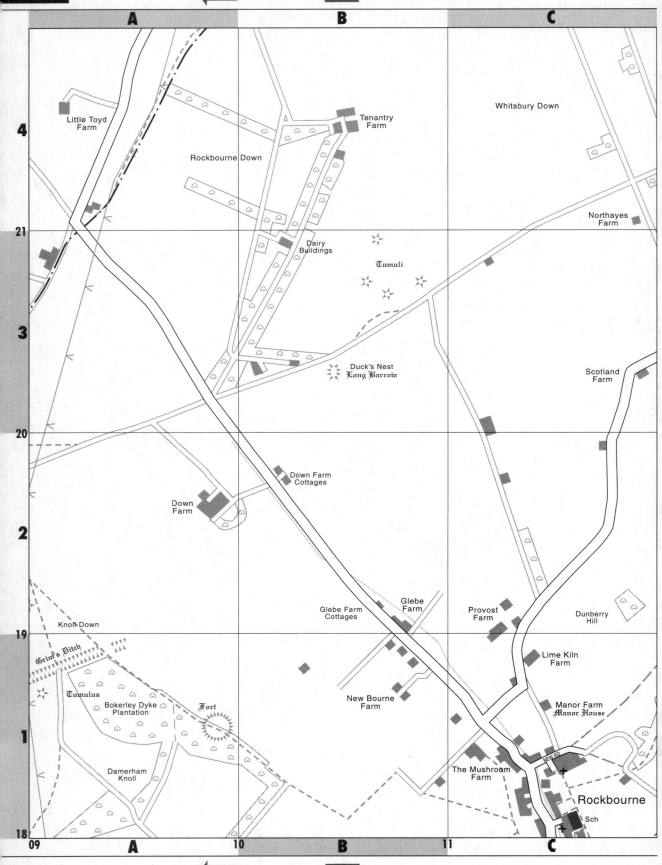

A B C

4

Little Toyd Farm

Rockbourne Down

Tenantry Farm

Whitsbury Down

21

Dairy Buildings

Northayes Farm

Tumuli

3

Duck's Nest Long Barrow

Scotland Farm

20

Down Farm Cottages

Down Farm

2

Glebe Farm Cottages

Glebe Farm

Provost Farm

Dunberry Hill

19

Knoll Down

New Bourne Farm

Lime Kiln Farm

Grim's Ditch

Tumulus

Bokerley Dyke Plantation

Fort

Manor Farm
Manor House

1

Damerham Knoll

The Mushroom Farm

NEW RD

Rockbourne

18

Sch

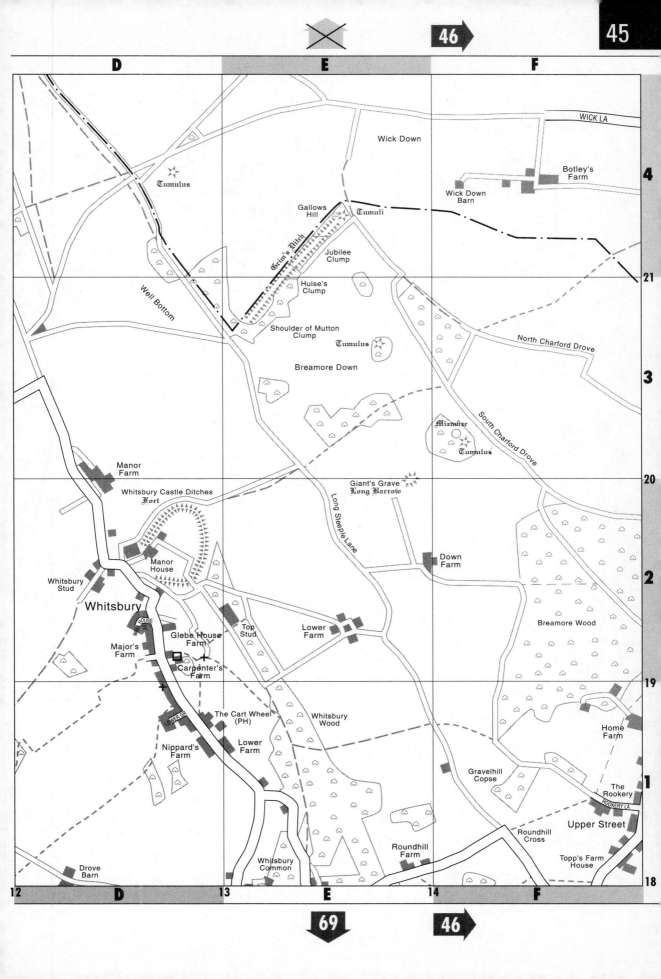

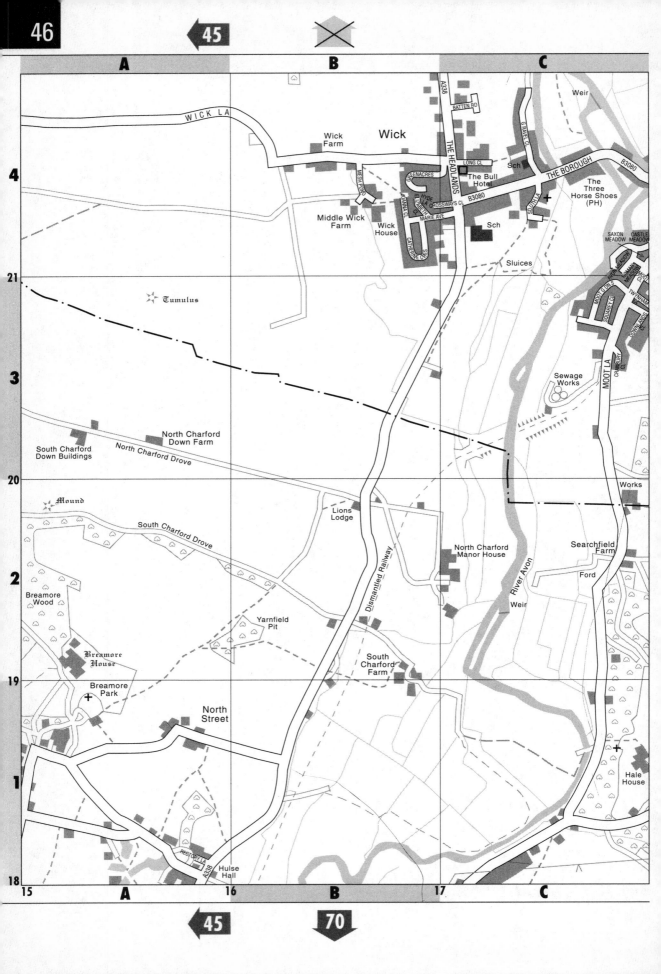

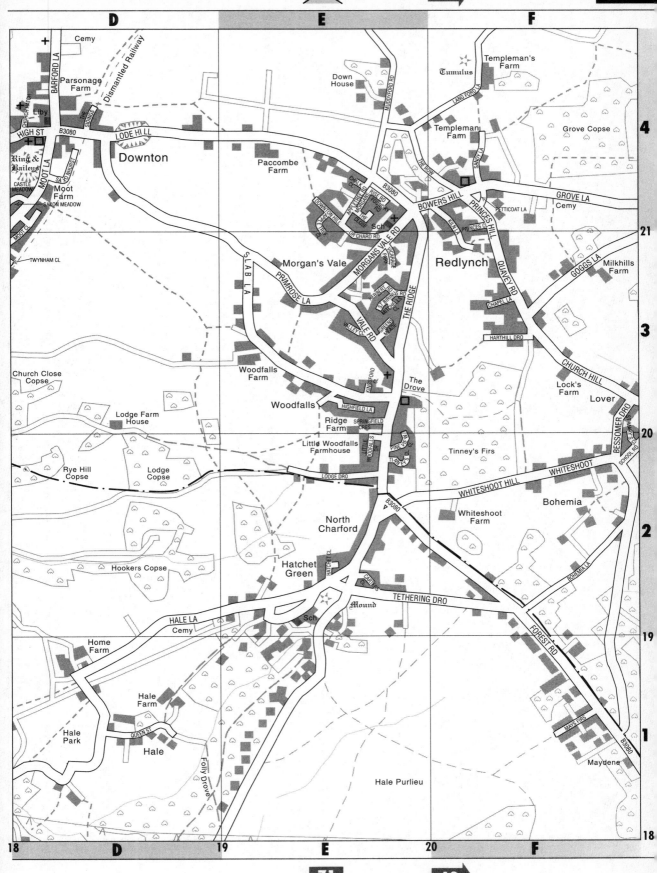

**D**      **E**      **F**

Cemy
+
BARFORD LA
Parsonage Farm
Dismantled Railway
Down House
Tumulus
Templeman's Farm
LANG FORD LA
+
Liby
THE SIDINGS
CHURCH MEAD
Grove Copse

**4**

HIGH ST
B3080
LODE HILL
Templeman Farm
SANDY LA
Ring & Baileys
MOOT LA
Downton
Paccombe Farm
B3080
THE ROW
BOWERS HILL
GROVE LA
Cemy
CASTLE MEADOW
SA ST HURST
Moot Farm
SAXON MEADOW
PETTICOAT LA

MOOT CL
TWYNHAM CL
Morgan's Vale
MORGANS VALE RD
Sch
PRINCES HILL
KILN LA
PRINCES CL
Redlynch
QUAVEY RD

**21**

SLAB LA
PRIMROSE LA
VICARAGE
THE RIDGE
CHALK
HERBERT RD
ST BRYANS RD
MITCHELLS
CHAPEL LA
HARTHILL DRO

**3**

Church Close Copse
VALE RD
VALLEY CL
GREENS MEAD
Woodfalls Farm
KNUDFORD
CHURCH HILL
Lock's Farm
Lover

Lodge Farm House
Woodfalls
HIGHFIELD LA
The Drove
BESSOMER DRO
SCHOOL RD
SA ST WN S

**20**

Rye Hill Copse
Lodge Copse
Ridge Farm
SPRINGFIELD CRES
LITTLE WOODFALLS
PINE VW
Tinney's Firs
WHITESHOOT
Bohemia

Little Woodfalls Farmhouse
LODGE DRO
WHITESHOOT HILL

Hookers Copse
North Charford
B3080
Whiteshoot Farm

**2**

HATCHET CL
BOHEMIA LA
HALE LA
Cemy
Hatchet Green
CARTERS
TETHERING DRO
FOREST RD

**19**

Home Farm
Sch
Mound

Hale Farm
Hale Park
QUEEN ST
Hale
Folly Drove
Hale Purlieu
MAYS FRS
B3080
Maydene

**1**

**18**

**D**      **E**      **F**

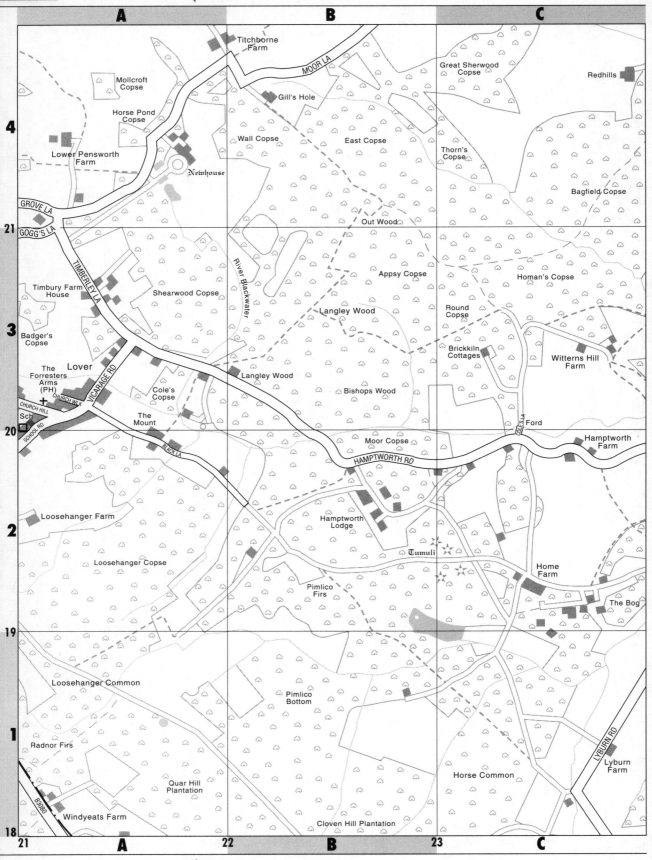

A B C

Titchborne Farm

MOOR LA

Great Sherwood Copse

Redhills

Mollcroft Copse

Gill's Hole

Horse Pond Copse

**4**

Wall Copse

East Copse

Thorn's Copse

Bagfield Copse

Lower Pensworth Farm

Newhouse

GROVE LA

**21**

GOGG'S LA

Out Wood

Appsy Copse

Homan's Copse

River Blackwater

TIMBERLEY LA

Timbury Farm House

Shearwood Copse

Langley Wood

Round Copse

**3**

Badger's Copse

Lover

VICARAGE RD

Langley Wood

Brickkiln Cottages

Witterns Hill Farm

The Forresters Arms (PH)

CHURCH WLK

Cole's Copse

Bishops Wood

CHURCH HILL

Sch

CHURCH HILL

SCHOOL RD

The Mount

BLACK LA

Moor Copse

COLE'S LA

Ford

Hamptworth Farm

**20**

HAMPTWORTH RD

Loosehanger Farm

Hamptworth Lodge

Home Farm

**2**

Loosehanger Copse

Tumuli

The Bog

Pimlico Firs

**19**

Loosehanger Common

Pimlico Bottom

LYBURN RD

**1**

Radnor Firs

Horse Common

Lyburn Farm

B3080

Quar Hill Plantation

Windyeats Farm

Cloven Hill Plantation

**18**

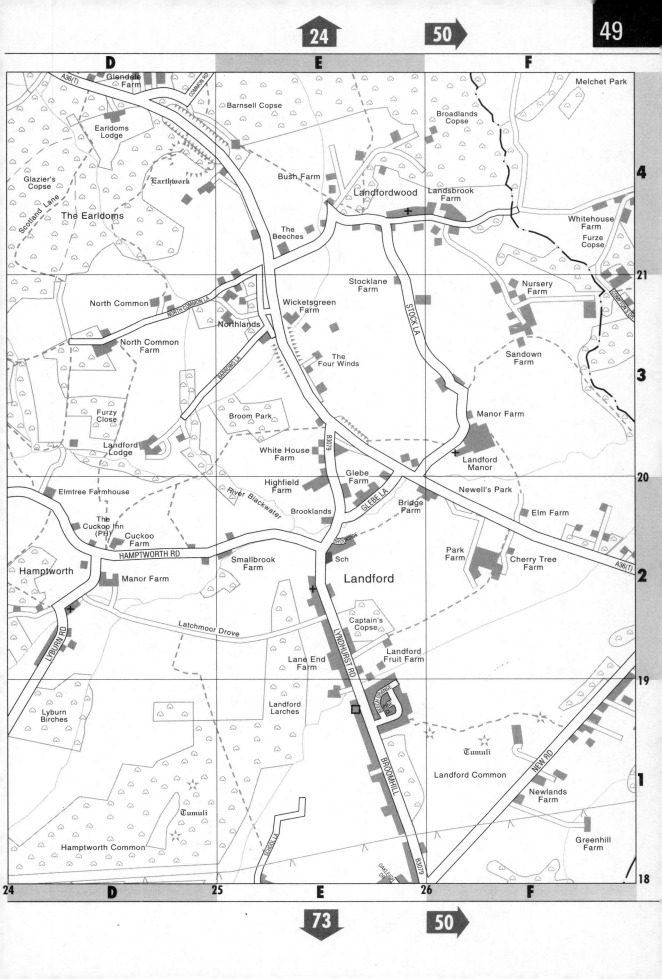

Melchetcourt
Farm

Sherfield
Mill

Dandy's
Ford

DANDY'S FORD LA

Plaitford
Wood

STEPLAKE LA

WELLOW WOOD RD

Wellow
Wood

Boulder Wood

Pilgrim's
Farm

Hazel
Wood

WELLOW DRO

Sinderkerkins
Farm

4

Plaitford
Green

Paddock
Farm

STEPLAKE RD

Yew Tree
Farm

Short's
Farm

BROAD WOODS LA

21

Fielder's
Farm

Cross Oak
Farm

Plaitford
Copse

FLOWERS LA

Gardiner's
Farm

Pinns
Farm

Bowls
Farm

SCALLOWS LA

FOXES LA

COMPTONS DR

New
Lodge

SPOUTS LA

3

Manor
Farm

SHERFIELD ENGLISH LA

Pound Hill

POUND LA

Gauntletts
Farm

Bower's
Farm

Ford

CHURCH LA

King's
Farm

Moat

Lower Bridge
Farm

Ford

River Blackwater

20

GILES LA

TUFT'S LA

Chapman's
Farm

Hatches
Farm

GROVES
DOWN

BOTTOM LA

Bottom Lane
Farm

Long's
Bridge

ROMSEY RD

Pyesmead
Farm

Pembroke
Farm

BARNES LA

BUTTON'S LA

Bridge
Farm

Plaitford

Ford

Redhouse
Farm

MAURY'S LA

SLAB LA

REEVES

Pottery
Farm

West
Wellow

Sch

The Shoe
(PH)

PEARTREE
CL

OLD
COTTAGE CL

MERRY TREE

YEARS DR

GODDARD
CL

2

A36(T)

TICHEY
CL

WARWICK
PL

GAZING LA

COUNTRY
VIEW

Oaklands

OLD FARM
COPSE

NEW RD

Partridge Hill
Farm

PURLEY WAY

SALISBURY RD

BROOKFIELDS

OSBOURNE
CL

NIGHTINGALE
CL

THE BREECHES

SCHOOL RD

LOWER COMMON RD

HOWDEN CL

THE DRONE

Red Rover
(PH)

QUENA'S MEAD

CRAWLEY HILL

19

A36(T)

1

Plaitford Common

Tumulus

West Wellow
Common

CANADA RD

Canada

Chatmohr

Abbotts
Farm

Sturtmoor Pond

ABBOTTS DRO

BLACK HILL
RD

18

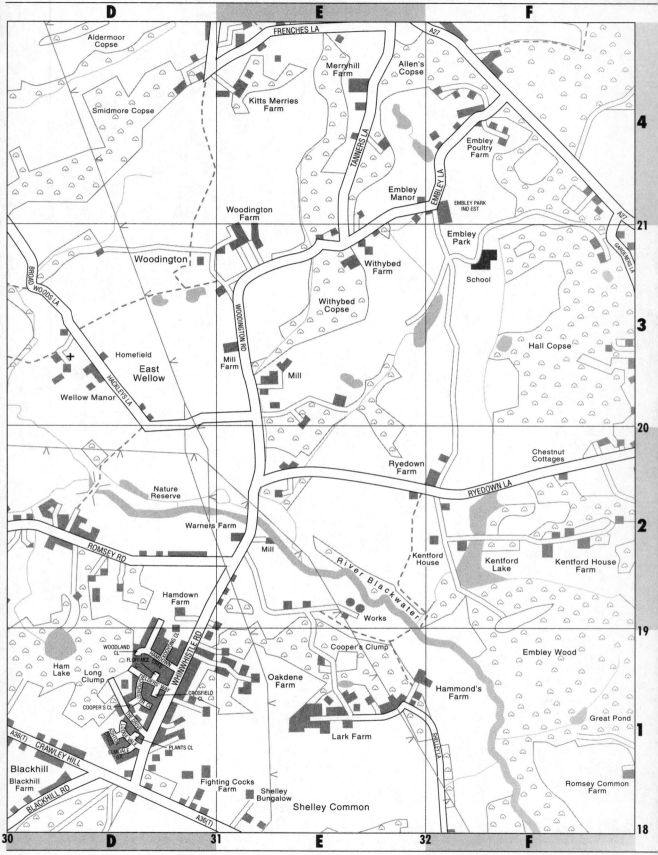

D

Aldermoor
Copse

Smidmore Copse

Kitts Merries
Farm

Merryhill
Farm

Allen's
Copse

A27

4

Embley
Poultry
Farm

TANNERS LA

Woodington
Farm

Embley
Manor

EMBLEY LA

EMBLEY PARK
IND EST

21

Woodington

Withybed
Farm

Embley
Park

School

A27

GARDENERS LA

BROAD
WOODS LA

Withybed
Copse

WOODINGTON RD

3

Hall Copse

Homefield

East
Wellow

Mill
Farm

Mill

HACKLEY'S LA

Wellow Manor

Chestnut
Cottages

20

Nature
Reserve

Ryedown
Farm

RYEDOWN LA

Warners Farm

2

Mill

River Blackwater

Kentford
House

Kentford
Lake

Kentford House
Farm

ROMSEY RD

Hamdown
Farm

Works

19

WHINWHISTLE RD

Cooper's Clump

Embley Wood

Ham
Lake

WOODLAND
CL

FLORENCE CL

Long
Clump

HAMDOWN

RODING'S CL

FIELDERS WAY

COOPER'S CL

THE DRIVE

BEL CL

CROSFIELD
CL

Oakdene
Farm

Hammond's
Farm

Great Pond

1

A36(T)

CRAWLEY HILL

ASHTON
CT

ELMDALE
PARK

ELMDALE
GR

PLANTS CL

Lark Farm

SHELLEY LA

Blackhill

Blackhill
Farm

BLACKHILL RD

Fighting Cocks
Farm

Shelley
Bungalow

Shelley Common

Romsey Common
Farm

A36(T)

18

30
D
31
E
32
F

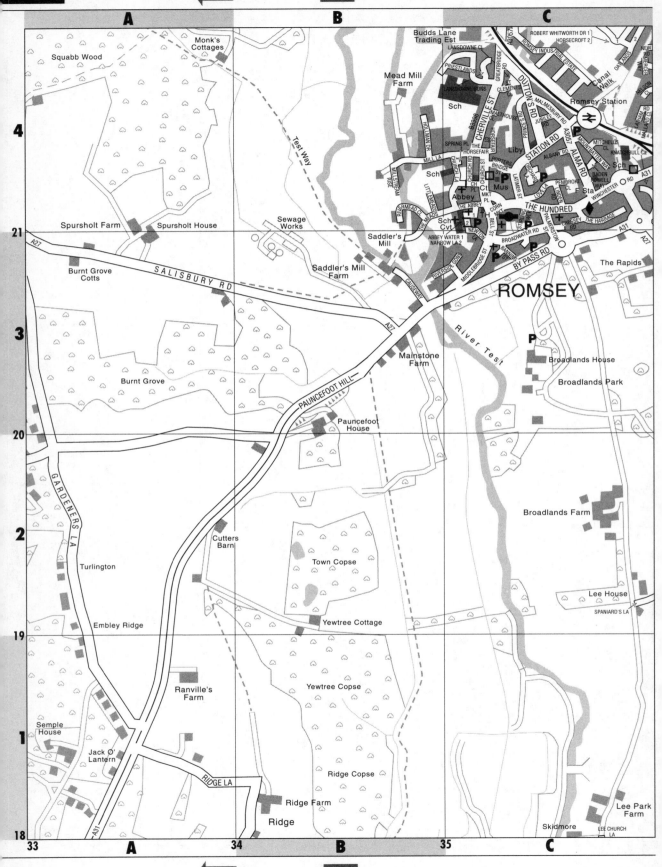

A

B

C

Squabb Wood

Monk's Cottages

**4**

Test Way

Budds Lane Trading Est

LANSDOWNE CL

Mead Mill Farm

ROBERT WHITWORTH DR 1
HORSCROFT 2

ROMSEY INDUSTRIAL ESTATE

Canal Walk

Romsey Station

PRIESTLANDS

GREATBRIDGE RD

DUTTON'S RD

MALMESBURY RD

CLEMENTS

Sch

CHERVILLE ST

MALTHOUSE LA

JUBILEE

A3057

STATION RD

ALMA RD

NELSON CL

NEW RD

A31

MITCHELLS CL

KNATCHBULL CL

BADEN POWELL WAY

Sch

SPRING PL

THE HORSEFAIR

MILL LA

CHURCH ST

HORSEFAIR

ALBANY RD

MOUNTBATTEN WAY

Liby

CHURCH LA

PORTERS

Sch

BRIDGE

LATIMER ST

P

P

PEMBROKE CL

LOVE L

LOADER

WINCHESTER RD

F Sta

A31

MILLSTREAM RISE

Abbey

LITTLEFIELDS

THE ABBEY

THE MEADS

MKT PL

Ct

Mus

MKT

CORN

BELL ST

BANNING

THE HUNDRED

PALMERSTON

CHERSEY RD

THE HARRAGE

**21**

Spursholt Farm

Spursholt House

Sewage Works

Saddler's Mill

Sch

2

ABBEY WATER 1
NARROW LA 2

BROADWATER RD

RIVERSIDE GDNS

MIDDLEBRIDGE ST

NEWTON

BY PASS RD

A31

A27

A27

Burnt Grove Cotts

SALISBURY RD

Saddler's Mill Farm

CAUSEWAY

RIVERSIDE GDNS

**ROMSEY**

The Rapids

**3**

Burnt Grove

A27

Mainstone Farm

River Test

Broadlands House

P

Broadlands Park

PAUNCEFOOT HILL

Pauncefoot House

**20**

GARDENERS LA

Broadlands Farm

**2**

Cutters Barn

Turlington

Town Copse

Lee House

SPANIARD'S LA

Embley Ridge

Yewtree Cottage

**19**

Ranville's Farm

Yewtree Copse

Semple House

Jack O' Lantern

**1**

RIDGE LA

Ridge Copse

A31

Ridge Farm

Ridge

Lee Park Farm

Skidmore

LEE CHURCH LA

**18**

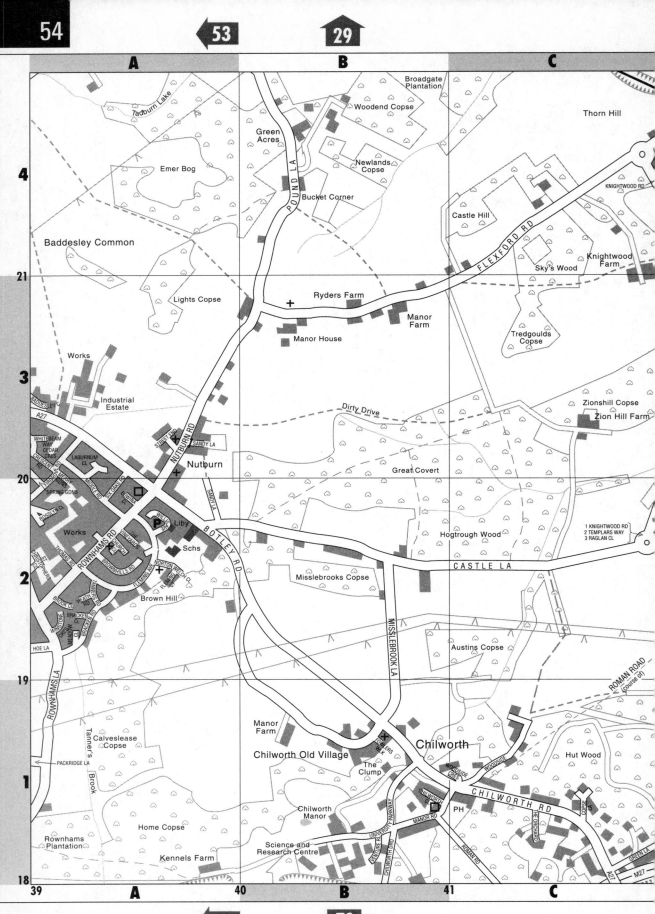

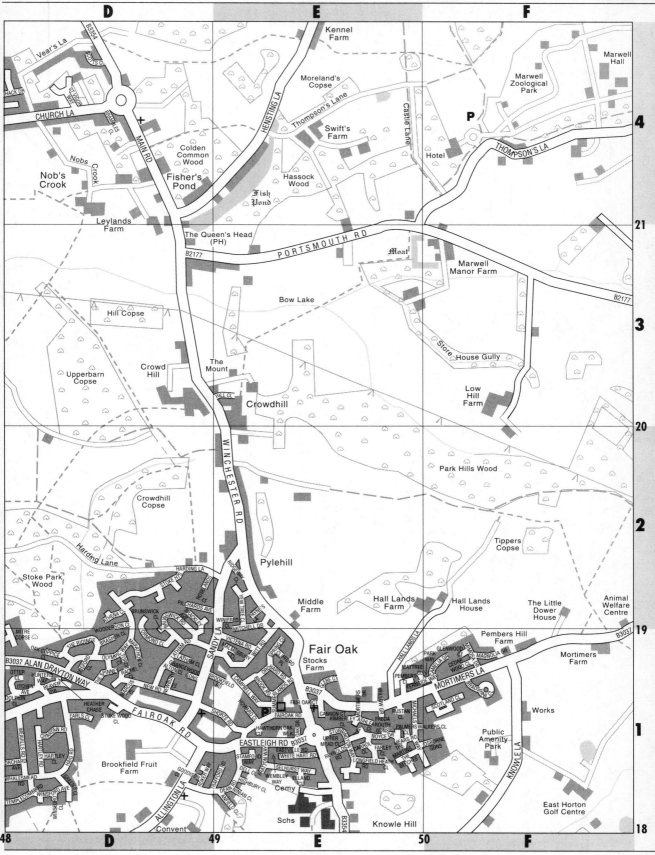

D

B3354

Vear's La

HACK DR

ST GILLES CL

SCOTTS CL

CHURCH LA

Nobs Crook

Nob's Crook

Leylands Farm

MAIN RD

BRAMBLES CL

Colden Common Wood

Fisher's Pond

Kennel Farm

Moreland's Copse

Thompson's Lane

Swift's Farm

HENSTING LA

Hassock Wood

Fish Pond

Castle Lane

Marwell Zoological Park

Marwell Hall

P

Hotel

THOMPSON'S LA

4

The Queen's Head (PH)

B2177

PORTSMOUTH RD

Moat

Marwell Manor Farm

21

B2177

Hill Copse

Bow Lake

Store House Gully

3

Upperbarn Copse

Crowd Hill

The Mount

HILL CL

Crowdhill

Low Hill Farm

Park Hills Wood

20

Crowdhill Copse

WINCHESTER RD

Harding Lane

HARDING LA

Pylehill

RIDGE WAY

PAW TREE CL

ROSE ARBS

Tippers Copse

The Little Dower House

Animal Welfare Centre

2

Stoke Park Wood

STOKE HEY

WINIFRED RD

MITCHELL DR

VICTENA RD

WILT RD

Middle Farm

Hall Lands Farm

Hall Lands House

Pembers Hill Farm

B3037

Mortimers Farm

19

MITRE COPSE

OAK COPPICE

THE RIDING

BRASHER CL

BRUNSWICK CL

BRUNSWICK RD

PACKLE

PILCHARDS AVE

WOODDERSON CL

ATHENA CL

OLYMPIC WAY

THE SPINNEY

RACHEL

LATHAM CL

ORMOND CL

GRANGEWOOD GDNS

ALTON CL

SANDY LA

NEW RD

BROOKFIELD CL

CAMPBELL WAY

MALMSBURY

GIFFORD

NORTHERN RD

PAYNE'S

LABURNUM

STANLES RD

Fair Oak

Stocks Farm

GLEBE CT

GLENWOOD

PARK WAY

AMELIA CL

CEDAR

MAGNOLIA GR

MAYTREE

PEMBERS CL

HALL LANDS LA

MICHAELS

SCOTLAND CL

BRADSON CL

Works

B3037 ALAN DRAYTON WAY

OTTER CL

HUNTER'S WAY

BEAVER CL

DOLPHIN CL

WEAVILLS RD

CHARIER RD

EARLS CL

HEATHER CHASE

STOKE WOOD CL

SHORTS RD

FAIROAK RD

P

FAIROAK RD

CANNON CL

KIMBERLEY CL

NOYCE DR

MORTIMERS

WILLOW GR

RUSTAN CL

FREDA ROUTH GDNS

ASHLEY

PALMERS WALKERS CL

OSBORNE GDNS

Public Amenity Park

KNOWLE LA

1

ORCHARD AVE

WHALESMEAD

TEMPLECOMBE

HAIN RD

HARTLEY

WINSFORD AVE

FAIROAK RD

GOODISON CL

BECKHAM LA

FREEFORD

ALLINGTON LA

Brookfield Fruit Farm

EASTLEIGH RD

STAMFORD WAY

DELL CL

HIGHBURY CL

WEMBLEY WAY

DEAN RD

VINIAN CL

ANFIELD CL

HAWTHORN OAK WLK

OAK WLK

WHITE HART RD

EASTVILLE RD

FENTON WAY

SELHURST WAY

Cemy

UPPER MEAD CL

B3037

STUBBINGTON WAY

REYNOLDS RD

CARROLL

FARLEY CL

LONGFIELD HEATH RD

YEARS RD

THE BEECHES

East Horton Golf Centre

Convent

Schs

B3354

Knowle Hill

48

D

49

E

50

F

18

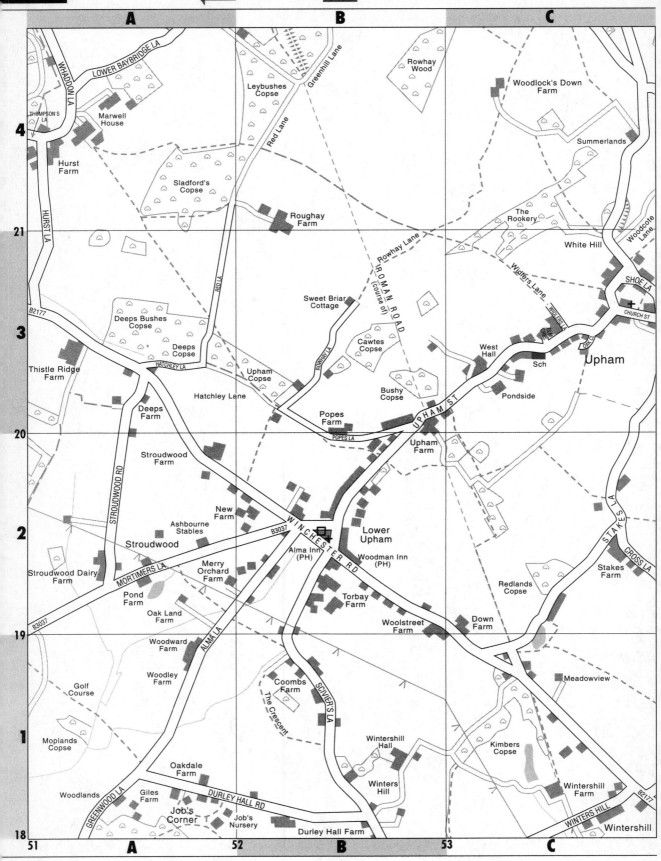

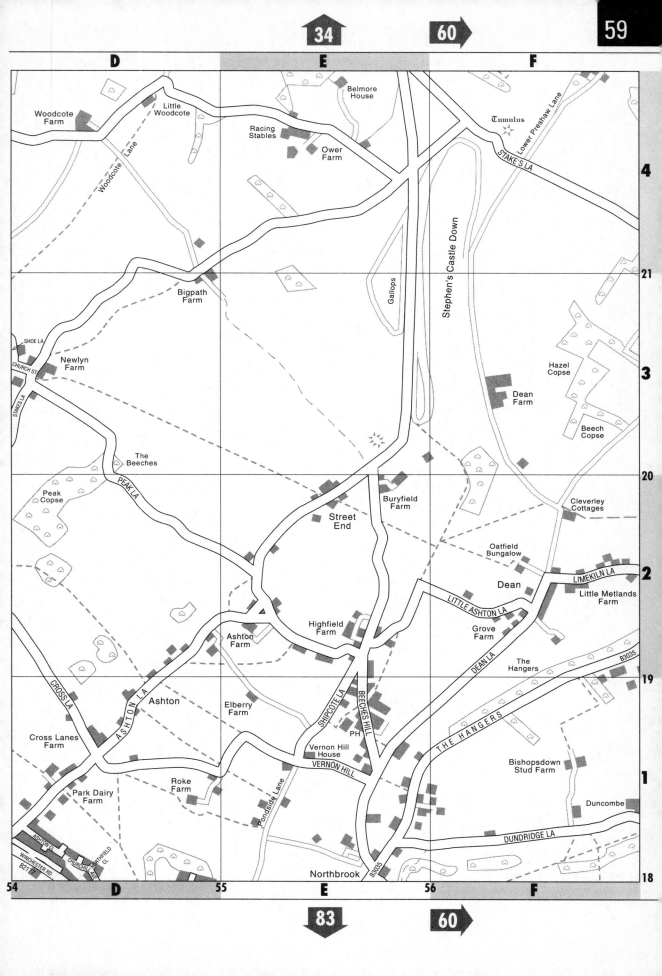

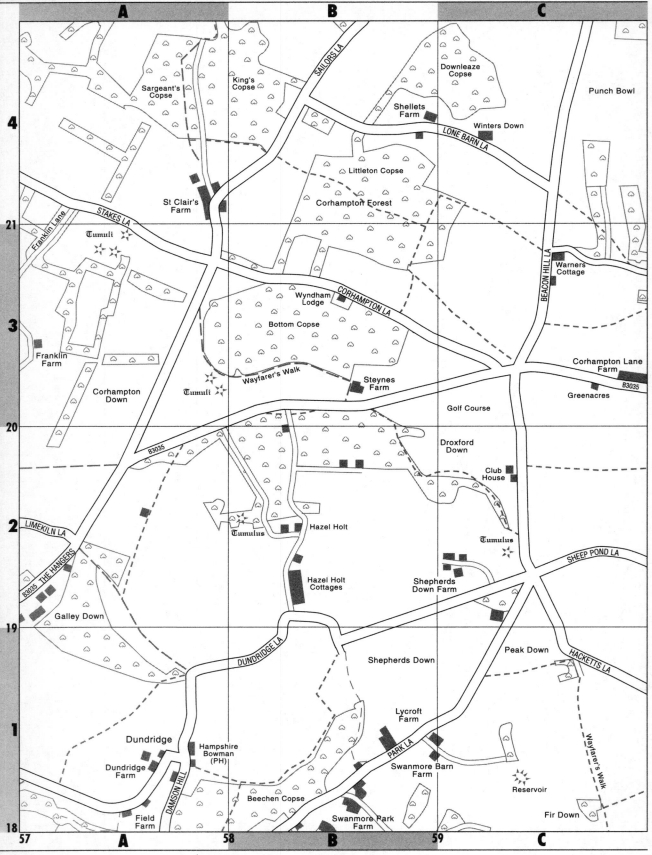

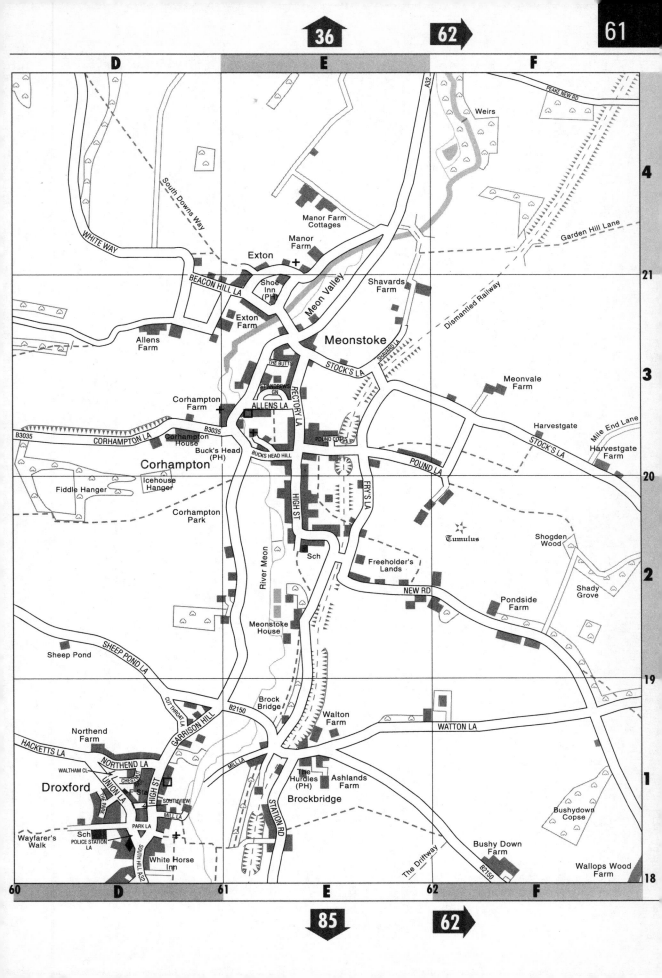

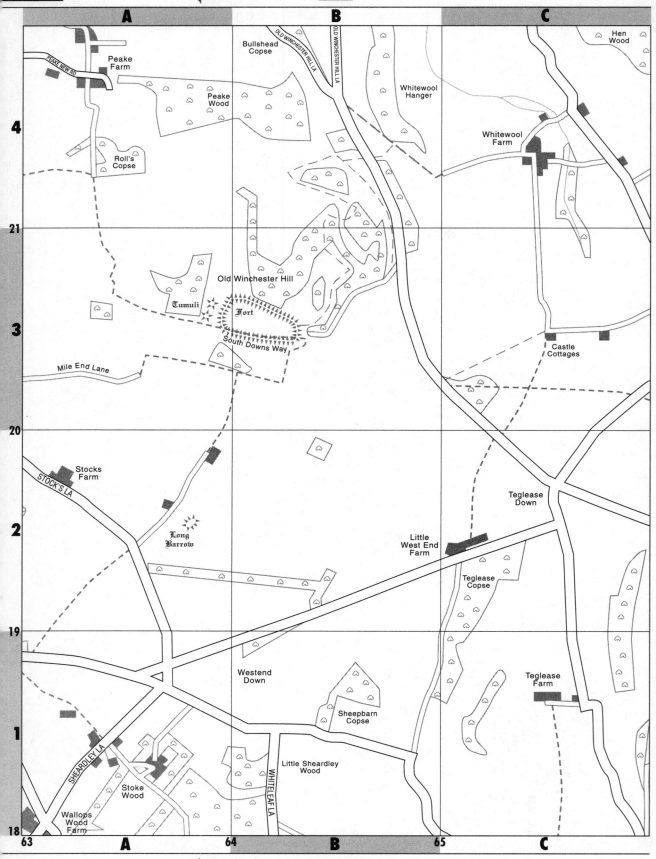

**A** **B** **C**

Hen Wood

Peake New Rd

Bullshead Copse

OLD WINCHESTER HILL LA

OLD WINCHESTER HILL LA

Peake Farm

Whitewool Hanger

Peake Wood

Whitewool Farm

**4**

Roll's Copse

**21**

Old Winchester Hill

Tumuli

Fort

Castle Cottages

**3**

South Downs Way

Mile End Lane

**20**

Stocks Farm

STOCK'S LA

Teglease Down

**2**

Long Barrow

Little West End Farm

Teglease Copse

**19**

Westend Down

Teglease Farm

Sheepbarn Copse

**1**

SHEARDLEY LA

WHITELEAF LA

Little Sheardley Wood

Stoke Wood

Wallops Wood Farm

**18**

**63** **A** **64** **B** **65** **C**

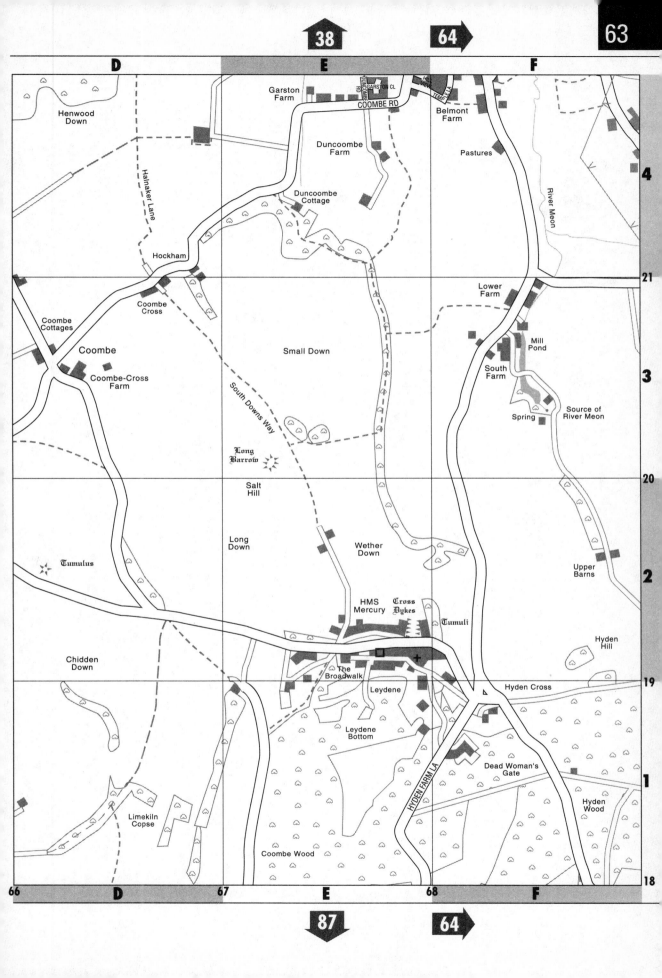

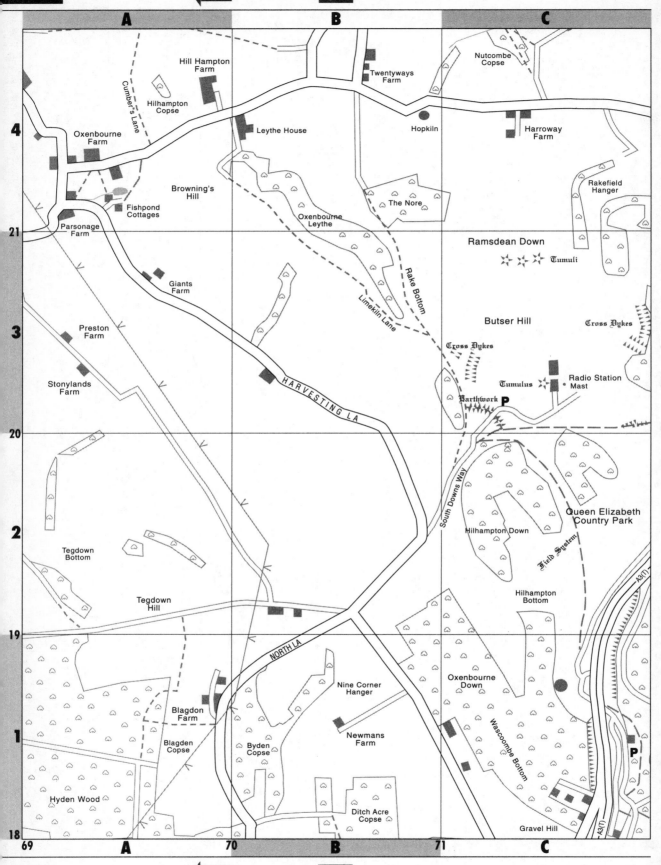

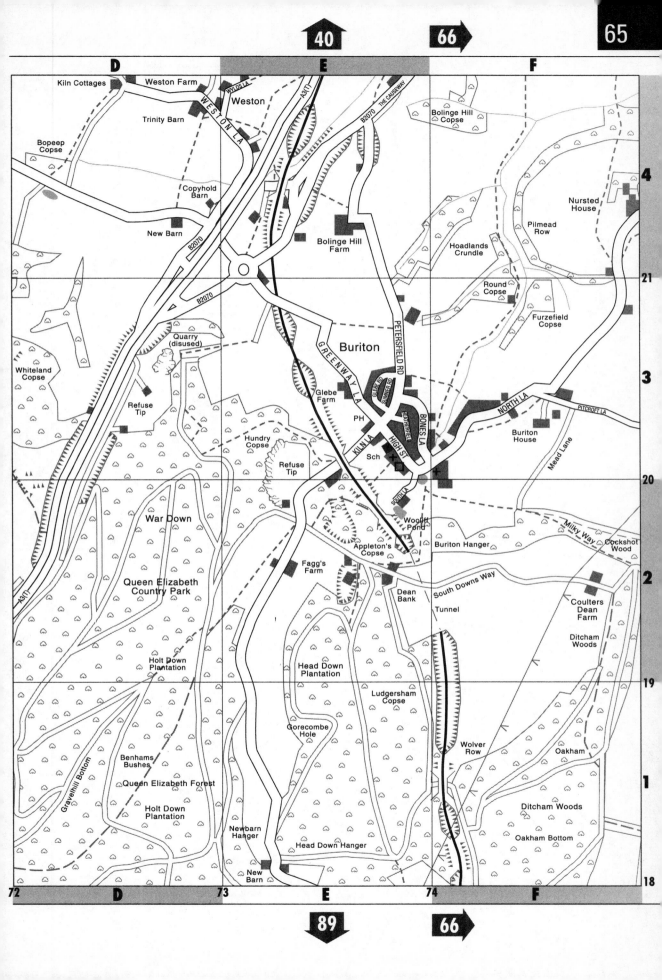

D          E          F

Kiln Cottages   Weston Farm

Weston

WESTON LA

WYLDS LA

A3(T)

B2070   THE CAUSEWAY

Bolinge Hill Copse

Trinity Barn

Bopeep Copse

Copyhold Barn

Bolinge Hill Farm

Nursted House

Pilmead Row

Hoadlands Crundle

New Barn

B2070

4

21

Round Copse

Furzefield Copse

Whiteland Copse

Quarry (disused)

GREENWAY LA

Buriton

PETERSFIELD RD

Refuse Tip

Glebe Farm

GLEBE RD

SUMMER RD

NORTH LA

PITCROFT LA

Buriton House

Mead Lane

3

PH

KILN LA

HEATHER RD

BONES LA

HIGH ST

Sch

Hundry Copse

Refuse Tip

SOUTH LA

20

War Down

Woolff Pond

Milky Way

Cockshot Wood

Buriton Hanger

A3(T)

Queen Elizabeth Country Park

Fagg's Farm

Appleton's Copse

South Downs Way

Dean Bank

Tunnel

Coulters Dean Farm

Ditcham Woods

2

Holt Down Plantation

Head Down Plantation

Ludgersham Copse

19

Gravelhill Bottom

Gorecombe Hole

Wolver Row

Oakham

Benhams Bushes

Queen Elizabeth Forest

Ditcham Woods

1

Holt Down Plantation

Newbarn Hanger

Oakham Bottom

Head Down Hanger

New Barn

18

72          D          73          E          74          F

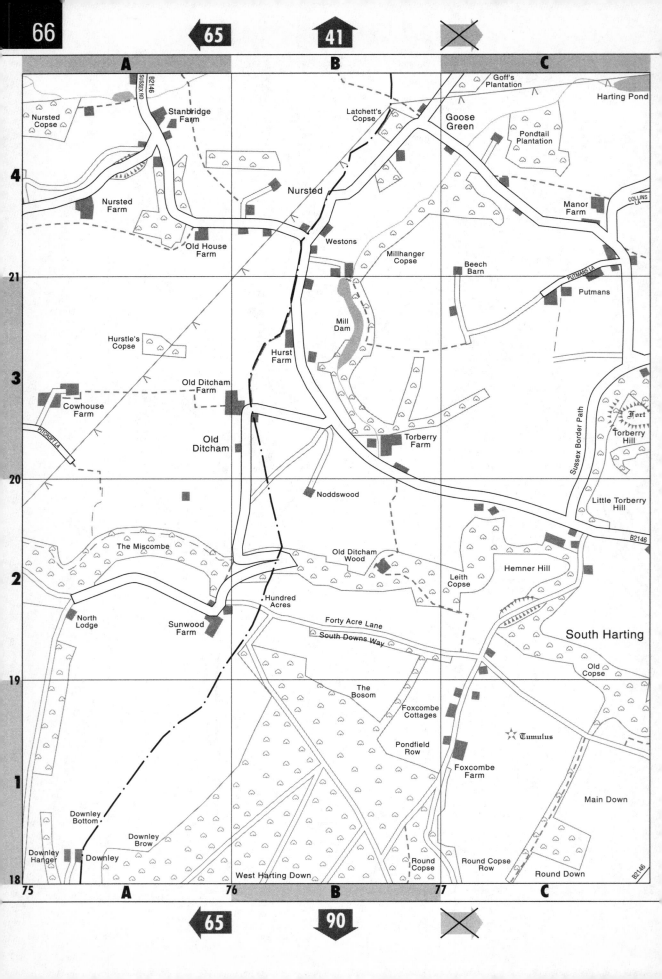

Nursted Copse

Stanbridge Farm

Nursted Farm

Old House Farm

Latchett's Copse

Goose Green

Goff's Plantation

Harting Pond

Pondtail Plantation

B2146

SUSSEX RD

Nursted

Westons

Millhanger Copse

Manor Farm

COLLINS LA

Beech Barn

PUTMANS LA

Putmans

Hurstle's Copse

Mill Dam

Hurst Farm

Old Ditcham Farm

Cowhouse Farm

PIGCROFT LA

Old Ditcham

Torberry Farm

Sussex Border Path

Fort

Torberry Hill

Noddswood

Little Torberry Hill

The Miscombe

Old Ditcham Wood

Leith Copse

Hemner Hill

B2146

North Lodge

Sunwood Farm

Hundred Acres

Forty Acre Lane

South Downs Way

South Harting

Old Copse

The Bosom

Foxcombe Cottages

Pondfield Row

Foxcombe Farm

Tumulus

Main Down

Downley Bottom

Downley Brow

Downley Hanger

Downley

Round Copse

West Harting Down

Round Copse Row

Round Down

B2146

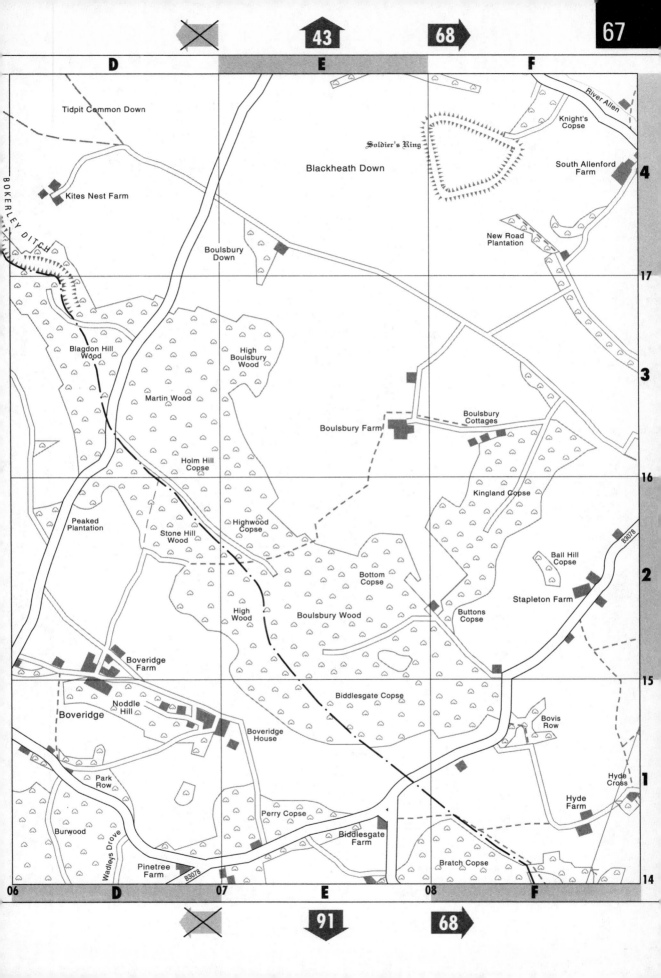

43
68

D
E
F

River Allen

Tidpit Common Down

Knight's Copse

Soldier's Ring

Blackheath Down

South Allenford Farm

4

BOKERLEY DITCH

Kites Nest Farm

New Road Plantation

Boulsbury Down

17

Blagdon Hill Wood

High Boulsbury Wood

3

Martin Wood

Boulsbury Cottages

Boulsbury Farm

Holm Hill Copse

16

Kingland Copse

Peaked Plantation

Highwood Copse

Stone Hill Wood

Ball Hill Copse

B3078

Bottom Copse

2

Stapleton Farm

High Wood

Boulsbury Wood

Buttons Copse

Boveridge Farm

15

Biddlesgate Copse

Noddle Hill

Bovis Row

Boveridge

Boveridge House

Park Row

Hyde Cross

1

Hyde Farm

Burwood

Wadleys Drove

Perry Copse

Biddlesgate Farm

Bratch Copse

Pinetree Farm

B3078

06
D
07
E
08
F
14

91
68

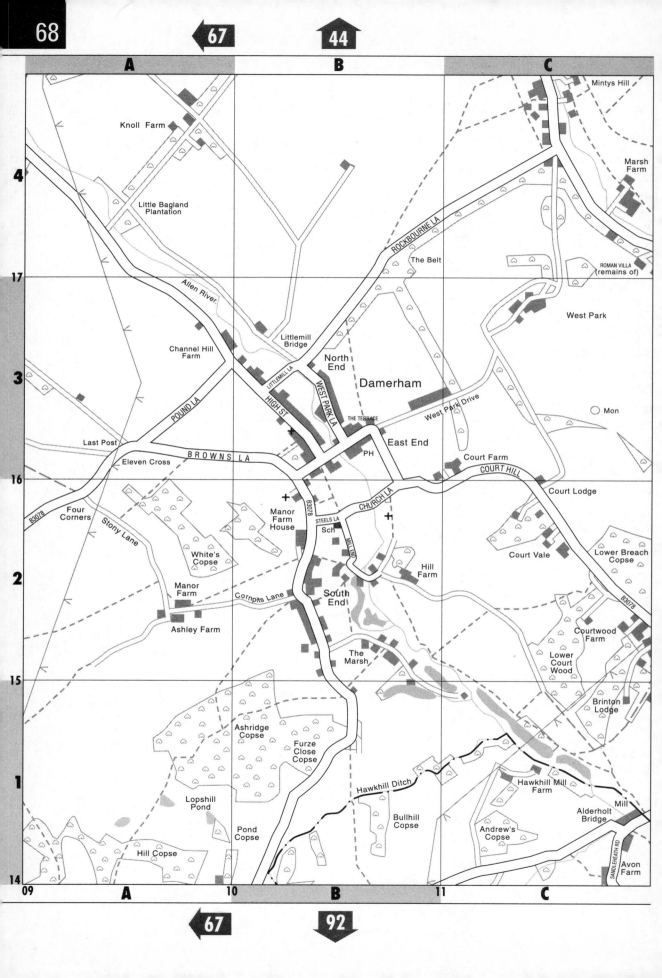

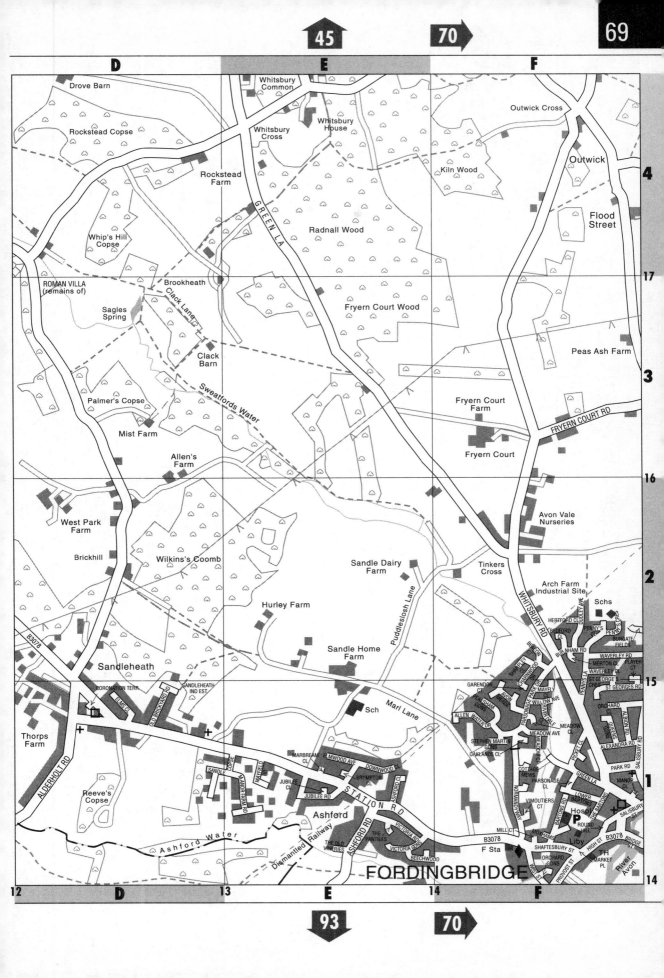

D E F

**4**

**17**

**3**

**16**

**2**

**15**

**1**

**14**

Drove Barn

Rockstead Copse

Whitsbury Common

Whitsbury Cross

Whitsbury House

Outwick Cross

Outwick

Rockstead Farm

Kiln Wood

Flood Street

Whip's Hill Copse

GREEN LA

Radnall Wood

ROMAN VILLA (remains of)

Brookheath

Clack Lane

Fryern Court Wood

Peas Ash Farm

Sagles Spring

Clack Barn

Palmer's Copse

Sweatfords Water

Fryern Court Farm

FRYERN COURT RD

Mist Farm

Fryern Court

Allen's Farm

West Park Farm

Brickhill

Wilkins's Coomb

Sandle Dairy Farm

Tinkers Cross

Avon Vale Nurseries

Arch Farm Industrial Site

Hurley Farm

Schs

WHITSBURY RD

HERTFORD CL

PENNY'S CL

PENNY'S CRES

BURGATE FIELDS

B3078

Sandleheath

Sandle Home Farm

Puddleslosh Lane

BURNHAM RD

WAVERLEY RD

MERTON CL

WAVERLEY CL

PLAYER CT

ST GEORGE'S CRES

ST GEORGES RD

GARENDON CT

CHARNWOOD

MAYELY

SHATTLE CL

AVON RD

WILLOW AVE

ORCHARD GDNS

ALBION RD

QUEENS GDNS

ALEXANDRA RD

SANDLEHEATH IND EST

CORONATION TERR

ELMS CL

OLD BRICKYARD RD

Sch

Marl Lane

PEASHAM GDNS

ALLEN WATER DR

MEADOW CL

MEADOW AVE

STEPHEN MARTIN GDNS

OAKLANDS CL

COTTAGE MEWS

PARSONAGE CL

GREEN LA

PICKET LA

ORCHARD GDNS

PARK RD

MANOR CL

SALISBURY RD

Thorps Farm

ALDERHOLT RD

Reeve's Copse

SANDLE CRES

MAYFIELD

NANDKE FARM RD

MARBREAM CL

ELMWOOD AVE

JUBILEE CL

JUBILEE RD

BRYMPTON CL

DOWNWOOD

ASHFORD CL

STATION RD

VIMOUTIERS CT

NORMANDY WAY

LOWER BARTONS

BARTONS RD

VICTORIA RD

BEECHWOOD

HIGHAMS CL

MILL CT

Hosp

ROUND HILL

P

Liby

HIGH ST

B3078

BRIDGE ST

River Avon

Ashford

Ashford Water

Dismantled Railway

THE OLD VINERIES

THE PANTILES

VICTORIA GDNS

B3078

F Sta

SHAFTESBURY ST

PROVOST ST

WEST ST

MARKET PL

TH

**FORDINGBRIDGE**

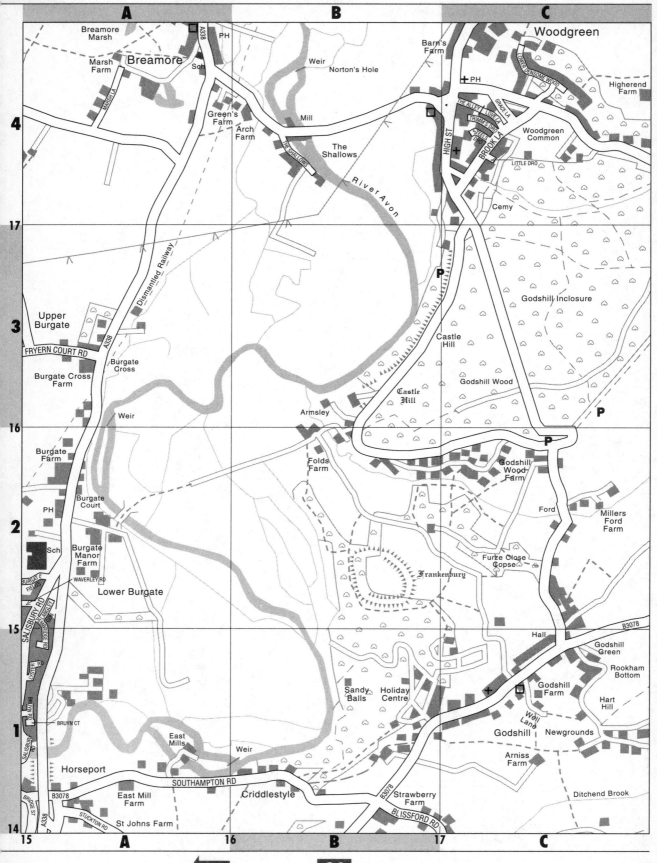

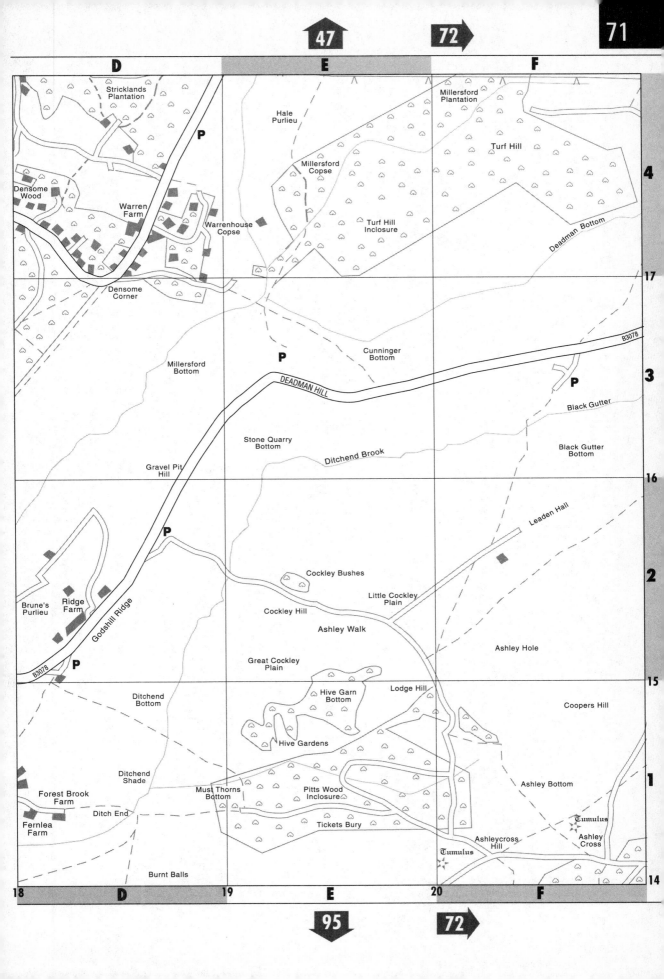

D E F

**Stricklands Plantation**

P

**Densome Wood**

**Warren Farm**

**Warrenhouse Copse**

**Densome Corner**

**Millersford Bottom**

P

**Millersford Plantation**

**Hale Purlieu**

**Millersford Copse**

**Turf Hill**

**Turf Hill Inclosure**

**Deadman Bottom**

4

17

**Cunninger Bottom**

B3078

P

3

**DEADMAN HILL**

**Stone Quarry Bottom**

**Black Gutter**

**Gravel Pit Hill**

**Ditchend Brook**

**Black Gutter Bottom**

16

**Leaden Hall**

**Cockley Bushes**

2

**Brune's Purlieu**

**Ridge Farm**

**Little Cockley Plain**

**Cockley Hill**

**Godshill Ridge**

**Ashley Walk**

**Ashley Hole**

P

B3078

P

**Great Cockley Plain**

15

**Lodge Hill**

**Ditchend Bottom**

**Hive Garn Bottom**

**Coopers Hill**

**Hive Gardens**

**Ditchend Shade**

1

**Forest Brook Farm**

**Must Thorns Bottom**

**Pitts Wood Inclosure**

**Ashley Bottom**

**Ditch End**

**Fernlea Farm**

**Tickets Bury**

𝕿umulus

**Ashley Cross**

**Ashleycross Hill**

𝕿umulus

**Burnt Balls**

14

18 D 19 E 20 F

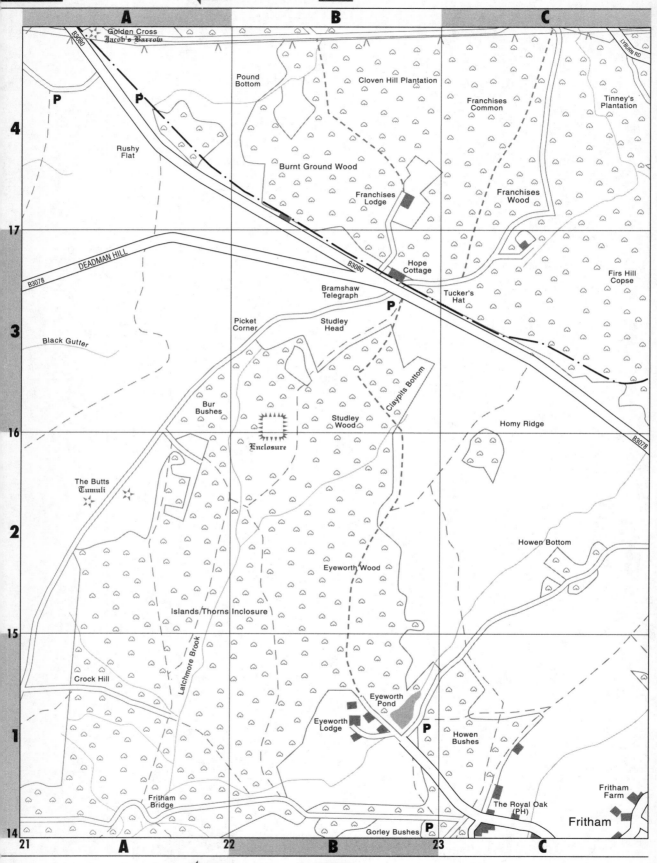

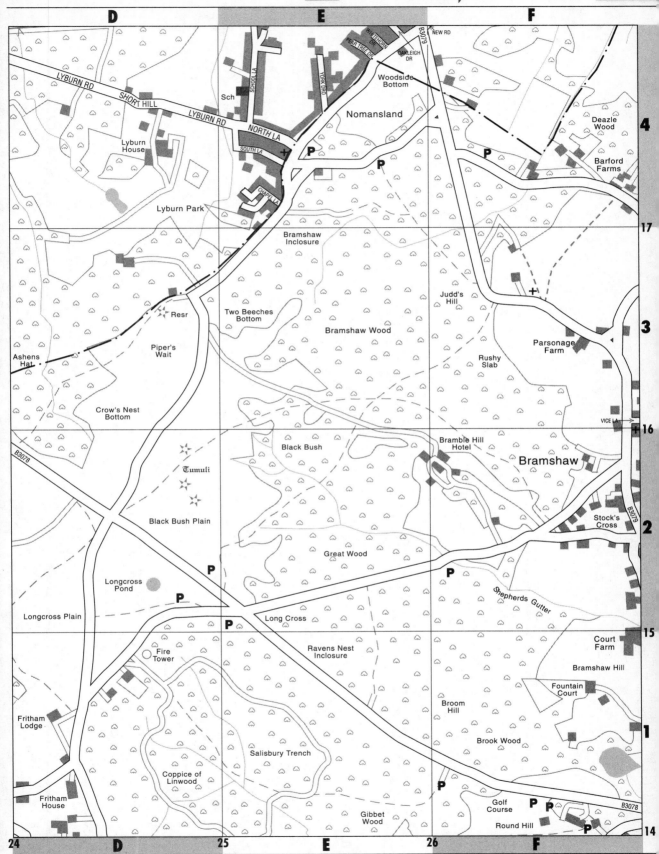

D     E     F

LYBURN RD

SHORT HILL

LYBURN RD

NORTH LA

SOUTH LA

SCHOOL LA

YORK GRO

PEAR TREE DR

WILTSHIRE DR

OAKLEIGH DR

B3079

NEW RD

Woodside Bottom

Nomansland

Deazle Wood

Barford Farms

Sch

Lyburn House

CHAPEL LA

Lyburn Park

**4**

Bramshaw Inclosure

**17**

Resr

Two Beeches Bottom

Bramshaw Wood

Judd's Hill

Parsonage Farm

Piper's Wait

Ashens Hat

Rushy Slab

**3**

Crow's Nest Bottom

VICE LA

**16**

Tumuli

Black Bush

Bramble Hill Hotel

Bramshaw

Black Bush Plain

B3078

Stock's Cross

B3079

**2**

Longcross Pond

Great Wood

Shepherds Gutter

Longcross Plain

Long Cross

**15**

Court Farm

Fire Tower

Ravens Nest Inclosure

Bramshaw Hill

Fountain Court

Fritham Lodge

Broom Hill

Brook Wood

**1**

Salisbury Trench

Coppice of Linwood

Golf Course

B3078

Fritham House

Gibbet Wood

Round Hill

**14**

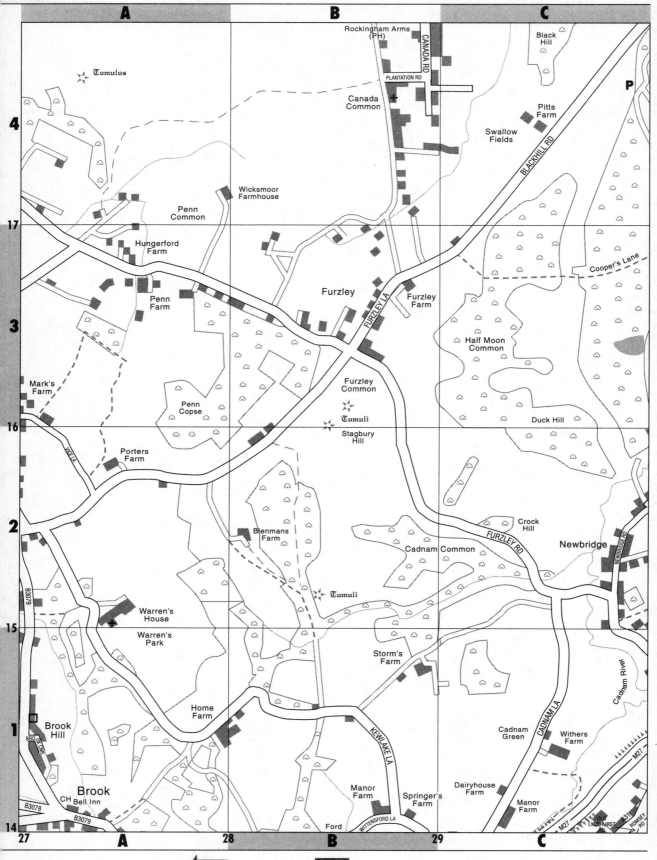

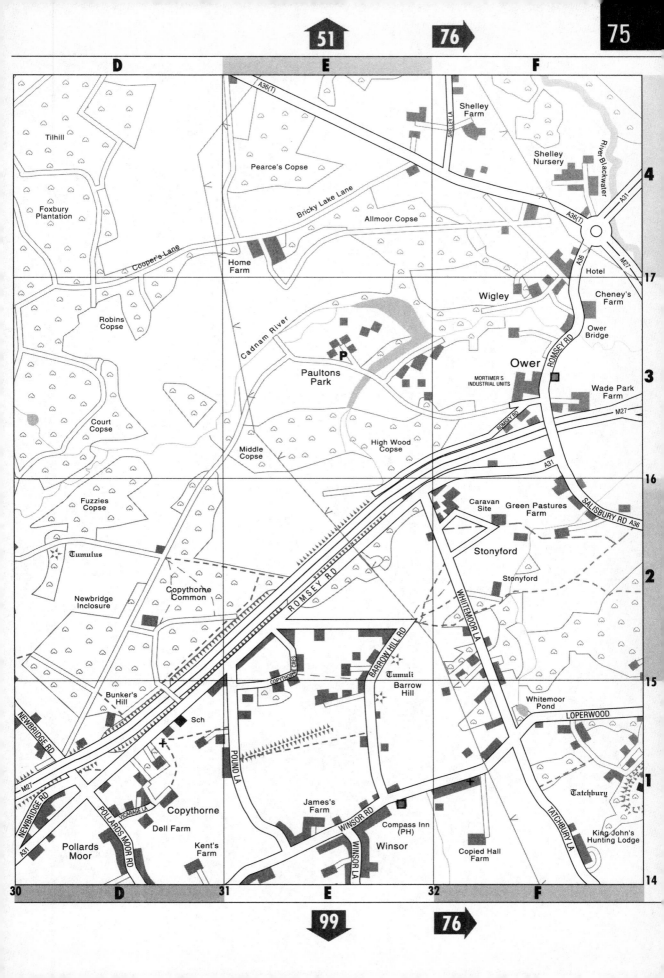

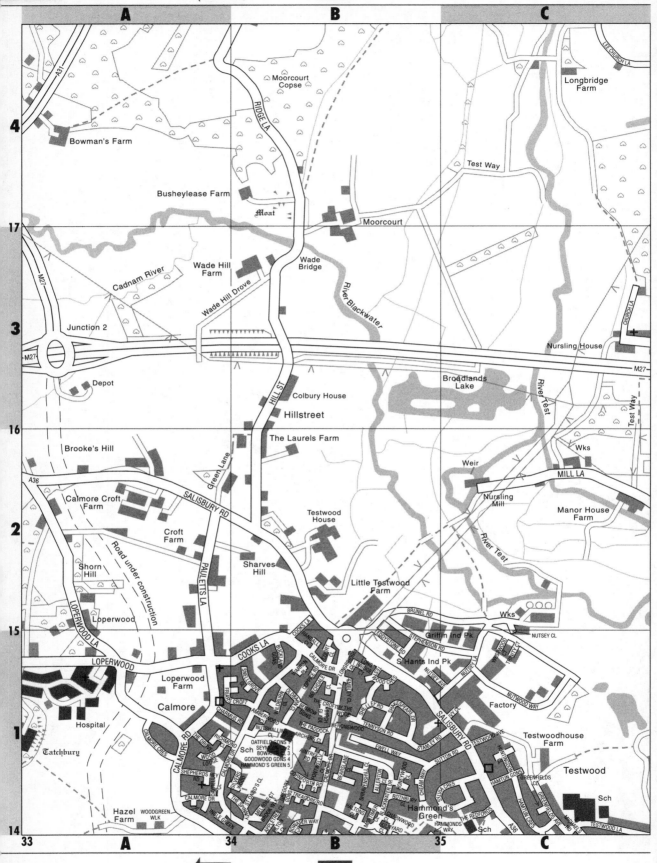

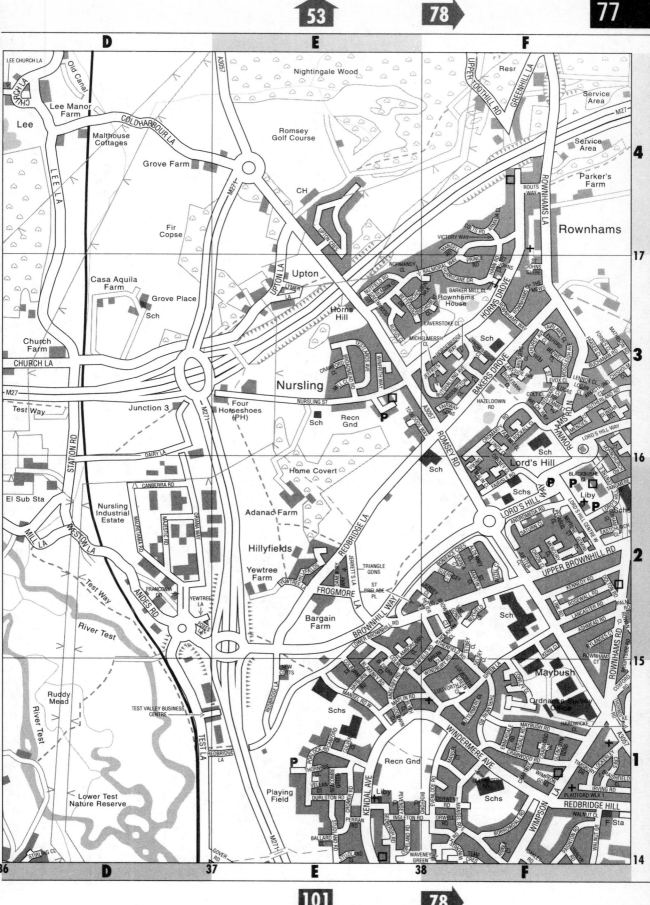

D
E
F

LEE CHURCH LA
Old Canal
Lee Manor Farm
Lee
CHURCH LA
Malthouse Cottages
COLDHARBOUR LA
Grove Farm
CH
Nightingale Wood
Romsey Golf Course
A3057
M27
LEE LA
Resr
UPPER TOOTHILL RD
GREENHILL LA
M27
Service Area
Service Area
Parker's Farm
Rownhams
ROWNHAMS LA

4

Casa Aquila Farm
Fir Copse
Grove Place
Sch
UPTON LA
Upton
LYMER LA
Horns Hill
UPTON CRES
Victory Way
ST JOHNS GLEBE
THE MEWS
HORNS DROVE
Rownhams House
Sch

17

Church Farm
CHURCH LA
M27
Test Way
STATION RD
Junction 3
Four Horseshoes (PH)
Nursling
NURSLING ST
Sch
Recn Gnd
P
Sch
BAKERS DROVE
ROMSEY RD
A3057
HAZELDOWN RD
Sch
Lord's Hill
Schs
LORD'S HILL WAY
Sch
BLACKBUSHE CL
Liby
P
P
P
Schs
LORD'S HILL CENTRE W
ROWNHAMS RD

3

16

El Sub Sta
DAIRY LA
CANBERRA RD
Nursling Industrial Estate
MAURETANIA RD
ORIANA WAY
MAJESTIC RD
M27
Home Covert
Adanac Farm
REDBRIDGE LA
Hillyfields
Yewtree Farm
FROGMORE LA
TRIANGLE GDNS
ST BRELADE PL
JERRETT'S LA
DANE DRV
YEW CLOS
YEWTREE LA
BROWNHILL WAY
UPPER BROWNHILL RD
Sch
KENNEDY RD
ROSEWALL RD
LANCASTER RD
ASHMEAD RD
ANDROMEDA RD
SATURN CL
EASTCHURCH CL

2

MILL LA
WESTON LA
ANDES RD
Test Way
FRANCONIA DR
YEWTREE LA
FOXES LA
River Test
Bargain Farm
LOWER BROWNHILL RD
WINDERMERE AVE
Schs
MANSEL RD W
LINDWORTH
GREEN LA
Maybush
Ordnance Survey Office
HARDWICKE

15

Ruddy Mead
River Test
TEST LA
REDBRIDGE LA
NEW COTTS
TEST VALLEY BUSINESS CENTRE
Recn Gnd
Schs
KENDAL AVE
Liby
Playing Field
MAYBUSH RD
WIMPSON
REDBRIDGE HILL
F Sta

1

Lower Test Nature Reserve
STIRLING CL
GOVER RD
M271
REDBRIDGE LA
Thorness
VELLAN CT
SEACOMBE GREEN
DURLSTON RD
PORLOCK RD
CRANFORD
CONISTON RD
PERRAN RD
BALLARD
SILKLAND CL
COPELAND RD
INGLETON RD
WAVENEY GREEN
WIMPSON

14

36
37
38

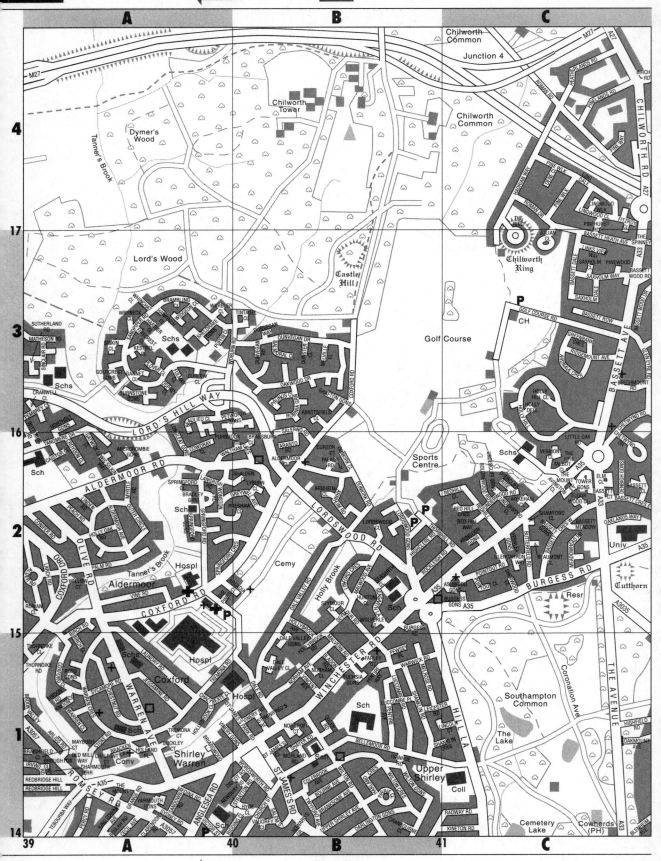

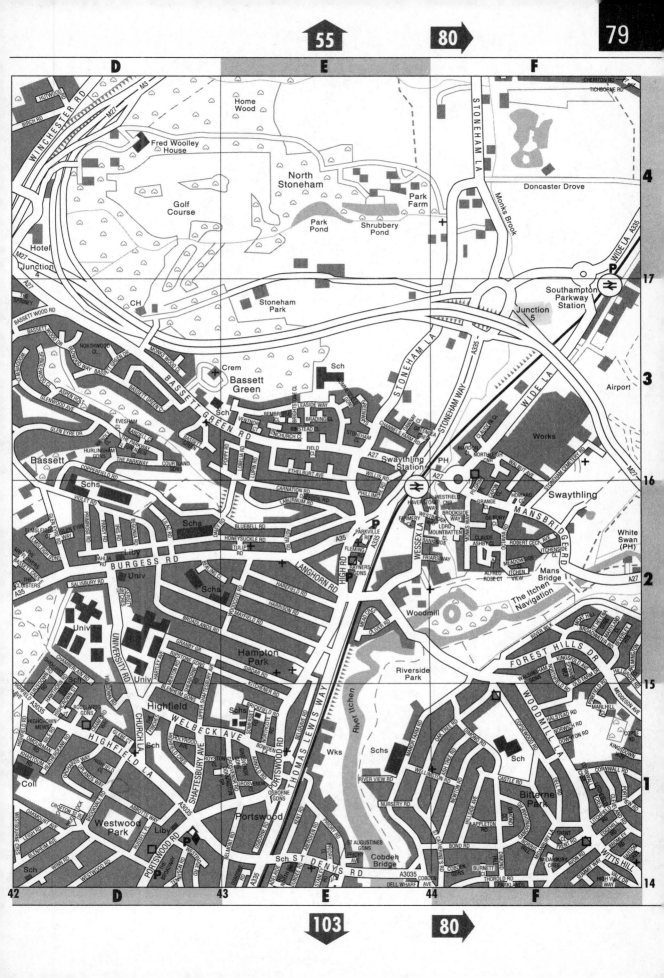

79 56

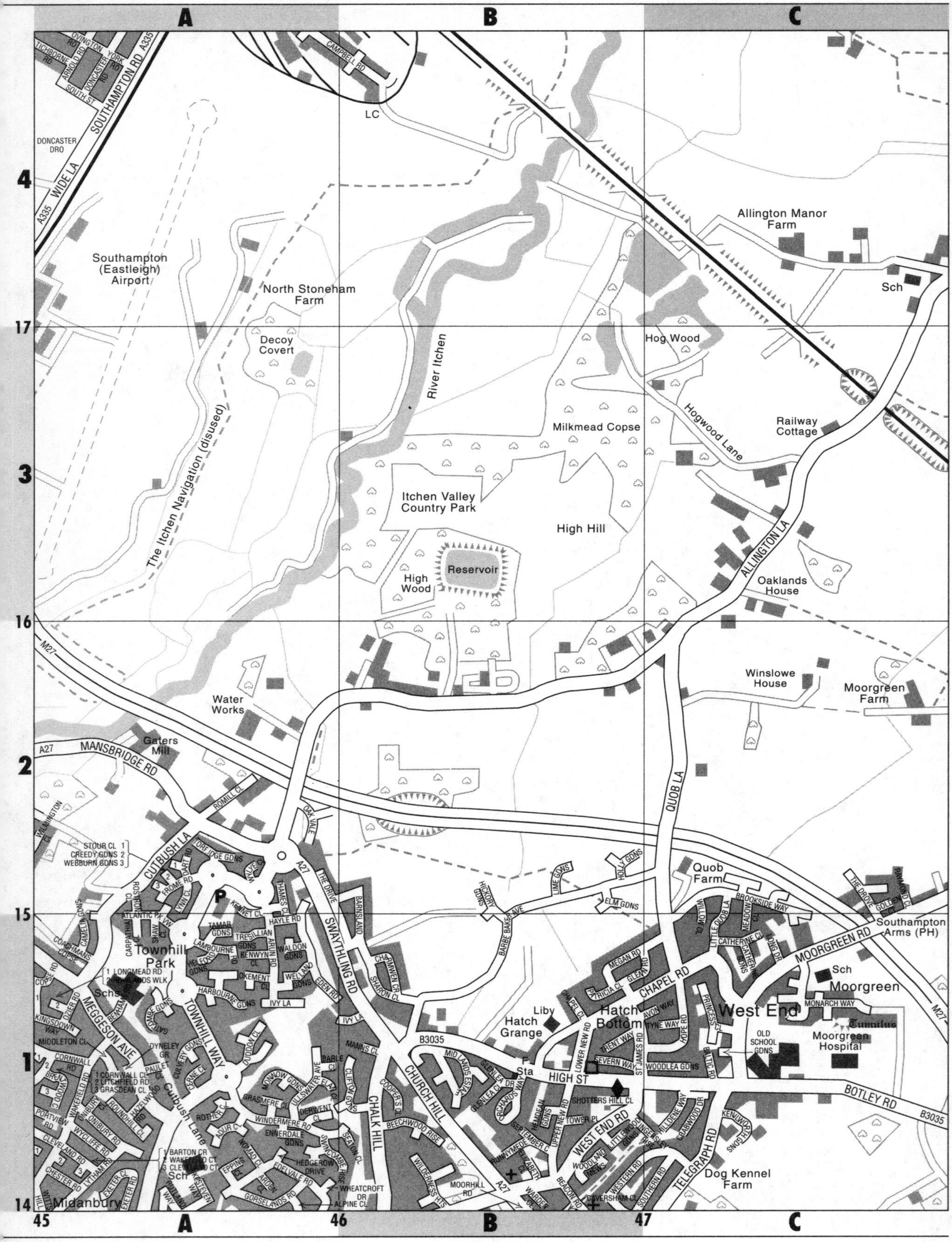

A  B  C

4

DONCASTER DRO

Southampton
(Eastleigh)
Airport

North Stoneham
Farm

Allington Manor
Farm

Sch

17

Decoy
Covert

River Itchen

Hog Wood

Hogwood Lane

Railway
Cottage

Milkmead Copse

3

The Itchen Navigation (disused)

Itchen Valley
Country Park

High Hill

High
Wood

Reservoir

High Hill

ALLINGTON LA

Oaklands
House

16

M27

Water
Works

Winslowe
House

Moorgreen
Farm

Gaters
Mill

A27  MANSBRIDGE RD

QUOB LA

Quob
Farm

Quob
Farm

BROOKSIDE WAY

2

STOUR CL 1
CREEDY GDNS 2
WEBBURN GDNS 3

CUTBUSH LA

LIME GDNS

ELM GDNS

Southampton
Arms (PH)

15

Townhill
Park

Sch

SWAYTHLING RD

MOORGREEN RD

Sch

Moorgreen

West End

Moorgreen
Hospital

MEGGESON AVE

TOWNHILL WAY

CHURCH HILL

CHALK HILL

Liby
Hatch
Grange

Hatch
Bottom

HIGH ST

P
Sta

B3035

Tumulus

OLD SCHOOL
GDNS

MONARCH WAY

1

CORNWALL
RD

B3035

WEST END RD

BOTLEY RD

B3035

Sch

Midanbury

MOORHILL
RD

A27

TELEGRAPH RD

Dog Kennel
Farm

14

45  A  46  B  47  C

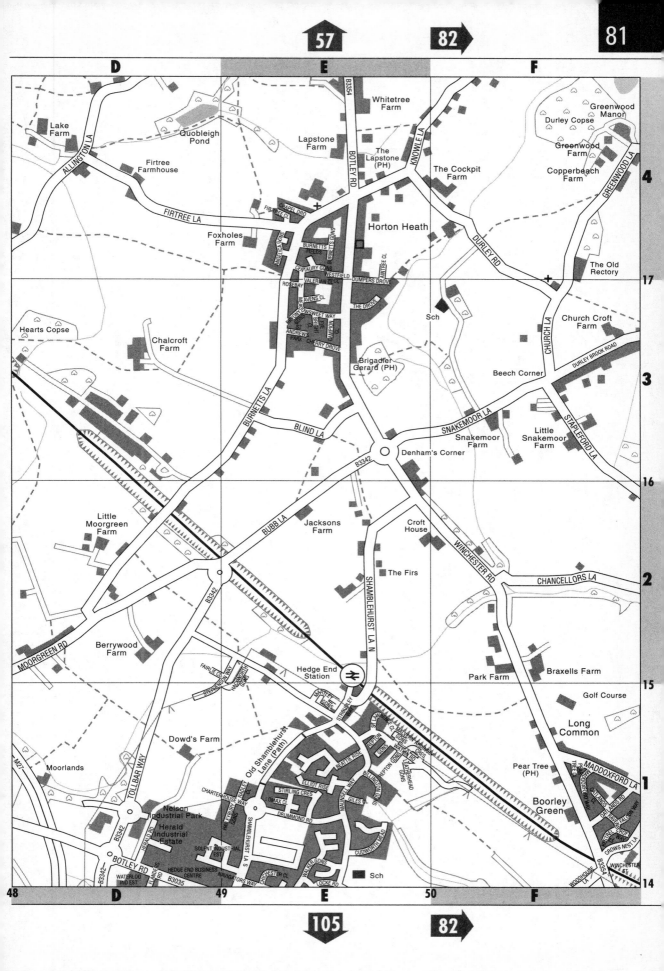

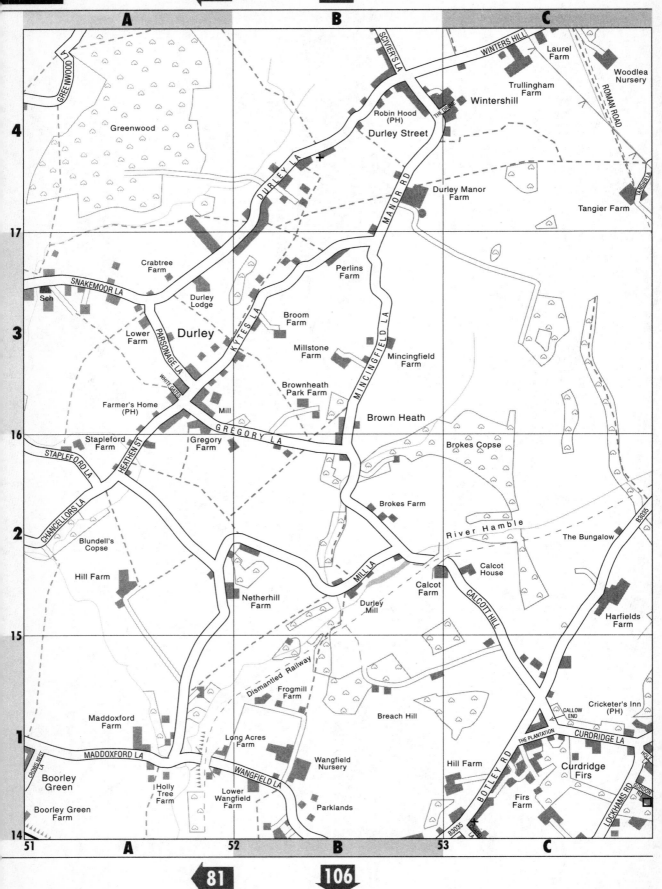

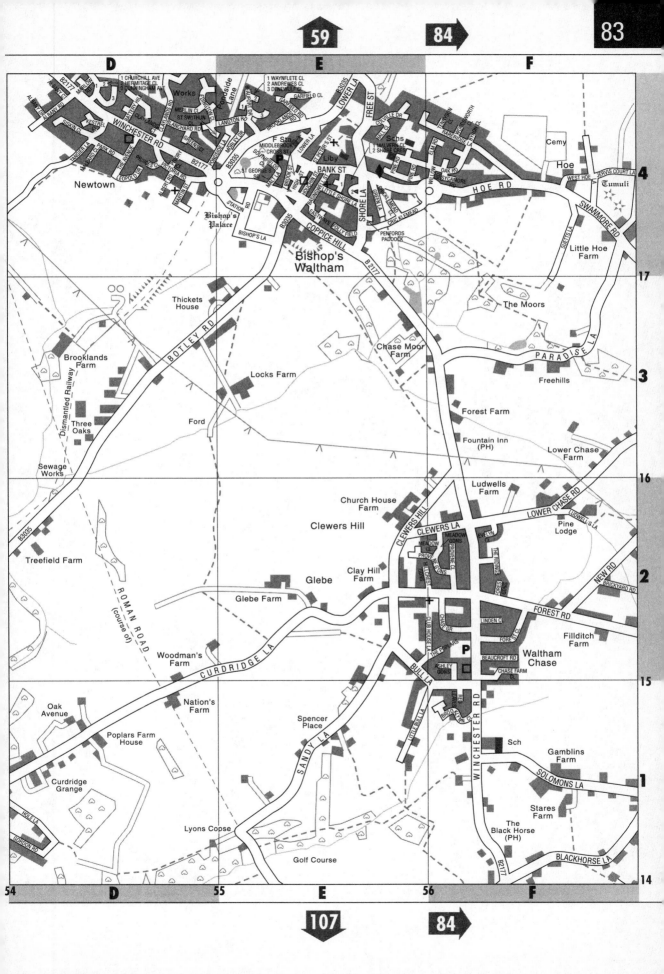

D       E       F

1 CHURCHILL AVE
2 HERMITAGE CL
3 DUNNINGHAM AVE

1 WAYNFLETE CL
2 ANDREWES CL
3 DENEWULF CL

Works

Pondside Lane

GARFIELD CL

FREE ST

LOWER LA

B3035

COLVILLE DR

Merlin CL
ST SWITHUN CL
BLANCHARD RD

LANGTON RD

BROOKLANDS RD

HALL CL

TRINGHAM CL
WAINSWORTH

RARERIDGE LA

Cemy

Hoe

WINCHESTER RD

GREENS CL

B2177

St George's

F Sta
MIDDLEBROOK
CROSS ST

Schs
1 MALVERN CL
2 SHORE CRES

Libby

PINE RD
OAK RD

WEST HOE
HOE RD

SWANMORE RD

4

Newtown

VICTORIA RD
LEOPOLD

BANK ST

Little Shore La

SYCAMORE

Tumuli

B3035

STATION RD

SHORE LA

CRICKLEMEAD

SUETTS LA

Little Hoe
Farm

Bishop's
Palace

BISHOP'S LA

COPPICE HILL

FOLLY FIELD

B2177

PENFORDS
PADDOCK

17

Bishop's
Waltham

The Moors

Thickets
House

BOTLEY RD

Chase Moor
Farm

PARADISE LA

Brooklands
Farm

Dismantled Railway

Locks Farm

Freehills

3

Three
Oaks

Ford

Forest Farm

Lower Chase
Farm

Sewage
Works

Fountain Inn
(PH)

16

Church House
Farm

Ludwells
Farm

LOWER CHASE RD

LUDWELL'S LA

Clewers Hill

CLEWERS HILL

CLEWERS LA

MEADOW
GDNS

Pine
Lodge

B3035

Treefield Farm

Glebe

Clay Hill
Farm

EVELYN CL

NEW RD

BRICKYARD RD

2

ROMAN ROAD
(course of)

Glebe Farm

FOREST RD

Woodman's
Farm

CURDRIDGE LA

CHASE GR

LINDEN CL

Fillditch
Farm

P

BEAUCROFT RD

Waltham
Chase

15

Oak
Avenue

Nation's
Farm

Spencer
Place

BULL LA

WINCHESTER RD

Sch

Gamblins
Farm

Poplars Farm
House

SANDY LA

LITTLE BULL LA

SOLOMONS LA

1

Curdridge
Grange

Stares
Farm

HOE LA
GORDON RD

Lyons Copse

Golf Course

The Black
Horse
(PH)

B2177

BLACKHORSE LA

14

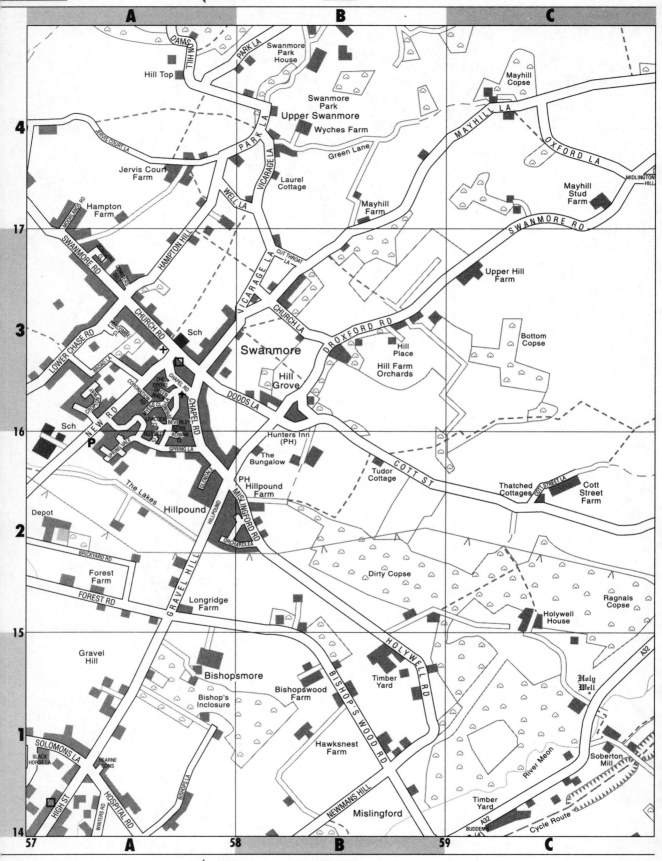

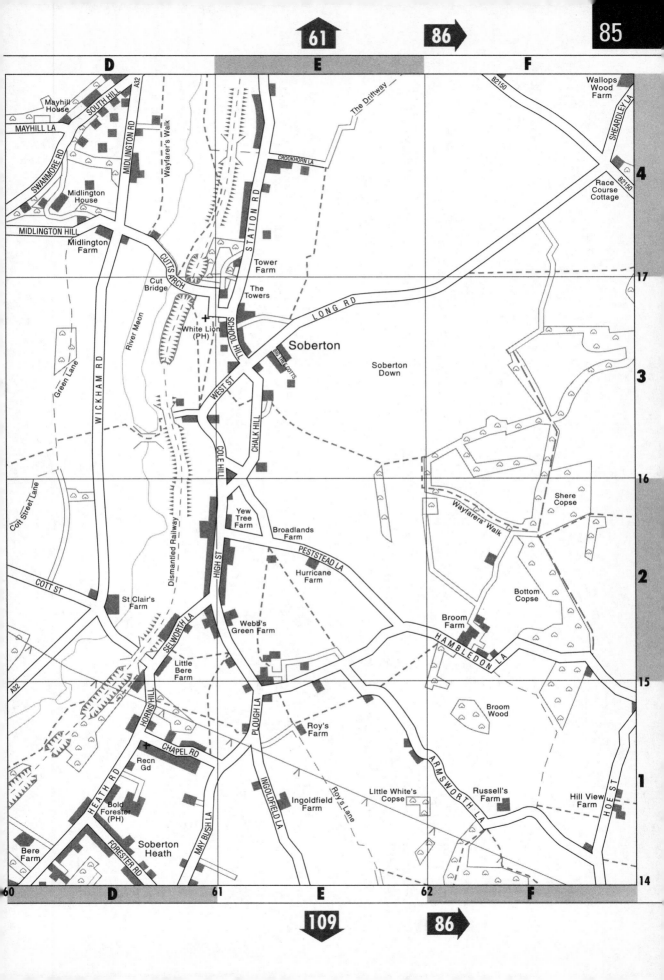

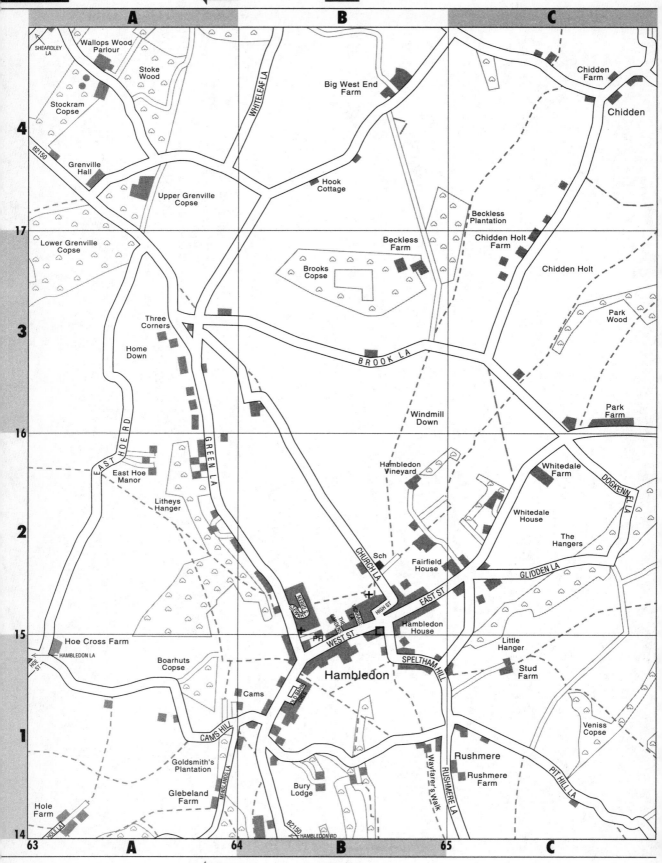

**A**   **B**   **C**

SHEARDLEY LA

Wallops Wood Parlour

Stoke Wood

Stockram Copse

B2150

Grenville Hall

Upper Grenville Copse

Big West End Farm

WHITELEAF LA

Hook Cottage

Chidden Farm

Chidden

Beckless Plantation

**4**

**17**

Lower Grenville Copse

Beckless Farm

Brooks Copse

Chidden Holt Farm

Chidden Holt

Three Corners

Home Down

EAST HOE RD

BROOK LA

Park Wood

**3**

Windmill Down

Park Farm

**16**

GREEN LA

Litheys Hanger

East Hoe Manor

Hambledon Vineyard

Whitedale Farm

DOGKENNEL LA

Whitedale House

The Hangers

**2**

CHURCH LA

Sch

Fairfield House

GLIDDEN LA

EAST ST

Hambledon House

Little Hanger

**15**

Hoe Cross Farm

HAMBLEDON LA

HOE ST

Boarhuts Copse

PH

WEST ST

HIGH ST

Stud Farm

SPELTHAM HILL

Cams

Hambledon

Veniss Copse

**1**

CAMS HILL

MERSCABS LA

Goldsmith's Plantation

Glebeland Farm

RUSHMERE LA

Bury Lodge

B2150 HAMBLEDON RD

Wayfarer's Walk

Rushmere

Rushmere Farm

PIT HILL LA

Hole Farm

HOLE LA

**14**

**63**   **A**   **64**   **B**   **65**   **C**

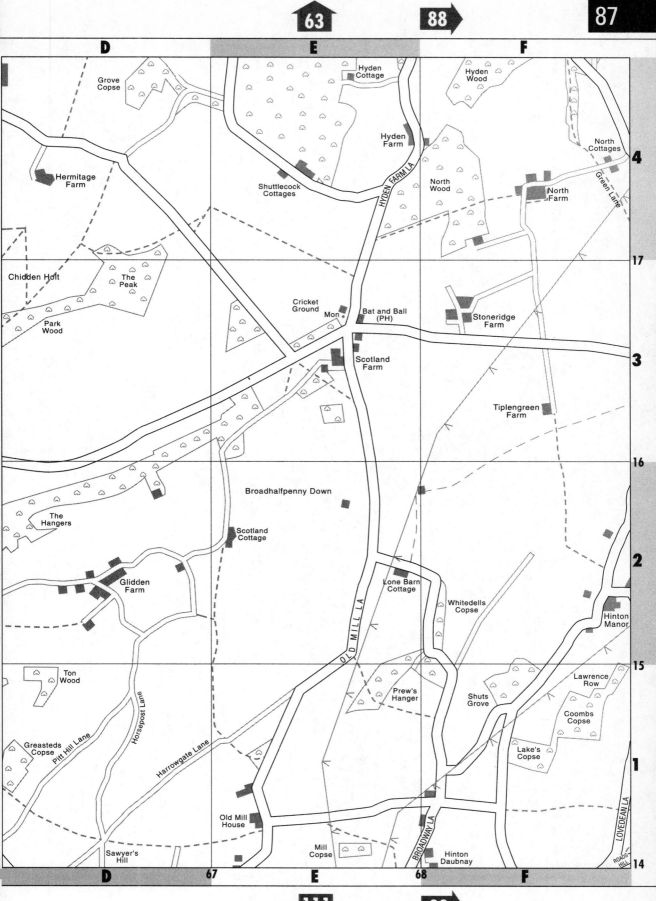

D E F

4

17

3

16

2

15

1

14

Grove
Copse

Hermitage
Farm

Chidden Holt

The
Peak

Park
Wood

Hyden
Cottage

Hyden
Farm

Shuttlecock
Cottages

Cricket
Ground

Mon

Bat and Ball
(PH)

Scotland
Farm

Broadhalfpenny Down

The
Hangers

Scotland
Cottage

Glidden
Farm

Ton
Wood

Greasteds
Copse

Old Mill
House

Sawyer's
Hill

Mill
Copse

Hyden
Wood

North
Cottages

North
Wood

North
Farm

Stoneridge
Farm

Tiplengreen
Farm

Lone Barn
Cottage

Whitedells
Copse

Hinton
Manor

Lawrence
Row

Shuts
Grove

Coombs
Copse

Lake's
Copse

Hinton
Daubnay

HYDEN FARM LA

Green Lane

OLD MILL LA

Horsepost Lane

Pitt Hill Lane

Harrowgate Lane

BROADWAY LA

LOVEDEAN LA

ROADS
HILL

Prew's
Hanger

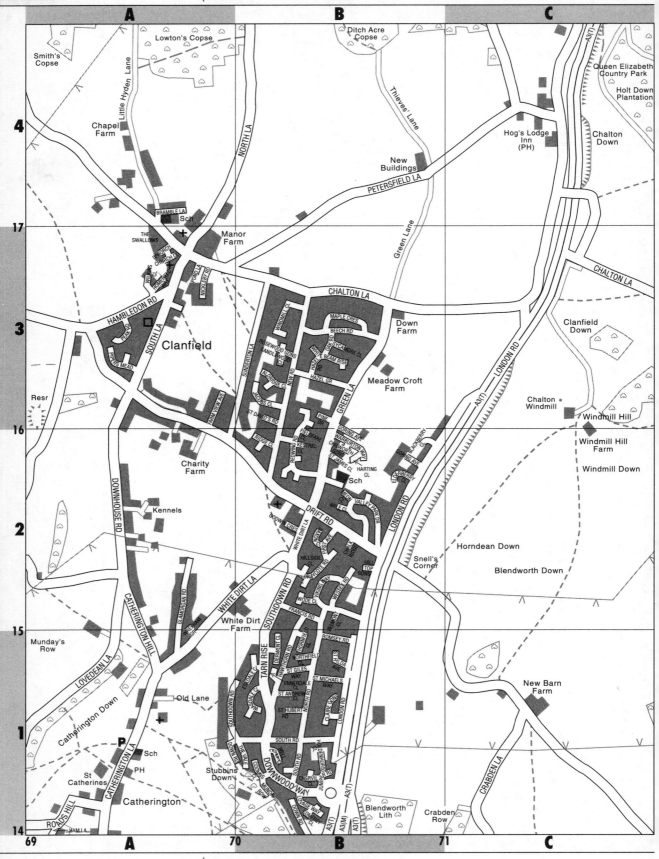

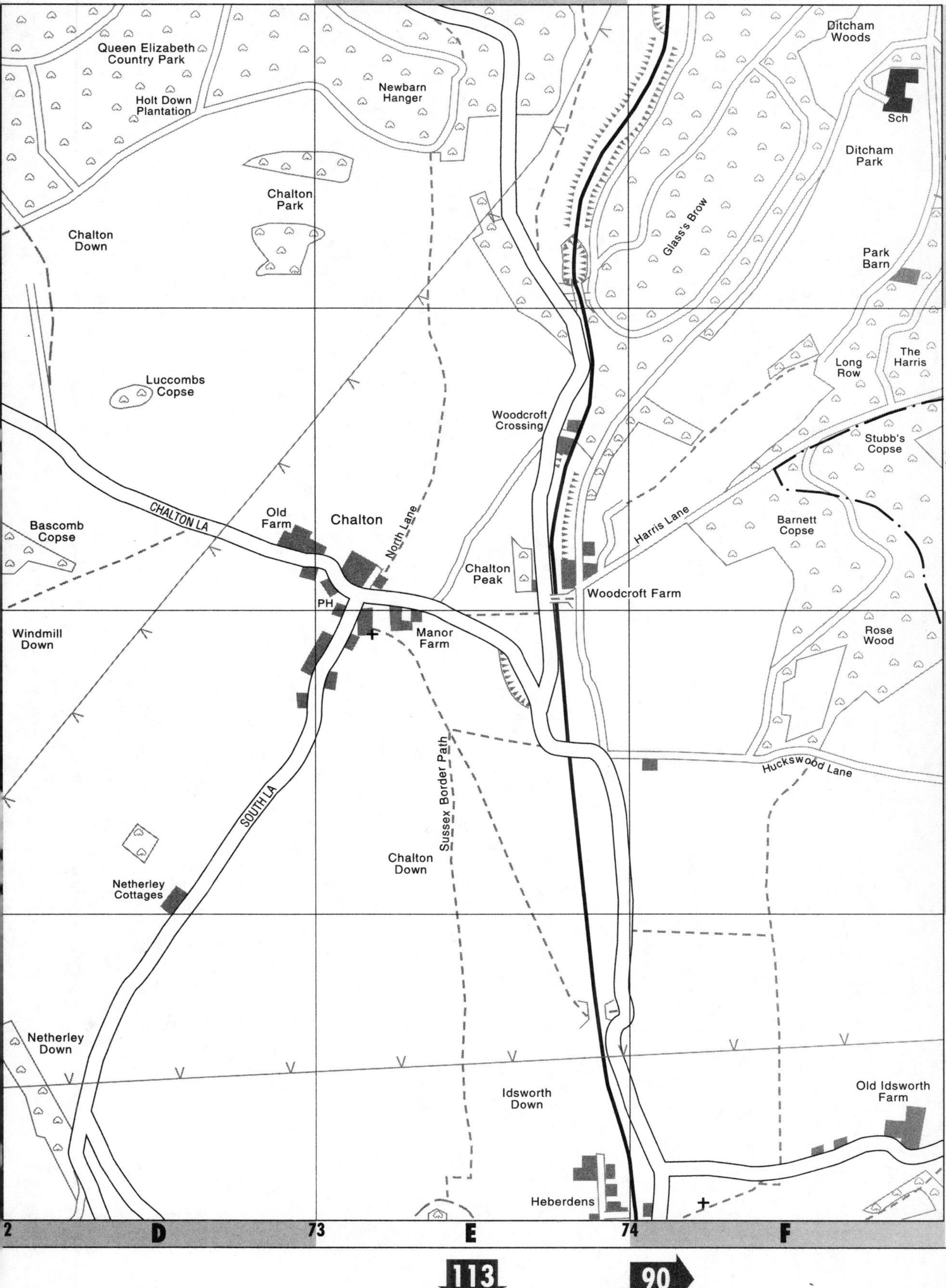

D
E
F

Queen Elizabeth
Country Park

Holt Down
Plantation

Newbarn
Hanger

Ditcham
Woods

Sch

Chalton
Park

Ditcham
Park

4

Chalton
Down

Glass's Brow

Park
Barn

17

Luccombs
Copse

Long
Row

The
Harris

Woodcroft
Crossing

Stubb's
Copse

3

Bascomb
Copse

CHALTON LA

Old
Farm

Chalton

North Lane

Harris Lane

Barnett
Copse

Chalton
Peak

Woodcroft Farm

16

PH

Windmill
Down

Manor
Farm

Rose
Wood

Sussex Border Path

Huckswood Lane

2

SOUTH LA

Chalton
Down

Netherley
Cottages

15

Netherley
Down

1

Idsworth
Down

Old Idsworth
Farm

Heberdens

14

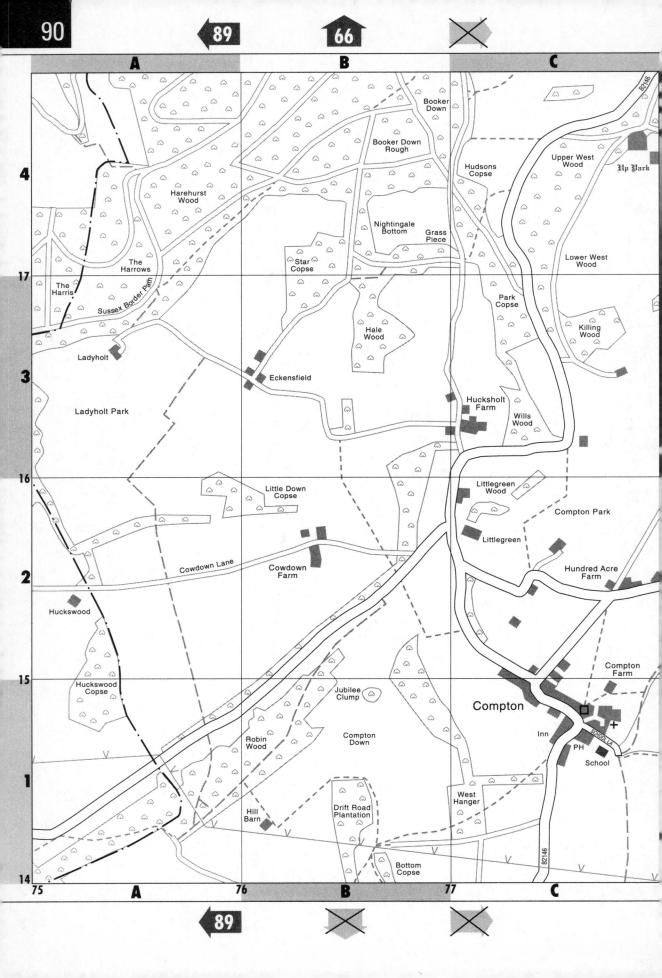

4

Harehurst
Wood

Booker
Down

Booker Down
Rough

Hudsons
Copse

Upper West
Wood

Up Park

The
Harrows

Nightingale
Bottom

Grass
Piece

Lower West
Wood

17

The
Harris

Star
Copse

Sussex Border Path

Park
Copse

Killing
Wood

Ladyholt

Hale
Wood

Eckensfield

Hucksholt
Farm

Wills
Wood

3

Ladyholt Park

16

Little Down
Copse

Littlegreen
Wood

Compton Park

Huckswood

Cowdown Lane

Cowdown
Farm

Littlegreen

Hundred Acre
Farm

2

Huckswood
Copse

Jubilee
Clump

Compton
Down

Compton

Compton
Farm

15

Robin
Wood

Inn

SCHOOL LA

PH

School

1

Hill
Barn

Drift Road
Plantation

West
Hanger

Bottom
Copse

14

B2146

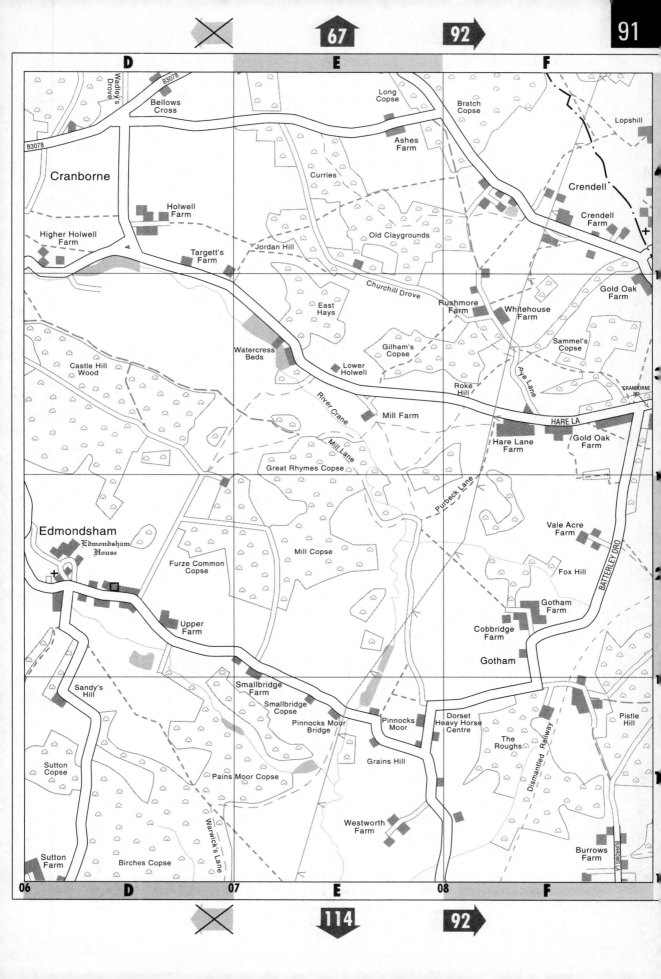

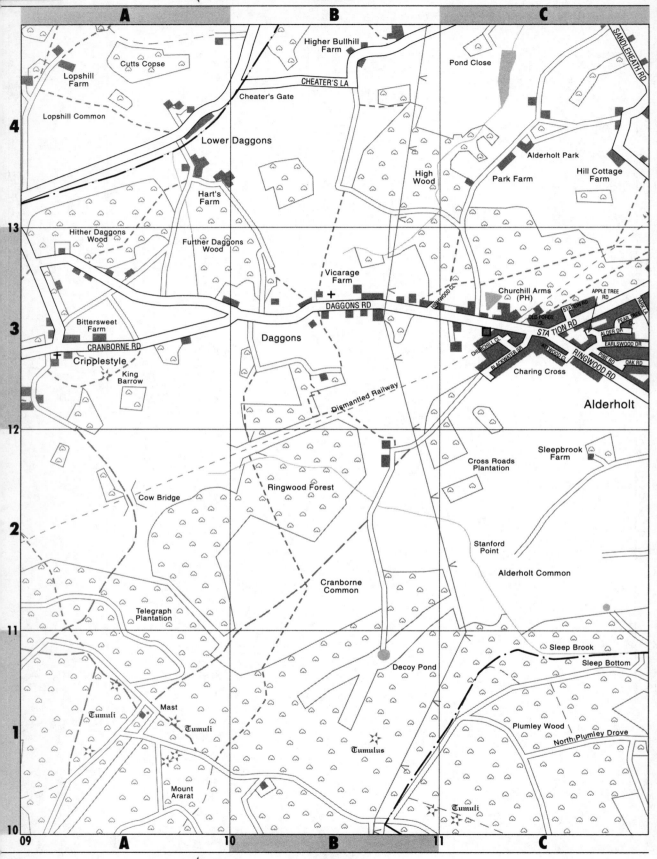

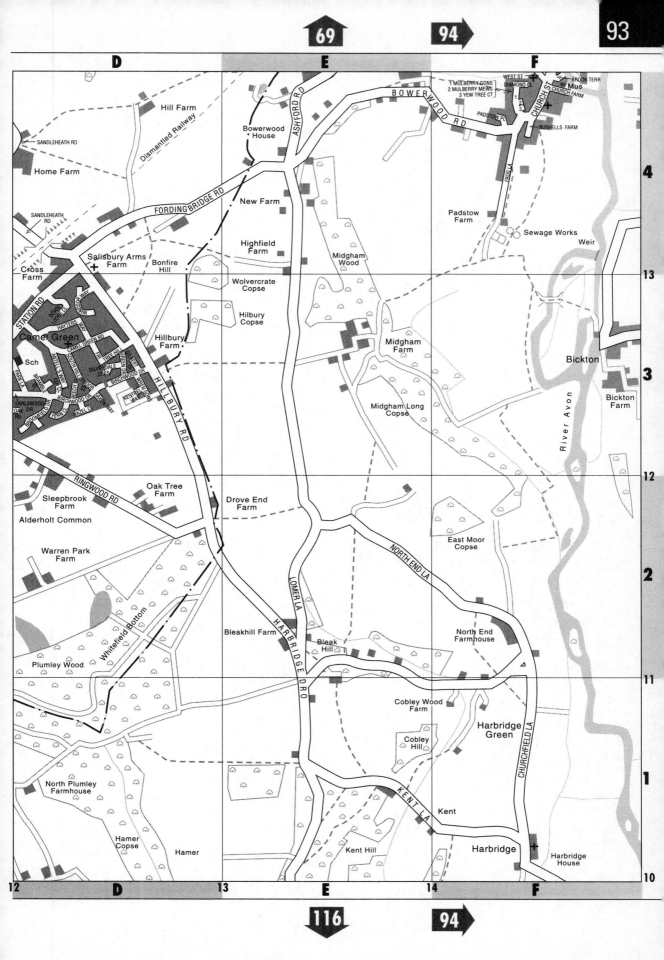

D
E
F

SANDLEHEATH RD
Hill Farm
Dismantled Railway
Bowerwood House
ASHFORD RD
BOWERWOOD RD
1 MULBERRY GDNS
2 MULBERRY MEWS
3 YEW TREE CT
WEST ST
DIAMOND CL
CHURCH ST
BROOK TERR
CHURCH FARM
Mus
BUSHELLS FARM
PADSTOW PL
FROG LA

Home Farm
SANDLEHEATH RD
FORDINGBRIDGE RD
New Farm
Highfield Farm
Midgham Wood
Padstow Farm
Sewage Works
Weir

4

Salisbury Arms Farm
Bonfire Hill
Cross Farm
Wolvercrate Copse
Hilbury Copse

13

STATION RD
DOWDS ORCHARD
CROSSWAY
HAYTERS
SOUTH HILL
ANTELL'S WAY
FIR TREE HILL
GREEN RD
SILVERDALE CRES
BILBERRY
BIRCHWOOD DR
WREN GDNS
Camel Green
CAMEL GREEN RD
Sch
PARK LA
BRAMBLE
BROOMFIELD
EARLSWOOD
OAK RD
DR
BIRCHWOOD DR
FERN CL
HAZEL CL
KESTREL
SAXON WAY
WAY
BEECH CL
Hillbury Farm
Midgham Farm
Bickton

HILLBURY RD
Midgham Long Copse
Bickton Farm
River Avon

3

RINGWOOD RD
Oak Tree Farm
Drove End Farm

12

Sleepbrook Farm
Alderholt Common
East Moor Copse

Warren Park Farm
NORTH END LA
North End Farmhouse

2

Whitefield Bottom
Plumley Wood
LOMER LA
Bleakhill Farm
HARBRIDGE DRO
Bleak Hill
North End Farmhouse

11

North Plumley Farmhouse
Cobley Wood Farm
Harbridge Green
CHURCHFIELD LA

1

Cobley Hill

Hamer Copse
Hamer
KENT LA
Kent Hill
Kent
Harbridge
Harbridge House

10

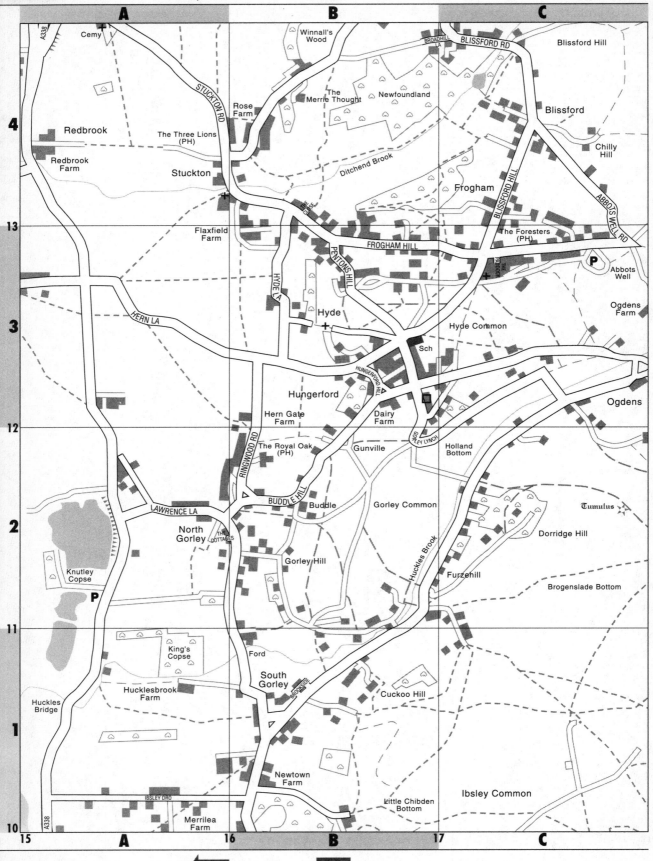

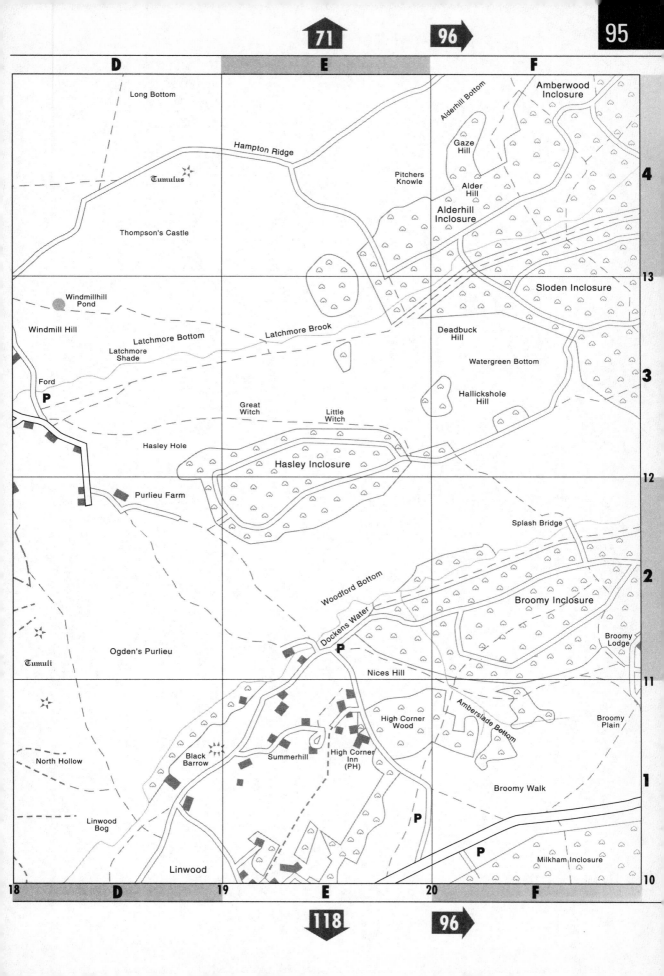

Long Bottom

Amberwood
Inclosure

Alderhill Bottom

Hampton Ridge

Gaze
Hill

Pitchers
Knowle

Alder
Hill

Tumulus

**4**

Alderhill
Inclosure

Thompson's Castle

13

Sloden Inclosure

Windmillhill
Pond

Windmill Hill

Latchmore Brook

Deadbuck
Hill

Latchmore Bottom

Watergreen Bottom

Latchmore
Shade

**3**

Ford

Hallickshole
Hill

P

Great
Witch

Little
Witch

Hasley Hole

Hasley Inclosure

12

Purlieu Farm

Splash Bridge

Woodford Bottom

**2**

Broomy Inclosure

Dockens Water

Broomy
Lodge

Tumuli

Ogden's Purlieu

P

Nices Hill

11

High Corner
Wood

Amberslade Bottom

Broomy
Plain

North Hollow

Black
Barrow

Summerhill

High Corner
Inn
(PH)

**1**

Broomy Walk

P

Linwood
Bog

P

Milkham Inclosure

Linwood

10

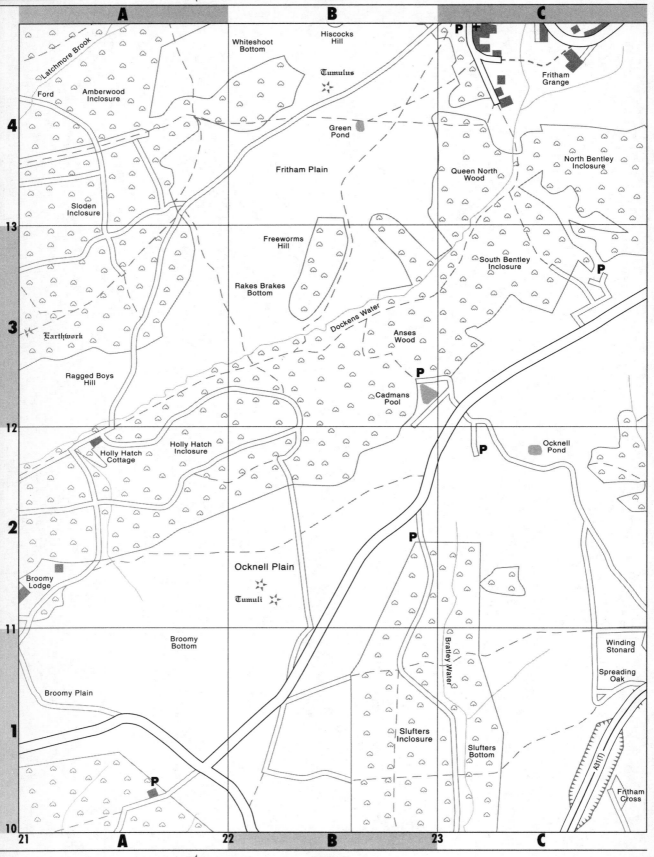

Whiteshoot
Bottom

Hiscocks
Hill

Tumulus

P +

Fritham
Grange

Ford

Latchmore Brook

Amberwood
Inclosure

Fritham Plain

Green
Pond

Queen North
Wood

North Bentley
Inclosure

4

Sloden
Inclosure

13

Freeworms
Hill

South Bentley
Inclosure

P

Rakes Brakes
Bottom

Dockens Water

Anses
Wood

3

Earthwork

Ragged Boys
Hill

P

Cadmans
Pool

12

Holly Hatch
Cottage

Holly Hatch
Inclosure

P

Ocknell
Pond

2

Broomy
Lodge

Ocknell Plain

Tumuli

P

11

Broomy
Bottom

Bratley Water

Winding
Stonard

Spreading
Oak

Broomy Plain

1

Slufters
Inclosure

Slufters
Bottom

A31(T)

Fritham
Cross

P

10

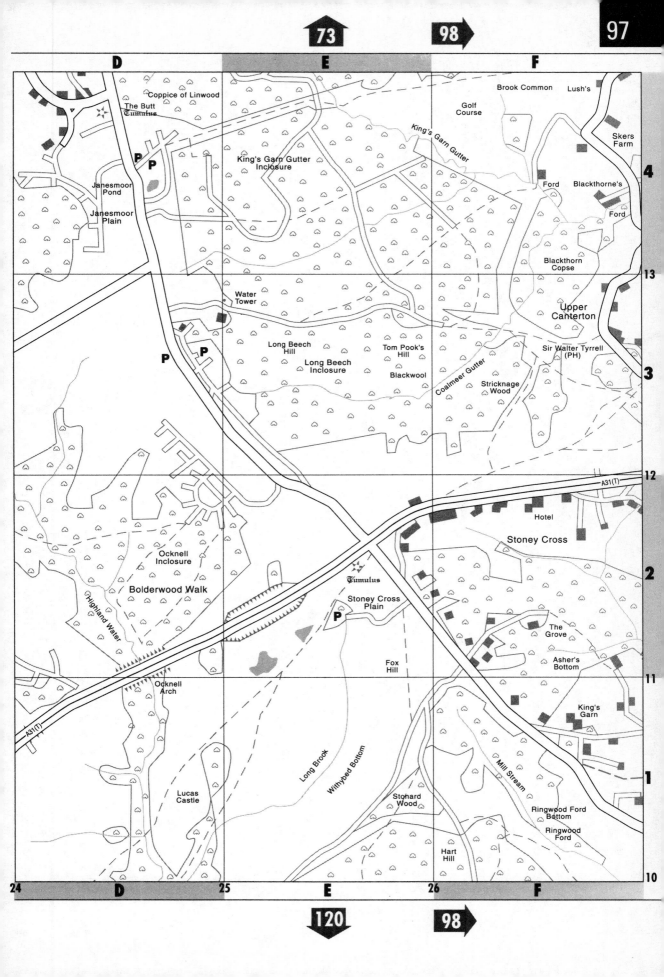

Coppice of Linwood

The Butt
Tumulus

4

King's Garn Gutter
Inclosure

King's Garn Gutter

Brook Common
Lush's

Golf
Course

Skers
Farm

P
P

Ford
Blackthorne's

Janesmoor
Pond

Ford

Janesmoor
Plain

Blackthorn
Copse

13

Water
Tower

Upper
Canterton

P
P

Long Beech
Hill

Tom Pook's
Hill

Sir Walter Tyrrell
(PH)

3

Long Beech
Inclosure

Blackwool

Coalmeer Gutter

Stricknage
Wood

A31(T)

12

Hotel

Stoney Cross

Ocknell
Inclosure

Bolderwood Walk

Tumulus

Stoney Cross
Plain

The
Grove

2

Highland Water

P

Asher's
Bottom

Fox
Hill

11

Ocknell
Arch

King's
Garn

A31(T)

Lucas
Castle

Long Brook

Withybed Bottom

Stonard
Wood

Mill Stream

1

Ringwood Ford
Bottom

Ringwood
Ford

Hart
Hill

10

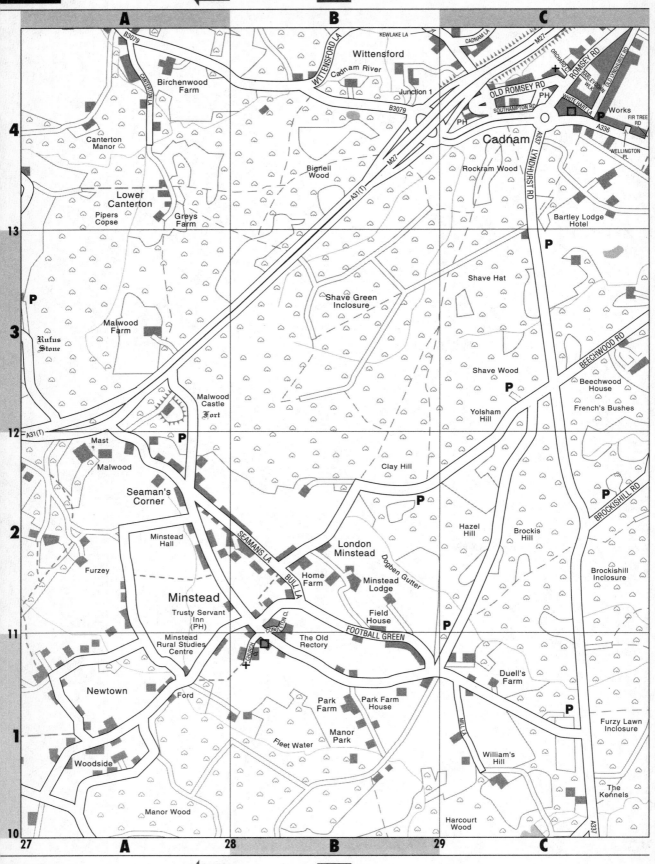

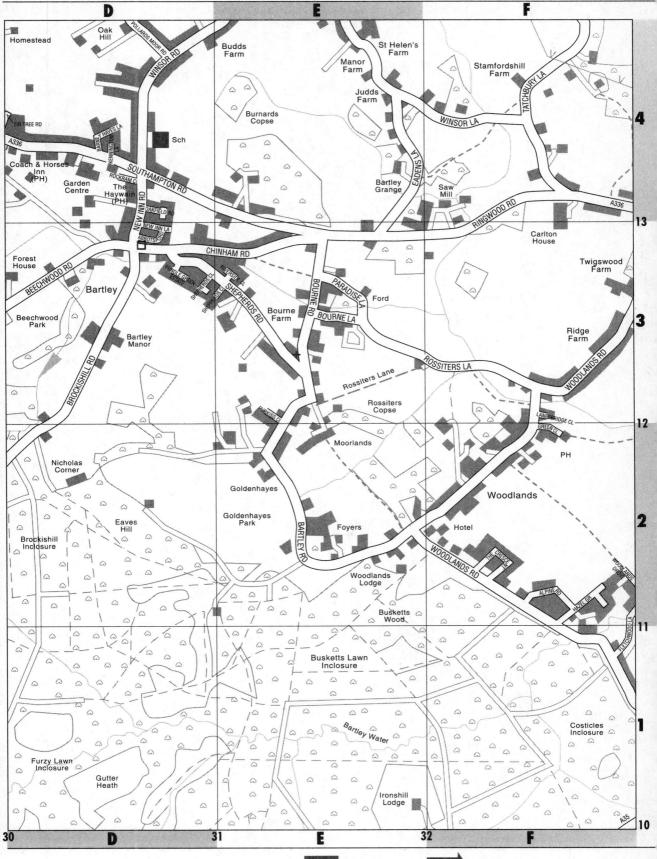

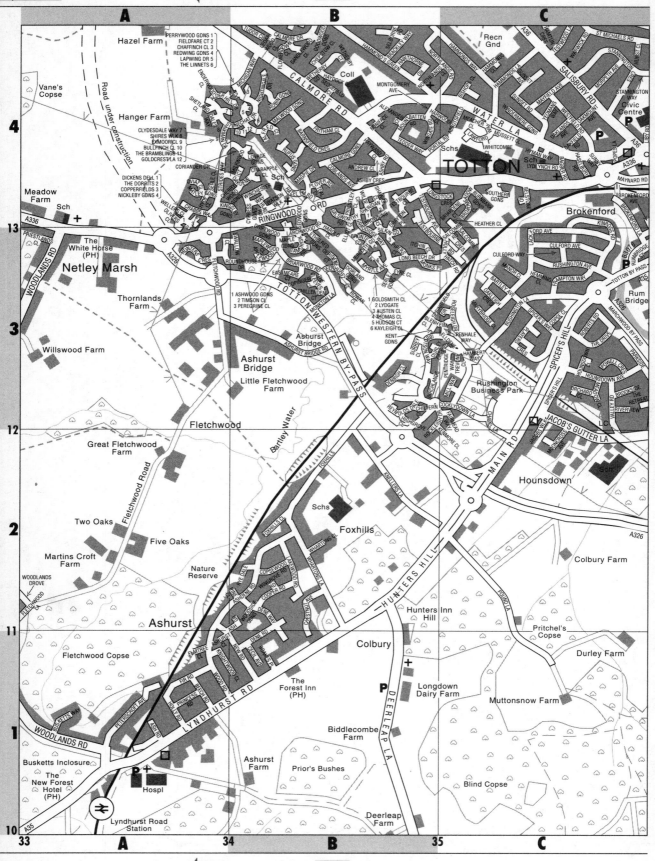

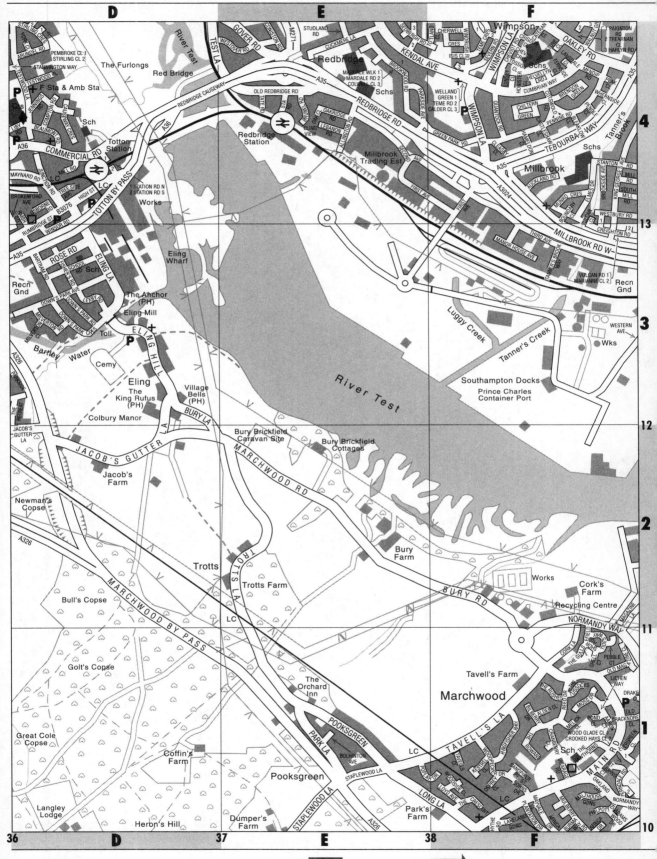

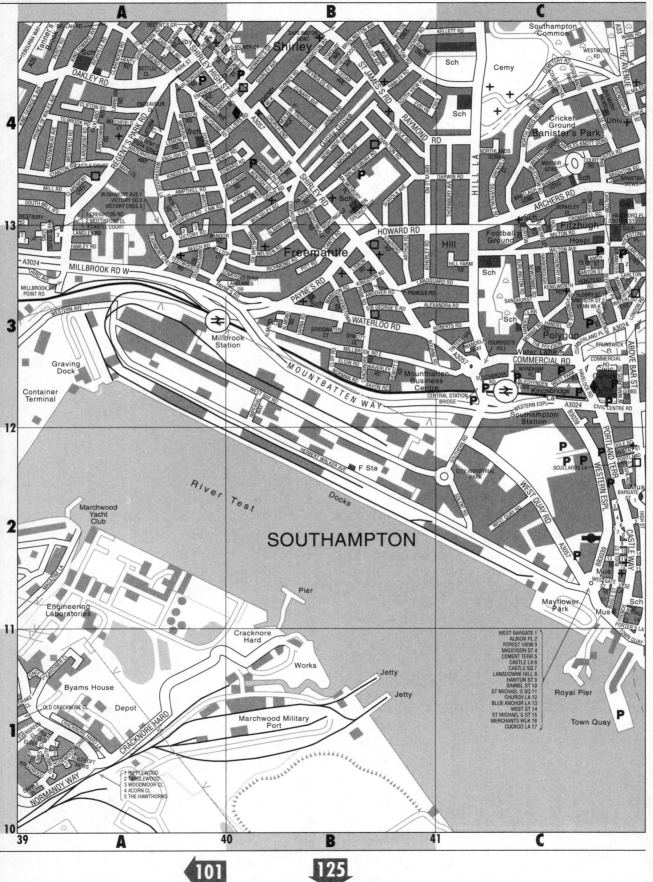

SOUTHAMPTON

WEST BARGATE 1
ALBION PL 2
FOREST VIEW 3
MADDISON ST 4
CEMENT TERR 5
CASTLE LA 6
CASTLE SQ 7
LANSDOWNE HILL 8
HAMTUN ST 9
SIMNEL ST 10
ST MICHAEL S SQ 11
CHURCH LA 12
BLUE ANCHOR LA 13
WEST ST 14
ST MICHAEL'S ST 15
MERCHANTS WLK 16
CUCKOO LA 17

1 RIPPLEWOOD
2 TANGLEWOOD
3 WOODMOOR CL
4 ACORN CL
5 THE HAWTHORNS

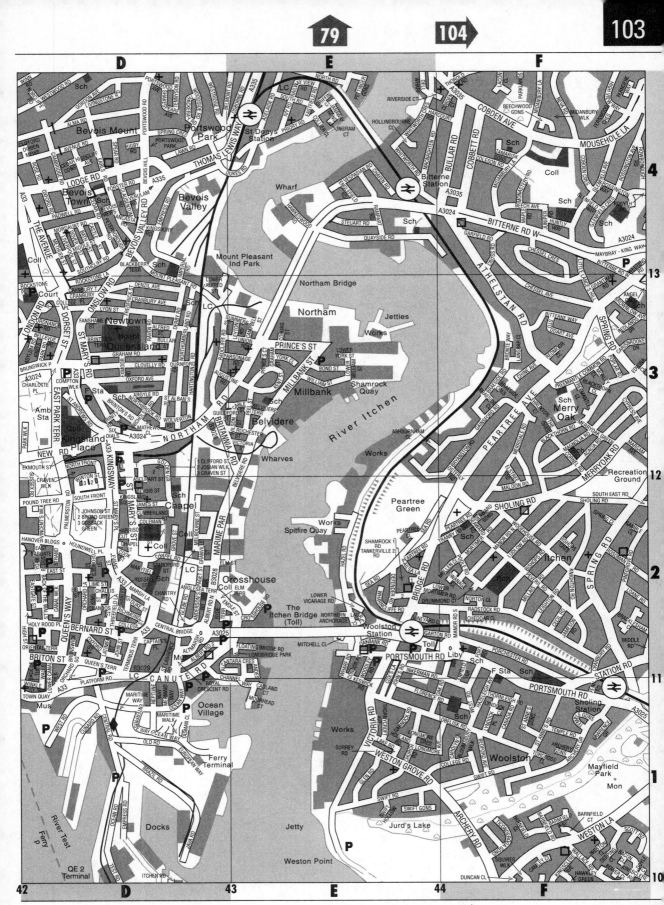

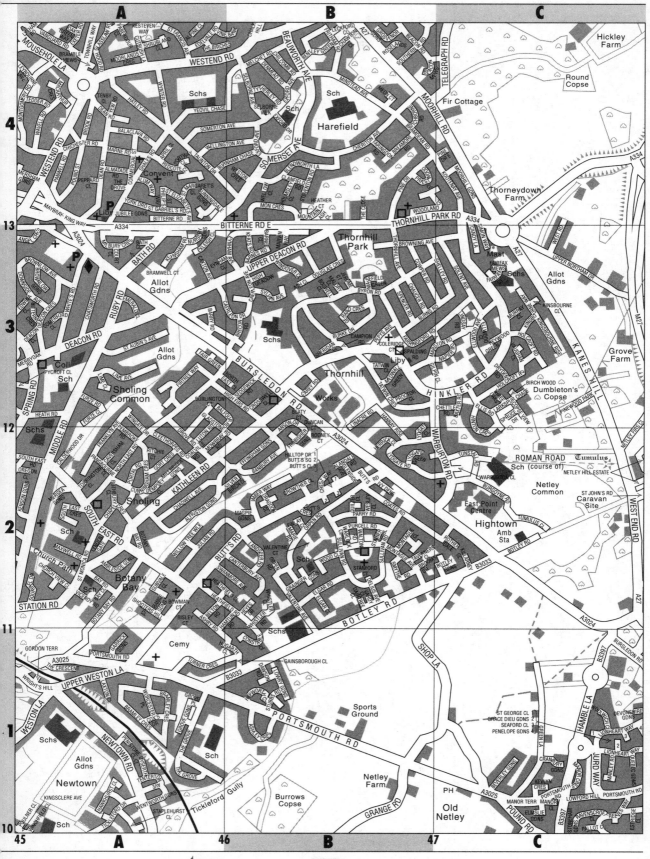

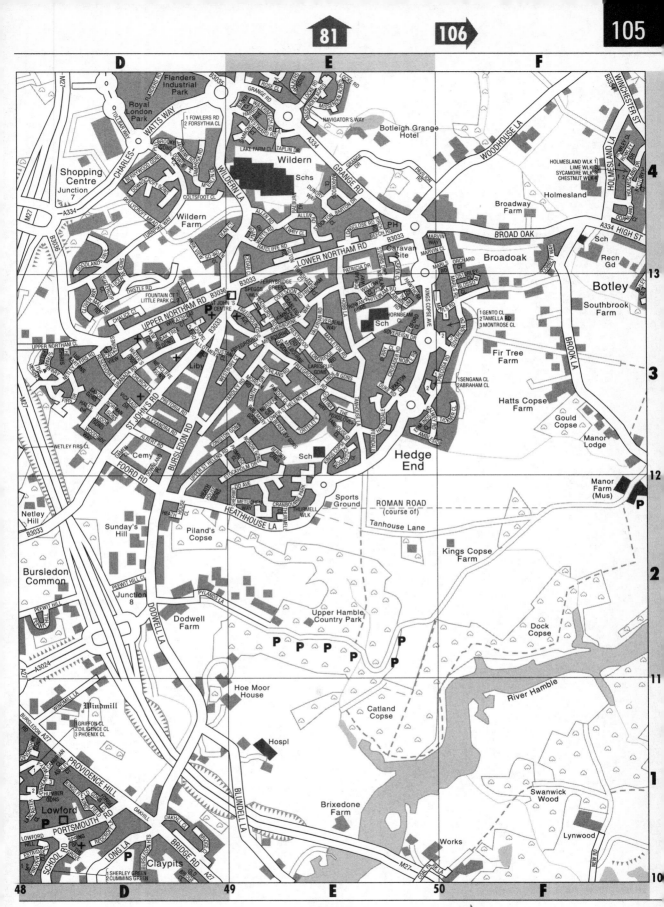

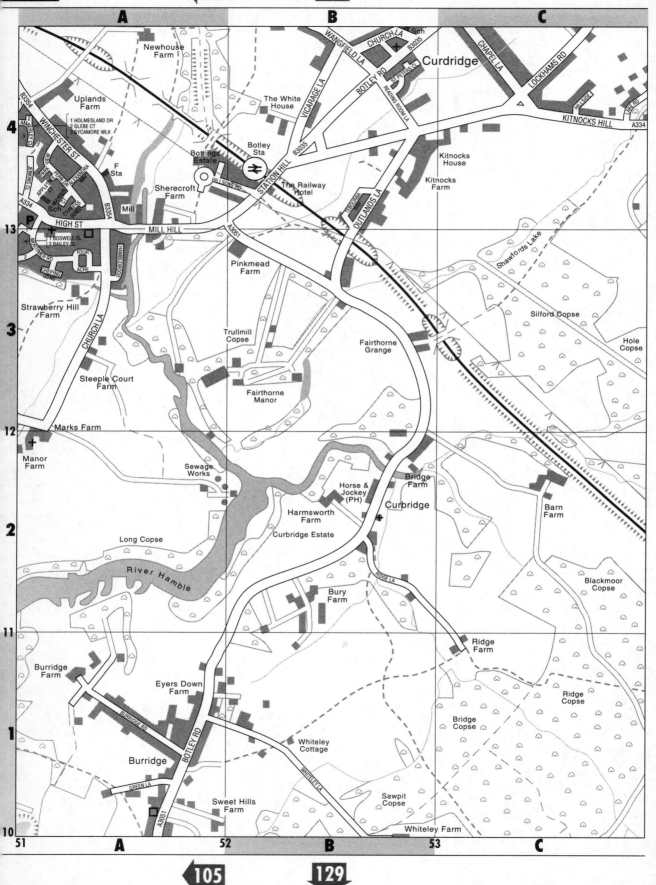

A            B            C

Newhouse Farm

Uplands Farm

1 HOLMESLAND DR
2 GLEBE CT
3 SYCAMORE WLK

WINCHESTER ST

B3354

AMPFIELD CL

JENKINS CL
PARK VIEW
FERN DR
ALEXANDRA WAY
APPLETON
MAPLE
KEY
CYPRESS GDNS

F Sta

Sch
A3354
HIGH ST

B3354

Mill

Bottings Estate

HILLSONS RD

Botley Sta

STATION HILL

B3035

The White House

WANGFIELD LA
CHURCH LA
Sch
B3035

BOTLEY RD

St PETERS CL
READING ROOM LA
VICARAGE LA

Curdridge

CHAPEL LA

LOCKHAMS RD

HILLSIDE
LAKE RD

KITNOCKS HILL
A334

Kitnocks House

Kitnocks Farm

Sherecroft Farm

**P**

1 BOSWELL CL
2 BAILEY CL

MORTIMER RD
CHEPING GDNS
FOUR ACRE

MILL HILL
A3051

The Railway Hotel

YEOVILTON
OUTLANDS LA

Shawfords Lake

HAMBLEWOOD
CHURCH LA

Strawberry Hill Farm

Pinkmead Farm

Trullmill Copse

Fairthorne Grange

Silford Copse

Hole Copse

Steeple Court Farm

Fairthorne Manor

Marks Farm

Manor Farm

Sewage Works

Horse & Jockey (PH)

Bridge Farm

Curbridge

Barn Farm

Harmsworth Farm

Curbridge Estate

Long Copse

River Hamble

Bury Farm

RIDGE LA

Blackmoor Copse

Ridge Farm

Burridge Farm

Eyers Down Farm

BURRIDGE RD

BOTLEY RD

Bridge Copse

Ridge Copse

Whiteley Cottage

WHITELEY LA

Burridge

GREEN LA
A3051

Sweet Hills Farm

Sawpit Copse

Whiteley Farm

51      A      52      B      53      C

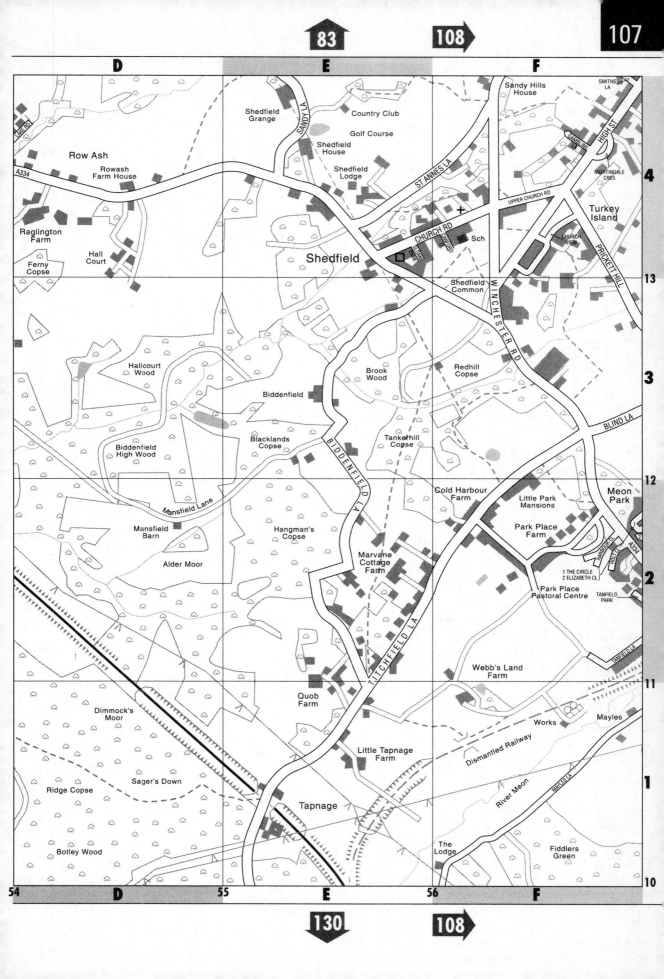

LAKE RD

Row Ash

A334

Rowash
Farm House

Raglington
Farm

Ferny
Copse

Hall
Court

Shedfield
Grange

SANDY LA

Country Club

Golf Course

Shedfield
House

Shedfield
Lodge

ST ANNES LA

Sandy Hills
House

SMITHS
LA

HIGH ST

GAMBLING

UPPER CHURCH RD

NIGHTINGALE
CRES

CHURCH RD

CANGRO

Sch

CHURCH
VIEW

Turkey
Island

Shedfield

STONE
PARK

4

PRICKETT HILL

Shedfield
Common

13

WINCHESTER RD

Hallcourt
Wood

Biddenfield

Brook
Wood

Redhill
Copse

3

Biddenfield
High Wood

Blacklands
Copse

Tankerhill
Copse

BLIND LA

BIDDENFIELD LA

Mansfield Lane

Cold Harbour
Farm

Little Park
Mansions

Meon
Park

12

Mansfield
Barn

Hangman's
Copse

Park Place
Farm

HARBOUR CL

HOLT CL

A334

Alder Moor

Marvane
Cottage
Farm

1 THE CIRCLE
2 ELIZABETH CL.

2

LITCHFIELD LA

Park Place
Pastoral Centre

TANFIELD
PARK

Webb's Land
Farm

TANFIELD LA

11

Dimmock's
Moor

Quob
Farm

Works

Mayles

Sager's Down

Little Tapnage
Farm

Dismantled Railway

MAYLES LA

Ridge Copse

River Meon

1

Botley Wood

Tapnage

The
Lodge

Fiddlers
Green

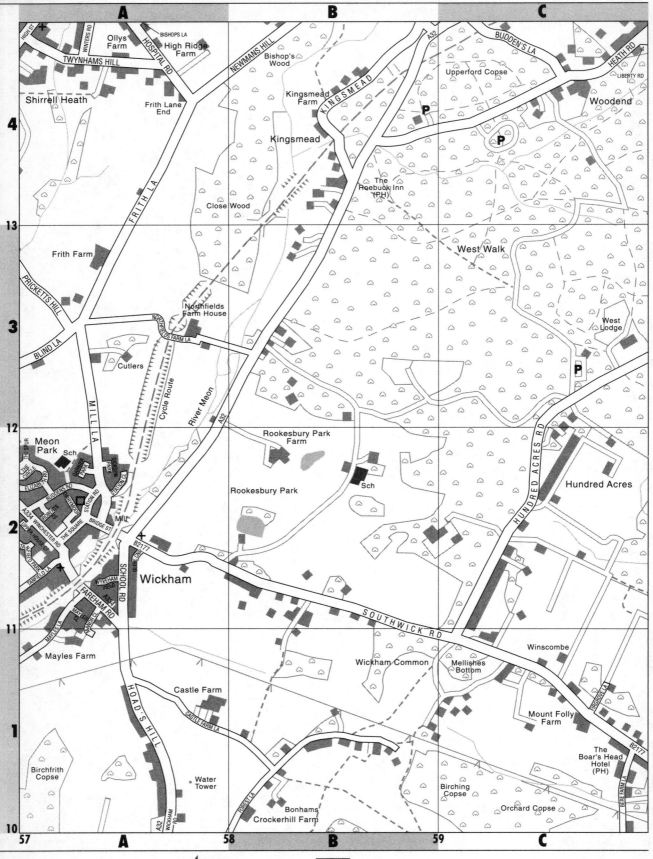

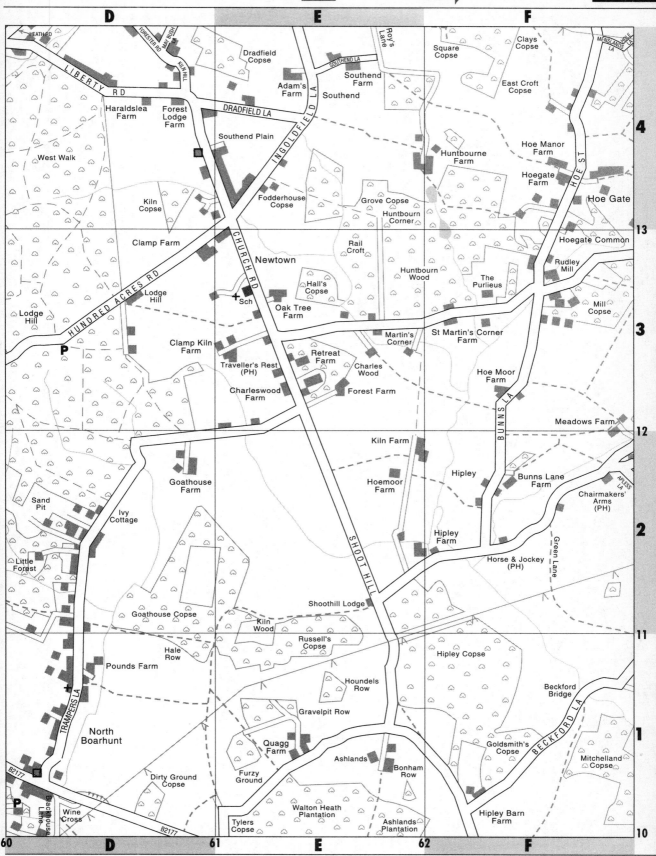

**D**     **E**     **F**

HEATH RD

FORRESTER RD

MAY BUSH

KILN HILL

LIBERTY RD

Haraldslea Farm

Forest Lodge Farm

Dradfield Copse

Adam's Farm

SOUTHEND LA

Southend Farm

Southend

Roy's Lane

Square Copse

Clays Copse

East Croft Copse

MENSLANDS LA

HOLE LA

HOE ST

Hoe Manor Farm

Hoegate Farm

Hoe Gate

**4**

DRADFIELD LA

INGOLDFIELD LA

West Walk

Southend Plain

Fodderhouse Copse

Grove Copse

Huntbourne Farm

Huntbourn Corner

Kiln Copse

**13**

Clamp Farm

CHURCH RD

Newtown

Rail Croft

Huntbourn Wood

The Purlieus

Hoegate Common

Rudley Mill

Mill Copse

Lodge Hill

Lodge Hill

HUNDRED ACRES RD

Sch

Hall's Copse

Oak Tree Farm

Martin's Corner

St Martin's Corner Farm

**P**

Clamp Kiln Farm

Traveller's Rest (PH)

Retreat Farm

Charles Wood

Hoe Moor Farm

**3**

Charleswood Farm

Forest Farm

BUNNS LA

Kiln Farm

Meadows Farm

**12**

Goathouse Farm

Hoemoor Farm

Hipley

Bunns Lane Farm

Chairmakers' Arms (PH)

APLESS LA

Sand Pit

Ivy Cottage

SHOOT HILL

Hipley Farm

Green Lane

**2**

Little Forest

Goathouse Copse

Kiln Wood

Shoothill Lodge

Horse & Jockey (PH)

**11**

Hale Row

Russell's Copse

Hipley Copse

Beckford Bridge

Pounds Farm

TRAMPERS LA

Houndels Row

**North Boarhunt**

Gravelpit Row

BECKFORD LA

Goldsmith's Copse

Mitchelland Copse

**1**

B2177

Dirty Ground Copse

Quagg Farm

Ashlands

Bonham Row

**P**

Blackhouse Lane

Wine Cross

Furzy Ground

Tylers Copse

Walton Heath Plantation

Ashlands Plantation

Hipley Barn Farm

B2177

**10**

**60**     **D**     **61**     **E**     **62**     **F**

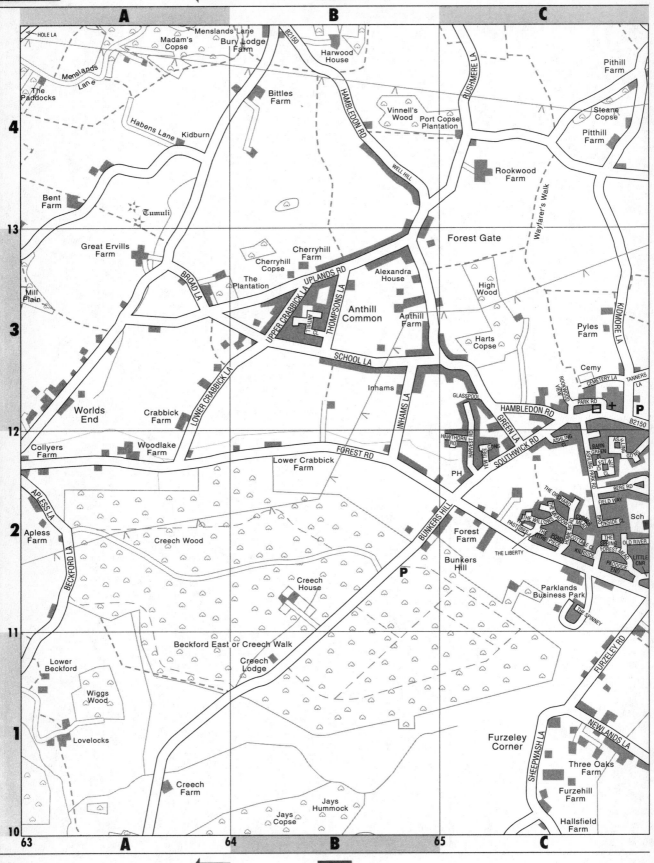

HOLE LA

Menslands Lane
Madam's Copse
Bury Lodge Farm
Mensland
Lane
Harwood House
Bittles Farm
The Paddocks
Habens Lane
Kidburn
Vinnell's Wood
Port Copse Plantation
Pithill Farm
Steane Copse
Pitthill Farm
Bent Farm
Tumuli
Rookwood Farm
Great Ervills Farm
Cherryhill Farm
Cherryhill Copse
The Plantation
Forest Gate
Mill Plain
Alexandra House
High Wood
Anthill Common
Anthill Farm
Pyles Farm
Harts Copse
Cemy
Worlds End
Crabbick Farm
Inhams
Glasspool
HAMBLEDON RD
Collyers Farm
Woodlake Farm
Forest Rd
Lower Crabbick Farm
PH
Apless Farm
Creech Wood
Bunkers Hill
Forest Farm
Bunkers Hill
Parklands Business Park
Creech House
Lower Beckford
Wiggs Wood
Beckford East or Creech Walk
Creech Lodge
Furzeley Corner
Newlands La
Lovelocks
Three Oaks Farm
Creech Farm
Jays Hummock
Furzehill Farm
Jays Copse
Hallsfield Farm

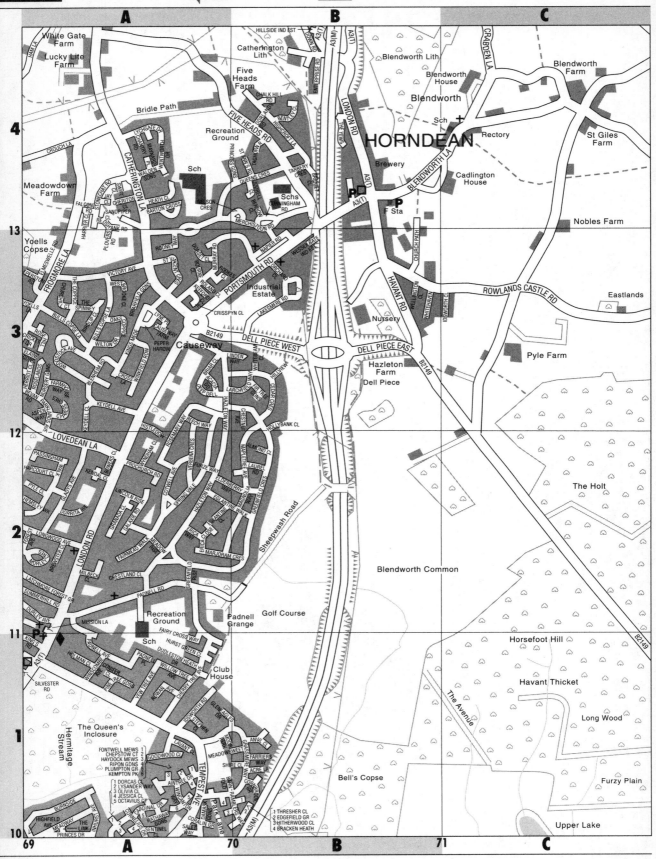

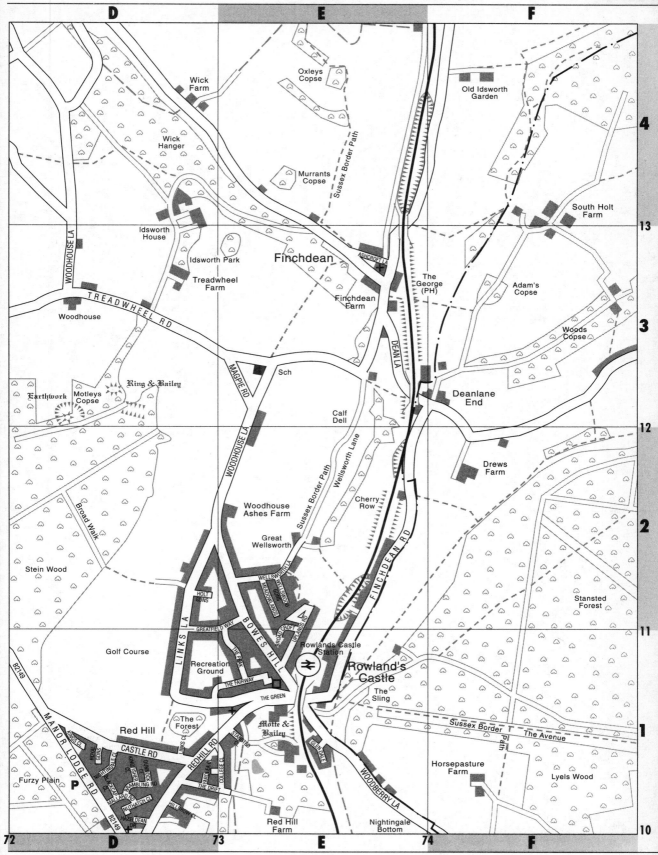

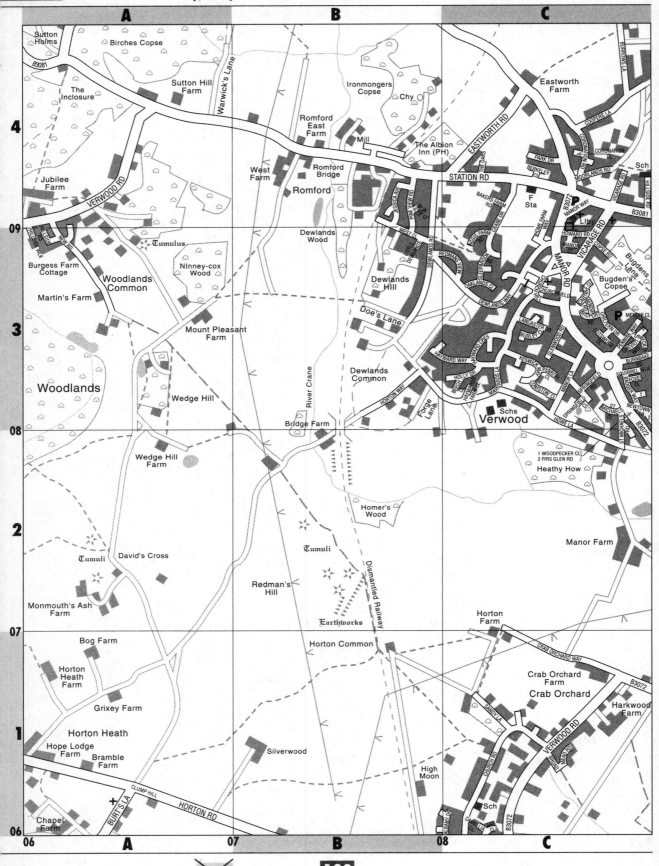

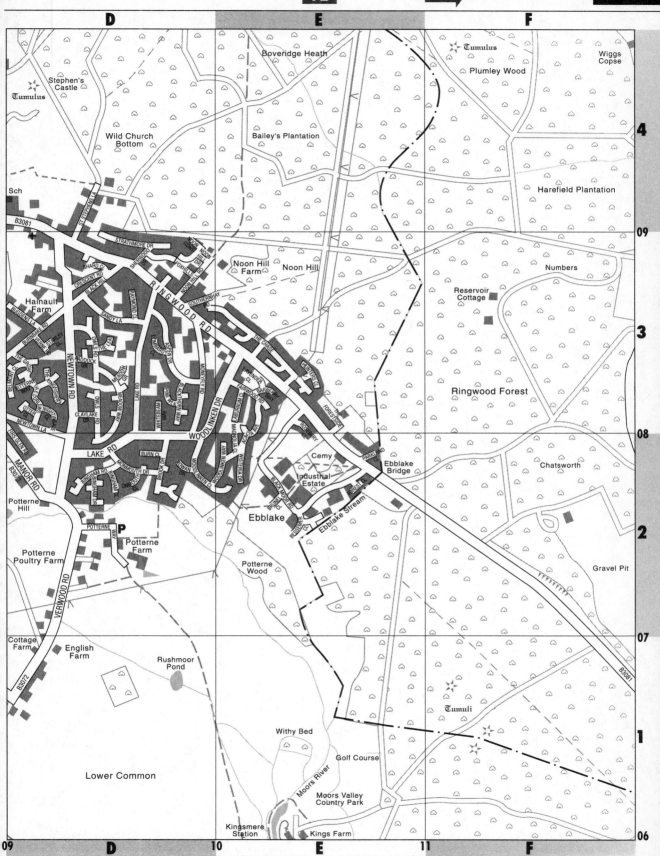

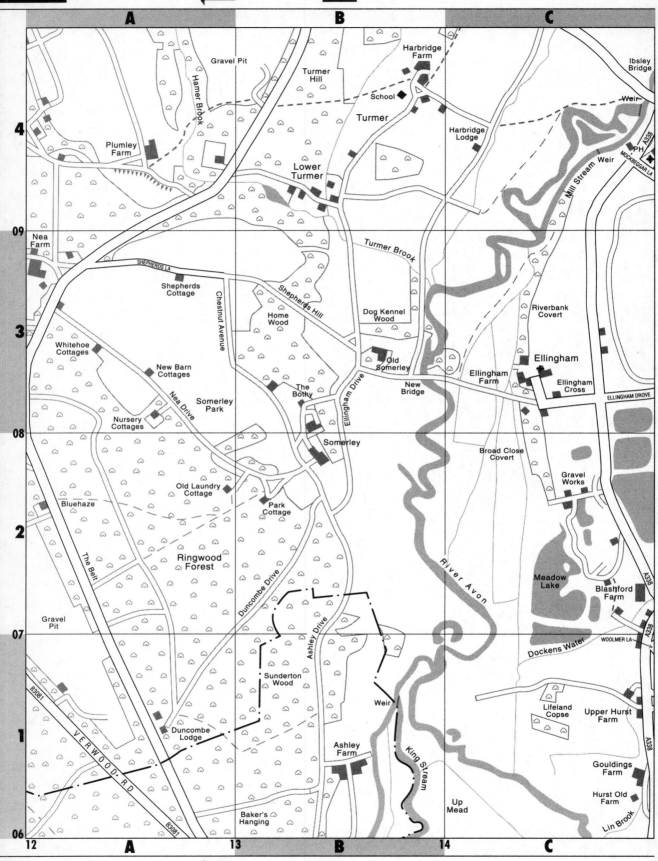

A

B

C

4

09

3

08

2

1

12

13

14

06

07

Gravel Pit

Hamer Brook

Turmer Hill

Turmer

Harbridge Farm

School

Ibsley Bridge

Weir

Plumley Farm

Lower Turmer

Harbridge Lodge

A338

Mill Stream

Weir

MOCKBEGGAR LA

PH

Nea Farm

SHEPHERDS LA

Shepherds Cottage

Turmer Brook

Chestnut Avenue

Shepherds Hill

Home Wood

Dog Kennel Wood

Riverbank Covert

Ellingham

Whitehoe Cottages

New Barn Cottages

Nea Drive

Somerley Park

The Bothy

Ellingham Drive

Old Somerley

New Bridge

Ellingham Farm

Ellingham Cross

ELLINGHAM DROVE

Nursery Cottages

Somerley

Old Laundry Cottage

Park Cottage

Bluehaze

Ringwood Forest

Duncombe Drive

Ashley Drive

Broad Close Covert

Gravel Works

The Bell

River Avon

Meadow Lake

Blashford Farm

A338

Gravel Pit

Sunderton Wood

Weir

Dockens Water

WOOLMER LA

A338

B3081

VERWOOD RD

Duncombe Lodge

Ashley Farm

King Stream

Lifeland Copse

Upper Hurst Farm

B3081

Baker's Hanging

Up Mead

Gouldings Farm

Hurst Old Farm

Lin Brook

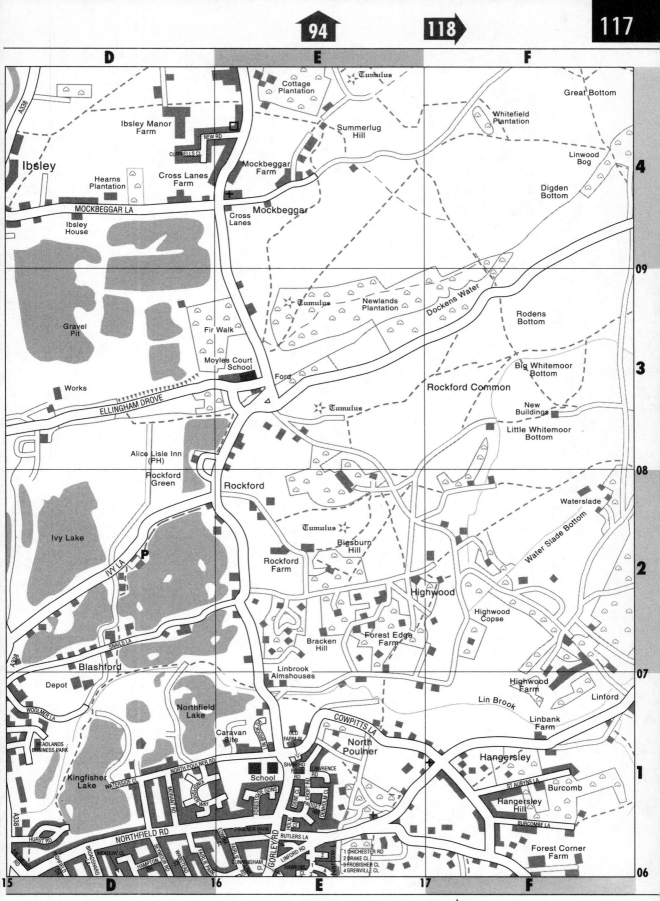

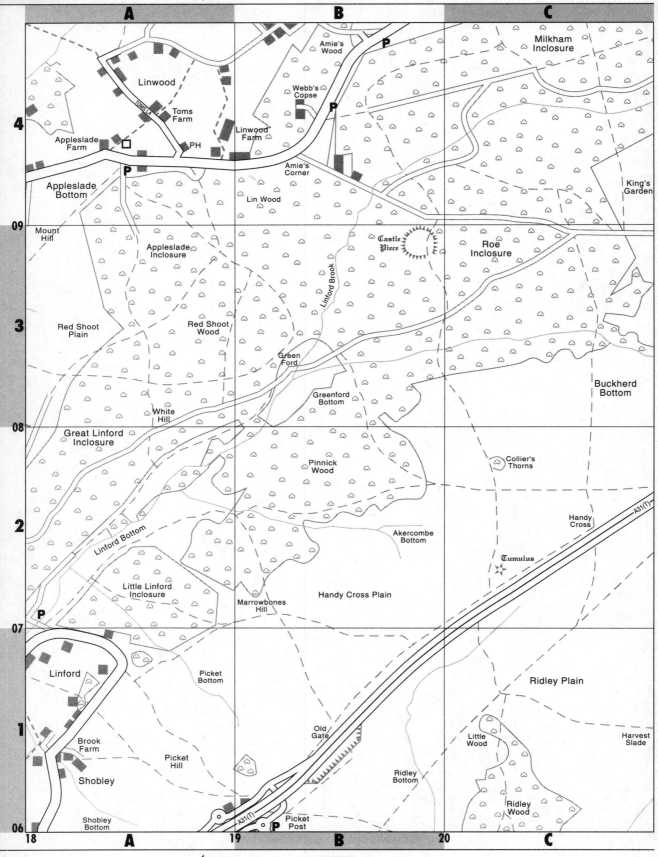

A      B      C

Linwood

Amie's Wood

**P**

Webb's Copse

Milkham Inclosure

Toms Farm

TOMS LA

Linwood Farm

King's Garden

Appleslade Farm

**P**

PH

**P**

Amie's Corner

Appleslade Bottom

Lin Wood

Mount Hill

Appleslade Inclosure

Castle Piece

Roe Inclosure

Linford Brook

Red Shoot Plain

Red Shoot Wood

Buckherd Bottom

Green Ford

White Hill

Greenford Bottom

Great Linford Inclosure

Pinnick Wood

Collier's Thorns

Linford Bottom

A31(T)

Handy Cross

Akercombe Bottom

Tumulus

Little Linford Inclosure

Marrowbones Hill

Handy Cross Plain

**P**

Ridley Plain

Linford

Picket Bottom

Old Gate

Little Wood

Harvest Slade

Brook Farm

Picket Hill

Ridley Bottom

Shobley

Ridley Wood

Shobley Bottom

A31(T)

Picket Post

**P**

18    A      19    B      20    C

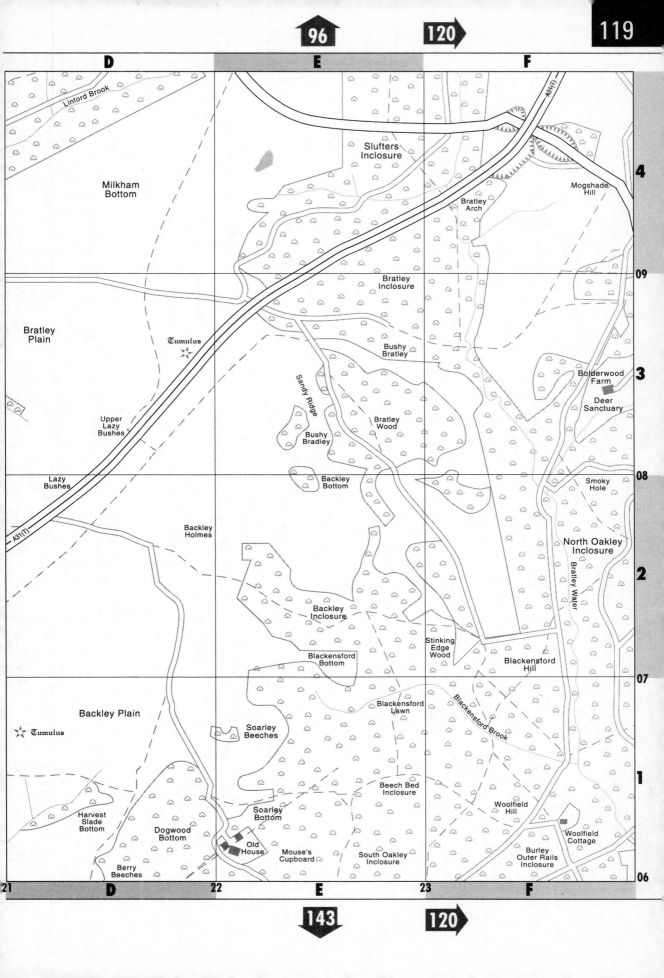

Linford Brook

Slufters
Inclosure

**4**

Milkham
Bottom

Mogshade
Hill

Bratley
Arch

A34(T)

**09**

Bratley
Inclosure

Bratley
Plain

Tumulus

Bushy
Bratley

Bolderwood
Farm

**3**

Sandy Ridge

Deer
Sanctuary

Bratley
Wood

Upper
Lazy
Bushes

Bushy
Bradley

Lazy
Bushes

Backley
Bottom

Smoky
Hole

**08**

A31(T)

North Oakley
Inclosure

Backley
Holmes

**2**

Bratley Water

Backley
Inclosure

Stinking
Edge
Wood

Blackensford
Bottom

Blackensford
Hill

**07**

Backley Plain

Blackensford
Lawn

Blackensford Brook

Tumulus

Soarley
Beeches

**1**

Beech Bed
Inclosure

Woolfield
Hill

Soarley
Bottom

Dogwood
Bottom

Old
House

Mouse's
Cupboard

South Oakley
Inclosure

Woolfield
Cottage

Burley
Outer Rails
Inclosure

Berry
Beeches

Harvest
Slade
Bottom

**06**

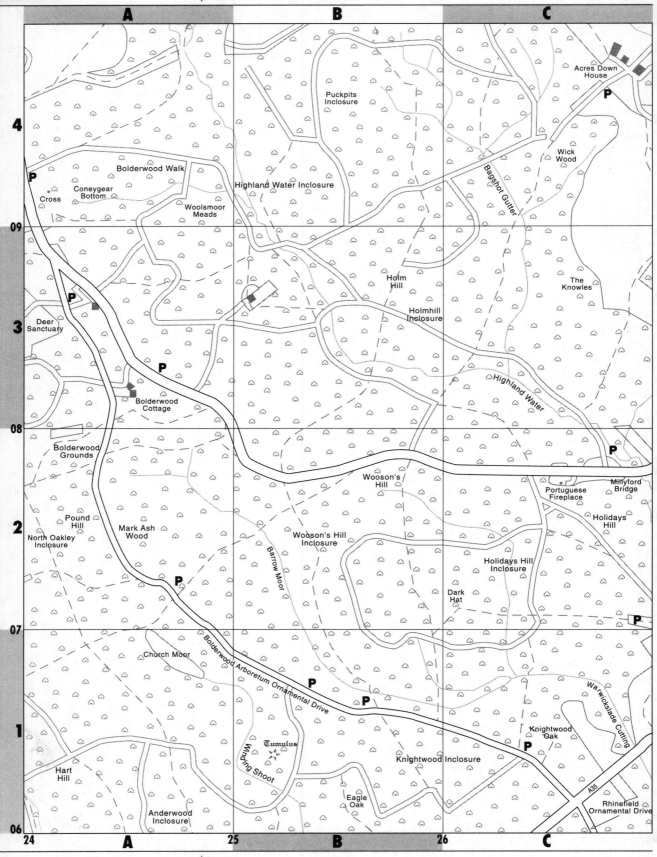

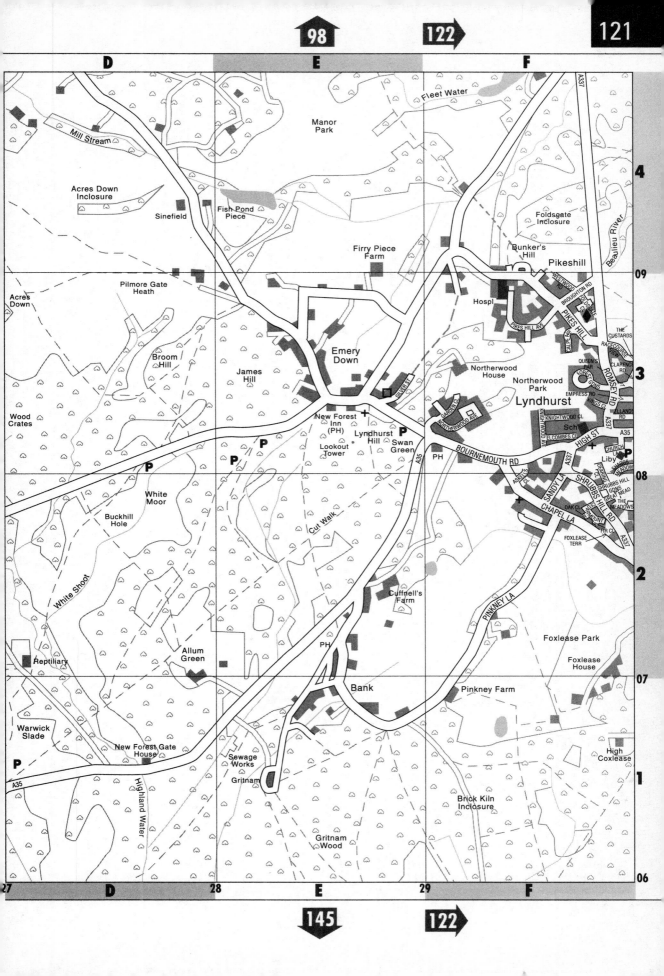

D   E   F

4

**Fleet Water**

Manor
Park

Acres Down
Inclosure

Mill Stream

Sinefield

Fish Pond
Piece

Firry Piece
Farm

Foldsgate
Inclosure

Bunker's
Hill

Pikeshill

Hospl

09

Acres
Down

Pilmore Gate
Heath

Broom
Hill

Emery
Down

James
Hill

Northerwood
House

Northerwood
Park

THE
CUSTARDS

RACECOURSE

QUEEN'S
PAR

CLARENCE
RD

**Lyndhurst**

Wood
Crates

New Forest
Inn
(PH)

Lyndhurst
Hill

Lookout
Tower

Swan
Green

P

PH

BOURNEMOUTH RD

HIGH ST

CHURCH

Liby

3

White
Moor

Buckhill
Hole

P

P

P

Cut Walk

P

SANDY LA

SHRUBBS HILL RD

CHAPEL LA

THE
MEADOWS

FOXLEASE
TERR

08

White Shoot

Allum
Green

Cuffnell's
Farm

PH

PINKNEY LA

Foxlease Park

Foxlease
House

2

Reptiliary

Bank

Pinkney Farm

07

Warwick
Slade

P

New Forest Gate
House

Sewage
Works

Gritnam

High
Coxlease

1

A35

Highland Water

Brick Kiln
Inclosure

Gritnam
Wood

06

121
99

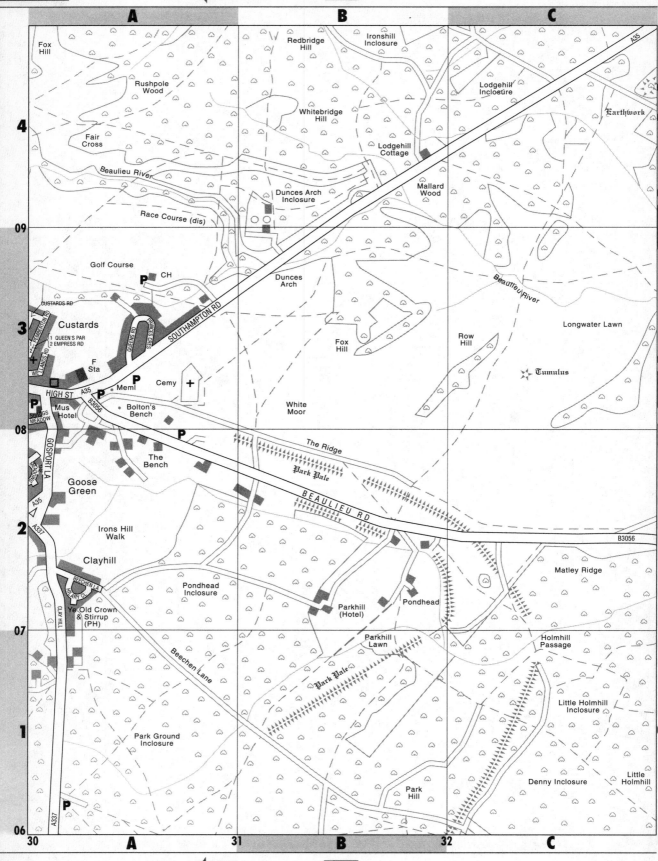

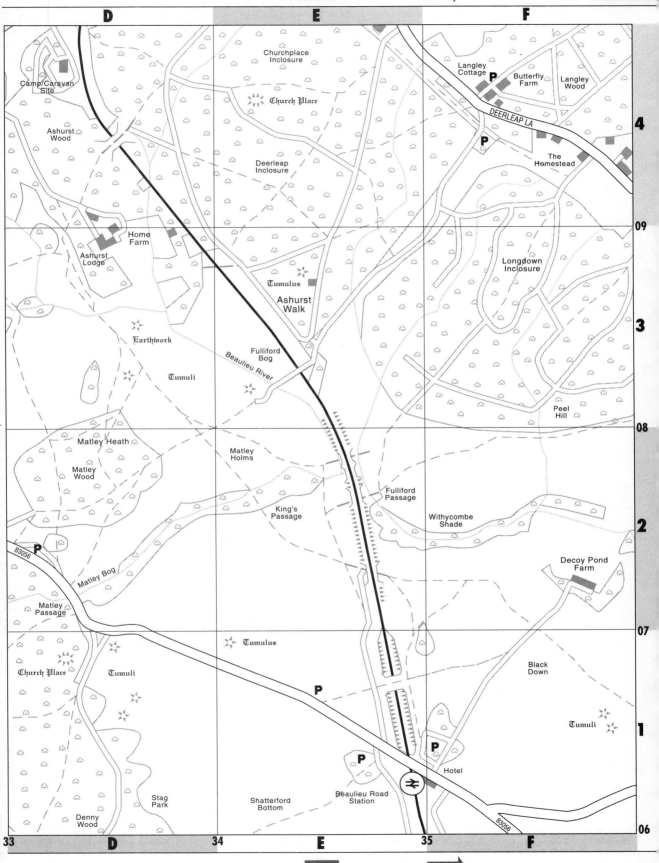

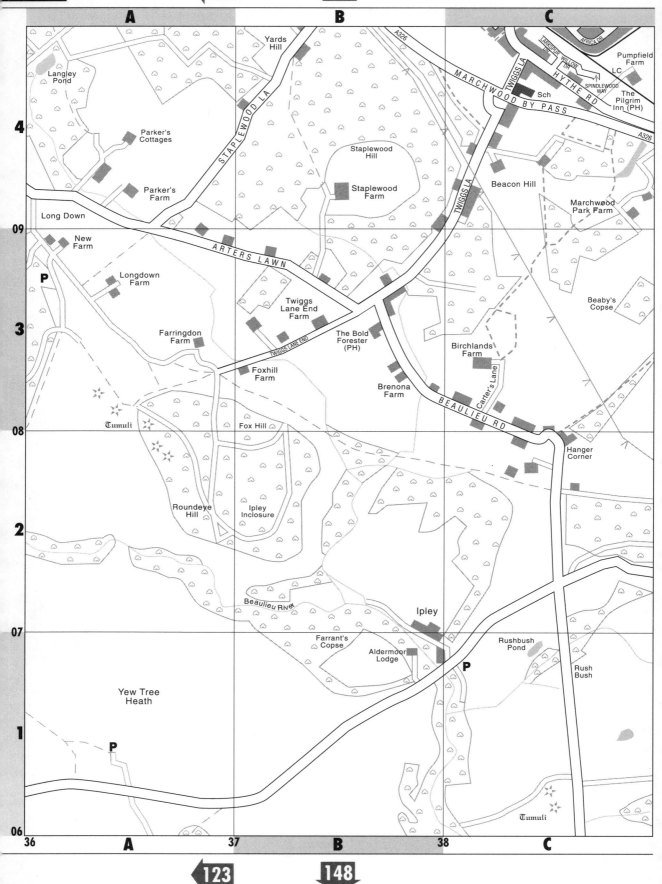

A B C

4

09

P

3

08

2

07

1

06

36 A 37 B 38 C

Langley Pond
Parker's Cottages
Parker's Farm
Long Down
New Farm
Longdown Farm
Farringdon Farm
Foxhill Farm
Tumuli
Fox Hill
Roundeye Hill
Ipley Inclosure
Beaulieu Rd
Farrant's Copse
Aldermoor Lodge
Yew Tree Heath
P

Yards Hill
STAPLEWOOD LA.
Staplewood Hill
Staplewood Farm
ARTERS LAWN
Twiggs Lane End Farm
TWIGGS LANE END
The Bold Forester (PH)
Brenona Farm
Ipley
P

A326
MARCHWOOD BY PASS
TWIGGS LA.
Beacon Hill
Marchwood Park Farm
Beaby's Copse
Birchlands Farm
Carter's Lane
BEAULIEU RD
Hanger Corner
Rushbush Pond
Rush Bush
Tumuli

LARKSPUR DR
WILLOW DR
AFRICA DR
SPINDLEWOOD WAY
HYTHE RD
Pumpfield Farm
LC
The Pilgrim Inn (PH)
Sch
A326

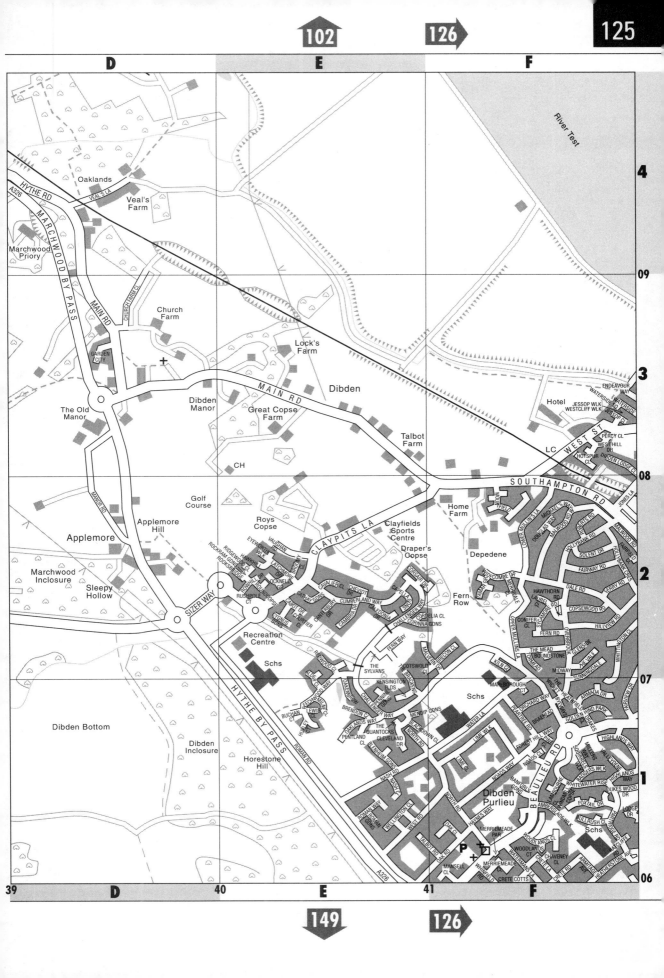

River Test

4

Oaklands
VEAL'S LA
Veal's Farm
HYTHE RD
A326
Marchwood Priory
MARCHWOOD BY PASS
MAIN RD
CHURCH FARM CL

09

Church Farm
GARDEN CITY
Lock's Farm

3

The Old Manor
MAIN RD
Dibden
ENDEAVOUR WAY
WATERSIDE
Hotel
Dibden Manor
Great Copse Farm
Talbot Farm
JESSOP WLK
WESTCLIFF WLK
PERCY CL
WEST HILL DR
LC
WEST ST
HOTSPUR CL
DIBDEN LODGE CL

08

CH
Golf Course
Roys Copse
Clayfields Sports Centre
Draper's Copse
Home Farm
SOUTHAMPTON RD
JONES LA
MOUNTFIELD
MICHAEL'S WAY
MALWOOD RD

Applemore Hill
Applemore
MANOR RD
Depedene
FERN ROW
FAIRWAY RD
DALE RD
KERRY RD
COPSEWOOD RD

2

Marchwood Inclosure
Sleepy Hollow
SIZER WAY
Recreation Centre
Schs
CLAYPITS LA
Fern Row
CONIFER CL
FERN RD
OVERBROOK
HILLVIEW RD
THE MEAD
BOUNDSTONE
MIDWAY
SUNNINGDALE

07

Dibden Bottom
HYTHE BY PASS
Dibden Inclosure
Horestone Hill
ROMAN RD
THE SYLVANS
KENSINGTON FLDS
Schs
MARLBOROUGH
KILN CL
ARMADA DR
GOLDEN HIND PARK
DRAKES

Dibden Purlieu
BEAULIEU RD
Schs
HIGHLANDS WAY

1

ROMAN WAY
WELLINGTON RD
WEST RD
NORTH RD
P
MERRIEMEADE PAR
MERRIEMEADE CL
CRETE COTTS

06

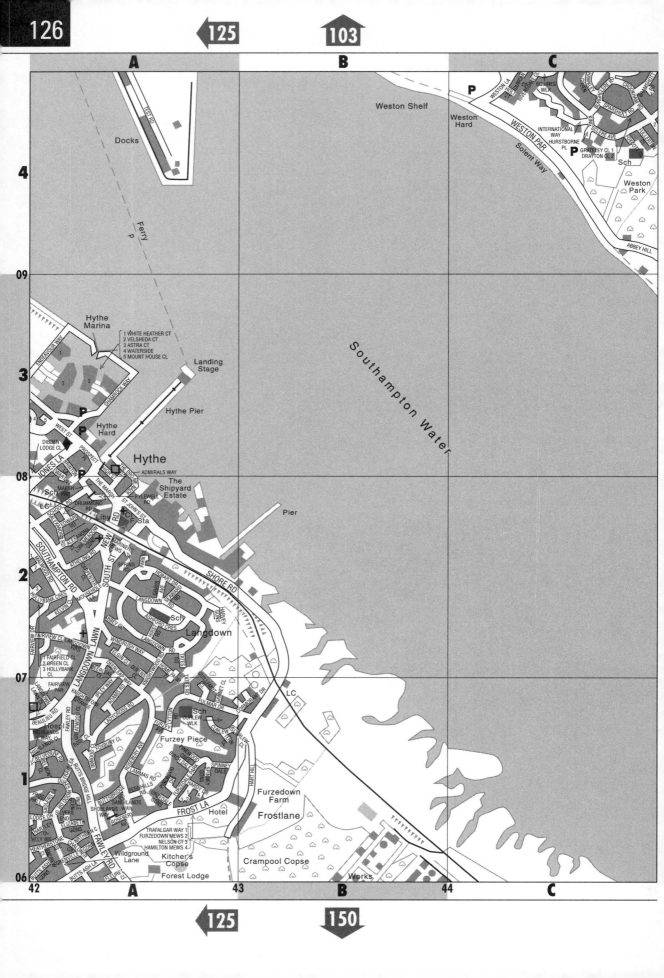

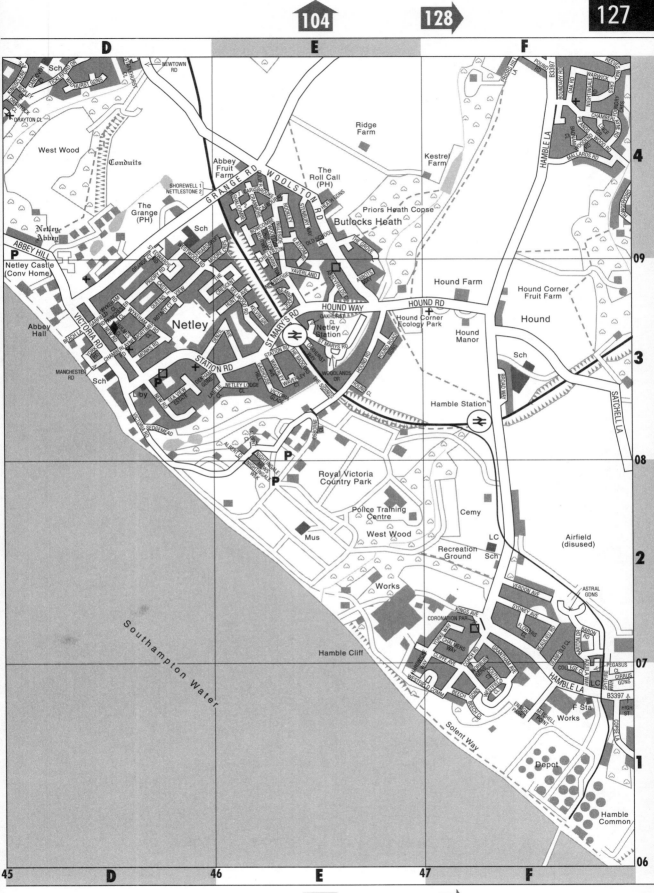

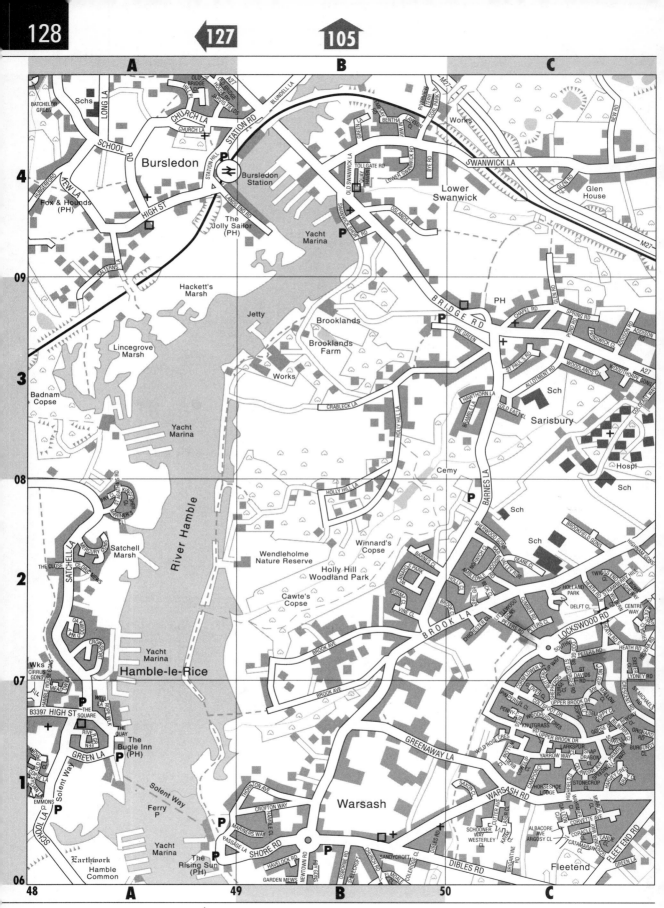

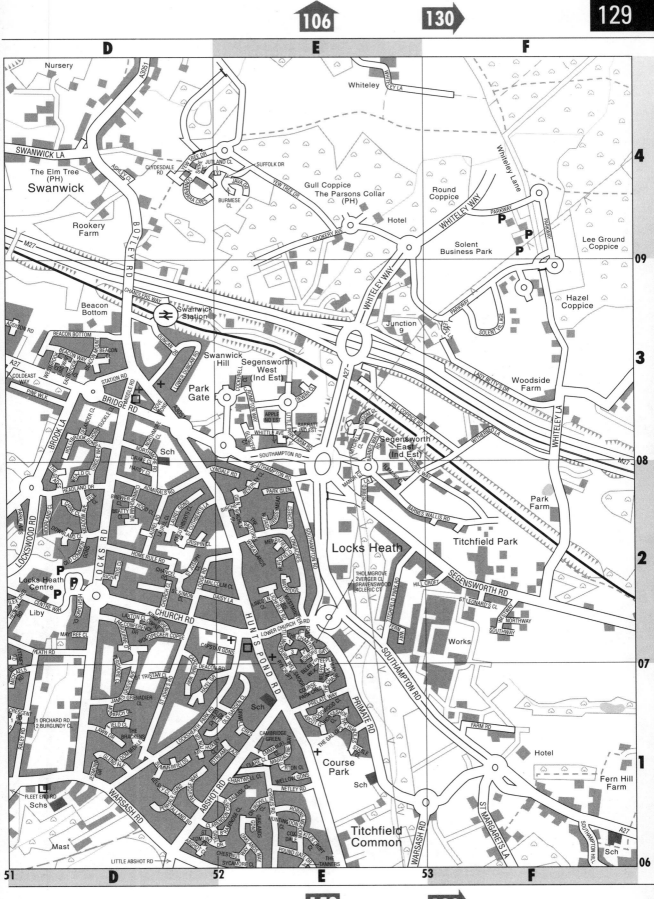

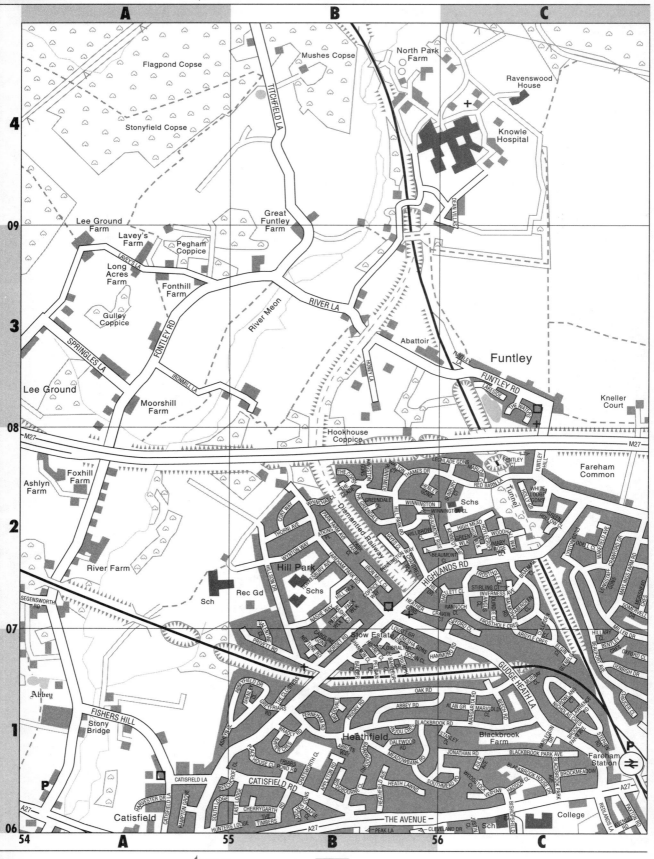

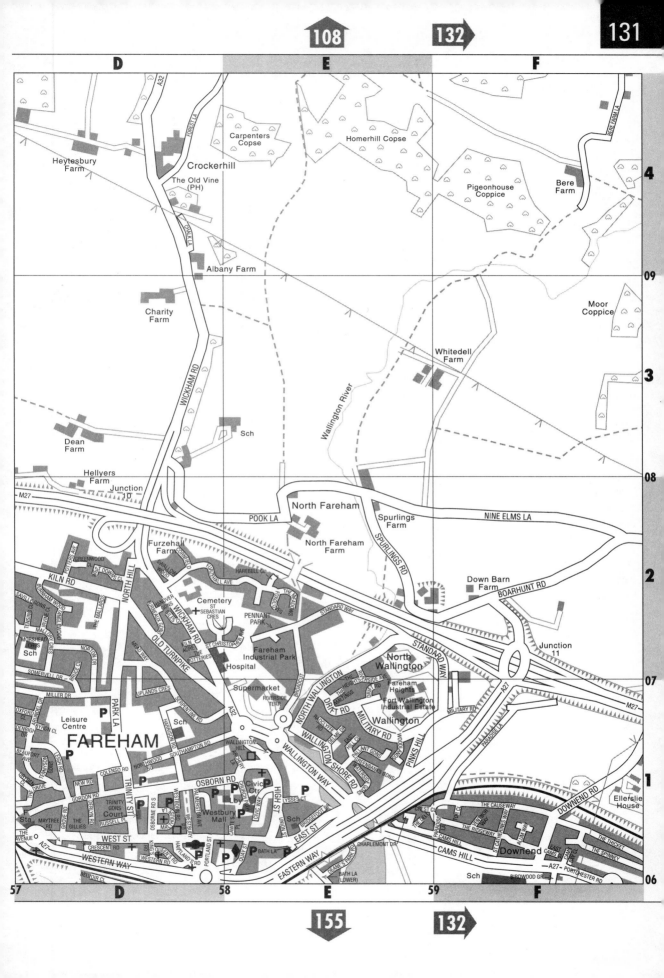

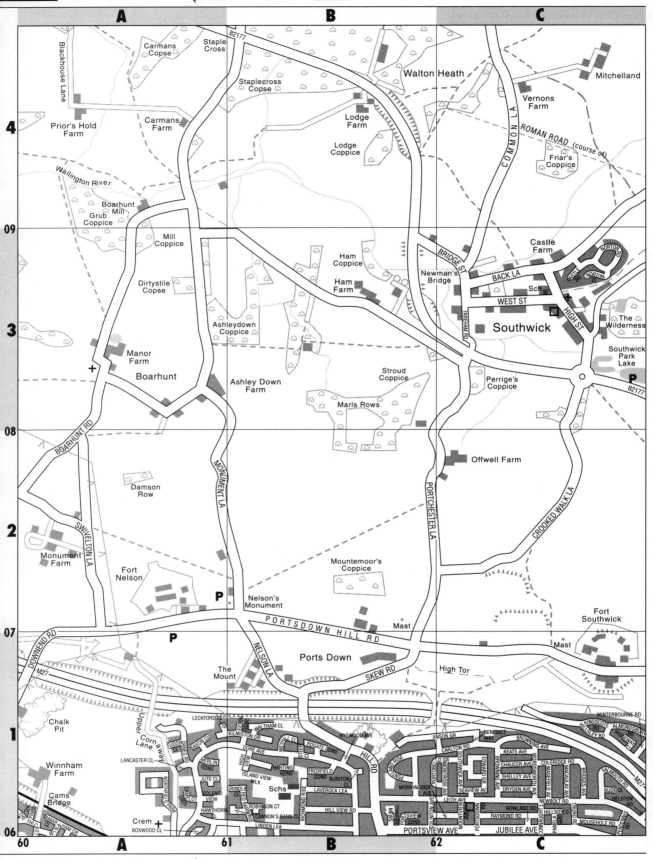

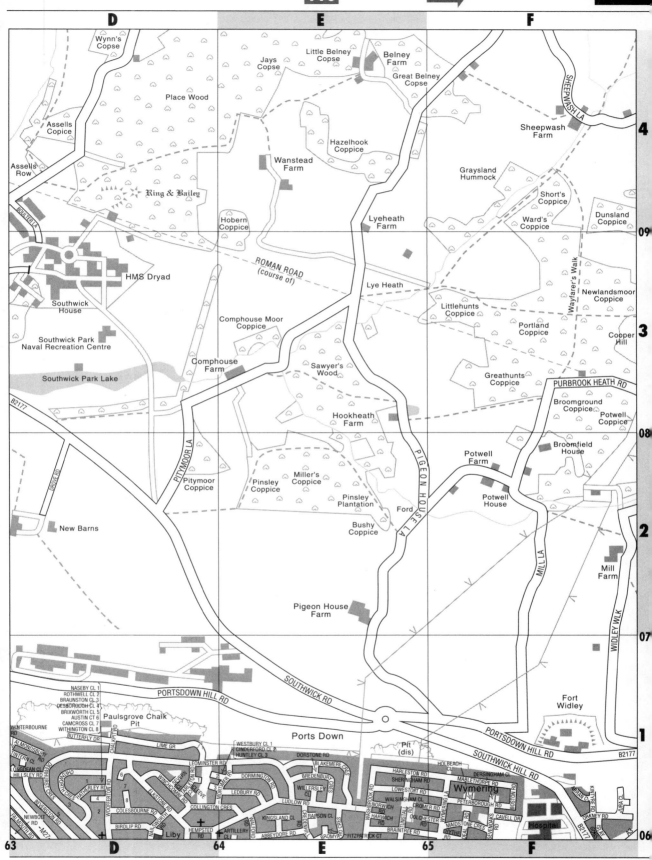

**D**

Wynn's Copse

Place Wood

Assells Copice

Assells Row

BOULTER LA

Ring & Bailey

Hobern Coppice

HMS Dryad

Southwick House

Southwick Park Naval Recreation Centre

Southwick Park Lake

B2177

Comphouse Farm

Comphouse Moor Coppice

PITYMOOR LA

Pitymoor Coppice

DROVE RD

New Barns

**E**

Jays Copse

Little Belney Copse

Belney Farm

Great Belney Copse

Hazelhook Coppice

Wanstead Farm

Lyeheath Farm

ROMAN ROAD (course of)

Lye Heath

Sawyer's Wood

Hookheath Farm

Pinsley Coppice

Miller's Coppice

Pinsley Plantation

Bushy Coppice

Ford

PIGEON HOUSE LA

Pigeon House Farm

**F**

SHEEPWASH LA

Sheepwash Farm

Graysland Hummock

Short's Coppice

Ward's Coppice

Dunsland Coppice

Wayfarer's Walk

Newlandsmoor Coppice

Littlehunts Coppice

Portland Coppice

Cooper Hill

Greathunts Coppice

PURBROOK HEATH RD

Broomground Coppice

Potwell Coppice

Broomfield House

Potwell Farm

Potwell House

MILL A

Mill Farm

WIDLEY WLK

**4**

**09**

**3**

**08**

**2**

**07**

SOUTHWICK RD

PORTSDOWN HILL RD

NASEBY CL 1
ROTHWELL CL 2
BRAUNSTON CL 3
DESBOROUGH CL 4
BRIXWORTH CL 5
AUSTIN CT 6
CAMCROSS CL 7
WITHINGTON CL 8

Paulsgrove Chalk Pit

WINTERBOURNE RD

BUTTERFLY DR

CHALK PIT RD

LIME GR

WESTBURY CL 1
CINDERFORD CL 2
HUNTLEY CL 3

Dorstone RD

LEOMINSTER RD

DORMINGTON RD

LEDBURY RD

LUDLOW RD

Ports Down

BLAKEMERE CRES

BREDENBURY CRES

WILLERSLEY CL

Pit (dis)

HOLBEACH CL

HARLESTON RD

SHERINGHAM RD

LOWESTOFT RD

NORWICH RD

WALSINGHAM CL

Fort Widley

PORTSDOWN HILL RD

SOUTHWICK HILL RD

DERSINGHAM CL

MABLETHORPE RD

PETERBOROUGH RD

BOSTON RD

**Wymering**

B2177

**1**

**06**

ALMONDSBURY RD

TINTERN CL

ORGREAN CL

HILLSLEY RD

NEWBOLT RD

M27

FALMOUTH RD

ORCHARD CRES

HURST CRES

WARLEY RD

BIRDLIP RD

COLESBOURNE RD

Liby

WINNALL CL

CHAWTON CL

NORTHOVER RD

ELKSTONE RD

WALFORD

COLLINGTON CRES

KINGSLAND CL

ABBEYDORE RD

HEMPSTED RD

ARTILLERY CL

FITZPATRICK CT

BROMYARD

CREDENHILL

RAPSON RD

HARWICH RD

BRAINTREE RD

WASHBROOK RD

COLCHESTER RD

WYCHE

MAIDSTONE CRES

BLYTHE

DEAL CRES

SEVENOAKS RD

CAVELL DR

Hospital

B2177

ARKNEY RD

KINTYRE RD

PERCY RD

**63** **D** **64** **E** **65** **F**

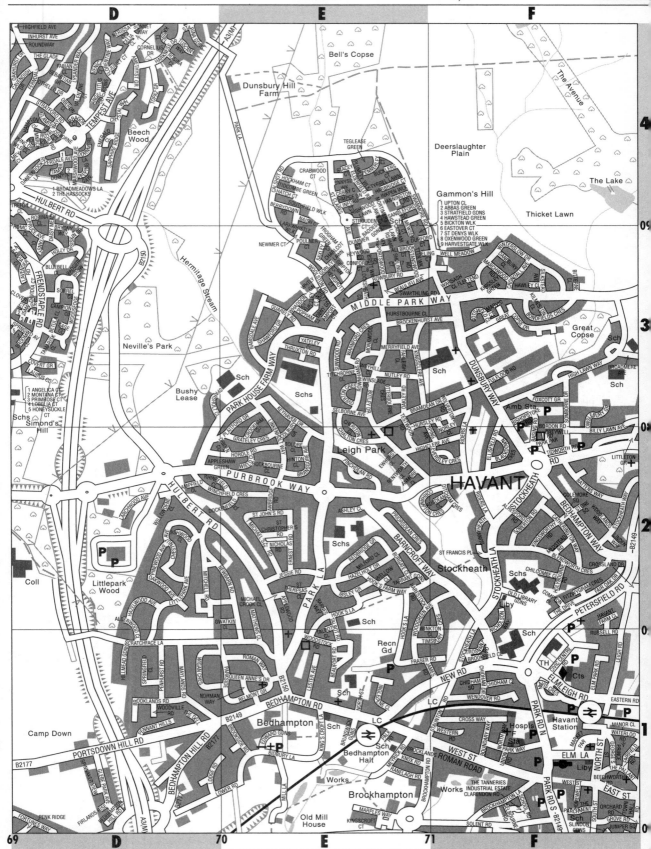

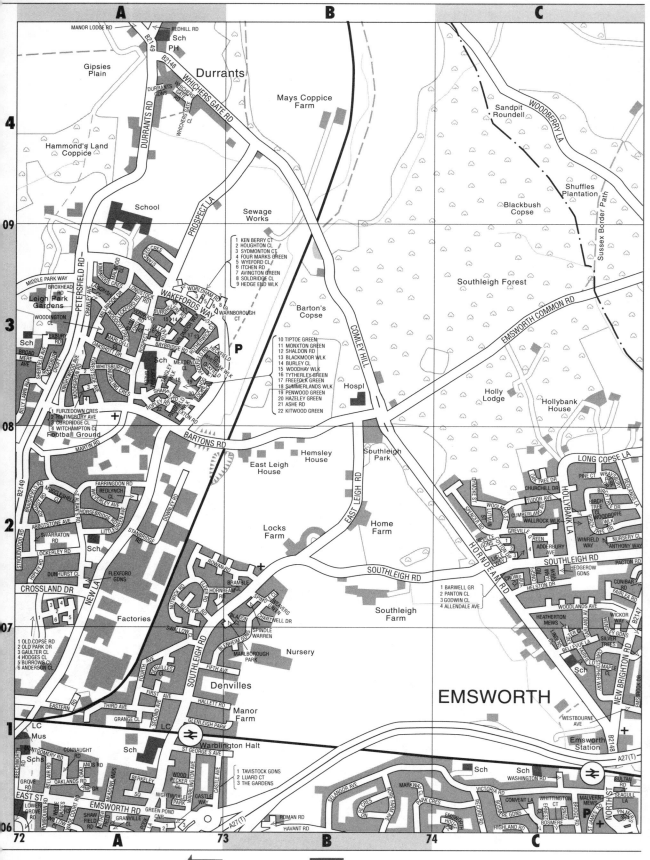

A      B      C

MANOR LODGE RD
REDHILL RD
Sch
PH
B2149

Gipsies Plain

WHICHERS GATE RD

Durrants

Mays Coppice Farm

4

Hammond's Land Coppice

WOODBERRY LA

Sandpit Roundell

Shuffles Plantation

School

DURRANTS RD

PROSPECT LA

Sewage Works

Blackbush Copse

Sussex Border Path

09

MIDDLE PARK WAY

Leigh Park Gardens

WAKEFORDS WAY

1 KEN BERRY CT
2 HOUGHTON CL
3 SYDMONTON CT
4 FOUR MARKS GREEN
5 WYEFORD CL
6 ITCHEN RD
7 AVINGTON GREEN
8 SOLDRIDGE CL
9 HEDGE END WLK

Southleigh Forest

Barton's Copse

COMLEY HILL

3

Sch

WARNBOROUGH CT

10 TIPTOE GREEN
11 MONXTON GREEN
12 SHALDON RD
13 BLACKMOOR WLK
14 BURLEY CL
15 WOODHAY WLK
16 TYTHERLEY GREEN
17 FREEFOLK GREEN
18 SUMMERLANDS WLK
19 PENWOOD GREEN
20 HAZELEY GREEN
21 ASHE RD
22 KITWOOD GREEN

Holly Lodge

Hollybank House

EMSWORTH COMMON RD

P

08

1 FURZEDOWN CRES
2 HILTINGBURY AVE
3 CURDRIDGE CL
4 WITCHAMPTON CL

Football Ground

MARTIN RD

BARTONS RD

Hemsley House

Southleigh Park

East Leigh House

LONG COPSE LA

B2149

Farringdon Rd
REDLYNCH CL

EAST LEIGH RD

CHURCHILL DR

TUDOR AVE

HOLLYBANK LA

2

Sch

STANBRIDGE RD

Locks Farm

Home Farm

HORNDEAN RD

CUMBERLAND

WALLROCK WLK

WINFIELD WAY

NURSERY CL
ANTHONY WAY

SOUTHLEIGH RD

CROSSLAND DR

NEW LA

FLEXFORD GDNS

SOUTHLEIGH RD

1 BARWELL GR
2 PANTON CL
3 GODWIN CL
4 ALLENDALE AVE

PACTON RD
B2147

07

1 OLD COPSE RD
2 OLD PARK DR
3 GAULTER CL
4 HODGES CL
5 BURROWS CL
6 ANDERSON CL

Factories

SOUTHLEIGH RD

SWALLOW

SPINDLE WARREN

BLENHEIM GDNS

MARLBOROUGH PARK

Southleigh Farm

Nursery

HEATHERTON MEWS

WICKOR WAY

SILVER TREES

Sch

NEW BRIGHTON RD

Denvilles

Manor Farm

EMSWORTH

WESTBOURNE AVE

1

LC
Mus

LC

Warblington Halt

Emsworth Station

A27(T)

Sch

Sch
WASHINGTON RD

Emsworth Station

SULTAN RD

SEAGULL RD

P

EAST ST

EMSWORTH RD

1 TAVISTOCK GDNS
2 LUARD CT
3 THE GARDENS

Sch
Sch

A27(T)

HAVANT RD

RDMAN RD

MARK WAY

PARK CRES

VICTORIA RD

CONVENT LA

WHITTINGTON CT

MALVERN MEWS

NORTHST

06

72      A      73      B      74      C

D E F

Holme Farm
Stubbermere
Racton Common
Pond Cottage
Pond Copse
Brickkiln Ponds
The Groves
Park Lane
Park Lane
Sindle's Farm
New Barn Cottage
Walderton
Racton Monument
Watercress Beds
Aldsworth
Ell Bridge
Ellbridge Buildings
WOODBERRY LA
Westbourne Common
Valley Farm
Cricket Ground
Aldsworth Manor
Aldsworth Common
COMMON RD
Longcopse Hill
Monk's Farm
MONK'S HILL
Didmans Copse
Hollybank Farm
COMMONSIDE
Commonside
River Ems
Woodmancote
LONG COPSE LA
Sch
River Ems
FOXBURY LA
Deepsprings
Woodmancote Farm
Bishop's Barn Farm
Manor House
PARADISE LA
NORTH ST
MILL RD
RIVER ST
Westbourne
1 NURSERY CL
2 SOUTHLEIGH RD
3 RACTON RD
THE SQUARE
King St
EAST ST
B2147
Cemy
CEMETERY LA
Woodmancote
WOODMANCOTE LA
Woodmancote (PH)
South Lane Farm
Hampshire Farm
Chantry Farm
WESTBOURNE RD
NEW RD
Lumley Farm
WHITECHIMNEY ROW
SOUTH LA
A27(T)
New Brighton
OLD FARM LA
SOUTH LA
Sussex Border Path
MILL LA
Lumley Croft
Lumley Mill Farm
Lumley
Seagull Lane
A27(T)
College
ST JOHN'S RD
PARK RD
STEIN RD
CHESHIRE WY
FRASER GDNS
BREACH AVE
Breach
Loveders Farm
PRIORS LEAZE LA
COOKS LA
HURSTWOOD AVE
Inlands Farm
Inlands
WOODFIELD PARK RD
THE ROOKERY

75 76 77
09 08 07 06
4 3 2 1

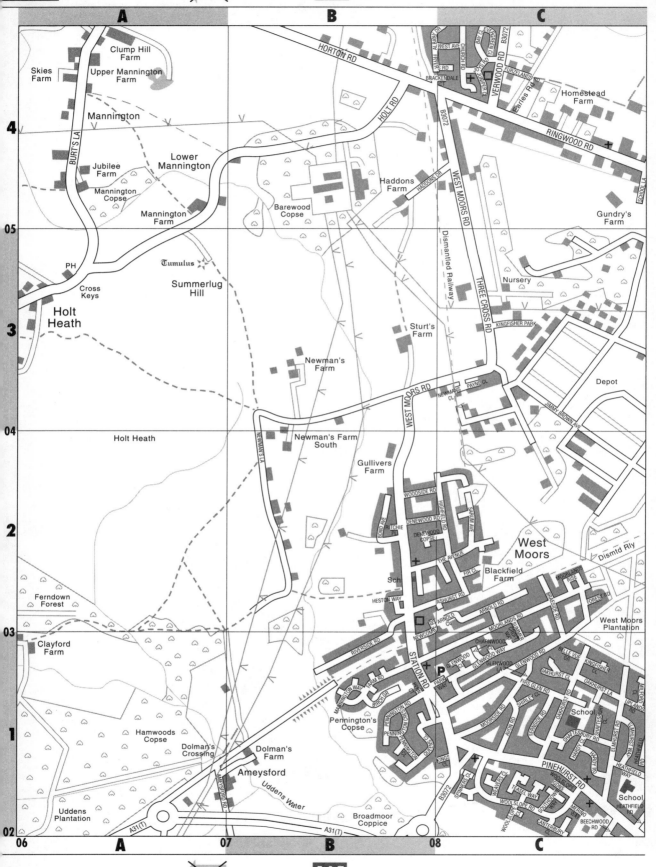

Holt Heath

Skies Farm

Clump Hill Farm

Upper Mannington Farm

Mannington

BURT'S LA

Jubilee Farm

Mannington Copse

Lower Mannington

Mannington Farm

HORTON RD

HOLT RD

Barewood Copse

Haddons Farm

HADDONS DR

WEST MOORS RD

B3072

ALBANY DR

WEST AVE

CHURCH RD

VERWOOD RD

FURZELANDS RD

Earles Rd

Homestead Farm

RINGWOOD RD

SCHOOL LA

Gundry's Farm

PH

Cross Keys

Holt Heath

Tumulus

Summerlug Hill

Dismantled Railway

THREE CROSS RD

Nursery

Kingfisher Park

KINGFISHER PARK

Sturt's Farm

Newman's Farm

WEST MOORS RD

Newman's Farm South

NEWMAN'S LA

Holt Heath

Gullivers Farm

Depot

Jimmy Brown Ave

JIMMY BROWN AVE

PAYNE CL

NEWMANS CL

WOODSIDE RD

RITCHIE

BOND AVE

DENEWOOD RD

HIGHFIELD RD

SARUM AVE

DENEWOOD COPSE

FIR CL

THE AVENUE

West Moors

MOORLANDS RISE

Ferndown Forest

Sch

Blackfield Farm

BRACKEN RD

FORES RD

West Moors Plantation

Dismtd Rly

HESTON WAY

ASHURST RD

ARNOLD RD

MOORLANDS RD

Clayford Farm

NEWCOMB

RIVERSIDE RD

STATION RD

ARNOLD CL

CHARNWOOD

GLENWOOD WAY

GLENWOOD RD

GLENWOOD RD

GLENWOOD RD

BELLE VUE

KINGFISHER

P

PARK WAY

FIRS GLEN RD

OAKHURST CL

OAKHURST LA

MILFORD RD

UPLANDS CL

School

Pennington's Copse

MANNINGTON WAY

FARM RD

SPRINGFIELD

BIRCH GR

PENNINGTON RD

KINGS CL

PENNINGTON RD

MOORSIDE RD

AVON RD

SHIRLEY CL

FERNDOWN RD

SHAFTESBURY CL

HARDY RD

ELMHURST RD

HEATHFIELD WAY

Hamwoods Copse

Dolman's Crossing

Dolman's Farm

Ameysford

AMEYSFORD RD

Uddens Water

PINEHURST RD

B3072

SPINNERS CL

WEAVERS CL

TEASEL WAY

WOOLSLOPE RD

WOOLSLOPE RD

CANTERBURY RD

SANDOWN RD

MERINO WAY

BEECHWOOD RD

HARDY RD

WOODSIDE CL

School

HEATHFIELD RD

Uddens Plantation

A31(T)

A31(T)

Broadmoor Coppice

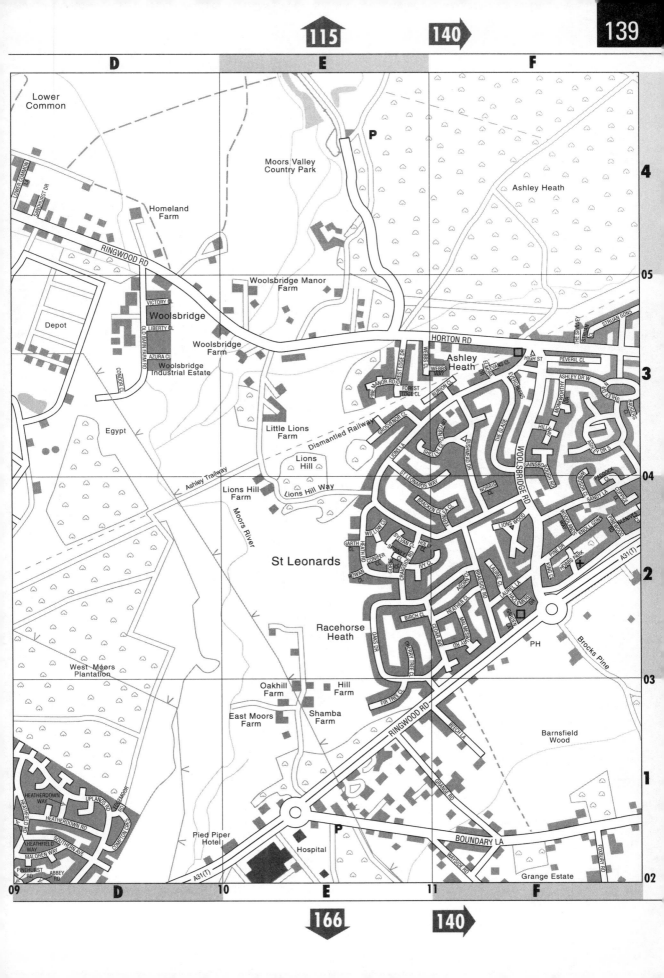

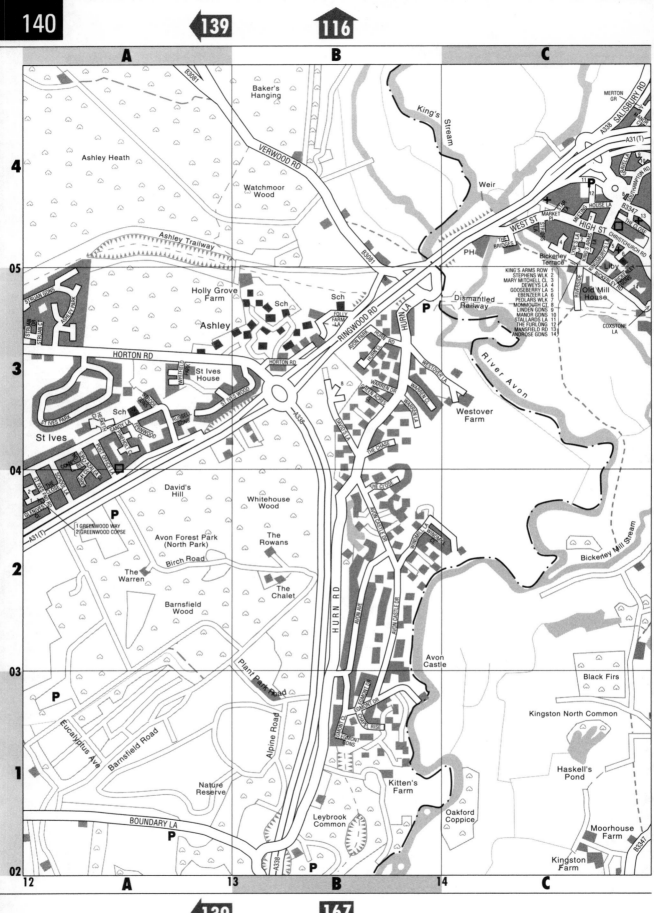

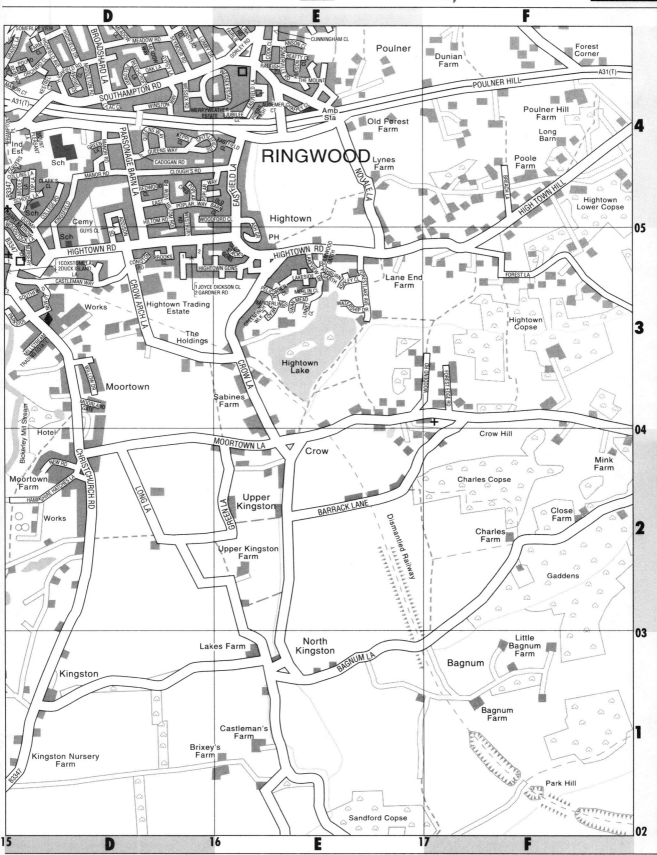

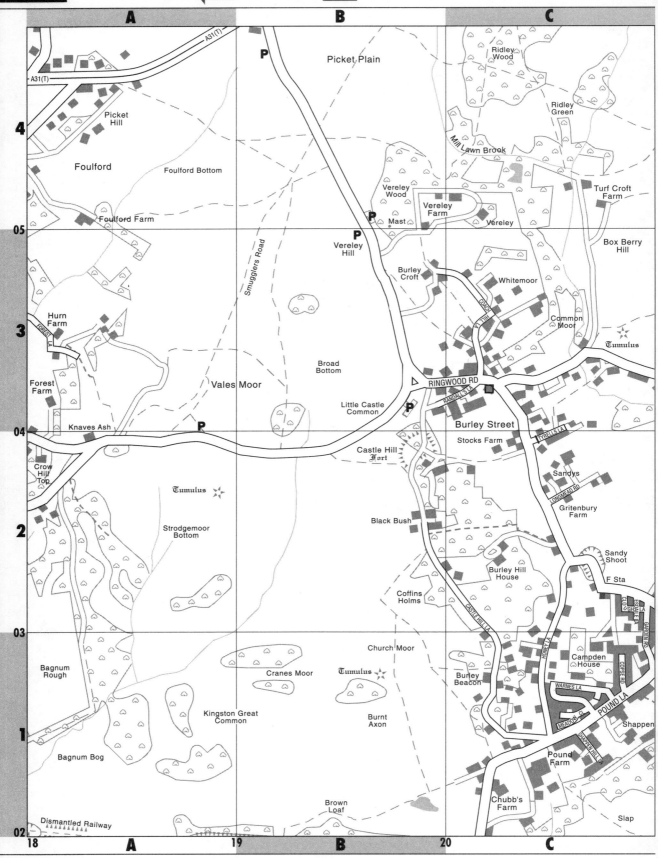

A31(T)

A31(T)

Picket Plain

Ridley
Wood

Ridley
Green

Picket
Hill

Mill Lawn Brook

Turf Croft
Farm

Foulford

Foulford Bottom

Vereley Wood

Vereley
Farm

Vereley

Box Berry
Hill

Foulford Farm

P

Mast

P

Vereley Hill

Smugglers Road

Burley
Croft

Whitemoor

Common
Moor

Tumulus

Hurn
Farm

Broad
Bottom

Vales Moor

Ringwood Rd

Forest
Farm

Little Castle
Common

P

Burley Street

Knaves Ash

P

Castle Hill
Fort

Stocks Farm

Crow
Hill
Top

Tumulus

Sandys

Gritenbury
Farm

Strodgemoor
Bottom

Black Bush

Sandy
Shoot

Burley Hill
House

F Sta

Coffins
Holms

Bagnum
Rough

Church Moor

Campden
House

Cranes Moor

Tumulus

Burley
Beacon

Kingston Great
Common

Burnt
Axon

WARNES LA

POUND LA

Shappen

Bagnum Bog

Pound
Farm

Chubb's
Farm

Slap

Dismantled Railway

Brown
Loaf

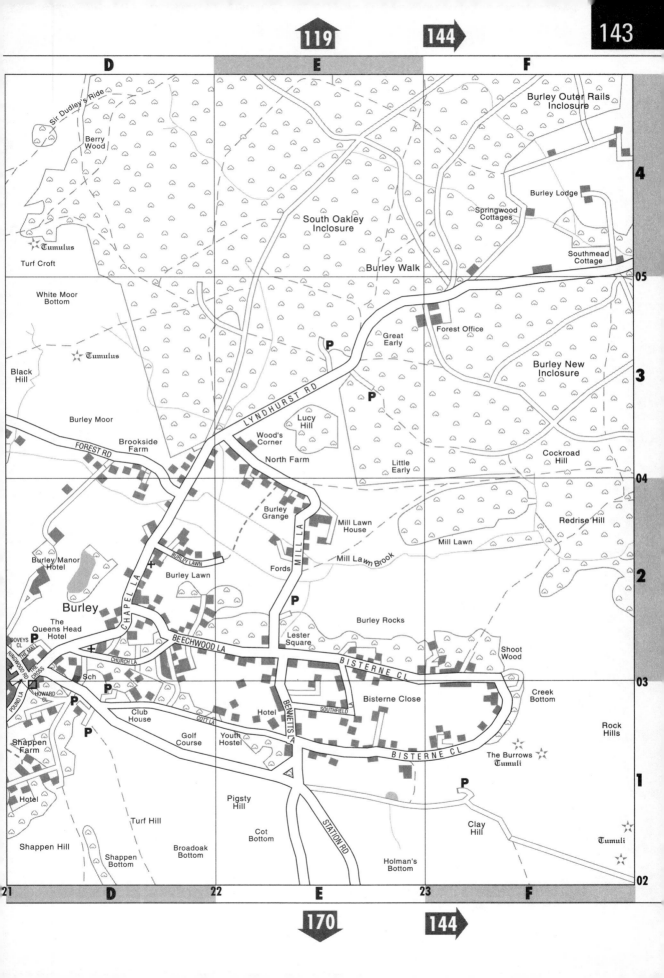

143
120

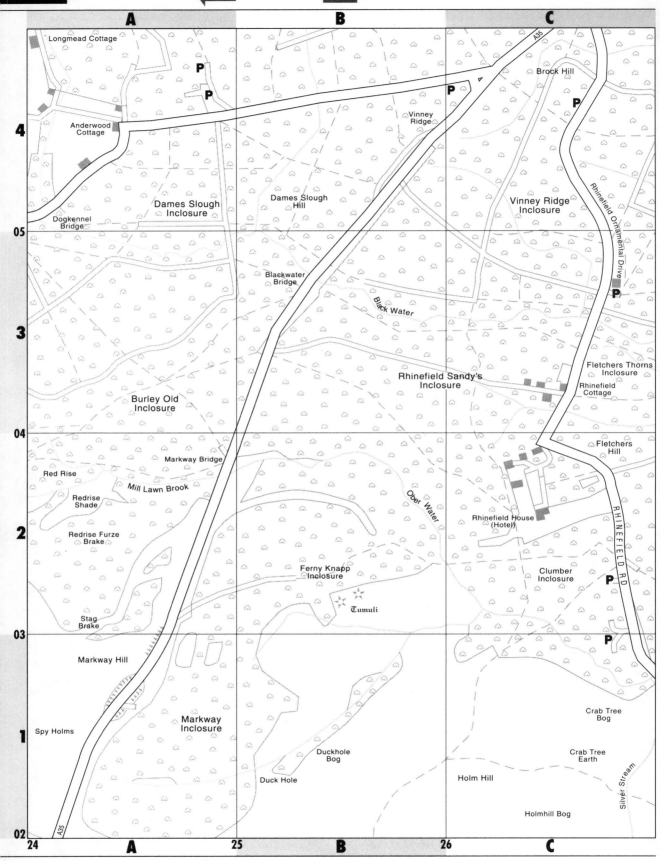

**A**      **B**      **C**

Longmead Cottage

P

P

Anderwood
Cottage

**4**

Dames Slough
Inclosure

Dames Slough
Hill

A35

Brock Hill

P

Vinney
Ridge

P

Vinney Ridge
Inclosure

Rhinefield Ornamental Drive

Dogkennel
Bridge

**05**

Blackwater
Bridge

Black Water

P

**3**

Fletchers Thorns
Inclosure

Rhinefield Sandy's
Inclosure

Rhinefield
Cottage

Burley Old
Inclosure

**04**

Fletchers
Hill

Markway Bridge

Red Rise

Mill Lawn Brook

Redrise
Shade

Ober Water

Rhinefield House
(Hotel)

RHINEFIELD RD

Redrise Furze
Brake

**2**

Ferny Knapp
Inclosure

Clumber
Inclosure

P

Stag
Brake

Tumuli

**03**

P

Markway Hill

Crab Tree
Bog

**1**

Spy Holms

Markway
Inclosure

Crab Tree
Earth

Duckhole
Bog

Silver Stream

Duck Hole

Holm Hill

A35

Holmhill Bog

**02**

24      **A**      25      **B**      26      **C**

143
171

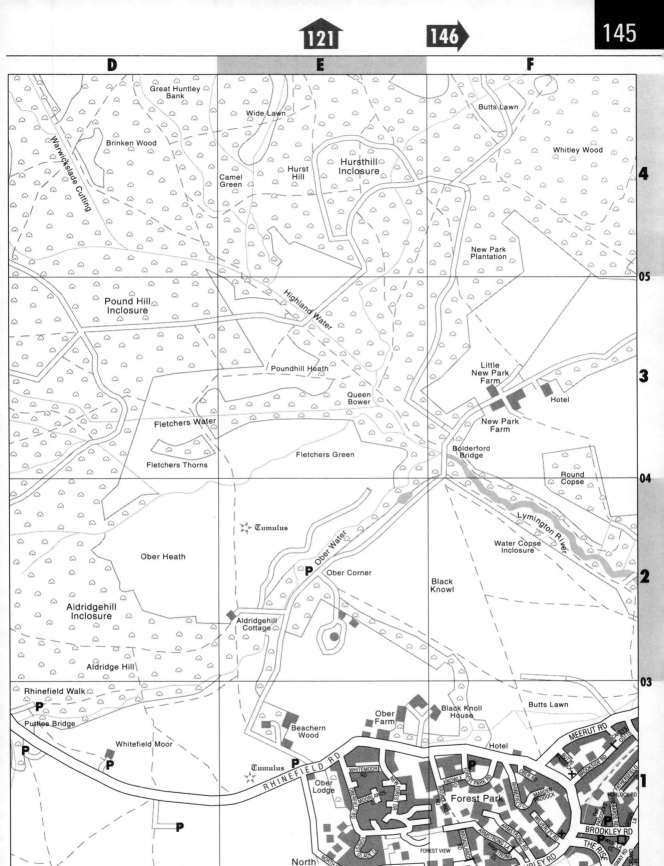

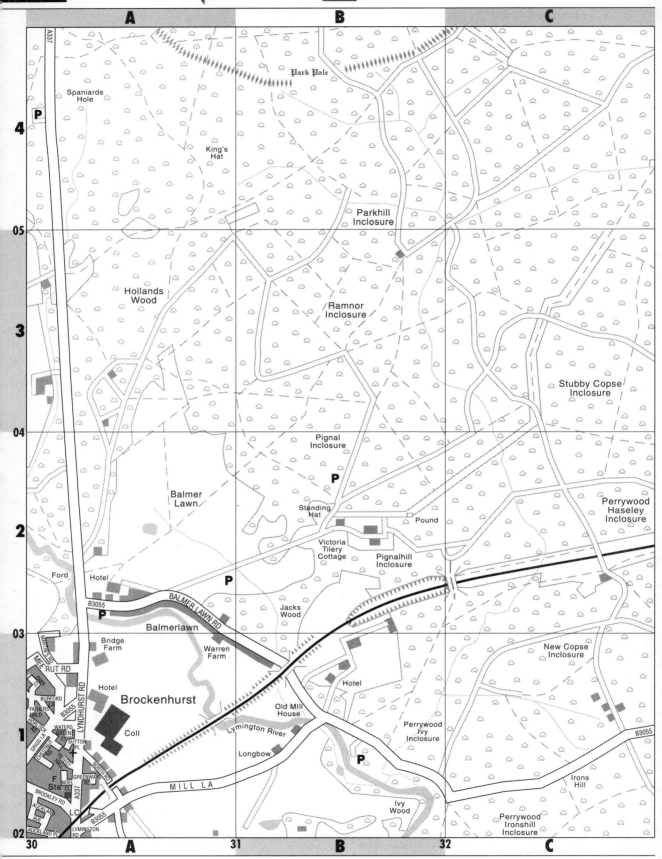

Park Pale

Spaniards
Hole

P

King's
Hat

Parkhill
Inclosure

Hollands
Wood

Ramnor
Inclosure

Stubby Copse
Inclosure

Pignal
Inclosure

P

Balmer
Lawn

Standing
Hat

Pound

Perrywood
Haseley
Inclosure

Victoria
Tilery
Cottage

Pignalhill
Inclosure

Ford

Hotel

P

BALMER LAWN RD

Jacks
Wood

B3055

P

Balmerlawn

New Copse
Inclosure

Bridge
Farm

Warren
Farm

Hotel

Brockenhurst

Hotel

Coll

Old Mill
House

Perrywood
Ivy
Inclosure

B3055

Lymington River

Longbow

P

Irons
Hill

F
Sta

MILL LA

Ivy
Wood

Perrywood
Ironshill
Inclosure

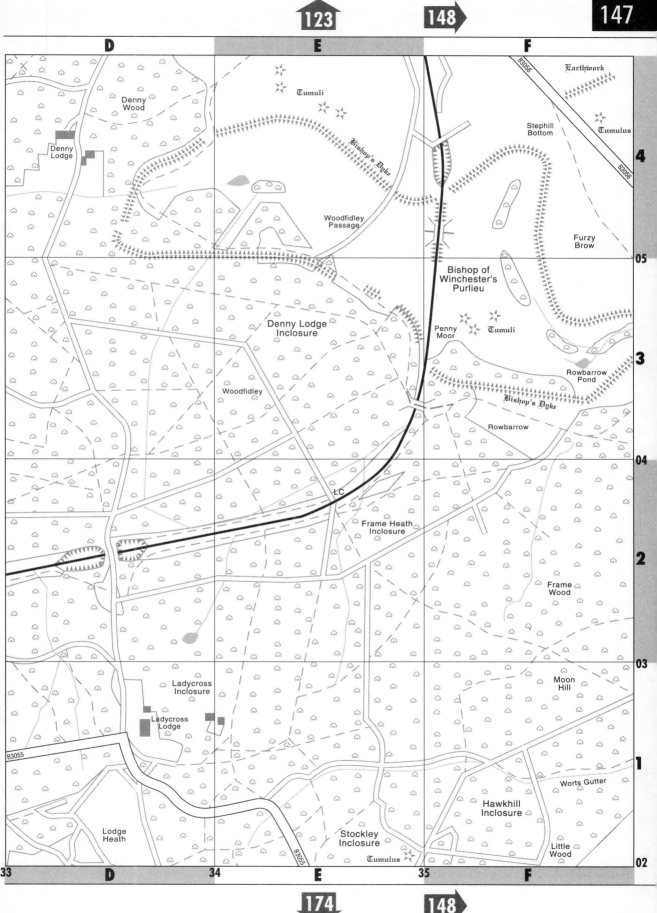

D
E
F

B3056

Earthwork

Denny
Wood

Tumuli

Stephill
Bottom

Tumulus

Denny
Lodge

B3056

4

Bishop's Dyke

Woodfidley
Passage

Furzy
Brow

05

Bishop of
Winchester's
Purlieu

Denny Lodge
Inclosure

Penny
Moor

Tumuli

3

Rowbarrow
Pond

Woodfidley

Bishop's Dyke

Rowbarrow

04

LC

Frame Heath
Inclosure

2

Frame
Wood

03

Ladycross
Inclosure

Moon
Hill

Ladycross
Lodge

B3055

1

Worts Gutter

Lodge
Heath

Hawkhill
Inclosure

Stockley
Inclosure

B3055

Little
Wood

Tumulus

02

33
D
34
E
35
F

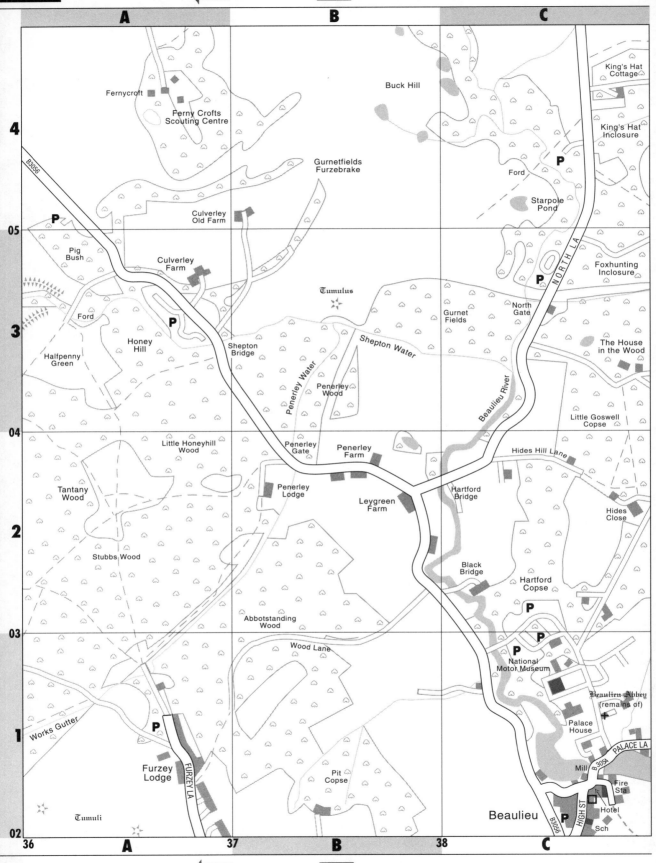

A    B    C

4

King's Hat
Cottage

Fernycroft

Ferny Crofts
Scouting Centre

Buck Hill

King's Hat
Inclosure

Gurnetfields
Furzebrake

Ford

P

05

P

Culverley
Old Farm

Starpole
Pond

Pig
Bush

Culverley
Farm

P

Foxhunting
Inclosure

Tumulus

Gurnet
Fields

North
Gate

3

Ford

P

Honey
Hill

Shepton
Bridge

Shepton Water

North LA

The House
in the Wood

Halfpenny
Green

Penerley Water

Penerley
Wood

Beaulieu River

Little Goswell
Copse

04

Little Honeyhill
Wood

Penerley
Gate

Penerley
Farm

Hides Hill Lane

Hides
Close

Tantany
Wood

Penerley
Lodge

Leygreen
Farm

Hartford
Bridge

2

Stubbs Wood

Black
Bridge

Hartford
Copse

P

Abbotstanding
Wood

03

P

P

Wood Lane

P

National
Motor Museum

Beaulieu Abbey
(remains of)

P

Palace
House

1

Works Gutter

P

Furzey
Lodge

FURZEY LA

Pit
Copse

Mill

B 3054

PALACE LA

Fire
Sta

Tumuli

Beaulieu

B 3056

HIGH ST

P

Hotel

Sch

02

36    A    37    B    38    C

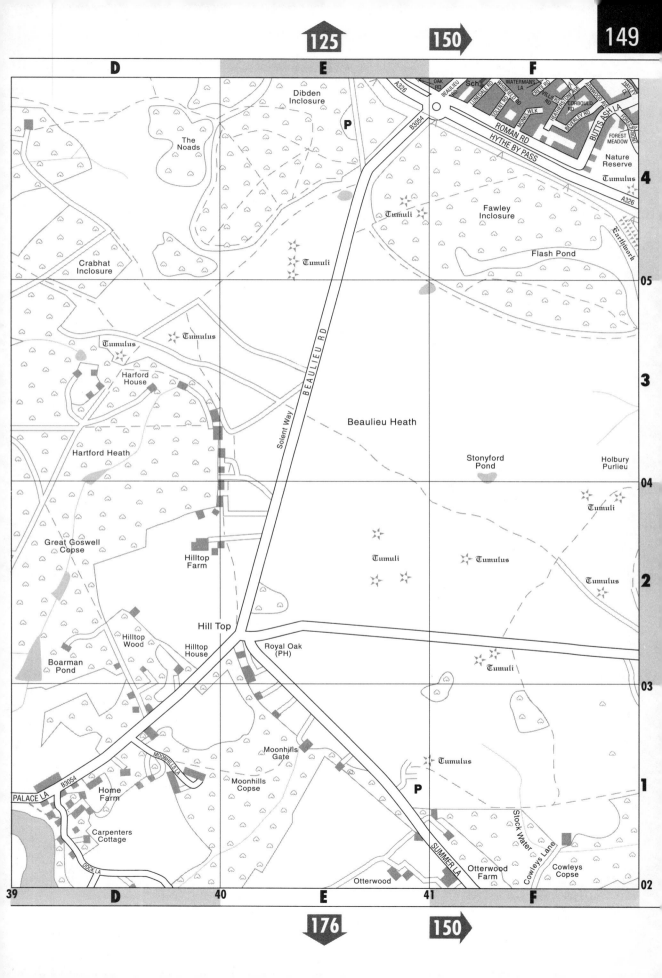

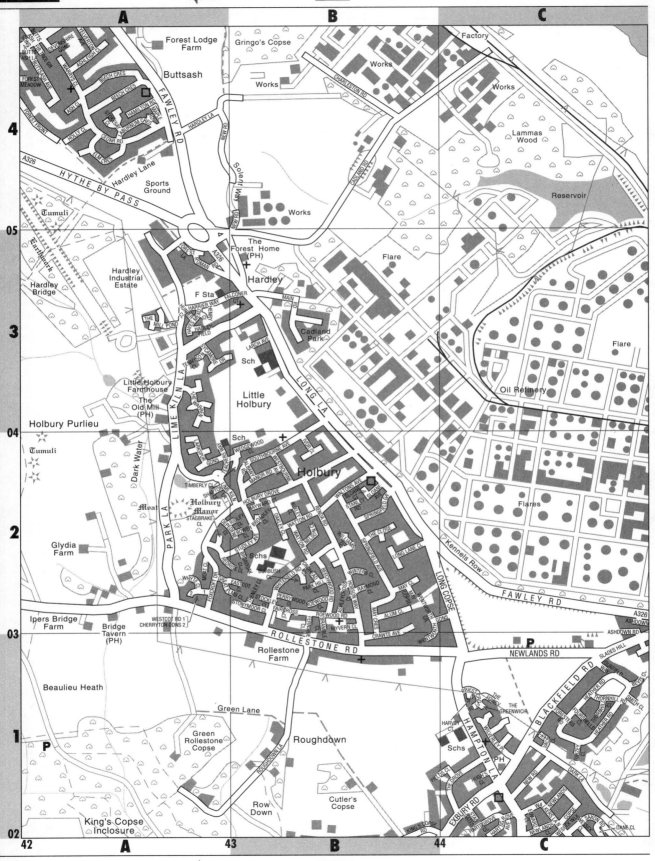

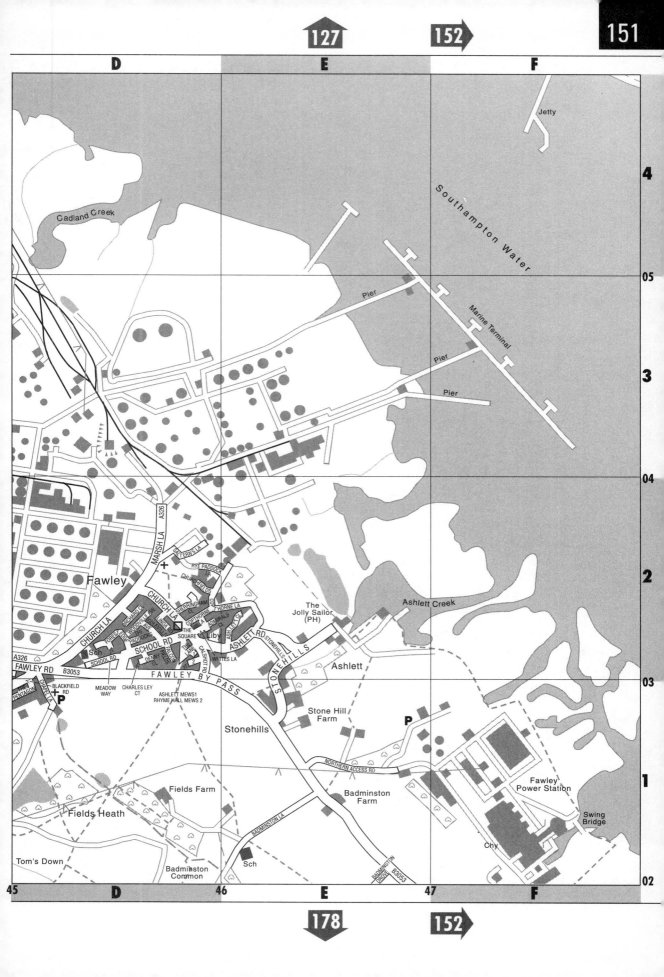

127
152

D

E

F

Jetty

4

Cadland Creek

Southampton Water

05

Pier

Marine Terminal

Pier

3

Pier

04

Fawley

MARSH LA
A326

SALTERN'S LA

RYE PADDOCK

CHURCHFIELDS

STERINGHAM CL

Ashlett Creek

The Jolly Sailor (PH)

2

CHURCH LA

COPTHORNE LA

THORNE LA

RICHARD CL
WOODHILL
DOE CT
THE PADDOCKS

ASHLETT CL
PRIMROSE CL

Liby

ASHLETT RD
STONEHILLS

Sch

FOREST FRONT

THE SQUARE

FALCON

CALSHOT RD

STONEHILLS

Ashlett

SCHOOL RD

DENNY FIELDS

WRITTES LA

A326

FAWLEY RD

B3053

FAWLEY BY PASS

03

PENTAGON

CHAPEL LA

BLACKFIELD RD

P

MEADOW WAY

CHARLES LEY CT

ASHLETT MEWS 1
RHYME HALL MEWS 2

Stonehills

Stone Hill Farm

P

Fawley Power Station

1

Fields Farm

NORTHERN ACCESS RD

Badminston Farm

Fields Heath

BADMINSTON LA

Chy

Swing Bridge

Tom's Down

Badminston Common

Sch

BADMINSTON BRIDGE
B3053

02

45

D

46

E

47

F

178
152

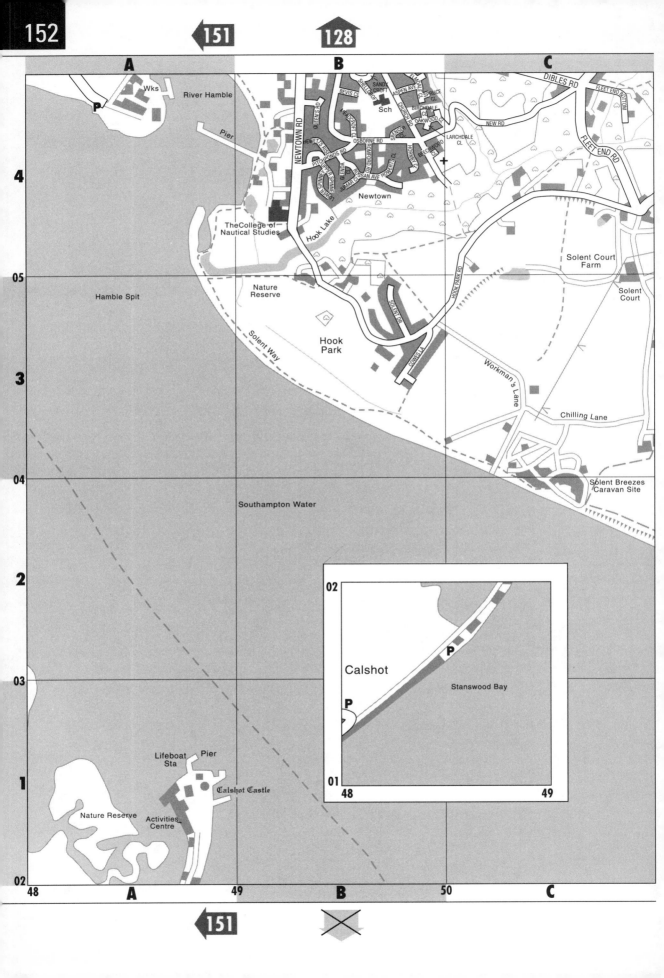

Wks

River Hamble

P

Pier

NEWTOWN RD

QUEEN'S RD

HEWETT'S RD

HUSBANDS RD

PITCHPONDS RD

LOWER SPINNEY

SPINNEY

DOWER SPINNEY

OSBORNE RD

JUMAR CLOSE

COSAN AVE

HUNGER CL

SANDY CROFT

SHELL CROFT

BEVIS CR

ASPEN AVE

SPRUCE CL

MAPLE CROFT

CHURCH RD

SPENSER

HORNBY CL

BIRCHDALE CL

OAKWOOD CL

BEECHWOOD CL

DIBLES RD

FLEET END BOTTOM

NEW RD

LARCHDALE CL

FLEET END RD

Sch

Newtown

The College of
Nautical Studies

Hook Lake

Solent Court
Farm

4

Hamble Spit

Nature
Reserve

Hook
Park

SOLENT DR

HOOK PARK RD

COWES LA

Solent
Court

05

Solent Way

Workman's Lane

3

Chilling Lane

04

Southampton Water

Solent Breezes
Caravan Site

2

Lifeboat
Sta

Pier

Calshot Castle

Nature Reserve

Activities
Centre

03

1

02

48          49          50

**Inset map:**

02

Calshot

P

P

Stanswood Bay

01

48                                    49

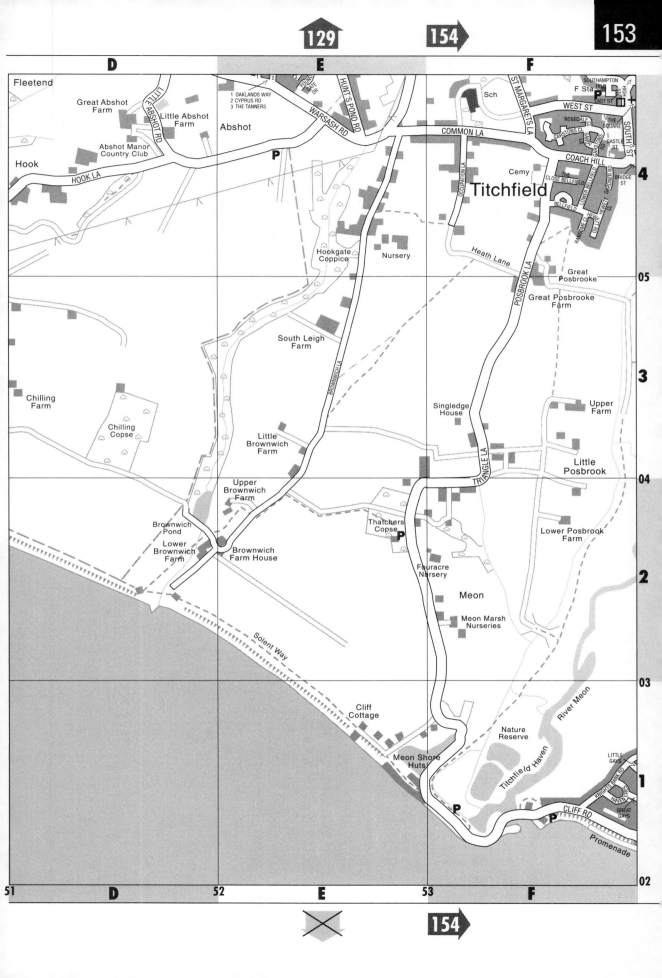

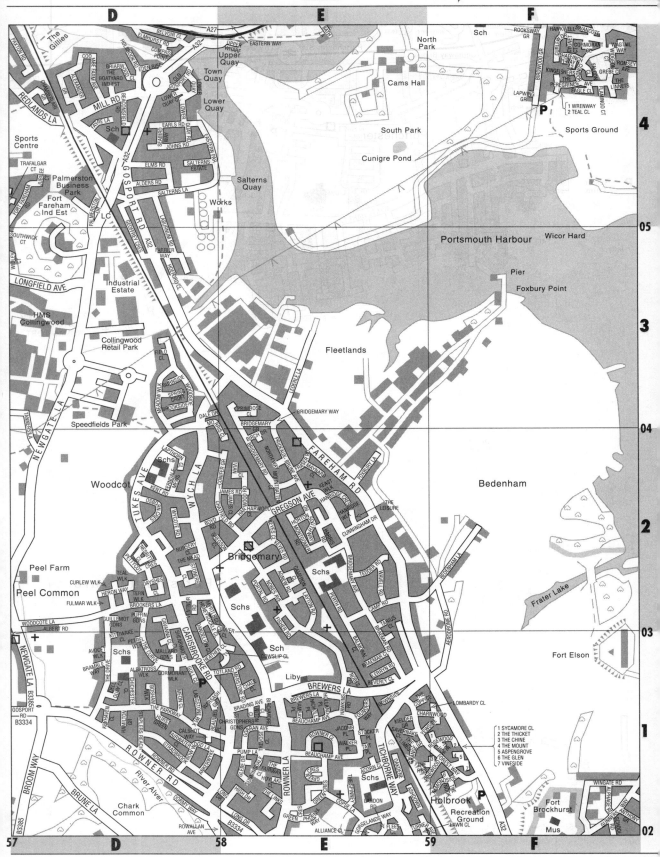

D E F

The Gillies

BELVOIR CL
A27
ELMHURST RD
COMPASS
POINT
Eastern Way
Bath
UPPER
WHARF
Upper
Quay

North
Park
Sch
ROOKSWAY GR
HAWKWELL SWANCOTE
CORMORANT
WAGTAIL
WAY
CURLEW GR
BIRDWOOD GR
HAFFINCH
WAY
WIDGEON
ROMSEY
AVE
GREBE CL
FLAMINGO CT
THE LINNETS

4

REDLANDS LA
BRIARWAY
THE BOATYARD IND EST
EDEN RISE
MILL RD
FARE LA
Sch
Town Quay
Lower
Quay
Lower
Quay
Cams Hall
KINGFISHERS
THE PEREGRINES
EAGLE CL

Sports
Centre
TRAFALGAR CT
Palmerston
Business
Park
Fort
Fareham
Ind Est
ALDERS RD
SALTERNS LA
Salterns
Estate
Salterns
Quay
Works
South Park
Cunigre Pond
LAPWING GR
P
1 WRENWAY
2 TEAL CL
Sports Ground

05
SOUTHWICK CT
GOSPORT RD A32
FARRIER WAY
Portsmouth Harbour
Wicor Hard

LONGFIELD AVE
Industrial
Estate
Pier
Foxbury Point

HMS
Collingwood
Collingwood
Retail Park
FIELD CL
Fleetlands

3

NEWGATE LA
Speedfields Park
DALE DR
PRIMROSE CL
BRIDGEMARY
Bridgemary Way

04
Woodcot
TUKES AVE
WYCH LA
Schs
CONIFER RD
FAREHAM RD
FOXBURY LA
Bedenham

2
KENT RD
JAMES RD
GREGSON AVE
CUNNINGHAM DR
THE LEISURE
BEDENHAM LA
Frater Lake

Peel Farm
CURLEW WLK
TEAL WLK
HERON WAY
FULMAR WLK
Schs
Schs
Schs
AERODROME RD

Peel Common
BROOKERS LA
GUILLEMOT GDNS
Sch
Bridgemary
TEDDER RD
WAVELL RD
CAMP RD

03
ALBERT RD
WOODCOTE LA
KITTIWAKE
CARISBROOKE RD
Sch
COWSLIP CL
Liby
BREWERS LA
Fort Elson

NEWGATE LA B3385
AVOCET WLK
ALBATROSS WLK
CORMORANT WLK
TOTLAND RD
Libby
BREWERS LA
LOMBARDY CL
CHARNWOOD

1
GOSPORT RD B3334
THE PARKWAY
CHICHESTER
MALLARD GDNS
BRADING AVE
BEAUCHAMP AVE
ST CHRISTOPHERS GDNS
JACOMB PL
STOCKER PL
WALKER RD
KIELDER GR
SAVERNAKE
ROSEWOOD
1 SYCAMORE CL
2 THE THICKET
3 THE CHINE
4 THE MOUNT
5 ASPENGROVE
6 THE GLEN
7 VINESIDE

BROOM WAY
BRUNE LA
B3385
ROWNER RD
River Alver
Chark
Common
ROWALLAN AVE
B3334
LONG DR
THE LINKS
ROWNER LA
BEAUCHAMP AVE
THE SPINNEY
GORSELANDS WAY
FLEET CL
ALLIANCE CL
Schs
TICHBORNE WAY
TURNER AVE
LAWN CL
Holbrook
Recreation
Ground
P
A32
Mus
Fort
Brockhurst
WINGATE RD

02
57 D 58 E 59 F

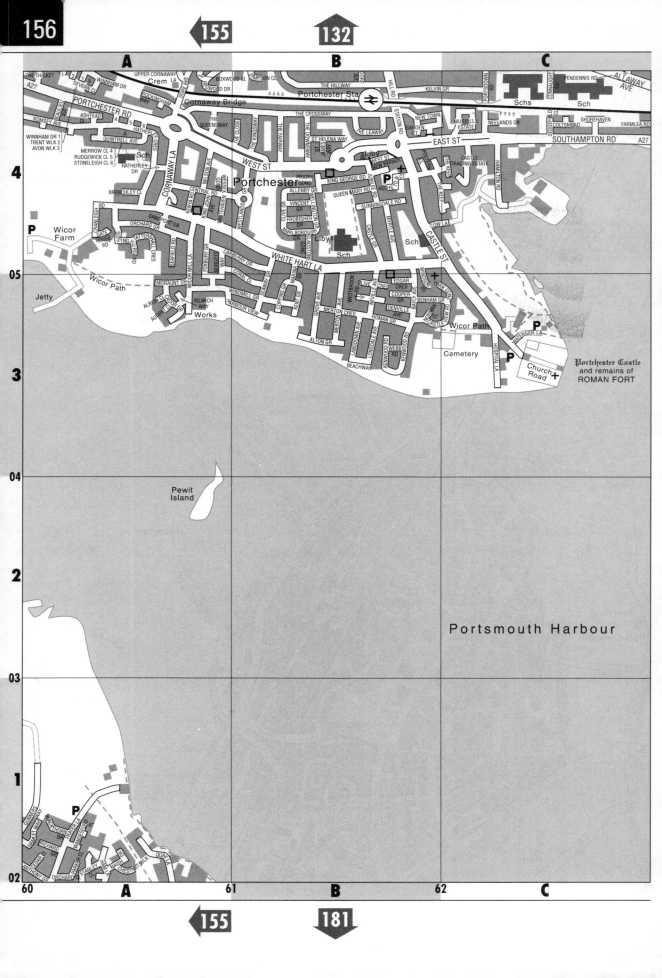

A                    B                    C

THE THICKET
A27
UPPER CORNAWAY LA
Crem    WINNHAM DR
SEVERN CL
PORTCHESTER RD
ROCKINGHAM WAY
BOXWOOD CL
THOMPSON CL
BOXWOOD DR
Cornaway Bridge
THE HILLWAY
Portchester Sta
HILL RD
MOORE
KELVIN GR
PORTSDOWN RD
CONNAUGHT LA
PENDENNIS RD
CALLAWAY AVE

ROMSEY AVE
RAVELEY AVE
ASHTEAD
HATHERLY CRES
THE QUEENSWAY
THE CLOSE
THE CROSSWAY
THE LEAWAY
STATION RD
NEW TOWN
GARDEN CT
MURRILLS ESTATE
NEELANDS GR
Schs
Sch
SEDGEFIELD
COLTSMEAD
SHOREHAVEN
FARMLEA RD

WINNHAM DR 1
TRENT WLK 2
AVON WLK 3
QUINTRELL AVE
THE FAIRWAY
THE KINGSWAY
ST HELENA WAY
EAST ST
CASTLE TRADING ESTATE
SOUTHAMPTON RD
A27

MERROW CL 4
RUDGEWICK CL 5
STONELEIGH CL 6
HATHERLEY DR
Sch
WEST ST
Portchester
PRIORY GDNS
KING GEORGE RD
Liby
NEW PARADE
P
THE KEEP
HAMILTON RD

4
BRENCHLEY CL
CORNAWAY LA
CENTRAL RD
ALLENBY GR
QUEEN MARY RD
SUNNINGDALE RD
CASTLE

FRANLEIGH RD
KENT RD
SANDPORT GR
CLIVE GR
VINCENT GR
FROBISHER GR
MARLBOROUGH GR
MYRTLE AVE
COW LA
Sch
CASTLE ST

P
Wicor Farm
GATE HOUSE RD
ORCHARD GR
SEAFIELD RD
HALL CRES
FOXBURY GR
MORGETT
CARBERRY DR
White Hart La
Liby
Sch

05
Wicor Path
MORAUNT GR
WICOR MILL LA
CORAL CL
SEAWAY GR
MARINA
GROVE AVE
WESTBROOK RD
OLIVE AVE
NEVILLE AVE
EDGAR CRES
COOPER GR
DENVILLE AVE
WINDSOR
YORK CRES
P

Jetty
ALBION CL
AURELIA GR
EXFORD DR
KILWICH WAY
Works
HARBOUR VIEW
WINDMILL GR
LOPPINS GR
MERTON CRES
ROMAN GR
BENHAM GR
CASTLE
Wicor Path
P

3
Pewit Island
ALTON GR
MERTON GR
LANSDOWNE AVE
LONSDALE AVE
WEBB RD
KENWOOD RD
HOSPITAL LA
Cemetery
Church Road
Portchester Castle
and remains of
ROMAN FORT

04

2
Portsmouth Harbour

03

1
P
GUNNERS
HAZEL WAY
HAWTHORN DR
WEDGEWOOD
RICHARD GR
CEDAR
PARISH
STANLEY
NASH
WALK
QUAY
CHESTERTON WALK

02
ANTHONY GR
ORCHARD

60        A        61        B        62        C

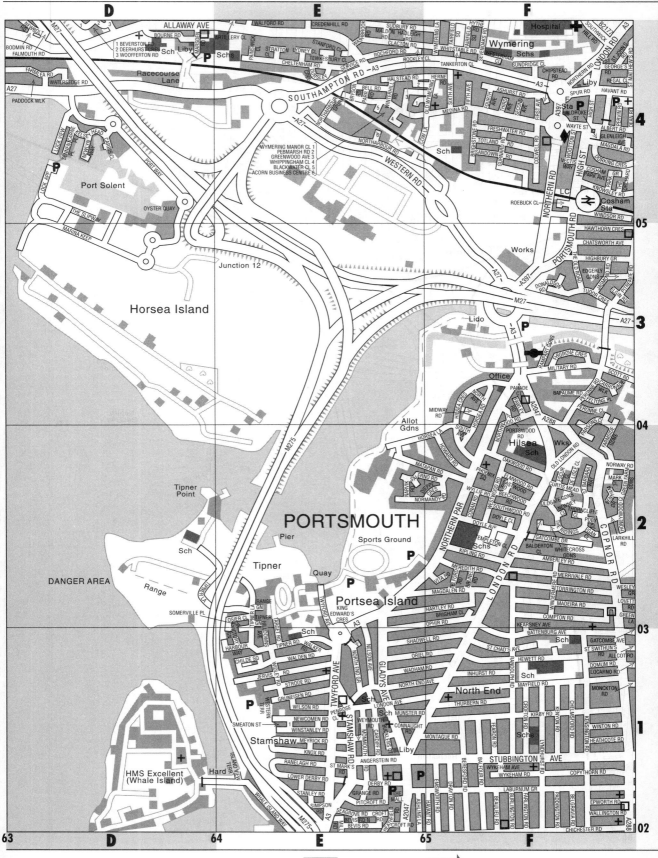

PORTSMOUTH

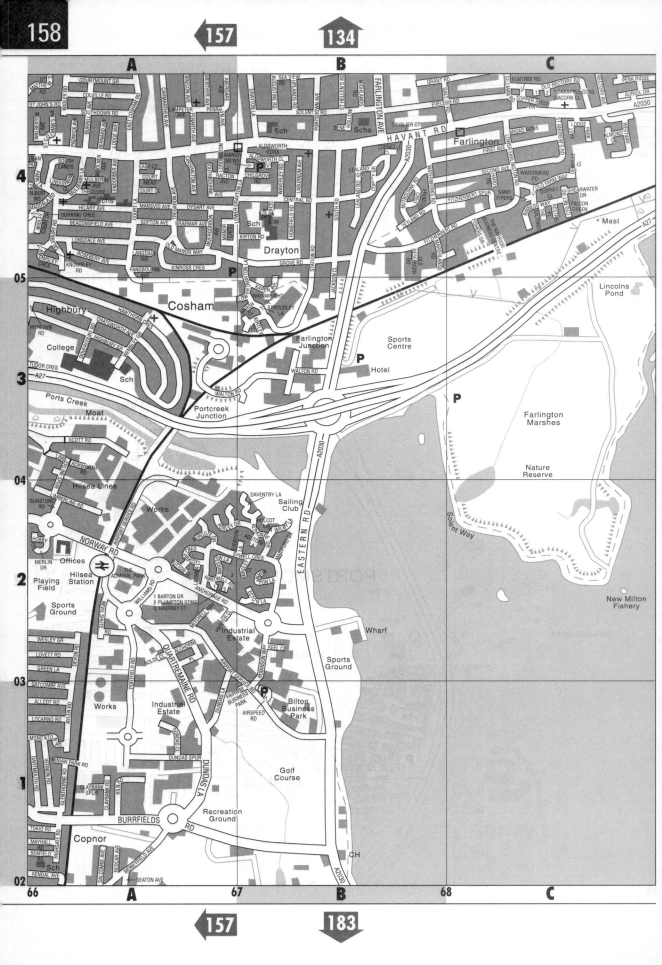

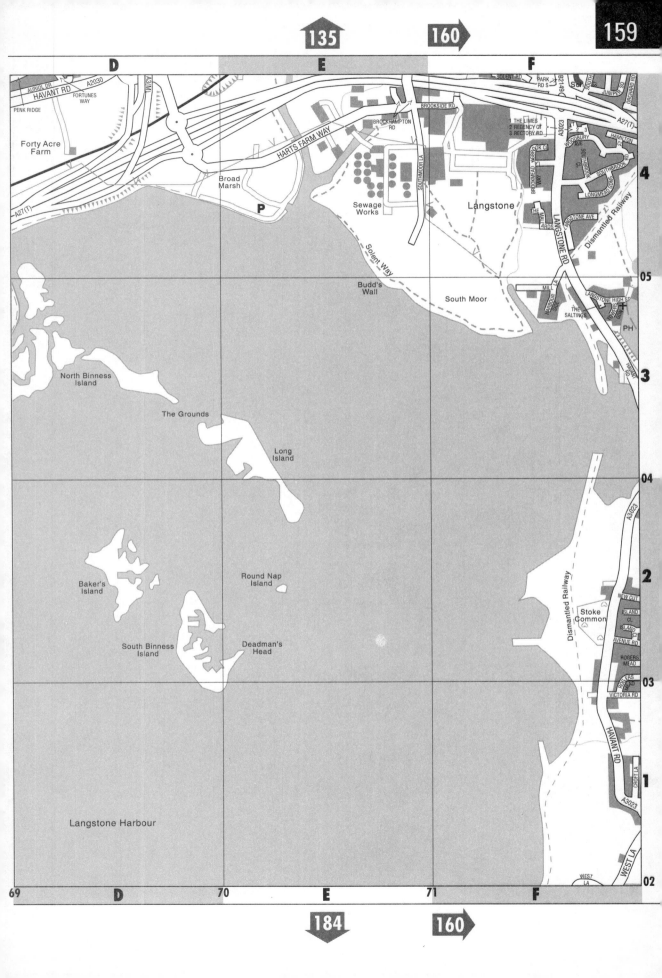

135
160

**D**
**E**
**F**

AURIOL DR
HAVANT RD
A2030
A3(M)
PENK RIDGE
FORTUNES WAY
SOLENT RD
PARK RD S
B2149
SGN
SOUTH
JUNIPER SQ
ORCHARD RD

BROOKSIDE RD

Forty Acre Farm

Broad Marsh

BROCKHAMPTON RD

1 THE LIMES
2 REGENCY CT
3 RECTORY RD

A3023

WOODBURY AVE

HAMILTON CL

A27(T)

**4**

A27(T)

Sewage Works

Langstone

BROOKFIELD

BROOK CL

SOUTHBROOK

LONGMEAD

SOUTHBROOK

LANGSTONE RD

THE MALLARDS

LANGSTONE AVE

Dismantled Railway

P

Solent Way

**05**

Budd's Wall

South Moor

MILL

HARBOUR SIDE

TOWERS GDNS

THE SALTINGS

LANGSTONE HIGH ST

PH

North Binness Island

HAVANT RD

**3**

The Grounds

Long Island

**04**

Baker's Island

Round Nap Island

A3023

Dismantled Railway

**2**

Stoke Common

NEW CUT

ISLAND CL

ISLAND AVENUE RD

ROGERS MEAD

South Binness Island

Deadman's Head

ROGERS MEAD

VICTORIA RD

**03**

HAVANT RD

CROFT LA

**1**

Langstone Harbour

A3023

WEST LA

WEST LA

**02**

69
**D**
70
**E**
71
**F**

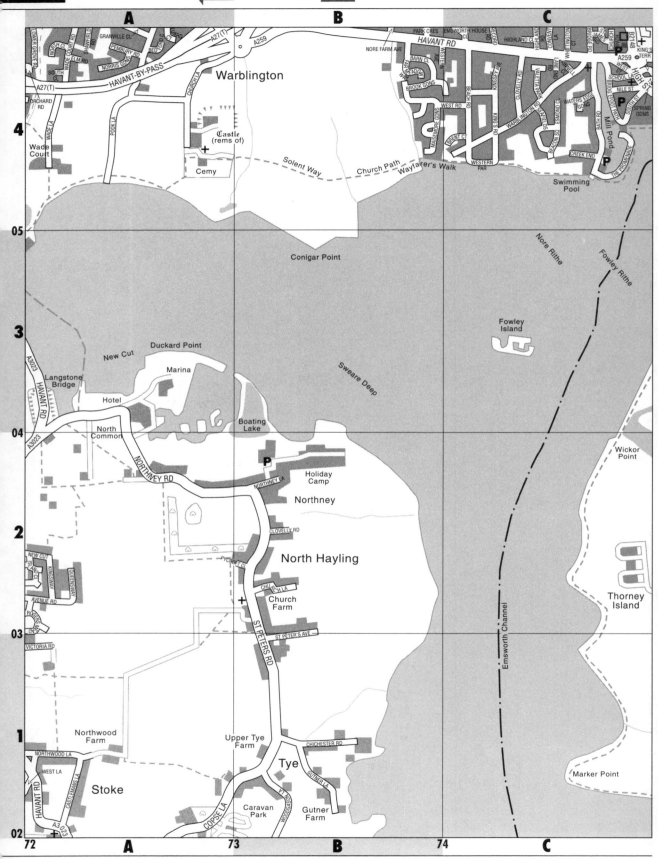

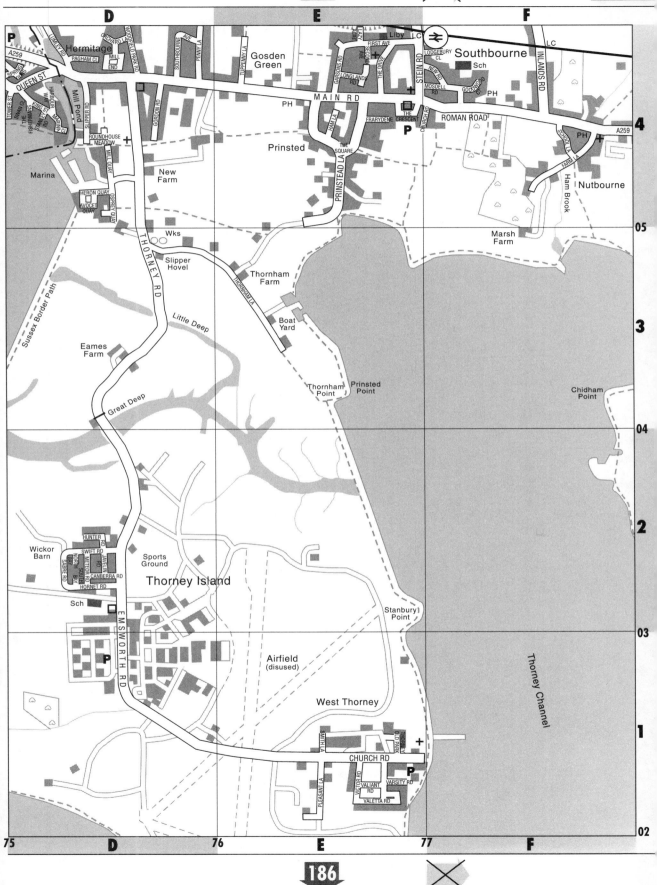

**D** **E** **F**

P
Hermitage
A259
Queen St
QUEEN ST
SPRING GDNS
TOWERS ST
THE FISHERMANS
SWAN CT
KING ST
STANLEY RD
MARINA GI
HARBOUR WAY
WOODFIELD RD
ORCHARD RD
LUMLEY RD
PAGHAM CL
MILL END
SOUTHBOURNE
PENNY LA
AVE
GORDON RD
MILL RD
BE HELPS
ROUNDHOUSE
MEADOW
MILL QUAY
OSPREY QUAY
HERON QUAY
AVOCET QUAY
Mill Pond
Marina
New Farm
Gosden
Green
TUPPENNY LA
GARSONS RD
LONGLANDS RD
HAM LA
AZZY RD
HARDY
FIRST AVE
THE DRIVE
Prinsted
PH
PH
MAIN RD
THE SQUARE
PRINSTEAD LA
FRARYDENE
THE CRESCENT
P
CHURCH RD
STEIN RD
Liby
LC
Southbourne
Sch
LODGEBURY CL
NEW RD
MOSDELL RD
GOODWOOD
PH
ROMAN ROAD
LC
INLANDS RD
A259
FARM LA
SCHOOL LA
PH
Nutbourne
Ham Brook
Marsh
Farm

**4**

**05**

THORNEY RD
Wks
Slipper
Hovel
THORNHAM LA
Thornham
Farm
Boat
Yard
Sussex Border Path
Little Deep
Eames
Farm
Great Deep
Thornham
Point
Prinsted
Point
Chidham
Point

**3**

**04**

Wickor
Barn
HUNTER RD
SWIFT RD
METEOR RD
NORTH BAY
SOUTH BAY
SABRE RD
JAVELIN RD
CANBERRA RD
HORNET RD
Sports
Ground
Thorney Island
Sch
EMSWORTH RD
P
Stanbury
Point

**2**

**03**

Airfield
(disused)
West Thorney
Thorney Channel

**1**

SMITH LA
CHURCH RD
PLEASANT LA
VICTOR RD
VALIANT RD
VALETTA RD
VARSITY RD
THORNEY
OLD PARK
P

**02**

**75** **D** **76** **E** **77** **F**

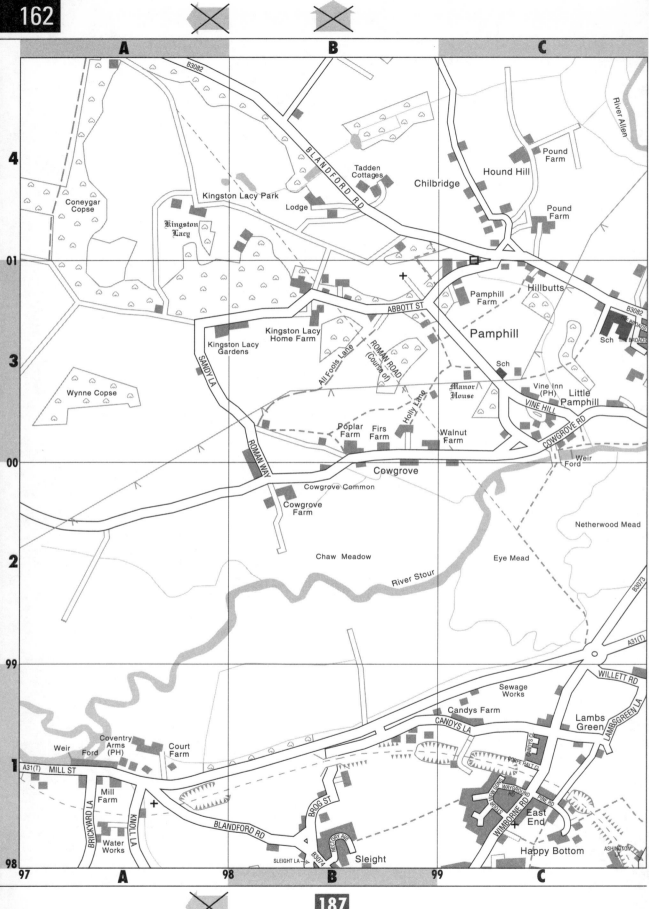

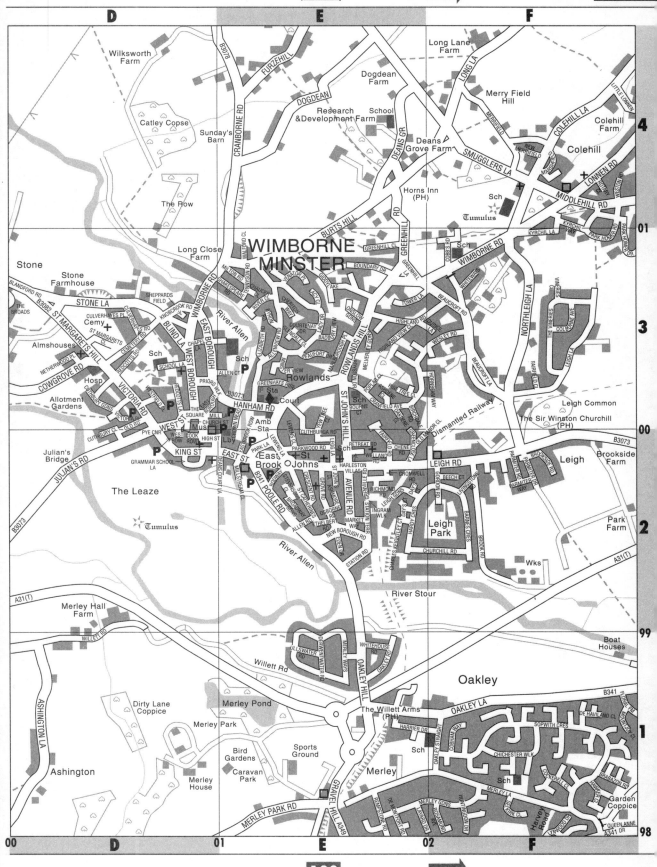

D     E     F

Wilksworth Farm

Catley Copse

Sunday's Barn

The Row

FURZEHILL

CRANBORNE RD

B3078

DOGDEAN

DEANS GR

Dogdean Farm

Research &Development Farm

School

Long Lane Farm

LONG LA

MERRIFIELD

Merry Field Hill

COLEHILL LA

Colehill Farm

Colehill

NEW MERRIFIELD

SMUGGLERS LA

Deans Grove Farm

Horns Inn (PH)

Tumulus

Sch

LONNEN RD

MIDDLEHILL RD

KYRCHIL LA

KYRCHIL WAY

Stone

Stone Farmhouse

Long Close Farm

BURTS HILL

WIMBORNE MINSTER

GREENHILL

GREENHILL CL

BOUNDARY DR

Sch

WIMBORNE RD

NORTHLEIGH LA

BLANDFORD RD

B3082

THE BROADS

STONE LA

ST MARGARET'S HILL

Cemy

Almshouses

SHEPPARDS FIELD

WIMBORNE RD

EAST BOROUGH

WEST BOROUGH

River Allen

Rowlands

ROWLANDS HILL

Leigh Common

The Sir Winston Churchill (PH)

B3073

COWGROVE RD

Hosp

VICTORIA RD

Sch

HANHAM RD

Court

St JOHN'S HILL

Sch

Dismantled Railway

Leigh

Brookside Farm

B3073

Allotment Gardens

Julian's Bridge

WEST ST

Mus

KING ST

EAST ST

Amb Sta

East Brook

St Johns

LEIGH RD

P

GRAMMAR SCHOOL LA

POOLE RD

AVENUE RD

Leigh Park

Park Farm

A31(T)

The Leaze

Tumulus

River Allen

STATION RD

CHURCHILL RD

Wks

River Stour

A31(T)

Merley Hall Farm

WILLETT RD

Willett Rd

OAKLEY HILL

Boat Houses

Oakley

OAKLEY LA

B341

ASHINGTON LA

Dirty Lane Coppice

Merley Park

Merley Pond

Bird Gardens

Sports Ground

The Willett Arms (PH)

HARRIER DR

COBHAM WAY

SOPWITH CRES

DE HAVILAND CL

Sch

CHICHESTER WLK

Ashington

Merley House

Caravan Park

Merley

Sch

GRAVEL HILL A349

MERLEY PARK RD

MERLEY GDNS

MERLEY LA

Garden Coppice

Harvey Road

QUEEN ANNE

A341 DR

00    D     01     E     02     F

4

01

3

00

2

99

1

98

**A**      **B**      **C**

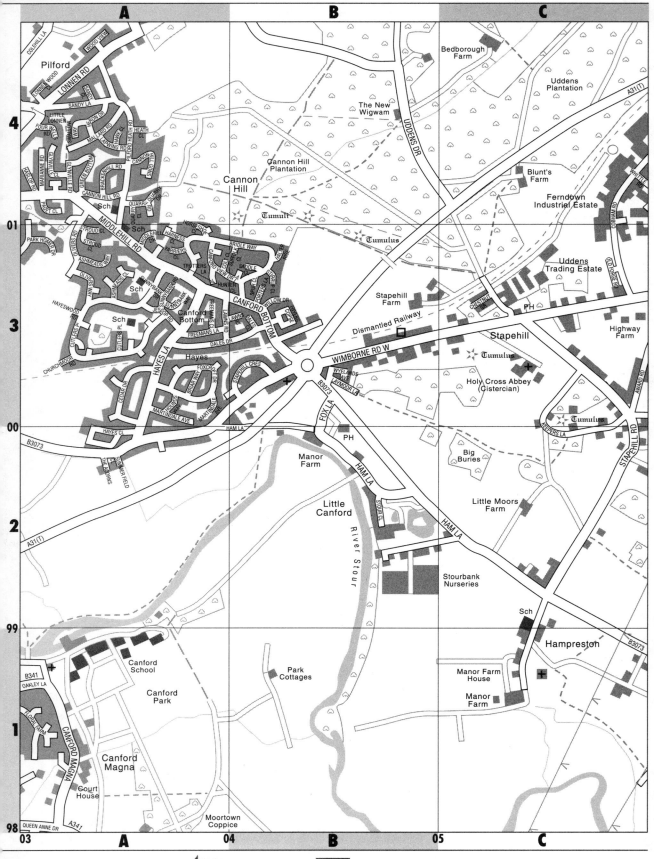

Pilford

COLEHILL LA
WOOD VIEW
LONNEN RD
FONDEL WOOD
SANDY LA
SANDY DR
LITTLE LONNEN
FOUR WELLS RD
HATON DR
MALLARD RD
LAPWING RD
HAWK LA
PILFORD HEATH RD
HEATH CL
CANNONS CL
MARRIANNE RD
GUTTMAN RD
GILBRIDE RD
GREEN BOTTOM
BLACKBULL RD
CANNON HILL RD
HASLOP RD
PAGET CL
CANNON HILL RD
QUARRY RD
Sch
Sch

Cannon Hill
Cannon Hill Plantation

MIDDLEHILL RD
PARK HOMER DR
SPROTT CL
STROUD CL
STROUD CL
ASHMEADS WAY
MIDDLEHILL RD
HARNESS CL
PARRIERS
BRIDLE WAY
SADDLE
CANFORD VIEW DR
TROTTERS LA
HUNTER
WALTER RISE
OLIVERS WAY
ASHMANS CL
Sch
JESSOPP
HAYESWOOD RD
CUTLERS PL
Sch
CUTLERS PL
CHURCHMOOR RD
CEDAR DR
HAYES LA
CANFORD BOTTOM
Hayes
BRIARWAY
HOLME RD
FOXCROFT DR
STAPEHILL CRES
MARTINDALE AVE
MARTINDALE
HAYES CL
HAM LA
THE ASPINS
SUMMER FIELD
B3073

Tumulus
Tumulus
Tumulus

The New Wigwam

UDDENS DR

Bedborough Farm

Uddens Plantation

A31(T)

Blunt's Farm

Ferndown Industrial Estate

Uddens Trading Estate

COBHAM RD
WHITTLE RD
OLD FORGE RD
WHITTLE RD

Stapehill Farm
CHESTNUT GR
PH
Stapehill

Dismantled Railway
WIMBORNE RD W
WYELANDS AVE
LAYMOOR LA
B3073
FOX LA
PH
Manor Farm

Little Canford
HAM LA
STOUR CL

River Stour

Holy Cross Abbey (Cistercian)
Tumulus

Highway Farm
AWARD RD

Tumulus
KEEPERS LA
STAPEHILL RD

Big Buries

Little Moors Farm

Stourbank Nurseries

Sch
Hampreston
B3073

B3073

A31(T)

Canford School
Canford Park

B341
OAKLEY LA
FLORAL FARM

Park Cottages

Manor Farm House
Manor Farm

CANFORD MAGNA
Canford Magna
Court House
QUEEN ANNE DR
A341
Moortown Coppice

98 99 00 01 2 3 4

03 A 04 B 05 C

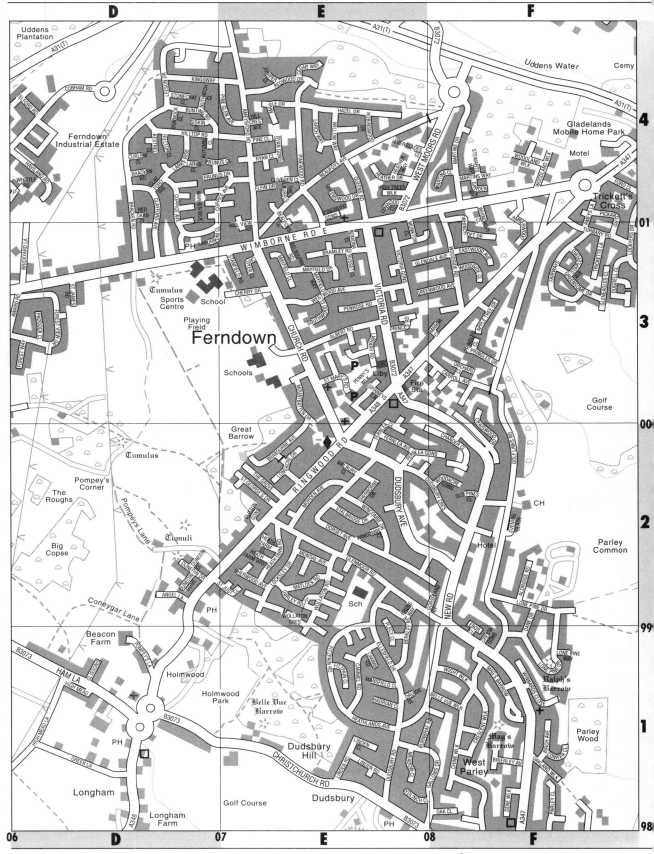

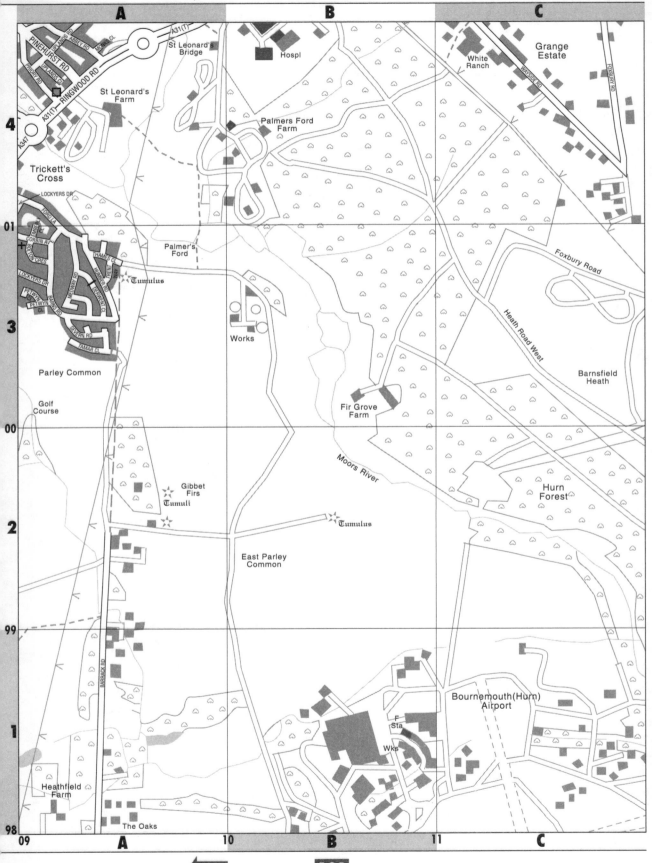

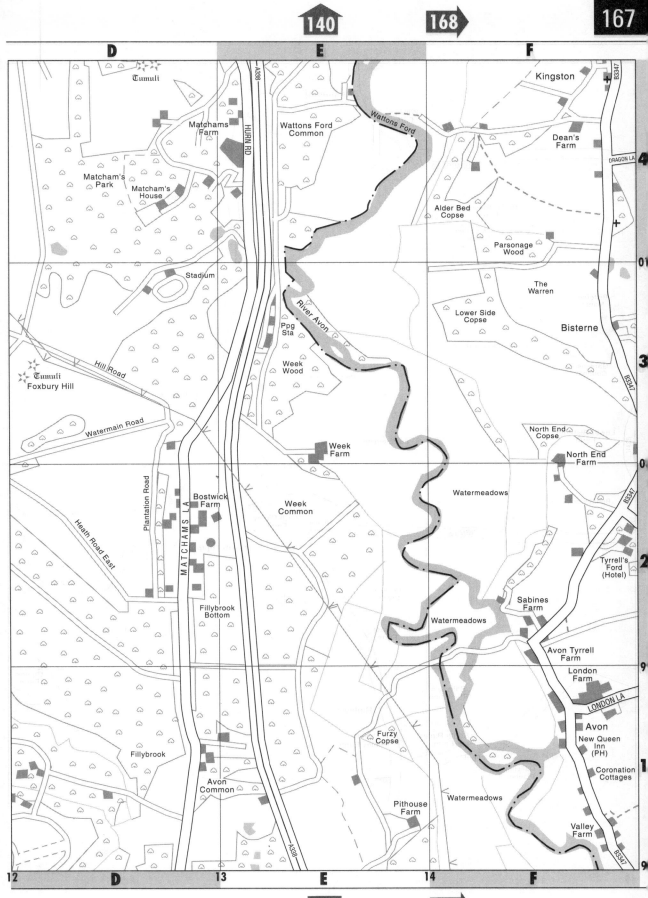

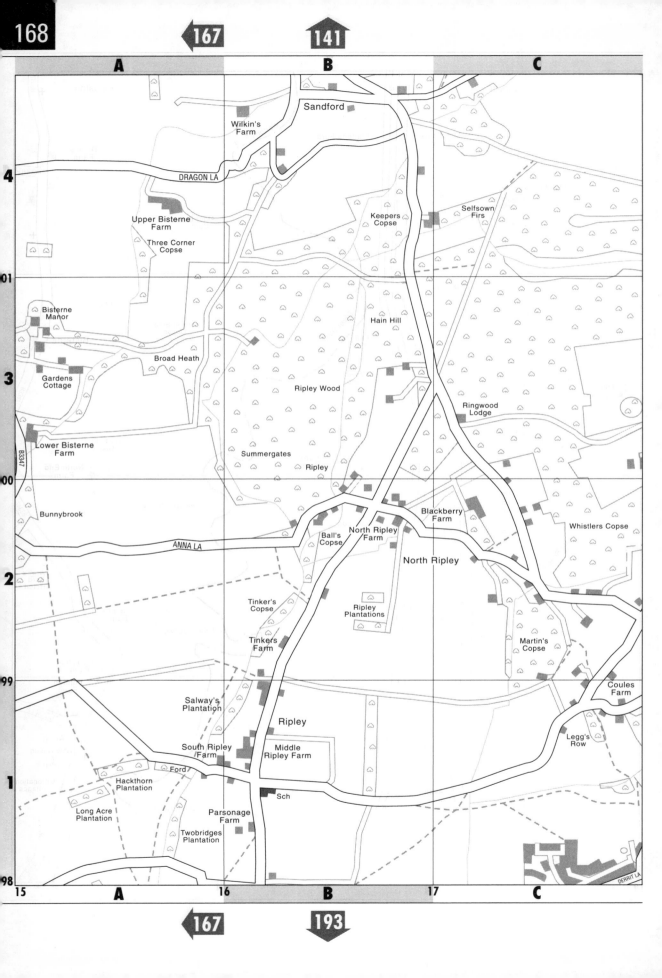

167
141

A B C

4

DRAGON LA

Wilkin's Farm

Sandford

Keepers Copse

Selfsown Firs

Upper Bisterne Farm

Three Corner Copse

01

Bisterne Manor

Hain Hill

Broad Heath

Gardens Cottage

Ripley Wood

Ringwood Lodge

B3347

Lower Bisterne Farm

Summergates

Ripley

00

Bunnybrook

Blackberry Farm

ANNA LA

Ball's Copse

North Ripley Farm

Whistlers Copse

North Ripley

2

Tinker's Copse

Ripley Plantations

Tinkers Farm

Martin's Copse

99

Coules Farm

Salway's Plantation

Ripley

Legg's Row

South Ripley Farm

Middle Ripley Farm

Ford

1

Hackthorn Plantation

Sch

Long Acre Plantation

Parsonage Farm

Twobridges Plantation

DERRIT LA

98

15 A 16 B 17 C

167
193

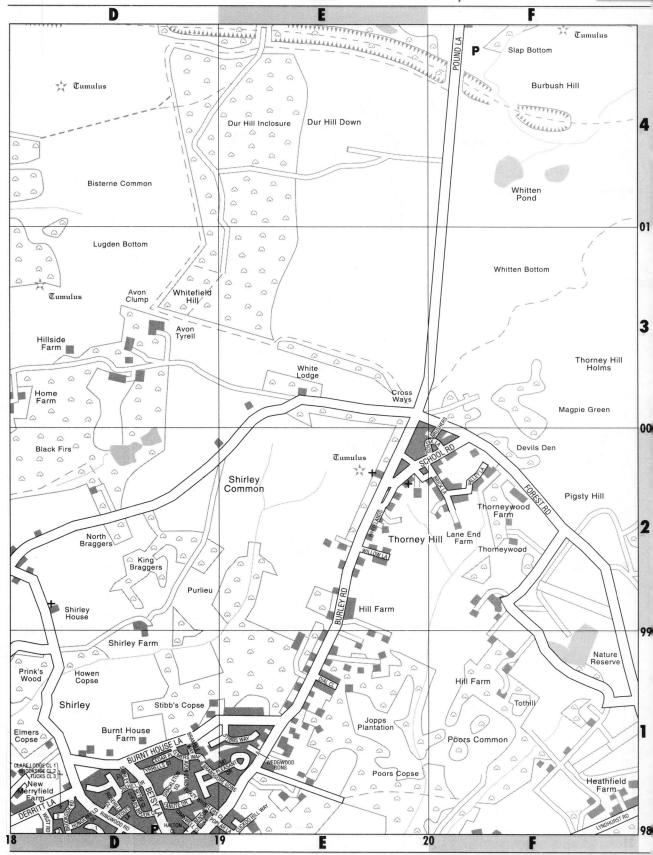

Tumulus

Slap Bottom

Burbush Hill

P

**4**

Dur Hill Inclosure    Dur Hill Down

Whitten Pond

Tumulus

Bisterne Common

**01**

Lugden Bottom

Whitten Bottom

Tumulus

Avon Clump

Whitefield Hill

**3**

Avon Tyrell

Thorney Hill Holms

Hillside Farm

White Lodge

Home Farm

Cross Ways

Magpie Green

SCHOOL RD

**00**

Black Firs

Devils Den

Tumulus

BRICK LA

VALLEY LA

Shirley Common

Pigsty Hill

FOREST RD

North Braggers

Thorneywood Farm

King Braggers

WHITELANDS

Thorney Hill

Lane End Farm

Thorneywood

**2**

WILLOW LA

Purlieu

BURLEY RD

Hill Farm

Shirley House

**99**

Shirley Farm

Nature Reserve

Prink's Wood

Howen Copse

DIAL CL

Hill Farm

Shirley

Stibb's Copse

Jopps Plantation

Tothill

Elmers Copse

Burnt House Farm

Poors Common

**1**

BURNT HOUSE LA

STIBBS WAY

WEDGWOOD GDNS

CLARE LODGE CL 1
BROOKSIDE CL 2
TUCKS CL 3

Poors Copse

New Merryfield Farm

BETSY LA

Heathfield Farm

DERRITT LA

WEST RD

RINGWOOD RD

CUCKOO HILL WAY

LYNDHURST RD

**98**

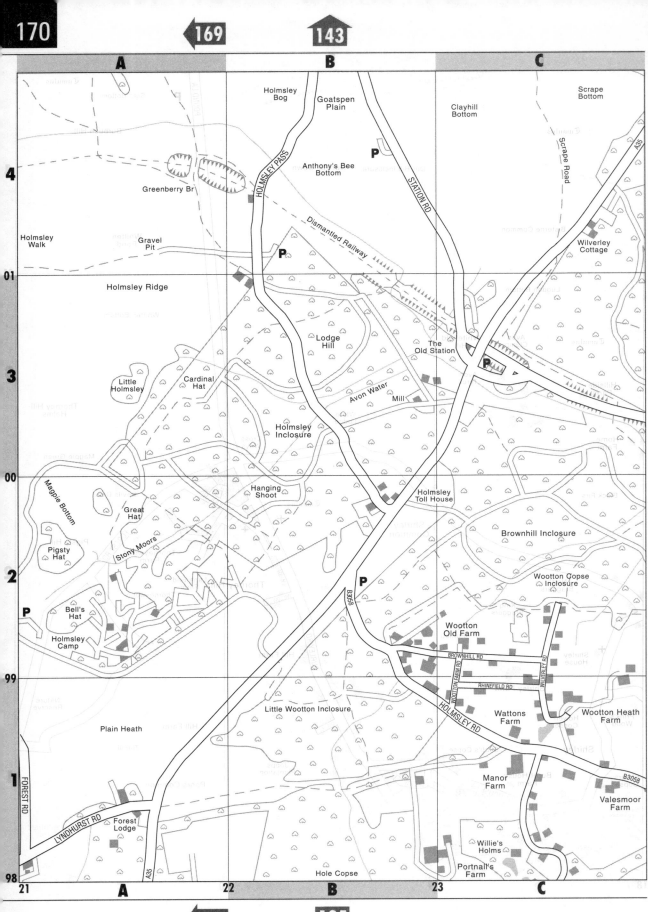

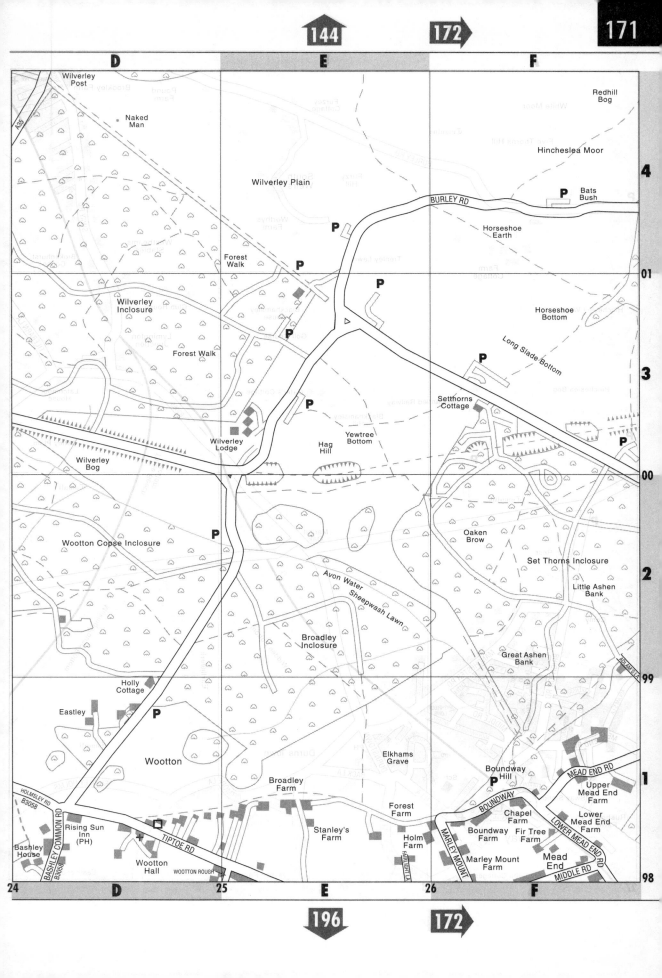

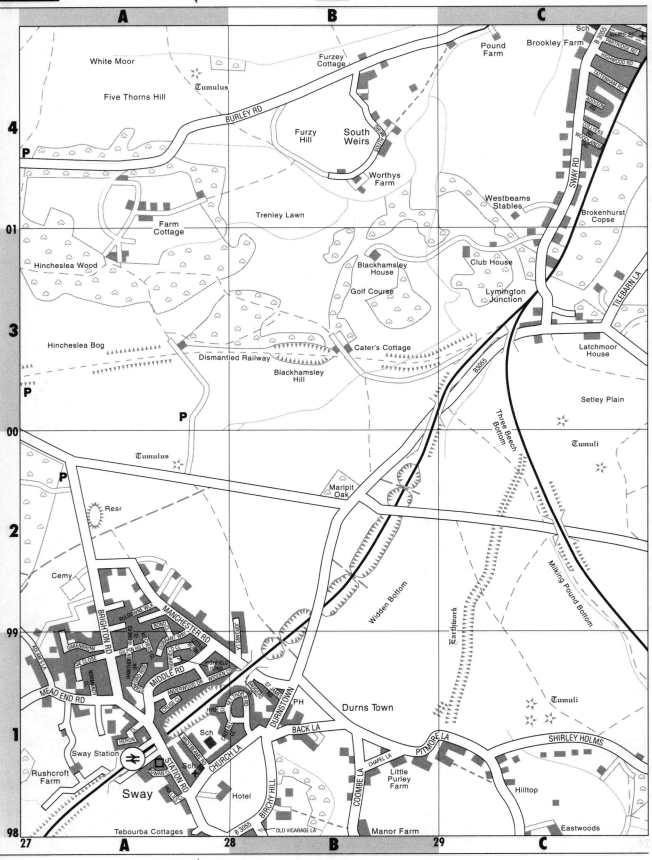

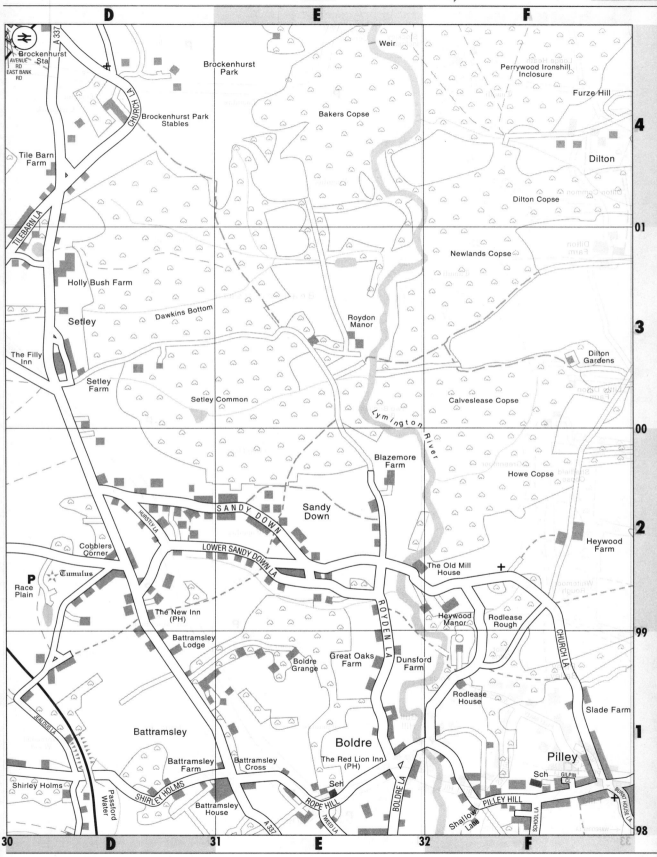

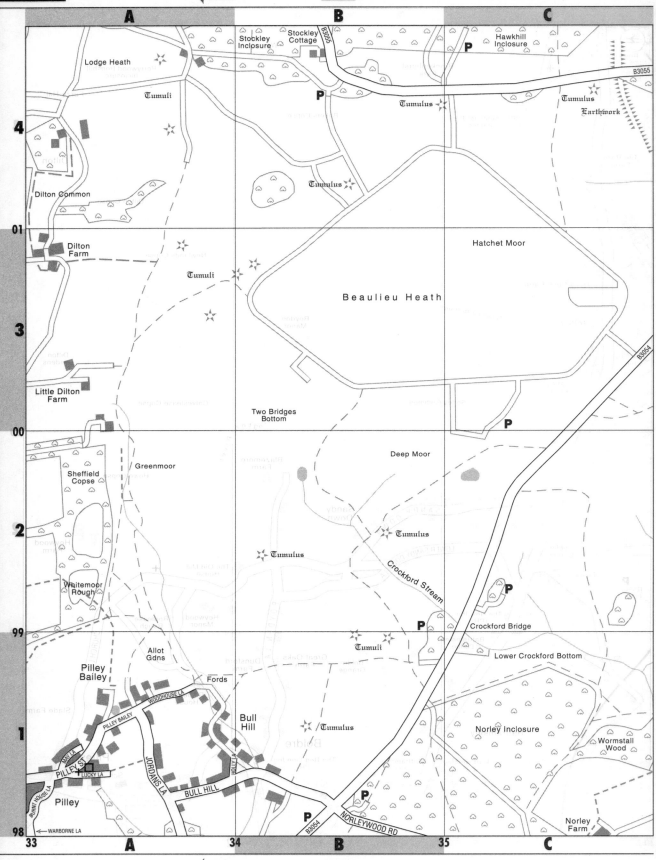

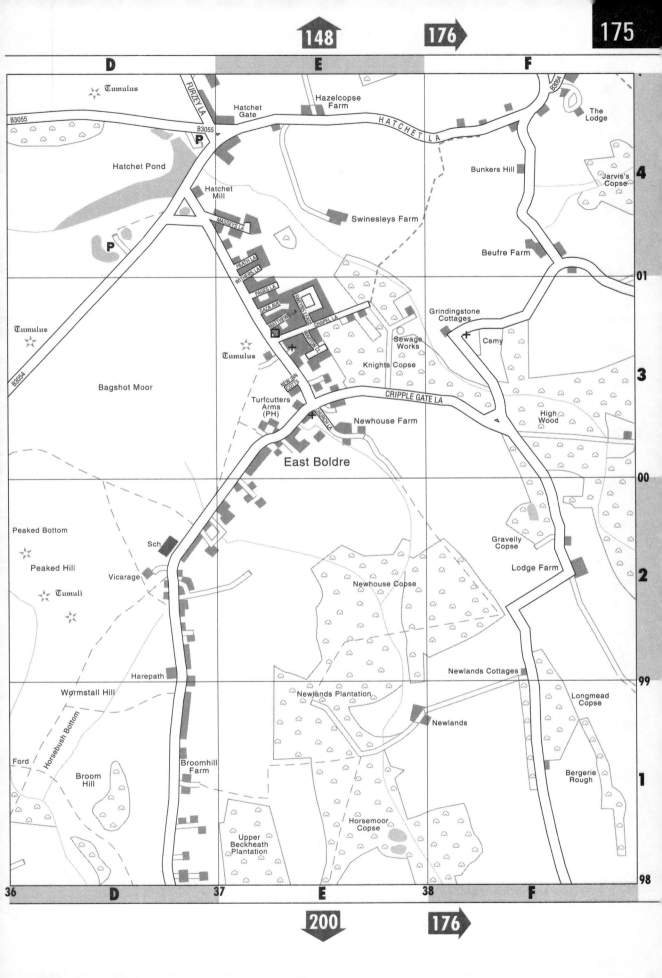

D     E     F

Tumulus

B3055

Hatchet Gate

Hazelcopse Farm

HATCHET LA

B3054

The Lodge

Bunkers Hill

Jarvis's Copse

4

Hatchet Pond

Hatchet Mill

Swinesleys Farm

Beufre Farm

P

MASSEYS LA

P

HEATH LA

WITHERS LA

01

Tumulus

PAGES LA

GAIA AVE

MATTHEWS LA

SWEENS EASE

CHAPEL LA

WARREN CL

Grindingstone Cottages

Cemy

Sewage Works

Knights Copse

3

B3054

Bagshot Moor

Tumulus

NEWLANN COTTS

CHURCH LA

CRIPPLE GATE LA

High Wood

Turfcutters Arms (PH)

Newhouse Farm

East Boldre

00

Peaked Bottom

Sch

Newhouse Copse

Gravelly Copse

Peaked Hill

Vicarage

Lodge Farm

2

Tumuli

Harepath

Newlands Cottages

99

Wormstall Hill

Newlands Plantation

Longmead Copse

Horsebush Bottom

Newlands

Ford

Broom Hill

Broomhill Farm

Bergerie Rough

1

Upper Beckheath Plantation

Horsemoor Copse

98

36     D     37     E     38     F

175
149

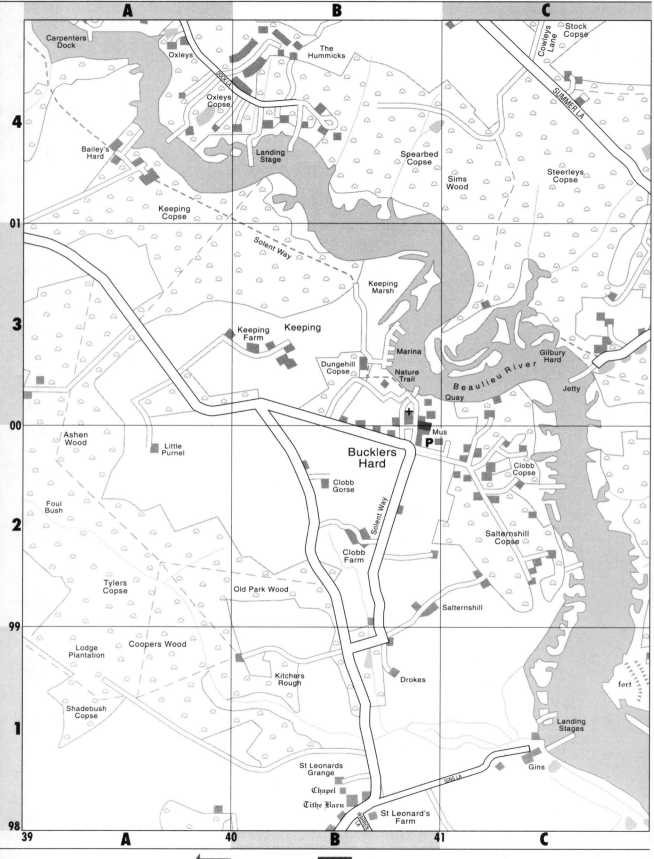

175
201

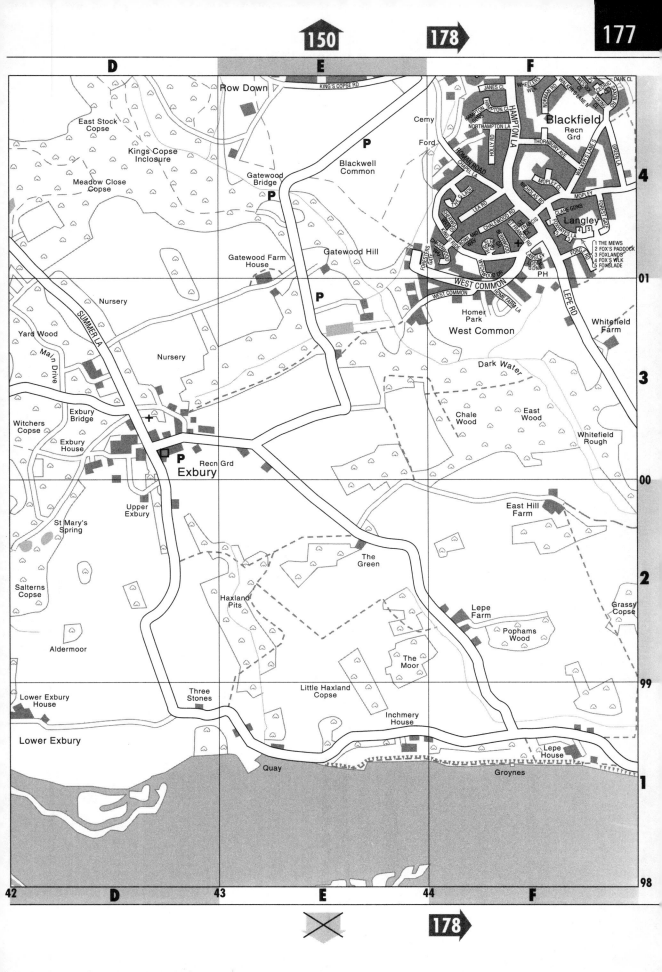

150
178

**D**

**E**

**F**

Row Down

KING'S COPSE RD

East Stock
Copse

Kings Copse
Inclosure

Meadow Close
Copse

Gatewood
Bridge

Blackwell
Common

**P**

Cemy

Ford

WHEELERS
WLK

JANES CL

NORMAN RD

HAMPTON CL

HAMPTON LA

WALTERS LANE N

CEDRIC
CL

DANE CL

Blackfield

Recn
Grd

NORTHAMPTON LA

HOWARD RD

CHAPEL LA

NICHOLAS RD

THORNBURY AVE

GREEN LA

WATERS LANE

MOPLEY CL

MOPLEY

**4**

Langley

FOREST GATE

Gatewood
Bridge

**P**

Gatewood Farm
House

Gatewood Hill

AVE G RD

LEA RD

CHALEWOOD RD

ST FRANCIS
AVE

BLUEBELL
WAY

CLARE GDNS

FOXLAYES LA

FORGE RD

1 THE MEWS
2 FOX'S PADDOCK
3 FOXLANDS
4 FOX'S WLK
5 FOXGLADE

LANGLEY
LODGE
GDNS

PH

Nursery

**P**

WEST COMMON

Homer
Park

WEST COMMON

HOME FARM LA

LEPE RD

Whitefield
Farm

**01**

Yard Wood

SUMMER LA

Main Drive

Nursery

Nursery

West Common

Dark Water

Chale
Wood

East
Wood

Whitefield
Rough

**3**

Witchers
Copse

Exbury
Bridge

Exbury
House

Exbury

**P**

Recn Grd

Upper
Exbury

St Mary's
Spring

East Hill
Farm

**00**

Salterns
Copse

The
Green

Haxland
Pits

The
Moor

Lepe
Farm

Pophams
Wood

Grassy
Copse

**2**

Aldermoor

Three
Stones

Little Haxland
Copse

Inchmery
House

**99**

Lower Exbury
House

Lower Exbury

Quay

Groynes

Lepe
House

**1**

**98**

**D**

**E**

**F**

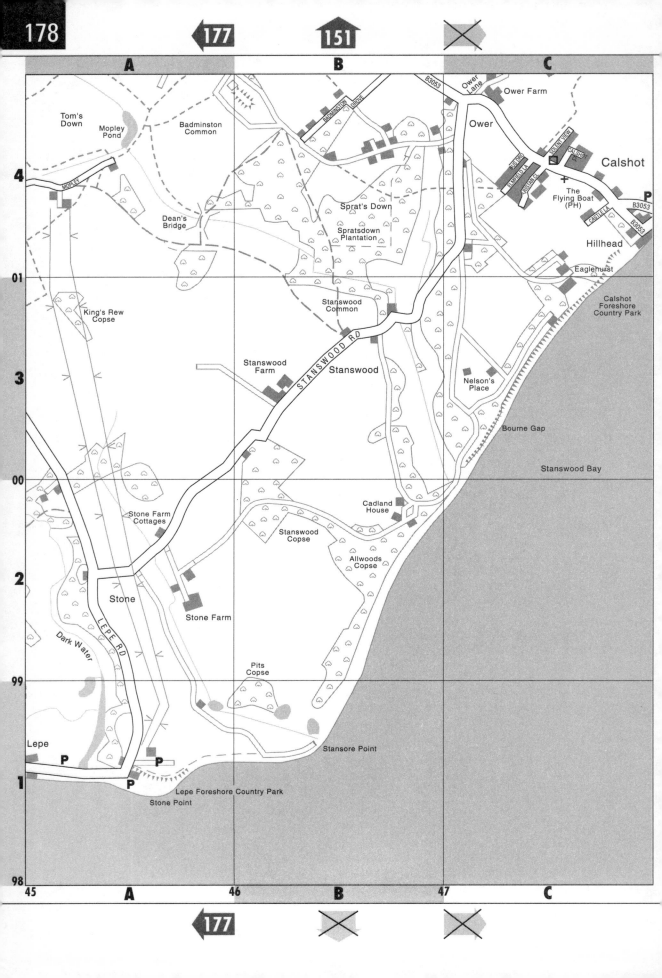

Tom's Down

Mopley Pond

Badminston Common

Ower Lane

B3053

Ower Farm

Ower

SOLENT VIEW

CALSHOT CR

Calshot

MOPLEY

4

Dean's Bridge

Sprat's Down

Spratsdown Plantation

EMPIRE LA

TISBRO

KOSTAN CL

The Flying Boat (PH)

CASTLE LA

B3053

P

B3053

Hillhead

01

King's Rew Copse

Stanswood Common

Eaglehurst

Calshot Foreshore Country Park

BADMINSTON GROVE

STANSWOOD RD

Stanswood Farm

Stanswood

Nelson's Place

3

Bourne Gap

Stanswood Bay

00

Stone Farm Cottages

Cadland House

2

Stone

LEPE RD

Stanswood Copse

Allwoods Copse

Stone Farm

Dark Water

Pits Copse

99

Lepe

P

P

P

Stansore Point

1

Lepe Foreshore Country Park

Stone Point

98

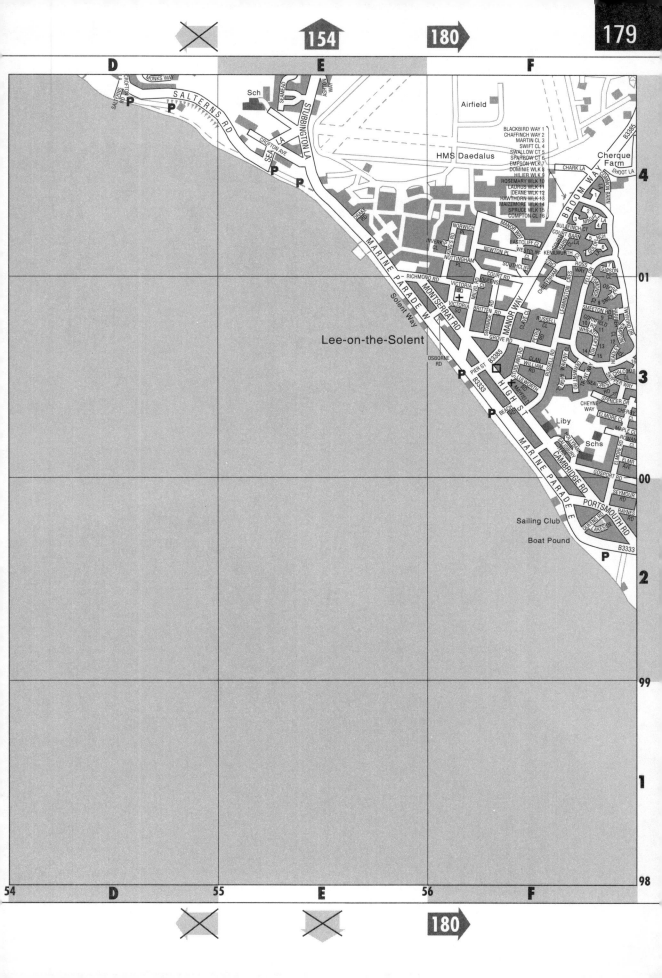

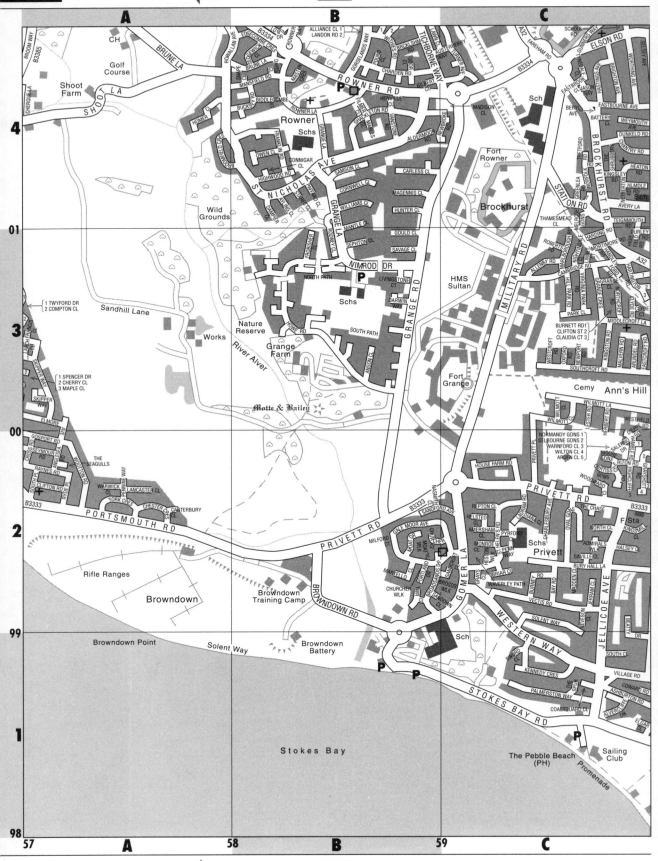

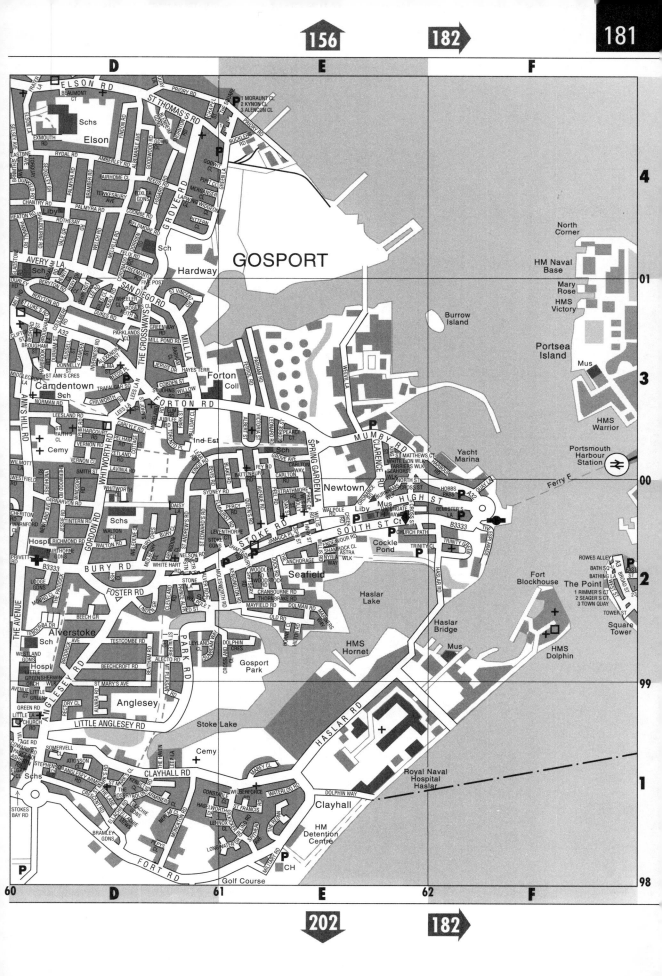

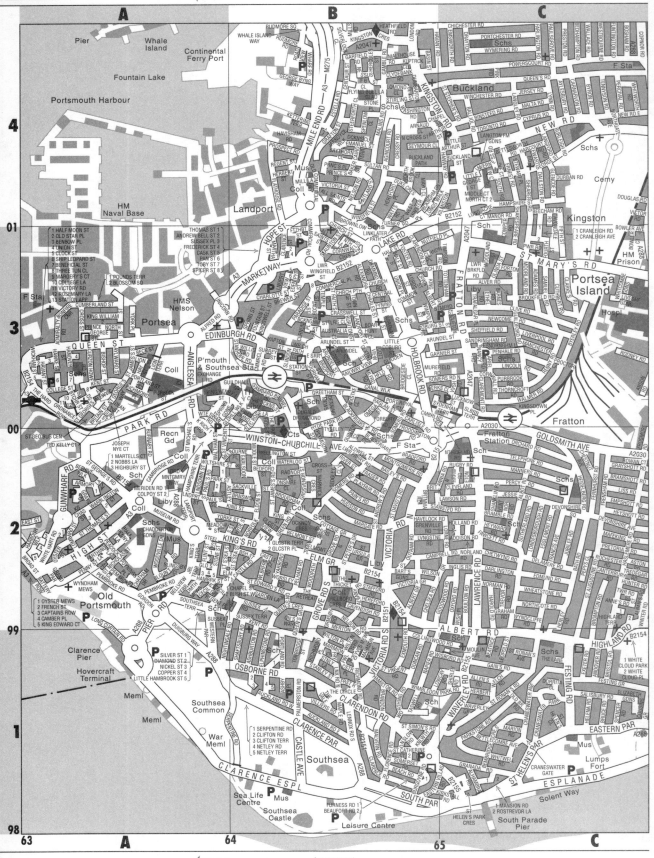

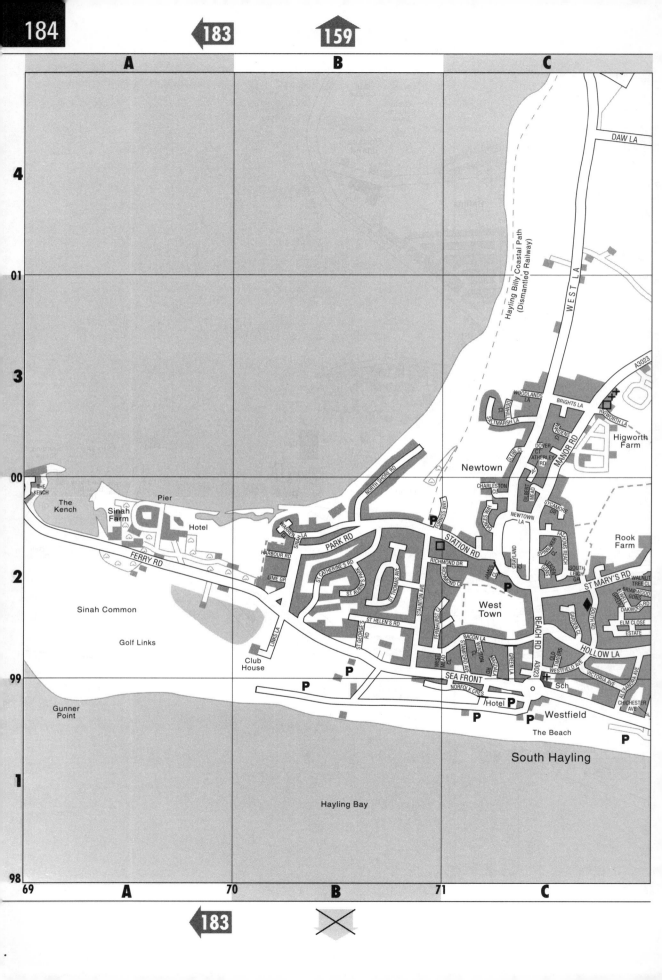

A    B    C

4

01

3

DAW LA

WEST LA

A3023

Hayling Billy Coastal Path
(Dismantled Railway)

WOODLANDS LA
TILLHARD

SALTMARSH LA

BRIGHTS LA

HIGWORTH LA

Higworth
Farm

MANOR RD

GLEBE CL

DOVER CT
ATHERLEY RD

GARDENS CL

Newtown

00

THE
KENCH

The
Kench

Pier

Sinah
Farm

Hotel

NORTH SHORE RD

CHARLESTON CL

GILBERT MEAD

NEWTOWN LA

SYCAMORE DR

Rook
Farm

WARREN LA

SINAH LA

FURNISS WAY

JAMES WAY

STATION RD

SOUTH
LEIGH

FERRY RD

HARBOUR RD

PARK RD

ST CATHERINE'S RD

RICHMOND DR

RICHMOND CT

GRAYLAND CL

SPINNAKER CL

FATHOMS REACH

LEVERS GDNS

St MARY'S RD

WALNUT
TREE CL

2

LIME GR

ST AUBIN'S RD

ST THOMAS AVE

STAUNTON AVE

JAMES CL

West
Town

BRIARWOOD

OAKWOOD CT

LOWER GDNS

Sinah Common

Golf Links

TINKS LA

ST HELEN'S RD

ST GEORGE'S RD

FERNHURST CL

BEACH RD

GARDEN CL

SCHOOL RD

ELM CLOSE
ESTATE

HOLLOW LA

Club
House

P

WEST
MEAD CL

BACON LA

STAMFORD AVE

WINSTON CL

MAGNOLIA RD

GREEN LA

A3023

OLD
TIMBERS

WESTFIELD AVE

VICTORIA AVE

ALEXANDRA AVE

CHICHESTER AVE

99

P

P

SEA FRONT

NORFOLK CRES

Hotel

P

P

Sch

Westfield

Gunner
Point

P

P

P

The Beach

South Hayling

1

Hayling Bay

98

69    A    70    B    71    C

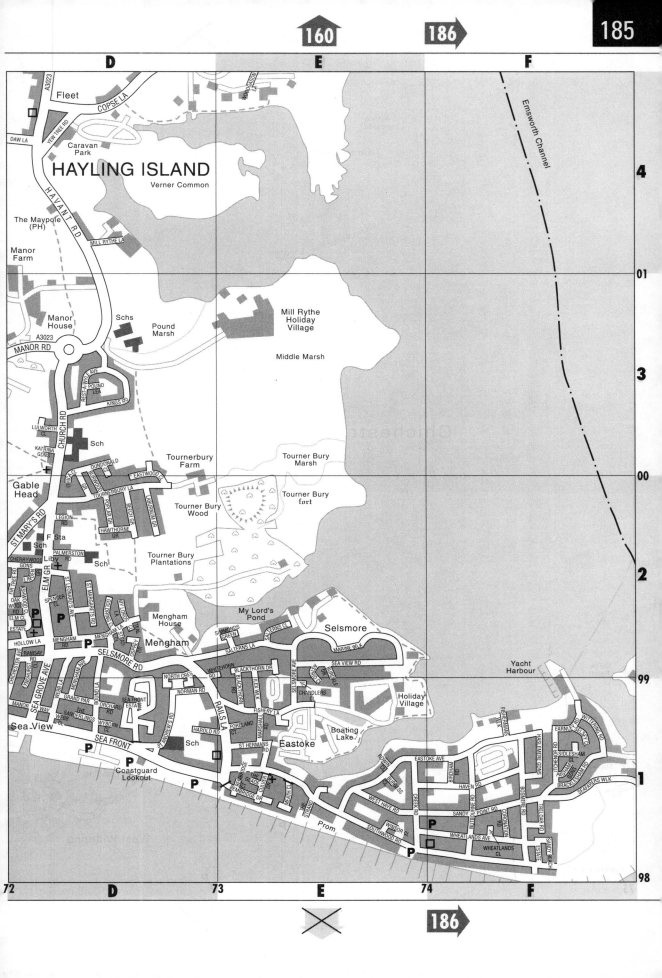

D
E
F

4

01

3

00

2

99

1

98

A3023
Fleet
COPSE LA
YEW TREE RD
DAW LA
Caravan Park
HAYLING ISLAND
Verner Common
The Maypole (PH)
MILL RYTHE LA
Manor Farm
HAVANT RD
Manor House
A3023
MANOR RD
Schs
Pound Marsh
Mill Rythe Holiday Village
Middle Marsh
REST-A-WYLE AVE
POUND LEA
KINGS RD
CHURCH RD
LULWORTH
KATRINA GDNS
Sch
Tournerbury Farm
Tourner Bury Marsh
Gable Head
ST MARY'S RD
LEGION RD
ITHICA CL
DUNDONALD CL
EASTWOOD
TOURNERBURY LA
POPLAR GR
BEECH GR
LABURNUM GR
HAWTHORNE GR
PALMERSTON
Sch
F Sta
Liby
ELM GR
ST LEONARDS AVE
ST MARGARETS RD
Tourner Bury Wood
Tourner Bury Plantations
Tourner Bury Fort
CHERRYWOOD GDNS
FIR TREE RD
LARCH GR
OAK WOOD RD
ELM CL
ESTATE
HOLLOW LA
SPENCER CL
MENGHAM LA
GOLDRING CL
MY LORDS
TIMSBURY
P
P
P
P
P
Mengham House
Mengham
SELSMORE RD
RAMSAY RD
LYNDHURST
CHICHESTER AVE
MANOR WAY
SEA GROVE AVE
WEBB LA
GRAND PAR
BOUND LA
THE SANDERLINGS
WEBB CL
MENGHAM AVE
My Lord's Pond
SIMMONDS GREEN
SALTERNS LA
SALTERNS CL
Selsmore
MARINE WLK
SEA VIEW RD
WHITETHORN RD
BLACKTHORN DR
BLACKTHORN RD
LEES WLK
SELSMORE AVE
BURRALE DR
ASTRID CL
Holiday Village
Yacht Harbour
NORTH CRES
NORMAN RD
ORCHARD RD
SEA FRONT ESTATE
WYBORN RD
FISHERY LA
FORELAND CT
MARSHALL RD
CHANDLERS CL
Sea View
SEA FRONT
HAROLD RD
ST HERMANS RD
Sch
ST ANDREW'S RD
RAILS LA
Eastoke
Boating Lake
FISHERMANS WALK
EARNLEY RD
SELSEY CT
WITTERING RD
P
P
P
Coastguard Lookout
BEMBRIDGE DR
THE GLADE
CULVER DR
HEATH CL
THE STRAND
Prom
WEST HAVE RD
CREEK RD
ROWAN CL
BURGESS
WINSOR CL
SOUTHWOOD RD
EASTOKE AVE
BIRDHAM RD
HAVEN RD
NUTBOURNE RD
SANDY POINT RD
CORONATION RD
BOSMERE RD
HASLEMERE GDNS
GROSVENOR RD
PAGHAM GDNS
SIDLESHAM CL
BRACKLESHAM RD
SEAFARERS WLK
TRELOAR RD
SANDY BEACH STAT
WHEATLANDS AVE
WHEATLANDS CL
Emsworth Channel
P
P

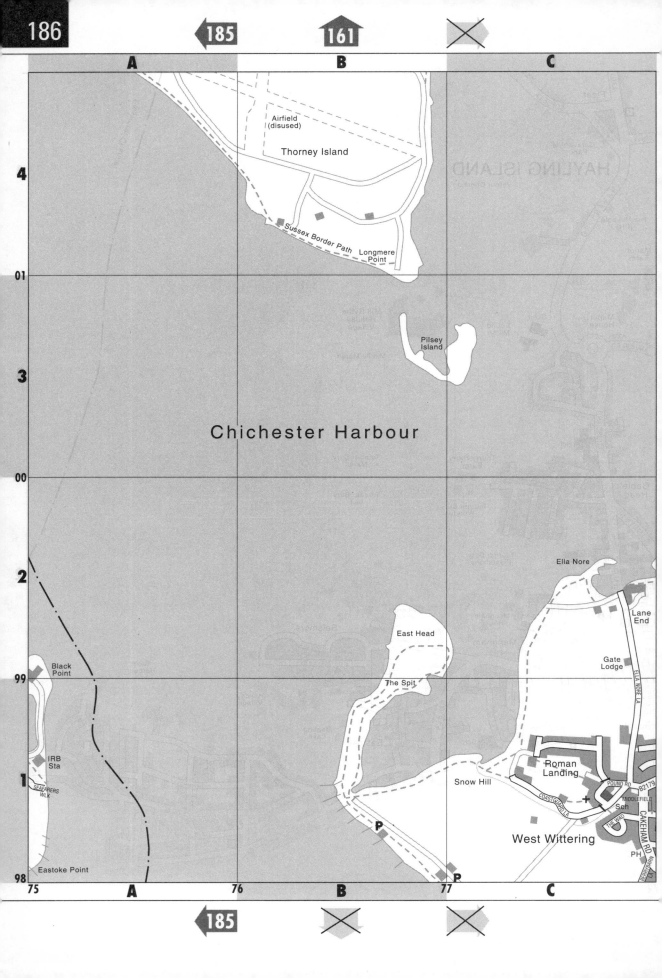

Airfield
(disused)

Thorney Island

Sussex Border Path

Longmere
Point

HAYLING ISLAND

Pilsey
Island

# Chichester Harbour

Ella Nore

Lane
End

East Head

Gate
Lodge

Black
Point

The Spit

IRB
Sta

SEAFARERS
WLK

Snow Hill

Roman
Landing

POUND RD

MIDDLEFIELD

COASTGUARD LA

ELLA NORE LA

Sch

P

West Wittering

THE WAD

CAKEHAM RD

PH

Eastoke Point

P

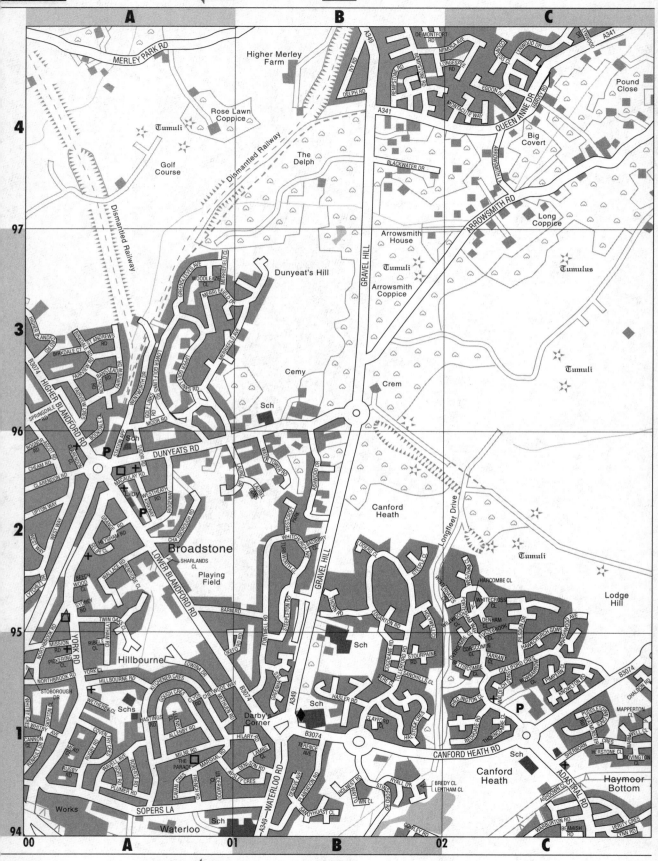

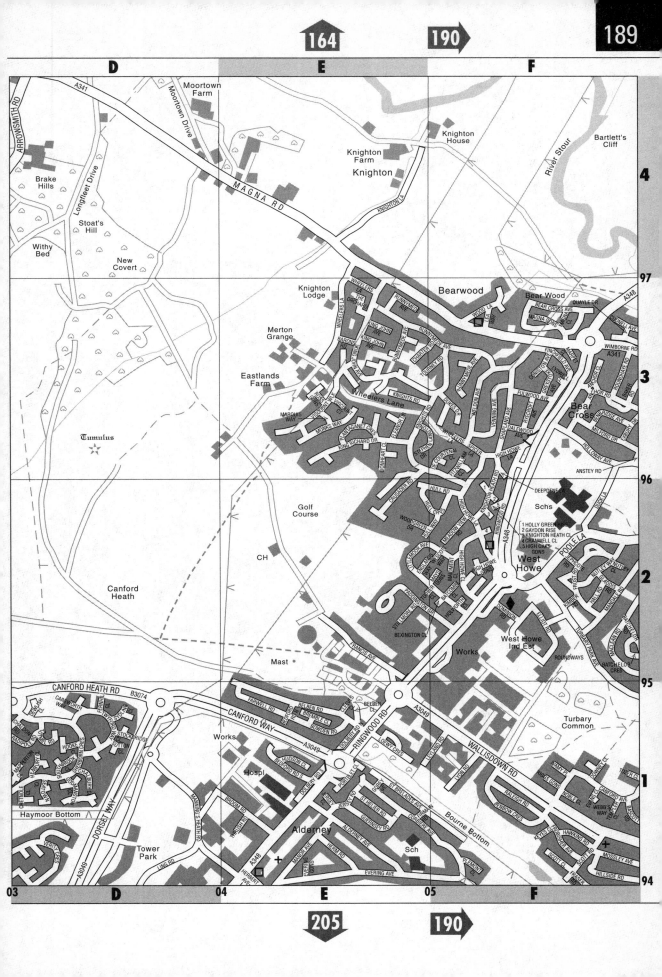

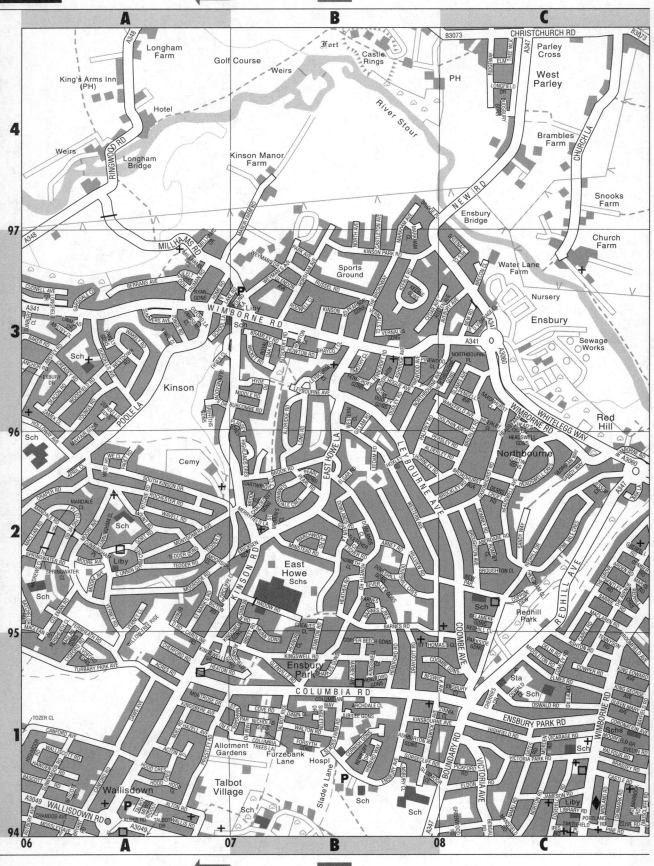

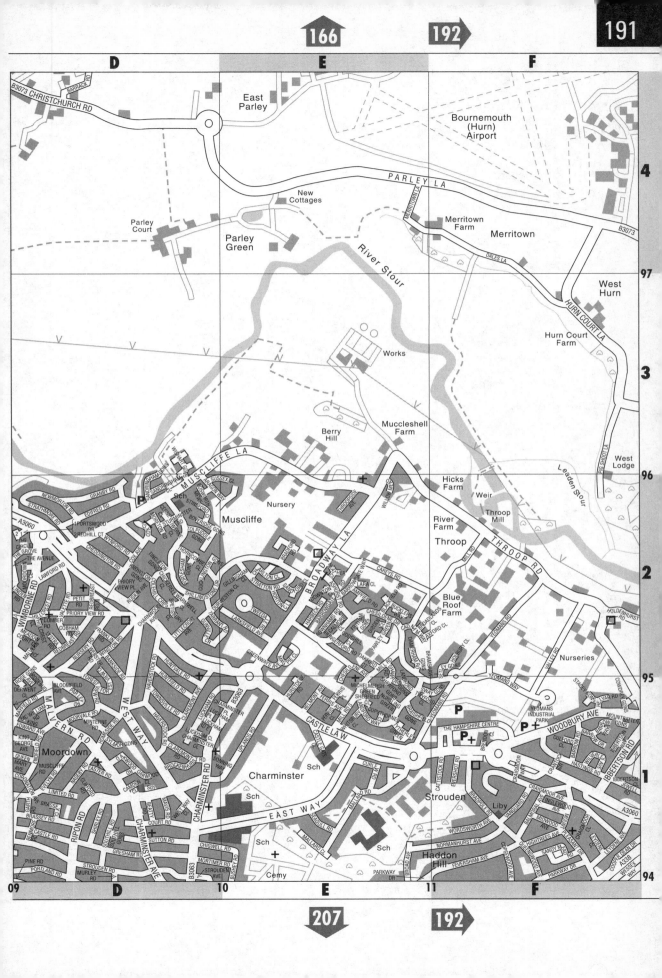

191
167

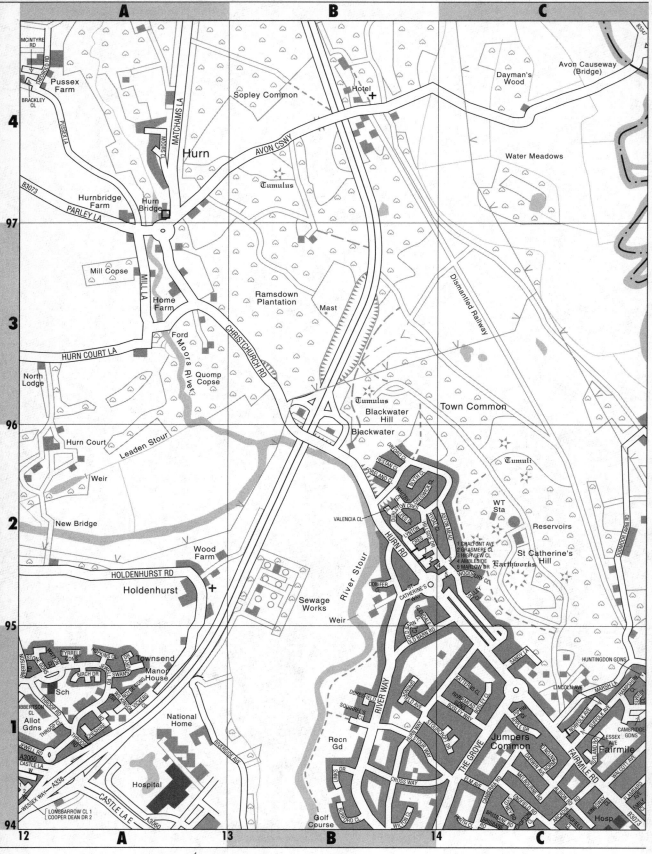

191
208

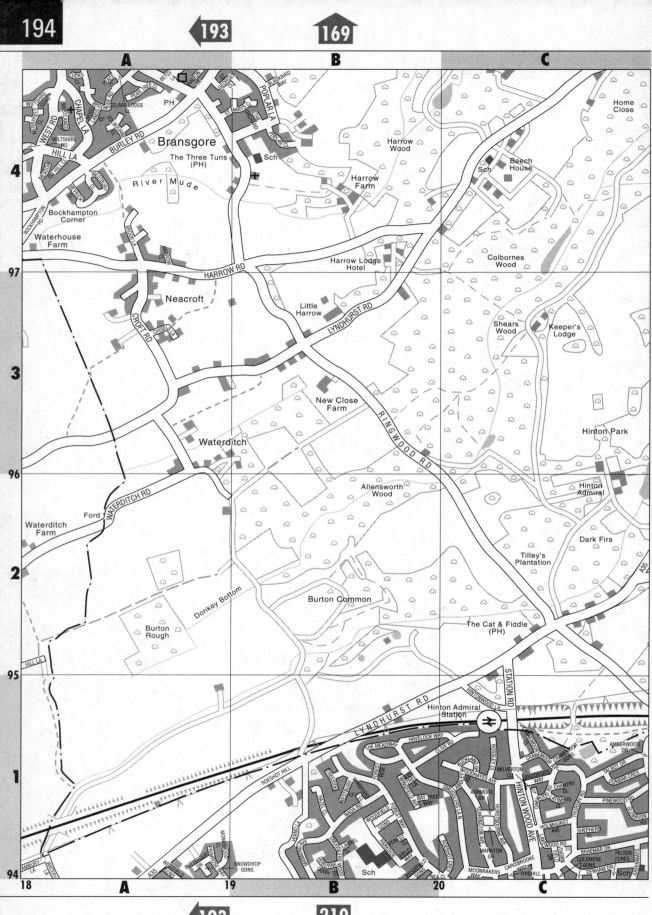

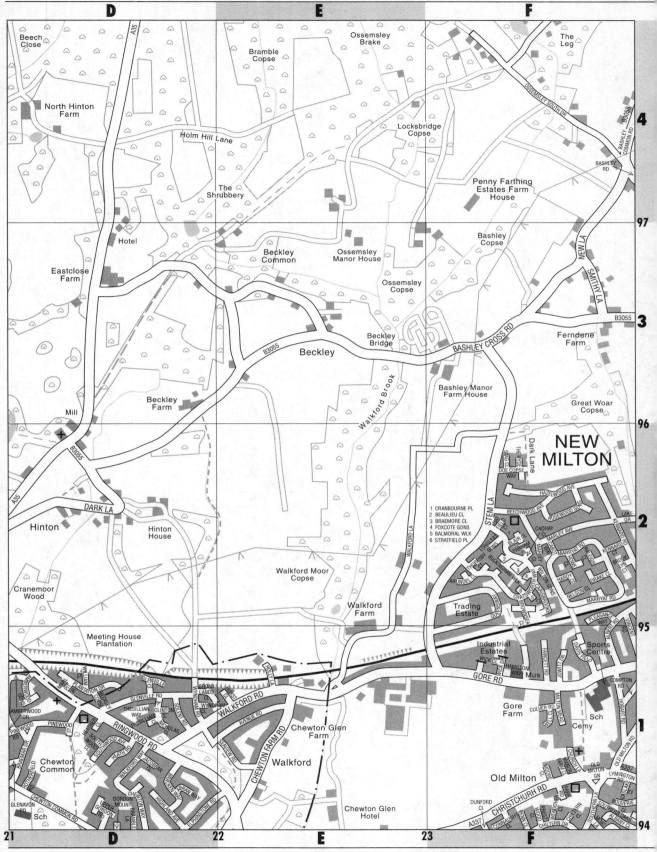

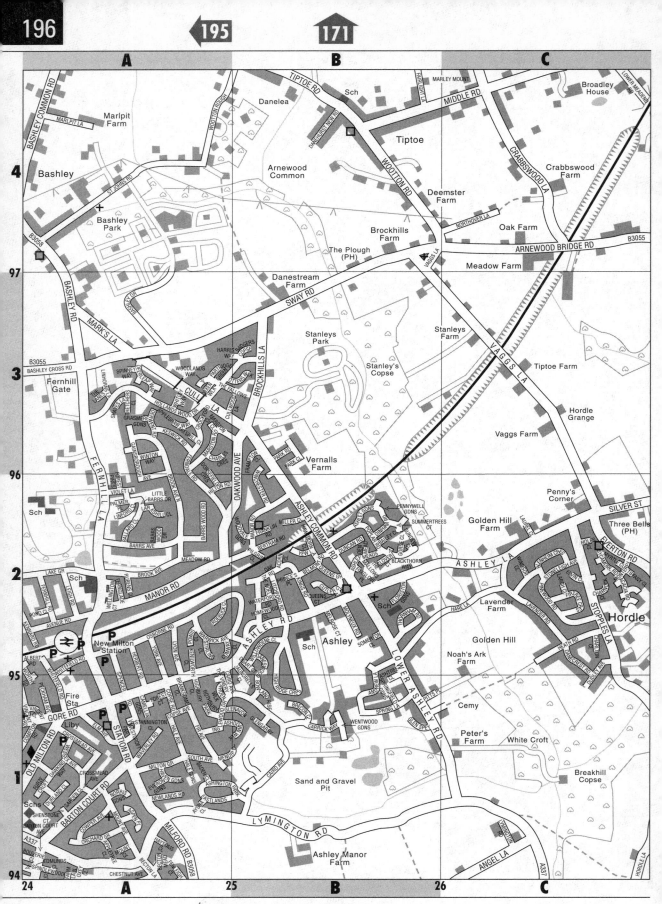

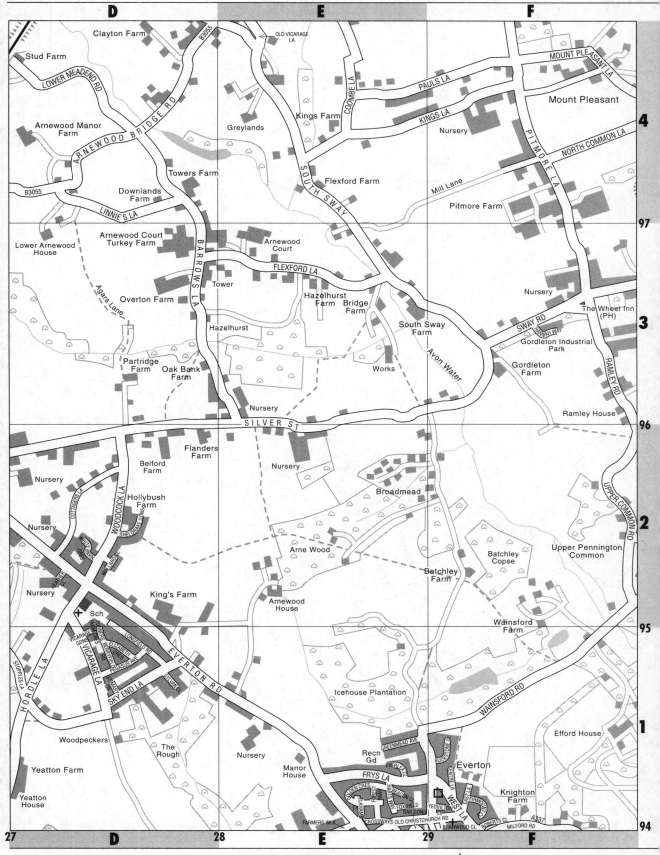

D     E     F

Clayton Farm

OLD VICARAGE LA

Stud Farm

LOWER MEADEND RD

MOUNT PLEASANT LA

PAULS LA

Mount Pleasant

Arnewood Manor Farm

Kings Farm

KINGS LA

Nursery

4

ARNEWOOD BRIDGE RD

Greylands

SOUTH SWAY

Flexford Farm

Mill Lane

NORTH COMMON LA

PITMORE LA

Towers Farm

Pitmore Farm

B3055

Downlands Farm

LINNIES LA

97

Lower Arnewood House

Arnewood Court Turkey Farm

Arnewood Court

Nursery

BARROWS LA

FLEXFORD LA

The Wheel Inn (PH)

SWAY RD

HANNAH WAY

3

Tower

Agars Lane

Overton Farm

Hazelhurst Farm

Bridge Farm

Gordleton Industrial Park

Gordleton Farm

Hazelhurst

South Sway Farm

Avon Water

Partridge Farm

RAMLEY RD

Oak Bank Farm

Works

Nursery

Ramley House

SILVER ST

96

Flanders Farm

Nursery

Belford Farm

WOODCOCK LA

Broadmead

COTTAGERS LA

Nursery

Hollybush Farm

UPPER COMMON RD

SHELDRAKE GDNS

Nursery

WHITE GATES CRES

Arne Wood

Batchley Copse

2

HEATHER CL

MT LARD

Upper Pennington Common

Nursery

King's Farm

Batchley Farm

Sch

VICARAGE GDNS

Arnewood House

Wainsford Farm

95

HORDLE LA

STOPPLES LA

VICARAGE LA

ELIZABETH CRES

LONGFIELD RD

PEGASUS AVE

EVERTON RD

SKY END LA

WAINSFORD RD

Woodpeckers

The Rough

Icehouse Plantation

Efford House

1

Yeatton Farm

Nursery

Manor House

GREENMEAD AVE

EVERLEA

Everton

A337

Yeatton House

Recn Gd

FRYS LA

YEOVILTON RD

BUCKLAND

CENTRAL LA

Knighton Farm

FIRMAN WAY

CADEN CRES

ELKHAM

FOREST

HARTS WAY

BEACON WAY

FOX FIELD

OAK GDNS

WEST LA

FARMERS WLK

CROSSWAYS

OLD CHRISTCHURCH RD

BRANWOOD CL

ROBERTS CL

MILFORD RD

94

27     D     28     E     29     F

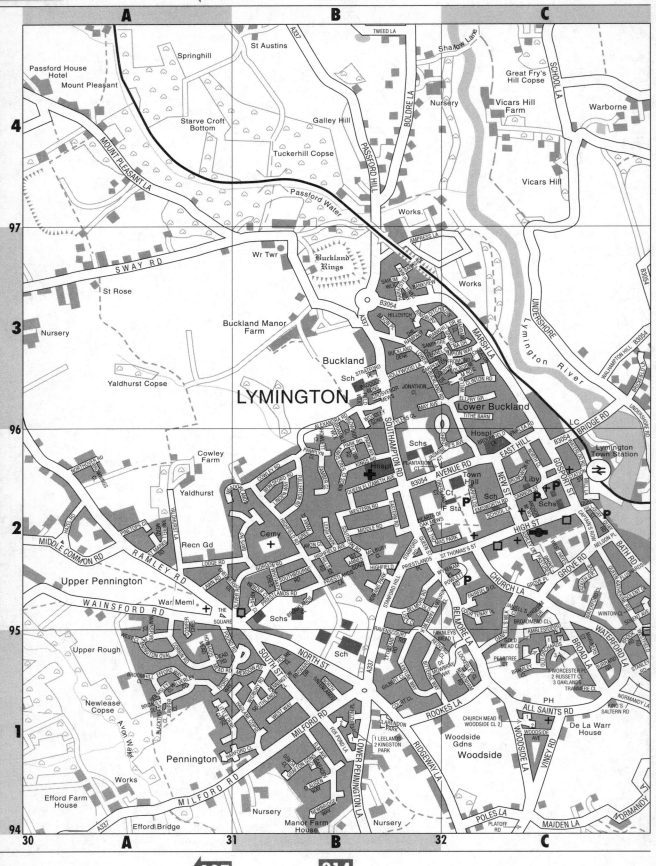

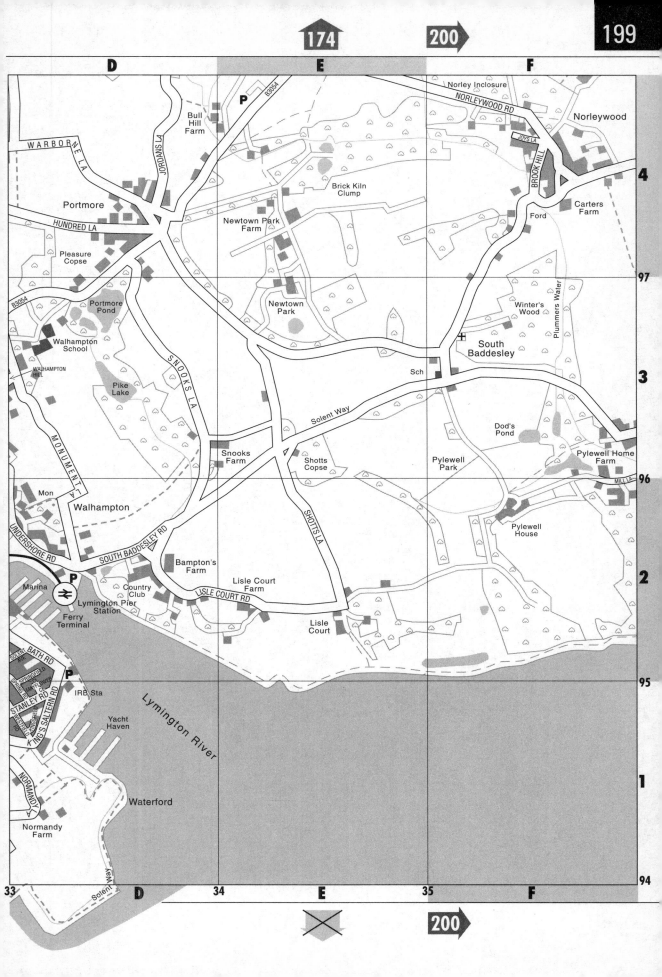

200

D  E  F

Norley Inclosure
NORLEYWOOD RD
Norleywood

P
B3054
Bull Hill Farm
JOYS LA
BROOK HILL

4

Brick Kiln Clump
Carters Farm
Ford

WARBORNE LA
JORDANS LA
Portmore
Newtown Park Farm

HUNDRED LA

Pleasure Copse
Winter's Wood
97

B3054
Newtown Park
Plummers Water
South Baddesley

Portmore Pond
Sch

Walhampton School
SNOOKS LA

WALHAMPTON HILL
3

Pike Lake
Solent Way
Dod's Pond

MONUMENT
Snooks Farm
Pylewell Park
Pylewell Home Farm
MILL LA
96

Mon
Shotts Copse
Pylewell House
Walhampton

SOUTH BADDESLEY RD
SHOTTS LA

UNDERSHORE RD
Bampton's Farm

P
Marina
Country Club
Lisle Court Farm
LISLE COURT RD
2

IRB Sta
Lymington Pier Station
Ferry Terminal
Lisle Court

BATH RD
SOLENT AVE
SPRINGFIELD
MAYFLOWER
95
P
STANLEY RD
KING'S SALTERN RD
WESTFIELD
KINGSFIELD

NORMANDY
Yacht Haven
Lymington River

1

Waterford

Normandy Farm

Solent Way

D  E  F
94

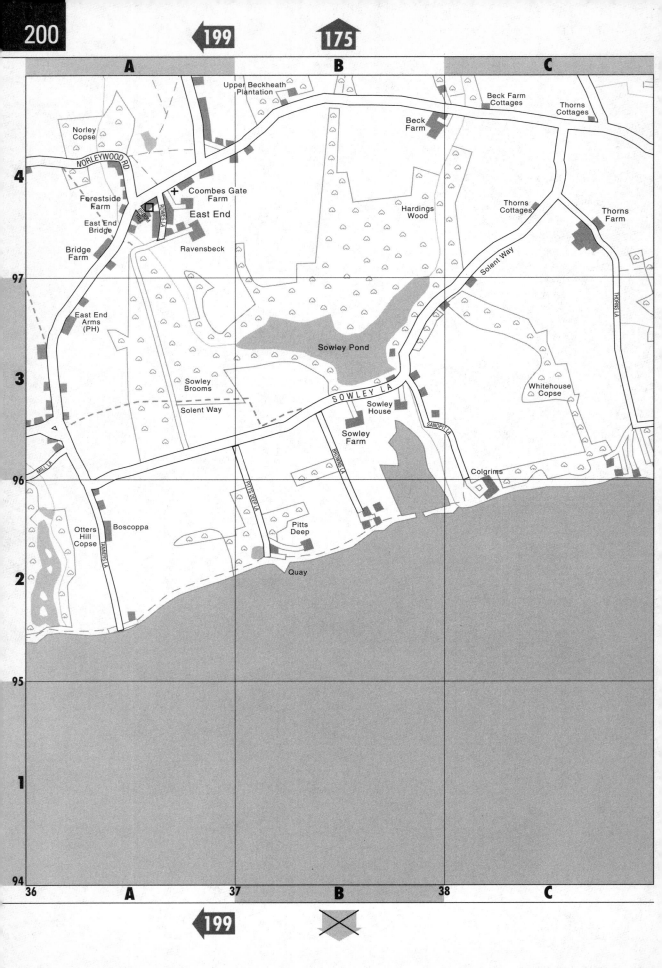

Upper Beckheath Plantation

Norley Copse

NORLEYWOOD RD

4

Forestside Farm

Coombes Gate Farm

East End

East End Bridge

Ravensbeck

Bridge Farm

Beck Farm

Beck Farm Cottages

Thorns Cottages

Hardings Wood

Thorns Cottages

Thorns Farm

THORNS LA

97

East End Arms (PH)

Solent Way

Sowley Pond

Solent Way

3

Sowley Brooms

Solent Way

SOWLEY LA

Sowley House

Sowley Farm

SANDPIT LA

Whitehouse Copse

MILL LA

96

Colgrims

Otters Hill Copse

Boscoppa

TANNERS LA

PITTS DEEP LA

BROWNS LA

Pitts Deep

2

Quay

95

1

94

36          A          37          B          38          C

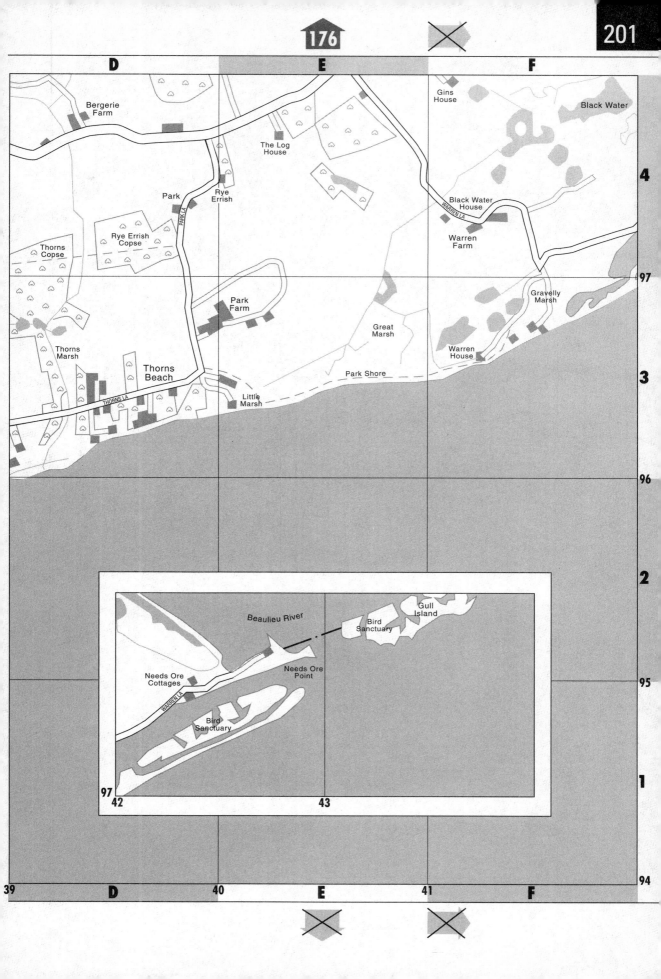

Bergerie Farm

Gins House

Black Water

The Log House

Park

Rye Errish

PARK LA

Black Water House

WARREN LA

Rye Errish Copse

Warren Farm

Thorns Copse

Gravelly Marsh

Park Farm

Great Marsh

Warren House

Thorns Marsh

Thorns Beach

Park Shore

THORNS LA

Little Marsh

Beaulieu River

Bird Sanctuary

Gull Island

Bird Sanctuary

Needs Ore Cottages

Needs Ore Point

WARREN LA

Bird Sanctuary

97

42

43

A

B

C

Golf Course

Solent Way

MILITARY RD

Fort
Gilkicker

Gilkicker
Point

Fort
Monkton

4

97

3

96

2

95

1

94

60

61

62

A

B

C

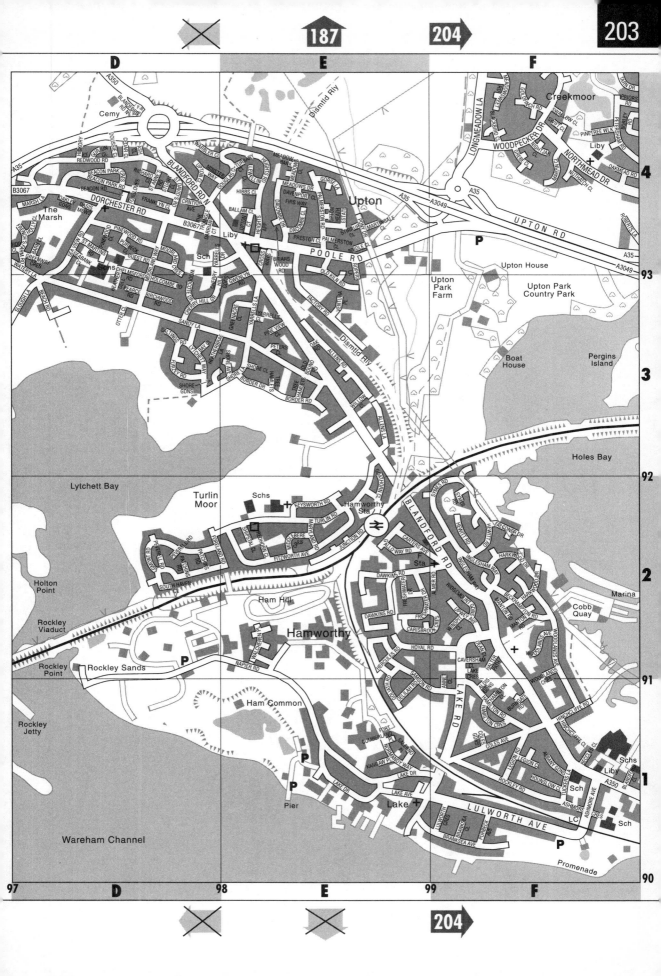

**D** **E** **F**

4

93

3

92

2

91

1

90

97 **D** 98 **E** 99 **F**

Creekmoor

LONGMEADOW LA
WOODPECKER DR
NORTHMEAD DR
Liby

UPTON RD
A35
A3049
Upton House
Upton Park Farm
Upton Park Country Park

Holes Bay
Boat House
Pergins Island

Cemy
Redwood Rd
BLANDFORD RD
DORCHESTER RD
The Marsh
B3067
Liby
Sch
Schs
Upton

POOLE RD
Dismtld Rly

Lytchett Bay
Turlin Moor
Schs
KEYSWORTH RD
Hamworthy Sta
BLANDFORD RD

Holton Point
Rockley Viaduct
Ham Hill
Hamworthy

Rockley Point
Rockley Sands
P
NAPIER RD
Ham Common
P
P

Rockley Jetty

Marina
Cobb Quay

LAKE RD

Pier
Lake
P
LULWORTH AVE
Schs
Liby
Sch
A350
LC
Sch

Wareham Channel
Promenade

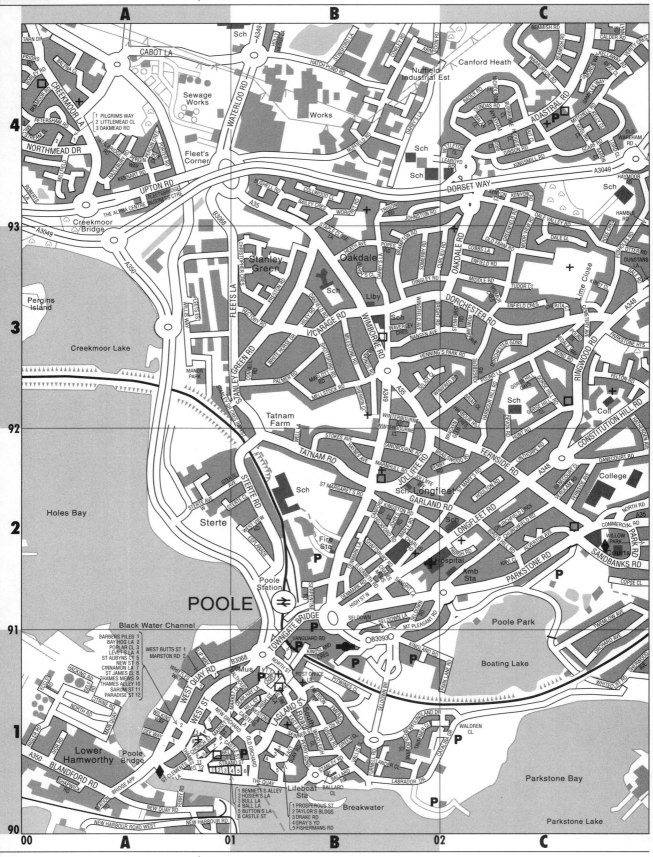

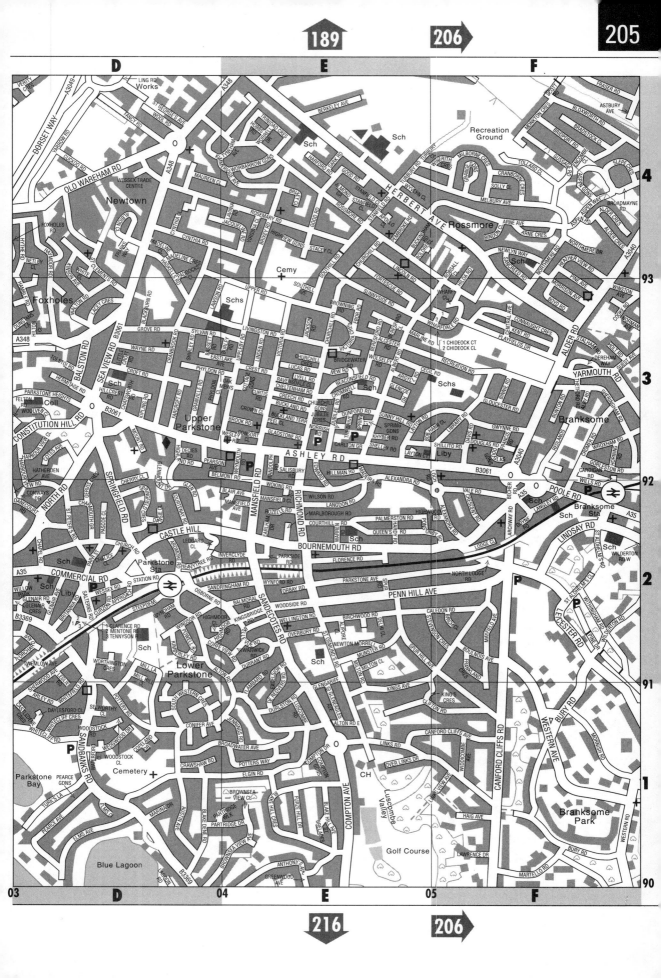

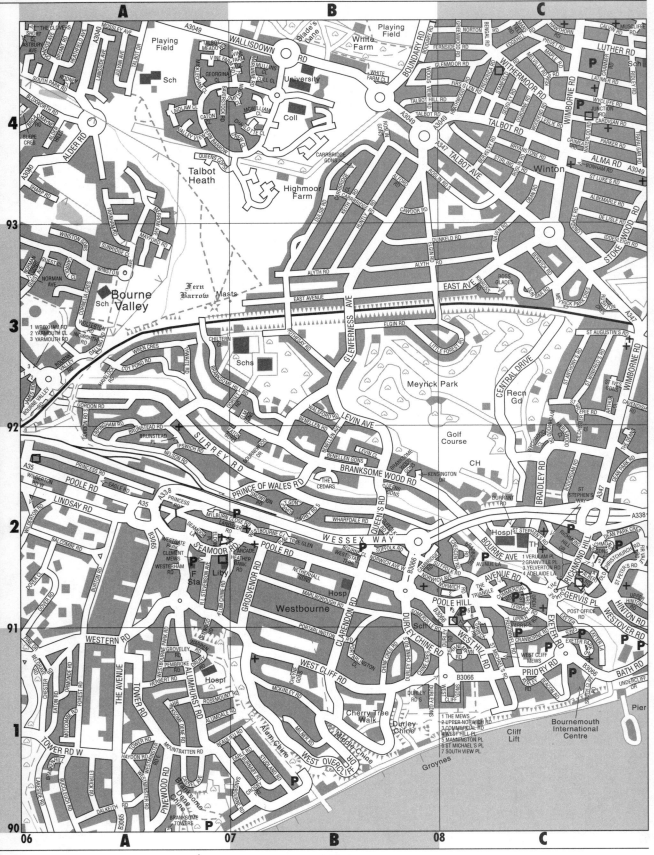

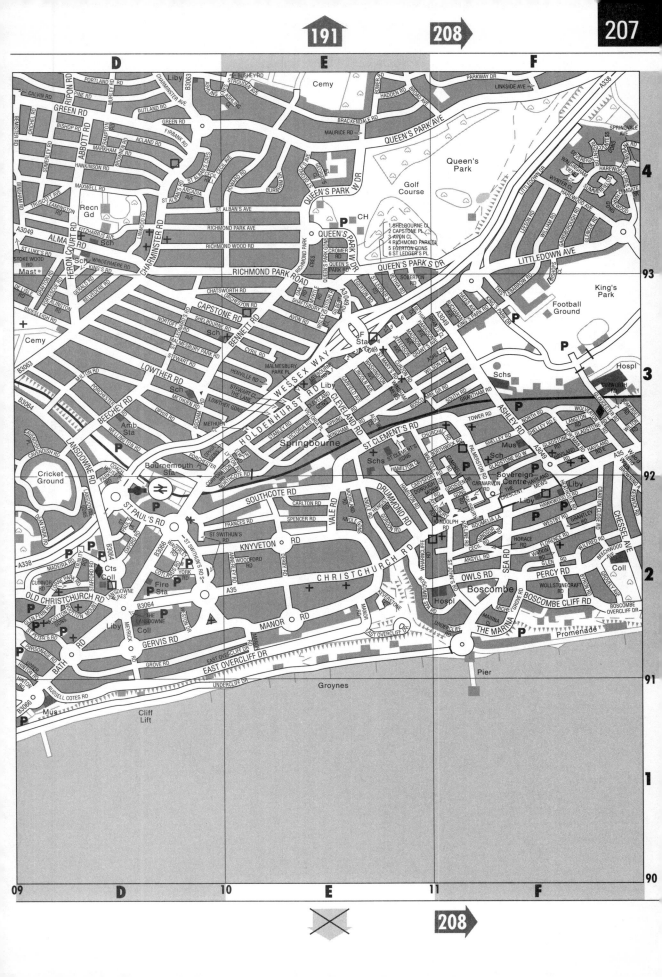

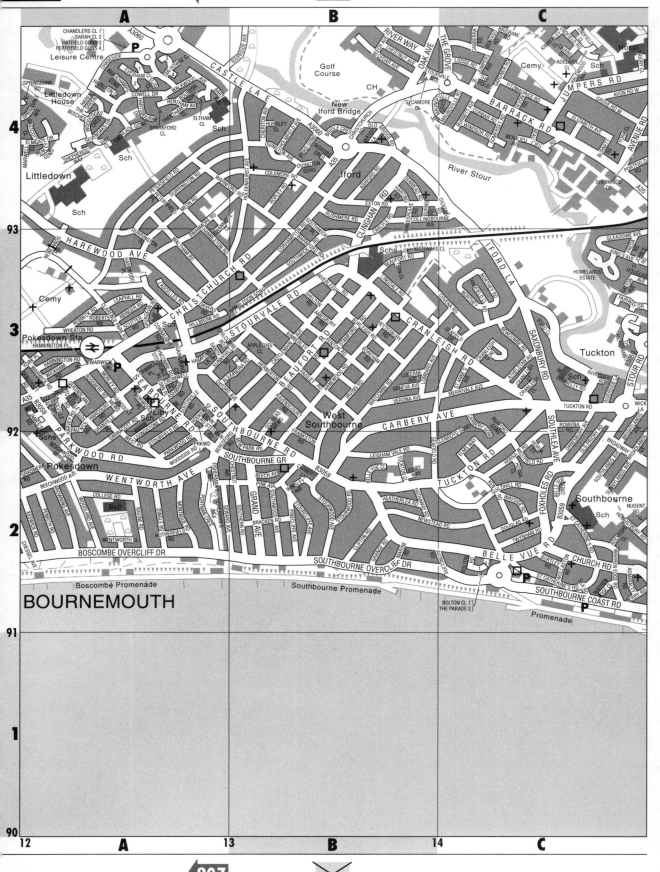

BOURNEMOUTH

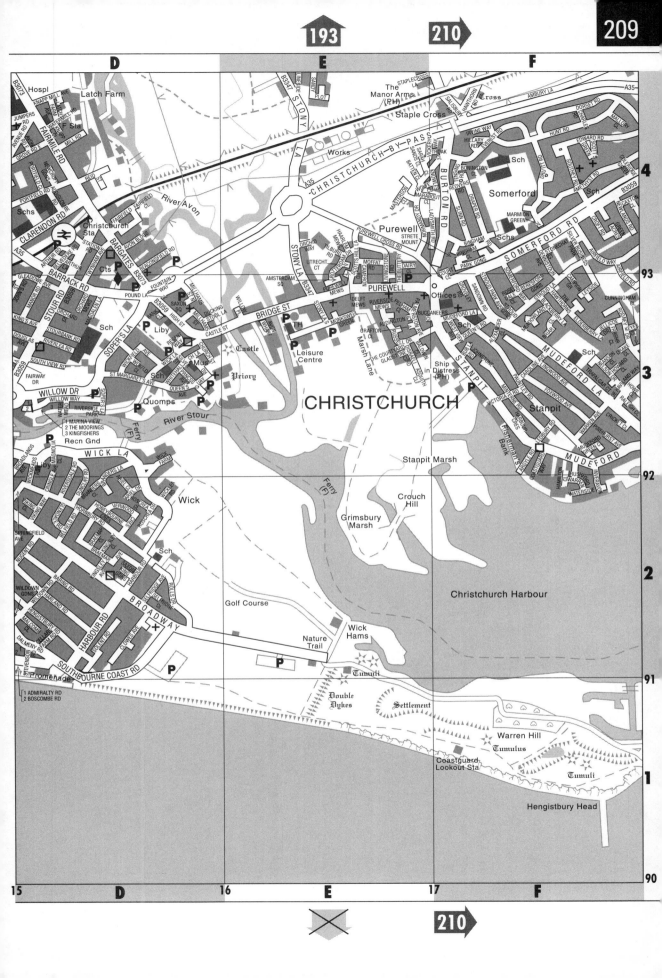

CHRISTCHURCH

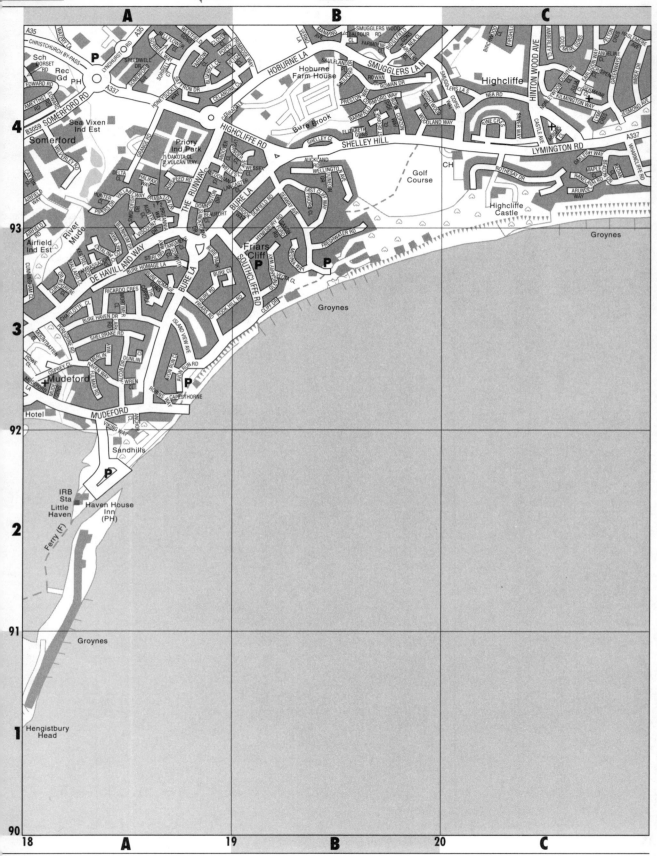

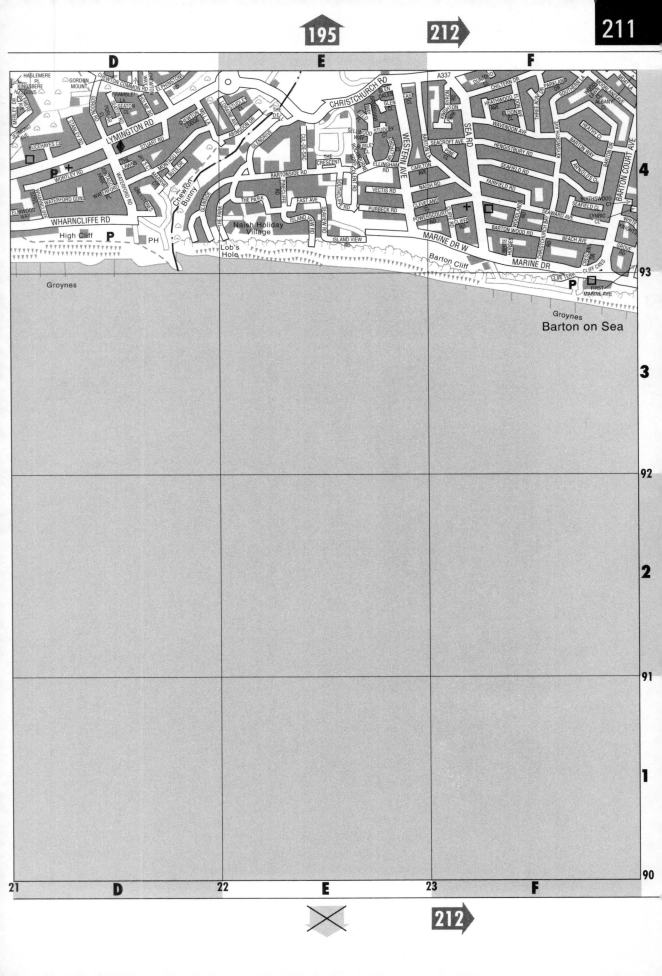

Barton on Sea

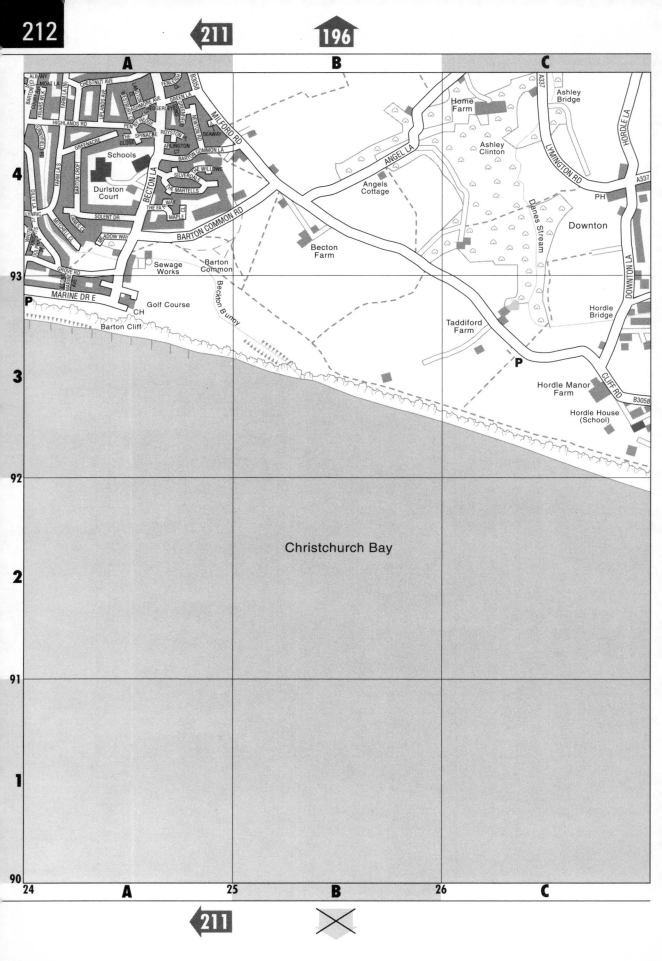

Christchurch Bay

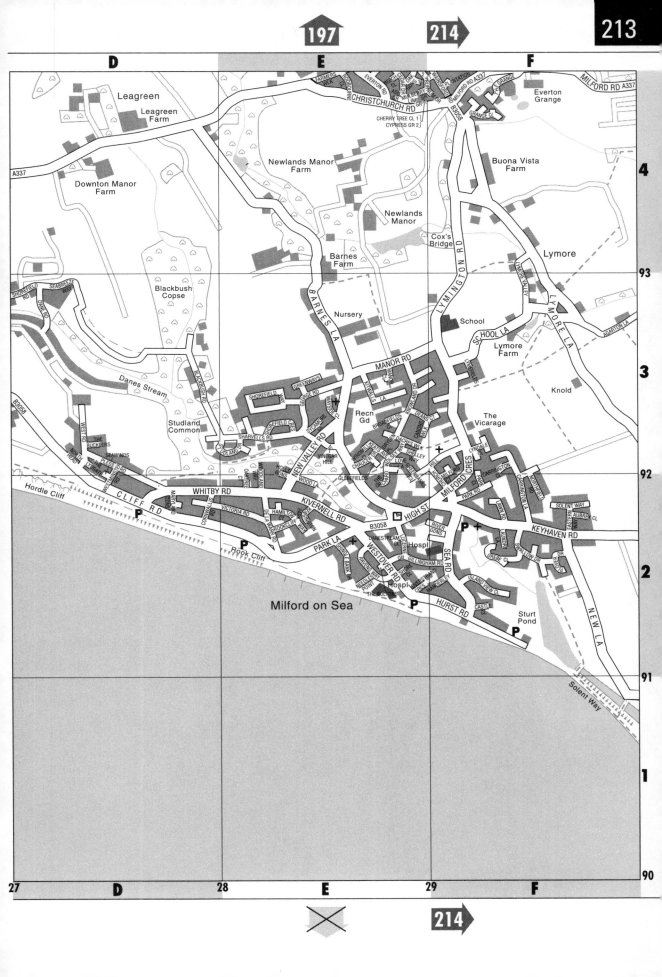

197
214

D

E

F

4

93

3

92

2

91

1

90

27  D  28  E  29  F

214

Leagreen

Leagreen
Farm

Downton Manor
Farm

A337

Blackbush
Copse

SHOREFIELD RD
SEABREEZE WAY
DALE RD

Danes Stream

Studland
Common

BLACKBUSH RD

WEST RD

B3058

NORTH HEAD
LYNDALE
PLESSEY RD
THE BUCKLERS
SEAWINDS
WESTMINSTER

Hordle Cliff

CLIFF RD

P

Rook Cliff

P

Milford on Sea

CHRISTCHURCH RD

FARMERS
BROOKDENE
ROSEDENE

EVERTON RD
BEECH CL
CEDAR GR
OAK
MULBERRY
LIME GR

MILFORD RD A337
B3058

PLANTATION

GRANGE CL

MILFORD RD A337

Everton
Grange

MILFORD RD A337

CHERRY TREE CL 1
CYPRESS GR 2

Newlands Manor
Farm

Newlands
Manor

Cox's
Bridge

Barnes
Farm

BARNES LA

Nursery

SHOREFIELD
GREENWAYS
WAY
GEORGE RD
SHOREFIELD CRES

SHARVELLS RD

STUDLAND

Manor RD

MANOR RD

WATSONS CL
SYCAMORE

NEW VALLEY RD

OAKTREE
WOODLAND
WAY
GDNS

VINEGAR
HILL

WOOD LA
GLEBEFIELDS

WHITBY RD

MARYLAND
CORNWALLIS
GDNS
VICTORIA RD
HAMILTON RD
BROOKCLIFF
WREN

KIVERNELL RD

PARK LA

SHURCE BANK RD

RAVENS WAY
NEEDLES
POINT
THE BOLTONS

WESTOVER RD

B3058

DANESTREAM
CT

GILLINGHAM RD

LUCERNE
RD

HIGH ST

KIVALLS
LA

BROADFIELDS

Recn
Gd

DACRES WLK
CHAUCER
WINDSOR
SMEATON
AVE
DRYDEN
WOODLANDS
THE
ORCHARD
LOVE
LA
SHELLEY
CL

DEANS CT

DEAN DR
CANDYS
WLK
MILFORD
HILL
RIVER
GDNS

CARINGTON
MILFORD

PARK RD

SEA RD

MANOR DR
LYNDALE

LITHFIELDS

LYMINGTON RD

LYMORE VALLEY
LYMORE LA

School

SCHOOL LA

Lymore
Farm

The Vicarage

Buona Vista
Farm

Lymore

93

LYMORE LA
AGARTON LA

Knold

CARRINGTON
CRES

CARRINGTON LA

NORTHFIELD

SOLENT WAY

KEYHAVEN RD

EASTERN
WAY
AUBREY CL

Hosp

P

LAUNDRY
LAWN RD

SWALLOW DR

GREBE CL

ISLAND VIEW CL

MANNERLY

HURST RD

CASTLE

Sturt
Pond

P

NEW LA

Solent Way

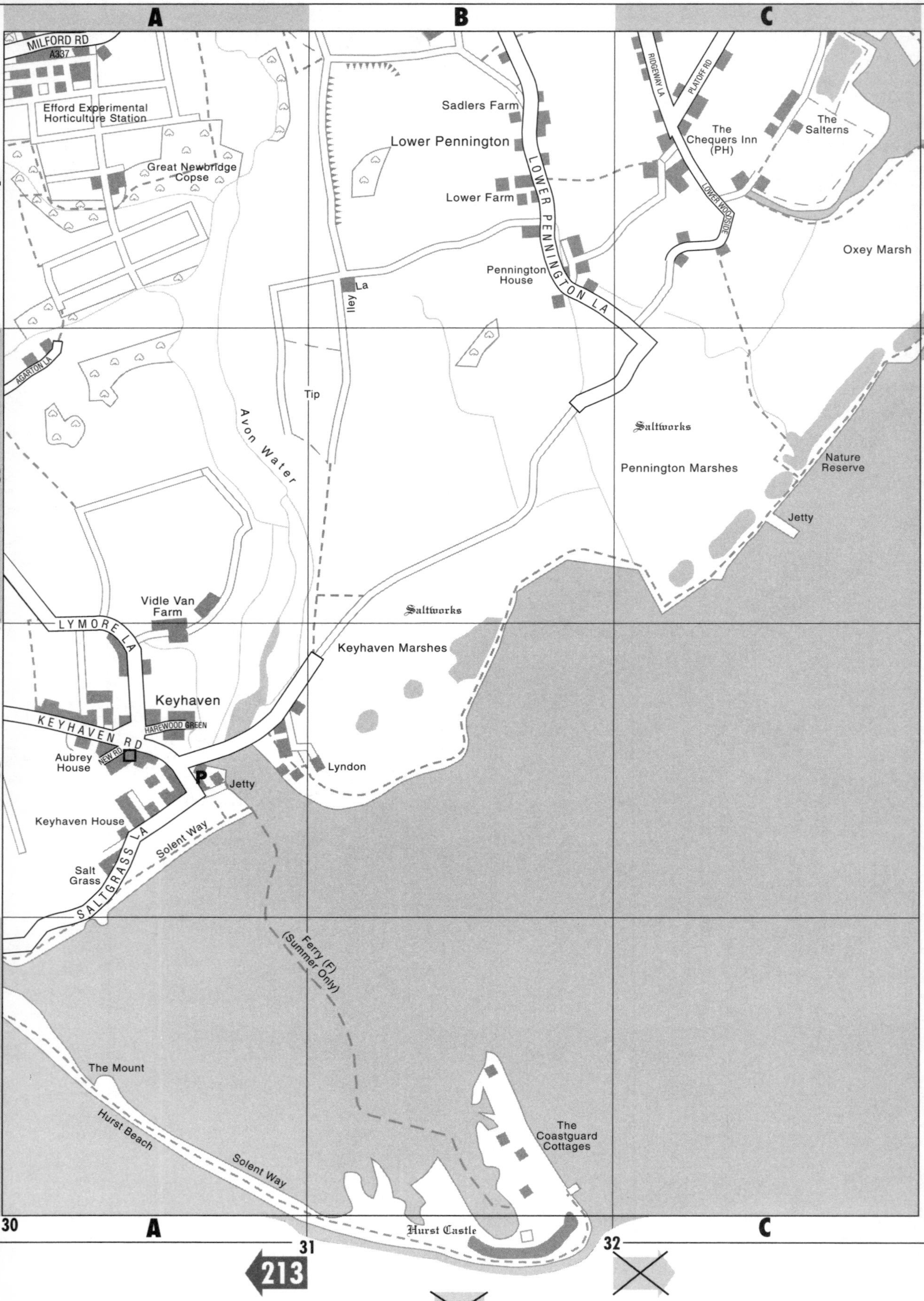

213
198

**A**

**B**

**C**

MILFORD RD
A337

Efford Experimental
Horticulture Station

Great Newbridge
Copse

Sadlers Farm

Lower Pennington

Lower Farm

LOWER PENNINGTON LA

RIDGEWAY LA

PLATOFF RD

The
Chequers Inn
(PH)

The
Salterns

**4**

Pennington
House

LOWER WOR LA

Oxey Marsh

**93**

AGARTON LA

Avon Water

Tip

La
Jelly

Saltworks

Pennington Marshes

Nature
Reserve

**3**

Jetty

Vidle Van
Farm

Saltworks

**92**

LYMORE LA

Keyhaven Marshes

Keyhaven

HAREWOOD GREEN

KEYHAVEN RD

NEW RD

Aubrey
House

**P**

Jetty

Lyndon

**2**

Keyhaven House

Solent Way

SALTGRASS LA

Salt
Grass

**91**

Ferry (F)
(Summer Only)

**1**

The Mount

Hurst Beach

The
Coastguard
Cottages

Solent Way

**90**

30

**A**

31

Hurst Castle

32

**C**

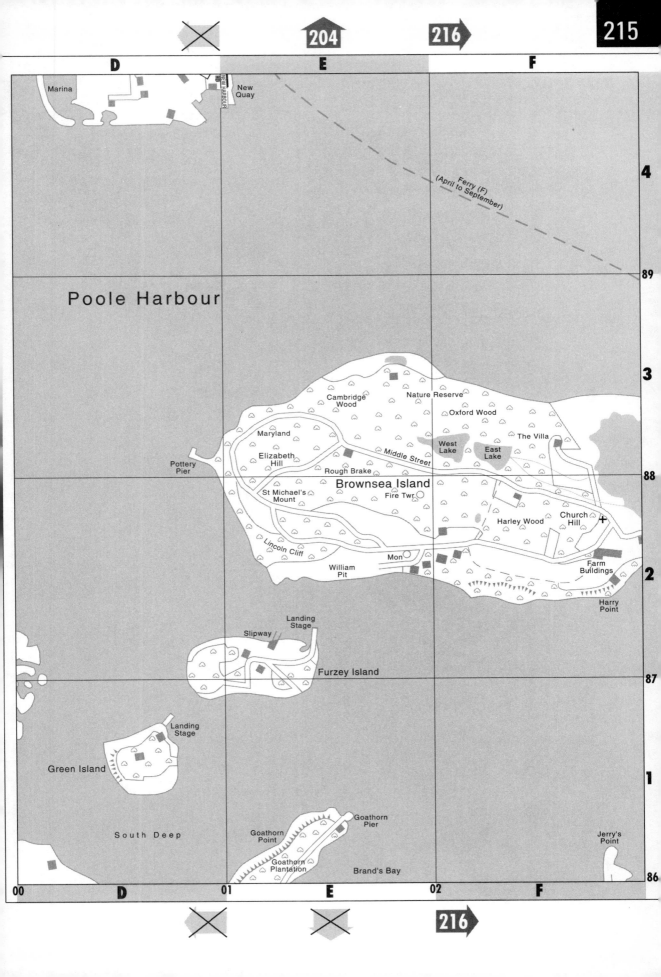

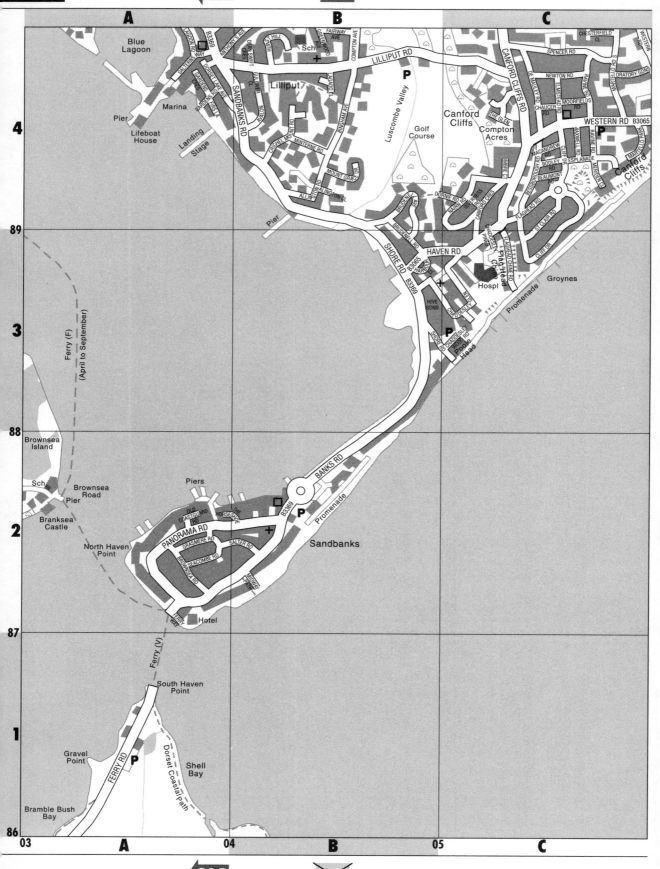

**A**

**B**

**C**

Blue
Lagoon

B3369

LAGOON RD

SALTERNS WAY

CORFE VIEW RD

BARCLAY RD

ANTHONY'S AVE

DEAN SWIFT CRES

GULL WAY

HIGH HILL

Sch

GREENWOOD

FAIRWAY AVE

COMPTON AVE

LILLIPUT RD

P

CANFORD CLIFFS RD

SPENCER RD

CHESTERFIELD CL

NEWTON RD

DE MAULEY RD

ELMSTEAD RD

WESTERN RD

S OLD ORATORY GDNS

ORATORY GDNS

Pier

Marina

SANDBANKS RD

Lilliput

LAGAGOL PL

LAKE RD

FLAGHEAD

BINGHAM AVE

Luscombe Valley

Golf
Course

Canford
Cliffs

THE GLEN

Compton
Acres

MOORFIELDS

RAVINE RD

CHAUCER RD

BODLEY RD

MAXWELL RD

RAVINE RD

WESTERN RD B3065

P

**4**

Lifeboat
House

Landing
Stage

CRICHEL MOUNT RD

MINTERNE RD

MOUNT GRACE DR

ALLINGTON CL

ALLINGTON

MOUNT RD

PINEWOOD RD

BRUDENELL RD

DORNIE RD

NAIRN RD

CANFORD CRES

ROSS GDNS

FLAGHEAD CHINE RD

BEAUMONT RD

MACANDREW RD

BESSBOROUGH RD

FLAGHEAD RD

CLIFF DR

ST CLAIR RD

MARTELLO RD

MARTELLO PARK

MERCER CT

Canford
Cliffs

**89**

Pier

SHORE RD

B3065

B3369

HARBOUR RD

HAVEN RD

CHADDESLEY GLEN RD

PINES

HAVEN RD

Flag Head

Hospl

Promenade

Groynes

**3**

Ferry (F)
(April to September)

HIVE
GDNS

CHADDESLEY

SHORE RD

CHADDESLEY

Poole
Head

P

**88**

Brownsea
Island

Sch

Brownsea
Road

Pier

BANKS RD

Promenade

**2**

Branksea
Castle

North Haven
Point

Piers

OLD COASTGUARD RD

PANORAMA RD

THE HORSESHOE

GRASMERE RD

SEACOMBE RD

BROWNSEA RD

SALTER RD

MIDWAY

B3369

P

Sandbanks

**87**

FERRY RD

Hotel

Ferry (V)

South Haven
Point

**1**

Gravel
Point

FERRY RD

P

Dorset Coastal Path

Shell
Bay

Bramble Bush
Bay

**86**

03 **A** 04 **B** 05 **C**

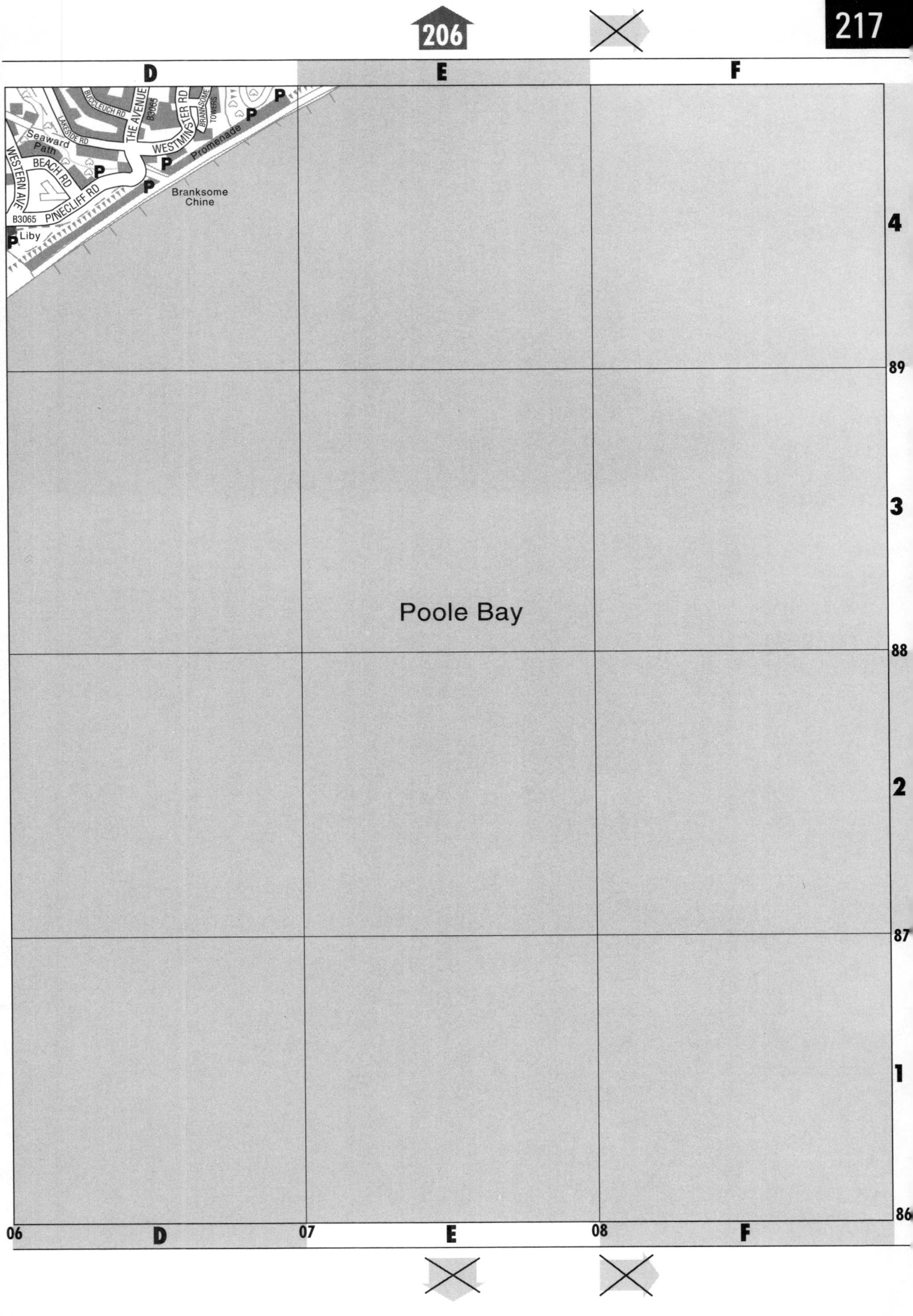
206
D
E
F
BUCCLEUCH RD
THE AVENUE
B3065
WESTMINSTER RD
BRANKSOME TOWERS
LAKESIDE RD
Seaward Path
WESTMINSTER
Promenade
WESTERN AVE
BEACH RD
PINECLIFF RD
Branksome Chine
B3065
Liby
P
4
89
3
Poole Bay
88
2
87
1
86
06
07
08
D
E
F

USER'S NOTES

# EXPLANATION OF THE STREET INDEX REFERENCE SYSTEM

Street names are listed alphabetically and show the locality, the page number and a reference to the square in which the name falls on the map page.

Example:          Abney Rd.   Bour.....................................................190   B2

Abney Rd          This is the full street name, which may have been abbreviated on the map.

Bour              This is the abbreviation for the town, village or locality in which the street falls.

190               This is the page number of the map on which the street name appears.

B2                The letter and figure indicate the square on the map in which the centre of the street falls. The square can be found at the junction of the vertical column carrying the appropriate letter and the horizontal row carrying the appropriate figure.

## ABBREVIATIONS USED IN THE INDEX
### Road Names

| | | | |
|---|---|---|---|
| Approach | App | Lane | La |
| Avenue | Ave | North | N |
| Boulevard | Bvd | Orchard | Orch |
| Broadway | Bwy | Parade | Par |
| By-Pass | By-Ps | Passage | Pas |
| Causeway | Cswy | Place | Pl |
| Common | Comm | Pleasant | Plea |
| Corner | Cnr | Precinct | Prec |
| Cottages | Cotts | Promenade | Prom |
| Court | Ct | Road | Rd |
| Crescent | Cres | South | S |
| Drive | Dri | Square | Sq |
| Drove | Dro | Street, Saint | St |
| East | E | Terrace | Terr |
| Gardens | Gdns | Walk | Wlk |
| Grove | Gr | West | W |
| Heights | Hts | Yard | Yd |

# Key to abbreviations of Town, Village and Rural Locality names used in the index of street names.

| Locality | Abbr | | |
|---|---|---|---|
| Abbotswood | Abb | 28 | A2 |
| Alderholt | Alderh | 92 | C3 |
| Ampfield | Ampf | 29 | E2 |
| Ashurst | Ashu | 100 | A2 |
| Awbridge | Awb | 26 | C2 |
| Barton on Sea | B on S | 211 | F3 |
| Beaulieu | Beaul | 148 | Cl |
| Beauworth | Beau | 35 | D4 |
| Bishop's Waltham | Bi Wa | 83 | E4 |
| Bishopstoke | Bish | 56 | C2 |
| Blackfield | Black | 177 | F4 |
| Boldre | Bold | 173 | El |
| Botley | Botl | 105 | F3 |
| Bournemouth | Bour | 208 | A2 |
| Braishfield | Brai | 28 | B4 |
| Bramdean | Bramd | 15 | E2 |
| Bramshaw | Bramsh | 73 | F2 |
| Bransgore | Bran | 194 | A4 |
| Breamore | Brea | 70 | A4 |
| Broadstone | Broa | 188 | A2 |
| Brockenhurst | Brock | 146 | Al |
| Brook | Bro | 74 | Al |
| Buriton | Buri | 65 | F3 |
| Burley | Bur | 143 | D2 |
| Bursledon | Burs | 128 | A4 |
| Burton | Burt | 193 | El |
| Cadnam | Cadn | 98 | C4 |
| Chandler's Ford | Ch Fo | 55 | E4 |
| Cheriton | Cher | 14 | B3 |
| Chilcomb | Chilc | 12 | A3 |
| Chilworth | Chilw | 54 | Bl |
| Christchurch | Christ | 209 | E3 |
| Clanfield | Clanf | 88 | A3 |
| Colden Common | Co Com | 32 | Al |
| Compton (Winchester) | Comp | 31 | E4 |
| Compton | Compt | 90 | Cl |
| Coombe Bisset | Co Bi | 23 | F4 |
| Cosham | Cos | 158 | A3 |
| Croucheston | Crouch | 22 | A4 |
| Curdridge | Curd | 106 | C4 |
| Damerham | Dame | 68 | B3 |
| Denmead | Den | 111 | D3 |
| Downton | Down | 47 | D4 |
| Droxford | Drox | 61 | Fl |
| Durley | Durl | 82 | A3 |
| East Boldre | E Bol | 175 | E3 |
| East Dean | E Dean | 4 | Al |
| East Meon | E Meo | 38 | Bl |
| East Tytherley | E Tyth | 4 | C4 |
| Eastleigh | Eastl | 55 | F2 |
| Edmondsham | Edmo | 91 | D2 |
| Emsworth | Ems | 136 | Cl |
| Exbury | Exb | 177 | D3 |
| Fair Oak | Fa Oa | 57 | El |
| Fareham | Fare | 131 | Dl |
| Fawley | Faw | 151 | D2 |
| Ferndown | Fern | 165 | E3 |
| Finchdean | Finc | 113 | E3 |
| Fordingbridge | Fordi | 69 | Fl |
| Fritham | Fri | 72 | Cl |
| Froxfield Green | Frox G | 39 | E4 |
| Gosport | Gos | 181 | E4 |
| Hamble | Hamble | 128 | A2 |
| Hambledon | Hambl | 86 | Bl |
| Hamworthy | Hamw | 203 | E2 |
| Havant | Hav | 135 | F2 |
| Hawkley | Hawk | 19 | F4 |
| Hedge End | He En | 105 | E3 |
| Hermitage | Herm | 137 | D4 |
| Hill Brow | Hill B | 21 | Dl |
| Holbury | Holb | 150 | B2 |
| Holt Heath | Holt | 138 | A3 |
| Hordle | Hord | 196 | C2 |
| Horndean | Horn | 112 | B4 |
| Hurn | Hurn | 192 | A4 |
| Hursley | Hurs | 30 | A4 |
| Hythe | Hyt | 126 | A3 |
| Ibsley | Ibs | 117 | D4 |
| Kilmeston | Kilm | 14 | Bl |
| Kings Worthy | Ki Wo | 2 | B3 |
| Landford | Lan | 49 | E2 |
| Langrish | Langr | 39 | E2 |
| Lee-on-the-Solent | L on S | 179 | E3 |
| Liss | Liss | 21 | D2 |
| Littleton | Litt | 1 | A3 |
| Lockerley | Locke | 4 | Cl |
| Locks Heath | Lo He | 129 | E2 |
| Lymington | Lym | 198 | B3 |
| Lyndhurst | Lyn | 121 | F3 |
| Marchwood | March | 101 | Fl |
| Martin | Mar | 43 | D2 |
| Meonstoke | Meons | 61 | E3 |
| Michelmersh | Miche | 6 | Bl |
| Milford on Sea | M on S | 213 | E2 |
| Minstead | Min | 98 | A2 |
| Mottisfont | Mott | 5 | Fl |
| Netley | Net | 127 | D3 |
| Netley Marsh | Ne Ma | 100 | A3 |
| New Milton | New M | 195 | F2 |
| North Baddesley | N Bad | 53 | F3 |
| North Hayling | N Hay | 160 | B2 |
| Nursling | Nur | 77 | E3 |
| Oakley | Oakl | 163 | Fl |
| Otterbourne | Ott | 31 | E2 |
| Ower | Ower | 75 | F3 |
| Owslebury | Ows | 33 | D2 |
| Pamphill | Pamp | 162 | C3 |
| Pentridge | Pent | 42 | Al |
| Petersfield | Pet | 40 | B2 |
| Plaitford | Plai | 50 | A2 |
| Poole | Poole | 204 | A2 |
| Portchester | Portc | 156 | B4 |
| Portsmouth | Ports | 157 | E2 |
| Rake | Ra | 21 | F2 |
| Redlynch | Red | 47 | F3 |
| Ringwood | Rin | 141 | E4 |
| Rockbourne | Rockb | 44 | Cl |
| Rogate | Roga | 41 | F3 |
| Romsey | Rom | 52 | C3 |
| Rowland's Castle | Ro Ca | 113 | El |
| Rownhams | Rown | 77 | F4 |
| Shedfield | Shed | 107 | E4 |
| Sherfield English | Sh En | 25 | El |
| Soberton | Sob | 85 | E3 |
| Sopley | Sop | 193 | D4 |
| South Harting | S Har | 66 | C2 |
| South Hayling | S Hay | 184 | Cl |
| Southampton | Southa | 102 | B2 |
| Southbourne | Southb | 161 | F4 |
| Southwick | Southw | 132 | C3 |
| St Leonards | St Le | 139 | E2 |
| Steep | Steep | 40 | B4 |
| Stubbington | Stubb | 154 | B2 |
| Swanmore | Swan | 84 | B3 |
| Swanwick | Swanw | 129 | D4 |
| Sway | Sway | 172 | A1 |
| Thorney Island | Th Is | 161 | D2 |
| Totton | Tot | 100 | C4 |
| Twyford | Twyf | 32 | A3 |
| Upham | Uph | 58 | C3 |
| Upton | Upt | 203 | E4 |
| Verwood | Ver | 114 | C3 |
| Walderton | Wal | 137 | F4 |
| Warnford | Warnf | 36 | C2 |
| Waterlooville | Wat | 134 | C4 |
| West Dean | W Dean | 3 | E2 |
| West End | W End | 80 | C1 |
| West Meon | W Meo | 37 | D2 |
| West Moors | W Moo | 138 | C2 |
| West Tisted | W Tis | 16 | B4 |
| West Wellow | W Wel | 50 | C2 |
| West Wittering | W Wit | 186 | C1 |
| Westbourne | Westb | 137 | D2 |
| Whiteparish | Whit | 24 | A2 |
| Whitsbury | Whits | 45 | D2 |
| Wickham | Wickh | 108 | A2 |
| Wimborne Minster | Wi Mi | 163 | E3 |
| Winchester | Winch | 10 | B3 |
| Woodgreen | Woodg | 70 | C4 |
| Woodlands | Woodl | 114 | A3 |

221

Aaron Cl. Poole — Ash Cl. Gos


Aaron Cl. Poole 204 C4
Aaron Ct. March 101 F1
Abbas Green. Hav 135 E4
Abbey Cl. Hyt 126 A2
Abbey Hill Cl. Winch 2 A1
Abbey Hill Rd. Winch 1 C1
Abbey Hill. Net 127 D4
Abbey Pas. Winch 11 D4
Abbey Rd. Fare 130 B1
Abbey Rd. W Moo 166 A4
Abbey The. Rom 52 C4
Abbey Water. Rom 52 C4
Abbeyfield Dr. Fare 130 B1
Abbeyfields Cl. Net 127 E3
Abbots Cl. Christ 210 C4
Abbots Cl. Wat 134 B2
Abbots Way. Fare 130 B1
Abbots Way. Net 127 E3
Abbots Well Rd. Fordi 94 C4
Abbotsbury Rd. Bish 56 C1
Abbotsbury Rd. Broa 187 F3
Abbotsfield Cl. Southa 78 B3
Abbotsfield. Tot 100 C4
Abbotsford. Cadn 99 D3
Abbotstone Ave. Hav 136 A2
Abbotswood Cl. Rom 28 B1
Abbott Rd. Bour 207 D4
Abbott St. Pamp 162 B3
Abbotts Ann Rd. Winch 1 B2
Abbotts Cl. Winch 2 A1
Abbotts Dro. W Wel 50 C1
Abbotts Rd. Eastl 55 F1
Abbotts Rd. Winch 2 A1
Abbotts Way. Southa 79 D1
Abercrombie Gdns. Southa 78 A2
Aberdare Ave. Cos 158 A4
Aberdare Rd. Bour 190 C2
Aberdeen Cl. Fare 130 C2
Aberdeen Rd. Southa 79 E1
Aberdour Cl. Southa 104 A4
Abingdon Cl. Gos 181 D2
Abingdon Dr. Christ 211 E4
Abingdon Gdns. Southa 78 C2
Abingdon Rd. Poole 204 B4
Abinger Rd. Bour 208 A3
Abney Rd. Bour 190 B2
Above Bar St. Southa 102 C3
Abraham Cl. He En 105 E3
Abshot Cl. Lo He 129 D1
Abshot Rd. Lo He 129 E1
Acacia Ave. Ver 115 E3
Acacia Gdns. Wat 112 A3
Acacia Rd. Hord 196 C2
Acacia Rd. Southa 103 F3
Ackworth Rd. Ports 158 A3
Acland Rd. Bour 207 D4
Acorn Bsns Centre. Cos 157 E4
Acorn Cl. Cos 158 B4
Acorn Cl. Gos 155 E1
Acorn Cl. March 102 A1
Acorn Cl. New M 196 B2
Acorn Cl. St Le 139 F2
Acorn Cl. Winch 1 B1
Acorns The. Wi Mi 164 A2
Acre La. Wat 112 B1
Acres Rd. Bour 190 A1
Acton Rd. Bour 190 A1
Adair Rd. Ports 183 D1
Adames Rd. Ports 182 C3
Adams Rd. Hyt 126 A1
Adams Wood Dr. March 101 F1
Adamsfield Gdns. Bour 190 B1
Adamson Cl. Ch Fo 55 E4
Adastral Rd. Poole 204 C4
Adderbury Ave. Ems 136 C2
Addington Pl. Christ 209 E3
Addiscombe Rd. Christ 209 D4
Addison Cl. Rom 28 A1
Addison Cl. Winch 10 B3
Addison Rd. Brock 172 C4
Addison Rd. Eastl 56 A3
Addison Rd. Lo He 128 C3
Addison Rd. Ports 182 C2
Addison Sq. Rin 141 D4
Adelaide Cl. Christ 208 C4
Adelaide La. Bour 206 C2
Adelaide Rd. Southa 103 E4
Adeline Rd. Bour 207 F2
Adlam's La. Sway 172 A1
Admiral Park The. Ports 158 A2
Admirals Cl. Faw 151 D2
Admirals Rd. Lo He 129 D2
Admirals Way. Hyt 126 A3
Admirals Wlk. Gos 180 C2
Admiralty Rd. Bour 208 C2
Admiralty Rd. Ports 182 A3
Adsdean Cl. Hav 135 F2
Adstone La. Ports 158 B2
Adur Cl. W End 80 A1
Aerodrome Rd. Gos 155 F2
Africa Dr. March 124 C4
Agarton La. M on S 213 F3
Aggis Farm Rd. Ver 114 C3
Agincourt Rd. Ports 182 B4
Agnew Rd. Gos 155 E2
Aikman La. Tot 100 A4
Ailsa La. Southa 103 E2
Ainsdale Rd. Cos 134 B1
Ainsley Gdns. Eastl 56 A3
Aintree Cl. Fa Oa 81 E4
Aintree Dr. Wat 112 A1
Aintree Rd. Tot 76 B1
Airfield Rd. Christ 209 F3
Airfield Way. Christ 209 F4
Airlie Rd. Winch 10 C3
Airport Service Rd. Ports 158 A2
Airspeed Rd. Ports 158 B1
Ajax Cl. Stubb 154 B1
Akeshill Cl. New M 196 A3
Alameda Rd. Wat 134 B2
Alameda Way. Wat 134 B2
Alan Drayton Way. Bish 56 C1
Alan Gr. Fare 130 C1
Albacore Ave. Lo He 128 C1
Albany Cl. B on S 195 F1
Albany Ct. Bi Wa 83 D4
Albany Dr. Bi Wa 83 D4
Albany Dr. W Moo 114 C1
Albany Gdns. Hamw 203 F1
Albany Rd. Bi Wa 83 D4
Albany Rd. Holb 150 B2
Albany Rd. Ports 182 B2
Albany Rd. Rom 52 C4
Albany Rd. Southa 102 B3
Albatross Wlk. Gos 155 D1
Albemarle Ave. Gosp 181 D4
Albemarle Rd. Bour 206 C4
Albert Cl. Net 127 E3
Albert Gr. Ports 182 B2
Albert Rd N. Southa 103 D2
Albert Rd S. Southa 103 D2
Albert Rd. Bi Wa 83 D4
Albert Rd. Bour 206 C2
Albert Rd. Broa 187 E3
Albert Rd. Cos 157 F4
Albert Rd. Eastl 56 A3
Albert Rd. Fern 165 E3
Albert Rd. He En 105 D3
Albert Rd. New M 195 F1
Albert Rd. Poole 205 E3
Albert Rd. Ports 182 C1
Albert Rd. Stubb 155 D1
Albert St. Gos 181 E3
Albion Cl. Poole 205 D4
Albion Cl. Portc 156 A3
Albion Pl. Southa 102 C2
Albion Rd. Christ 192 C1
Albion Rd. Fordi 69 F1
Albretia Ave. Wat 111 F2
Albury Pl. Ch Fo 30 A1
Alby Rd. Poole 205 F3
Alcantara Cres. Southa 103 D2
Alcester Rd. Poole 205 E3
Alchorne Pl. Ports 158 A2
Alder Cl. Burt 193 E1
Alder Cl. Hyt 125 E2
Alder Cl. March 101 F1
Alder Cl. Rom 53 E3
Alder Cres. Poole 205 F4
Alder Dr. Alderh 92 C3
Alder Hill Dr. Tot 100 A4
Alder Hills. Poole 206 A4
Alder Rd. Poole 205 F3
Alder Rd. Southa 78 A2
Alderfield. Pet 40 C2
Alderholt Rd. Fordi 69 D1
Alderley Rd. Bour 190 C2
Aldermoor Ave. Southa 78 A2
Aldermoor Cl. Southa 78 B2
Aldermoor Rd E. Wat 134 B3
Aldermoor Rd. Gos 180 B4
Aldermoor Rd. Southa 78 A2
Aldermoor Rd. Wat 134 B2
Alderney Ave. Poole 189 E1
Alderney Cl. Southa 77 F2
Alders Rd. Fare 155 D4
Alderwood Ave. N Bad 55 D3
Alderwood Cl. Hav 135 D2
Aldis Gdns. Hamw 203 F1
Aldridge Cl. Clanf 88 B3
Aldridge Rd. Bour 190 B3
Aldridge Rd. Fern 165 F2
Aldroke St. Cos 157 F4
Aldsworth Cl. Cos 158 B4
Aldsworth Gdns. Cos 158 B4
Aldwell St. Ports 182 B2
Alec Rose La. Ports 182 B3
Alecto Rd. Gos 181 D2
Alencon Cl. Gosp 181 E4
Alexander Cl. Christ 209 F3
Alexander Cl. Tot 100 B4
Alexander Cl. Wat 134 B3
Alexander Gr. Fare 155 D4
Alexander Rd. Ch Fo 55 F4
Alexandra Ave. S Hay 184 C1
Alexandra Cl. Hyt 126 A2
Alexandra Rd. Bour 208 B3
Alexandra Rd. Fordi 69 F1
Alexandra Rd. He En 105 D3
Alexandra Rd. Hyt 126 A2
Alexandra Rd. Lym 198 B3
Alexandra Rd. Poole 205 F2
Alexandra Rd. Ports 182 B3
Alexandra Rd. Southa 102 C3
Alexandra St. Gos 181 D3
Alexandra Terr. Winch 10 C4
Alexandra Way. Botl 106 A4
Alford Rd. Bour 206 B4
Alfred Cl. Tot 100 B4
Alfred Rd. Ports 182 A3
Alfred Rd. Stubb 154 B2
Alfred Rose Ct. Southa 79 F2
Alfred St. Southa 103 D3
Alfriston Gdns. Southa 104 A2
Algiers Rd. Ports 183 D4
Alhambra Rd. Ports 182 C1
Alington Cl. Poole 216 B4
Alington Rd. Bour 207 D3
Alipore Cl. Poole 205 E2
All Saints Rd. Lym 198 C1
All Saints' Rd. Ports 182 B4
All Saints' St. Ports 182 B3
Allan Gr. Rom 53 D4
Allaway Ave. Cos 157 D4
Allaway Ave. Portc 157 D4
Allbrook Ct. Hav 135 E3
Allbrook Hill. Eastl 56 A4
Allbrook Hill. Ott 56 A4
Allbrook Knoll. Eastl 56 A4
Allcot Rd. Ports 158 A1
Allen Ct. Wi Mi 163 E3
Allen Rd. He En 105 E4
Allen Rd. Wi Mi 163 E2
Allen Water Dr. Fordi 69 F1
Allen's Rd. Ports 182 C1
Allenby Cl. Broa 188 A1
Allenby Gr. Portc 156 B4
Allenby Rd. Broa 188 A1
Allenby Rd. Gos 180 C3
Allendale Ave. Ems 136 C2
Allens La. Meons 61 E3
Allens La. Upt 203 E3
Allens Rd. Upt 203 E3
Allenview Rd. Wi Mi 163 E3
Allerton Cl. Tot 76 B1
Alliance Cl. Gos 180 B4
Allington La. W End 80 C3
Allington Rd. Poole 216 B4
Allington Rd. Southa 101 E4
Allmara Dr. Wat 134 C2
Allotment Rd. He En 105 D3
Allotment Rd. Lo He 128 C3
Alma La. Uph 58 A1
Alma Rd. Bour 207 D4
Alma Rd. Rom 52 C4
Alma Rd. Southa 103 D4
Alma St. Gos 181 D3
Alma Terr. Ports 183 D2
Almatade Rd. Southa 104 A4
Almer Rd. Hamw 203 F2
Almond Cl. Cos 158 B4
Almond Cl. Wat 112 B2
Almond Ct. Southa 102 B3
Almond Gr. Poole 205 E4
Almond Rd. Southa 102 B3
Almondsbury Rd. Cos 132 C1
Almondside. Gos 155 F1
Alpha Centre The. Broa 204 A4
Alphage Rd. Gos 155 F1
Alpine Cl. Southa 104 A4
Alpine Rd. Ashu 99 F2
Alresford Rd. Chilc 12 B4
Alresford Rd. Hav 135 F2
Alresford Rd. It Ab 12 B4
Alresford Rd. Ovin 12 B4
Alresford Rd. Tich 12 B4
Alresford Rd. Winch 11 E4
Alresford Rd. Winch 12 B4
Alsford Rd. Wat 134 B3
Alten Rd. Wat 111 E1
Althorpe Dr. Ports 158 B2
Alton Cl. Fa Oa 57 E1
Alton Gr. Portc 156 B3
Alton Rd E. Poole 205 E1
Alton Rd. Bour 190 A1
Alum Chine Rd. Bour 206 A2
Alum Cl. Holb 150 B2
Alum Way. Portc 131 F1
Alum Way. Southa 104 A4
Alumdale Rd. Bour 206 A1
Alumhurst Rd. Bour 206 A1
Alvara Rd. Gos 181 D1
Alver Rd. Gos 181 D2
Alver Rd. Ports 182 C3
Alvercliffe Dr. Gos 180 C1
Alverstone Rd. Ports 183 D3
Alverton Ave. Poole 204 C2
Alveston Ave. Fare 154 B4
Alyth Rd. Bour 206 B3
Ambassador Cl. Christ 210 A3
Amber Rd. Broa 187 E2
Amberley Cl. Botl 106 A4
Amberley Cl. Christ 210 C4
Amberley Cl. N Bad 53 F3
Amberley Rd. Gosp 181 D4
Amberley Rd. Ports 157 F2
Amberslade Wlk. Hyt 125 F1
Amberwood Cl. Tot 76 B1
Amberwood Dr. Christ 194 C1
Amberwood Gdns. Christ 195 D1
Amberwood. Fern 165 F3
Ambledale. Lo He 128 C2
Ambleside Gdns. Southa 104 A2
Ambleside Rd. Lym 198 C2
Ambleside. Christ 192 C2
Ambleside. He En 105 E3
Ambury La. Burt 209 F4
Amersham Cl. Gos 180 C2
Amesbury Rd. Bour 208 B3
Amethyst Gr. Wat 135 D4
Amethyst Rd. Christ 209 F4
Amey Ind Est. Pet 40 C2
Ameys La. Fern 165 F4
Ameysford Rd. Fern 138 A1
Ameysford Rd. Fern 165 E4
Amoy St. Southa 102 C3
Ampfield Cl. Hav 135 D2
Ampfield Rd. Bour 191 E2
Amport Cl. Winch 1 B2
Amport Ct. Hav 135 E3
Ampress La. Bold 198 B3
Ampthill Rd. Southa 102 A4
Amsterdam Sq. Christ 209 E3
Amyas Ct. Ports 183 E2
Ancasta Rd. Southa 103 D4
Anchor Cl. Bour 189 F3
Anchor Cl. Christ 210 A3
Anchor Mews. Lym 198 C2
Anchor Rd. Bour 189 F3
Anchorage Rd. Ports 158 A2
Anchorage The. Gos 181 E2
Anderby Rd. Southa 77 E1
Anderson Cl. Hav 136 A2
Anderson Cl. Rom 28 B1
Anderson's Rd. Southa 103 D2
Anderwood Dr. Sway 172 A1
Andes Cl. Southa 103 E2
Andes Rd. Nur 77 D2
Andlers Ash Rd. Liss 20 C2
Andover Cl. Christ 210 A4
Andover Rd N. Winch 1 C2
Andover Rd. Ports 182 C1
Andover Rd. Southa 102 B3
Andover Rd. Winch 1 C1
Andrew Bell St. Ports 182 B3
Andrew Cl. Hyt 126 A1
Andrew Cl. Tot 100 B4
Andrew Cres. Wat 111 E1
Andrew La. New M 196 B1
Andrew Pl. Stubb 154 A1
Andrewes Cl. Bi Wa 83 E4
Andrews Cl. Bour 190 A2
Andromeda Rd. Southa 77 F2
Androse Gdns. Rin 140 C4
Anfield Cl. Fa Oa 57 E1
Angel Cres. Southa 104 A3
Angel La. B on S 212 B4
Angel La. Fern 165 D2
Angelica Ct. Wat 135 D3
Angelica Gdns. Fa Oa 81 E4
Angeline Cl. Christ 210 C4
Angelo Cl. Wat 135 D4
Angelus Cl. Stubb 154 B1
Angerstein Rd. Ports 157 E1
Anglesea Rd. Lon S 180 A2
Anglesea Rd. Ports 182 A3
Anglesea Rd. Southa 78 A1
Anglesea Terr. Southa 103 D2
Anglesey Arms Rd. Gos 181 D1
Anglesey Rd. Gos 181 D1
Angus Cl. Fare 130 C2
Anjou Cres. Fare 130 B1
Anker La. Stubb 154 B2
Ankerwyke. Gos 155 D1
Anmore Cl. Hav 135 E2
Anmore Dr. Wat 111 E1
Anmore La. Horn 111 E3
Anmore Rd. Den 111 D2
Ann's Hill Rd. Gos 181 D3
Anna La. Sop 168 A2
Anne Cl. Christ 193 D1
Anne Cres. Wat 134 C3
Annerley Rd. Bour 207 E2
Annet Cl. Hamw 203 F1
Anson Cl. Christ 209 F3
Anson Cl. Gos 180 B3
Anson Cl. Rin 141 E4
Anson Dr. Southa 104 B3
Anson Gr. Portc 132 C1
Anson Rd. Ports 183 D3
Anstey Cl. Bour 190 A3
Anstey Rd. Bour 190 D3
Anstey Rd. Rom 28 A1
Antell's Way. Alderh 93 D3
Anthill Cl. Den 110 B3
Anthony Gr. Gos 156 A1
Anthony Way. Ems 136 C2
Anthony's Ave. Poole 205 E1
Anton Cl. Rom 53 E4
Anvil Cl. Wat 112 B1
Anvil Cres. Broa 187 F3
Anzac Cl. Stubb 154 B2
Apless La. Den 110 A2
Apollo Cl. Poole 205 E4
Apollo Dr. Wat 134 C2
Apollo Rd. Ch Fo 55 F4
Apple Gr. Christ 192 C1
Apple Ind Est. Lo He 129 E3
Apple Tree Cl. Red 47 E4
Apple Tree Gr. Fern 165 F3
Apple Tree Rd. Alderh 92 C3
Appleshaw Cl. Winch 1 B2
Appleshaw Green. Hav 135 E2
Appleshaw Way. New M 196 A3
Appleton Rd. Fare 130 B1
Appleton Rd. Southa 79 F1
Appletree Cl. Bour 208 B3
Appletree Cl. New M 196 A1
Appletree Cl. Tot 76 B1
Appletree Ct. Botl 106 A4
Appletree Rd. Red 47 E4
Applewood Gr. Wat 134 B2
Applewood Pl. Tot 100 B3
Approach Rd. Poole 205 D2
April Cl. Bour 190 A2
April Cl. Southa 104 A4
April Gr. Lo He 128 C2
Apsley Cres. Broa 188 B1
Apsley Pl. Ch Fo 30 A1
Apsley Rd. Ports 183 D2
Aquila Way. Hamble 127 F1
Aragon Way. Bour 191 D2
Arcade. Bour 206 A2
Arcadia Ave. Bour 207 D4
Arcadia Cl. Southa 78 B2
Arcadia Rd. Christ 192 C1
Archdale Cl. Bour 190 B1
Archers Cl. Tot 76 B1
Archers Rd. Eastl 56 A2
Archers Rd. Southa 102 C4
Archery Gdns. Southa 103 F1
Archery Gr. Southa 103 F1
Archery La. Fare 131 E1
Archery Rd. Southa 103 F1
Archway Rd. Poole 205 F2
Arden Cl. Gos 180 C2
Arden Cl. Southa 80 A1
Arden Rd. Bour 190 C2
Arden Wlk. New M 196 A1
Ardingly Cres. He En 81 E1
Ardington Rise. Wat 134 C2
Ardmore Rd. Poole 205 D2
Ardnave Cres. Southa 78 C3
Argyle Cres. Fare 130 C1
Argyle Rd. Christ 209 F3
Argyle Rd. Southa 103 D3
Argyll Rd. Bour 207 F2
Argyll Rd. Poole 205 E3
Ariel Cl. Bour 209 D2
Ariel Dr. Bour 209 D2
Ariel Rd. Ports 182 C3
Arle Cl. Clanf 88 B2
Arley Rd. Poole 205 D1
Arlington Ct. B on S 212 A4
Arliss Rd. Southa 78 A1
Armada Cl. Rown 77 F4
Armada Dr. Hyt 125 F1
Arminers Cl. Gos 181 D1
Armitage Ave. Hyt 125 F1
Armory La. Ports 182 A2
Armstrong Cl. Brock 145 F1
Armstrong Cl. Wat 111 E1
Armstrong Ct. Southa 77 F3
Armstrong La. Brock 145 F1
Armstrong Rd. Brock 145 F1
Armsworth La. Sob 85 F1
Arnaud Cl. Ports 182 B4
Arne Ave. Poole 205 F4
Arne Cres. Poole 205 F4
Arnewood Bridge Rd. Sway 197 D4
Arnewood Rd. Bour 208 B3
Arnheim Cl. Southa 78 B2
Arnheim Rd. Southa 78 B2
Arnold Cl. W Moo 138 C2
Arnold Rd. Eastl 80 A4
Arnold Rd. Southa 79 E1
Arnold Rd. W Moo 138 C2
Arnolds Cl. B on S 211 F4
Arnside Rd. Wat 134 C4
Arnwood Ave. Hyt 149 F4
Arragon Ct. Wat 135 D4
Arran Cl. Cos 133 F1
Arran Way. Christ 195 D1
Arreton. Net 127 E3
Arrow Cl. Eastl 56 A2
Arrowsmith La. Oakl 188 C4
Arrowsmith Rd. Oakl 188 C4
Arters Lawn. Ashu 124 B3
Arthur Cl. Bour 206 C3
Arthur La. Christ 209 D4
Arthur Rd. Christ 209 D4
Arthur Rd. Eastl 56 A2
Arthur Rd. Southa 102 B3
Arthur Rd. Winch 2 A1
Arthur St. Ports 182 C4
Artillery Cl. Cos 157 E4
Arun Rd. W End 80 A1
Arun Way. W Wel 50 B2
Arundel Cl. New M 195 F2
Arundel Dr. Fare 131 D1
Arundel Pl. Ports 182 B3
Arundel Rd. Eastl 56 A3
Arundel Rd. Gos 180 C3
Arundel Rd. Tot 101 D4
Arundel St. Ports 182 B3
Arundel Way. Christ 210 C4
Ascham Rd. Bour 207 D3
Ascot Cl. Lo He 129 E1
Ascot Rd. Broa 188 A2
Ascot Rd. Ports 183 D4
Ascupart St. Southa 103 D2
Asford Gr. Bish 56 B2
Ash Cl. Alderh 93 D3
Ash Cl. Fare 154 C4
Ash Cl. Gos 181 D2

## Ash Cl. Hyt

Ash Cl. Hyt .................. 150 A4
Ash Cl. N Bad .............. 53 F3
Ash Cl. Rom ................ 53 E3
Ash Cl. Southa ............. 104 B3
Ash Cl. Upt ................. 203 D4
Ash Cl. Wat ................ 111 F1
Ash Gr. Ashu ............... 100 B2
Ash Gr. Hord ............... 213 E4
Ash Gr. Rin ................ 141 E4
Ash Rd. Ashu ............... 100 A1
Ash Tree Rd. Southa ........ 79 F1
Ashbarn Cres. Winch ........ 10 C3
Ashbourne Rd. Bour ........ 208 A3
Ashbridge Rise. Ch Fo ...... 30 A1
Ashburn Garth. Rin ......... 141 E3
Ashburnham Cl. Southa ...... 103 E3
Ashburton Gdns. Bour ...... 190 B1
Ashburton Rd. Gos ......... 180 C1
Ashburton Rd. Ports ........ 182 B1
Ashby Cres. Tot ............ 100 B4
Ashby Pl. Ports ............ 182 B1
Ashby Rd. Southa ........... 104 A2
Ashby Rd. Tot .............. 100 B4
Ashcroft La. Finc .......... 113 E3
Ashdene Cl. Wi Mi .......... 163 E3
Ashdene Rd. Ashu ........... 100 B2
Ashdown Cl. Ch Fo .......... 30 B1
Ashdown Cl. Poole .......... 188 C1
Ashdown Dr. Ch Fo .......... 30 B1
Ashdown Rd. Black .......... 150 C1
Ashdown Rd. Ch Fo ......... 30 B1
Ashdown Way. Rom .......... 53 D4
Ashdown. Faw .............. 150 C2
Ashdown. Gos .............. 155 E1
Ashe Rd. Hav .............. 136 A3
Ashford Cl. Fordi .......... 69 E1
Ashford Cres. Hyt .......... 126 A2
Ashford Rd. Bour ........... 208 B4
Ashford Rd. Fordi .......... 93 E4
Ashington La. Oakl ......... 163 D1
Ashington Park. New M ...... 196 B1
Ashlea Cl. Fa Oa ........... 57 E1
Ashleigh Cl. Hyt ........... 150 A4
Ashlett Cl. Faw ............ 151 E2
Ashlett Lawn. Hav .......... 135 E3
Ashlett Mews. Faw .......... 151 D2
Ashlett Rd. Faw ............ 151 E2
Ashley Cl. Bour ............ 207 F3
Ashley Cl. Hav ............. 135 E2
Ashley Cl. Horn ............ 111 F3
Ashley Cl. Rin ............. 141 E3
Ashley Cl. Swanw ........... 129 D4
Ashley Cl. Winch ........... 1 B2
Ashley Common Rd. New M .... 196 B2
Ashley Cres. Southa ........ 104 B1
Ashley Ct. Burs ............ 105 D1
Ashley Drive N. St Le ...... 139 F3
Ashley Drive S. St Le ...... 139 F3
Ashley Drive W. St Le ...... 139 F3
Ashley Gdns. Ch Fo ......... 55 F3
Ashley Gdns. New M ......... 196 B2
Ashley Gdns. Shed .......... 83 F2
Ashley La. Hord ............ 196 C2
Ashley La. Lym ............. 198 C2
Ashley La. New M ........... 196 C2
Ashley Meadows. Rom ........ 53 D4
Ashley Meads. New M ........ 196 B2
Ashley Park. St Le ......... 140 A3
Ashley Rd. Bour ............ 207 E3
Ashley Rd. New M ........... 196 B2
Ashley Rd. Poole ........... 205 E3
Ashleycross Cl. Holb ....... 150 B2
Ashling Cl. Bour ........... 207 E4
Ashling Cl. Den ............ 110 C2
Ashling Cres. Bour ......... 207 D4
Ashling Gdns. Den .......... 110 C2
Ashling La. Ports .......... 157 E1
Ashling Park Rd. Den ....... 110 C2
Ashlyn Cl. Fare ............ 130 B1
Ashmead Rd. Southa ......... 77 F2
Ashmeads Cl. Wi Mi ......... 164 A3
Ashmeads Way. Wi Mi ........ 164 A3
Ashmore Ave. Hamw .......... 203 F1
Ashmore Cl. Whit ........... 24 A2
Ashmore Cres. Hamw ......... 203 F1
Ashmore Gr. Christ ......... 194 C1
Ashmore La. W Dean ......... 24 A3
Ashmore La. Whit ........... 24 A3
Ashmore Rd. Winch .......... 1 B1
Ashmore. Wi Mi ............. 163 E2
Ashridge Ave. Bour ......... 190 B3
Ashridge Cl. Southa ........ 102 C4
Ashridge Gdns. Bour ........ 190 B3
Ashtead Cl. Portc .......... 156 A4
Ashton Cl. Bi Wa ........... 59 D1
Ashton Cross. W Wel ........ 51 D1
Ashton La. Bi Wa ........... 59 D1
Ashton Rd. Bour ............ 190 C1
Ashton Way. Stubb .......... 179 E4
Ashtree Cl. New M .......... 196 B1
Ashurst Bridge Rd. Ne Ma ... 100 B3
Ashurst Bridge Rd. Tot ..... 100 B3
Ashurst Cl. Ashu ........... 100 A1
Ashurst Cl. Winch .......... 1 B1
Ashurst Rd. Bour ........... 191 E2
Ashurst Rd. Cos ............ 157 F4
Ashurst Rd. W Moo .......... 138 C2

Ashwood Cl. Hav ............ 135 D2
Ashwood Cl. S Hay .......... 185 D2
Ashwood Dr. Broa ........... 188 B2
Ashwood Gdns. Tot .......... 100 B4
Aspen Ave. Lo He ........... 152 B4
Aspen Cl. He En ............ 105 E4
Aspen Dr. Ver .............. 115 D3
Aspen Gdns. Poole .......... 205 F4
Aspen Holt. Southa ......... 79 D3
Aspen Pl. New M ............ 196 A1
Aspen Rd. Poole ............ 205 F4
Aspen Way. Poole ........... 205 F4
Aspen Way. Wat ............. 112 A3
Aspengrove. Gos ............ 155 F1
Asquith Cl. Christ ......... 209 E3
Assheton Ct. Portc ......... 156 B4
Astbury Ave. Poole ......... 190 A1
Aster Rd. Southa ........... 79 E2
Astley St. Ports ........... 182 B2
Aston Mead. Christ ......... 192 C2
Aston Rd. Ports ............ 182 C2
Aston Rd. Wat .............. 134 B4
Astra Ct. Hyt .............. 126 A3
Astra Wlk. Gos ............. 181 E2
Astral Gdns. Hamble ........ 127 F2
Astrid Cl. S Hay ........... 185 E2
Asylum Rd. Southa .......... 103 D3
Atalanta Cl. Ports ......... 183 E3
Atheling Rd. Hyt ........... 126 A2
Athelstan Rd. Bour ......... 208 C3
Athelstan Rd. Southa ....... 103 F3
Athena Ave. Wat ............ 134 C2
Athena Cl. Fa Oa ........... 57 D2
Atherfield Rd. Southa ...... 77 F2
Atherley Rd. S Hay ......... 184 C3
Atherley Rd. Southa ........ 102 B3
Atkins Pl. Fare ............ 130 B2
Atkinson Cl. Gos ........... 181 D1
Atlantic Park View. W End .. 80 A1
Atlantis Ave. Wat .......... 134 C1
Attwood Cl. Alderh ......... 92 C3
Attwoods Dro. Comp ......... 31 E4
Aubrey Cl. M on S .......... 213 F2
Auckland Ave. Brock ........ 146 A1
Auckland Pl. Brock ......... 146 A1
Auckland Rd E. Ports ....... 182 B1
Auckland Rd W. Ports ....... 182 B1
Auckland Rd. Christ ........ 210 B4
Auckland Rd. Southa ........ 101 F4
Audemer Ct. Rin ............ 141 E4
Augustine Rd. Cos .......... 158 B4
Augustine Rd. Southa ....... 103 D3
Augustus Cl. Ch Fo ......... 55 F4
Augustus Way. Ch Fo ........ 55 F4
Auriol Dr. Hav ............. 159 D4
Aust Rd. Fare .............. 154 B4
Austen Ave. Bour ........... 190 C3
Austen Ave. Winch .......... 10 B2
Austen Cl. Tot ............. 100 B3
Austen Cl. Winch ........... 2 A1
Auster Cl. Christ .......... 210 A4
Austerberry Way. Gos ....... 180 C4
Austin Ave. Poole .......... 205 D1
Austin Cl. Bour ............ 207 E3
Austin Ct. Cos ............. 133 D1
Australia Cl. Ports ........ 182 B3
Autumn Cl. Fern ............ 165 D4
Autumn Rd. March ........... 102 A1
Avalon. Poole .............. 216 B4
Avebury Ave. Bour .......... 190 C3
Avebury Gdns. Ch Fo ........ 30 A1
Avenger Cl. Ch Fo .......... 55 D3
Avens Cl. Fa Oa ............ 81 E3
Avenue Ct. Gos ............. 181 D1
Avenue La. Bour ............ 206 C2
Avenue Rd. Bour ............ 206 C2
Avenue Rd. Brock ........... 172 C4
Avenue Rd. Christ .......... 195 E1
Avenue Rd. Christ .......... 208 C4
Avenue Rd. Fare ............ 130 C1
Avenue Rd. Gos ............. 181 E2
Avenue Rd. Lym ............. 198 C2
Avenue Rd. N Hay ........... 160 A2
Avenue Rd. New M ........... 196 A2
Avenue Rd. Southa .......... 103 D4
Avenue Rd. Wi Mi ........... 163 E2
Avenue The. Bi Wa .......... 83 D4
Avenue The. Bour ........... 190 C2
Avenue The. Fare ........... 130 B1
Avenue The. Gos ............ 181 D2
Avenue The. Pet ............ 40 C2
Avenue The. Southa ......... 102 C4
Avenue The. Twyf ........... 32 A3
Avenue The. W Moo .......... 138 C2
Avery La. Gosp ............. 181 D4
Avington Cl. Bish .......... 56 B3
Avington Cl. Southa ........ 78 C2
Avington Green. Hav ........ 136 A3
Avocet Quay. Herm .......... 161 D4
Avocet Wlk. Gos ............ 155 D1
Avon Ave. St Le ............ 140 B2
Avon Bldgs. Christ ......... 209 D4
Avon Castle Dr. St Le ...... 140 B2
Avon Cl. Bour .............. 207 E3
Avon Cl. L on S ............ 179 F3
Avon Cl. Lym ............... 198 B2
Avon Cres. Rom ............. 53 E4
Avon Cswy. Hurn ............ 192 B4
Avon Gdns. Bran ............ 169 D1

Avon Green. Ch Fo .......... 55 E3
Avon Meade. Fordi .......... 69 F1
Avon Meadow. Down .......... 46 C4
Avon Park. St Le ........... 140 B3
Avon Rd E. Christ .......... 209 D4
Avon Rd W. Christ .......... 208 C4
Avon Rd. Bour .............. 207 E3
Avon Rd. Christ ............ 79 F1
Avon Rd. W Moo ............. 138 C1
Avon Run Cl. Christ ........ 210 A3
Avon Run Rd. Christ ........ 210 A3
Avon View Par. Burt ........ 193 E2
Avon View Rd. Burt ......... 193 E2
Avon Way. W End ............ 80 C1
Avon Wharf. Christ ......... 209 E3
Avon Wlk. Portc ............ 156 A4
Avoncliffe Rd. Bour ........ 208 C3
Avondale Rd. Ports ......... 182 C4
Avondale Rd. Wat ........... 134 C4
Award Rd. Fern ............. 164 C3
Awbridge Rd. Hav ........... 135 E2
Axford Cl. Bour ............ 191 E2
Aylen Rd. Ports ............ 158 A1
Aylesbury Rd. Bour ......... 207 F2
Aylesbury Rd. Ports ........ 182 C4
Ayling Cl. Gos ............. 180 B4
Aylward St. Ports .......... 182 A3
Aysha Cl. New M ............ 196 A1
Aysgarth Rd. Wat ........... 134 C4
Azalea Cl. St Le ........... 140 A3
Azura Cl. W Moo ............ 139 D3

Back La. Mott .............. 5 F3
Back La. Southw ............ 132 C3
Back La. Sway .............. 172 B1
Back Of The Walls. Southa .. 103 D2
Back St. Winch ............. 10 C2
Bacon Cl. Southa ........... 103 F1
Bacon La. S Hay ............ 184 C2
Badbury Cl. Broa ........... 188 B2
Badbury View Rd. Broa ...... 187 E4
Badbury View. Wi Mi ........ 163 E3
Baddesley Cl. N Bad ........ 53 F3
Baddesley Gdns. Hav ........ 135 E4
Baddesley Rd. Ch Fo ........ 30 A1
Baden Cl. New M ............ 196 A1
Baden Powell Way. Rom ...... 52 C4
Bader Cl. He En ............ 105 E4
Bader Rd. Poole ............ 204 C4
Badger Brow. Wat ........... 135 D3
Badger Cl. Bish ............ 56 C1
Badger Cl. Fare ............ 130 B1
Badger Farm Rd. Winch ...... 10 B2
Badger Way. Ver ............ 114 C3
Badgers Cl. St Le .......... 139 F3
Badgers Cl. Sway ........... 172 B1
Badgers Copse. New M ....... 196 B3
Badgers The. Net ........... 127 E3
Badgers Wlk. Hyt ........... 125 F1
Badminton Drove. Faw ....... 178 B4
Badminton La. Faw .......... 151 E1
Badnam Cl. Burs ............ 127 F4
Badshear La. Cher .......... 14 C4
Baffins Rd. Ports .......... 183 D4
Bagber Rd. Tot ............. 100 C4
Bagnum La. Rin ............. 141 E1
Baigent Cl. Winch .......... 11 D4
Baigent Rd. Winch .......... 11 E4
Bailey Cl. Botl ............ 106 A3
Bailey Cl. New M ........... 196 B2
Bailey Cl. Winch ........... 10 B3
Bailey Cres. Poole ......... 204 B4
Bailey's Rd. Ports ......... 182 B2
Baker Rd. Bour ............. 190 D3
Baker St. Ports ............ 182 B4
Bakers Dro. Rown ........... 77 F3
Bakers Farm Rd. Ver ........ 114 C4
Balaclava Rd. Southa ....... 104 A4
Balcombe Rd. Poole ......... 206 A2
Balderton Cl. Ports ........ 157 F2
Baldwin Cl. Christ ......... 209 E3
Balena Cl. Broa ............ 204 A4
Balfour Cl. Christ ......... 210 B4
Balfour Rd. Bour ........... 190 C1
Balfour Rd. Ports .......... 157 F1
Balfour Rd. Southa ......... 104 B3
Ball La. Poole ............. 204 B1
Ballam Cl. Upt ............. 203 E4
Ballard Cl. New M .......... 196 A2
Ballard Cl. Poole .......... 204 B1
Ballard Cl. Southa ......... 77 E1
Ballard Rd. Poole .......... 204 B1
Balliol Cl. Lo He .......... 129 E1
Balliol Rd. Ports .......... 182 C4
Balmer Lawn Rd. Brock ...... 146 A2
Balmoral Ave. Bour ......... 191 F1
Balmoral Cl. Ch Fo ......... 55 D4
Balmoral Cl. Gos ........... 155 E1
Balmoral Cl. Southa ........ 78 B3
Balmoral Dr. Wat ........... 134 B2
Balmoral Rd. Fare .......... 130 C2
Balmoral Rd. Poole ......... 205 E2
Balmoral Way. Pet .......... 40 C2
Balmoral Way. Rown ......... 77 F3
Balmoral Wlk. New M ........ 195 F2
Balston Rd. Poole .......... 205 D3
Baltic Rd. W End ........... 80 C1
Banbury Ave. Southa ........ 104 B2

Banfurly Gdns. Hyt ......... 125 F1
Bangor Rd. Southa .......... 102 A3
Banister Gdns. Southa ...... 102 C4
Banister Mews. Southa ...... 102 C4
Banister Rd. Southa ........ 102 C4
Bank Cl. Christ ............ 209 D3
Bank Side. Southa .......... 79 E2
Bank St. Bi Wa ............. 83 E4
Bankhill Dr. Lym ........... 198 B3
Banks The. Locke ........... 26 A3
Bankside Rd. Bour .......... 191 D2
Bankside. Lym .............. 198 B3
Bankview. Lym .............. 198 B3
Bannerman Rd. Pet .......... 40 C2
Banning St. Rom ............ 52 C3
Banstead Rd. Broa .......... 188 A3
Bapaume Rd. Ports .......... 157 F3
Bar End Rd. Winch .......... 11 D3
Barbe Baker Ave. W End ..... 80 B1
Barberry Way. Ver .......... 115 E3
Barbers Piles. Poole ....... 204 A1
Bardon Way. Fare ........... 154 B4
Barfield Cl. Winch ......... 11 D3
Barfields. Lym ............. 198 C2
Barfleur Cl. Fare .......... 130 C1
Barford Cl. Ch Fo .......... 55 D4
Barford La. Down ........... 47 D4
Bargate St. Southa ......... 102 C2
Bargates. Christ ........... 209 D4
Barham Cl. Gos ............. 181 D3
Barham Rd. Pet ............. 40 C2
Baring Rd. Bour ............ 209 D2
Baring Rd. Winch ........... 11 D4
Barker Mill Cl. Rown ....... 77 F3
Barlands Cl. Burt .......... 193 E1
Barle Cl. W End ............ 80 A1
Barley Down Dr. Winch ...... 10 B2
Barleycorn Wlk. Cadn ....... 98 C4
Barlow Cl. Stubb ........... 154 A1
Barn Cl. Ems ............... 160 B4
Barn Cl. Upt ............... 203 D4
Barn Fold. Wat ............. 112 B1
Barn Rd. Broa .............. 188 B3
Barnbrook Rd. Lo He ........ 128 C2
Barncroft Way. Hav ......... 135 E2
Barnes Cl. Bour ............ 190 B2
Barnes Cl. Christ .......... 192 B2
Barnes Cl. Lo He ........... 128 B2
Barnes Cl. Southa .......... 104 B3
Barnes Cl. W Wel ........... 50 C1
Barnes Cl. Winch ........... 10 C3
Barnes Cres. Bour .......... 190 B2
Barnes Cres. Wi Mi ......... 163 F2
Barnes La. Lo He ........... 128 C3
Barnes La. M on S .......... 213 E3
Barnes Rd. Bour ............ 190 B2
Barnes Rd. Ports ........... 182 C3
Barnes Rd. Southa .......... 104 B3
Barnes Wallis Rd. Lo He .... 129 E2
Barnes Way. Hav ............ 135 E2
Barnet Side La. Frox G ..... 18 B3
Barney Evans Cres. Wat ..... 111 E2
Barney Hayes La. Cadn ...... 99 D4
Barnfield Cl. Southa ....... 103 F1
Barnfield Cl. Southb ....... 137 F1
Barnfield Ct. Southa ....... 103 F1
Barnfield Rd. Pet .......... 40 C2
Barnfield Rd. Southa ....... 103 F1
Barnfield Way. Southa ...... 103 F1
Barnfield Wlk. Fare ........ 154 C4
Barns Rd. Fern ............. 166 A3
Barnsfield Cres. Tot ....... 100 B4
Barnside Way. Liss ......... 20 C2
Barnsland. W End ........... 80 B2
Barnwood Rd. Fare .......... 130 B1
Baron Rd. Hamble ........... 127 F2
Barons Rd. Bour ............ 189 E3
Barrack La. Rin ............ 141 E2
Barrack Rd. Christ ......... 208 C4
Barrack Rd. Fern ........... 166 A1
Barratt Ind Est. Lo He ..... 129 E3
Barrie Rd. Bour ............ 190 C2
Barrington Cl. Eastl ....... 55 F3
Barrow Dr. Bour ............ 191 F1
Barrow Hill Rd. Cadn ....... 75 C2
Barrow Rd. Bour ............ 191 F1
Barrow Way. Bour ........... 191 F1
Barrowgate Rd. Bour ........ 191 E2
Barrowgate Way. Bour ....... 191 E2
Barrows La. Lan ............ 49 E3
Barrows La. Sway ........... 197 D3
Barrs Ave. New M ........... 196 A2
Barrs Wood Dr. New M ....... 196 A2
Barrs Wood Rd. New M ....... 196 A2
Barry Gdns. Broa ........... 187 F3
Barry Rd. Southa ........... 104 A3
Barters La. Broa ........... 187 F2
Bartlett Ave. Bour ......... 208 A4
Bartlett Cl. Fare .......... 130 C2
Bartley Ave. Tot ........... 100 C3
Bartley Rd. Ne Ma .......... 99 E2
Barton Cl. Rom ............. 53 D4
Barton Common La. B on S ... 212 A4
Barton Common Rd. B on S ... 212 A4
Barton Court Ave. B on S ... 212 A4
Barton Court Rd. New M ..... 196 A1
Barton Croft. B on S ....... 212 A4
Barton Dr. B on S .......... 211 F4

## Beacon Rd. W End

Barton Dr. Hamble .......... 127 F2
Barton Dr. He En ........... 105 E4
Barton Gr. Ports ........... 158 A2
Barton La. B on S .......... 211 F4
Barton Park Ind Est. Eastl . 56 B1
Barton Rd. Bish ............ 56 B2
Barton Way. B on S ......... 211 F4
Barton Wood Rd. B on S ..... 211 F4
Bartons Rd. Fordi .......... 69 F1
Bartons Rd. Hav ............ 136 A2
Bartons The. Fordi ......... 69 F1
Bartons The. He En ......... 105 D3
Bartonside Rd. B on S ...... 211 E4
Bartram Rd. Tot ............ 101 D3
Barwell Gr. Ems ............ 136 C2
Bascott Cl. Bour ........... 190 A1
Bascott Rd. Bour ........... 190 A1
Bashley Cross Rd. New M .... 195 F3
Bashley Dr. New M .......... 196 A3
Bashley Rd. New M .......... 196 A3
Basin St. Ports ............ 182 B4
Basing Dean. Frox G ........ 17 F2
Basing Rd. Hav ............. 135 F3
Basing Way. Ch Fo .......... 55 D2
Basingstoke Rd. Ki Wo ...... 2 B4
Basingwell St. Bi Wa ....... 83 E4
Bassett Ave. Southa ........ 78 C3
Bassett Cl. Southa ......... 78 C2
Bassett Cres E. Southa ..... 78 C2
Bassett Cres W. Southa ..... 78 C2
Bassett Ct. Southa ......... 78 C3
Bassett Dale. Southa ....... 78 C3
Bassett Gdns. Southa ....... 78 C2
Bassett Green Cl. Southa ... 79 D3
Bassett Green Dr. Southa ... 79 D3
Bassett Green Rd. Southa ... 79 D3
Bassett Green. Southa ...... 79 D3
Bassett Heath Ave. Southa .. 78 C3
Bassett Meadow. Southa ..... 78 C2
Bassett Rd. Poole .......... 205 D3
Bassett Row. Southa ........ 78 C3
Bassett Wlk. Hav ........... 135 E3
Bassett Wood Dr. Southa .... 79 D3
Bassett Wood Rd. Southa .... 79 D3
Batchelor Cres. Bour ....... 189 F2
Batchelor Green. Burs ...... 128 A4
Batchelor Rd. Bour ......... 189 F2
Batcombe Cl. Bour .......... 189 F2
Bath Cl. Southa ............ 104 A3
Bath La (Lower). Fare ...... 131 E1
Bath La. Fare .............. 131 E1
Bath Rd. Bour .............. 207 D2
Bath Rd. Ems ............... 160 C4
Bath Rd. Lym ............... 198 C2
Bath Rd. Ports ............. 182 C2
Bath Rd. Southa ............ 104 A3
Bath Sq. Ports ............. 181 F2
Bath St. Southa ............ 103 D4
Bathing La. Ports .......... 181 F2
Batten Cl. Christ .......... 209 E4
Batten Rd. Down ............ 46 C4
Battenburg Ave. Ports ...... 157 F1
Battenburg Rd. Gos ......... 181 E3
Battens Way. Hav ........... 135 F2
Batterley Dro. Alderh ...... 91 F2
Battery Hill. Bi Wa ........ 83 D4
Battery Hill. Winch ........ 10 B3
Battery Row. Ports ......... 182 A2
Baverstock Rd. Poole ....... 206 A4
Baxter Rd. Southa .......... 104 C3
Bay Cl. Southa ............. 104 A2
Bay Cl. Upt ................ 203 D3
Bay Cl. W Moo .............. 138 C2
Bay Hog La. Poole .......... 204 A1
Bay Rd. Gos ................ 180 C2
Bay Rd. Southa ............. 104 A2
Bay Tree Way. Christ ....... 194 B1
Baybridge La. Ows .......... 33 E2
Baybridge Rd. Hav .......... 136 A3
Bayly Ave. Portc ........... 156 B3
Bays Rd. Lym ............... 198 B2
Baythorn Cl. Ports ......... 182 B4
Beach Ave. B on S .......... 211 F4
Beach La. Net .............. 127 F2
Beach Rd. Ems .............. 160 C4
Beach Rd. L on S ........... 179 F3
Beach Rd. Ports ............ 182 B1
Beach Rd. S Hay ............ 184 C2
Beach Rd. Upt .............. 203 D3
Beachway. Portc ............ 156 B3
Beacon Bottom. Lo He ....... 129 D3
Beacon Cl. Hord ............ 197 E1
Beacon Cl. Lo He ........... 129 D3
Beacon Cl. Rown ............ 77 E3
Beacon Cl. Fordi ........... 69 F2
Beacon Dr. Christ .......... 210 D4
Beacon Gdns. Broa .......... 187 F2
Beacon Hill La. Drox ....... 60 C3
Beacon Hill La. Meons ...... 61 E3
Beacon Mews. W End ......... 104 B4
Beacon Mount. Lo He ........ 129 D3
Beacon Park Cres. Upt ...... 203 D4
Beacon Park Rd. Upt ........ 203 D4
Beacon Rd. Bour ............ 206 C2
Beacon Rd. Broa ............ 187 F2
Beacon Rd. Upt ............. 203 D4
Beacon Rd. W End ........... 104 B4

223

Beacon Sq. Ems

Blyth Cl. Southa

Beacon Sq. Ems 160 C4
Beacon Way. Broa 187 F2
Beacon Way. Lo He 129 D3
Beaconsfield Ave. Cos 158 A4
Beaconsfield Rd. Christ 209 D4
Beaconsfield Rd. Fare 155 D4
Beaconsfield Rd. Poole 205 E3
Beaconsfield Rd. Wat 134 C4
Bealing Cl. Southa 79 D2
Beamish Rd. Poole 204 C4
Bear Cross Ave. Bour 189 F3
Bearslane Cl. Tot 76 B1
Beatrice Rd. Ports 182 C1
Beatrice Rd. Southa 102 B4
Beattie Rise. He En 81 E1
Beatty Cl. Lo He 129 D2
Beatty Cl. Rin 141 E4
Beatty Dr. Gos 180 C2
Beatty Rd. Bour 191 D1
Beaty Ct. Southa 104 B3
Beauchamp Ave. Gos 155 E1
Beauchamps Gdns. Bour 208 A4
Beaucroft La. Wi Mi 163 F3
Beaucroft Rd. Shed 83 F2
Beaucroft Rd. Wi Mi 163 F3
Beaufort Ave. Fare 130 C1
Beaufort Cl. Christ 210 A4
Beaufort Dr. Bi Wa 83 E4
Beaufort Rd. Bour 208 B3
Beaufort Rd. Hav 135 E1
Beaufort Rd. Ports 182 B1
Beaufort Rd. Winch 10 C3
Beaufoys Ave. Fern 165 E4
Beaufoys Cl. Fern 165 E4
Beaulieu Ave. Christ 208 C4
Beaulieu Ave. Hav 135 E3
Beaulieu Ave. Portc 156 A4
Beaulieu Cl. New M 195 F2
Beaulieu Cl. Southa 78 A3
Beaulieu Cl. Winch 1 B2
Beaulieu Pl. Gos 155 D1
Beaulieu Rd. Beaul 122 B2
Beaulieu Rd. Beaul 149 E3
Beaulieu Rd. Bour 206 B1
Beaulieu Rd. Christ 208 C4
Beaulieu Rd. Eastl 56 A2
Beaulieu Rd. Hamble 127 F2
Beaulieu Rd. Hyt 149 F4
Beaulieu Rd. Lyn 122 B2
Beaulieu Rd. March 124 C3
Beaulieu Rd. Ports 157 F1
Beaumaris Cl. Ch Fo 55 D2
Beaumont Cl. Fare 130 B2
Beaumont Cl. Southa 78 C2
Beaumont Ct. Gosp 181 D4
Beaumont Rd. Poole 216 C4
Beaumont Rd. Tot 101 D4
Beaumont Rise. Fare 130 B2
Beauworth Ave. Southa 104 B4
Beaver Dr. Bish 57 D1
Beccles Cl. Hamw 203 F1
Becher Rd. Poole 205 F2
Beck Cl. Lo He 128 C2
Beck St. Ports 182 A3
Beckford La. Southw 109 F1
Beckham La. Pet 40 B2
Beckhampton Rd. Hamw 203 F2
Beckley Copse. Christ 195 D1
Becton La. B on S 212 A4
Becton Mead. B on S 196 A1
Bedale Way. Poole 204 C3
Bedenham La. Gos 155 F2
Bedfield La. Ki Wo 2 A3
Bedford Ave. Southa 103 F1
Bedford Cl. Fordi 69 F2
Bedford Cl. Hav 160 A4
Bedford Cl. He En 105 E3
Bedford Cres. Bour 208 B4
Bedford Pl. Southa 102 C3
Bedford Rd N. Poole 189 E1
Bedford Rd S. Poole 189 E1
Bedford Rd. Pet 40 C2
Bedford St. Gos 181 D3
Bedford St. Ports 182 B2
Bedhampton Hill Rd. Hav 135 D1
Bedhampton Rd. Hav 135 E1
Bedhampton Rd. Ports 182 C4
Bedhampton Way. Hav 135 F2
Bedwell Cl. Rown 77 F3
Beech Ave. Bour 208 B2
Beech Ave. Christ 208 B4
Beech Ave. Southa 103 F4
Beech Cl. Alderh 93 D3
Beech Cl. Broa 187 F2
Beech Cl. Ch Fo 30 B1
Beech Cl. Hamble 127 F1
Beech Cl. Hord 213 E4
Beech Cl. Rom 53 E3
Beech Cl. Ver 114 C3
Beech Cl. Wat 111 F1
Beech Cl. Winch 10 A2
Beech Copse. Winch 1 A1
Beech Cres. Hyt 150 A4
Beech Gdns. Hamble 127 F1
Beech Gr. Gos 181 D2
Beech Gr. Ows 33 D2
Beech Gr. S Hay 185 D2
Beech Grange. Lan 49 E1
Beech La. St Le 139 F1
Beech Rd. Ashu 100 A1
Beech Rd. Ch Fo 55 E4
Beech Rd. Clanf 88 B3
Beech Rd. Fare 130 C1
Beech Rd. He En 105 E4
Beech Rd. Southa 102 A3
Beech Way. Wat 112 A3
Beech Wood Cl. Broa 188 A2
Beecham Rd. Ports 182 C4
Beechbank Ave. Broa 187 F1
Beechcroft Cl. Ch Fo 55 E3
Beechcroft Cl. Fare 130 B1
Beechcroft La. Rin 141 D4
Beechcroft Rd. Gos 181 D2
Beechcroft Way. Ch Fo 55 E3
Beechdale Cl. Tot 76 B1
Beechen La. Lyn 122 A2
Beeches Hill. Bi Wa 59 E1
Beeches The. Bour 208 A4
Beeches The. Fa Oa 57 E1
Beeches The. W Wel 50 B2
Beechey Rd. Bour 207 D3
Beechfield Ct. Southa 102 A4
Beechmount Rd. Southa 78 C3
Beechwood Ave. Bour 207 F2
Beechwood Ave. New M 195 F2
Beechwood Ave. Wat 134 C3
Beechwood Cl. Ch Fo 30 A1
Beechwood Cl. Lo He 152 B4
Beechwood Cres. Ch Fo 30 A1
Beechwood Gdns. Bour 208 A2
Beechwood Gdns. Southa 103 F4
Beechwood La. Bur 143 D2
Beechwood Rd. Cadn 99 D3
Beechwood Rd. Holb 150 B2
Beechwood Rd. Ports 157 F2
Beechwood Rd. W Moo 138 C1
Beechwood Rise. W End 80 B1
Beechwood Way. Hyt 125 E1
Beechwood. Fordi 69 E1
Beechworth Rd. Hav 136 A1
Beehive Wlk. Ports 182 A2
Beggar's La. Winch 11 D4
Begonia Rd. Southa 79 D2
Behrendt Cl. Gosp 181 D3
Belben Cl. Poole 189 E1
Belben Rd. Poole 189 E1
Belbins. Abb 27 F2
Belfield Rd. Bour 209 D2
Belfry Wlk. Lo He 129 E2
Belgrave Rd. Poole 206 A1
Belgrave Rd. Southa 79 E1
Belgravia Rd. Ports 157 F1
Bell Cres. Wat 134 C3
Bell Davies Rd. Stubb 154 A1
Bell Hill Ridge. Pet 40 C3
Bell Hill. Pet 40 C3
Bell La. Poole 204 A1
Bell Rd. Cos 157 E4
Bell St. Rom 52 C4
Bell St. Southa 103 D2
Bellair Rd. Hav 136 A1
Belle Vue Cl. Bour 208 B2
Belle Vue Cres. Bour 208 C2
Belle Vue Gr. W Moo 138 C1
Belle Vue Rd. Bour 208 C2
Belle Vue Rd. Poole 205 E2
Belle Vue Wlk. Fern 165 F1
Bellemoor Rd. Southa 78 B1
Bellevue La. Ems 136 C1
Bellevue Rd. Eastl 56 A2
Bellevue Rd. Southa 103 D3
Bellfield. Lo He 153 F4
Bellflower Cl. Christ 210 A4
Bells La. Stubb 154 B1
Bellview Terr. Ports 182 A2
Belmont Ave. Bour 191 E1
Belmont Cl. Horn 88 B2
Belmont Cl. Hyt 126 A1
Belmont Cl. Stubb 154 B2
Belmont Cl. Ver 115 D3
Belmont Gr. Hav 135 E1
Belmont Pl. Ports 182 B2
Belmont Rd. Ch Fo 55 E2
Belmont Rd. New M 196 B2
Belmont Rd. Poole 205 E3
Belmont Rd. Southa 103 D4
Belmont St. Ports 182 B2
Belmore La. Lym 198 C2
Belmore La. Ows 33 F2
Belmore La. Uph 34 A2
Belmore Rd. Lym 198 B2
Belstone Rd. Tot 100 C4
Belton Rd. Southa 104 A2
Belvedere Pl. Pet 40 C2
Belvedere Rd. Bour 207 D3
Belvedere Rd. Christ 209 D4
Belvedere Rd. Hyt 126 A1
Belvidere Rd. Southa 103 E3
Belvidere Terr. Southa 103 E3
Belvoir Cl. Fare 155 D4
Bembridge Cl. Southa 79 E3
Bembridge Cres. Ports 182 C1
Bembridge Ct. S Hay 185 E1
Bembridge Dr. S Hay 185 E1
Bembridge. Net 127 E3
Bemister Rd. Bour 207 D4
Bemister's La. Gos 181 F2
Benbow Cl. Horn 112 B4
Benbow Cres. Poole 189 F1
Benbow Gdns. Tot 76 B1
Benbow Pl. Ports 182 A3
Benbridge Ave. Bour 189 F3
Bendigo Rd. Christ 208 C4
Benedict Cl. Rom 53 E4
Benedict Way. Portc 132 C1
Beneficial St. Ports 182 A3
Benellen Ave. Bour 206 B2
Benellen Gdns. Bour 206 B2
Benellen Rd. Bour 206 B3
Bengal Rd. Bour 206 C4
Benger's La. Mott 5 E1
Benham Dr. Ports 157 F2
Benham Gr. Portc 156 B3
Benhams Rd. Southa 80 A1
Benmoor Rd. Broa 204 A4
Benmore Gdns. Ch Fo 55 D4
Benmore Rd. Bour 191 D1
Bennett Rd. Bour 207 E3
Bennett's Alley. Poole 204 A1
Bennetts La. Bur 143 E1
Bennion Rd. Bour 190 B2
Benridge Cl. Broa 188 A2
Benson Cl. Bran 169 D1
Bentham Rd. Gos 181 D2
Bentham Way. Swanw 128 B4
Bentley Cl. Horn 112 B4
Bentley Cl. Ki Wo 2 A3
Bentley Cres. Fare 130 C1
Bentley Green. Southa 104 B4
Bentley Rd. Bour 190 C2
Bentworth Cl. Hav 135 E2
Bepton Down. Pet 41 D2
Bercote Cl. Litt 1 A3
Bere Cl. Broa 188 B1
Bere Cl. N Bad 55 D4
Bere Cl. Winch 1 B1
Bere Farm La. Southw 131 F4
Bere Rd. Den 110 C2
Beresford Cl. Ch Fo 55 F3
Beresford Cl. Poole 205 E3
Beresford Cl. Wat 134 C3
Beresford Gdns. Ch Fo 55 F3
Beresford Gdns. Christ 209 F3
Beresford Rd. Bour 208 A2
Beresford Rd. Ch Fo 55 F3
Beresford Rd. Lym 198 B2
Beresford Rd. Poole 205 E3
Beresford Rd. Ports 157 F1
Beresford Rd. Stubb 154 B2
Bereweeke Ave. Winch 1 C1
Bereweeke Cl. Winch 1 C1
Bereweeke Rd. Winch 1 C1
Bereweeke Way. Winch 1 C1
Bergen Cres. He En 105 E3
Berkeley Ave. Poole 205 E4
Berkeley Cl. Southa 102 C4
Berkeley Cl. Stubb 154 A1
Berkeley Cl. Ver 114 C4
Berkeley Gdns. He En 105 E3
Berkeley Rd. Bour 206 C4
Berkeley Rd. Southa 102 C3
Berkeley Sq. Hav 136 A1
Berkley Ave. Fern 165 E1
Berkshire Cl. Ports 182 C3
Bernard Ave. Cos 158 A4
Bernard St. Southa 103 D2
Berney Rd. Ports 183 E2
Bernina Ave. Wat 111 E1
Bernina Cl. Wat 111 E1
Bernwood Gr. Black 177 F4
Berrans Ave. Bour 190 D3
Berry Cl. He En 105 E3
Berry La. Stubb 154 A1
Berry La. Twyf 32 A4
Berrybarn La. W Wit 186 C1
Berrydown Rd. Hav 135 E4
Berryfield Rd. Hord 197 D1
Berrylands. Liss 21 D4
Berrywood Gdns. He En 105 D4
Bertie Rd. Ports 183 D2
Bertram Rd. New M 196 B2
Berwick Rd. Bour 206 C3
Berwyn Wlk. Fare 154 C4
Beryl Ave. Gos 180 C4
Beryton Cl. Gosp 181 D3
Beryton Rd. Gosp 181 D3
Besomer Dro. Red 47 F3
Bessborough Rd. Poole 216 C4
Bessemer Cl. Ver 115 E2
Beswick Ave. Bour 190 B1
Bethia Cl. Bour 207 E3
Bethia Rd. Bour 207 E3
Betsy Cl. Bran 169 D1
Betsy La. Bran 169 D1
Betteridge Dr. Rown 77 E3
Bettesworth Rd. Ports 182 C4
Bettiscombe Cl. Broa 188 C1
Betula Cl. Wat 135 D3
Beulah Rd. Southa 78 A1
Bevan Rd. Wat 112 A3
Beverley Cl. Lo He 129 E2
Beverley Gdns. Bour 190 B2
Beverley Gdns. Burs 104 C1
Beverley Gdns. Southa 79 E2
Beverley Gdns. Swan 84 A3
Beverley Gr. Cos 134 C1
Beverley Hts. Southa 79 F2
Beverley Rd. Hyt 149 F4
Beverley Rd. Stubb 154 B1
Beverly Cl. Gos 155 E1
Beverston Rd. Cos 133 D1
Bevis Cl. Black 150 C1
Bevis Cl. Lo He 152 B4
Bevis Rd North. Ports 157 E1
Bevis Rd. Gos 181 D3
Bevis Rd. Ports 157 E1
Bevois Hill. Southa 103 D4
Bevois Mews. Southa 103 D4
Bevois St. Southa 103 D2
Bevois Valley Rd. Southa 103 D4
Bexington Cl. Bour 189 F2
Beyne Rd. Winch 10 A2
Bickerley Gdns. Rin 140 C3
Bickerley Rd. Rin 140 C3
Bickton Wlk. Hav 135 E3
Bicton Rd. Bour 190 A2
Bidbury La. Hav 135 E1
Biddenfield La. Shed 107 E3
Biddenfield La. Wickh 107 E3
Biddlecombe Cl. Gos 180 B4
Bideford Cl. Southa 77 F1
Big Tree Cotts. Sob 85 E3
Biggin Wlk. Fare 154 C4
Bilberry Cl. Lo He 128 C1
Bilberry Dr. March 101 F1
Billett Ave. Wat 134 C4
Billington Gdns. He En 81 E1
Billy Lawn Ave. Hav 135 F3
Bindon Cl. Poole 205 F4
Bindon Cl. Southa 78 A1
Bindon Rd. Southa 78 A1
Bingham Ave. Poole 216 B4
Bingham Cl. Christ 209 F4
Bingham Cl. Ver 115 D2
Bingham Dr. Lym 198 C2
Bingham Rd. Bour 207 D4
Bingham Rd. Christ 209 F4
Bingham Rd. Ver 115 D2
Binness Way. Cos 158 C4
Binnie Rd. Poole 205 F3
Binstead Cl. Southa 79 E3
Binsteed Rd. Ports 182 C4
Birch Ave. Burt 193 E2
Birch Ave. Fern 165 F1
Birch Cl. Broa 187 E3
Birch Cl. Liss 21 D2
Birch Cl. Poole 205 F2
Birch Cl. Rom 53 E3
Birch Cl. Southa 78 A1
Birch Cl. St Le 139 E2
Birch Cl. Wat 111 F2
Birch Dale. Hyt 126 A1
Birch Dr. Bour 192 A1
Birch Dr. Gos 155 E2
Birch Gr. Eastl 56 A3
Birch Gr. W Moo 138 B1
Birch Rd. Chilw 79 D4
Birch Rd. He En 105 E4
Birch Rd. Southa 78 A2
Birch Tree Cl. Ems 136 C2
Birch Tree Dr. Ems 136 C2
Birch Wood. Southa 104 C3
Birchdale Cl. Lo He 152 B4
Birchdale Rd. Wi Mi 163 E3
Birchen Cl. Lo He 129 E2
Birchen Rd. Lo He 129 E2
Birches Cl The. N Bad 53 F3
Birches The. Southa 104 A4
Birchglade. Tot 76 B1
Birchlands. Tot 100 B3
Birchmore Cl. Gos 155 E1
Birchwood Cl. Christ 210 C4
Birchwood Dr. Alderh 93 D3
Birchwood Rd. Poole 205 E2
Birchwood Rd. Upt 203 D3
Birchy Hill. Sway 172 B1
Bird's Hill Rd. Poole 204 C2
Birdham Rd. S Hay 185 F1
Birdlip Cl. Wat 112 A3
Birdlip Rd. Cos 133 D1
Birdwood Gr. Portc 155 F4
Birinus Rd. Winch 2 A1
Birkdale Ave. Cos 134 B1
Birkdale Ct. Broa 188 A3
Birkdale Rd. Broa 188 A3
Biscay Cl. Stubb 154 A2
Bishearne Gdns. Liss 20 C3
Bishop Rd. Bour 207 D4
Bishop St. Ports 182 A3
Bishop's La. Bi Wa 83 E4
Bishop's Wood Rd. Shed 84 B1
Bishops Cl. Bour 207 F4
Bishops Cl. Tot 100 C4
Bishops Cres. Southa 103 F2
Bishops Ct. Bish 56 B3
Bishops Gate. Lo He 129 E2
Bishops La. Shed 84 A1
Bishops Rd. Southa 103 F2
Bishopsfield Rd. Fare 154 C4
Bishopstoke Rd. Bish 56 B2
Bishopstoke Rd. Co Com 56 C4
Bishopstoke Rd. Hav 135 F3
Bisley Ct. Southa 104 A2
Bisterne Cl. Bur 143 E2
Bittern Cl. Gosp 181 D4
Bitterne Cl. Hav 135 F3
Bitterne Cres. Southa 104 A3
Bitterne Rd E. Southa 104 B4
Bitterne Rd W. Southa 103 F4
Bitterne Way. Lym 198 B1
Bitterne Way. Southa 103 F3
Bitterne Way. Ver 115 D3
Black Hill. Ver 115 D3
Black La. Red 48 A2
Black Moor Rd. Ver 115 E2
Blackberry Cl. Clanf 88 B2
Blackberry La. Christ 209 F3
Blackberry Terr. Southa 103 D4
Blackbird Cl. Broa 203 F4
Blackbird Cl. Wat 111 F2
Blackbird Rd. Eastl 55 E1
Blackbird Way. Bran 194 B4
Blackbird Way. L on S 179 F4
Blackbrook House Dr. Fare 130 C1
Blackbrook Park Ave. Fare 130 C1
Blackburn Rd. Poole 205 D3
Blackbush Rd. M on S 213 D3
Blackbushe Cl. Southa 77 F3
Blackcap Cl. Ro Ca 113 D1
Blackdown Cl. Hyt 125 E2
Blackdown Cres. Hav 135 F2
Blackfield Rd. Black 150 C1
Blackfield Rd. Bour 191 E2
Blackfriars Cl. Ports 182 B2
Blackfriars Rd. Ports 182 B3
Blackhill Rd. Ower 74 C4
Blackhorse La. Shed 83 F1
Blackmoor Wlk. Hav 136 A3
Blackmore La. Frox G 18 C2
Blacksmith Cl. Broa 187 E3
Blackthorn Cl. Lym 198 A1
Blackthorn Cl. Southa 103 F3
Blackthorn Dr. Gos 156 A1
Blackthorn Dr. S Hay 185 E2
Blackthorn Rd. S Hay 185 E1
Blackthorn Rd. Southa 103 F3
Blackthorn Way. New M 196 B2
Blackthorn Way. Ver 115 D3
Blackwater Cl. Cos 157 E4
Blackwater Dr. Oakl 188 B4
Blackwater Dr. Tot 76 B1
Blackwater Gr. Alderh 92 C3
Bladon Cl. Hav 136 B2
Bladon Rd. Southa 78 B1
Blair Ave. Poole 205 E2
Blair Cl. New M 195 F2
Blake Dene Rd. Poole 205 D1
Blake Hill Ave. Poole 205 E1
Blake Hill Cres. Poole 205 E1
Blake Rd. Cos 134 B1
Blake Rd. Gos 181 E3
Blakemere Cres. Cos 133 E1
Blakeney Rd. Southa 77 E1
Blanchard Rd. Bi Wa 83 D4
Blandford Cl. Hamw 203 F1
Blandford Rd N. Upt 203 D4
Blandford Rd. Broa 187 E4
Blandford Rd. Co Bi 23 E4
Blandford Rd. Hamw 203 E2
Blandford Rd. Pamp 162 B4
Blandford Rd. Upt 203 E2
Blaney Way. Broa 187 E3
Blankney Cl. Stubb 154 A1
Blaven Wlk. Fare 154 C4
Bleaklow Cl. Southa 101 F4
Blechynden Terr. Southa 102 C3
Blendworth Cres. Hav 135 F2
Blendworth La. Horn 112 C4
Blendworth La. Southa 104 B4
Blendworth Rd. Ports 183 D3
Blenheim Ave. Southa 79 D1
Blenheim Cl. Tot 100 C3
Blenheim Cres. Hord 196 C2
Blenheim Ct. Ports 183 D2
Blenheim Dr. Christ 210 A3
Blenheim Gdns. Gosp 181 D4
Blenheim Gdns. Hav 136 B1
Blenheim Gdns. Hyt 125 E2
Blenheim Gdns. Southa 79 D1
Blenheim Rd. Eastl 56 A1
Blenheim Rd. Wat 112 A3
Blighmont Ave. Southa 102 A3
Blighmont Cres. Southa 102 A3
Blind La. Fa Oa 81 E3
Blind La. W End 81 E3
Blind La. Wi Mi 163 D3
Blind La. Wickh 107 F3
Bliss Cl. Wat 134 C3
Blissford Cl. Hav 136 A3
Blissford Hill. Fordi 94 C4
Blissford Rd. Fordi 94 C4
Bloomsbury Wlk. Southa 103 F1
Blossom Cl. He En 105 F3
Blount Rd. Ports 182 A2
Bloxworth Rd. Poole 205 F4
Blue Anchor La. Southa 102 C2
Blue Ball Hill. Winch 11 D4
Bluebell Cl. Christ 210 A4
Bluebell Cl. Wat 135 D3
Bluebell Copse. Lo He 128 C1
Bluebell La. Broa 187 F1
Bluebell Rd. Southa 79 E2
Blundell La. Burs 105 E1
Blyth Cl. Christ 192 B2
Blyth Cl. Southa 77 E1

# 224

**Blythe Rd. Broa**

**Brooks Cl. Rin**

Blythe Rd. Broa ................ 187 E3
Blythswood Ct. B on S ........ 211 F4
Boakes Pl. Ashu ................ 100 B1
Boarhunt Cl. Ports ............. 182 B3
Boarhunt Rd. Fare .............. 131 F2
Boatyard Ind Est The. Fare ... 155 D4
Bob Hann Cl. Poole ............ 205 F3
Bockhampton Rd. Bran ......... 193 F3
Bockhampton Rd. Burt .......... 193 F3
Bodley Rd. Poole .............. 216 C4
Bodmin Rd. Bish ................ 56 C1
Bodmin Rd. Portc .............. 157 D4
Bodorgan Rd. Bour ............ 206 C2
Bodowen Rd. Burt .............. 193 E1
Bodowen Rd. Burt .............. 193 E1
Bodycoats Rd. Ch Fo ........... 55 E3
Bognor Rd. Broa ............... 187 F2
Bohemia La. Red ................ 47 F2
Bolde Cl. Ports ................ 158 A2
Boldens Rd. Gos ............... 181 D1
Bolderwood Cl. Bish ............ 56 C1
Boldre Cl. Hav ................ 135 E2
Boldre Cl. Poole .............. 205 E4
Boldre La. Bold ............... 198 B4
Boldrewood Rd. Southa ......... 78 C2
Bolhinton Ave. March ......... 101 E1
Bolton Cl. Bour ............... 208 C2
Bolton Cres. Fern ............. 166 A3
Bolton Rd. Bour ............... 208 C2
Boltons The. Wat .............. 134 C2
Boltons The. M on S ........... 213 E2
Bonchurch Cl. Southa ........... 79 E3
Bonchurch Rd. Ports ........... 183 D3
Bond Ave. W Moo ............... 138 B2
Bond Cl. Sway ................ 172 A2
Bond Rd. Poole ............... 204 C3
Bond Rd. Southa ................ 79 F1
Bondfields Cres. Hav .......... 135 F3
Bones La. Buri ................. 65 E3
Bonfire Cnr. Ports ............ 182 A3
Bonham Rd. Bour .............. 206 C4
Boniface Cl. Tot .............. 100 B4
Boniface Cres. Southa .......... 77 F2
Bonington Cl. Christ .......... 209 F4
Bookdale Cl. Broa ............. 188 A2
Border Dr. Upt ................ 203 E3
Border Rd. Upt ................ 203 E3
Bordon Rd. Hav ................ 135 F3
Boredean La. Frox G ............ 39 E3
Boredean La. Langr ............. 39 E3
Boreham Rd. Bour .............. 208 B3
Borley Rd. Broa ............... 204 A4
Borough Gr. Pet ................ 40 C1
Borough Hill. Pet .............. 40 C2
Borough Rd. Pet ................ 40 B1
Borough The. Down .............. 46 C4
Borrowdale Rd. Southa .......... 77 F1
Borthwick Rd. Bour ............ 207 E3
Boscobel Rd. Winch ............. 1 C1
Boscombe Cliff Rd. Bour ....... 207 F2
Boscombe Gr Rd. Bour .......... 207 E4
Boscombe Overcliff Dr. Exb ... 208 A2
Boscombe Rd. Bour ............. 209 D2
Boscombe Spa Rd. Bour ......... 207 E2
Bosham Rd. Ports .............. 182 C4
Bosham Wlk. Gos ............... 155 D1
Bosley Cl. Christ ............. 192 C1
Bosley Way. Christ ............ 192 C1
Bosmere Gdns. Ems ............. 136 C1
Bosmere Rd. S Hay ............. 185 F1
Bossington Cl. Rown ............ 77 F3
Boston Rd. Cos ................ 133 F1
Bosville. Eastl ................ 56 A3
Boswell Cl. Botl .............. 106 A3
Boswell Cl. Southa ............ 104 B3
Bosworth Mews. Bour ........... 191 D2
Botany Bay Rd. Southa ......... 104 A2
Botley Dr. Hav ................ 135 E3
Botley Gdns. Southa ........... 104 C2
Botley Rd. Bi Wa ............... 82 C1
Botley Rd. Chilw .............. 53 E3
Botley Rd. Curd ................ 82 C1
Botley Rd. Fa Oa ............... 81 E4
Botley Rd. He En ............... 81 D1
Botley Rd. Lo He .............. 129 D4
Botley Rd. N Bad ............... 53 E3
Botley Rd. Rom ................. 53 E3
Botley Rd. Southa ............. 104 B2
Botley Rd. Swanw .............. 106 A1
Botley Rd. Swanw .............. 129 D4
Botley Rd. W End ............... 81 D1
Bottom La. W Wel ............... 50 C2
Boulnois Ave. Poole ........... 205 F2
Boulter La. Southw ............ 133 D4
Boulton Rd. Ports ............. 182 C2
Bound La. S Hay ............... 185 D1
Boundary Cl. Southa ........... 101 F4
Boundary Dr. Wi Mi ............ 163 D3
Boundary La. St Le ............ 139 F1
Boundary Rd. Bour ............. 190 C1
Boundary Rd. Burs ............. 127 F4
Boundary Way. Hav ............. 135 F1
Boundary Way. Wat ............. 134 C4
Boundstone. Hyt ............... 125 F2
Boundway. Sway ................ 171 F1
Bourne Ave. Bour .............. 206 C2
Bourne Ave. Southa ............. 78 B1
Bourne Cl. Bour ............... 206 B2

Bourne Cl. Horn ............... 112 A3
Bourne Cl. Ott ................. 31 E2
Bourne Cl. W Wel ............... 50 B2
Bourne Ct. Wi Mi .............. 163 E3
Bourne La. Ne Ma ............... 99 E3
Bourne La. Twyf ................ 32 A3
Bourne Rd. Cos ................ 157 D4
Bourne Rd. Ne Ma ............... 99 E3
Bourne Rd. Southa ............. 102 B3
Bourne Valley Rd. Poole ....... 206 A3
Bourne View. Southb ........... 137 E1
Bournefields. Twyf ............. 32 A4
Bournemouth Ave. Gosp ........ 181 D4
Bournemouth Rd. Ch Fo .......... 55 E2
Bournemouth Rd. Chilw .......... 55 E2
Bournemouth Rd. Lyn .......... 121 F3
Bournemouth Rd. Poole ......... 205 E2
Bournewood Dr. Bour ........... 206 B2
Bourton Gdns. Bour ............ 208 A4
Boveridge Gdns. Bour .......... 191 D2
Bovington Cl. Poole ........... 188 C1
Bowater Way. Tot ............... 76 B1
Bowater Way. Tot ............... 76 B1
Bowden La. Southa .............. 79 E1
Bowden Rd. Poole .............. 189 E1
Bower Cl. Holb ................ 150 B2
Bower Cl. Southa .............. 103 F1
Bower Rd. Bour ................ 207 E4
Bowers Cl. Wat ................ 112 A2
Bowers Hill. Red ............... 47 F4
Bowerwood Rd. Fordi ............ 93 E4
Bowes Hill. Ro Ca ............. 113 E2
Bowland Rise. N Bad ............ 55 D4
Bowland Rise. New M ........... 196 B1
Bowland Way. Black ............ 177 F4
Bowler Ave. Ports ............. 182 C3
Bowler Ct. Ports .............. 182 C3
Bowman Ct. Southa ............. 104 A2
Box Cl. Broa .................. 204 A4
Boxwood Cl. Portc ............. 132 A1
Boxwood Cl. Wat ............... 134 C3
Boyatt La. Eastl ............... 56 A4
Boyatt La. Ott ................. 56 A4
Boyd Cl. Stubb ................ 154 A1
Boyd Rd. Gos .................. 155 D2
Boyd Rd. Poole ................ 205 F3
Boyes La. Co Com ............... 58 A1
Boyle Cres. Wat ............... 134 B3
Boyne Mead Rd. Ki Wo ........... 2 A4
Boyne Rise. Ki Wo .............. 2 A4
Boynton Cl. Ch Fo .............. 55 D4
Brabazon Dr. Christ ........... 210 A4
Brabazon Rd. Oakl ............. 163 F1
Brabourne Ave. Fern ........... 165 E2
Bracken Cl. N Bad .............. 54 A2
Bracken Cl. Pet ................ 41 E1
Bracken Cl. St Le ............. 139 E2
Bracken Cres. Bish ............. 56 C1
Bracken Glen. Poole ........... 204 C3
Bracken La. Southa ............. 78 A1
Bracken Pl. Chilw .............. 79 D4
Bracken Rd. Bour .............. 208 B2
Bracken Rd. Fern .............. 165 D4
Bracken Rd. N Bad .............. 54 A2
Bracken Way. Christ ........... 195 D1
Brackendale Ct. W Moo ......... 138 C4
Brackendale Rd. Bour .......... 207 E4
Brackenhill Rd. Wi Mi ......... 164 A4
Brackenhill. Poole ............ 206 A1
Brackens The. Hyt ............. 125 E2
Brackens The. Lo He ........... 129 D1
Brackenway Rd. Ch Fo ........... 55 E4
Bracklesham Cl. Southa ........ 103 F2
Bracklesham Rd. Gos ........... 180 B4
Bracklesham Rd. S Hay ......... 185 F1
Brackley Ave. Fa Oa ............ 57 D2
Brackley Cl. Hurn ............. 192 A4
Brackley Way. Tot ............. 100 B4
Bradbourne Rd. Bour ........... 206 C2
Bradford Rd. Bour ............. 191 E2
Bradford Rd. Ports ............ 182 B2
Brading Ave. Gos .............. 155 E1
Brading Ave. Ports ............ 183 D1
Brading Cl. Southa ............. 79 E3
Bradley Grn. Southa ............ 78 A2
Bradley Peak. Winch ............ 1 B1
Bradley Rd. Winch .............. 1 B2
Bradly Rd. Fare ............... 130 B1
Bradpole Rd. Bour ............. 191 F1
Bradshaw Cl. Fa Oa ............. 57 F1
Bradstock Cl. Poole ........... 205 F4
Braehead. Hyt ................. 125 F1
Braemar Ave. Bour ............. 209 D2
Braemar Ave. Cos .............. 158 A4
Braemar Cl. Bour .............. 209 D2
Braemar Cl. Fare .............. 130 C2
Braemar Cl. Gos ............... 155 E1
Braemar Dr. Christ ............ 194 C1
Braemar Rd. Gos ............... 155 E1
Braemore Cl. New M ............ 195 F2
Braeside Cl. Southa ........... 103 F3
Braeside Cl. Winch ............. 10 A2
Braeside Cres. Southa ......... 103 F3
Braeside Rd. Southa ........... 103 F3
Braeside Rd. St Le ............ 139 F2
Braeside Rd. W Moo ............ 138 C2
Braidley Rd. Bour ............. 206 C2
Brailswood Rd. Poole .......... 204 C2
Braintree Cl. Cos ............. 133 E1

Braishfield Cl. Southa ......... 77 F1
Braishfield Gdns. Bour ........ 191 E1
Braishfield Rd. Abb ............ 28 B2
Braishfield Rd. Brai ............ 7 E1
Braishfield Rd. Brai ........... 28 B2
Braishfield Rd. Hav ........... 136 A2
Braishfield Rd. Rom ............ 28 B2
Bramber Rd. Gosp .............. 181 D4
Bramble Cl. Alderh ............. 93 D3
Bramble Cl. Eastl .............. 56 A3
Bramble Cl. Hav ............... 136 B2
Bramble Cl. Holb .............. 150 B2
Bramble Cl. Stubb ............. 154 A1
Bramble Dr. Rom ................ 28 B1
Bramble La. Christ ............ 195 D1
Bramble La. Clanf .............. 88 A4
Bramble La. Lo He ............. 128 C3
Bramble Mews. Southa .......... 104 A4
Bramble Rd. Pet ................ 41 E2
Bramble Rd. Ports ............. 182 C2
Bramble Way. Bran ............. 169 D1
Bramble Way. Gos .............. 155 D1
Bramble Wlk. Lym .............. 198 B3
Brambles Cl. Co Com ............ 57 D4
Brambling Cl. Southa ........... 78 A3
Brambling Rd. Ro Ca ........... 113 D1
Bramblings The. Tot ........... 100 B4
Brambridge Rd. Co Com .......... 31 F1
Brambridge Rd. Twyf ............ 31 F1
Brambridge. Co Com ............. 56 C4
Bramdean Dr. Hav .............. 135 F3
Bramdean Rd. Southa ........... 104 B4
Bramham Moor. Stubb ........... 154 A1
Bramley Cl. Lym ............... 198 C1
Bramley Cl. Wat ............... 134 C4
Bramley Cres. Southa .......... 104 A1
Bramley Gdns. Gos ............. 181 D1
Bramley Rd. Bour .............. 190 B3
Bramley Rd. Fern .............. 165 E3
Brampton La. Ports ............ 158 B2
Brampton Rd. Poole ............ 204 B3
Bramshaw Cl. Winch ............. 1 B2
Bramshaw Gdns. Bour ........... 191 E2
Bramshaw Way. B on S .......... 211 E4
Bramshott Rd. Ports ........... 182 C2
Bramshott Rd. Southa .......... 126 C4
Bramston Rd. Southa ........... 102 B4
Bramwell Ct. Southa ........... 104 A3
Branches La. Sh En ............. 25 F2
Branders Cl. Bour ............. 209 D2
Branders La. Bour ............. 209 D3
Brandon Rd. Ports ............. 182 B1
Branksea Ave. Hamw ........... 203 F1
Branksea Cl. Hamw ............ 203 F1
Branksome Ave. Southa .......... 78 B1
Branksome Cl. New M ........... 196 A1
Branksome Dene Rd. Bour ...... 206 A4
Branksome Hill Rd. Bour ...... 206 A3
Branksome Towers. Poole ...... 217 D4
Branksome Wood Gdns. Bour 206 B2
Branksome Wood Rd. Bour .. 206 B2
Branksome Wood Rd. Poole .206 B2
Bransbury Cl. Southa ........... 78 B2
Bransbury Rd. Ports ........... 183 D2
Bransgore Ave. Hav ............ 135 E2
Bransgore Gdns. Bran .......... 169 E1
Bransley Cl. Rom ............... 28 A1
Branwell Cl. Christ ........... 193 D1
Branwood Cl. Hord ............. 197 F1
Brasenose Cl. Lo He ........... 129 E1
Brasher Cl. Fa Oa .............. 57 D1
Brassey Cl. Bour .............. 191 D1
Brassey Rd. Bour .............. 191 D1
Brassey Rd. Winch .............. 1 C1
Braunston Cl. Cos ............. 133 F1
Brazil Rd. Southa ............. 103 D1
Breach Ave. Southb ............ 137 F1
Breach La. Rin ................ 141 F4
Breamore Cl. Eastl ............. 56 A3
Breamore Rd. Southa ........... 104 B4
Brean Cl. Southa ............... 77 F1
Brecon Ave. Cos ............... 158 A4
Brecon Cl. Bour ............... 190 C3
Brecon Cl. Ch Fo ............... 55 D2
Brecon Cl. Fare ............... 154 C2
Brecon Cl. New M .............. 196 B1
Brecon Rd. Southa ............. 104 B3
Bredenbury Cres. Cos .......... 133 E1
Bredon Wlk. Fare .............. 154 C4
Bredy Cl. Poole ............... 188 B1
Bremble Cl. Poole ............. 189 E1
Brenchley Cl. Portc ........... 156 A4
Brendon Cl. Bour .............. 191 F1
Brendon Cl. Hyt ............... 125 E2
Brendon Green. Southa ......... 101 F4
Brendon Rd. Fare .............. 154 B4
Brent Ct. Ems ................. 160 C4
Brentwood Cres. Southa ......... 80 A1
Brewells La. Ra ................ 21 F2
Brewer Cl. Lo He .............. 129 D2
Brewer St. Ports .............. 182 B3
Brewers La. Gos ............... 155 E1
Brewers La. W Tis .............. 17 E4
Brewster Cl. Wat .............. 112 A2
Briar Cl. Christ .............. 209 F3
Briar Cl. Gos ................. 180 C3
Briar Cl. Poole ............... 204 C3
Briar Cl. Wat ................. 112 A3

Briar Way. Rom ................. 28 B1
Briar Way. Wi Mi .............. 164 A3
Briar Wood. Liss .............. 21 D4
Briar's The. Wat .............. 111 E1
Briardene Ct. Tot ............. 100 C4
Briarfield Gdns. Wat .......... 112 A3
Briarswood Rd. Upt ............ 203 E4
Briarswood. Southa ............. 78 A1
Briarwood Cl. Fare ............ 155 D4
Briarwood Gdns. S Hay ......... 184 C2
Briarwood Rd. Tot ............. 100 B3
Brick Kiln La. W Tis ........... 17 D4
Brick La. Bran ................ 169 F2
Brickfield La. Ch Fo ........... 55 E3
Brickfield La. Lym ............ 198 C3
Brickfield Rd. Southa .......... 79 E1
Brickmakers Rd. Co Comm ....... 56 C4
Brickworth Rd. Whit ............ 24 A2
Brickyard La. Broa ............ 162 A1
Brickyard La. Fern ............ 165 D3
Brickyard Rd. Swan ............. 84 A2
Bridefield Cl. Wat ............ 111 E2
Bridefield Cres. Wat .......... 111 E2
Bridge App. Hamw .............. 204 A1
Bridge Cl. Burs ............... 105 D1
Bridge Meadows. Liss ........... 20 C2
Bridge Pl. Fern ............... 190 B4
Bridge Rd. Burs ............... 128 B4
Bridge Rd. Ems ................ 136 C1
Bridge Rd. Lo He .............. 128 B4
Bridge Rd. Lym ................ 198 C3
Bridge Rd. Rom ................. 53 D4
Bridge Rd. Southa ............. 103 D2
Bridge Rd. Swanw .............. 128 B4
Bridge St. Fordi ............... 69 F1
Bridge St. Lo He .............. 154 A4
Bridge St. Southw ............. 132 C3
Bridge St. Wickh .............. 108 A2
Bridge St. Winch ............... 11 D4
Bridgefoot Dr. Fare ........... 131 E1
Bridgefoot Hill. Fare ......... 131 E1
Bridgefoot Path. Ems .......... 160 C4
Bridgemary Ave. Gos ........... 155 E2
Bridgemary Gr. Gos ............ 155 E2
Bridgemary Rd. Gos ............ 155 E2
Bridgemary Way. Gos ........... 155 E3
Bridgers Cl. Rown .............. 77 F3
Bridges Ave. Portc ............ 132 C1
Bridges Cl. Eastl .............. 55 F2
Bridges The. Rin .............. 140 C4
Bridgeside Cl. Ports .......... 182 B3
Bridget Cl. Horn .............. 112 B4
Bridgewater Rd. Poole ......... 205 E3
Bridgwater Ct. Southa ......... 102 B3
Bridle Cl. Upt ................ 203 E4
Bridle Cres. Bour ............. 208 B4
Bridle Way. Wi Mi ............. 164 B3
Bridlington Ave. Southa ....... 102 B4
Bridport Rd. Poole ............ 205 F4
Bridport St. Ver .............. 114 C3
Bridport St. Ports ............ 182 B3
Brierley Ave. Fern ............ 165 F1
Brierley Cl. Bour ............. 190 C3
Brierley Rd. Bour ............. 190 C2
Brigantine Rd. Lo He .......... 128 C1
Brigham Cl. Ports ............. 157 F2
Bright Rd. Poole .............. 204 C3
Brightlands Ave. Bour ......... 208 C3
Brighton Ave. Gos ............. 180 C4
Brighton Rd. Southa ........... 102 C4
Brighton Rd. Sway ............. 172 A1
Brights La. S Hay ............. 184 C3
Brightside Rd. Southa .......... 77 F1
Brightside. Wat ............... 134 B3
Brightstone Cl. Southa ......... 79 E3
Brightstone Rd. Cos ........... 157 F4
Brindle Cl. Southa ............. 79 D3
Brinsons Cl. Burt ............. 193 E2
Brinton La. Hyt ............... 126 A3
Brinton's Rd. Southa .......... 103 D3
Brinton's Terr. Southa ........ 103 D3
Brisbane Rd. Christ ........... 192 C1
Bristol Rd. Ports ............. 182 C1
Britain St. Ports ............. 182 A3
Britannia Rd N. Ports ......... 182 B2
Britannia Rd. Poole ........... 205 D2
Britannia Rd. Ports ........... 182 B2
Britannia Rd. Southa .......... 103 D3
Britannia Way. Christ ......... 210 A4
Briton St. Southa ............. 103 D2
Britten Rd. L on S ............ 179 F3
Britten Way. Wat .............. 134 C2
Brixey Cl. Poole .............. 205 E4
Brixey Rd. Poole .............. 205 E4
Brixworth Cl. Cos ............. 133 D1
Broad Ave. Bour ............... 207 E4
Broad Chalke Down. Winch .... 10 B2
Broad Croft. Ro Ca ............ 113 E2
Broad Gdns. Cos ............... 158 C4
Broad Green. Southa ........... 103 D2
Broad La. Den ................. 110 A3
Broad La. Lym ................. 198 C1
Broad La. N Bad ................ 53 F3
Broad La. Southa .............. 102 C2
Broad La. Swan ................. 84 A3
Broad Mead Rd. W Moo ......... 114 C1
Broad Oak. Botl ............... 105 F4
Broad St. Ports .............. 181 F2

Broad View La. Winch ........... 10 A2
Broad Way. Frox G .............. 39 F4
Broad Way. Hamble ............. 127 F3
Broad Woods La. W Wel .......... 51 D3
Broadbent Cl. Rown ............. 77 F3
Broadcut. Fare ................ 131 E1
Broadfields Cl. M on S ........ 213 E3
Broadhill La. Fordi ............ 94 B4
Broadhurst Ave. Bour .......... 190 C2
Broadlands Ave. Bour .......... 208 C2
Broadlands Ave. Eastl .......... 56 A3
Broadlands Ave. Wat ........... 134 C4
Broadlands Cl. Bour ........... 191 E2
Broadlands Cl. Christ ......... 195 D1
Broadlands Rd. Brock .......... 145 F1
Broadlands Rd. Southa .......... 79 D2
Broadlaw Wlk. Fare ............ 154 C4
Broadley Cl. Holb ............. 150 B2
Broadly Cl. Lym ............... 198 A1
Broadmayne Rd. Poole .......... 206 A4
Broadmead Cl. Lym ............. 198 C2
Broadmead Rd. Nur .............. 77 E3
Broadmeadow Cl. Tot ........... 100 C4
Broadmeadows La. Wat .......... 135 D4
Broadmere Ave. Hav ............ 135 F3
Broadmoor Rd. Broa ............ 187 D4
Broadoak Cl. Holb ............. 150 B2
Broads The. Pamp ............. 163 D3
Broadsands Dr. Gos ............ 180 B2
Broadsands Wlk. Gos ........... 180 C2
Broadshard La. Rin ............ 141 D4
Broadwater Ave. Poole ......... 205 E1
Broadwater Rd. Rom ............. 52 C3
Broadwater Rd. Southa .......... 79 F2
Broadway Gdns. Wi Mi .......... 163 E2
Broadway La. Bour ............. 191 E2
Broadway La. Horn ............. 111 E4
Broadway The. Bour ............ 190 B3
Broadway The. Southa .......... 79 D1
Broadway The. Winch ............ 11 D4
Broadway. Bour ................ 209 D2
Brockenhurst Ave. Hav ......... 135 E3
Brockenhurst Rd. Bour ......... 191 D1
Brockhampton La. Hav .......... 135 F1
Brockhampton Rd. Hav .......... 135 E1
Brockhills La. New M .......... 196 B3
Brockhurst Rd. Gos ............ 180 C4
Brockishill Rd. Cadn ........... 99 D3
Brocklands. Hav ............... 135 E1
Brockley Rd. Bour ............. 190 C2
Brockmeadow. Fare ............. 130 C1
Brockwood Bottom. Bramd ....... 36 C4
Brodrick Ave. Gos ............. 181 D2
Brog St. Broa ................. 162 B1
Brokenford Ave. Tot ........... 100 C4
Brokenford La. Tot ............ 100 C4
Bromley Rd. Southa ............. 79 F1
Brompton Rd. Ports ............ 182 C2
Bromyard Cres. Cos ............ 133 E1
Bronte Ave. Christ ............ 193 D1
Bronte Cl. Tot ................ 100 B3
Bronte Way. Southa ............ 103 F3
Brook Ave N. New M ............ 196 A2
Brook Ave. New M .............. 196 A2
Brook Cl. Bour ................ 190 B2
Brook Cl. Lo He ............... 128 C2
Brook Cl. N Bad ................ 54 A2
Brook Cnr. Bro ................. 74 A1
Brook Dr. Ver ................. 115 D2
Brook Farm Ave. Fare .......... 130 C2
Brook Gdns. Ems ............... 160 B4
Brook Hill. Bold .............. 199 F4
Brook La. Botl ................ 105 F3
Brook La. Bran ................ 194 A4
Brook La. Broa ................ 187 E3
Brook La. Hambl ................ 86 B3
Brook La. Lo He ............... 128 B2
Brook La. Woodg ................ 70 C4
Brook Rd. Bour ................ 190 B2
Brook Rd. Fa Oa ................ 57 E1
Brook Rd. Lym ................. 198 C1
Brook Rd. Poole ............... 205 E3
Brook Rd. Southa .............. 104 A4
Brook Rd. Wi Mi ............... 163 E3
Brook St. Bi Wa ................ 83 E4
Brook Terr. Fordi .............. 93 F4
Brook Valley. Southa ........... 78 A1
Brook Way. Christ ............. 210 B4
Brook Way. Rom ................. 28 A1
Brook Wlk. Tot ................. 76 B1
Brookdale Cl. Wat ............. 134 C4
Brooke Cl. Ki Wo ............... 2 A4
Brookers La. Gos .............. 155 D2
Brookfield Cl. Hav ............ 135 F1
Brookfield Gdns. Lo He ........ 128 C2
Brookfield Rd. Fa Oa ........... 57 E1
Brookfield Rd. Ports .......... 182 C3
Brookfields. W Wel ............. 50 B2
Brooklands Cl. Lym ............ 198 B2
Brooklands Rd. Bi Wa ........... 83 E4
Brooklands Rd. Hav ............ 135 D1
Brooklyn Cl. Ott ............... 31 E2
Brooklyn Ct. New M ............ 195 F2
Brooklyn Dr. Wat .............. 134 C4
Brooklynn Cl. Shed ............. 83 F1
Brookmead Way. Hav ............ 159 F4
Brooks Cl. Rin ................ 141 D3

225

Brookside Ave. Southa

Carrol Cl. Fa Oa

Brookside Ave. Southa 101 F4
Brookside Cl. Bran 169 D1
Brookside Cl. Den 110 C2
Brookside Rd. Bran 194 A4
Brookside Rd. Brock 145 F1
Brookside Rd. Hav 135 E1
Brookside Rd. Hav 159 F4
Brookside Rd. Wi Mi 163 F2
Brookside Way. Christ 194 C1
Brookside Way. Southa 79 F2
Brookside Way. W End 80 C2
Brookside. Gos 155 D3
Brookside. Ibs 55 B1
Brookside. Lan 49 E2
Brookside. Tot 100 C3
Brookvale Rd. Southa 79 D1
Brookwood Ave. Eastl 55 F2
Brookwood Rd. Southa 101 E4
Broom Cl. Ports 183 E2
Broom Cl. Wat 135 D3
Broom Hill Way. Eastl 56 A4
Broom Hill. E Bol 200 A4
Broom Rd. Pet 41 E1
Broom Rd. Poole 189 E1
Broom Sq. Ports 183 E2
Broom Way. L on S 179 F4
Broom Way. Stubb 179 F4
Broomfield Ave. Bour 190 C1
Broomfield Cres. Gos 180 A4
Broomfield Dr. Alderh 93 D3
Broomfield La. Lym 198 C2
Broomhill Cl. Lym 198 A1
Broomhill. Lan 49 E1
Brooms Gr. Southa 104 B2
Broomy Cl. Hyt 125 E2
Brougham La. Gos 181 D3
Brougham Rd. Ports 182 B2
Brougham St. Gos 181 D3
Broughton Ave. Bour 190 C2
Broughton Cl. Bour 190 C2
Broughton Cl. Southa 78 A1
Broughton Rd. Lyn 121 F3
Brow The. Wat 134 B1
Browndown Rd. Gos 180 B2
Brownen Rd. Bour 207 D4
Brownhill Cl. Ch Fo 55 E4
Brownhill Ct. Southa 77 F2
Brownhill Gdns. Ch Fo 55 E4
Brownhill Rd. Brock 170 C2
Brownhill Rd. Ch Fo 55 E4
Brownhill Rd. N Bad 54 A2
Brownhill Way. Nur 77 E2
Brownhill Way. Southa 77 E2
Browning Ave. Bour 208 A2
Browning Ave. Portc 132 C1
Browning Ave. Southa 104 B3
Browning Cl. Eastl 55 F2
Browning Cl. Tot 100 B4
Browning Dr. Winch 10 B4
Browning Rd. Poole 205 E3
Brownings Cl. Lym 198 A2
Brownlow Ave. Southa 104 A3
Brownlow Cl. Ports 182 B4
Brownlow Gdns. Southa 104 A3
Browns La. Beaul 200 B3
Browns La. Dame 68 A3
Brownsea Ave. Broa 187 E3
Brownsea Cl. New M 195 F2
Brownsea Rd. Poole 216 A2
Brownsea View Ave. Poole 205 E1
Brownsea View Cl. Poole 205 E1
Brownsholme Cl. Eastl 56 A3
Brownwich La. Lo He 153 E3
Broxburn Cl. Ch Fo 30 C1
Broxhead Rd. Hav 136 A3
Bruce Cl. Fare 131 D2
Bruce Rd. Ports 182 C1
Brudenell Ave. Poole 216 B4
Brudenell Rd. Poole 216 B3
Brue Cl. N Bad 55 D4
Brune La. Stubb 155 D1
Brune Way. Fern 165 E2
Brunel Cl. Ver 115 E2
Brunel Rd. Ports 157 F2
Brunel Rd. Southa 101 E4
Brunel Rd. Tot 76 B2
Brunel Way. Lo He 129 E2
Brunstead Pl. Poole 206 A2
Brunstead Rd. Poole 206 A2
Brunswick Cl. Fa Oa 57 D2
Brunswick Gdns. Hav 135 E1
Brunswick Pl. Lym 198 C2
Brunswick Pl. Southa 103 D3
Brunswick Rd. Fa Oa 57 D2
Brunswick Sq. Southa 103 D2
Brunswick St. Ports 182 B2
Brushers. Bran 169 F2
Bruyn Ct. Fordi 70 A1
Bruyn Rd. Fordi 70 A1
Bryanston Rd. Southa 103 F3
Bryanstone Rd. Bour 206 C4
Bryant Rd. Poole 206 A4
Brympton Cl. Fordi 69 E1
Bryony Cl. Lo He 128 C1
Bryony Gdns. Fa Oa 81 E3
Bryony Way. Wat 135 D4
Bryson Rd. Cos 157 E4
Bub La. Christ 209 F3
Bubbs La. W End 81 E2
Buccaneers Cl. Christ 209 F3
Buccleuch Rd. Poole 206 A1
Bucehayes Cl. Christ 211 D4
Buchan Ct. Hyt 125 E1
Buchanan Ave. Bour 207 F3
Buchanan Rd. Southa 77 F3
Buckingham Green. Ports 182 B4
Buckingham Rd. Pet 40 B2
Buckingham Rd. Poole 205 E4
Buckingham St. Ports 182 B3
Buckingham Wlk. New M 195 F2
Buckland Cl. Eastl 56 A3
Buckland Cl. Wat 111 E1
Buckland Dene. Lym 198 B3
Buckland Gdns. Tot 76 B1
Buckland Gr. Christ 194 C1
Buckland Path. Ports 182 B4
Buckland Rd. Poole 205 E3
Buckland St. Ports 182 C4
Buckland Terr. Poole 205 E3
Bucklers Ct. Hav 135 E4
Bucklers Ct. Ports 157 E1
Bucklers Rd. Gosp 181 E4
Bucklers The. M on S 213 D3
Bucklers Way. Bour 191 E2
Buckley Ct. Southa 78 A1
Buckmore Ave. Pet 40 B2
Bucks Head Hill. Meons 61 E3
Bucksey Rd. Gos 180 B4
Buckstone Cl. Hord 197 F1
Buckthorn Cl. Broa 187 F1
Budden's La. Sob 108 C4
Buddens Rd. Wickh 108 A2
Buddle Hill. Fordi 94 B2
Budds La. Rom 27 F1
Bude Cl. Portc 132 C1
Bugle St. Southa 102 C2
Bulbarrow Wlk. Fare 154 C4
Buldowne Wlk. Sway 172 A2
Bull Drove. Winch 11 D3
Bull Hill. Bold 174 A1
Bull La. Min 98 B2
Bull La. Poole 204 B1
Bull La. Shed 83 E2
Bullar Rd. Southa 103 F4
Bullar St. Southa 103 D3
Bullfinch Cl. Broa 187 F1
Bullfinch Cl. Tot 100 B4
Bullfinch Ct. L on S 179 F4
Bullrush Cl. Hyt 125 F1
Bulls Copse La. Wat 112 A3
Bulls Drove. W Tyth 4 A3
Bunkers Hill. Den 110 B2
Bunns La. Hambl 109 F3
Bunny La. Mich 27 F3
Bunny La. Sh En 25 D2
Bunstead La. Hurs 30 B4
Bunting Gdns. Wat 111 F2
Bunting Rd. Fern 165 D4
Burbidge Gr. Ports 183 D1
Burbush Cl. Holb 150 B2
Burcombe La. Rin 117 F1
Burcombe Rd. Bour 190 B3
Burcote Dr. Ports 158 A2
Burdale Dr. S Hay 185 E2
Bure Cl. Christ 210 A3
Bure Haven Dr. Christ 210 A3
Bure Homage Gdns. Christ 210 A3
Bure Homage La. Christ 210 A3
Bure La. Christ 210 A3
Bure Park. Christ 210 A3
Bure Rd. Christ 210 A3
Burford Cl. Christ 192 B1
Burford La. Brock 146 A1
Burgate Cl. Hav 135 E2
Burgate Fields. Fordi 70 A2
Burgess Cl. S Hay 185 E1
Burgess Gdns. Southa 78 C2
Burgess Rd. Southa 79 D2
Burghclere Rd. Hav 136 A3
Burghclere Rd. Southa 126 C4
Burgoyne Rd. Ports 182 C1
Burgoyne Rd. Southa 104 C2
Burgundy Cl. Lo He 128 C1
Burion Cl. St Le 139 F3
Buriton Cl. Portc 132 B1
Buriton Rd. Winch 1 B2
Buriton St. Ports 182 B3
Burke Dr. Southa 104 B3
Burleigh Rd. Bour 208 B3
Burleigh Rd. Ports 182 C4
Burley Cl. B on S 211 E4
Burley Cl. Ch Fo 55 D2
Burley Cl. Hav 136 A3
Burley Cl. Ver 114 C3
Burley Down. Ch Fo 55 D2
Burley Lawn. Bur 143 D2
Burley Rd. Bran 194 A4
Burley Rd. Brock 172 C4
Burley Rd. Burt 193 E3
Burley Rd. Poole 205 E3
Burley Rd. Winch 1 B2
Burlington Ct. Southa 104 A3
Burlington Rd. Ports 157 F1
Burlington Rd. Southa 102 C3
Burmese Cl. Swanw 129 E4
Burn Cl. Ver 115 D2
Burnaby Rd. Bour 206 B1
Burnaby Rd. Ports 182 A2
Burnbake Rd. Ver 115 D3
Burnbank Gdns. Tot 100 C4
Burnbrae Rd. Fern 165 E1
Burnett Ave. Christ 208 C4
Burnett Cl. Southa 79 F1
Burnett Cl. Winch 1 B1
Burnett Rd. Christ 208 C4
Burnett Rd. Gos 180 C3
Burnetts Flds. Fa Oa 81 E4
Burnetts Gdns. Fa Oa 81 E4
Burnetts La. Fa Oa 81 E3
Burnetts La. W End 81 E3
Burney Rd. Gos 180 C2
Burngate Rd. Hamw 203 F1
Burnham Beeches. N Bad 55 D3
Burnham Chase. Southa 104 B4
Burnham Dr. Bour 207 E4
Burnham Rd. Burt 193 E1
Burnham Rd. Cos 134 B1
Burnham Rd. Fordi 69 F2
Burnham Wood. Fare 131 D2
Burnhams Wlk. Gos 181 E2
Burns Cl. Eastl 55 F1
Burns Rd. Bour 208 B4
Burns Rd. Eastl 55 F1
Burns Rd. Southa 104 B3
Burnside. Christ 210 B4
Burnside. Gos 155 D3
Burnside. Wat 112 A1
Burnt House La. Bold 174 A1
Burnt House La. Bran 169 D1
Burnt House La. Stubb 154 B2
Burr Cl. Co Com 56 C4
Burrard Gr. Lym 198 C1
Burrfields Rd. Ports 158 A1
Burridge Rd. Swanw 106 A1
Burrill Ave. Cos 158 A4
Burrows Cl. Hav 136 A2
Burrows La. Ver 114 C4
Bursledon Hts. Burs 105 D1
Bursledon Pl. Wat 134 B3
Bursledon Rd. He En 105 D3
Bursledon Rd. Southa 104 B3
Bursledon Rd. Wat 134 B3
Burt's La. Holt 138 A4
Burt's La. Ver 138 A4
Burtley Rd. Bour 208 C2
Burton Cl. Burt 193 E1
Burton Hall Pl. Burt 193 E2
Burton Rd. Christ 209 F4
Burton Rd. Poole 206 A2
Burton Rd. Southa 102 C3
Burtoncroft. Burt 193 E2
Burts Hill. Wi Mi 163 E3
Burwood Gr. S Hay 185 D2
Bury Cl. Gos 181 D2
Bury Cres. Gos 181 D2
Bury Hall La. Gos 180 C2
Bury La. Tot 101 D3
Bury Rd. Gos 181 D2
Bury Rd. March 101 F2
Bury Rd. Poole 205 F1
Bus Dro. Faw 178 C4
Bush St E. Ports 182 B2
Bush St W. Ports 182 B2
Bushell Rd. Poole 204 B4
Bushey Rd. Bour 191 E1
Bushmead Dr. St Le 139 F3
Bushy Mead. Wat 134 B2
Busket La. Winch 11 D4
Busketts Way. Ashu 100 A1
Butcher St. Ports 182 A3
Bute Dr. Christ 211 D4
Butlers Cl. Locke 4 C1
Butlers La. Rin 117 E1
Butser Wlk. Fare 154 C4
Butser Wlk. Pet 41 D2
Butt's Cl. Southa 104 B2
Butt's Cres. Southa 104 B2
Butt's Rd. Southa 104 B2
Butt's Sq. Southa 104 B2
Buttercup Cl. He En 105 D3
Buttercup Dr. Christ 194 A1
Buttercup Way. Lo He 128 C2
Butterfield Rd. Southa 78 C2
Butterfly Dr. Cos 133 D1
Buttermere Cl. Southa 77 F1
Buttery The. Christ 209 E4
Button's La. Poole 204 B1
Button's La. W Wel 50 C2
Butts Ash Gdns. Hyt 126 A1
Butts Ash La. Hyt 149 F4
Butts Bridge Hill. Hyt 126 A1
Butts Paddock. Brock 145 F1
Butts The. Meons 61 E3
Buttsash Ave. Hyt 150 A4
Buttsbridge Rd. Hyt 126 A1
By Pass Rd. Rom 52 C3
By The Wood. Tot 76 B1
Bye Rd. Swanw 128 B4
Byerley Cl. Westb 137 D3
Byerley Rd. Ports 182 C3
Byeways. Hyt 125 F1
Byers The. Stubb 154 B2
Byrd Cl. Wat 134 C3
Byron Ave. Winch 10 B4
Byron Cl. Bi Wa 83 F4
Byron Cl. Fare 131 D1
Byron Rd. B on S 211 F4
Byron Rd. Bour 207 F2
Byron Rd. Eastl 56 A2
Byron Rd. Ports 182 C4
Byron Rd. Southa 104 B3
Byron Rd. Wi Mi 163 E3
Cable St. Southa 103 E3
Cabot Dr. Hyt 125 E2
Cabot La. Broa 204 A4
Cabot Way. New M 195 F2
Cadhay Cl. New M 195 F2
Cadland Ct. Southa 103 E1
Cadland Rd. Faw 150 B4
Cadnam La. Cadn 74 C1
Cadnam Lawn. Hav 135 E4
Cadnam Rd. Ports 183 D2
Cadnam Way. Bour 191 E2
Cadogan Rd. Rin 141 D4
Cador Dr. Portc 156 A3
Caerleon Ave. Southa 104 B3
Caerleon Dr. Southa 104 B3
Caernarvon Gdns. Ch Fo 55 D2
Caesar's Way. Broa 187 F2
Cains Cl. Stubb 154 B2
Caird Ave. New M 196 B1
Cairns Cl. Christ 208 C4
Cairo Terr. Ports 182 B4
Caister Cl. Fern 165 E3
Caistor Cl. Southa 78 A2
Cakeham Rd. W Wit 186 C1
Calbourne. Net 127 E4
Calcott Hill. Curd 82 C2
Calder Cl. Southa 101 F4
Calder Rd. Poole 204 C4
Calderwood Dr. Southa 104 A2
Caledon Rd. Poole 205 F2
Caledonia Dr. Hyt 125 E2
Caledonian Cl. Christ 210 A4
Callow End. Curd 82 C1
Calmore Cl. Bour 191 E2
Calmore Cres. Tot 76 A1
Calmore Dr. Tot 76 B1
Calmore Gdns. Tot 100 B4
Calmore Rd. Tot 100 B4
Calpe Ave. Lyn 121 F3
Calshot Cl. Faw 178 C4
Calshot Dr. Ch Fo 55 D2
Calshot Rd. Faw 151 D1
Calshot Rd. Hav 135 E4
Calshot Way. Gos 155 D1
Calvin Rd. Bour 206 C4
Camber Pl. Ports 182 A2
Cambria Dr. Hyt 125 E2
Cambrian Cl. Burs 105 D1
Cambrian Wlk. Fare 154 C4
Cambridge Dr. Ch Fo 55 E2
Cambridge Gdns. Christ 192 C1
Cambridge Green. Ch Fo 55 E1
Cambridge Green. Lo He 129 E1
Cambridge Rd. Bour 206 B2
Cambridge Rd. Gos 180 C3
Cambridge Rd. L on S 179 F3
Cambridge Rd. Ports 182 A2
Cambridge Rd. Southa 103 D4
Camcross Cl. Cos 133 D1
Camden Cl. Bour 191 D1
Camden St. Gos 181 D3
Camel Green Rd. Alderh 93 D3
Camelia Gdns. Southa 80 A1
Camelia Gr. Fa Oa 57 F1
Camellia Cl. W Moo 114 C1
Camellia Gdns. New M 196 A1
Camelot Cres. Portc 132 A1
Cameron Cl. Gos 155 E2
Cameron Rd. Christ 209 E4
Camley Cl. Southa 103 F1
Cammel Rd. Fern 165 E1
Camp Rd. Gos 155 E2
Campbell Cres. Wat 134 B3
Campbell Rd. Bour 207 E3
Campbell Rd. Burt 193 E2
Campbell Rd. Eastl 56 A1
Campbell Rd. Ports 182 C2
Campbell St. Southa 103 E3
Campbell Way. Fa Oa 57 E1
Campion Cl. Fa Oa 81 E3
Campion Cl. Lo He 128 C1
Campion Cl. Wat 135 D3
Campion Dr. Rom 28 B1
Campion Gr. Christ 209 F3
Campion Rd. Southa 104 B3
Campion Way. Ki Wo 2 B4
Campion Way. Lym 198 C3
Cams Bay Cl. Portc 131 F1
Cams Hill. Hambl 86 A1
Cams Hill. Portc 131 F1
Canada Rd. Southa 103 F1
Canada Rd. W Wel 50 B1
Canal Cl. Rom 28 A1
Canal Wlk. Ports 182 B3
Canal Wlk. Southa 103 D2
Canberra Rd. Christ 192 C1
Canberra Rd. Nur 77 D2
Canberra Rd. Th Is 161 D2
Cande Cl. Lo He 128 C1
Candover Ct. Southa 127 D4
Candy La. Southa 104 C3
Candys Cl. Broa 162 C1
Candys La. Broa 162 C1
Canford Ave. Bour 190 A1
Canford Bottom. Wi Mi 164 B3
Canford Cl. Shed 107 F4
Canford Cl. Southa 77 E1
Canford Cliffs Ave. Poole 205 F1
Canford Cres. Poole 216 C4
Canford Heath Rd. Broa 188 C1
Canford Heath Rd. Poole 188 C1
Canford Magna. Oakl 164 A1
Canford Rd. Bour 190 A1
Canford Rd. Poole 204 B2
Canford View Dr. Wi Mi 164 A3
Canford Way. Poole 189 E1
Canhouse La. Ra 21 F2
Cannock Wlk. Fare 154 C4
Cannon Cl. Broa 188 A1
Cannon Ct. Fa Oa 57 E1
Cannon Hill Gdns. Wi Mi 164 A4
Cannon Hill Rd. Wi Mi 164 A4
Cannon St. Lym 198 C2
Cannon St. Southa 102 B4
Cannon's Barn Cl. Portc 132 B1
Canon St. Winch 10 C4
Canons Wlk. M on S 213 E3
Canterbury Ave. Southa 104 B2
Canterbury Cl. Lon S 180 A2
Canterbury Cl. W Moo 138 C1
Canterbury Dr. Hyt 125 E2
Canterbury Rd. Ports 182 C2
Canterbury Rd. Stubb 154 B2
Canterton La. Bro 98 A4
Canton St. Southa 102 C3
Canute Dr. Bran 169 D1
Canute Rd. Southa 103 D2
Canute Rd. Winch 11 D3
Capel Ley. Wat 134 C2
Capella Gdns. Hyt 125 E2
Capesthorne. Christ 210 A3
Capon Cl. Southa 79 F2
Capstan Gdns. Lo He 129 E2
Capstone Pl. Bour 207 E3
Capstone Rd. Bour 207 D3
Captain's Pl. Southa 103 D2
Captain's Row. Lym 198 C2
Captains Row. Ports 182 A2
Carberry Dr. Portc 156 B4
Carbery Ave. Bour 208 B3
Carbery Ct. Hav 135 E4
Carbery Gdns. Bour 208 C3
Carbery La. Bour 208 B2
Carbis Cl. Ports 157 D4
Cardew Rd. Liss 21 D2
Cardiff Rd. Ports 157 E1
Cardigan Rd. Bour 206 C4
Cardinal Dr. Wat 112 A1
Cardinal Way. Lo He 129 D1
Carey Rd. Bour 190 C2
Carey Rd. Southa 104 B3
Careys Cotts. Brock 145 F1
Careys Rd. Bour 191 E2
Carisbrook Cres. Hamw 203 E2
Carisbrooke Ave. Stubb 154 A1
Carisbrooke Cres. Ch Fo 55 F3
Carisbrooke Ct. New M 195 F2
Carisbrooke Ct. Rom 28 A1
Carisbrooke Dr. Southa 103 F3
Carisbrooke Rd. Gos 155 D1
Carisbrooke Rd. Ports 183 D2
Carisbrooke Way. Christ 194 C1
Carisbrooke. Net 127 E4
Carless Cl. Gos 180 B4
Carlisle Rd. Ports 182 B3
Carlisle Rd. Southa 102 A4
Carlton Ave. B on S 211 F4
Carlton Cres. Southa 102 C3
Carlton Gr. Poole 205 E3
Carlton Pl. Southa 102 C3
Carlton Rd. Bour 207 E2
Carlton Rd. Gos 181 E3
Carlton Rd. Portc 132 C1
Carlton Rd. Southa 102 C4
Carlton Way. Gos 181 E3
Carlyle Rd. Bour 208 B3
Carlyle Rd. Gos 181 D3
Carlyn Dr. Ch Fo 55 E4
Carmans La. Comp 31 E4
Carmarthen Ave. Cos 158 A4
Carnarvon Rd. Bour 207 F2
Carnarvon Rd. Gos 181 D2
Carnarvon Rd. Ports 182 C4
Carnation Rd. Southa 79 E2
Carne Cl. Ch Fo 55 E4
Carne Pl. Ports 157 D4
Caroline Ave. Christ 209 F3
Caroline Gdns. Fare 130 B1
Caroline Rd. Bour 190 A2
Carolyn Cl. Southa 103 F1
Carpathia Cl. W End 80 A1
Carpenter Cl. Hyt 126 A2
Carpenter Cl. Lym 198 B3
Carradale. Christ 210 A4
Carran Wlk. Fare 154 C4
Carrbridge Cl. Bour 206 B4
Carrbridge Gdns. Bour 206 B4
Carrbridge Rd. Bour 206 B4
Carrick Way. New M 196 B1
Carrington Cl. M on S 213 F3
Carrington La. M on S 213 F2
Carrol Cl. Fa Oa 57 E1

Carroll Ave. Fern ............ 165 F3
Carroll Cl. Poole ............ 206 A3
Carronade Wlk. Ports ........ 157 F3
Carshalton Ave. Cos ......... 158 A4
Carsworth Way. Poole ........ 189 D1
Carter's Clay Rd. Locke ...... 26 A3
Carters Ave. Hamw .......... 203 E2
Carters Cl. Woodg ........... 47 E2
Carters La. Poole ........... 204 B1
Carthage Cl. Ch Fo .......... 55 F4
Cartref Cl. Ver ............. 114 C3
Cartwright Cl. Bour ......... 190 B2
Carvers La. Rin ............. 141 D4
Carysfort Rd. Bour .......... 207 E2
Cask St. Ports .............. 182 B3
Caslake Cl. B on S .......... 195 F1
Caspar John Cl. Stubb ....... 154 A1
Cassel Ave. Bour ............ 206 A1
Castle Ave. Christ .......... 210 C4
Castle Ave. Hav ............. 136 A1
Castle Ave. Ports ........... 182 B1
Castle Ave. Winch ........... 10 C4
Castle Cl. M on S ........... 213 F2
Castle Cl. Ports ............ 182 B2
Castle Court. Southa ........ 102 A4
Castle Farm La. Wickh ....... 108 A1
Castle Gate Cl. Bour ........ 191 E1
Castle Gdn. Pet ............. 40 C2
Castle Hill La. Bur ......... 142 C2
Castle Hill. Poole .......... 205 D2
Castle Hill. Winch .......... 10 C4
Castle La E. Bour ........... 208 B4
Castle La W. Bour ........... 191 E1
Castle La. Ch Fo ............ 55 D2
Castle La. Faw .............. 178 C4
Castle La. N Bad ............ 54 B2
Castle La. Southa ........... 102 C2
Castle Meadow. Down ......... 46 C4
Castle Rd. Bour ............. 191 D1
Castle Rd. Net .............. 127 D3
Castle Rd. Ports ............ 182 B2
Castle Rd. Ro Ca ............ 113 D1
Castle Rd. Southa ........... 79 F1
Castle Rd. Southw ........... 132 C3
Castle Sq. Southa ........... 102 C2
Castle St. Christ ........... 209 E3
Castle St. Lo He ............ 154 A4
Castle St. Poole ............ 204 B1
Castle St. Portc ............ 156 B4
Castle St. Southa ........... 103 D4
Castle View Rd. Portc ....... 156 C4
Castle Way. Hav ............. 136 A1
Castle Way. Southa .......... 102 C2
Castledene Cres. Poole ...... 205 D1
Castlemain Ave. Bour ........ 208 B3
Castleman Way. Rin .......... 141 D3
Castlemans La. N Hay ........ 160 A1
Castleshaw Cl. Southa ....... 101 F4
Castleton Ave. Bour ......... 190 B3
Catalina Cl. Christ ......... 210 A3
Catalina Dr. Poole .......... 204 C1
Catamaran Cl. Lo He ......... 128 C1
Cateran Cl. Southa .......... 101 F4
Cathay Gdns. Hyt ............ 125 E2
Cathedral View. Winch ....... 11 D3
Catherine Cl. W End ......... 80 C1
Catherine Cres. Down ........ 46 B4
Catherine Gdns. W End ....... 80 C1
Catherington Hill. Horn ..... 88 A1
Catherington La. Horn ....... 112 A4
Catherington La. Wat ........ 112 A4
Catherington Way. Hav ....... 135 F2
Catisfield La. Fare ......... 130 A1
Catisfield Rd. Fare ......... 130 B1
Catisfield Rd. Ports ........ 183 D2
Caton Cl. Poole ............. 206 A4
Cattistock Rd. Bour ......... 191 F1
Causeway Cres. Tot .......... 101 D4
Causeway Farm. Wat .......... 112 A3
Causeway The. Pet ........... 40 C1
Causeway The. Portc ......... 131 F1
Causeway. Rom ............... 52 B3
Cavalier Gdns. Hyt .......... 125 E2
Cavalier Cl. Cos ............ 158 B4
Cavan Cres. Broa ............ 188 A1
Cavanna Cl. Gos ............. 155 D1
Cavell Dr. Cos .............. 133 F1
Cavendish Cl. Rom ........... 28 A1
Cavendish Cl. Wat ........... 134 C4
Cavendish Dr. Wat ........... 134 C4
Cavendish Gr. Southa ........ 102 C4
Cavendish Gr. Winch ......... 2 A2
Cavendish Mews. Southa ...... 102 C4
Cavendish Pl. Bour .......... 207 D3
Cavendish Rd. Bour .......... 207 D3
Cavendish Rd. Ports ......... 182 B2
Caversham Cl. Hamw .......... 203 F2
Caversham Cl. Southa ........ 104 A2
Caversham Cl. W End ......... 80 B1
Cawdor Rd. Bour ............. 206 B4
Cawte Rd. Southa ............ 102 B3
Cawte's Pl. Fare ............ 88 B1
Caxton Ave. Southa .......... 104 A3
Caxton Cl. Christ ........... 210 A4
Cecil Ave. Ashu ............. 100 B1
Cecil Ave. Bour ............. 207 E4
Cecil Ave. Southa ........... 78 A1

Cecil Cl. Broa .............. 187 F3
Cecil Gr. Ports ............. 182 A2
Cecil Hill. Bour ............ 207 D4
Cecil Pl. Ports ............. 182 A2
Cecil Rd. Bour .............. 207 F2
Cecil Rd. Poole ............. 205 E3
Cecil Rd. Southa ............ 103 F2
Cedar Ave. Bour ............. 190 B3
Cedar Ave. Christ ........... 208 B4
Cedar Ave. Southa ........... 102 B4
Cedar Ave. St Le ............ 139 F2
Cedar Cl. Gos ............... 156 A1
Cedar Cl. He En ............. 105 E4
Cedar Cl. Ki Wo ............. 2 A4
Cedar Cl. Upt ............... 203 D4
Cedar Cl. Wat ............... 134 C3
Cedar Cres. N Bad ........... 53 F3
Cedar Cres. Wat ............. 112 B3
Cedar Cl. Winch ............. 10 C3
Cedar Dr. Hord .............. 213 E4
Cedar Dr. Wi Mi ............. 164 A3
Cedar Gdns. Southa .......... 103 D4
Cedar Gr. Ports ............. 183 D4
Cedar Lawn. Rom ............. 28 B1
Cedar Pl. Bran .............. 169 D1
Cedar Rd. Eastl ............. 55 F1
Cedar Rd. Hyt ............... 150 A4
Cedar Rd. Southa ............ 103 D4
Cedar Way. Fare ............. 154 C4
Cedar Way. Fern ............. 165 E4
Cedar Wood Cl. Fa Oa ........ 57 F1
Cedar Wood Cl. Tot .......... 100 B4
Cedarmount. Lyn ............. 121 F2
Cedars The. Bour ............ 206 B2
Cedric Cl. Black ............ 177 F4
Celandine Ave. Lo He ........ 128 C1
Celandine Cl. Christ ........ 210 A4
Celia Cl. Wat ............... 135 D4
Cellars Farm Rd. Bour ....... 209 D2
Cement Terr. Southa ......... 102 C2
Cemetery Ave. Poole ......... 204 C3
Cemetery La. Den ............ 110 C3
Cemetery La. Westb .......... 137 E2
Cemetery Rd. Southa ......... 102 C4
Cemetery Rd. Wi Mi .......... 163 D3
Centaur St. Ports ........... 182 B4
Central Ave. Broa ........... 187 E4
Central Ave. Poole .......... 205 F3
Central Bridge. Southa ...... 103 D2
Central Drive. Bour ......... 206 C3
Central Rd. Cos ............. 158 B4
Central Rd. Portc ........... 156 A4
Central Rd. Southa .......... 103 D1
Central St. Ports ........... 182 B3
Central Station Bridge. Southa 102 C4
Centre La. Hord ............. 197 F1
Centre Way. Lo He ........... 129 D2
Cerne Cl. Bour .............. 191 D2
Cerne Cl. N Bad ............. 53 F2
Cerne Cl. W End ............. 80 A1
Chadderton Gdns. Ports ...... 182 A2
Chaddesley Glen. Poole ...... 216 C3
Chaddesley Pines. Poole ..... 216 C3
Chaddesley Wood Rd. Poole ... 216 C3
Chadwell Ave. Southa ........ 104 A2
Chadwick Rd. Eastl .......... 55 F1
Chafen Rd. Southa ........... 103 E4
Chaffey Cl. Rin ............. 141 E4
Chaffinch Cl. Broa .......... 187 F1
Chaffinch Cl. Tot ........... 100 B4
Chaffinch Green. Wat ........ 111 F2
Chaffinch Way. Lo S ......... 179 F4
Chaffinch Way. Portc ........ 155 F4
Chalbury Cl. Poole .......... 189 D1
Chaldecott Gdns. Bour ....... 190 B2
Chaldon Rd. Southa .......... 188 C1
Chale Cl. Gos ............... 155 E1
Chalewood Rd. Black ......... 177 F4
Chalfont Ave. Christ ........ 192 B2
Chalfont Ct. Southa ......... 78 A1
Chalice Cl. Poole ........... 205 D2
Chalice Ct. He En ........... 105 D3
Chalk Cl. Red ............... 47 E4
Chalk Hill Rd. Horn ......... 112 B4
Chalk Hill. Sob ............. 85 E3
Chalk Hill. W End ........... 80 B1
Chalk La. Fare .............. 131 D4
Chalk Ridge. Horn ........... 88 B2
Chalkpit Rd. Cos ............ 133 D1
Chalkridge Rd. Cos .......... 134 A1
Challenger Way. Hyt ......... 125 E1
Challis Ct. Southa .......... 103 D2
Chalmers Way. Hamble ........ 127 F2
Chaloner Cres. Hyt .......... 126 A1
Chalton Cres. Hav ........... 135 E2
Chalton La. Clanf ........... 88 B3
Chalvington Rd. Ch Fo ....... 55 E2
Chalybeate Cl. Southa ....... 78 A1
Chamberlain Gr. Fare ........ 155 D4
Chamberlain Rd. Southa ...... 79 D2
Chamberlayne Rd. Burs ....... 127 F4
Chamberlayne Rd. Eastl ...... 56 A1
Chamberlayne Rd. Net ........ 127 E2
Chambers Ave. Rom ........... 53 D4
Chancel Rd. Lo He ........... 129 D2
Chancellors Lane. Durl ...... 81 F2
Chander Cl. Fern ............ 165 F2
Chandlers Cl. Bour .......... 208 A4

Chandlers Cl. S Hay ......... 185 E1
Chandlers Way. Swanw ........ 129 D3
Chandos Ave. Poole .......... 206 A4
Chandos St. Southa .......... 103 D2
Channel Way. Southa ......... 103 E2
Channels Farm Rd. Southa .... 79 E3
Chantrell Wlk. Fare ......... 130 B2
Chantry Cl. Christ .......... 194 C1
Chantry Rd. Gosp ............ 181 D4
Chantry Rd. Horn ............ 112 A4
Chantry Rd. Southa .......... 103 D2
Chantry The. Lo He .......... 129 E2
Chapel Cl. Broa ............. 187 E3
Chapel Cres. Southa ......... 104 A2
Chapel Dro. Fa Oa ........... 81 E4
Chapel Dro. He En ........... 105 D3
Chapel La. Black ............ 151 D1
Chapel La. Black ............ 177 F4
Chapel La. Bran ............. 194 A4
Chapel La. Broa ............. 187 E3
Chapel La. Bur .............. 143 D2
Chapel La. Curd ............. 106 C4
Chapel La. E Bol ............ 175 E3
Chapel La. Locke ............ 26 A3
Chapel La. Lyn .............. 121 F3
Chapel La. Mich ............. 27 E4
Chapel La. Ott .............. 31 D1
Chapel La. Poole ............ 204 B1
Chapel La. Red .............. 47 F3
Chapel La. Red .............. 73 E4
Chapel La. Sway ............. 172 B1
Chapel La. Tot .............. 100 C3
Chapel La. Wat .............. 134 C4
Chapel La. Wi Mi ............ 163 D3
Chapel Rd. Lo He ............ 128 C3
Chapel Rd. Poole ............ 205 D2
Chapel Rd. Sob .............. 85 D1
Chapel Rd. Southa ........... 103 D2
Chapel Rd. Swan ............. 84 A3
Chapel Rd. W End ............ 80 C1
Chapel Rise. St Le .......... 140 B1
Chapel St. E Meo ............ 38 B1
Chapel St. Gosp ............. 181 D4
Chapel St. Pet .............. 40 C2
Chapel St. Ports ............ 182 A2
Chapel St. Ports ............ 182 C4
Chapel St. Southa ........... 103 D2
Chapelside. Lo He ........... 154 A4
Chaplains Ave. Wat .......... 111 E2
Chaplains Cl. Wat ........... 111 E2
Charborough Rd. Broa ........ 188 A2
Charden Rd. Bish ............ 57 D1
Charden Rd. Gos ............. 180 B4
Charfield Cl. Fare .......... 154 B4
Charfield Cl. Winch ......... 10 C3
Chark La. L on S ............ 179 F4
Charlcot Lawn. Hav .......... 135 E3
Charlecote Dr. Ch Fo ........ 55 D4
Charlemont Dr. Portc ........ 131 E1
Charles Cl. Wat ............. 134 B3
Charles Cl. Winch ........... 2 A1
Charles Cres. New M ......... 196 A3
Charles Dickens St. Ports ... 182 B3
Charles Gdns. Bour .......... 190 B1
Charles Keightley Ct. Wi Mi . 163 E2
Charles Knott Gdns. Southa . 102 C4
Charles Ley Ct. Faw ......... 151 D2
Charles Rd. Christ .......... 209 F4
Charles Rd. Poole ........... 204 B2
Charles St. Pet ............. 40 C2
Charles St. Ports ........... 182 B3
Charles St. Southa .......... 103 D3
Charles Watts Way. He En .... 105 D4
Charlesbury Ave. Gos ........ 180 C2
Charleston Cl. S Hay ........ 184 C2
Charleston Rd. Faw .......... 150 B4
Charlesworth Dr. Wat ........ 111 E1
Charlesworth Gdns. Wat ...... 111 E1
Charlotte Cl. Christ ........ 210 A3
Charlotte Cl. Poole ......... 206 B4
Charlotte Pl. Southa ........ 103 D3
Charlotte St. Ports ......... 182 B3
Charlton Cl. Bour ........... 191 E2
Charlton Cl. Hord ........... 196 C2
Charlton Rd. Southa ......... 102 B4
Charminster Ave. Bour ....... 191 D1
Charminster Cl. Bour ........ 191 D1
Charminster Cl. Wat ......... 134 C4
Charminster Pl. Bour ........ 191 E1
Charminster Rd. Bour ........ 207 D4
Charmouth Gr. Poole ......... 205 D2
Charmouth Terr. Southa ...... 76 A1
Charmus Rd. Tot ............. 76 A1
Charmwen Cres. W End ........ 80 B1
Charnock Rd. Hord ........... 196 C2
Charnwood Ave. Bour ......... 191 D2
Charnwood Cl. Ch Fo ......... 30 B1
Charnwood Cl. Tot ........... 100 B4
Charnwood Cl. W Moo ......... 138 C1
Charnwood Cres. Ch Fo ....... 30 B1
Charnwood Dr. Fordi ......... 69 F2
Charnwood Gdns. Ch Fo ....... 30 B1
Charnwood Way. Black ........ 177 F4
Charnwood. Gos .............. 155 F1
Charter Rd. Bour ............ 189 E3
Charterhouse Way. He En ..... 81 E1
Chartwell Cl. Eastl ......... 56 A1
Chartwell Cl. Lo He ......... 129 E1
Chartwell Dr. Hav ........... 136 B2

Chase Cl. Liss .............. 21 D2
Chase Farm Cl. Shed ......... 83 F2
Chase Gr. Shed .............. 83 F2
Chase Rd. Liss .............. 21 D2
Chase The. Gos .............. 180 C2
Chase The. Lo He ............ 129 E1
Chase The. St Le ............ 140 B3
Chase The. Ver .............. 115 E3
Chaseside. Bour ............. 208 A4
Chasewater Ave. Ports ....... 183 D4
Chatburn Ave. Wat ........... 111 F2
Chatfield Rd. Gos ........... 155 E2
Chatham Dr. Ports ........... 182 A2
Chatham Rd. Winch ........... 10 B3
Chatsworth Ave. Cos ......... 158 A3
Chatsworth Cl. Fare ......... 130 B1
Chatsworth Rd. Bour ......... 207 E3
Chatsworth Rd. Eastl ........ 56 A3
Chatsworth Rd. Poole ........ 205 D3
Chatsworth Rd. Southa ....... 104 A3
Chatsworth Way. New M ....... 195 F2
Chaucer Ave. Portc .......... 132 C1
Chaucer Cl. Fare ............ 130 C1
Chaucer Cl. Wat ............. 111 F1
Chaucer Cl. Wi Mi ........... 163 E3
Chaucer Dr. M on S .......... 213 E3
Chaucer Rd. Poole ........... 216 C4
Chaucer Rd. Southa .......... 104 B3
Chaundler Rd. Winch ......... 2 A1
Chaveney Cl. Hyt ............ 125 F1
Chawton Cl. Southa .......... 104 B4
Chawton Cl. Winch ........... 1 B2
Cheam Rd. Broa .............. 187 F2
Cheam Way. Tot .............. 76 B1
Cheater's Farm La. Alderh ... 92 B4
Cheddar Cl. Southa .......... 103 F2
Cheddington Rd. Bour ........ 191 D1
Chedington Cl. Broa ......... 188 C1
Chedworth Cres. Cos ......... 133 D1
Chelmsford Rd. Ports ........ 157 F1
Chelmsford Rd. Upt .......... 203 D3
Chelsea Rd. Ports ........... 182 B2
Cheltenham Cres. L on S ..... 179 F4
Cheltenham Rd. Cos .......... 157 E4
Cheltenham Rd. Poole ........ 205 E3
Chene Rd. Wi Mi ............. 163 E2
Cheping Gdns. Botl .......... 106 A3
Chepstow Cl. N Bad .......... 55 D3
Chepstow Cl. Tot ............ 100 B4
Chepstow Court. Wat ......... 111 F1
Chequers Cl. Lym ............ 198 B2
Cherbourg Rd. Eastl ......... 56 A1
Cherford Rd. Bour ........... 190 A1
Cherita Ct. Poole ........... 204 C3
Cheriton Ave. Bour .......... 208 B4
Cheriton Ave. Southa ........ 104 B4
Cheriton Cl. Hav ............ 135 F2
Cheriton Cl. Winch .......... 1 B1
Cheriton Rd. Eastl .......... 55 F1
Cheriton Rd. Gos ............ 180 C2
Cheriton Rd. Winch .......... 10 C4
Cheriton Way. Wi Mi ......... 163 E2
Cherque La. Stubb ........... 180 A4
Cherries Dr. Bour ........... 190 C1
Cherry Cl. Poole ............ 205 D2
Cherry Cl. L on S ........... 180 A3
Cherry Drove. Fa Oa ......... 81 E3
Cherry Gr. Fern ............. 165 E3
Cherry Hill Gr. Upt ......... 203 D3
Cherry Hill Rd. Upt ......... 203 D3
Cherry Tree Ave. Fare ....... 154 B4
Cherry Tree Ave. Wat ........ 112 A4
Cherry Tree Cl. Hord ........ 213 E4
Cherry Tree Cl. St Le ....... 139 E2
Cherry Wlk. Southa .......... 102 B4
Cherrygarth Rd. Fare ........ 130 B1
Cherryton Gdns. Holb ........ 150 A2
Cherrywood Gdns. S Hay ...... 185 D2
Cherrywood Gdns. Tot ........ 100 B4
Chervil Cl. Horn ............ 88 B1
Cherville St. Rom ........... 52 C4
Cherwell Cres. Southa ....... 101 F4
Cherwell Gdns. Ch Fo ........ 55 E3
Cheshire Dr. Bour ........... 192 A1
Cheshire Way. Southb ........ 137 F1
Chesil St. Winch ............ 11 D4
Chesildene Ave. Bour ........ 191 E2
Chesildene Dr. Bour ......... 191 E2
Cheslyn Rd. Ports ........... 183 D3
Chessel Ave. Bour ........... 207 F2
Chessel Ave. Southa ......... 103 F3
Chessel Cres. Southa ........ 103 F4
Chester Cres. L on S ........ 180 A2
Chester Pl. Ports ........... 182 B1
Chester Rd. Poole ........... 206 A1
Chester Rd. Southa .......... 80 A1
Chester Rd. Winch ........... 11 D4
Chesterfield Cl. Poole ...... 216 C4
Chesterfield Rd. Ports ...... 183 D3
Chesterton Gdns. Wat ........ 111 F2
Chestnut Ave. Ashu .......... 100 B2
Chestnut Ave. B on S ........ 212 A4
Chestnut Ave. Bour .......... 208 B2
Chestnut Ave. Ch Fo ......... 55 E1
Chestnut Ave. Christ ........ 208 B4
Chestnut Ave. Eastl ......... 55 E1
Chestnut Ave. Hav ........... 135 D2
Chestnut Ave. Litt .......... 1 A2

Chestnut Ave. Ports ......... 182 C2
Chestnut Ave. Wat ........... 112 B3
Chestnut Cl. Ch Fo .......... 55 E2
Chestnut Cl. Den ............ 110 C2
Chestnut Cl. Rom ............ 53 E3
Chestnut Gr. Fern ........... 164 C3
Chestnut Rd. Brock .......... 146 A1
Chestnut Rd. Southa ......... 78 A1
Chestnut Rise. Drox ......... 61 D1
Chestnut Rise. Eastl ........ 55 E1
Chestnut Way. Burt .......... 193 E2
Chestnut Way. Lo He ......... 129 E1
Chestnut Wlk. Botl .......... 105 F4
Chetnole Cl. Poole .......... 189 D1
Chettle Rd. Southa .......... 104 C3
Chetwode Way. Broa .......... 188 A1
Chetwynd Dr. Southa ......... 78 C2
Chetwynd Rd. Ports .......... 182 C2
Chetwynd Rd. Southa ......... 78 C3
Cheviot Cres. Southa ........ 101 F4
Cheviot Dr. Hyt ............. 125 E2
Cheviot Rd. Southa .......... 101 F4
Cheviot Way. Ver ............ 114 C3
Cheviot Wlk. Fare ........... 154 C4
Chewton Common Rd. Christ ... 211 D4
Chewton Farm Rd. Christ ..... 195 E1
Chewton Lodge. Christ ....... 211 D4
Chewton Way. Christ ......... 195 D1
Cheyne Gdns. Bour ........... 206 B1
Cheyne Way. L on S .......... 179 F3
Chichester Ave. S Hay ....... 185 D2
Chichester Cl. Gos .......... 155 D1
Chichester Cl. He En ........ 81 E1
Chichester Cl. Lo He ........ 128 C2
Chichester Cl. W Wel ........ 51 D1
Chichester Rd. N Hay ........ 160 B3
Chichester Rd. Ports ........ 182 C4
Chichester Rd. Rin .......... 117 E1
Chichester Rd. Southa ....... 104 A4
Chichester Wlk. Oakl ........ 163 F1
Chicken Hall La. Eastl ...... 56 B1
Chickerell Cl. Bour ......... 191 D2
Chidden Cl. E Meo ........... 38 B1
Chidden Holt. N Bad ......... 55 D3
Chideock Cl. Poole .......... 205 F3
Chideock Ct. Poole .......... 205 F3
Chidham Cl. Hav ............. 135 F1
Chidham Dr. Hav ............. 135 F1
Chidham Rd. Cos ............. 134 A1
Chidham Sq. Hav ............. 135 F1
Chigwell Rd. Bour ........... 191 D1
Chilbolton Ave. Winch ....... 10 B4
Chilcomb Cl. L on S ......... 179 F3
Chilcomb La. Chilc .......... 11 F3
Chilcomb La. Winch .......... 11 E3
Chilcomb Rd. Southa ......... 104 B4
Chilcombe Cl. Hav ........... 135 F2
Chilcombe Rd. Bour .......... 208 A3
Chilcote Rd. Ports .......... 157 D4
Childe Sq. Ports ............ 157 E1
Chilgrove Rd. Cos ........... 158 B4
Chilham Cl. Eastl ........... 56 A4
Chillenden Ct. Tot .......... 100 B3
Chillerton. Net ............. 127 E4
Chillington Gdns. Ch Fo ..... 30 A1
Chilsdown Way. Wat .......... 134 C2
Chiltern Cl. B on S ......... 195 F1
Chiltern Cl. Poole .......... 206 A3
Chiltern Cl. Tot ............ 100 B3
Chiltern Dr. B on S ......... 211 F4
Chiltern Dr. Ver ............ 114 C3
Chiltern Green. Southa ...... 101 F4
Chiltern Wlk. Fare .......... 154 C4
Chilworth Cl. Chilw ......... 54 B1
Chilworth Gdns. Clanf ....... 88 B2
Chilworth Gr. Gos ........... 181 D3
Chilworth Rd. Chilw ......... 54 C1
Chine Ave. Southa ........... 103 F3
Chine Cl. Lo He ............. 129 D2
Chine Cres Rd. Bour ......... 206 B1
Chine Cres. Bour ............ 206 B1
Chine The. Gos .............. 155 F1
Chine Wlk. Fern ............. 165 F1
Chinham Rd. Ne Ma ........... 99 E3
Chipstead Rd. Cos ........... 157 F4
Chisels La. Bran ............ 194 A3
Chisholm Cl. Southa ......... 77 F3
Chitty Rd. Ports ............ 183 D1
Chivers Cl. Ports ........... 182 B2
Christchurch Bay Rd. B on S . 211 F4
Christchurch By Pass. Christ  209 E4
Christchurch Gdns. Wat ...... 134 A1
Christchurch Gdns. Winch .... 10 C3
Christchurch Rd. B on S ..... 211 E4
Christchurch Rd. Bour ....... 207 E2
Christchurch Rd. Fern ....... 165 E1
Christchurch Rd. Hord ....... 213 E4
Christchurch Rd. Hurn ....... 192 A3
Christchurch Rd. Rin ........ 141 D2
Christchurch Rd. Winch ...... 10 C3
Christopher Cres. Poole ..... 204 B3
Christopher Way. Ems ........ 136 C1
Church Cl. Bish ............. 56 B2
Church Cl. Clanf ............ 88 A3
Church Cl. Lo He ............ 129 D2
Church Cl. Min .............. 98 B1
Church Cl. N Bad ............ 54 A2
Church End. Southa .......... 102 B4

Church Farm Cl. Hyt .............. 125 D3
Church Hatch. Down .............. 47 D4
Church Hill. M on S ............... 213 F2
Church Hill. Red ..................... 47 F3
Church Hill. Ver ..................... 114 C3
Church Hill. W End ................. 80 B1
Church La. Awb ....................... 26 B2
Church La. Bold ..................... 173 F1
Church La. Botl ...................... 106 A3
Church La. Brai ....................... 28 B4
Church La. Bramd ................... 15 E2
Church La. Brock ................... 173 D4
Church La. Bur ...................... 143 D2
Church La. Burs .................... 128 A4
Church La. Christ .................. 209 D3
Church La. Co Com ................ 56 C4
Church La. Dame ..................... 68 B2
Church La. Durl ....................... 81 E3
Church La. E Bol ................... 175 E3
Church La. Faw ..................... 151 D2
Church La. Fern ..................... 190 C4
Church La. Frox G ................... 17 E2
Church La. Hambl .................... 86 B2
Church La. Hav ..................... 160 A4
Church La. He En .................. 105 D3
Church La. It Ab ........................ 2 C3
Church La. Ki Wo ...................... 2 B3
Church La. Litt .......................... 1 A3
Church La. Lym .................... 198 C2
Church La. Lyn ..................... 121 F3
Church La. N Hay .................. 160 B2
Church La. New M ................ 195 F1
Church La. Nur ....................... 76 C3
Church La. Plai ....................... 50 A3
Church La. Rom ....................... 52 C4
Church La. Rom ....................... 54 D4
Church La. Sh En .................... 25 E2
Church La. Southa ................... 79 D1
Church La. Southa ................. 102 C2
Church La. Swan ..................... 84 B3
Church La. Sway ................... 172 A1
Church La. Twyf ...................... 32 A4
Church La. W Meo ................... 37 E3
Church Mead. Lym ................ 198 C1
Church Path. Ems ................. 160 C4
Church Path. Fare ................. 131 E1
Church Path. Gos .................. 181 E2
Church Path. Horn ................. 112 B3
Church Path. Lo He ............... 154 A4
Church Pl. Rom ....................... 52 C4
Church Rd. Bish ...................... 56 B3
Church Rd. Bour ................... 208 C2
Church Rd. Fern ................... 165 E3
Church Rd. Gos ..................... 181 D1
Church Rd. Liss ...................... 20 C3
Church Rd. Lo He .................. 129 D2
Church Rd. Lo He .................. 152 B4
Church Rd. Miche ...................... 6 B1
Church Rd. Poole .................. 205 D2
Church Rd. Ports .................. 182 B3
Church Rd. Rom ...................... 52 C4
Church Rd. S Hay .................. 185 D3
Church Rd. Shed ................... 107 F4
Church Rd. Sob ..................... 109 E3
Church Rd. Southa ................ 103 E1
Church Rd. Southb ................ 161 F4
Church Rd. Steep .................... 40 C4
Church Rd. Swan ..................... 84 A3
Church Rd. Th Is ................... 161 E1
Church Rd. W Moo ................ 114 C1
Church Rd. Westb ................. 137 D2
Church St. Christ .................. 209 D3
Church St. E Meo .................... 38 C1
Church St. Fordi ...................... 93 F4
Church St. Lo He ................... 154 A4
Church St. Poole ................... 204 A1
Church St. Ports ................... 182 B3
Church St. Rom ....................... 52 C4
Church St. Southa ................... 78 B1
Church St. Uph ........................ 58 C3
Church View Cl. Southa ......... 104 A2
Church View. Ports ............... 183 D3
Church View. Shed ................ 107 F4
Church View. Westb .............. 137 D2
Church Wlk. Red ..................... 48 A3
Churcher Cl. Gos .................. 180 B2
Churcher Rd. Westb .............. 137 D2
Churcher Wlk. Gos ................ 180 B2
Churchfield Cres. Poole ........ 204 C2
Churchfield La. Ibs .................. 93 F1
Churchfield Rd. Pet ................. 41 D2
Churchfield Rd. Poole ........... 204 C2
Churchfield. Ver .................... 114 C3
Churchfields Rd. Twyf ............ 32 A3
Churchfields. Faw ................. 151 D2
Churchill Ave. Bi Wa ............... 59 D1
Churchill Cl. Alderh ................. 92 C3
Churchill Cl. Lo He ................ 129 E1
Churchill Cres. Poole ............ 205 E3
Churchill Ct. Wat .................. 112 A3
Churchill Dr. Ems .................. 136 C2
Churchill Gdns. Poole ........... 205 E3
Churchill Rd. Bour ................. 207 E3
Churchill Rd. Poole ............... 205 E3
Churchill Rd. Wi Mi ............... 163 F2
Churchmoor Rd. Wi Mi .......... 164 A3
Cinderford Cl. Cos ................ 133 E1
Cinnamon La. Poole .............. 204 A1

Circle The. Bour .................... 191 D2
Circle The. Ports .................. 182 B1
Circle The. Wickh ................. 108 A2
Cirrus Gdns. Hamble ............ 127 F1
Citrine Rd. Hamw ................. 204 A1
City Ind Park. Southa ............ 102 C2
City Rd. Winch ......................... 10 C4
Civic Centre Rd. Hav ............ 135 F1
Civic Centre Rd. Southa ....... 102 C3
Civic Way. Fare .................... 131 E1
Clacton Rd. Cos ................... 157 E4
Claire Gdns. Horn ................... 88 B1
Clamp Green. Co Com ............ 56 C4
Clandon Dr. Eastl .................... 55 F3
Clanfield Cl. Ch Fo .................. 55 E3
Clanfield Dr. Ch Fo .................. 55 E3
Clanfield Rd. Southa .............. 104 B4
Clanfield Way. Ch Fo ............... 55 E3
Clanwilliam Rd. L on S .......... 179 F3
Clare Cl. Lo He ..................... 129 E1
Clare Gdns. Black ................. 177 F4
Clare Gdns. Pet ...................... 41 E2
Clare Lodge Cl. Bran ............. 169 D1
Claremont Ave. Bour ............ 191 D1
Claremont Cl. Eastl ................. 56 A3
Claremont Cres. Southa ........ 102 A4
Claremont Rd. Bour .............. 191 D1
Claremont Rd. Ports ............. 182 C3
Claremont Rd. Southa ........... 102 A4
Clarence Espl. Ports ............. 182 B1
Clarence Par. Ports .............. 182 B1
Clarence Park Rd. Bour ........ 208 A3
Clarence Rd. Gos .................. 181 E3
Clarence Rd. Lyn .................. 121 F3
Clarence Rd. Poole ............... 205 D2
Clarence Rd. Ports ............... 182 B1
Clarendon Cl. Broa ............... 188 A2
Clarendon Cl. Rom .................. 28 A1
Clarendon Cres. Lo He .......... 129 E1
Clarendon Park. Lym ............ 198 B1
Clarendon Pl. Ports .............. 182 B3
Clarendon Rd. Bour .............. 206 B2
Clarendon Rd. Broa .............. 187 F2
Clarendon Rd. Christ ............ 209 D4
Clarendon Rd. Hav ............... 135 F1
Clarendon Rd. Ports ............. 182 B1
Clarendon Rd. Southa ........... 102 A4
Clarendon St. Ports .............. 182 B3
Clark's Rd. Rin ..................... 141 D4
Clarke's Rd. Ports ................ 182 C3
Claude Ashby Cl. Southa ........ 79 F2
Claudeen Cl. Southa ............... 79 F3
Claudia Ct. Gos .................... 180 C3
Claudius Cl. Ch Fo .................. 55 F4
Claudius Gdns. Ch Fo ............. 55 F4
Clausen Way. Lym ................ 198 B1
Clausentum Cl. Fo ................... 55 F4
Clausentum Rd. Southa ......... 103 D4
Clausentum Rd. Winch ............ 10 C3
Clave Cl. L on S .................... 179 F3
Claxton St. Ports .................. 182 B3
Clay Hill. Lyn ........................ 122 A2
Clay St. Whit .......................... 24 A2
Claybank Rd. Ports ............... 158 A1
Claybank Rd. Ports ............... 158 A1
Claydon Ave. Ports ............... 183 D2
Clayford Ave. Fern ................ 165 D4
Clayford Cl. Broa .................. 188 B1
Clayhall Rd. Gos ................... 181 D1
Claylake Dr. Ver .................... 115 D3
Claylands Ct. Curd .................. 83 D4
Claylands Rd. Bi Wa ............... 83 D4
Claypits La. Hyt .................... 125 E2
Claypitt La. Frox G .................. 18 B3
Cleasby Cl. Southa ................ 101 F4
Clease Way. Comp ................... 31 E4
Clee Ave. Fare ....................... 154 B4
Cleethorpes Rd. Southa ........ 104 A2
Cleeve Cl. Cos ...................... 133 D1
Cleeves Cl. Poole .................. 189 E1
Cleeves The. Tot ................... 100 B3
Clegg Rd. Ports .................... 183 D2
Clement Mews. Bour ............. 206 A2
Cleric Ct. Lo He .................... 129 E2
Cleveland Cl. B on S ............. 211 E4
Cleveland Ct. Southa ............... 80 A1
Cleveland Dr. Fare ................ 154 B4
Cleveland Dr. Hyt .................. 125 E2
Cleveland Gdns. Bour ........... 207 E3
Cleveland Rd. Bour ............... 207 E3
Cleveland Rd. Gos ................ 181 D2
Cleveland Rd. Ports .............. 182 C2
Cleveland Rd. Southa .............. 79 F1
Clevelands Cl. Ch Fo ............... 30 A1
Clewers Hill. Shed ................... 83 E2
Clewers La. Shed .................... 83 F2
Cliff Cres. B on S .................. 211 F4
Cliff Dr. Christ ...................... 210 B3
Cliff Dr. Poole ...................... 216 C3
Cliff Rd. M on S .................... 213 D2
Cliff Rd. Southa .................... 102 B3
Cliff Rd. Stubb ..................... 153 F1
Cliff Terr. B on S .................. 211 F3
Cliff Way. Comp ..................... 31 E4
Cliffe Ave. Hamble ................ 127 F2
Cliffe Rd. B on S ................... 211 F4
Clifford Dibben Mews. Southa 103 D4
Clifford Pl. Fa Oa ................... 57 E1

Clifford Rd. Bour .................. 191 D1
Clifford St. Southa ................ 103 D3
Clifton Cres. Den .................. 111 D2
Clifton Gdns. Fern ................ 165 E2
Clifton Gdns. W End ................ 80 B1
Clifton Hill. Winch ................... 10 C4
Clifton Rd. Bour ................... 208 B2
Clifton Rd. Lon S .................. 180 A2
Clifton Rd. Poole .................. 205 F1
Clifton Rd. Ports .................. 182 B1
Clifton Rd. Southa ................ 102 A4
Clifton Rd. Winch ................... 10 C4
Clifton St. Gos ..................... 180 C3
Clifton St. Ports ................... 182 C3
Clifton Terr. Ports ................ 182 B1
Clifton Terr. Winch .................. 10 C4
Clinghan Rd. Bour ................ 208 B4
Clinton St. Christ .................. 195 D1
Clinton Rd. Lym .................... 198 C3
Clinton Rd. Wat .................... 111 E1
Clive Gr. Portc ...................... 156 B4
Clive Rd. Bour ...................... 190 C1
Clive Rd. Christ .................... 194 C1
Clive Rd. Ports ..................... 182 C3
Cliveden Cl. Fern .................. 165 E4
Clock St. Ports ..................... 182 A3
Cloisters The. Fare ............... 130 B1
Cloisters The. Southa .............. 79 D2
Close Bellfield The. Lo He ..... 153 F4
Close. B on S ....................... 212 A4
Close The. Broa .................... 187 F2
Close The. Cos ..................... 158 A4
Close The. Fordi ..................... 94 B4
Close The. Hamble ................ 128 A2
Close The. He En .................. 105 D3
Close The. Holb ..................... 150 B2
Close The. Langr ..................... 39 E2
Close The. Portc ................... 156 B4
Close The. Red ....................... 47 E4
Close The. Rin ...................... 140 C4
Close The. Southa ................. 104 B4
Close The. St Le .................... 140 A2
Close The. St Le .................... 140 B2
Close,The. Sway ................... 172 A1
Closewood Rd. Den ............... 111 F1
Clough La. Bur ...................... 142 C2
Clough's Rd. Rin ................... 141 D4
Clovelly Rd. Ems .................. 160 C4
Clovelly Rd. N Hay ................ 160 B2
Clovelly Rd. Ports ................. 183 D2
Clovelly Rd. Southa .............. 103 D3
Clovelly Rd. Southb .............. 137 E1
Clover Cl. Christ .................... 210 A4
Clover Cl. Gos ...................... 155 E2
Clover Cl. Lo He .................... 128 C1
Clover Ct. New M .................. 196 B2
Clover Cl. Wat ...................... 135 D3
Clover Dr. Broa ..................... 187 F1
Clover Way. He En ................ 105 D3
Clover Way. Rom .................... 53 E4
Clovers The. Poole ................ 206 A4
Clowes Ave. Bour ................. 209 D2
Club House La. Shed ............... 83 F2
Clump Hill. Ver ..................... 114 A1
Clyde Ct. Gos ....................... 180 C3
Clyde Rd. Broa ..................... 188 A1
Clyde Rd. Gos ...................... 180 C3
Clydebank Rd. Ports ............. 182 B4
Clydesdale Rd. Swanw .......... 129 D4
Clydesdale Way. Tot ............. 100 A4
Coach Hill Cl. Ch Fo ................ 55 D4
Coach Hill La. Bur ................. 142 C3
Coach Hill. Lo He .................. 153 F4
Coach House Pl. Bour ........... 207 D3
Coach Rd. Hamble ................ 127 F2
Coachmans Copse. Southa ...... 80 A1
Coal Park La. Swanw ............ 128 B4
Coalville Rd. Southa .............. 104 A2
Coastguard Cl. Gos ............... 180 C1
Coastguard La. S Wit ............ 186 C1
Coastguard Way. Christ ........ 209 F3
Coates Rd. Southa ................ 104 B2
Coates Way. Wat ................... 134 C3
Cobb's Rd. Wi Mi .................. 163 F3
Cobbett Cl. Winch ................... 10 B3
Cobbett Rd. Southa .............. 103 F4
Cobbett Way. Botl ................ 105 F4
Cobbs La. Poole ................... 204 C3
Cobden Ave. Ports ................ 183 D4
Cobden Ave. Southa .............. 103 F4
Cobden Cres. Southa ............ 103 F4
Cobden Cl. Southa ................ 103 F4
Cobden Gdns. Southa .............. 79 F1
Cobden St. Gos ..................... 181 D3
Cobham Rd. Bour .................. 191 D2
Cobham Rd. Fern .................. 165 D4
Cobham Way. Oakl ............... 163 F1
Coblands Ave. Tot ................ 100 B4
Coburg St. Ports ................... 182 B3
Coburg St. Southa ................ 103 E3
Cockerell Cl. Oakl ................. 163 F1
Cockleshell Gdns. Ports ....... 183 E2
Cocklydown La. Tot ............... 100 B3
Cockshott La. Frox G .............. 19 E1
Cogdean Cl. Broa .................. 187 F4
Cogdean Way. Broa .............. 187 F4
Cogdean Wlk. Broa ............... 187 F4
Cogdeane Rd. Broa ............... 188 B1
Coker Cl. Winch ...................... 10 C4

Colborne Ave. Wi Mi ............ 163 F3
Colborne Cl. Lym .................. 198 C3
Colbourne Cl. Bran ............... 194 A4
Colbourne Cl. Poole .............. 204 B1
Colburn Cl. Southa .................. 77 E1
Colbury Gr. Hav .................... 135 E3
Colchester Rd. Bish ................ 56 C2
Colchester Rd. Cos ............... 133 F1
Cold East Cl. Lo He ............... 128 C3
Coldeast Way. Lo He ............. 128 C3
Coldharbour La. Nur ................ 77 D4
Coldhill La. Horn ................... 111 F4
Coldhill La. Wi Mi .................. 163 F4
Cole Hill. Sob ......................... 85 E3
Cole's La. Red ........................ 48 C2
Colebrook Ave. Ports ............ 183 D4
Colebrook Ave. Southa ............ 78 B1
Colebrook Pl. Winch ................ 11 D4
Colebrook St. Winch ................ 11 D4
Colehill Cres. Bour ............... 191 D2
Colehill La. Wi Mi .................. 163 F4
Coleman Rd. Bour ................. 190 A2
Coleman St. Southa ............... 103 D2
Colemore Rd. Bour ............... 208 B4
Colemore Sq. Hav ................. 135 F2
Colenso Rd. Fare .................. 131 D1
Coleridge Cl. Lo He ............... 128 B1
Coleridge Ct. Southa ............. 104 B3
Coleridge Gdns. Wat ............. 111 F2
Coleridge Green. Christ ........ 209 F4
Coleridge Rd. Portc .............. 132 C1
Coles Ave. Hamw .................. 203 F1
Coles Cl. Twyf ........................ 32 A4
Coles Gdns. Hamw ............... 203 F1
Colesbourne Rd. Cos ............ 133 D1
Coleson Rd. Southa ............... 103 F4
Coleville Ave. Faw ................ 151 D2
Colin Cl. Broa ....................... 187 E3
Colinton Ave. Portc ............... 132 B1
Coll Ave. Poole ..................... 205 D1
College Cl. Hamble ............... 127 F1
College Cl. Ro Ca .................. 113 E1
College La. Ports .................. 182 A3
College Pl. Southa ................ 103 D3
College Rd. Bour .................. 208 A2
College Rd. Rin .................... 141 D4
College Rd. Southa ............... 103 F1
College Rd. Wat .................... 134 C1
College St. Pet ....................... 40 C2
College St. Ports .................. 182 A3
College St. Southa ................ 103 D2
College St. Winch ................... 11 D4
College Wlk. Winch .................. 11 D3
Colley Cl. Winch ....................... 2 A2
Collier Cl. Southa .................. 103 E4
Collingbourne Ave. Bour ....... 208 B3
Collingbourne Dr. N Bad ......... 55 D3
Collingwood Rd. Ports .......... 182 B1
Collins La. Rin ...................... 141 D4
Collins La. S Har .................... 66 C4
Collins Rd. Ports .................. 183 D1
Collins' La. Hurs .................... 30 B4
Collis Rd. Ports .................... 183 D4
Collwood Cl. Poole ............... 204 B4
Collyers Rd. Brock ................ 172 C4
Colne Ave. Southa ................... 77 E1
Colonnade Rd. Bour .............. 208 A3
Colpoy St. Ports ................... 182 A2
Colson Cl. Winch ..................... 11 D4
Colson Rd. Winch .................... 11 D4
Colt Cl. Southa ....................... 77 F3
Colt Cl. Wi Mi ....................... 164 A3
Colts Rd. Rown ....................... 77 F4
Coltsfoot Cl. He En ............... 105 D4
Coltsfoot Dr. Lo He ............... 128 C1
Coltsfoot Dr. Wat .................. 134 C3
Coltsfoot Wlk. Rom ................ 28 B1
Coltsmead. Portc .................. 156 C4
Columbia Rd. Bour ............... 190 B1
Columbia Trees La. Bour ...... 190 B1
Columbian Way. Bour ........... 190 B1
Colvedene Cl. Comp ............... 31 F1
Colville Cl. Bour ................... 208 A3
Colville Dr. Bi Wa ................... 83 E4
Colville Rd. Bour .................. 208 A3
Colville Rd. Cos ................... 158 A4
Colwell Cl. Southa ................ 101 E4
Colwell Rd. Cos .................... 157 F4
Combe Rd. Hill B ..................... 21 D1
Comber Rd. Bour .................. 191 D2
Comet Way. Christ ................ 210 A3
Comfrey Cl. Horn .................... 88 B1
Comfrey Cl. Rom ..................... 28 B1
Comley Hill. Ro Ca ................ 136 B3
Comley Rd. Bour .................. 190 C1
Commercial Pl. Ports ............ 182 B3
Commercial Rd. Bour ........... 206 C2
Commercial Rd. Poole ........... 205 D2
Commercial Rd. Ports ........... 182 B3
Commercial Rd. Southa ........ 102 C3
Commercial Rd. Tot .............. 101 D4
Commercial St. Southa ......... 104 A4
Common Barn La. L on S ...... 179 F4
Common Cl. Ch Fo .................. 55 E4
Common Gdns. Ch Fo ............. 55 E4
Common Hill Rd. Brai .............. 28 B3
Common La. Lo He ............... 153 F4
Common La. Southw ............. 132 C4
Common Rd. Ch Fo ................. 55 E4

Common Rd. Westb ............... 137 F3
Common Rd. Whit .................... 24 A1
Common St. Ports .................. 182 B3
Commonside. Westb ............... 137 D3
Compass Point. Fare ............. 155 D4
Compton Ave. Poole .............. 205 E1
Compton Beeches. St Le ....... 140 A3
Compton Cl. Eastl .................... 55 F3
Compton Cl. Hav ................... 135 F2
Compton Cl. L on S ............... 179 F3
Compton Cl. Winch .................. 10 A2
Compton Cres. W Moo ........... 139 D1
Compton Dr. Poole ................ 205 E1
Compton Gdns. Poole ........... 205 E1
Compton Rd. New M ............. 196 A1
Compton Rd. Ports ............... 157 F2
Compton Rd. Tot .................. 101 D4
Compton Rd. Winch ................ 10 C4
Compton St. Comp ................. 31 E4
Compton Way. Winch .............. 10 A2
Compton Wlk. Southa ............ 103 D3
Compton's Dr. Plai ................... 50 A3
Conan Rd. Ports .................... 157 F2
Condor Ave. Portc ................. 155 F4
Condor Cl. W Moo ................. 139 D3
Condor Rd. Southa ................ 103 E2
Conference Dr. Lo He ............ 129 D2
Conford Ct. Hav .................... 135 E3
Congleton Cl. Min .................... 98 B2
Conibar Rd. Ems ................... 136 C2
Conifer Ave. Poole ................ 205 D1
Conifer Cl. Christ .................. 192 B2
Conifer Cl. Fern .................... 165 F1
Conifer Cl. Hyt ...................... 125 F2
Conifer Cl. St Le ................... 139 E2
Conifer Cl. Wat ..................... 112 A1
Conifer Cl. Winch ...................... 1 C1
Conifer Cres. Lym ................. 198 A2
Conifer Gr. Gos .................... 155 E2
Conifer Mews. Portc ............. 132 B1
Conifer Rd. Southa .................. 78 A2
Coniston Ave. Bour ............... 189 F3
Coniston Ave. Ports .............. 183 D4
Coniston Cl. Ver ................... 114 C3
Coniston Gdns. He En ........... 105 E3
Coniston Rd. Eastl ................... 55 F1
Coniston Rd. Rin ................... 141 D3
Coniston Rd. Southa ............. 101 E4
Coniston Wlk. Fare ............... 154 C4
Connaught Cl. B on S ........... 195 F1
Connaught Cres. Poole ......... 205 F3
Connaught La. Portc .............. 156 C4
Connaught Rd. Bour ............. 208 A3
Connaught Rd. Hav ............... 136 A1
Connaught Rd. Ports ............ 157 E1
Connell Rd. Poole ................. 204 B3
Connemara Cres. Swanw ...... 129 D4
Connigar Cl. Gos .................. 180 B4
Conqueror Way. Stubb .......... 154 B1
Consort Cl. Eastl ..................... 56 A3
Consort Cl. Poole .................. 205 E3
Consort Rd. Eastl .................... 56 A3
Constable Cl. Gos ................. 181 E4
Constable Cl. Southa ............ 104 B1
Constantine Ave. Ch Fo .......... 55 F3
Constantine Cl. Ch Fo ............. 55 F3
Constitution Hill Rd. Poole .... 205 D3
Convent La. Ems ................... 160 C4
Conway Cl. Ch Fo ................... 55 D2
Conway Cl. New M ................ 196 A2
Conways Dr. Poole ................ 205 D2
Cook Cl. Rin .......................... 141 E4
Cook Row. Wi Mi ................... 163 D2
Cook St. Southa .................... 103 D2
Cooke Rd. Poole ................... 205 F3
Cooks La. Locke ..................... 25 F4
Cooks La. Southb .................. 137 F1
Cooks La. Tot .......................... 76 B1
Coombe Ave. Bour ................ 190 C2
Coombe Ave. Fare. Fare ....... 155 D4
Coombe Gdns. Bour .............. 190 C1
Coombe La. Sway ................. 197 E4
Coombe Rd. E Meon ................ 63 E4
Coombe Rd. Gosp ................. 181 D4
Coombedale. Lo He ............... 129 D1
Coombs Cl. Horn ..................... 88 B1
Cooper Dean Dr. Bour .......... 191 F4
Cooper Gr. Portc .................. 156 B3
Cooper Rd. Ashu ................... 100 A4
Cooper Rd. Ports .................. 183 D4
Cooper's Cl. W End ................ 80 B1
Cooper's Cl. W Wel ................. 51 D1
Coopers La. Ver .................... 114 C4
Copeland Rd. Southa ............... 77 E1
Copinger Cl. Tot .................... 100 B3
Copnor Rd. Ports .................. 157 F2
Copper Beech Dr. Cos .......... 158 B4
Copper Beech Gdns. Bour .... 190 B1
Copper St. Ports ................... 182 A2
Copperfield Rd. Southa ........... 79 D3
Copperfields. Tot .................. 100 A4
Coppice Ave. Fern ................ 165 D4
Coppice Cl. St Le .................. 139 D4
Coppice Cl. Winch ..................... 1 B1
Coppice Hill. Bi Wa ................. 83 E4
Coppice Rd. Tot ...................... 76 B1
Coppice The. Christ .............. 210 A3
Coppice The. Gos ................. 155 E1
Coppice The. Wat ................. 112 A3

Coppice View. Bour ....... 190 C2
Coppice Way. Fare ....... 130 B2
Coppins Gr. Portc ....... 156 B3
Copse Ave. New M ....... 196 A1
Copse Cl. Liss ....... 21 D2
Copse Cl. N Bad ....... 53 F2
Copse Cl. Ott ....... 31 E2
Copse Cl. Pet ....... 41 E2
Copse Cl. Poole ....... 204 C2
Copse Cl. Tot ....... 100 C3
Copse Cl. Wat ....... 134 B3
Copse La. Chilw ....... 54 C1
Copse La. Gos ....... 155 E1
Copse La. Hamble ....... 127 F1
Copse La. N Hay ....... 160 A1
Copse Rd. Bur ....... 142 C1
Copse Rd. New M ....... 196 A1
Copse Rd. Southa ....... 80 A1
Copse Rd. Ver ....... 114 C3
Copse The. Ch Fo ....... 55 F3
Copse The. Fare ....... 130 B2
Copse The. Rom ....... 28 B1
Copse View. Southa ....... 104 C3
Copse Way. Christ ....... 210 C4
Copsewood Ave. Bour ....... 191 F1
Copsewood Rd. Ashu ....... 100 B2
Copsewood Rd. Hyt ....... 125 F2
Copsewood Rd. Southa ....... 79 F1
Copsey Cl. Cos ....... 158 B4
Copsey Gr. Cos ....... 158 B4
Copthorne La. Faw ....... 151 E2
Copythorn Rd. Ports ....... 157 F1
Copythorne Cl. Bour ....... 191 E1
Copythorne Cres. Cadn ....... 75 E2
Coracle Cl. Lo He ....... 128 C1
Coral Cl. Portc ....... 156 B3
Coralin Gr. Wat ....... 112 A1
Coram Cl. Winch ....... 2 A1
Corbar Rd. Christ ....... 208 C4
Corbett Rd. Wat ....... 134 B3
Corbiere Ave. Poole ....... 189 F1
Corbin Ave. Fern ....... 166 A3
Corbin Rd. Lym ....... 198 A1
Corbould Rd. Hyt ....... 149 F4
Corby Cres. Ports ....... 158 A2
Cordelia Cl. Hyt ....... 125 E2
Corfe Cl. Stubb ....... 154 A1
Corfe Halt Cl. Broa ....... 162 C1
Corfe Lodge Rd. Broa ....... 187 E2
Corfe View Rd. Broa ....... 187 E3
Corfe View Rd. Poole ....... 205 E2
Corfe Way. Broa ....... 135 F2
Corhampton Cres. Hav ....... 135 E2
Corhampton La. Drox ....... 60 B3
Corhampton Rd. Bour ....... 208 B4
Coriander Dr. Tot ....... 100 B4
Corinna Gdns. Hyt ....... 125 E2
Corinthian Rd. Ch Fo ....... 55 F4
Cork La. March ....... 101 F1
Cormorant Cl. Portc ....... 155 F4
Cormorant Dr. Hyt ....... 126 B1
Cormorant Wlk. Gos ....... 155 D1
Corn Market. Rom ....... 52 C4
Cornaway La. Portc ....... 156 A4
Combrook Gr. Wat ....... 112 B1
Cornel Rd. Southa ....... 103 F3
Cornelia Cres. Poole ....... 206 A3
Cornelius Dr. Wat ....... 112 A1
Corner Mead. Den ....... 110 C2
Cornfield Rd. L on S ....... 179 F3
Cornfield. Fare ....... 131 D2
Cornflower Cl. Lo He ....... 128 C2
Cornford Way. Christ ....... 210 B4
Cornforth Rd. Tot ....... 76 B1
Cornish Gdns. Bour ....... 190 B1
Cornwall Cl. Southa ....... 80 A1
Cornwall Cres. Southa ....... 79 F1
Cornwall Rd. Ch Fo ....... 55 E2
Cornwall Rd. Ports ....... 182 C3
Cornwall Rd. Southa ....... 79 F1
Cornwallis Cres. Ports ....... 182 B3
Cornwallis Rd. M on S ....... 213 D2
Cornwell Cl. Gos ....... 180 B4
Coronado Rd. Gosp ....... 181 D4
Coronation Ave. Bour ....... 190 C1
Coronation Ave. Upt ....... 203 D4
Coronation Cl. Ver ....... 114 C4
Coronation Par. Hamble ....... 127 F2
Coronation Rd. S Hay ....... 185 F1
Coronation Rd. Swan ....... 84 A3
Coronation Rd. Ver ....... 114 C4
Coronation Terr. Fordi ....... 69 D1
Corporation Rd. Bour ....... 207 E3
Corsair Dr. Hyt ....... 125 E2
Corscombe Cl. Broa ....... 188 C1
Cort Way. Fare ....... 130 B2
Cortina Way. He En ....... 105 E3
Corvette Ave. Lo He ....... 128 C1
Cosford Cl. Fa Oa ....... 57 D1
Cosham Park Ave. Cos ....... 157 F4
Cossack Green. Southa ....... 103 D2
Cossack La. Winch ....... 11 D4
Cotes Ave. Poole ....... 205 D3
Cotlands Rd. Bour ....... 207 D2
Cotswold Cl. Hav ....... 135 F3
Cotswold Cl. Hyt ....... 125 E2
Cotswold Cl. Ver ....... 114 C3
Cotswold Rd. Southa ....... 101 F4
Cotswold Wlk. Fare ....... 154 C4

Cott La. Bur ....... 143 D1
Cott St. Swan ....... 84 B2
Cott Street La. Swan ....... 84 C2
Cottage Cl. Den ....... 110 C2
Cottage Gdns. Poole ....... 205 E3
Cottage Gr. Gos ....... 181 D3
Cottage Gr. Ports ....... 182 B2
Cottage La. Hawk ....... 19 F2
Cottage Mews. Fordi ....... 69 F1
Cottage View. Ports ....... 182 B3
Cottagers La. Hord ....... 197 D2
Cottages The. Fordi ....... 94 A2
Cottes Way. Stubb ....... 154 A1
Cottesway E. Stubb ....... 154 A1
Cotton Cl. Bish ....... 56 C2
Cotton Cl. Broa ....... 187 F3
Cotton Dr. Ems ....... 136 C2
Cotwell Ave. Wat ....... 112 A2
Coulmere Rd. Gosp ....... 181 D3
Coulsdon Rd. He En ....... 105 E3
Coultas Rd. Ch Fo ....... 30 C1
Countess Cl. Oakl ....... 188 C4
Countess Gdns. Bour ....... 207 F4
Country View. Stubb ....... 154 A2
Country View. W Wel ....... 50 C2
Course Park Cres. Lo He ....... 129 E1
Court Barn Cl. L on S ....... 179 F4
Court Barn La. L on S ....... 179 F4
Court Cl. Christ ....... 209 F4
Court Cl. Cos ....... 158 A4
Court Cl. Lym ....... 198 B1
Court Cl. Southa ....... 104 A3
Court Cl. Tot ....... 76 B1
Court Hill. Dame ....... 68 C3
Court La. Cos ....... 158 A4
Court Mead. Cos ....... 158 A4
Court Rd. Bour ....... 191 D1
Court Rd. Ki Wo ....... 2 B3
Court Rd. L on S ....... 179 F4
Court Rd. Southa ....... 102 C4
Court Royal Mews. Southa ....... 102 C3
Courtenay Dr. Wi Mi ....... 163 E3
Courtenay Pl. Lym ....... 198 C2
Courtenay Rd. Poole ....... 205 D2
Courtenay Rd. Winch ....... 2 A2
Courthill Rd. Poole ....... 205 E2
Courtier Cl. Hyt ....... 125 E2
Courtland Gdns. Southa ....... 79 D3
Courtmount Gr. Cos ....... 158 A4
Courtyard The. Christ ....... 209 E3
Cousins Gr. Ports ....... 183 D1
Cove Rd. Bour ....... 190 B1
Covena Rd. Bour ....... 208 C3
Coventry Cl. Broa ....... 187 E2
Coventry Cres. Broa ....... 188 A1
Coventry Rd. Southa ....... 102 C3
Covert Gr. Wat ....... 135 D3
Covert The. Rom ....... 53 D3
Covington Rd. Westb ....... 137 D3
Cow La. Cos ....... 157 E4
Cow La. Portc ....... 156 B4
Cowan Rd. Wat ....... 134 B3
Coward Rd. Gos ....... 181 D1
Cowdray Cl. Bish ....... 56 C1
Cowdray Cl. Southa ....... 78 A2
Cowdray Park. Stubb ....... 154 A1
Cowdrey Gdns. Bour ....... 191 F1
Cowell Dr. Bour ....... 208 A4
Cowes La. Lo He ....... 152 B3
Cowgrove Rd. Pamp ....... 162 C3
Cowleas Cotts. Awb ....... 26 C3
Cowley Cl. Southa ....... 77 F1
Cowley Rd. Lym ....... 198 B2
Cowley Rd. Poole ....... 204 B4
Cowleys Rd. Burt ....... 193 E1
Cowper Ave. New M ....... 196 A1
Cowper Rd. Bour ....... 190 C1
Cowper Rd. Ports ....... 182 C4
Cowper Rd. Southa ....... 104 B3
Cowpitts La. Rin ....... 117 E1
Cowslip Cl. Gos ....... 155 E1
Cowslip Cl. Lo He ....... 128 C1
Cowslip Cl. Broa ....... 187 F1
Cox Ave. Bour ....... 191 D2
Cox Cl. Bour ....... 191 D2
Cox Dale. Lo He ....... 129 E1
Cox Row. Ch Fo ....... 55 E2
Cox's Dr. Southa ....... 104 A1
Cox's La. Southa ....... 103 E2
Coxes Meadows. Pet ....... 40 C3
Coxford Cl. Southa ....... 78 A1
Coxford Dro. Southa ....... 78 A2
Coxs Hill. Twyf ....... 32 A4
Coxstone La. Rin ....... 141 D3
Coy Pond Rd. Poole ....... 206 A3
Crab Orchard Way. W Moo ....... 114 C1
Crabapple Cl. Tot ....... 100 B4
Crabbs Way. Tot ....... 100 A4
Crabbswood La. Sway ....... 196 C4
Crabden La. Horn ....... 88 C1
Crableck La. Lo He ....... 128 B3
Crabthorne Farm La. Stubb ....... 154 A2
Crabton Close Rd. Bour ....... 207 F2
Crabtree Cl. Burt ....... 193 E1
Crabtree. Southa ....... 77 F1
Crabwood Cl. Southa ....... 77 F1
Crabwood Ct. Hav ....... 135 E4
Crabwood Dr. W End ....... 80 C1
Crabwood Rd. Southa ....... 77 F1

Cracknore Hard. March ....... 102 A1
Cracknore Rd. Southa ....... 102 B3
Craigmoor Ave. Bour ....... 191 F1
Craigmoor Cl. Bour ....... 191 F1
Craigmoor Way. Bour ....... 191 F1
Craigside Rd. St Le ....... 139 E2
Craigwell Rd. Wat ....... 134 B2
Craigwood Dr. Fern ....... 165 F2
Crampmoor La. N Bad ....... 28 C1
Cranberry Cl. March ....... 101 F1
Cranborne Cres. Poole ....... 205 F4
Cranborne Gdns. Ch Fo ....... 30 A1
Cranborne Rd. Alderh ....... 92 A3
Cranborne Rd. Bour ....... 206 C1
Cranborne Rd. Cos ....... 134 A1
Cranborne Rd. Wi Mi ....... 163 E4
Cranborne Wlk. Fare ....... 154 C4
Cranbourne Cl. Southa ....... 78 B1
Cranbourne Dr. Ott ....... 31 D2
Cranbourne Park. He En ....... 105 E2
Cranbourne Pl. New M ....... 195 F2
Cranbourne Rd. Gos ....... 181 D3
Cranbrook Rd. Poole ....... 205 D3
Cranbury Ave. Southa ....... 103 D3
Cranbury Cl. Down ....... 46 C3
Cranbury Cl. Ott ....... 31 D2
Cranbury Ct. Eastl ....... 56 A1
Cranbury Gdns. Burs ....... 104 C1
Cranbury Pl. Southa ....... 103 D3
Cranbury Rd. Eastl ....... 56 A1
Cranbury Rd. Southa ....... 103 F2
Cranbury Terr. Southa ....... 103 D3
Crane Dr. Ver ....... 114 C4
Cranemoor Ave. Christ ....... 194 C1
Cranemoor Cl. Christ ....... 194 C1
Cranemoor Gdns. Christ ....... 194 C1
Cranes Mews. Poole ....... 204 B2
Craneswater Ave. Ports ....... 182 C1
Craneswater Gate. Ports ....... 182 C1
Craneswater Park. Ports ....... 182 C1
Cranfield Ave. Wi Mi ....... 163 E3
Cranford Cl. Ch Fo ....... 55 D4
Cranford Rd. Pet ....... 40 C1
Cranford Way. Southa ....... 79 D1
Cranleigh Ave. Ports ....... 182 C3
Cranleigh Cl. Bour ....... 208 C3
Cranleigh Ct. Bour ....... 208 C3
Cranleigh Gdns. Bour ....... 208 C3
Cranleigh Rd. He En ....... 105 E3
Cranleigh Rd. Portc ....... 156 A4
Cranleigh Rd. Ports ....... 182 C3
Cranmer Rd. Bour ....... 206 C4
Cranmore. Net ....... 127 E4
Crantock Gr. Bour ....... 191 F2
Cranwell Cl. Bour ....... 189 F2
Cranwell Cl. Bran ....... 169 D1
Cranwell Cl. Southa ....... 78 A3
Cranworth Rd. Winch ....... 1 C1
Crasswell St. Ports ....... 182 B3
Craven Ct. Fare ....... 130 C2
Craven Rd. Ch Fo ....... 55 E3
Craven St. Southa ....... 103 D3
Craven Wlk. Southa ....... 103 D3
Crawford Cl. Nur ....... 77 E3
Crawford Dr. Fare ....... 130 C2
Crawley Ave. Hav ....... 136 A3
Crawley Hill. W Wel ....... 50 C1
Crawshaw Rd. Poole ....... 205 D1
Crawte Ave. Holb ....... 150 B1
Creasey Rd. Bour ....... 190 D3
Credenhill Rd. Cos ....... 133 E1
Creedy Gdns. W End ....... 80 A2
Creek End. Ems ....... 160 C4
Creek Gdns. Gos ....... 181 E2
Creek Rd. S Hay ....... 185 E1
Creekmoor La. Broa ....... 204 A4
Creighton Rd. Southa ....... 101 F3
Cremyll Cl. Stubb ....... 154 B1
Crescent Cl. Winch ....... 10 A2
Crescent Dr. B on S ....... 211 F4
Crescent Rd. Fare ....... 131 D1
Crescent Rd. Gos ....... 181 D1
Crescent Rd. Lo He ....... 128 C1
Crescent Rd. N Bad ....... 53 F2
Crescent Rd. Poole ....... 205 F2
Crescent Rd. Ver ....... 115 D3
Crescent Rd. Wi Mi ....... 163 E2
Crescent The. B on S ....... 211 E4
Crescent The. Bour ....... 207 F2
Crescent The. Eastl ....... 56 A2
Crescent The. March ....... 101 F1
Crescent The. Ne Ma ....... 99 F2
Crescent The. Net ....... 127 E3
Crescent The. Rom ....... 53 D4
Crescent The. Southa ....... 104 A1
Crescent The. Southb ....... 161 E4
Crescent The. Twyf ....... 32 A3
Crescent The. Wat ....... 134 B1
Crescent Wlk. Fern ....... 165 F2
Cressey Rd. Rom ....... 52 C4
Cressy Rd. Ports ....... 182 B4
Crest Cl. Portc ....... 131 E1
Crest Rd. Poole ....... 205 D1
Crest The. Wat ....... 134 B1
Crest Way. Southa ....... 104 B2
Cresta Gdns. Fern ....... 165 F2
Crestland Cl. Wat ....... 112 A2
Crete Cotts. Hyt ....... 125 F1

Crete La. Hyt ....... 125 F1
Crete Rd. Hyt ....... 125 F1
Cribb Cl. Poole ....... 204 C4
Crichel Mount Rd. Poole ....... 216 B4
Crichel Rd. Bour ....... 207 D4
Cricket Cl. Christ ....... 209 F3
Cricket Dr. Wat ....... 112 A3
Cricklemead Cl. Bi Wa ....... 83 E4
Cricklemead. Bi Wa ....... 83 E4
Crigdon Cl. Southa ....... 101 F4
Crimea Rd. Bour ....... 206 C4
Cringle Ave. Bour ....... 209 D2
Cripple Gate La. Beaul ....... 175 E3
Cripple Gate La. E Bol ....... 175 E3
Cripstead La. Winch ....... 10 C3
Crispen Cl. Christ ....... 210 C4
Crispin Cl. Lo He ....... 129 D2
Crisspyn Cl. Horn ....... 112 A3
Crittall Cl. Sway ....... 172 B1
Crockford Cl. New M ....... 196 A3
Crockford Rd. Westb ....... 137 D2
Croft Cl. Broa ....... 187 E4
Croft Hts. Whit ....... 24 A2
Croft La. N Hay ....... 159 F1
Croft Rd. Bour ....... 190 C1
Croft Rd. Bran ....... 169 A3
Croft Rd. Christ ....... 209 F4
Croft Rd. Poole ....... 205 D3
Croft Rd. Ports ....... 157 E1
Croft Rd. Rin ....... 117 E1
Croft The. Ch Fo ....... 55 E2
Croft The. Crouch ....... 22 B4
Croft The. Stubb ....... 154 B2
Croft The. Tot ....... 76 B1
Croftlands Ave. Stubb ....... 154 B2
Crofton Ave. Stubb ....... 179 E4
Crofton Cl. Christ ....... 192 C1
Crofton Cl. Southa ....... 79 D1
Crofton Cl. Wat ....... 134 B3
Crofton La. Stubb ....... 154 A1
Crofton Rd. Ports ....... 157 F1
Crofton Rd. Ports ....... 183 D3
Crofton Way. Lo He ....... 128 B1
Crofton Way. Swan ....... 84 A3
Cromarty Ave. Ports ....... 183 D2
Cromarty Cl. Stubb ....... 154 A2
Cromarty Rd. Southa ....... 77 F3
Crombie Cl. Wat ....... 111 F2
Cromer Rd. Bour ....... 207 E4
Cromer Rd. Cos ....... 133 F1
Cromer Rd. Poole ....... 205 F3
Cromer Rd. Southa ....... 77 E1
Cromhall Cl. Fare ....... 154 B4
Crompton Way. Lo He ....... 129 E3
Cromwell Pl. Bour ....... 208 A3
Cromwell Rd. Bour ....... 208 A3
Cromwell Rd. Poole ....... 205 E3
Cromwell Rd. Ports ....... 183 D1
Cromwell Rd. Southa ....... 102 C4
Cromwell Rd. Wi Mi ....... 163 E2
Cromwell Rd. Winch ....... 10 C3
Crondall Ave. Hav ....... 135 F3
Crooked Hays Cl. March ....... 55 F1
Crooked Walk La. Southw ....... 132 C2
Crookham Cl. Hav ....... 135 E2
Crookham Rd. Southa ....... 126 C4
Crookhorn La. Sob ....... 85 E4
Crookhorn La. Wat ....... 134 C2
Crosby Rd. Bour ....... 206 B1
Crosfield Cl. W Wel ....... 51 D1
Cross La. Bi Wa ....... 59 D1
Cross Rd. L on S ....... 180 A2
Cross Rd. Southa ....... 103 F4
Cross St. Bi Wa ....... 83 E4
Cross St. Ports ....... 182 A3
Cross St. Ports ....... 182 B2
Cross St. Winch ....... 10 C4
Cross The. Bur ....... 143 D2
Cross The. E Meo ....... 38 B1
Cross Way. Christ ....... 192 B1
Cross Way. Comp ....... 31 E3
Cross Way. Hav ....... 135 F1
Crossfell Wlk. Fare ....... 154 C4
Crosshouse Rd. Southa ....... 103 E2
Crossland Cl. Gos ....... 181 E2
Crossland Dr. Hav ....... 136 A2
Crossmead Ave. New M ....... 196 A1
Crossway The. Portc ....... 156 B4
Crossways Cl. Down ....... 46 C4
Crossways The. Gos ....... 181 D3
Crossways. Hord ....... 197 E1
Crossways. Upt ....... 203 E4
Crosswell Cl. Southa ....... 104 B3
Crouch La. Horn ....... 112 A4
Crow Arch La. Rin ....... 141 D3
Crow La. Rin ....... 141 E3
Crowder Terr. Winch ....... 10 C4
Crowders Green. Co Com ....... 56 C4
Crown Cl. Poole ....... 205 E3
Crown Cl. Wat ....... 134 C2
Crown Mead. Wi Mi ....... 163 E3
Crown St. Ports ....... 182 B3
Crown St. Southa ....... 102 A4
Crows Nest La. Botl ....... 81 F1
Crowsbury Cl. Ems ....... 136 C2
Crowsport. Hamble ....... 128 A2
Crowther Cl. Southa ....... 104 B3
Croydon Cl. Southa ....... 78 A2

Crummock Rd. N Bad ....... 55 D4
Crusader Rd. Bour ....... 189 E2
Crusader Rd. He En ....... 105 E3
Cruse Cl. Sway ....... 172 A1
Crystal Way. Wat ....... 135 D4
Cucklington Gdns. Bour ....... 191 D2
Cuckmere La. Southa ....... 101 E4
Cuckoo Bushes La. Ch Fo ....... 55 E4
Cuckoo Hill Way. Bran ....... 169 E1
Cuckoo La. Southa ....... 102 C2
Cuckoo La. Stubb ....... 154 A2
Cudnell Ave. Bour ....... 190 A3
Cudworth Mead. He En ....... 81 E1
Cuffnells Cl. Ibs ....... 117 D4
Cul-de-sac. B on S ....... 211 E4
Culford Ave. Tot ....... 100 C3
Culford Cl. Bour ....... 191 F1
Culford Way. Tot ....... 100 C3
Cull Cl. Poole ....... 206 B4
Cull La. New M ....... 196 A3
Culliford Cres. Broa ....... 188 C1
Culloden Cl. Fare ....... 130 C3
Cullwood La. New M ....... 196 B3
Culver Cl. Southa ....... 77 E1
Culver Dr. S Hay ....... 185 E1
Culver Rd. New M ....... 195 F1
Culver Rd. Ports ....... 183 D1
Culver. Net ....... 127 E4
Culverhayes Rd. Wi Mi ....... 163 D3
Culverley Cl. Brock ....... 145 F1
Culverwell Gdns. Winch ....... 10 C4
Culvery Gdns. W End ....... 80 A1
Cumber Rd. Lo He ....... 128 C2
Cumberland Ave. Ch Fo ....... 55 F3
Cumberland Ave. Ems ....... 136 C2
Cumberland Cl. Ch Fo ....... 55 F3
Cumberland Pl. Southa ....... 102 C3
Cumberland Rd. Ports ....... 182 C3
Cumberland St. Ports ....... 182 A3
Cumberland St. Southa ....... 103 D2
Cumberland Way. Hyt ....... 125 E2
Cumbrian Way. Southa ....... 101 F4
Cummins Green. Burs ....... 105 D3
Cumnor Rd. Bour ....... 207 D2
Cunard Ave. Southa ....... 102 B4
Cunard Rd. Southa ....... 103 D1
Cundellway. Ki Wo ....... 2 A4
Cunningham Ave. Bi Wa ....... 83 D4
Cunningham Cl. Bour ....... 190 A2
Cunningham Cl. Christ ....... 210 A3
Cunningham Cl. Rin ....... 141 E4
Cunningham Cres. Southa ....... 104 A2
Cunningham Dr. Gos ....... 155 E2
Cunningham Dr. Lo He ....... 129 D2
Cunningham Pl. Bour ....... 190 A2
Cunningham Rd. Horn ....... 112 B4
Cunningham Rd. Wat ....... 134 B3
Cupernham Cl. Rom ....... 28 A1
Cupernham La. Abb ....... 28 A1
Cupernham La. Rom ....... 28 A1
Curdridge Cl. Hav ....... 136 A3
Curdridge La. Curd ....... 83 E2
Curdridge La. Shed ....... 83 E2
Curlew Cl. Fern ....... 165 D4
Curlew Cl. Hyt ....... 126 B1
Curlew Cl. Southa ....... 78 A3
Curlew Dr. Hyt ....... 126 B1
Curlew Dr. Portc ....... 155 F4
Curlew Gdns. Wat ....... 111 F2
Curlew Path. Ports ....... 183 D3
Curlew Rd. Bour ....... 191 E1
Curlew Rd. Christ ....... 210 A3
Curlew Sq. Eastl ....... 55 F1
Curlew Wlk. Gos ....... 155 D2
Curlew Wlk. Hyt ....... 126 A1
Curlews The. Ver ....... 115 D3
Curlieu Rd. Poole ....... 204 B3
Curtis Mead. Ports ....... 157 F2
Curtis Rd. Poole ....... 205 E3
Curtiss Gdns. Gos ....... 180 C2
Curve The. Gos ....... 155 D1
Curve The. Horn ....... 111 F3
Curzon Ct. Southa ....... 78 B2
Curzon Howe Rd. Ports ....... 182 A3
Curzon Pl. Lym ....... 198 B1
Curzon Rd. Bour ....... 207 E3
Curzon Rd. Poole ....... 205 D2
Curzon Rd. Wat ....... 134 C4
Curzon Way. Christ ....... 210 B4
Custards Rd. Lyn ....... 122 A3
Custards The. Lyn ....... 121 F3
Cut Throat La. Drox ....... 61 D1
Cut Throat La. Swan ....... 84 B3
Cutbush La. Southa ....... 80 A2
Cutbush La. Southa ....... 104 A4
Cutbush La. W End ....... 80 A2
Cuthbert Rd. Ports ....... 182 C3
Cuthburga Rd. Wi Mi ....... 163 D2
Cuthbury Cl. Wi Mi ....... 163 D2
Cuthbury Gdns. Wi Mi ....... 163 D3
Cutler Cl. New M ....... 196 B2
Cutlers La. Stubb ....... 154 B2
Cutlers Pl. Wi Mi ....... 164 A3
Cutter Ave. Lo He ....... 128 C1
Cutts Arch. Drox ....... 85 D3
Cutts Arch. Sob ....... 85 D3
Cygnet Ct. Portc ....... 155 F4
Cygnet Rd. Cos ....... 158 C4

Cygnus Gdns. Hyt ............ 125 D2
Cynthia Cl. Poole ............ 205 D4
Cynthia Rd. Poole ............ 205 D4
Cypress Ave. Southa ......... 103 F3
Cypress Cres. Wat ........... 112 A3
Cypress Gdns. Botl .......... 106 A4
Cypress Gdns. Tot ........... 100 B4
Cypress Gr. Hord ............ 213 E4
Cyprus Rd. Lo He ............ 129 E1
Cyprus Rd. Ports ............ 182 C4
Cyril Rd. Bour ............... 207 E3

Dacombe Cl. Upt ............. 203 E4
Dacombe Dr. Upt ............. 203 E4
Dacres Wlk. M on S .......... 213 E3
Daffodil Rd. Southa ......... 79 E2
Daggons Rd. Alderh ......... 92 B3
Dahlia Rd. Southa ........... 79 D2
Daintree Cl. Southa ......... 104 B2
Dairy Cl. Christ ............. 209 E4
Dairy La. Hur ............... 77 D3
Dairymoor. Wickh ............ 108 A2
Daisy La. Gos ............... 181 D2
Daisy La. Lo He ............. 129 E2
Daisy Mead. Wat ............. 135 D4
Daisy Rd. Southa ............ 79 D2
Dakota Cl. Christ ........... 210 A4
Dale Cl. Litt ............... 1 A3
Dale Cl. Poole .............. 204 C3
Dale Dr. Gos ................ 155 D3
Dale Rd. Hyt ................ 125 F2
Dale Rd. Poole .............. 204 C3
Dale Rd. Southa ............. 78 B1
Dale Rd. Stubb .............. 154 B2
Dale The. Wat ............... 134 B1
Dale Valley Cl. Southa ...... 78 B1
Dale Valley Gdns. Southa .... 78 B1
Dale Valley Rd. Poole ....... 204 C4
Dale Valley Rd. Southa ...... 78 B2
Dales Cl. Wi Mi ............. 164 B3
Dales Dr. Wi Mi ............. 164 A3
Dales La. Hurn .............. 191 F4
Dales Way. Tot .............. 100 A4
Dalewood Ave. Bour .......... 189 F3
Dalewood Rd. Fare ........... 130 B1
Dalkeith Rd. Broa ........... 187 E2
Dalkeith Rd. Bour ........... 206 A1
Dalling Rd. Poole ........... 206 A3
Dallington Cl. Stubb ........ 154 B1
Dalmeny Rd. Bour ............ 209 D2
Damask Gdns. Wat ............ 112 A1
Damen Cl. He En ............. 105 D3
Damerham Rd. Bour ........... 191 E2
Dampier Cl. Gos ............. 180 B4
Damson Hill. Bi Wa .......... 60 A1
Damson Hill. Swan ........... 60 A1
Danbury Ct. Ems ............. 137 D1
Dances Way. S Hay ........... 184 C2
Dandelion Cl. Gos ........... 155 D1
Dando Rd. Den ............... 111 D2
Dandy's Ford La. Sh En ...... 25 F1
Dane Cl. Black .............. 150 C1
Dane Dr. Fern ............... 165 F2
Dane Rd. M on S ............. 213 D3
Danebury Cl. Hav ............ 135 F3
Danebury Gdns. Ch Fo ........ 55 D2
Danebury Way. Nur ........... 77 E2
Danecourt Cl. Poole ......... 204 C2
Danecourt Rd. Poole ......... 204 C2
Danecrest Rd. Hord .......... 196 C2
Danehurst New Rd. New M ..... 196 B4
Danes Cl. B on S ............ 212 A4
Danes Rd. Awb ............... 26 B2
Danes Rd. Portc ............. 132 A1
Danes Rd. Winch ............. 2 A1
Danesbrook La. Wat .......... 135 D4
Danesbury Ave. Bour ......... 208 C2
Danestream Cl. M on S ....... 213 E2
Daneswood Rd. New M ......... 196 B2
Daniell's Cl. Lym ........... 198 C2
Daniell's Wlk. Lym .......... 198 C2
Dansie Cl. Poole ............ 205 D2
Dapple Pl. March ............ 102 A1
Darby's Cl. Poole ........... 204 B3
Darby's La. Poole ........... 204 B3
Darby's La. Poole ........... 204 B4
Dark La. Black .............. 150 C1
Dark La. Bran ............... 195 D2
Darley Rd. Fern ............. 165 E2
Darlington Gdns. Southa ..... 78 B1
Darlington Rd. Ports ........ 182 C2
Darracott Rd. Bour .......... 208 A3
Darren Cl. Stubb ............ 154 B2
Darrian Ct. Upt ............. 203 D4
Dart Rd. W End .............. 80 A2
Dartington Rd. Bish ......... 56 B3
Dartmouth Mews. Ports ....... 182 A2
Dartmouth Rd. Ports ......... 158 A4
Darwin Ave. Christ .......... 192 C1
Darwin Rd. Eastl ............ 56 A2
Darwin Rd. Southa ........... 102 C4
Darwin Way. Gos ............. 180 B3
Daubney Gdns. Hav ........... 135 E3
Daulston Rd. Ports .......... 182 C4
Davenport Cl. Upt ........... 203 E4
Daventry La. Ports .......... 158 B2
David Ct. Rom ............... 53 D3
David's La. St Le ........... 140 B3
Davidia Ct. Wat ............. 135 D3

Davis Cl. Gos ............... 180 B4
Davis Field. New M .......... 195 F1
Davis Rd. Poole ............. 205 F3
Daw La. N Hay ............... 184 C4
Dawkins Rd. Hamw ............ 203 E2
Dawkins Way. New M .......... 196 A1
Dawlish Ave. Southa ......... 102 B4
Dawn Cl. Bour ............... 190 B1
Dawn Gdns. Winch ............ 10 B3
Dawnay Cl. Southa ........... 79 E3
Daws Ave. Bour .............. 190 A1
Dawson Rd. Southa ........... 104 B1
Day La. Horn ................ 111 F4
Day's Ct. Wi Mi ............. 163 E2
Daylesford Cl. Poole ........ 205 D1
Dayrell Cl. Tot ............. 76 A1
Dayshes Cl. Gos ............. 155 D2
Dayslondon Rd. Wat .......... 134 B3
De Courtenai Cl. Bour ....... 189 F3
De Haviland Cl. Oakl ........ 163 F1
De Havilland Way. Christ .... 210 A3
De La Warr Rd. M on S ....... 213 E2
De Lisle Cl. Ports .......... 157 F2
De Lisle Rd. Bour ........... 206 C4
De Mauley Rd. Poole ......... 216 C4
De Montfort Rd. Oakl ........ 163 E1
De Mowbray Way. Lym ......... 198 B1
De Redvers Rd. Poole ........ 205 E1
Deacon Cl. Southa ........... 104 A3
Deacon Cres. Southa ......... 104 A3
Deacon Rd. Bour ............. 190 D3
Deacon Rd. Lo He ............ 129 D1
Deacon Rd. Southa ........... 104 A3
Deadman Hill. Fordi ......... 71 E3
Deal Cl. Stubb .............. 154 B2
Deal Rd. Cos ................ 133 F1
Dean Cl. Hamw ............... 203 F2
Dean Cl. Winch .............. 1 B1
Dean Ct. He En .............. 105 E4
Dean La. Bi Wa .............. 59 F2
Dean La. Ro Ca .............. 113 E3
Dean La. Spar ............... 1 A1
Dean La. Whit ............... 24 A2
Dean La. Winch .............. 1 A1
Dean Park Cres. Bour ........ 206 C2
Dean Park Rd. Bour .......... 206 C2
Dean Rd. Cos ................ 157 F4
Dean Rd. Fa Oa .............. 57 E1
Dean Rd. Southa ............. 104 A4
Dean Rd. W Dean ............. 3 D1
Dean Rd. W Tyth ............. 3 F3
Dean St. Ports .............. 182 A3
Dean Swift Cres. Poole ...... 216 B4
Dean Villas. Wickh .......... 130 C4
Dean's Rd. Bour ............. 208 A3
Deane Cl. Lo He ............. 128 C2
Deane Down Dro. Litt ........ 1 A2
Deane Gdns. L on S .......... 179 F3
Deane's Park Rd. Fare ....... 131 E1
Deanery The. Ch Fo .......... 55 D4
Deanfield Cl. Hamble ........ 127 F1
Deans Court La. Wi Mi ....... 163 E2
Deans Ct. M on S ............ 213 E3
Deans Gate. Stubb ........... 154 B1
Deans Gr. Wi Mi ............. 163 E4
Deans The. Bour ............. 206 C2
Deanscroft Rd. Bour ......... 190 C2
Deanswood Dr. Wat ........... 111 F1
Dear Hay La. Poole .......... 204 B1
Dearing Cl. Lyn ............. 121 F3
Decies Rd. Poole ............ 205 D3
Dee Way. Poole .............. 204 A1
Deep Dell. Wat .............. 112 A3
Deepdene La. Bour ........... 189 F3
Deeping Cl. Southa .......... 103 F1
Deeping Gate. Wat ........... 135 D4
Deerhurst Cl. Tot ........... 100 B3
Deerhurst Cres. Cos ......... 133 D1
Deerleap Cl. Hyt ............ 126 A2
Deerleap La. Ashu ........... 100 B1
Deerleap Way. Hyt ........... 126 A2
Deerleap Way. New M ......... 196 A3
Defender Rd. Southa ......... 103 E2
Delamere Gdns. Bour ......... 190 C2
Delamere Rd. Ports .......... 182 C2
Delft Cl. Lo He ............. 128 C2
Delft Gdns. Wat ............. 111 E1
Delft Mews. Hello ........... 209 C3
Delhi Cl. Poole ............. 205 E2
Delhi Rd. Bour .............. 190 C1
Delilah Rd. Hamw ............ 203 E1
Delius Ave. Southa .......... 104 B2
Delius Wlk. Wat ............. 134 C3
Dell Cl. Broa ............... 187 F2
Dell Cl. Fa Oa .............. 57 E1
Dell Cl. Wat ................ 134 A1
Dell Piece East. Horn ....... 112 B3
Dell Piece West. Horn ....... 112 B3
Dell Quay Cl. Gos ........... 155 D1
Dell Rd. Southa ............. 79 F1
Dell Rd. Winch .............. 11 B3
Dell The. B on S ............ 211 E4
Dell The. Hav ............... 135 D1
Dell The. Portc ............. 131 E1
Dell Wharf. Southa .......... 103 E4
Dellfield. Frox G ........... 18 C1
Delme Dr. Fare .............. 131 E1
Delph Rd. Oakl .............. 188 B4

Delphi Way. Wat ............. 134 C1
Delta Cl. Christ ............ 210 A4
Dempsey Cl. Southa .......... 104 A2
Denbigh Cl. Eastl ........... 55 F3
Denbigh Cl. Tot ............. 100 B3
Denbigh Dr. Fare ............ 130 C1
Denbigh Gdns. Southa ........ 78 C2
Denby Rd. Poole ............. 204 C2
Dene Cl. Rin ................ 117 E1
Dene Cl. Rown ............... 78 C4
Dene Hollow. Cos ............ 158 B4
Dene Rd. Ashu ............... 100 B1
Dene Way. Ashu .............. 100 B2
Dene Wlk. Fern .............. 165 F1
Deneve Ave. Broa ............ 188 B1
Denewood Copse. W Moo ....... 138 B2
Denewood Rd. W Moo .......... 138 B2
Denewulf Cl. Bi Wa .......... 83 E4
Denham Cl. Broa ............. 188 C2
Denham Cl. Stubb ............ 154 A1
Denham Cl. Winch ............ 1 C1
Denham Dr. Christ ........... 194 C1
Denham Gdns. Net ............ 127 D3
Denhill Cl. S Hay ........... 184 C3
Denholm Cl. Rin ............. 117 E1
Denison Rd. Southa .......... 104 B4
Denmark La. Poole ........... 204 B2
Denmark Rd. Bour ............ 190 C1
Denmark Rd. Poole ........... 204 B2
Denmead Rd. Bour ............ 208 B4
Denmead Rd. Southa .......... 104 B4
Denmead. New M .............. 196 B2
Denning Mews. Ports ......... 182 B3
Dennis Rd. Broa ............. 187 E3
Dennis Way. Liss ............ 21 D2
Dennistoun Ave. Christ ...... 209 F4
Denny Cl. Faw ............... 151 D2
Denville Ave. Portc ......... 156 B3
Denville Cl. Cos ............ 158 C4
Denvilles Cl. Hav ........... 136 A1
Denwood Rd. Bour ............ 206 A2
Denzil Ave. Net ............. 127 E3
Denzil Ave. Southa .......... 103 D3
Depedene Cl. Holb ........... 150 B2
Derby Cl. Bour .............. 207 E2
Derby Rd. Bour .............. 207 E2
Derby Rd. Eastl ............. 56 A1
Derby Rd. Ports ............. 157 E1
Derby Rd. Southa ............ 103 D3
Dereham Way. Poole .......... 205 F3
Derlyn Rd. Fare ............. 131 D1
Derritt La. Bran ............ 193 E4
Derritt La. Sop ............. 193 E4
Dersingham Cl. Cos .......... 133 F1
Derwent Cl. Bour ............ 191 D1
Derwent Cl. Fern ............ 166 A3
Derwent Cl. Horn ............ 88 B1
Derwent Cl. Stubb ........... 154 B2
Derwent Cl. W End ........... 80 A1
Derwent Rd. L on S .......... 179 F3
Derwent Rd. New M ........... 196 A3
Derwent Rd. Southa .......... 77 F1
Derwentwater Rd. Oakl ....... 163 E1
Desborough Cl. Cos .......... 133 D1
Desborough Ct. Eastl ........ 56 A1
Desborough Rd. Eastl ........ 56 A1
Devenish Rd. Winch .......... 1 B1
Deverall Pl. Wat ............ 134 B2
Devine Gdns. Bish ........... 56 C1
Devon Cl. Ch Fo ............. 55 C2
Devon Dr. Ch Fo ............. 55 E2
Devon Rd. Christ ............ 208 C4
Devon Rd. Poole ............. 204 C3
Devon Rd. Ports ............. 158 A2
Devonshire Ave. Ports ....... 183 D2
Devonshire Gdns. Burs ....... 105 D1
Devonshire Gdns. Hyt ........ 150 A4
Devonshire Rd. Southa ....... 102 C3
Devonshire Sq. Ports ........ 182 C2
Devonshire Way. Fare ........ 154 B4
Dew La. Eastl ............... 55 F2
Dewar Cl. Lo He ............. 129 E3
Deweys La. Rin .............. 140 C4
Dewlands Cl. Bour ........... 114 B3
Dewlands Way. Ver ........... 114 C3
Dewlish Cl. Poole ........... 189 D1
Dial Cl. Bran ............... 169 E1
Diamond Cl. Fordi ........... 93 F4
Diamond St. Ports ........... 182 A2
Diana Cl. Gos ............... 180 C2
Diana Way. Broa ............. 187 F4
Dibben Wlk. Rom ............. 28 B1
Dibble Dr. N Bad ............ 53 F2
Dibden Cl. Bour ............. 191 E2
Dibden Cl. Hav .............. 135 E2
Dibles Rd. Lo He ............ 128 C1
Dickens Cl. Ports ........... 182 B4
Dickens Dell. Tot ........... 100 A4
Dickens Rd. Bour ............ 208 C4
Dickson Park. Wickh ......... 108 A2
Didcot Rd. Southa ........... 78 B1
Dieppe Cres. Ports .......... 157 F2
Dieppe Gdns. Gos ............ 180 C2
Diligence Cl. Burs .......... 105 D1
Dilly La. B on S ............ 212 A4
Dimond Cl. Southa ........... 79 F1

Dimond Hill. Southa ......... 79 F1
Dimond Rd. Southa ........... 79 F1
Dingle Rd. Bour ............. 208 A2
Dingle Way. Lo He ........... 129 D2
Dingley Rd. Poole ........... 204 B3
Dinham Rd. New M ............ 196 B2
Dinsey Cl. Southa ........... 101 F4
Diprose Rd. Broa ............ 187 F4
Discovery Cl. Stubb ......... 154 B3
Disraeli Rd. Christ ......... 209 E3
Ditcham Cres. Hav ........... 135 F2
Ditchbury. Lym .............. 198 B3
Ditton Cl. Stubb ............ 154 B2
Dock La. Beaul .............. 149 D1
Dock Rd. Gos ................ 181 E2
Dockenfield Cl. Hav ......... 135 E2
Doctor's Hill. Sh En ........ 26 A2
Doctors La. W Meo ........... 37 E3
Dodds La. Swan .............. 84 B3
Dodwell La. Burs ............ 105 D2
Doe Copse Way. New M ........ 195 F2
Dogdean. Wi Mi .............. 163 E4
Dogkennel La. Hambl ......... 86 C2
Dogwood Dell. Wat ........... 134 C3
Dogwood Rd. Bour ............ 187 F1
Dolbery Rd N. Poole ......... 189 E1
Dolbery Rd S. Poole ......... 189 E1
Dolman Rd. Gos .............. 181 E2
Dolphin Ave. Bour ........... 190 C3
Dolphin Cl. Bish ............ 56 C1
Dolphin Cres. Gos ........... 181 E2
Dolphin Cl. Stubb ........... 154 A2
Dolphin Hill. Twyf .......... 32 A3
Dolphin Pl. B on S .......... 212 A4
Dolphin Way. Gos ............ 181 E1
Dolton Rd. Southa ........... 77 F2
Dome Al. Winch .............. 11 D4
Dominie Wlk. L on S ......... 179 F3
Dominion Rd. Bour ........... 189 F2
Domum Rd. Ports ............. 157 F1
Domum Rd. Winch ............. 11 D3
Donaldson Rd. Cos ........... 157 F3
Doncaster Dr. Eastl ......... 79 F4
Doncaster Rd. Eastl ......... 80 A4
Donigers Cl. Swan ........... 84 A3
Donigers Dell. Swan ......... 84 A3
Donnelly Rd. Bour ........... 208 C3
Donnelly St. Gos ............ 181 D3
Donnington Dr. Ch Fo ........ 55 D2
Donnington Dr. Christ ....... 210 A4
Donnington Gr. Southa ....... 79 E1
Donoughmore Rd. Bour ........ 207 F2
Dorcas Cl. Wat .............. 112 A1
Dorchester Gdns. Poole ...... 204 C3
Dorchester Rd. Poole ........ 204 C3
Dorchester Rd. Upt .......... 203 D4
Dore Ave. Portc ............. 132 B1
Dores La. Brai .............. 29 D4
Dores La. Hurs .............. 29 D4
Doric Cl. Ch Fo ............. 55 F4
Dorking Cres. Cos ........... 157 F4
Dorland Gdns. Tot ........... 100 B3
Dorlands Rd. Horn ........... 112 B4
Dormington Rd. Cos .......... 133 E1
Dormy Cl. Lo He ............. 128 B2
Dormy Way. Gos .............. 155 D1
Dornie Rd. Poole ............ 216 C4
Dorothy Dymond St. Ports .... 182 B3
Dorrien Rd. Gosp ............ 181 D4
Dorrita Cl. Wat ............. 112 A2
Dorrita Cl. Ports ........... 182 C1
Dorrits The. Tot ............ 100 A4
Dorset Ave. Fern ............ 165 E2
Dorset Cl. Horn ............. 112 A3
Dorset Lake Ave. Poole ...... 216 A4
Dorset Rd. Bour ............. 206 B3
Dorset Rd. Ch Fo ............ 55 E2
Dorset Rd. Christ ........... 209 F4
Dorset St. Southa ........... 103 D3
Dorstone Rd. Cos ............ 133 E1
Douglas Ave. Christ ......... 209 D3
Douglas Cres. Southa ........ 104 B3
Douglas Gdns. Poole ......... 205 F3
Douglas Mews. Bour .......... 208 B3
Douglas Rd. Bour ............ 208 C2
Douglas Rd. Poole ........... 205 F3
Douglas Way. Hyt ............ 125 E2
Doussiec Cl. Upt ............ 203 D4
Dove Cl. Wat ................ 111 F2
Dove Dale. Eastl ............ 55 E1
Dove Gdns. Lo He ............ 129 D3
Dove La. Hurs ............... 29 D4
Dover Cl. Poole ............. 206 A2
Dover Cl. Stubb ............. 154 A2
Dover Ct. S Hay ............. 184 C3
Dover Rd. Poole ............. 206 A2
Dover Rd. Ports ............. 183 D4
Dover St. Southa ............ 103 D4
Dovercourt Rd. Cos .......... 158 A3
Doveshill Cres. Bour ........ 190 B2
Doveshill Gdns. Bour ........ 190 B2
Doveys Cl. Bour ............. 143 D2
Dowds Cl. He En ............. 105 D4
Dowlands Cl. Bour ........... 190 B2
Dowlands Rd. Bour ........... 190 B2
Down End Rd. Cos ............ 134 B1
Down End. Cos ............... 134 B1

Down Farm La. Ki Wo ......... 1 C4
Down Lodge Cl. Alderh ....... 93 D3
Down Rd. Horn ............... 88 A1
Down's Park Ave. Tot ........ 101 D3
Down's Park Cres. Tot ....... 101 D3
Down's Park Rd. Tot ......... 101 D3
Downend Rd. Portc ........... 131 F1
Downham Cl. Wat ............. 111 F2
Downhouse Rd. Horn .......... 88 A2
Downland Cl. Botl ........... 105 F4
Downland Cl. Lo He .......... 129 D2
Downland Pl. He En .......... 105 D3
Downlands Cl. Down .......... 46 C3
Downlands Rd. Winch ......... 10 A2
Downley Rd. Hav ............. 136 A2
Downs Cl. Cos ............... 134 C2
Downscroft Gdns. He En ...... 105 D4
Downside Ave. Southa ........ 104 A3
Downside Rd. Wat ............ 134 B2
Downside Rd. Winch .......... 1 A1
Downside. Gos ............... 155 E1
Downsway The. Portc ......... 156 B4
Downton Cl. Bour ............ 191 E2
Downton Hill. Red ........... 47 E4
Downton La. M on S .......... 212 C4
Downton Rd. Southa .......... 79 F1
Downview Rd. Mar ............ 43 D2
Downwood Cl. Fordi .......... 69 E1
Downwood Way. Horn .......... 88 B1
Doyle Ave. Ports ............ 157 F2
Doyle Cl. Ports ............. 157 F2
Doyle Cl. Southa ............ 103 F1
Doyne Rd. Poole ............. 205 F2
Dradfield La. Sob ........... 109 E4
Dragon La. Rin .............. 168 A4
Dragon St. Pet .............. 40 C2
Dragoon Cl. Southa .......... 104 B2
Drake Cl. Christ ............ 209 F3
Drake Cl. Lo He ............. 129 D3
Drake Cl. March ............. 102 A1
Drake Cl. New M ............. 195 F2
Drake Cl. Rin ............... 117 E1
Drake Rd. Bish .............. 56 C2
Drake Rd. L on S ............ 179 E4
Drakes Cl. Hyt .............. 125 F1
Draper Rd. Bour ............. 190 A2
Draper Rd. Christ ........... 209 F4
Draycote Rd. Horn ........... 88 B2
Draycott Rd. Bour ........... 190 B1
Drayton Cl. Southa .......... 127 D4
Drayton La. Cos ............. 134 A1
Drayton Pl. Tot ............. 100 B4
Drayton Rd. Ports ........... 157 F1
Drayton St. Winch ........... 10 B3
Dresden Dr. Wat ............. 111 E2
Dreswick Cl. Christ ......... 192 B2
Drew Cl. Poole .............. 206 B4
Drift Rd. Clanf ............. 88 B2
Drift Rd. Fare .............. 131 E1
Drift The. Ro Ca ............ 113 D1
Driftwood Gdns. Ports ....... 183 E1
Driftwood Gdns. Tot ......... 100 B3
Drinkwater Cl. Eastl ........ 55 F2
Drive The. Fare ............. 131 D1
Drive The. Gos .............. 155 D1
Drive The. Hav .............. 135 F2
Drive The. Plai ............. 25 D1
Drive The. Poole ............ 205 E3
Drive The. Sh En ............ 25 D1
Drive The. Southb ........... 161 E4
Drive The. Tot .............. 100 C3
Drive The. W End ............ 80 A2
Drive The. W Wel ............ 51 D1
Drove Cl. Twyf .............. 31 F3
Drove Rd. Southa ............ 104 A2
Drove Rd. Southw ............ 133 D2
Drove The. Black ............ 150 C1
Drove The. Durl ............. 82 B4
Drove The. Fa Oa ............ 81 E3
Drove The. Southa ........... 104 A4
Drove The. Swan ............. 84 A3
Drove The. Tot .............. 76 A1
Drove The. Twyf ............. 31 F3
Drove The. W End ............ 80 C2
Drove The. W Wel ............ 50 C2
Droxford Rd. Bour ........... 208 A3
Droxford Rd. Swan ........... 84 B3
Druids Cl. Fern ............. 165 E1
Druitt Rd. Christ ........... 209 F4
Drum La. Pet ................ 40 C2
Drum Mead. Pet .............. 40 C2
Drummond Cl. Winch .......... 10 C3
Drummond Ct. Southa ......... 103 F2
Drummond Rd. Bour ........... 207 E2
Drummond Rd. He En .......... 81 E1
Drummond Rd. Hyt ............ 126 A2
Drummond Rd. Ports .......... 182 B3
Drummond Way. Ch Fo ......... 55 D4
Drury La. Pet ............... 40 C2
Drury Rd. Bour .............. 206 A1
Dryden Ave. Portc ........... 132 C1
Dryden Cl. Fare ............. 131 D1
Dryden Cl. St Le ............ 139 F3
Dryden Cl. Wat .............. 111 F1
Dryden Pl. M on S ........... 213 E3
Dryden Rd. Southa ........... 104 C3
Duart Ct. New M ............. 196 B2
Duck Island La. Rin ......... 141 D3
Duck La. Bour ............... 189 F2

Ducking Stool La. Christ ........ 209 D3
Duckmead La. Liss ................ 21 D3
Duddon Cl. W End ................ 80 A1
Dudleston Heath Dr. Wat .. 112 A1
Dudley Ave. Fordi ................ 69 F2
Dudley Ave. Hord ................ 196 C2
Dudley Gdns. Bour .............. 190 B3
Dudley Rd. Bour .................. 190 B3
Dudley Rd. Ports ................ 183 D4
Dudmoor Farm Rd. Christ .. 192 C2
Dudsbury Ave. Fern ............ 165 E2
Dudsbury Cres. Fern .......... 165 F2
Dudsbury Gdns. Fern .......... 190 C4
Dudsbury Rd. Fern .............. 165 E1
Duffield La. Westb .............. 137 F2
Dugald Drummond St. Ports .182 B3
Dugdell Cl. Fern ................ 165 F3
Duisburg Way. Ports .......... 182 A1
Duke Cres. Ports ................ 182 B4
Duke Rd. He En .................. 105 E3
Duke St. Southa .................. 103 D2
Dukes Cl. Pet ...................... 40 B2
Dukes Dr. Bour .................. 189 F3
Dukes Rd. Gosp .................. 181 D3
Dukes Rd. Southa ................ 103 E4
Dukes Wood Dr. Hyt .......... 126 A1
Dukesfield. Christ .............. 192 B1
Dulsie Rd. Bour .................. 206 B4
Dumbarton Cl. Ports .......... 182 B4
Dummer Ct. Hav ................ 135 E3
Dummer Rd. Brai ................ 28 B4
Dumpers Drove. Fa Oa ........ 81 E4
Dunbar Cl. Southa ................ 77 F3
Dunbar Cres. Christ ............ 194 C1
Dunbar Rd. Bour ................ 206 C3
Dunbar Rd. Ports ................ 183 D2
Dunbridge La. Awb .............. 26 C3
Dunbridge La. Mott .............. 26 C4
Duncan Cl. Southa .............. 126 C4
Duncan Ct. Southa .............. 104 B3
Duncan Rd. Lo He .............. 129 D3
Duncan Rd. New M .............. 196 B2
Duncan Rd. Ports ................ 182 B1
Duncans Dr. Fare ................ 154 A4
Duncliff Rd. Bour ................ 209 D2
Duncombe Rd. E Meon ........ 63 E4
Dundas Cl. Ports ................ 158 A1
Dundas La. Ports ................ 158 A1
Dundas Rd. Poole .............. 204 C4
Dundas Spur. Ports ............ 158 A1
Dundee Cl. Fare .................. 130 C2
Dundee Rd. Southa .............. 79 E1
Dundonald Cl. S Hay .......... 185 D3
Dundridge La. Drox .............. 60 B1
Dundry Way. He En ............ 105 E4
Dunedin Cl. Fern ................ 165 D2
Dunedin Dr. Fern ................ 165 D2
Dunedin Gdns. Fern .......... 165 D2
Dunedin Gr. Christ ............ 210 B4
Dunfield Way. Black .......... 150 C1
Dunford Cl. B on S ............ 211 F4
Dunford Cl. New M .............. 195 F1
Dunford Rd. Poole .............. 205 E3
Dunhurst Cl. Hav ................ 136 A2
Dunkeld Rd. Bour .............. 206 C3
Dunkeld Rd. Gosp .............. 181 D4
Dunkirk Cl. Southa .............. 78 B2
Dunkirk Rd. Southa .............. 78 B2
Dunlin Cl. Christ ................ 210 A3
Dunlin Cl. Ports ................ 183 E3
Dunnings La. N Bad ............ 53 F3
Dunnock Cl. Fern ................ 165 D4
Dunnock Cl. Ro Ca .............. 113 D1
Dunsbury Way. Hav ............ 135 F3
Dunsmore Cl. Ports ............ 182 B2
Dunster Cl. Southa .............. 78 B3
Dunstable Wlk. Fare .......... 154 B4
Dunstans Cl. Poole ............ 205 D3
Dunvegan Dr. Southa .......... 78 B3
Dunvegan Rd. Southa .......... 78 B3
Dunvegan Way. Southa ........ 78 B3
Dunville Cres. Bour ............ 191 D2
Dunyeats Rd. Broa .............. 188 A2
Durban Cl. Rom .................. 28 A1
Durban Rd. Ports ................ 182 C4
Durdells Ave. Bour ............ 190 D3
Durdells Gdns. Bour .......... 190 D3
Durford Ct. Hav .................. 135 E3
Durford Rd. Pet .................. 41 E2
Durham Gdns. Wat .............. 134 C3
Durham St. Gos .................. 181 D3
Durham St. Ports ................ 182 B3
Durland Cl. New M .............. 196 A1
Durley Ave. Wat ................ 111 F2
Durley Brook Road. Durl ...... 81 F3
Durley Chine Rd S. Bour .... 206 B1
Durley Chine Rd. Bour ...... 206 B1
Durley Cres. Tot ................ 100 B3
Durley Gdns. Bour .............. 206 B1
Durley Hall Rd. Durl ............ 58 B1
Durley La. Durl .................. 82 B4
Durley Rd S. Bour .............. 206 B1
Durley Rd. Bour .................. 206 C1
Durley Rd. Durl .................. 81 F4
Durley Rd. Fa Oa ................ 81 F4
Durley Rd. Gosp ................ 181 D3
Durlston Cres. Christ .......... 192 B2
Durlston Rd. Poole .............. 205 E1
Durlston Rd. Southa ............ 77 E1

Dumford Rd. Southa ............ 103 D3
Dumgate Pl. Winch .............. 11 D4
Dumgate Terr. Winch .......... 11 D4
Dumstown. Sway ................ 172 B1
Durrant Rd. Bour ................ 206 C2
Durrant Rd. Poole .............. 205 E2
Durrant Way. Sway .............. 172 A1
Durrants Gdns. Ro Ca ........ 136 A4
Durrants Rd. Ro Ca ............ 136 A4
Durrington Pl. Bour ............ 208 A3
Durrington Rd. Bour .......... 208 A4
Dursley Cres. Cos .............. 157 E4
Durweston Cl. Bour ............ 191 D2
Dutton La. Eastl .................. 56 A2
Dutton's Rd. Rom ................ 52 C4
Dyer Rd. Southa .................. 102 B4
Dymoke St. Ems ................ 136 C2
Dymott Cl. Southa .............. 102 B3
Dyneley Gr. Southa .............. 80 A1
Dyram Cl. Eastl .................. 55 F3
Dysart Ave. Cos ................ 158 A4
Dyserth Cl. Southa ............ 104 A1
Dyson Dr. Winch .................. 2 A1

Eadens La. Ne Ma ................ 99 E4
Eagle Ave. Wat .................. 111 F2
Eagle Cl. Ch Fo .................. 55 D2
Eagle Cl. Portc .................. 155 F4
Eagle Rd. Poole .................. 206 A2
Eames La. Hawk .................. 19 F4
Earl's Rd. Southa ................ 103 D4
Earle Rd. Bour .................. 206 B1
Earlham Dr. Poole .............. 205 E2
Earls Cl. Bish ...................... 57 D1
Earls Rd. Fare .................... 155 D4
Earlsdon St. Ports .............. 182 B2
Earlsdon Way. Christ ........ 210 C4
Earlswood Dr. Alderh .......... 92 C3
Earnley Rd. S Hay .............. 185 F1
East Ave. B on S ................ 211 E4
East Avenue. Bour .............. 206 C3
East Bank Rd. Brock .......... 173 D4
East Bargate. Southa .......... 103 D2
East Borough. Wi Mi .......... 163 D3
East Cams Cl. Portc .......... 131 F1
East Cl. B on S .................. 211 E4
East Cliff Way. Christ ........ 210 B4
East Cosham Rd. Cos ........ 158 A4
East Cl. Cos ...................... 158 A4
East Ct. Ports .................... 182 C4
East Dean Rd. Locke ............ 4 C1
East Dr. Bish ...................... 56 C2
East Field Cl. Southb .......... 137 F1
East Hill Cl. Fare ................ 131 E1
East Hill Dr. Liss ................ 21 D2
East Hill. Lym .................... 198 C2
East Hoe Rd. Sob ................ 86 A2
East House Ave. Stubb ...... 154 B1
East Howe Gdns. Bour ........ 190 B2
East La. Hord .................... 197 F1
East Leigh Rd. Hav ............ 136 B2
East Lodge Park. Cos ........ 158 B4
East Lodge. Fare ................ 130 B1
East Overcliff Dr. Bour ...... 207 E2
East Park Terr. Southa ........ 103 D3
East Quay Rd. Poole .......... 204 B1
East St. Fare ...................... 131 E1
East St. Hambl .................... 86 B2
East St. Hav ...................... 135 F1
East St. Lo He .................... 154 A4
East St. Poole .................... 204 B1
East St. Portc .................... 156 C4
East St. Ports .................... 182 A2
East St. Southa .................. 103 D2
East St. Westb .................... 137 D2
East St. Wi Mi .................... 163 E2
East Surrey St. Ports .......... 182 B3
East View Rd. Rin .............. 141 D4
East Way. Bour .................. 191 E1
East Way. Broa .................. 187 E3
East Woodhay Rd. Winch ...... 1 B2
Eastbourne Ave. Gos .......... 180 C4
Eastbourne Ave. Southa .... 102 B4
Eastbourne Rd. Ports ........ 183 D4
Eastbrook Cl. Gos .............. 180 C4
Eastbrook Cl. Lo He .......... 129 D3
Eastbrook Row. Wi Mi ...... 163 E2
Eastchurch Cl. Southa ........ 77 F2
Eastcliff Cl. L on S ............ 179 F4
Eastcot Cl. Holb ................ 150 B2
Eastcott Cl. Bour .............. 208 A4
Easter Rd. Bour ................ 191 D1
Eastern Ave. Ports ............ 183 D3
Eastern Par. Fare .............. 155 D4
Eastern Par. Ports .............. 182 C1
Eastern Rd. Cos ................ 158 B2
Eastern Rd. Hav ................ 136 A1
Eastern Rd. Lym ................ 198 B2
Eastern Rd. Ports .............. 158 B2
Eastern Villas Rd. Ports .... 182 C1
Eastern Way. M on S .......... 213 F2
Eastfield Ave. Fare ............ 154 C4
Eastfield Cl. Rin ................ 141 E4
Eastfield La. Rin ................ 141 E4
Eastfield Rd. Ports ............ 183 D2
Eastfield Rd. Southa .......... 103 E4
Eastgate St. Southa ............ 103 D2
Eastgate St. Winch .............. 11 D4

Eastlake Ave. Poole .......... 205 E3
Eastlake Cl. Pet .................. 41 E2
Eastlake Hts. Ports ............ 183 E2
Eastlands. New M .............. 196 A1
Eastleigh Rd. Fa Oa ............ 57 E1
Eastmeare Ct. Tot .............. 100 B3
Eastney Farm Rd. Ports .... 183 E2
Eastney Rd. Ports .............. 183 D2
Eastney St. Ports ................ 183 D1
Eastoke Ave. S Hay ............ 185 E1
Easton La. It Ab .................... 2 C2
Eastover Ct. Hav ................ 135 E3
Eastville Rd. Fa Oa .............. 57 E1
Eastways. Bi Wa .................. 83 E4
Eastwood Ave. Fern .......... 165 F3
Eastwood Cl. S Hay .......... 185 D3
Eastwood Rd. Ports ............ 157 F2
Eastworth Rd. Ver .............. 114 C4
Eaton Gdns. Bour .............. 206 B2
Eaton Rd. Poole ................ 206 A1
Ebden Rd. Winch ................ 11 D4
Ebenzeer La. Rin ................ 140 C4
Ebery Gr. Ports .................. 183 E4
Ebor Cl. Fern .................... 165 F1
Ebor Rd. Poole .................. 205 E3
Eccles Rd. Poole ................ 204 A1
Ecton La. Ports .................. 158 B2
Eddystone Rd. Tot .............. 76 B1
Edelvale Rd. Southa ............ 80 A1
Eden Gr. Wi Mi .................. 163 E2
Eden Rd. W End .................. 80 A1
Eden Rise. Fare .................. 155 D4
Eden St. Ports .................... 182 B3
Eden Wlk. N Bad ................ 55 D3
Edgar Cres. Portc .............. 156 B3
Edgar Rd. Winch ................ 10 C4
Edgarton Rd. Broa .............. 188 B2
Edgecombe Cres. Gos ...... 180 B4
Edgehill Rd. Bour .............. 190 C1
Edgehill Rd. Southa ............ 79 F1
Edgell Rd. Westb ................ 137 D2
Edgemoor Rd. W Moo ........ 139 D1
Edgerly Gdns. Cos ............ 157 F3
Edgeware Rd. Ports .......... 183 D3
Edifred Rd. Bour ................ 191 D2
Edinburgh Rd. Ports .......... 182 B3
Edington Cl. Bi Wa .............. 83 D4
Edington Rd. Winch .............. 2 A1
Edmund Rd. Ports .............. 182 C2
Edmunds Cl. He En ............ 105 E3
Edneys La. Den .................. 111 D3
Edward Ave. Bish ................ 56 B2
Edward Cl. Black ................ 150 C1
Edward Gdns. Hav .............. 135 E1
Edward Gr. Portc ................ 132 C1
Edward Rd. Bour ................ 190 A2
Edward Rd. Christ .............. 209 F4
Edward Rd. Hyt .................. 126 A2
Edward Rd. Poole .............. 205 E3
Edward Rd. Southa ............ 102 B4
Edward Rd. Winch ................ 10 C3
Edward St. Southa .............. 103 D2
Edwards Cl. Wat ................ 111 F2
Edwina Cl. N Bad ................ 54 A2
Edwina Cl. Rin .................. 117 E1
Edwina Cl. Southa .............. 104 A3
Edwina Dr. Broa ................ 188 A1
Effingham Gdns. Southa .... 104 B2
Efford Way. Lym ................ 198 A1
Egan Cl. Ports .................... 157 F2
Egbert Rd. Winch .................. 2 A1
Egdon Dr. Oakl .................. 188 C4
Egerton Gdns. Bour .......... 207 E3
Egerton Rd. Bour .............. 207 E3
Eglantine Cl. Wat .............. 112 A2
Eglantine Walk. Wat .......... 112 B2
Egmont Cl. St Le ................ 140 B1
Egmont Dr. St Le ................ 140 B1
Egmont Gdns. St Le .......... 140 B1
Egmont Rd. Hamw .............. 203 D2
Eight Acres. Rom ................ 53 D4
Elaine Gdns. Wat ................ 112 A3
Elan Cl. W End .................... 80 A1
Elcombes Cl. Lyn .............. 121 F3
Elder Cl. March ................ 102 A1
Elder Cl. Winch .................. 10 B2
Elder Rd. Hav .................... 136 A2
Elderberry Cl. Clanf ............ 88 B2
Elderberry La. Christ ........ 209 F3
Elderberry Way. Wat .......... 112 B2
Elderfield Cl. Ems .............. 137 D2
Elderfield Rd. Hav .............. 135 E4
Eldon Ave. B on S .............. 211 F4
Eldon Cl. B on S ................ 211 F4
Eldon Pl. Bour .................... 206 A2
Eldon Rd. Bour .................. 190 C1
Eldon Rd. Brai ...................... 7 D3
Eldon Rd. Brai .................... 28 A4
Eldon Rd. Ki So .................... 7 D3
Eldon St. Ports .................. 182 B2
Eleanor Dr. Bour ................ 189 E3
Electron Way. Ch Fo ............ 55 E3
Eletra Ave. Wat .................. 134 B4
Elfin Dr. Fern .................... 165 E4
Elgar Cl. Gos .................... 181 D1
Elgar Rd. Southa ................ 104 B2
Elgar Rd. Southa ................ 190 B2
Elgar Rd. Southa ................ 104 B2
Elgar Wlk. Wat .................. 134 C3

Elgin Cl. Fare .................... 130 C1
Elgin Cl. Hyt ...................... 126 A2
Elgin Rd. Bour .................. 206 B3
Elgin Rd. Cos .................... 157 F3
Elgin Rd. Poole .................. 205 E1
Elgin Rd. Southa ................ 102 B3
Eling Cl. Winch .................... 1 B2
Eling Hill. Tot .................... 101 D3
Eling La. Tot ...................... 101 D3
Eling View. Southa ............ 101 E4
Elise Cl. Bour .................... 208 A4
Elizabeth Ave. Christ ........ 208 C4
Elizabeth Cl. Down .............. 46 B4
Elizabeth Cl. W End ............ 80 B1
Elizabeth Cres. Hord .......... 197 D1
Elizabeth Ct. Fare .............. 154 C4
Elizabeth Gdns. Christ ...... 210 B4
Elizabeth Gdns. Hyt .......... 126 A1
Elizabeth Gdns. Ports ...... 182 C1
Elizabeth Rd. Poole .......... 204 B2
Elizabeth Rd. Stubb .......... 154 B1
Elizabeth Rd. Wat .............. 134 C3
Elizabeth Rd. Wi Mi .......... 163 E3
Elizabeth Rd. Wickh .......... 108 A2
Elizabeth Way. Eastl .......... 56 A3
Elkhams Cl. Hord .............. 197 E1
Elkstone Rd. Cos .............. 133 D1
Ella Nore La. W Wit .......... 186 C1
Ellachie Gdns. Gos ............ 181 D1
Ellachie Mews. Gos .......... 181 D1
Ellachie Rd. Gos ................ 181 D1
Elland Cl. Fa Oa .................. 57 E1
Ellcombe Cl. Poole ............ 205 F4
Elldene Ct. Tot .................. 100 C3
Ellen Gdns. N Bad .............. 55 D3
Ellerslie Cl. Stubb ............ 154 A1
Ellery Gr. Lym .................... 198 C3
Ellesfield Dr. Fern .............. 165 E1
Ellesmere Orch. Westb ...... 137 D3
Ellingham Dro. Rin ............ 117 D3
Ellingham Rd. B on S ........ 211 E4
Elliot Cl. Tot ...................... 100 B4
Elliot Rd. Bour .................. 189 F2
Elliot Rise. He En ................ 81 E1
Ellis Rd. Southa ................ 104 C3
Ellisfield Rd. Hav .............. 135 F2
Ellwood Ave. Southa .......... 104 C3
Ellwood Cl. Southa ............ 104 C3
Elm Av. Lo He .................... 129 D1
Elm Ave. Christ .................. 192 C1
Elm Ave. Lym .................... 198 B1
Elm Ave. New M ................ 196 A1
Elm Cl. Southa .................... 78 C2
Elm Close Estate. S Hay .... 184 C2
Elm Cres. Hyt .................... 150 A4
Elm Cres. Uph .................... 58 C3
Elm Gdns. Bour .................. 206 B3
Elm Gdns. W End ................ 80 B2
Elm Gr. Eastl ...................... 55 F1
Elm Gr. Gos ...................... 181 D3
Elm Gr. Ports .................... 182 B2
Elm Gr. S Hay .................... 185 D2
Elm Park Rd. Hav .............. 135 F1
Elm Rd. Bi Wa ...................... 83 F4
Elm Rd. Hav ...................... 160 A4
Elm Rd. Winch .................... 10 C4
Elm St. Ports .................... 182 A2
Elm St. Southa .................. 103 D2
Elm Terr. Southa ................ 103 D2
Elm Tree Wlk. Fern ............ 190 C4
Elmdale Gr. W Wel .............. 51 D1
Elmers Way. Bran .............. 169 D1
Elmes Dr. Southa .............. 101 F4
Elmes Rd. Bour .................. 190 C1
Elmeswelle Rd. Wat .......... 112 A3
Elmfield La. Faw ................ 178 A4
Elmgate Dr. Bour .............. 208 A4
Elmhurst Rd. Fare ............ 155 D4
Elmhurst Rd. Gos .............. 181 E2
Elmhurst Rd. W Moo .......... 138 C1
Elmhurst Way. W Moo ........ 138 C1
Elmleigh Rd. Hav .............. 135 F1
Elmore Ave. Lon S .......... 180 A3
Elmore Cl. L on S .............. 179 F3
Elmore Dr. St Le ................ 139 F3
Elmore Rd. L on S ............ 179 F3
Elms Ave. Poole ................ 205 D1
Elms Cl. Fordi .................... 69 D1
Elms Cl. Poole .................. 205 D1
Elms Rd. Fare .................... 155 D4
Elms Way. Bour ................ 208 C2
Elmsleigh Ct. Southa .......... 79 D2
Elmsleigh Gdns. Southa ...... 79 D2
Elmslie Gdns. Burs ............ 104 C1
Elmstead Rd. Poole .......... 216 C4
Elmtree Cl. Ashu .............. 100 A1
Elmtree Gdns. Rom ............ 53 E3
Elmtree Rd. Cos ................ 158 B4
Elmwood Ave. Fordi ............ 69 E1
Elmwood Ave. Wat ............ 134 C3
Elmwood Rd. Ports ............ 157 F2
Elmwood. Christ ................ 211 D4
Elphinstone Rd. Christ ...... 195 D1
Elphinstone Rd. Ports ...... 182 B1
Elsfred Rd. Stubb .............. 154 A1
Elson La. Gosp .................. 181 D4
Elson Rd. Gos .................... 180 C4
Elson Rd. Gosp ................ 181 D4
Elstead Gdns. Wat ............ 134 B2

Elstree Rd. Southa ............ 103 F3
Eltham Cl. Bour .................. 208 A4
Elvin Cl. Hord .................... 196 C2
Elwell Gn. S Hay .............. 184 C2
Elwyn Rd. Bour ................ 207 E3
Emanuel St. Ports .............. 182 B4
Emberly Cl. Fern .............. 166 A4
Embley Cl. Tot .................... 76 B1
Embley La. W Wel .............. 51 F4
Embley Park Ind Est. W Wel .. 51 F4
Embsay Rd. Swanw .......... 128 B4
Emerald Cl. Southa ............ 104 A3
Emerald Cl. Wat ................ 135 D4
Emerson Cl. Poole ............ 204 B1
Emerson Rd. Poole ............ 204 B1
Emily Cl. Christ .................. 193 D1
Emmanuel Cl. Lo He ........ 129 E1
Emmett Rd. Southa ............ 77 F3
Emmons Cl. Hamble .......... 128 A1
Empress Rd. Lyn .............. 121 F3
Empress Rd. Southa .......... 103 D1
Empress Rd. Southa .......... 103 D4
Empshott Rd. Ports .......... 182 C2
Empson Wlk. L on S .......... 179 F4
Emsbrook Dr. Ems ............ 136 C1
Emsworth Common Rd. Ems . 136 B3
Emsworth House Cl. Ems .. 136 C1
Emsworth Rd. Hav ............ 136 A1
Emsworth Rd. Lym ............ 198 C2
Emsworth Rd. Ports .......... 157 F1
Emsworth Rd. Southa ........ 102 A4
Emsworth Rd. Th Is .......... 161 E2
Encombe Cl. Poole ............ 205 F4
Endeavour Cl. Southa ........ 102 A4
Endeavour Rd. Gos .......... 181 E2
Endeavour Way. Hyt ........ 126 A3
Enderwood Cl. Tot ............ 100 A4
Endfield Cl. Christ ............ 192 C1
Endfield Rd. Bour .............. 191 D1
Endfield Rd. Christ ............ 192 C1
Endle St. Southa ................ 103 E2
Endofield Cl. Gos .............. 154 C3
Enfield Cres. Poole .......... 204 C3
Enfield Gr. Southa ............ 103 F2
Enfield Rd. Poole .............. 204 C3
Englands Way. Bour .......... 189 E2
Englefield Rd. Southa ........ 103 E4
English Rd. Southa ............ 102 A4
Enmill La. Hurs .................... 9 F3
Ennerdale Cl. Horn ............ 88 B1
Ennerdale Gdns. W End ...... 80 A1
Ennerdale Rd. Southa ........ 77 F1
Ennerdale Rd. Stubb ........ 154 B2
Ensbury Ave. Bour ............ 190 B1
Ensbury Cl. Bour .............. 190 B1
Ensbury Ct. Bour .............. 190 C1
Ensbury Park Rd. Bour ...... 190 C1
Ensign Park. Hamble ........ 127 F1
Enterprise Rd. Horn .......... 112 B4
Enterprise Way. Southa .... 103 D1
Eperston Rd. Wat .............. 112 A3
Epping Cl. Southa ................ 80 A1
Epworth Rd. Ports ............ 157 F1
Eric Rd. Stubb .................... 154 B1
Erica Cl. Lo He .................. 128 C2
Erica Cl. Wat .................... 112 A2
Erica Dr. Broa .................. 187 E3
Erica Way. Wat .................. 112 A2
Ericksen Rd. Bour ............ 190 B2
Ernest Cl. Ems .................. 136 C1
Ernest Rd. Hav .................. 135 E2
Ernest Rd. Ports ................ 182 C4
Erpingham Rd. Poole ........ 206 A3
Erskine Rd. Winch .............. 10 C4
Escombe Rd. Bish .............. 56 B2
Escur Cl. Ports .................. 157 F2
Esdaile La. Bur ................ 142 C2
Esher Gr. Wat .................... 111 E1
Eskdale Cl. Horn ................ 88 B1
Esmond Cl. Ems ................ 160 C4
Esmonde Cl. L on S .......... 179 F3
Esmonde Way. Poole ........ 204 C4
Esplanade Gdns. Ports .... 183 E1
Esplanade The. Gos .......... 181 F2
Esplanade. B on S ............ 216 C4
Esplanade. Poole .............. 204 B2
Esplanade. Ports .............. 183 D1
Essex Ave. Christ .............. 192 C1
Essex Green. Ch Fo ............ 55 E1
Essex Rd. Ports ................ 183 D2
Essex Rd. Ports ................ 182 C2
Esslemont Rd. Ports ........ 182 B4
Estella Rd. Ports .............. 182 B4
Estridge Cl. Burs .............. 105 D1
Ethel Rd. Ports .................. 182 C3
Ethelbert Rd. Wi Mi .......... 163 E2
Ethelburt Ave. Southa ........ 79 E3
Ethelred Gdns. Tot ............ 100 B3
Eton Rd. Ports .................. 182 C2
Ettrick Rd. Poole .............. 206 A1
European Way. Southa ...... 103 D1
Euston Rd. Ports .............. 183 D3
Eva Allaway Ct. Ports ...... 182 A3
Evans Cl. Bour .................. 189 F1
Evans Cl. St Le .................. 139 F3
Evans Rd. Ports ................ 183 D2
Evans St. Southa .............. 103 D2
Evelegh Rd. Cos ................ 158 B4
Evelyn Cl. Shed .................. 83 F2
Evelyn Cres. Southa .......... 102 B4

Evelyn Rd. Bour ................ 191 D1
Evening Glade. Fern ......... 165 F2
Evenlode Rd. Southa .......... 77 F1
Everdon La. Ports ............ 158 B2
Everest Rd. Christ ............ 209 F4
Everglade Ave. Wat .......... 111 F2
Everglades Cl. Fern .......... 165 E4
Evergreen Cl. March .......... 101 F1
Evergreen Cl. W Moo ........ 138 C4
Evergreen Cl. Wat ............ 134 B4
Evergreens. St Le ............ 139 F3
Evering Ave. Poole .......... 189 E1
Evering Gdns. Poole ......... 189 E1
Everlea Cl. Hord .............. 197 E1
Everon Gdns. New M ........ 196 A1
Evershot Rd. Bour ........... 191 F1
Eversley Cres. Hav ......... 135 F2
Eversley Pl. Winch ............. 10 B3
Everton Rd. Hord ............. 197 D1
Evesham Cl. Bour ............ 208 A4
Evesham Cl. Southa .......... 79 D3
Ewart Ct. Hyt ................. 126 A3
Ewart Rd. Ports .............. 182 C4
Ewell Way. Tot ................. 76 B1
Ewhurst Cl. Hav .............. 135 E2
Exbury Cl. Bish ................ 56 C1
Exbury Dr. Bour .............. 189 F3
Exbury Rd. Black ............. 150 C1
Exbury Rd. Hav ............... 136 A3
Excelsior Rd. Poole .......... 205 E2
Exchange Rd. Ports ......... 182 A3
Exeter Cl. Eastl ................ 55 F3
Exeter Cl. Ems ............... 136 C2
Exeter Cl. Lo He ............. 128 C2
Exeter Cl. Southa .............. 80 A1
Exeter Cres. Bour ........... 206 A1
Exeter La. Bour .............. 206 C1
Exeter Park Rd. Bour ....... 206 C1
Exeter Rd. Bour .............. 206 C1
Exeter Rd. Ports ............. 182 C1
Exeter Rd. Southa ........... 104 A4
Exford Ave. Southa .......... 104 B4
Exford Dr. Southa ............ 104 B4
Exleigh Cl. Southa ........... 104 A3
Exmoor Cl. Tot ............... 100 A4
Exmoor Rd. Southa .......... 103 D3
Exmouth Rd. Gosp .......... 181 D4
Exmouth Rd. Ports ......... 182 B1
Exmouth St. Southa ........ 103 D3
Exton Gdns. Portc ......... 132 B1
Exton Rd. Bour .............. 208 B4
Exton Rd. Hav ............... 136 A3
Eyeworth Wlk. Hyt ......... 125 E2
Eynham Ave. Southa ....... 104 B3
Eynham Cl. Southa ......... 104 B3
Eyre Cl. Tot .................. 100 B3

Fabian Cl. Wat ............... 135 D4
Factory Rd. Eastl ............. 56 A1
Factory Rd. Upt ............. 203 E3
Fair Field. Rom ................ 28 A1
Fair Green. Southa .......... 104 A3
Fair Isle Cl. Stubb ........... 154 A2
Fair Oak Ct. Fa Oa ........... 57 E1
Fair Oak Dr. Hav ............ 135 F2
Fairacre Rise. Fare ......... 154 A4
Fairbourne Cl. Wat ......... 111 F1
Fairclose Dr. Litt ................ 1 A3
Faircross Cl. Holb .......... 150 B2
Fairdown Cl. Winch .......... 11 E4
Fairfax Cl. Winch ............. 10 A3
Fairfax Ct. Southa .......... 104 C3
Fairfax Mews. Southa ...... 104 C3
Fairfield Ave. Fare .......... 154 C4
Fairfield Cl. Christ .......... 209 D4
Fairfield Cl. Ems ............ 136 C1
Fairfield Cl. Hyt ............. 126 A2
Fairfield Cl. Lym ............ 198 C2
Fairfield Cl. Wi Mi .......... 163 F3
Fairfield Rd. Comp ........... 31 E3
Fairfield Rd. Hav ............ 135 F1
Fairfield Rd. Wi Mi ......... 163 E2
Fairfield Rd. Winch ............ 1 C1
Fairfield Sq. Cos ............ 157 F4
Fairfield. Christ .............. 209 D4
Fairhome Cl. Gosp ......... 181 D4
Fairisle Rd. Southa ........... 77 F2
Fairlawn Cl. Rown ........... 77 F3
Fairlea Rd. Ems ............. 136 C2
Fairlea Rd. Lym ............. 198 C3
Fairlie Cl. He En .............. 81 D2
Fairlie Park. Rin ............. 117 D1
Fairlie. Rin ................... 117 E1
Fairlight La. Sway .......... 196 B4
Fairmead Walk. Wat ....... 112 A2
Fairmead Way. Tot ......... 100 C3
Fairmile Rd. Christ ......... 192 C1
Fairoak Rd. Bish .............. 57 D1
Fairoak Rd. Fa Oa ........... 57 D1
Fairthorne Gdns. Gos ..... 181 D2
Fairview Cl. Hyt ............. 126 A2
Fairview Cl. Rom .............. 28 A1
Fairview Cres. Broa ........ 188 A3
Fairview Dr. Broa ........... 188 A3
Fairview Dr. Hyt ............. 126 A2
Fairview Dr. Rom .............. 28 A1
Fairview Par. Hyt ........... 126 A1
Fairview Rd. Broa ........... 188 A3
Fairwater Rd. Gos .......... 155 D1

Fairway Ave. Poole ........ 216 B4
Fairway Bsns Park. Ports ... 158 B1
Fairway Dr. Christ .......... 208 C3
Fairway Gdns. Rown ......... 77 F3
Fairway Rd. Hyt ............ 125 F2
Fairway The. B on S ....... 212 A4
Fairway The. Gos ........... 155 E1
Fairway The. Portc ......... 156 B4
Fairway The. Ro Ca ........ 113 E1
Fairways. Fern ............... 165 F3
Fairwood Rd. Ver ........... 115 E3
Fairy Cross Way. Wat ...... 112 A1
Falaise Rd. Southa ........... 78 B2
Falcon Cl. Portc ............ 155 F4
Falcon Dr. Christ ........... 210 A3
Falcon Fields. Faw ......... 151 D2
Falcon Green. Cos .......... 158 C4
Falcon Rd. Horn ............ 112 A4
Falcon Sq. Eastl .............. 55 F1
Falcon View. Winch .......... 10 B2
Falcon Way. Botl ............. 81 F1
Falconer Ct. Faw ........... 150 B3
Falconer Dr. Hamw ........ 203 F2
Falkland Rd. Ch Fo .......... 55 E2
Falkland Rd. Southa ....... 102 A4
Fallow Field. Winch .......... 10 B2
Fallows The. New M ....... 196 A3
Fancy Rd. Poole ............ 205 D4
Fanshawe St. Southa ...... 103 D3
Far Meadow Way. Ems ... 160 B4
Farcroft Rd. Poole .......... 205 D3
Fareham Park Rd. Fare .... 130 B2
Fareham Rd. Gos ........... 155 E2
Fareham Rd. Southw ....... 132 C3
Fareham Rd. Wickh ........ 108 A2
Faringdon Rd. Southa ..... 104 B4
Farleigh Cl. Hav ............ 135 E3
Farley Cl. Fa Oa .............. 57 E1
Farley Cl. Winch ............. 10 A2
Farley Ct. Southa ............ 78 B1
Farley La. Brai .................. 7 F1
Farley La. Hurs ................ 7 F1
Farley Mount Rd. Hurs ...... 9 D2
Farlington Ave. Cos ........ 134 B1
Farlington Rd. Ports ....... 157 F1
Farnham Rd. Liss ............ 20 B2
Farnham Rd. Poole ......... 206 A4
Farnham Rd. Steep .......... 20 B2
Farnleys Mead. Lym ....... 198 C1
Faroes Cl. Stubb ............ 154 A2
Farrier Way. Fare ........... 155 D3
Farriers Cl. Wi Mi .......... 164 A3
Farriers Way. Wat .......... 112 B1
Farriers Wlk. Gos ........... 181 E3
Farringdon Rd. Hav ........ 136 A2
Farringford Rd. Southa .... 104 B3
Farthing La. Ports .......... 182 A2
Farthings Gate. Wat ....... 134 C2
Farwell Cl. Burt ............. 193 E2
Farwell Rd. Poole .......... 189 E1
Fastnet Cl. Southa ........... 77 F3
Fastnet Way. Stubb ........ 154 A2
Fathersfield. Brock ......... 145 F1
Fathoms Reach. S Hay .... 184 C2
Fawcett Rd. New M ........ 195 F1
Fawcett Rd. Ports .......... 182 C2
Fawley By Pass. Faw ...... 151 D2
Fawley Green. Bour ....... 191 E2
Fawley La. Frox G ........... 17 D2
Fawley La. Ows ............... 33 D4
Fawley Rd. Hav ............. 150 C2
Fawley Rd. Hyt .............. 150 A4
Fawley Rd. Ports ........... 157 F3
Fawley Rd. Southa ......... 102 A3
Fay Cl. Stubb ................ 154 B1
Fayre La. Fare ............... 155 D4
Fearon Rd. Ports ........... 157 F1
Felix Rd. Gosp .............. 181 D4
Fell Cl. Lo He ............... 129 D2
Fell Dr. L on S .............. 179 F4
Felmer Dr. Ki Wo .............. 2 B4
Feltham Cl. Rom ............. 53 E4
Felton Cres. Christ ......... 210 C4
Felton Rd. Poole ........... 204 C3
Feltons Pl. Ports ........... 157 F3
Fenleigh Cl. B on S ........ 196 A1
Fennel Gdns. Lym .......... 198 C3
Fennell Cl. Wat ............. 111 E1
Fenton Rd. Bour ............ 208 B3
Fern Barrow. Poole ........ 206 A4
Fern Cl. Alderh ............... 93 D3
Fern Cl. Burt ................ 193 E1
Fern Cl. Pet .................... 41 E2
Fern Rd. Hyt ................. 125 F2

Fern Rd. Southa ............ 103 F1
Fern Way. Hyt ............... 125 E2
Fern Way. Lo He ........... 129 E2
Ferncroft Cl. Stubb ........ 154 B1
Ferncroft Gdns. Bour ..... 190 B3
Ferncroft Rd. Bour ........ 190 B3
Ferndale Mews. Gos ...... 155 D2
Ferndale Rd. March ........ 101 F1
Ferndale Rd. New M ...... 196 A3
Ferndale. He En ............ 105 E3
Ferndale. Wat ............... 135 D4
Ferndene Way. Southa ... 103 F4
Ferneham Rd. Fare ........ 130 B1
Fernglade. New M .......... 196 A2
Fernheath Cl. Bour ........ 190 A2
Fernheath Rd. Bour ....... 190 A2
Fernhill Cl. Poole ........... 189 D1
Fernhill La. New M ........ 196 A2
Fernhill Rd. New M ........ 196 A2
Fernhills Rd. Hyt ........... 126 A1
Fernhurst Cl. S Hay ........ 184 B2
Fernhurst Rd. Ports ....... 182 C2
Fernie Cl. Stubb ............ 154 A1
Fernlea Ave. Fern .......... 165 E1
Fernlea Cl. Fern ............ 165 E2
Fernlea Cl. St Le ........... 139 F2
Fernlea Gdns. Fern ........ 165 E2
Fernlea Gdns. Southa ....... 78 C2
Fernside Ave. Poole ....... 204 C2
Fernside Cl. Holb .......... 150 B2
Fernside Cl. Southa ....... 101 F4
Fernside Rd. Bour ......... 206 C4
Fernside Rd. Poole ........ 204 C2
Fernside Rd. W Moo ...... 138 C1
Fernside Way. Fa Oa ....... 57 F1
Fernwood Cl. St Le ........ 140 A3
Fernwood Cres. Southa ... 103 F4
Fernyhurst Ave. Rown ...... 77 F3
Ferris Ave. Bour ........... 191 E1
Ferris Cl. Bour .............. 191 E1
Ferris Pl. Bour .............. 191 E1
Ferrol Rd. Gos .............. 181 E3
Ferry Rd. Bour .............. 208 C2
Ferry Rd. Br Is .............. 216 A1
Ferry Rd. Hamw ............ 204 A1
Ferry Rd. Hyt ............... 125 F2
Ferry Rd. Ports ............. 183 E2
Ferry Rd. S Hay ............ 184 A2
Ferry Way. Poole .......... 216 A2
Ferrybridge Green. He En ... 105 E3
Festing Gr. Ports ........... 183 D1
Festing Rd. Ports .......... 182 C1
Feversham Ave. Bour ..... 191 F1
Fey Rd. Gos ................. 181 D3
Fibbards Rd. Brock ........ 145 F1
Field Cl. Comp ................ 31 E3
Field Cl. Gos ................. 155 D3
Field Cl. Lo He .............. 129 D1
Field Cl. Rom .................. 53 D4
Field Cl. Southa .............. 79 E3
Field End. Ki Wo ............... 2 B4
Field Way. Christ ........... 194 B1
Field Way. Comp ............. 31 E3
Field Way. Den .............. 110 C2
Field Wlk. Lym .............. 198 B3
Fielden Cl. N Bad ............ 53 F2
Fielders' Way. W Wel ....... 51 D1
Fieldfare Cl. Clanf ........... 88 B2
Fieldfare Ct. Tot ............ 100 B4
Fieldmore Rd. Gosp ....... 181 D4
Fields Cl. Black ............. 150 C1
Fieldway. Rin ............... 141 D4
Fifth Ave. Cos .............. 157 F4
Fifth Ave. Hav .............. 136 A1
Fifth St. Ports .............. 182 C3
Filmer Cl. Gos .............. 180 B4
Filmorehill La. Frox G ...... 17 D2
Filton Cl. Tot ................. 76 B1
Filton Rd. Lym .............. 198 B2
Finch Rd. Ports ............ 183 E2
Finchdean Rd. Hav ........ 135 E2
Finchdean Rd. Ro Ca ..... 113 E2
Finches The. Southa ........ 79 D1
Finchfield Ave. Bour ...... 189 F3
Finchmead La. Pet .......... 40 A2
Findon Rd. Gosp ........... 181 D4
Finisterre Cl. Stubb ....... 154 A2
Finlay Cl. Southa ........... 104 B2
Fiona Cl. Winch .............. 11 E4
Fir Ave. New M ............. 196 A1
Fir Cl. Lyn ................... 121 F2
Fir Cl. W Moo ............... 138 C2
Fir Copse Rd. Wat ......... 134 B2
Fir Rd. Ashu ................. 100 A1
Fir Tree Cl. Fa Oa ........... 81 E4
Fir Tree Cl. St Le ........... 139 E1
Fir Tree Gdns. Wat ........ 112 B3
Fir Tree Gr. Hyt ............ 150 A4
Fir Tree La. Christ ......... 194 B1
Fir Tree Rd. Cadn ........... 99 D4
Fir Tree Rd. S Hay ......... 185 D2
Fir Vale Rd. Bour .......... 206 C2
Firbank Rd. Bour .......... 207 D4
Firecrest Cl. Southa ......... 78 A3
Firgrove Cl. N Bad ........... 53 F2
Firgrove Cres. Ports ...... 157 F3

Firgrove La. Southw ....... 108 C1
Firgrove Rd. N Bad .......... 54 A3
Firgrove Rd. Southa ....... 102 B4
Firlands Rise. Cos ......... 135 D1
Firmain Rd. Poole .......... 189 E1
Firmount Cl. Hord ......... 197 F1
Firs Ave. Wat ............... 111 F1
Firs Cres. Ki Wo ............... 2 A4
Firs Dr. He En .............. 105 D3
Firs Glen Rd. Bour ........ 206 C4
Firs Glen Rd. Ver .......... 115 D2
Firs Glen Rd. W Moo ..... 138 C1
Firs La. Poole .............. 216 A4
Firs The. Gos ............... 155 E1
Firs The. Southa ............. 78 C2
Firs Way. Upt .............. 203 E4
Firshill. Christ .............. 210 C4
Firside Rd. Broa ........... 187 E2
First Ave. Cos .............. 157 F4
First Ave. Hav .............. 136 A1
First Ave. Horn ............... 88 B2
First Ave. Southa .......... 101 E4
First Ave. Southb .......... 161 E4
First Marine Ave. B on S ... 211 F4
Firtree Cres. Hord ......... 196 C2
Firtree La. Fa Oa ............ 81 D4
Firtree Way. Southa ....... 104 A3
Fisgard Rd. Gosp .......... 181 D4
Fisher Cl. Stubb ............ 154 A2
Fisher Rd. Bos .............. 155 E2
Fisher's Rd. Tot ............ 101 D3
Fisherman's Ave. Bour ... 208 A2
Fisherman's Wlk. Bour ... 208 A2
Fishermans Rd. Poole .... 204 B1
Fishermans The. Ems ..... 161 D4
Fishermans Wlk. S Hay ... 185 F1
Fishers Gr. Cos ............. 158 C4
Fishers Hill. Fare .......... 130 A1
Fishers Rd. S Hay ......... 185 E1
Fishery La. S Hay .......... 185 E1
Fishlake Meadows. Rom .... 28 A1
Fitzharris Ave. Bour ...... 207 D4
Fitzherbert Rd. Cos ....... 158 C4
Fitzherbert St. Ports ...... 182 B3
Fitzhugh Pl. Southa ....... 102 C4
Fitzmaurice Rd. Christ .... 208 C4
Fitzpain Cl. Fern ........... 165 E1
Fitzpain Rd. Fern .......... 165 E1
Fitzpatrick Ct. Cos ........ 133 E1
Fitzroy Cl. Rown ............. 78 C4
Fitzwilliam Ave. Stubb .... 154 A1
Fitzwilliam Cl. Bour ....... 189 F3
Fitzworth Ave. Hamw ..... 203 E2
Fitzwygram Cres. Hav .... 135 F2
Five Elms Dr. Rom ........... 53 E3
Five Heads Rd. Horn ...... 112 A4
Five Post La. Gos .......... 181 D3
Fivefields Cl. Winch ......... 11 E4
Fivefields Rd. Winch ........ 11 E4
Flag Wlk. Wat ............... 111 F2
Flaghead Chine Rd. Poole ... 216 C3
Flambard Ave. Christ ...... 193 D1
Flambard Rd. Poole ....... 205 E2
Flamborough Cl. Southa .... 77 E2
Flamingo Ct. Portc ........ 155 F4
Flamston St. Crouch ........ 22 A4
Flanders Rd. He En ....... 105 D4
Flathouse Rd. Ports ....... 182 B4
Fleet Cl. Gos ................ 155 E1
Fleet End Bottom. Lo He ... 152 C4
Fleet End Rd. Lo He ....... 152 C4
Fleetend Cl. Hav ........... 135 F3
Fleets Est. Poole ........... 204 A3
Fleets La. Poole ............ 204 B3
Fleetsbridge Bsns Ctre. Broa ... 204 A4
Fleming Ave. N Bad ......... 54 A2
Fleming Cl. Lo He .......... 129 E2
Fleming Cl. N Bad ........... 54 A2
Fleming Pl. Co Com .......... 31 F1
Fletcher Cl. Bour .......... 190 B2
Fletcher Rd. Bour ......... 190 B2
Fletchwood La. Ashu ....... 99 F1
Fletchwood Rd. Tot ....... 100 A3
Fleuret Cl. Hyt ............. 126 A1
Flexford Cl. Ch Fo ........... 30 A1
Flexford Gdns. Hav ....... 136 A2
Flexford La. Sway ......... 197 E3
Flexford Rd. N Bad .......... 54 C4
Flint St. Ports .............. 182 A2
Floating Bridge Rd. Southa ... 103 E2
Floral Farm. Oakl .......... 164 A1
Florence Cl. W Wel .......... 51 D1
Florence Rd. Bour ......... 207 F2
Florence Rd. Poole ........ 205 E2
Florence Rd. Ports ........ 182 B1
Florence Rd. Southa ...... 103 E1
Florentine Way. Wat ...... 135 D4
Florins The. Wat ........... 134 C2
Floriston Gdns. New M ... 196 B2
Flowerdown Cl. Tot ....... 100 B4
Flowers Cl. Hamble ....... 127 F2
Flowers La. Plai .............. 50 B3
Flushards. Lym ............. 198 C2
Flying Bull Cl. Ports ....... 182 B4
Flying Bull La. Ports ...... 182 B4
Foldsgate Cl. Lyn .......... 121 F3
Folkestone Rd. Ports ..... 183 D4
Folly Farm La. St Le ...... 140 B3

Folly Field. Bi Wa ............ 83 E4
Folly La. Pet .................. 40 C2
Font Cl. Lo He ............... 129 E2
Fontley Rd. Swanw ........ 130 A3
Fontmell Rd. Broa ......... 188 B2
Fontwell Cl. Tot .............. 76 B1
Fontwell Mews. Wat ...... 112 A1
Fontwell Rd. Ports ........ 182 B1
Foord Rd. He En ........... 105 D2
Football Green. Min ......... 98 B2
Footner Cl. Rom .............. 28 B1
Footners La. Burt .......... 193 E1
Forbes Cl. Southa ........... 77 F3
Forbes Rd. Ki Wo .............. 2 A4
Forbury Rd. Ports ......... 182 B2
Ford Ave. Ch Fo ............. 55 E2
Ford Cl. Fern ............... 165 F4
Ford Rd. Gos ............... 180 C3
Fordingbridge Rd. Alderh ... 93 D4
Fordingbridge Rd. Fordi ... 93 D4
Fordingbridge Rd. Ports ... 183 D2
Fordington Ave. Winch ..... 10 C4
Fordington Rd. Winch ........ 1 C1
Foreland Cl. Christ ........ 192 B2
Foreland Ct. S Hay ........ 185 E1
Foreland Rd. Hamw ....... 203 E2
Forest Ave. Wat ............ 112 A2
Forest Cl. Ch Fo ............. 55 E4
Forest Cl. Christ ........... 194 B1
Forest Cl. N Bad ............. 53 F3
Forest Cl. Shed .............. 83 F2
Forest Cl. Ver ............... 115 E2
Forest Cl. Wat .............. 111 F2
Forest Cnr. Liss .............. 21 D4
Forest Ct. New M .......... 196 A1
Forest Edge Cl. St Le ..... 139 E3
Forest Edge Dr. St Le ..... 139 E3
Forest Edge Rd. Rin ...... 141 F3
Forest Edge. Faw .......... 151 D2
Forest End. Wat ........... 134 B4
Forest Front. Hyt .......... 150 A4
Forest Gate. Black ........ 177 F4
Forest Gdns. Lyn .......... 121 F3
Forest Gdns. Shed .......... 83 F2
Forest Glade Cl. Brock ... 145 E1
Forest Hall. Brock ......... 146 A1
Forest Hill Way. Hyt ...... 125 F1
Forest Hills Dr. Southa ..... 79 F2
Forest La. Fare ............. 131 D4
Forest La. Holb ............ 150 A3
Forest La. Rin .............. 141 F3
Forest Mead. Den .......... 110 C2
Forest Meadow. Hyt ...... 150 A4
Forest Park Rd. Brock .... 145 F1
Forest Pines. New M ...... 196 A2
Forest Rd. Bran ............ 169 F2
Forest Rd. Bur ............. 143 D3
Forest Rd. Ch Fo ............ 55 E4
Forest Rd. Den ............. 110 B2
Forest Rd. Greath ........... 20 C4
Forest Rd. Liss .............. 21 D3
Forest Rd. Poole ........... 206 A1
Forest Rd. Red ............... 47 F2
Forest Rd. Shed ............. 83 F2
Forest Rd. Swan ............. 83 F2
Forest Rd. W Moo ......... 138 C2
Forest Rd. Wat ............. 134 B4
Forest Rd. Woodg ........... 47 F2
Forest Rise. Christ ........ 194 B1
Forest Rise. Liss ............ 21 D3
Forest View Cl. Bour ...... 191 D1
Forest View Dr. Fern ...... 165 D3
Forest View Rd. Bour ..... 191 D1
Forest View. Brock ........ 145 E1
Forest View. Southa ...... 102 C2
Forest Way. Christ ........ 194 B1
Forest Way. Fern .......... 165 D3
Forest Way. Gos ........... 155 F1
Forest Way. Hord ......... 197 E1
Forester Rd. Sob ............ 85 D1
Foresters Gate. Black .... 177 E4
Foresters Rd. Black ....... 150 C1
Forestlake Ave. Rin ....... 141 E3
Forestside Ave. Hav ...... 136 A3
Forestside Gdns. Rin ..... 117 E1
Forestside The. Ver ....... 115 E3
Forge Cl. Burs .............. 105 D1
Forge Rd. Black ........... 177 F4
Forneth Gdns. Fare ....... 154 A4
Forster Rd. Southa ........ 103 D4
Forsyth Gdns. Bour ....... 190 B1
Forsythia Cl. He En ....... 105 D4
Fort Cumberland Pl. Hamw ... 203 E1
Fort Cumberland Rd. Ports ... 183 E2
Fort Fareham Rd. Fare ... 154 C3
Fort Rd. Gos ................ 181 D1
Fort Rd. Southa ............ 103 F2
Fortescue Rd. Bour ....... 207 D3
Fortescue Rd. Poole ...... 205 E4
Forth Cl. N Bad .............. 55 D3
Forth Cl. Stubb ............. 154 A2
Forties Cl. Stubb .......... 154 A2
Forton Rd. Gos ............. 181 D3
Forton Rd. Ports ........... 182 C3
Fortunes Way. Cos ........ 134 C1
Forward Dr. Lym ........... 198 B1
Foster Cl. Stubb ........... 154 B2
Foster Rd. Gos ............. 181 D2

# Foster Rd. Ports

Foster Rd. Ports .................. 182 B3
Founders Way. Gos .............. 155 E1
Foundry Cres. Burs ............. 127 F4
Foundry La. Southa ............. 102 A4
Foundry Rd. Red ................... 47 E4
Fountain Ct. He En .............. 105 D3
Fountain St. Ports ............... 182 B3
Fountain Way. Christ ........... 209 D3
Four Acre. Botl .................... 106 A3
Four Marks Green. Hav ....... 136 A3
Four Wells Rd. Wi Mi .......... 164 A4
Fourpost Hill. Southa ........... 102 C3
Fourshells Cl. Black ............ 150 C1
Fourth Ave. Cos ................... 157 F4
Fourth Ave. Hav .................. 136 A1
Fourth St. Ports ................... 182 C3
Fowey Cl. N Bad ................... 55 D3
Fowey The. Black ................ 150 C1
Fowlers Rd. He En ............... 105 D4
Fowlers Wlk. Chilw .............. 54 B1
Fox Cl. Bish ........................... 56 C1
Fox Field. Hord ................... 197 E1
Fox La. Fern ........................ 164 B3
Fox La. Winch ........................ 10 B3
Fox Pond La. Lym ............... 198 B3
Fox's Paddock. Black .......... 177 F4
Fox's Wlk. Black .................. 177 F4
Foxbury Cl. Hyt ................... 126 A1
Foxbury Gr. Portc ............... 156 A4
Foxbury La. Westb .............. 137 E2
Foxbury La. Westb .............. 137 E2
Foxbury Rd. St Le ............... 166 C4
Foxcombe Cl. Swan .............. 84 A3
Foxcote Gdns. New M ......... 195 F2
Foxcott Cl. Southa .............. 126 C4
Foxcott Gr. Hav .................. 135 F3
Foxcroft Dr. Holb ............... 150 A2
Foxcroft Dr. Wi Mi ............. 164 A3
Foxes Cl. Ver ...................... 114 C3
Foxes Cl. Wat ..................... 134 C3
Foxes La. Nur ....................... 77 D2
Foxes La. Plai ........................ 50 C3
Foxglade. Black ................... 177 F4
Foxglove Pl. New M ............ 196 B2
Foxgloves. Fare ................... 131 E2
Foxgloves. Upt ................... 203 D4
Foxhayes La. Black ............. 177 F4
Foxhills Cl. Ashu ................. 100 B2
Foxhills. Ashu ..................... 100 B2
Foxhills. Ver ....................... 115 D3
Foxholes Rd. Bour .............. 208 C2
Foxholes Rd. Poole ............. 204 C3
Foxlands. Black .................... 77 F4
Foxlea Gdns. Gosp ............. 181 D4
Foxlease Terr. Lyn .............. 121 F2
Foxley Dr. Ports .................. 158 A2
Foxtail Dr. Hyt ................... 125 F1
Foxwood Ave. Christ .......... 209 F3
Foy Gdns. Lo He ................. 128 B1
Foyle Rd. N Bad ................... 55 D3
Frampton Cl. Co Com ........... 31 F1
Frampton Cl. New M ........... 196 B3
Frampton Pl. Rin ................ 141 D4
Frampton Rd. Bour ............. 207 D4
Frampton Way. Ki Wo ............ 2 B4
Frampton Way. Tot ............. 100 C3
Frances Rd. Bour ................ 207 E2
Frances Rd. Wat ................. 134 B2
Francis Ave. Bour ............... 189 E2
Francis Ave. Ports .............. 182 C2
Francis Cl. Lon S ................ 180 A3
Francis Gdns. Winch .............. 2 A2
Francis Pl. Stubb ................ 154 B1
Francis Rd. Horn ................... 88 B2
Francis Rd. Poole ............... 205 F3
Franconia Dr. Nur ................ 77 D2
Frankland Cres. Poole ........ 205 F2
Franklin Rd. Bour ............... 191 D2
Franklin Rd. Gos ................. 180 B4
Franklin Rd. New M ............ 196 B2
Franklin Rd. Twyf ................. 32 A4
Franklyn Ave. Southa ......... 104 A2
Franklyn Cl. Upt ................. 203 D4
Franks Way. Poole .............. 205 D4
Frankston Rd. Bour ............ 208 B2
Frarydene. Southb .............. 161 E4
Fraser Cl. Southa .................. 77 F3
Fraser Gdns. Southb ........... 137 F1
Fraser Rd. Gos ................... 155 E2
Fraser Rd. Hav ................... 135 E1
Fraser Rd. Ki Wo .................... 2 B4
Fraser Rd. Poole ................ 205 F4
Fraser Rd. Ports ................. 182 B2
Frater La. Gos .................... 156 A1
Fratton Rd. Ports ............... 182 C3
Fratton Way. Fa Oa .............. 57 E1
Frayslea. Hyt ...................... 126 A1
Freda Rd. Christ .................. 208 C3
Freda Routh Gdns. Fa Oa ..... 57 E1
Frederica Rd. Bour ............. 206 C4
Frederick St. Ports ............. 182 B3
Frederick St. Southa ........... 103 D3
Free St. Bi Wa ...................... 83 E4
Freefolk Green. Hav ........... 136 A3
Freegrounds Ave. He En ..... 105 E3
Freegrounds Cl. He En ........ 105 E3
Freegrounds Rd. He En ....... 105 E3
Freemans Cl. Wi Mi ............ 164 A3

Freemans La. Wi Mi ............ 164 A3
Freemantle Cl. Southa ........ 103 F3
Freemantle Cmn Rd. Southa 103 F3
Freemantle Rd. Gosp .......... 181 D4
Freestone Rd. Ports ............ 182 B1
French Rd. Broa .................. 188 A1
French St. Ports .................. 182 A2
French St. Southa ............... 102 C2
French's Farm Rd. Upt ....... 203 D4
Frenches La. W Wel .............. 51 E4
Frenchmans Rd. Pet ............. 40 C2
Frenchmoor La. E Dean .......... 3 F2
Frenchmoor La. W Tyth ......... 3 F2
Frendstaple Rd. Wat ........... 135 D3
Frensham Cl. Bour .............. 190 C2
Frensham Cl. He En ............ 105 E3
Frensham Ct. He En ............ 105 E3
Frensham Rd. Ports ............ 182 C2
Freshfield Gdns. Wat .......... 134 C4
Freshfield Rd. Southa ......... 102 A4
Freshfield Sq. Southa .......... 102 A4
Freshwater Dr. Hamw ......... 203 E2
Freshwater Rd. Christ ......... 210 B3
Freshwater Rd. Cos ............ 157 F4
Friars Croft. Tot ................... 76 B1
Friars Pond Rd. Fare ........... 130 B1
Friars Rd. Eastl ..................... 55 F1
Friars Rd. Christ ................. 210 A3
Friars Way. Southa ............... 79 E2
Friars Wlk. B on S .............. 212 A4
Friarscroft. Net .................. 127 D4
Friarsgate. Winch ................. 11 D4
Friary Cl. Ports .................. 182 B1
Frith La. Wickh ................... 108 A4
Fritham Cl. Tot ................... 100 B4
Fritham Gdns. Bour ............ 191 E2
Fritham Rd. Southa ............. 104 B4
Frobisher Ave. Poole .......... 189 F1
Frobisher Cl. Christ ............ 209 F3
Frobisher Cl. Gos ............... 180 B3
Frobisher Cl. Rin ............... 117 E1
Frobisher Gdns. Southa ...... 104 B2
Frobisher Gr. Portc ............ 156 B4
Froddington Rd. Ports ........ 182 B2
Frog La. Fordi ...................... 93 F4
Froghall. Hyt ..................... 126 A1
Frogham Green. Hav ........... 135 E3
Frogham Hill. Fordi .............. 94 B3
Frogmore La. Horn ............. 112 A3
Frogmore La. Nur ................. 77 E2
Frogmore La. Wat .............. 112 A3
Frogmore Rd. Ports ............ 183 D3
Frogmore. Fare .................. 154 B4
Frome Cl. March ................ 102 A1
Fromond Cl. Lym ................ 198 C3
Fromond Rd. Winch ................ 1 B2
Frost La. Hyt ...................... 126 A1
Frost Rd. Bour ................... 189 F2
Frosthole Cl. Fare .............. 130 C2
Frosthole Cres. Fare .......... 130 C2
Froud Way. Broa ................ 187 E2
Froxfield Cl. Winch ................ 1 B2
Froxfield Gdns. Portc .......... 132 B1
Fry Cl. Hamble .................. 128 A2
Fry's La. Meons ................... 61 E2
Fryer Cl. Bour ................... 190 A3
Fryern Cl. Ch Fo ................... 55 F3
Fryern Court Rd. Fordi .......... 69 F3
Fryers Copse. Wi Mi ........... 164 B3
Fryers Rd. W Moo ............... 138 B4
Frys La. Hord ..................... 197 E1
Fuchsia Gdns. Southa ........... 78 B3
Fulflood Rd. Hav ................ 135 F3
Fullerton Cl. Hav ............... 136 A3
Fullerton Cl. Southa ........... 126 C4
Fullerton Rd. Lym .............. 198 B2
Fulmar Cl. Southa ................ 78 A3
Fulmar Rd. Christ ............... 210 A3
Fulmar Wlk. Gos ................ 155 D2
Fulmer Wlk. Wat ................ 111 F2
Fulwood Ave. Bour ............ 189 F3
Funtington Rd. Ports .......... 182 C4
Funtley Ct. Fare ................. 130 C2
Funtley Hill. Fare ............... 130 C2
Funtley La. Fare ................. 130 C3
Funtley Rd. Fare ................ 130 C3
Furley Cl. Winch ................... 11 D4
Furlong The. Rin ................ 140 C4
Furneaux Gdns. Fare .......... 131 D2
Furnell Rd. Poole ............... 204 B1
Furness Rd. Ports .............. 182 B1
Furniss Way. S Hay ............ 184 B2
Furnston Gr. Southb ........... 137 F1
Fury Way. Stubb ................ 154 A2
Furze Cl. Southa ................ 104 A3
Furze Croft. New M ............ 196 A1
Furze Hill Dr. Poole ........... 205 E1
Furze La. Ports .................. 183 E2
Furze Rd. Southa ............... 104 A3
Furze Way. Wat ................. 112 A2
Furzebrook Cl. Broa ........... 188 C2
Furzedale Gdns. Hyt .......... 126 A1
Furzedale Park. Hyt ........... 126 A1
Furzedown Cres. Hav ......... 136 A3
Furzedown Mews. Hyt ....... 126 A1
Furzedown Rd. Ki So ............. 7 D4
Furzedown Rd. Southa .......... 79 D1
Furzehall Ave. Fare ............ 131 D2
Furzehill. WI MI .................. 163 E4

Furzelands Rd. W Moo ....... 138 C4
Furzeley Rd. Den ............... 110 C1
Furzey Ave. Hyt ................. 126 A1
Furzey Cl. Black ................. 150 C1
Furzey La. E Bol ................ 148 A1
Furzey Rd. Upt ................... 203 D3
Furzley Cl. Hav .................. 135 E3
Furzley La. Bramsh .............. 74 B3
Furzley Rd. Cadn .................. 74 B2
Furzy Whistlers Cl. Bran .... 169 D1
Fye Bright Cl. Fa Oa ............ 81 E3
Fyeford Cl. Rown .................. 77 F3
Fyfield Way. Litt ..................... 1 A3
Fyning St. Ports ................. 182 B3

Gage Cl. March .................. 102 A1
Gain's Rd. Ports ................. 182 C1
Gainsborough Ave. New M .. 196 A3
Gainsborough Cl. Southa .... 104 B1
Gainsborough Ct. Bour ....... 208 A3
Gainsborough Rd. Bour ...... 207 F4
Gainsborough Rd. St Le ..... 139 F3
Gainsford Rd. Southa ......... 103 F3
Galaxie Rd. Wat ................. 112 A2
Gale Moor Ave. Gos ........... 180 B2
Galleon Cl. Lo He ............... 128 C1
Gallops The. Lo He ............ 129 E1
Galloway Rd. Hamw ........... 203 E2
Gallows Dr. Fern ................ 165 F1
Galsworthy Rd. Tot ............ 100 B4
Galt Rd. Cos ...................... 158 C4
Galton Ave. Christ .............. 208 C3
Gamble Cl. Southa .............. 103 F2
Gamble Rd. Ports ............... 182 B4
Gamblins La. Shed ............. 107 F4
Ganger Farm La. Rom ......... 28 B1
Ganger Rd. Rom ................... 28 B1
Gannet Cl. Hyt ................... 126 A1
Gannet Cl. Southa ................ 78 A3
Gannets The. Stubb ............ 154 A2
Garbett Rd. Winch ............... 11 E4
Garden Cl. Hyt ................... 125 D3
Garden Cl. Lyn ................... 121 F3
Garden Cl. New M .............. 196 A1
Garden Cl. Portc ................ 156 B4
Garden Cl. St Le ................ 139 F2
Garden La. Ports ................ 182 B2
Garden La. St Le ................ 139 F2
Garden La. Winch ................. 11 D4
Garden Mews. Lo He .......... 128 B1
Garden Rd. Bur .................. 142 C2
Garden Wlk. Fern ............... 165 F4
Gardeners La. Awb .............. 52 A2
Gardeners La. Rom .............. 52 A2
Gardens Cres. Poole .......... 216 A4
Gardens Rd. Poole ............. 216 A4
Gardens The. Hambl ............ 86 B2
Gardens The. Hav .............. 136 A1
Gardiner Cl. March ............. 102 A1
Gardner Rd. Christ ............. 208 C4
Gardner Rd. Lo He ............. 153 F4
Gardner Rd. Rin ................. 141 D3
Garendon Cl. Fordi .............. 69 F1
Garfield Ave. Bour ............. 207 E4
Garfield Cl. Bi Wa ................ 83 E4
Garfield Rd. Bi Wa ............... 83 E4
Garfield Rd. Net ................ 127 D3
Garfield Rd. Ports .............. 182 B4
Garfield Rd. Southa ............ 103 F4
Garland Av. Ems ................ 136 C2
Garland Rd. Poole .............. 204 B2
Garnett Cl. Stubb ............... 154 B2
Garnier Park. Wickh ........... 108 A2
Garnier Rd. Winch ............... 11 D3
Garnier St. Ports ................ 182 C3
Garnock Rd. Southa ........... 103 E1
Garrick Gdns. Southa ......... 104 A1
Garrison Hill. Drox .............. 61 D1
Garrow Dr. Lym ................. 198 C1
Garsdale Cl. Bour .............. 190 A3
Garsons Rd. Southb ........... 161 E4
Garston Cl. E Meon .............. 63 E4
Garstons Cl. Lo He ............. 153 F4
Garstons Rd. Lo He ............ 153 F4
Garth Cl. St Le .................. 139 E2
Garth Rd. Bour .................. 191 D1
Garton Rd. Southa .............. 103 E2
Gashouse Hill. Net ............. 127 E3
Gatcombe Ave. Ports ......... 158 A1
Gatcombe Dr. Ports ........... 157 F2
Gatcombe Gdns. Fare ......... 154 A4
Gatcombe Gdns. W End ....... 80 A1
Gatcombe. Net .................. 127 E4
Gate House Rd. Portc ......... 156 A4
Gatwick Cl. Southa .............. 78 A2
Gaulter Cl. Hav .................. 136 A2
Gaydon Rise. Bour ............. 189 F2
Gaylyn Way. Fare .............. 154 A4
Gaza Ave. E Bol ................ 175 E3
Gazing La. W Wel ................ 50 C2
Geddes Way. Pet ................ 41 E2
Gemini Cl. Southa ................ 77 F2
Geneva Ave. Bour .............. 208 B3
Genoa Cl. Lym .................. 198 B1
Gento Cl. He En ................. 105 F3
Geoffrey Ave. Wat ............. 134 A1
Geoffrey Cres. Fare ............ 155 D3
George Byng Way. Ports .... 182 B4
George Eyston Dr. Winch ...... 10 B3

George Rd. M on S ............. 213 E3
George St. Eastl ................... 56 A2
George St. Gos .................. 181 E3
George St. Ports ................ 182 C4
Georges Mews. Broa .......... 187 E4
Georgian Cl. Rin ................ 141 D4
Georgian Way. Bour .......... 190 C2
Georgina Cl. Poole ............. 206 B4
Gerald Rd. Bour ................. 207 D3
Gerard Cres. Southa ........... 104 B3
Germaine Cl. Christ ............ 210 C4
Gervis Cres. Poole ............. 205 D2
Gervis Pl. Bour .................. 206 C2
Gervis Rd. Bour ................. 207 D2
Gibbs Rd. Southa ............... 102 C3
Gibraltar Cl. Fare ............... 130 B1
Gibraltar Rd. Ports ............ 183 E2
Gibson Cl. L on S ............... 179 F4
Gibson Rd. Poole ............... 204 C4
Giddylake. Wi Mi ............... 163 E3
Gifford Cl. Fare .................. 130 C2
Gilbert Cl. Alderh ................ 93 D3
Gilbert Cl. Gos .................. 180 B4
Gilbert Cl. Lym .................. 198 B1
Gilbert Mead. S Hay ........... 184 C2
Gilbert Rd. Bour ................ 207 E3
Gilbert Way. Wat ............... 134 C3
Gilbury Cl. Southa ............... 79 F2
Giles Cl. Fare .................... 131 D2
Giles Cl. Gos .................... 181 D3
Giles Cl. He En .................... 81 E1
Giles Hill. Winch ................. 11 D4
Giles La. Lan ...................... 50 A2
Gilkicker Rd. Gos ............... 181 E1
Gillam Rd. Bour ................. 190 B3
Gillcrest. Lo He .................. 129 E2
Gillies The. Fare ................ 131 D1
Gillingham Cl. Bour ............ 191 E2
Gillingham Cl. Ki Wo ............. 2 B4
Gillingham Rd. M on S ........ 213 E2
Gillman Rd. Cos ................. 134 C1
Gilpin Cl. Bold ................... 173 F1
Gilpin Cl. Southa ................ 104 C3
Gilpin Hill. Sway ................ 172 A1
Gins La. Beaul ................... 176 C1
Girton Cl. Lo He ................. 129 E1
Gitsham Gdns. Wat ............ 134 B2
Gladdis Rd. Bour ............... 189 F2
Glade Cl. The. Ch Fo ............ 30 C1
Glade The. Fare ................. 130 B2
Glade The. S Hay ............... 185 E1
Glade The. St Le ................ 139 D4
Glade The. Wat .................. 135 D4
Gladelands Cl. Broa ........... 187 F2
Gladelands Way. Broa ........ 187 F2
Glades The. Lo He .............. 129 D2
Gladstone Cl. Christ ........... 209 E3
Gladstone Pl. Portc ............ 156 B4
Gladstone Rd E. Bour ......... 207 F3
Gladstone Rd W. Bour ........ 207 F3
Gladstone Rd. Bour ............ 207 F3
Gladstone Rd. Gos ............. 181 D4
Gladstone Rd. Poole ........... 205 E3
Gladstone Rd. Southa ......... 104 A3
Gladys Ave. Ports .............. 157 E1
Gladys Ave. Wat ................ 112 A2
Glamis Ave. Bour .............. 190 C3
Glamis Cl. Wat ................... 135 D4
Glamorgan Rd. Horn ............ 88 A2
Glasgow Rd. Ports ............. 183 D2
Glasslaw Rd. Southa ........... 104 A4
Glasspool. Den .................. 110 C3
Gleadowe Ave. Christ ......... 208 C3
Glebe Cl. S Hay ................. 184 C3
Glebe Cnr. Wickh ............... 108 A2
Glebe Ct. Botl ................... 106 A4
Glebe Ct. Fa Oa ................... 57 E1
Glebe Ct. Southa .................. 79 D1
Glebe Dr. Gos .................... 155 E1
Glebe La. Lan ...................... 49 E2
Glebe Meadow. E Dean .......... 4 A1
Glebe Park Ave. Cos .......... 135 D1
Glebe Rd. Buri ..................... 65 E3
Glebe Rd. Southa ............... 103 D2
Glebe The. Stubb ............... 154 B1
Glebefields. M on S ............ 213 E3
Glen Cl. B on S .................. 211 E4
Glen Dale. Ro Ca ............... 113 E1
Glen Eyre Dr. Southa ........... 79 D3
Glen Eyre Rd. Southa ........... 78 C3
Glen Eyre Way. Southa ......... 79 D2
Glen Fern Rd. Bour ............ 207 D2
Glen Rd. Bour .................... 207 F2
Glen Rd. Lo He ................... 128 C3
Glen Rd. Lo He ................... 128 C4
Glen Rd. Poole .................. 205 D2
Glen Rd. Southa ................. 103 E1
Glen Rd. Swanw ................ 128 C4
Glen Spey. New M ............. 196 B1
Glen The. Gos ................... 155 F1
Glen The. Poole ................. 216 C4
Glenair Ave. Poole ............. 205 D2
Glenair Cres. Poole ............ 205 D2
Glenair Rd. Poole .............. 205 D2
Glenavon Rd. Christ ........... 194 C1
Glenavon. New M ............... 196 B1
Glenbrook Wlk. Fare .......... 154 B4

# Goodlands Vale. He En

Glencarron Way. Southa ....... 78 C2
Glencoe Rd. Bour ............... 207 F4
Glencoe Rd. Poole ............. 205 E3
Glencoe Rd. Ports .............. 182 C4
Glencoyne Gdns. Southa ....... 77 F1
Glenda Cl. Lo He ................ 152 B4
Glendale Ave. Fern ............ 165 F3
Glendale Cl. Christ ............. 192 B2
Glendale Cl. Wi Mi ............ 163 E3
Glendale Rd. Bour ............. 209 D2
Glendale. Lo He ................. 129 D1
Glendale. Swan .................... 84 A2
Glendales. B on S .............. 211 E4
Glendon Ave. Bour ............ 190 B3
Glendowan Rd. N Bad .......... 55 D4
Glendrive. B on S .............. 211 E4
Gleneagles Ave. Poole ....... 205 E1
Gleneagles Cl. Fern ........... 165 F3
Gleneagles Dr. Wat ............ 112 A1
Glenelg. Fare ..................... 130 C1
Glenesha Gdns. Fare .......... 130 C1
Glenferness Ave. Bour ....... 206 B3
Glenfield Ave. Southa ......... 103 F4
Glenfield Cres. Southa ....... 103 F4
Glenfield Way. Southa ........ 103 F4
Glengariff Rd. Poole .......... 205 E2
Glengarry Way. Christ ........ 210 B3
Glengarry. New M .............. 196 B1
Glenives Cl. St Le .............. 140 A2
Glenlea Cl. W End ............... 80 B1
Glenlea Dr. W End ............... 80 B1
Glenleigh Ave. Cos ............ 157 F4
Glenleigh Park. Hav ........... 136 A1
Glenmeadows Dr. Bour ...... 190 D3
Glenmoor Cl. Bour ............. 190 B1
Glenmoor Rd. Bour ............ 207 F2
Glenmoor Rd. Fern ............ 165 E2
Glenmount Dr. Poole .......... 205 D2
Glenn Rd. W End .................. 80 B1
Glenroyd Gdns. Bour .......... 208 C2
Glenside Ave. Southa ......... 104 B2
Glenside. Christ ................. 211 D4
Glenside. Hyt ..................... 125 F2
Glenthorne Cl. Stubb ......... 154 B1
Glenthorne Meadow. E Meo ... 38 C1
Glenthorne Rd. Ports ......... 158 A1
Glenville Cl. Christ ............. 195 D1
Glenville Rd. Bour ............. 190 B1
Glenville Rd. Christ ............ 195 D1
Glenwood Ave. Southa ......... 79 D3
Glenwood Cl. W Moo .......... 138 C1
Glenwood Cl. Fa Oa ............. 57 F1
Glenwood Gdns. Wat .......... 111 F2
Glenwood La. W Moo ......... 138 C1
Glenwood Rd. Southb ......... 137 F1
Glenwood Rd. Ver .............. 114 C3
Glenwood Rd. W Moo ......... 138 C1
Glenwood Way. W Moo ...... 138 C1
Glidden Cl. Ports ............... 182 B3
Glidden La. Hambl ............... 86 C2
Glissons. Fern ................... 165 D1
Globe La. Poole ................. 204 B1
Gloster Ct. Lo He ............... 129 E3
Gloucester Cl. Pet ............... 40 B2
Gloucester Pl. Ports ........... 182 B2
Gloucester Rd. Bour .......... 207 F3
Gloucester Rd. Poole ......... 205 F3
Gloucester Rd. Wat ............ 134 C3
Gloucester Terr. Ports ........ 182 B2
Gloucester View. Ports ....... 182 B2
Glyn Dr. Stubb ................... 154 B1
Glyn Way. Stubb ................ 154 B1
Glynville Cl. Wi Mi ............ 164 A4
Glynville Rd. Wi Mi ........... 164 A4
Goathorn Cl. Hamw ........... 203 E2
Goddard Cl. W Wel .............. 50 C2
Godiva Lawn. Ports ............ 183 D2
Godmanston Cl. Poole ........ 189 D1
Godshill Cl. Bour ............... 191 D2
Godwin Cl. Ems ................. 136 C2
Godwin Cl. Winch .................. 1 B1
Godwin Cres. Horn .............. 88 B2
Godwit Cl. Gos .................. 181 D4
Godwit Rd. Ports ............... 183 E3
Gofton Ave. Cos ................ 158 A4
Goggs La. Red ..................... 47 F3
Gold Mead Cl. Lym ............ 198 C1
Gold St. Ports .................... 182 A2
Goldcrest Gdns. Southa ........ 78 A3
Goldcrest La. Tot ............... 100 B4
Golden Cres. Hord ............. 197 E1
Golden Ct. W End ................ 80 C2
Golden Gr. Southa .............. 103 D3
Golden Hind Park. Hyt ........ 125 F1
Goldfinch La. L on S ........... 179 F4
Goldfinch Rd. Broa ............ 203 F4
Goldring Cl. S Hay ............. 185 D2
Goldsmith Ave. Ports ......... 182 C2
Goldsmith Cl. Tot .............. 100 B4
Goldsmith Rd. Eastl ............ 55 F1
Golf Course Rd. Southa ........ 78 C3
Golf Links Rd. Broa ........... 188 A3
Golf Links Rd. Fern ............ 165 F2
Goliath Rd. Hamw .............. 203 E1
Gomer La. Gos ................... 180 C2
Good Rd. Poole .................. 205 E4
Goodens The. Cher .............. 14 B3
Goodison Cl. Fa Oa .............. 57 D1
Goodlands Vale. He En ....... 105 D4

233

Goodsell Cl. Stubb Handley Rd. Gos


Goodsell Cl. Stubb 154 A1
Goodwin Cl. Southa 77 E1
Goodwood Cl. Gos 181 D4
Goodwood Cl. Lo He 129 E1
Goodwood Cl. Wat 112 A1
Goodwood Ct. Southb 161 F4
Goodwood Gdns. Tot 100 B4
Goodwood Rd. Eastl 55 F2
Goodwood Rd. Gos 181 D4
Goodwood Rd. Ports 182 C2
Gooseberry La. Rin 140 C4
Gordon Ave. Southa 103 D4
Gordon Ave. Winch 11 E3
Gordon Mount. Christ 211 D4
Gordon Rd S. Poole 206 A3
Gordon Rd. Bour 207 E2
Gordon Rd. Ch Fo 30 B1
Gordon Rd. Christ 211 D4
Gordon Rd. Curd 83 D1
Gordon Rd. Fare 131 D1
Gordon Rd. Gos 181 D2
Gordon Rd. Herm 161 D4
Gordon Rd. Lym 198 B2
Gordon Rd. Poole 206 A3
Gordon Rd. Ports 182 A2
Gordon Rd. Wat 134 B3
Gordon Rd. Wi Mi 163 F2
Gordon Rd. Winch 11 D4
Gordon Terr. Southa 104 A1
Gordon Way. Burt 193 E1
Gore Rd. New M 195 F1
Gorey Ave. Poole 189 E1
Goring Ave. Clanf 88 B2
Goring Field. Winch 1 B1
Gorleston Rd. Poole 205 F3
Gorley Ct. Hav 135 E3
Gorley Lynch. Fordi 94 B2
Gorley Rd. Rin 117 E1
Gorran Ave. Gos 155 E1
Gorse Cl. Lo He 128 C1
Gorse Cl. New M 196 B2
Gorse Cl. St Le 139 E2
Gorse Hill Cl. Poole 204 C3
Gorse Hill Cres. Poole 204 C3
Gorse Hill Rd. Poole 204 C3
Gorse La. Upt 203 E4
Gorse Rd. Broa 187 E3
Gorse Rd. Pet 41 E2
Gorsecliff Rd. Bour 190 B1
Gorsefield Cres. New M 196 A2
Gorseland Ct. Fern 165 F2
Gorselands Rd. Southa 80 A1
Gorselands Way. Gos 180 B4
Gort Cres. Southa 104 A2
Gort Rd. Bour 190 A2
Gort Rd. Broa 188 A1
Gosling Cl. Poole 204 C4
Gosport La. Lyn 122 A2
Gosport Rd. Fare 155 D4
Gosport Rd. L on S 179 F3
Gosport Rd. Stubb 154 C1
Gosport St. Lym 198 C2
Gough Cres. Broa 188 A1
Gould Cl. Gos 180 B3
Gover Rd. Southa 101 E4
Grace Dieu Gdns. Burs 104 C1
Grace La. Woodg 70 C4
Graddidge Way. Tot 100 B3
Graemar La. Sh En 25 E1
Grafton Cl. Christ 209 E3
Grafton Gdns. Lym 198 B1
Grafton Gdns. Southa 78 B3
Grafton Rd. Bour 207 D3
Grafton Rd. Winch 10 C3
Graham Rd. Gos 181 D4
Graham Rd. Ports 182 C2
Graham Rd. Southa 103 D3
Graham St. Southa 103 E3
Grainger Gdns. Southa 104 B2
Grammar School La. Wi Mi 163 D2
Granada Cl. Wat 112 A2
Granada Rd. He En 105 D3
Granada Rd. Ports 182 C1
Granby Gr. Southa 79 D2
Granby Rd. Bour 191 D2
Grand Ave. Bour 208 B2
Grand Par. Ports 182 A2
Grand Par. S Hay 185 D1
Grange Cl. Gos 180 C3
Grange Cl. Hav 136 A1
Grange Cl. Hord 213 F4
Grange Cl. Southa 79 F2
Grange Cl. Winch 10 C2
Grange Cres. Gos 180 C3
Grange Ct. Net 127 D4
Grange Dr. He En 105 E4
Grange Gr. Gos 155 E1
Grange La. Gos 180 B4
Grange Rd. Bour 208 B2
Grange Rd. Broa 188 A2
Grange Rd. Christ 210 A4
Grange Rd. Gos 180 B3
Grange Rd. He En 105 E4
Grange Rd. Net 127 E4
Grange Rd. Pet 40 C1
Grange Rd. Ports 157 E1
Grange Rd. Southa 78 A1
Grange Rd. St Le 139 F1
Grange Rd. Winch 10 C2
Grange The. Hord 213 F4
Grangewood Gdns. Fa Oa 57 D1
Grant Rd. Cos 158 B4
Grant's Ave. Bour 207 E3
Grantham Ave. Hamble 127 F2
Grantham Ct. Eastl 56 A1
Grantham Rd. Bour 207 E3
Grantham Rd. Eastl 56 A1
Grantham Rd. Southa 103 F3
Grantley Rd. Bour 207 F2
Grants Cl. Bour 207 F3
Granville Cl. Hav 136 A1
Granville Pl. Bour 206 C2
Granville Pl. Winch 11 D3
Granville Rd. Bour 208 A3
Granville Rd. Poole 205 D3
Granville St. Southa 103 D2
Grasdean Cl. Southa 80 A1
Grasmere Cl. Christ 192 B2
Grasmere Cl. W End 80 A1
Grasmere Gdns. New M 196 A3
Grasmere Rd. Bour 208 A2
Grasmere Rd. Poole 216 A2
Grasmere Way. Stubb 154 B2
Grasmere. Eastl 55 F1
Grassmere Way. Wat 112 B1
Grassymead. Lo He 129 E2
Grateley Cl. Southa 126 C4
Grateley Cres. Hav 135 E2
Gravel Cl. Down 46 C4
Gravel Hill. Broa 188 B3
Gravel Hill. Oakl 188 B3
Gravel Hill. Shed 84 A2
Gravel Hill. Swan 84 A2
Gravel La. Rin 140 C4
Gray Cl. Lo He 128 C1
Gray Cl. Poole 204 C4
Gray's Yd. Poole 204 B1
Graycot Cl. Bour 190 B3
Grayland Cl. S Hay 184 C2
Grays Ave. Hyt 126 A2
Grays Cl. Co Com 56 C4
Grays Cl. Gos 180 C2
Grays Cl. Rom 53 D4
Grays Ct. Ports 182 A2
Grayshott Cl. Winch 1 B2
Grayshott Rd. Gos 180 C2
Grayshott Rd. Ports 182 C2
Great Copse Dr. Hav 135 F3
Great Elms Cl. Holb 150 A2
Great Field Rd. Winch 1 B2
Great Gays. Stubb 154 A1
Great Hanger. Pet 41 D2
Great Mead. Den 111 D2
Great Mead. Lyn 121 F2
Great Minster St. Winch 11 D4
Great Southsea St. Ports 182 B2
Great Well Dr. Rom 53 D4
Greatbridge Rd. Awb 27 F1
Greatbridge Rd. Rom 27 F1
Greatfield Way. Ro Ca 113 D2
Greatwood Cl. Hyt 126 A1
Greaves Cl. Bour 190 B2
Grebe Cl. Broa 203 F4
Grebe Cl. Christ 210 A3
Grebe Cl. M on S 213 F2
Grebe Cl. Portc 155 F4
Grebe Cl. Wat 111 F2
Green Acres Cl. St Le 140 B3
Green Acres. Christ 209 F4
Green Bottom. Wi Mi 164 A4
Green Cl. Hyt 126 A2
Green Cl. Ne Ma 99 F2
Green Cl. Poole 204 B1
Green Cl. Whit 24 A2
Green Cres. Gos 155 E1
Green Dr. Alderh 93 D3
Green Farm Gdns. Ports 157 F2
Green Hollow Cl. Fare 130 C2
Green Jacket Cl. Winch 10 C3
Green La. Ampf 29 D1
Green La. B on S 212 A4
Green La. Bi Wa 83 E4
Green La. Black 177 F4
Green La. Bour 190 B2
Green La. Burs 104 C1
Green La. Chilw 54 C1
Green La. Clanf 88 B3
Green La. Den 110 C2
Green La. Fern 165 D1
Green La. Fordi 69 F1
Green La. Frox G 18 C3
Green La. Gos 181 E4
Green La. Hamble 128 A1
Green La. Lo He 128 C1
Green La. Ports 158 A2
Green La. Rin 141 D4
Green La. Rin 141 E2
Green La. Rockb 69 E4
Green La. S Hay 184 C2
Green La. Sob 86 A3
Green La. Southa 77 F1
Green La. Swanw 106 A1
Green La. Swanw 128 B4
Green Park Cl. Winch 2 A1
Green Park Rd. Southa 101 F4
Green Pond La. Ampf 29 E2
Green Rd. Bour 207 D4
Green Rd. Gos 181 D1
Green Rd. Poole 204 B1
Green Rd. Ports 182 B2
Green Rd. Stubb 154 B2
Green The. Liss 20 C3
Green The. Lo He 128 C3
Green The. Ro Ca 113 E1
Green The. Rom 28 B1
Green The. Whit 24 A2
Green Ways. Swan 84 A3
Green Wlk. Fare 130 C2
Green's Cl. Bish 57 D1
Greenacre Cl. Upt 203 E3
Greenacre Gdns. Wat 134 B2
Greenacre. B on S 212 A4
Greenacres Cl. Bour 190 C3
Greenacres Dr. Ott 31 E2
Greenacres. Down 46 B4
Greenaway La. Lo He 128 B1
Greenbank Cres. Southa 78 C3
Greenbanks Cl. M on S 213 E2
Greenbanks Gdns. Fare 131 E1
Greenclose La. Wi Mi 163 E2
Greendale Cl. Ch Fo 55 F3
Greendale The. Fare 130 B2
Greenfield Gdns. B on S 212 A4
Greenfield Rd. Poole 204 C4
Greenfield Rise. Wat 112 A2
Greenfields Ave. Tot 76 C1
Greenfields Cl. Tot 76 C1
Greenfields. Liss 21 D2
Greenfinch Cl. Broa 187 F1
Greenfinch Cl. Eastl 55 E1
Greenfinch Wlk. Rin 141 E3
Greenhayes. Broa 188 B1
Greenhays Rise. Wi Mi 163 E3
Greenhill Cl. Wi Mi 163 E3
Greenhill Cl. Winch 10 C4
Greenhill La. Rown 77 F4
Greenhill La. Wi Mi 163 E3
Greenhill Rd. Wi Mi 163 E3
Greenhill Rd. Winch 10 B4
Greenhill Terr. Winch 10 C4
Greenlea Cl. Wat 134 A1
Greenlea Cres. Southa 79 E3
Greenlea Rd. Gos 180 C4
Greenmead Ave. Hord 197 E1
Greens Cl. Bi Wa 83 D4
Greens Meade. Red 47 E3
Greensleeves Ave. Broa 188 A3
Greensome Dr. Fern 165 F3
Greenway Cl. Lym 198 B2
Greenway Cres. Upt 203 D4
Greenway La. Buri 65 E3
Greenway Rd. Gos 181 D3
Greenway. E Meo 38 C1
Greenways Ave. Bour 191 E2
Greenways Rd. Brock 146 A1
Greenways. Ch Fo 55 F3
Greenways. Christ 210 C4
Greenways. M on S 213 E3
Greenways. Southa 79 E3
Greenwich The. Black 150 C1
Greenwood Ave. Cos 157 E4
Greenwood Ave. Fern 165 F3
Greenwood Ave. Poole 216 E4
Greenwood Ave. Rown 77 E3
Greenwood Cl. Eastl 55 F1
Greenwood Cl. Fare 131 D2
Greenwood Cl. Rom 53 D4
Greenwood Copse. St Le 140 A2
Greenwood La. Durl 82 F4
Greenwood Rd. Bour 206 C4
Greenwood Way. St Le 140 A2
Greetham St. Ports 182 B3
Gregory Gdns. Tot 76 B1
Gregory La. Durl 82 B3
Gregson Ave. Gos 155 E2
Gregson Cl. Gos 155 E2
Grenadier Cl. Lo He 129 D1
Grendon Cl. Southa 79 D3
Grenehurst Way. Pet 40 C2
Grenfell Rd. Bour 190 C2
Grenville Cl. Rin 117 E1
Grenville Ct. Southa 102 C4
Grenville Gdns. Hyt 126 A1
Grenville Rd. Ports 182 C2
Grenville Rd. Wi Mi 163 E2
Gresham Rd. Bour 191 D1
Greville Green. Ems 136 C2
Greville Rd. Southa 102 B4
Greyfriars Rd. Fare 130 B1
Greyshott Ave. Fare 154 B4
Greystoke Ave. Bour 189 F3
Greystones. Christ 211 D4
Greywell Ave. Southa 78 B2
Greywell Rd. Hav 135 F2
Griffin Ct. Southa 103 E4
Griffiths Gdns. Bour 190 A3
Griffon Cl. Burs 105 D1
Grigg La. Brock 146 A1
Grindle Cl. Portc 132 B1
Gritanwood Rd. Ports 183 D2
Grosvenor Cl. Southa 79 E1
Grosvenor Cl. St Le 139 E3
Grosvenor Dr. Winch 2 A1
Grosvenor Gdns. Bour 207 F2
Grosvenor Gdns. Southa 79 E1
Grosvenor Gdns. W End 104 B4
Grosvenor Mews. Lym 198 B3
Grosvenor Rd. Bour 206 B2
Grosvenor Rd. Ch Fo 30 C1
Grosvenor Rd. Southa 79 E1
Grosvenor Sq. Southa 102 C3
Grosvenor St. Ports 182 B2
Grove Ave. Gos 181 E3
Grove Ave. Portc 156 B3
Grove Gdns. Southa 104 A1
Grove La. Red 47 F4
Grove Pastures. Lym 198 C2
Grove Pl. Lym 198 C2
Grove Pl. Southa 104 A1
Grove Rd E. Christ 209 D4
Grove Rd N. Ports 182 B2
Grove Rd S. Ports 182 B2
Grove Rd W. Christ 208 C4
Grove Rd. B on S 212 A4
Grove Rd. Bour 207 D2
Grove Rd. Comp 31 E3
Grove Rd. Cos 158 B4
Grove Rd. Fare 131 D1
Grove Rd. Gos 181 D4
Grove Rd. Hav 135 F1
Grove Rd. L on S 179 F3
Grove Rd. Lym 198 C2
Grove Rd. Poole 205 D3
Grove Rd. Southa 102 B4
Grove Rd. Twyf 31 F3
Grove Rd. Wi Mi 163 E2
Grove St. Southa 103 D2
Grove The. Bour 190 C2
Grove The. Burs 105 D1
Grove The. Christ 192 C1
Grove The. Fern 165 E2
Grove The. Net 127 E4
Grove The. Southa 104 A1
Grove The. Stubb 154 A1
Grove The. Ver 115 D3
Grove The. Westb 137 D2
Grovelands Rd. Winch 1 A1
Groveley Rd. Bour 206 A1
Groveley Rd. Christ 209 F3
Groveley Way. N Bad 28 C1
Grovely Ave. Bour 207 F2
Groves Down. W Wel 50 C2
Grundles. Pet 41 D2
Gruneisen Rd. Ports 157 E1
Gudge Heath La. Fare 130 C1
Guelders The. Wat 134 C2
Guernsey Cl. Southa 77 F2
Guernsey Rd. Poole 189 E1
Guest Ave. Poole 206 A3
Guest Cl. Poole 206 A3
Guest Rd. Bish 56 B2
Guest Rd. Upt 203 D4
Guildford Dr. Ch Fo 55 D2
Guildford Rd. Ports 182 C3
Guildford St. Southa 103 D3
Guildhall Sq. Ports 182 B3
Guildhall Wlk. Ports 182 B3
Guildhill Rd. Bour 208 C2
Guilford Ct. Southb 137 F1
Guillemot Cl. Hyt 126 A1
Guillemot Gdns. Gos 155 D2
Gull Cl. Gos 155 D1
Gulliver Cl. Poole 216 B4
Gulls The. March 101 F1
Gullycroft Mead. He En 105 D4
Gunners Way. Gos 155 F1
Gunstore Rd. Ports 158 A2
Gunwharf Rd. Ports 182 A2
Gurjun Cl. Upt 203 D4
Gurnard Rd. Cos 157 F4
Gurnays Mead. W Wel 50 C2
Gurney Rd. Broa 187 F3
Gurney Rd. Ports 183 D2
Gurney Rd. Southa 102 B4
Gussage Rd. Poole 205 F4
Gutner La. N Hay 160 B1
Guys Cl. Rin 141 D3
Gwatkin Cl. Hav 135 E2
Gwenlyn Rd. Upt 203 E3
Gwynne Rd. Poole 205 F3
Gypsy La. Rin 141 D4

Haarlem Mews. Christ 209 E4
Hack Dr. Co Com 57 D4
Hacketts La. Drox 60 C1
Hacking Rd. Poole 204 A1
Hackleys La. W Wel 51 D3
Hackupps La. Miche 6 B1
Hackworth Gdns. He En 81 E2
Hadden Rd. Bour 207 E4
Haddon Cl. Fare 130 C1
Haddon Dr. Eastl 56 A3
Haddons Dr. W Moo 138 B4
Hadleigh Gdns. Eastl 56 A3
Hadleigh Rd. Cos 157 E4
Hadley Field. Holb 150 A3
Hadley Way. Broa 187 F2
Hadow Rd. Bour 190 B2
Hadrian Cl. Fern 165 E1
Hadrian Way. Broa 187 F4
Hadrian Way. Rown 78 C4
Hadrians Cl. Ch Fo 55 F4
Haglane Copse. Lym 198 B1
Hahnemann Rd. Bour 206 C1
Haig Ave. Poole 205 F1
Haig Rd. Bish 57 D1
Haileybury Gdns. He En 81 E1
Halden Cl. Rom 28 A1
Hale Ave. New M 196 A1
Hale Gdns. New M 196 A1
Hale La. Woodg 47 D2
Hale St N. Ports 182 B3
Hale St S. Ports 182 B3
Hales Dr. He En 105 D3
Halewood Way. Christ 208 C4
Half Moon St. Ports 182 A3
Halfpenny Dell. Wat 134 C2
Halfpenny La. Ports 182 A2
Halifax Rise. Wat 134 C4
Halifax Way. Christ 210 A4
Hall Cl. Bi Wa 83 E4
Hall Lands La. Fa Oa 57 E1
Hall Rd. Bour 189 F2
Hall Way The. Litt 1 A3
Hallet Cl. Southa 80 A1
Hallett Rd. Hav 136 A1
Halletts Cl. Stubb 154 B2
Halliday Cl. Gos 181 D3
Halliday Cres. Ports 183 E2
Halls Farm Close. Winch 1 C2
Halsey Cl. Gos 180 C2
Halstead Rd. Cos 157 E4
Halstead Rd. Southa 79 F1
Halstock Cres. Broa 188 B1
Halter Path. Hamw 203 F2
Halter Rise. Wi Mi 164 B3
Halterworth Cl. Rom 53 D4
Halterworth La. Rom 53 E4
Halton Cl. Bran 194 A4
Haltons Cl. Tot 76 B1
Ham La. Fern 164 C2
Ham La. Gos 156 A1
Ham La. Horn 112 A4
Ham La. Southb 161 E4
Ham La. Wi Mi 164 C2
Hambert Way. Tot 100 C3
Hamble Cl. Lo He 128 B1
Hamble Ct. Ch Fo 55 E3
Hamble House Gdns. Hamble 128 A1
Hamble La. Burs 127 F4
Hamble La. Hamble 127 F4
Hamble La. Wat 134 C3
Hamble Rd. Gos 180 C2
Hamble Rd. Poole 205 D3
Hambledon Cl. Winch 1 B2
Hambledon Gdns. Bour 208 B3
Hambledon La. Sob 85 F2
Hambledon Par. Wat 111 E1
Hambledon Rd. Clanf 88 A3
Hambledon Rd. Den 110 D2
Hambledon Rd. Hambl 110 B4
Hambledon Rd. Wat 111 D2
Hambleton Rd. Bour 208 A3
Hamblewood. Botl 106 A3
Hambrook Rd. Gos 181 D3
Hambrook St. Ports 182 A2
Hamdown Cres. W Wel 51 D1
Hameldon Cl. Southa 101 F4
Hamilton Cl. Bour 207 E3
Hamilton Cl. Hamw 203 F1
Hamilton Cl. Hav 159 F4
Hamilton Cres. Hamw 203 F1
Hamilton Ct. M on S 213 E2
Hamilton Gr. Gos 155 D1
Hamilton Mews. Hyt 126 A1
Hamilton Rd. Bish 56 B2
Hamilton Rd. Bour 207 F2
Hamilton Rd. Broa 187 F3
Hamilton Rd. Hamw 203 F1
Hamilton Rd. Hyt 150 A4
Hamilton Rd. Portc 156 C4
Hamilton Rd. Ports 182 B1
Hamilton Way. New M 195 F1
Hamlet Way. Gos 156 A1
Hamlets. Upt 203 E3
Hammond's Green. Tot 100 B4
Hammonds Cl. Tot 100 C4
Hammonds La. Tot 100 C4
Hammonds Way. Tot 100 C4
Hampage Green. Hav 135 E4
Hampden La. Bour 208 A3
Hampshire Centre The. Bour 191 F1
Hampshire Cl. Christ 192 C1
Hampshire Hatches La. Rin 141 D2
Hampshire St. Ports 182 C4
Hampshire Terr. Ports 182 A2
Hampton Cl. Black 177 F4
Hampton Cl. Wat 135 D4
Hampton Dr. Rin 117 D1
Hampton Gdns. Black 177 F4
Hampton Gr. Fare 130 A1
Hampton Hill. Swan 84 A3
Hampton La. Black 150 C1
Hampton La. Winch 1 B1
Hamptworth Rd. Red 48 B2
Hamtun Cres. Tot 76 C1
Hamtun Gdns. Tot 76 C1
Hamtun Rd. Southa 104 B2
Hamtun St. Southa 102 C2
Hanbidge Cres. Gos 155 E2
Hanbidge Wlk. Gos 155 E2
Handel Rd. Southa 102 C3
Handel Terr. Southa 102 C3
Handford Pl. Southa 102 C3
Handley Rd. Gos 180 C3

Hanger Way. Pet ..................... 41 D2
Hangers The. Bi Wa ................. 59 F1
Hanham Rd. Broa ................... 187 E3
Hanham Rd. Wi Mi ................. 163 E3
Hankinson Rd. Bour ............... 207 D4
Hanley Rd. Southa .................. 102 B4
Hann Rd. Rown ........................ 77 F3
Hannah Gdns. Wat .................. 134 C4
Hannah Way. Hord .................. 197 F3
Hannay Rise. Southa ............... 104 B3
Hannington Pl. Bour ............... 208 A3
Hannington Rd. Bour ............... 208 A3
Hannington Rd. Hav ............... 135 E4
Hanover Lodge. Winch .............. 10 C3
Hanover Bldgs. Southa ........... 103 D2
Hanover Gdns. Fare ............... 131 D2
Hanover St. Ports ................... 182 A3
Hants Corporate Pk. Chilw ....... 55 D1
Hanway Rd. Ports .................. 182 C4
Harbeck Rd. Bour .................. 191 E2
Harborough Rd. Southa .......... 102 C3
Harbour Cl. Poole .................. 216 B3
Harbour Cl. Wickh .................. 107 F2
Harbour Cres. Christ .............. 209 F3
Harbour Hill Cres. Poole ....... 204 C3
Harbour Hill Rd. Poole .......... 204 C3
Harbour Rd. Bour .................. 209 D2
Harbour Rd. Gos ................... 181 F3
Harbour Rd. S Hay ................ 184 B2
Harbour View Cl. Poole ......... 205 D3
Harbour View Rd. Poole ........ 205 D2
Harbour View. Portc .............. 156 B3
Harbour Way. Ems ................ 161 D4
Harbour Way. Ports ............... 157 E1
Harbourne Gdns. W End .......... 80 A1
Harbourside. Hav ................... 159 F3
Harbridge Ct. Hav ................. 135 E4
Harbridge Dro. Ibs .................. 93 E2
Harcombe Cl. Broa ................ 188 C2
Harcourt Cl. Wat ................... 112 A2
Harcourt Mews. Bour ............ 208 A3
Harcourt Rd. Bour ................. 208 A3
Harcourt Rd. Fare .................. 154 A4
Harcourt Rd. Gos ................... 181 D3
Harcourt Rd. Ports ................ 182 C4
Harcourt Rd. Southa ............. 103 F4
Hard The. Ports ..................... 182 A3
Harding La. Fa Oa ................... 57 D2
Harding Rd. Gos .................... 180 C3
Hardley La. Hyt ..................... 150 A4
Hardwick Rd. Ch Fo ................ 55 E3
Hardwicke Cl. Southa .............. 77 F1
Hardwicke Way. Hamble ......... 127 F2
Hardy Cl. Lo He ..................... 129 D2
Hardy Cl. New M .................... 195 F2
Hardy Cl. W Moo ................... 138 C1
Hardy Cres. Wi Mi ................ 163 E2
Hardy Dr. Hyt ....................... 126 A1
Hardy Rd. Cos ....................... 158 C4
Hardy Rd. Eastl ....................... 56 A1
Hardy Rd. Poole .................... 205 E2
Hardy Rd. W Moo .................. 138 C1
Hare La. Alderh ....................... 91 F3
Hare La. Hord ....................... 196 C2
Hare La. New M ..................... 196 C2
Harebell Cl. Fare ................... 131 E2
Harefield Ct. Rom ................... 53 D4
Harefield Rd. Southa ............... 79 E2
Hares Green. Bour ................. 208 A4
Harestock Cl. Litt ..................... 1 B3
Harestock Rd. Hav ................ 135 E2
Harestock Rd. Winch ................. 1 B2
Harewood Ave. Bour .............. 208 A3
Harewood Cl. Eastl .................. 56 A3
Harewood Cres. Bour ............ 207 F4
Harewood Gdns. Bour ........... 207 F4
Harewood Green. M on S ....... 214 A2
Harewood Pl. Bour ................. 208 A3
Harford Cl. Lym ..................... 198 B1
Harford Rd. Poole .................. 205 E4
Harkness Dr. Wat .................. 135 D4
Harkwood Dr. Hamw .............. 203 F2
Harland Cres. Southa .............. 78 B1
Harland Rd. Bour .................. 209 D2
Harlech Dr. Ch Fo .................... 55 D2
Harlequin Gr. Fare ................. 130 C1
Harleston Rd. Cos ................. 133 E1
Harleston Villas. Wi Mi ......... 163 E2
Harlyn Rd. Southa ................... 77 F1
Harness Cl. Wi Mi ................. 164 A3
Harold Cl. Tot ....................... 100 B3
Harold Rd. Ports ................... 182 C2
Harold Rd. S Hay .................. 185 D1
Harold Rd. Southa ................. 102 B4
Harold Rd. Stubb .................. 154 B2
Harold Rd. Westb .................. 137 D2
Harpway La. Burt ................... 193 E3
Harpway La. Sop ................... 193 E3
Harrage The. Rom ................... 52 C4
Harrier Cl. Horn .................... 112 A4
Harrier Cl. L on S ................. 179 F3
Harrier Cl. Southa ................... 78 A3
Harrier Dr. Oakl .................... 163 E1
Harrier Way. Faw .................. 150 A3
Harrier Way. Pet ..................... 41 E1
Harriers Cl. Christ ................. 210 B4
Harriet Cl. Stubb .................. 154 A1
Harris Ave. He En ................. 105 E4

Harris Rd. Gos ...................... 155 E2
Harris Way. New M ............... 196 B3
Harrison Ave. Bour ............... 207 E3
Harrison Cl. Burt .................. 193 E2
Harrison Rd. Fare ................. 131 D1
Harrison Rd. Southa ................ 79 E2
Harrison's Cut. Southa .......... 103 D2
Harrow Cl. Bran .................... 194 A4
Harrow Down. Winch ............... 10 B2
Harrow La. Pet ....................... 40 C3
Harrow Rd. Bran .................... 194 A4
Harrow Rd. Ports .................. 182 C2
Harry Barrow Cl. Rin ............ 141 D3
Hart Hill. Hyt ....................... 126 B1
Hart Plain Ave. Wat .............. 111 F2
Harthill Dro. Red .................... 47 F3
Harting Cl. Clanf ..................... 88 B2
Harting Down. Pet ................... 41 D2
Harting Gdns. Portc .............. 132 B1
Harting Rd. Bour ................... 208 B4
Hartington Rd. Gos ............... 180 C3
Hartington Rd. Southa ........... 103 D3
Hartland Ct. Southb .............. 137 E1
Hartland's Rd. Fare ............... 131 D1
Hartley Ave. Southa ................ 79 D2
Hartley Cl. Bish ...................... 57 D1
Hartley Cl. Hyt ..................... 126 A1
Hartley Rd. Bish ..................... 57 D1
Hartley Rd. Ports .................. 157 F2
Hartley Wlk. Hyt ................... 126 A1
Harts Farm Way. Hav ............ 159 E4
Harts Way. Hord ................... 197 E1
Hartsbourne Dr. Bour ........... 208 A4
Hartsgrove Ave. Black .......... 150 C1
Hartsgrove Cl. Black ............. 150 C1
Hartwell Rd. Ports ................ 158 A4
Harvest Cl. Winch ................... 10 B2
Harvest Rd. Den .................... 110 C2
Harvester Dr. Fare ................ 130 A1
Harvester Way. Lym .............. 198 B3
Harvestgate Wlk. Hav ........... 135 E3
Harvesting La. E Meo .............. 64 B3
Harvey Cres. Lo He ............... 128 C1
Harvey Ct. Black ................... 150 C1
Harvey Gdns. Hyt .................. 126 A2
Harvey Rd. Bish ..................... 56 C1
Harvey Rd. Bour ................... 208 A3
Harvey Rd. Oakl .................... 188 C4
Harwich Rd. Cos ................... 133 E1
Harwood Cl. Gos ................... 155 E2
Harwood Cl. Tot .................... 100 B4
Harwood Pl. Ki Wo ................... 2 B4
Harwood Rd. Gos .................. 155 E2
Haselbury Rd. Tot ................. 100 C4
Haselworth Dr. Gos .............. 181 D1
Haskells Cl. Lyn .................... 121 F2
Haskells Rd. Poole ............... 205 D4
Haslar Cres. Wat ................... 111 E1
Haslar Rd. Gos ..................... 181 E1
Haslemere Ave. Christ .......... 211 D4
Haslemere Gdns. S Hay ........ 185 F1
Haslemere Pl. Christ ............. 211 D4
Haslemere Rd. Ports ............. 182 C2
Haslemere Rd. Southb ........... 137 E1
Hasler Rd. Broa .................... 188 B1
Haslop Rd. Wi Mi .................. 164 A4
Hassocks The. Wat ............... 135 D4
Hastings Ave. Gos ................ 180 C4
Hastings Rd. Bour ................ 191 F1
Hastings Rd. Broa ................ 188 A1
Hatch Cl. Hav ....................... 135 E4
Hatch La. Liss ......................... 21 E2
Hatch Pond Rd. Poole .......... 204 B4
Hatchers Cl. Ows .................... 33 D3
Hatchet Cl. Woodg .................. 47 E2
Hatchet La. E Bol .................. 175 E4
Hatchley La. Ows .................... 58 A3
Hatfield Ct. New M ............... 195 F2
Hatfield Gdns. Bour .............. 208 A4
Hatfield Rd. Ports ................. 183 D2
Hathaway Cl. Eastl .................. 56 A2
Hathaway Gdns. Wat ............ 112 A1
Hathaway Rd. Bour ............... 208 B2
Hatherden Ave. Poole ........... 204 C3
Hatherley Cres. Portc ........... 156 A4
Hatherley Dr. Portc .............. 156 A4
Hatherley Rd. Cos ................ 133 D1
Hatherley Rd. Winch ................ 1 C1
Hatley Rd. Southa ................. 104 A4
Hatt La. Mott ........................... 5 F1
Havant Farm Cl. Hav ........... 135 F2
Havant Rd. Cos ..................... 158 B4
Havant Rd. Ems .................... 160 C4
Havant Rd. Horn ................... 112 B3
Havant Rd. N Hay ................. 159 F1
Havant Rd. Ports .................. 182 C4
Havant St. Ports ................... 182 A3
Havant-by-pass. Hav ............ 160 A4
Havelock Rd. Lo He .............. 128 B1
Havelock Rd. Poole .............. 206 A3
Havelock Rd. Ports ............... 182 B2
Havelock Rd. Southa ............. 102 C2
Havelock Way. Christ ............ 194 B1
Haven Cres. Stubb ................ 153 F1
Haven Gdns. New M .............. 196 A1
Haven Rd. Broa .................... 187 E3
Haven Rd. Poole ................... 216 B3
Haven Rd. S Hay ................... 185 F1

Haven The. Eastl ..................... 56 A3
Haven The. Gos .................... 181 D1
Haven The. Ports .................. 183 D3
Havendale. He En ................. 105 E3
Haverstock Rd. Bour ............ 191 D2
Haverstone Way. Southa ......... 79 E2
Haviland Mews. Bour ............ 207 F3
Haviland Rd E. Bour ............. 207 F3
Haviland Rd. Bour ................ 207 F3
Haviland Rd. Fern ................. 165 D4
Havisham Rd. Ports .............. 182 B4
Hawden Rd. Bour .................. 190 A1
Hawfinch Cl. Southa ............... 78 A3
Hawk Cl. Stubb ..................... 154 A1
Hawk Cl. Wi Mi ..................... 164 A4
Hawkchurch Gdns. Broa ....... 188 C1
Hawke St. Ports .................... 182 A3
Hawker Cl. Oakl .................... 163 F1
Hawkeswood Rd. Southa ....... 103 E4
Hawkewood Ave. Wat ........... 111 E1
Hawkhill. Hyt ........................ 125 E2
Hawkhurst Cl. Southa ........... 104 A1
Hawkins Cl. Rin .................... 117 E1
Hawkins Rd. Gos ................... 155 E1
Hawkins Rd. Poole ................ 189 F1
Hawkley Green. Southa ......... 126 C4
Hawkley Rd. Hawk .................. 20 B3
Hawkley Rd. Liss .................... 20 B3
Hawkwell. Portc .................... 155 F4
Hawkwood Rd. Bour .............. 207 F2
Hawley Cl. Hav ..................... 135 F3
Haworth Cl. Christ ................ 193 D1
Hawstead Green. Hav ........... 135 E3
Hawthorn Cl. Fa Oa ................ 57 E1
Hawthorn Cl. He En .............. 105 E3
Hawthorn Cl. New M ............. 196 B2
Hawthorn Cres. Cos ............. 158 A3
Hawthorn Dr. Broa ............... 187 F1
Hawthorn Dr. Sway ............... 172 A1
Hawthorn La. Lo He .............. 128 C3
Hawthorn Rd. Bour ............... 206 C4
Hawthorn Rd. Burt ................ 193 F2
Hawthorn Rd. Den ................ 110 C2
Hawthorn Rd. Horn ................. 88 B1
Hawthorn Rd. Hyt .................. 125 F2
Hawthorn Rd. Southa .............. 79 D1
Hawthorn Wlk. L on S ........... 179 F3
Hawthorne Gr. S Hay ............ 185 D2
Hawthorne Rd. Tot ............... 100 B4
Hawthorns The. March .......... 101 F1
Hawthorns The. March .......... 102 A1
Hay St. Ports ........................ 182 A3
Hayburn Rd. Southa ................ 77 E1
Haydn Cl. Ki Wo ....................... 2 A4
Haydock Cl. Tot .................... 100 B4
Haydock Mews. Wat .............. 112 A1
Haydon Rd. Poole ................. 206 A1
Hayes Ave. Bour ................... 207 F3
Hayes Cl. Fare ...................... 130 B2
Hayes Cl. Wi Mi .................... 164 A2
Hayes La. Wi Mi ................... 164 A3
Hayes Mead. Holb ................. 150 A3
Hayes Terr. Gos .................... 181 D3
Hayeswood Rd. Wi Mi ........... 164 A3
Hayle Rd. W End ..................... 80 A1
Hayley Cl. Hyt ...................... 149 F4
Hayling Ave. Ports ................ 183 D4
Hayling Cl. Fare .................... 154 B4
Haymoor Rd. Poole ............... 205 D4
Haynes Ave. Poole ................ 204 B2
Haynes Way. Hyt .................. 125 F1
Hays Cotts. Steep ................... 40 B4
Haysoms Cl. B on S .............. 196 A1
Hayter Gdns. Rom .................. 53 D4
Hayters Way. Alderh .............. 93 D3
Hayward Cl. Tot .................... 100 B4
Hayward Cres. Ver ................ 114 C3
Hayward Ct. Holb .................. 150 B2
Hayward Way. Ver ................ 114 C3
Haywards Farm Cl. Ver ......... 114 C3
Haywards La. Broa ................ 187 E4
Hazel Cl. Alderh ..................... 93 D3
Hazel Cl. Ch Fo ...................... 30 B1
Hazel Cl. Christ .................... 194 B1
Hazel Dr. Fern ...................... 165 E4
Hazel Farm Rd. Tot .............. 100 B4
Hazel Gr. Ashu ....................... 99 F2
Hazel Gr. Clanf ...................... 88 B3
Hazel Gr. Lo He .................... 129 D1
Hazel Gr. Winch ..................... 10 B3
Hazel Rd. Clanf ...................... 88 B3
Hazel Rd. Lym ...................... 198 A2
Hazel Rd. Southa .................. 103 E2
Hazelbank Cl. Pet ................... 41 D2
Hazeldean Dr. Ro Ca ............ 113 D1
Hazeldown Rd. Rown .............. 77 F3
Hazeleigh Ave. Southa .......... 103 F1
Hazeley Green. Hav .............. 136 A3
Hazeley Rd. Twyf .................... 32 B4
Hazelholt Dr. Hav ................. 135 E2
Hazell Ave. Bour ................... 190 A1
Hazelton Cl. Bour ................. 208 A4
Hazelwood Ave. Hav ............. 135 D2
Hazelwood Ave. New M ......... 195 F2
Hazelwood Rd. Southa ............ 80 A1
Hazelwood. Stubb ................. 154 A3
Hazlebury Rd. Broa .............. 204 A4
Hazlemere Dr. St Le .............. 139 F2

Hazleton Way. Wat ............... 112 A3
Head Down. Pet ...................... 41 D2
Head's La. Bour .................... 190 C3
Headland Dr. Lo He .............. 129 D2
Headlands Bsns Park. Rin .... 117 D1
Headlands The. Down ............. 46 C4
Headley Cl. L on S ................ 179 F3
Headon View. W Meo .............. 37 E3
Heads Farm Cl. Bour ............ 190 C3
Headswell Ave. Bour ............ 190 C2
Headswell Cres. Bour ........... 190 C2
Headswell Gdns. Bour .......... 190 C2
Heanor Cl. Bour .................... 190 B1
Hearne Gdns. Shed ................. 84 A1
Hearts Of Oak Mews. Lym ..... 198 B2
Heath Ave. Poole .................. 204 B3
Heath Cl. Fa Oa ...................... 57 E1
Heath Cl. Horn ...................... 112 A4
Heath Cl. Wi Mi .................... 164 A4
Heath Farm Cl. Fern ............ 165 E2
Heath Farm Rd. Fern ........... 165 E2
Heath Farm Way. Fern ......... 165 E2
Heath Gdns. Net ................... 127 E4
Heath House Cl. He En ......... 105 D2
Heath La. E Bol .................... 175 E4
Heath Lawns. Fare ............... 130 B1
Heath Rd E. Pet ..................... 41 D1
Heath Rd N. Lo He ............... 128 C2
Heath Rd S. Lo He ............... 128 C2
Heath Rd W. Pet ..................... 41 D1
Heath Rd. Christ ................... 195 D1
Heath Rd. Hord .................... 196 C2
Heath Rd. Lo He ................... 129 D2
Heath Rd. N Bad .................... 54 A2
Heath Rd. Pet ......................... 41 D2
Heath Rd. Sob ........................ 85 D1
Heath Rd. Southa .................. 104 A3
Heath Rd. St Le .................... 139 E2
Heath The. Den ..................... 111 D2
Heath Dell. Upt ..................... 203 D3
Heather Chase. Bish .............. 57 D1
Heather Cl. Broa ................... 187 F3
Heather Cl. Christ ................. 195 D1
Heather Cl. Gos .................... 155 D1
Heather Cl. Hord .................. 197 D2
Heather Cl. St Le .................. 139 F2
Heather Cl. Tot ..................... 100 C4
Heather Cl. Wat .................... 134 C3
Heather Ct. Southa ............... 104 B4
Heather Dell. Upt .................. 203 D3
Heather Dr. Fern .................. 165 E4
Heather Gdns. Fare .............. 130 B2
Heather Rd. Black ................ 150 C1
Heather Rd. Bour .................. 190 B2
Heather Rd. Pet ...................... 41 E2
Heather View Rd. Poole ........ 205 F4
Heather Way. Fern ................ 165 E4
Heatherbank Rd. Bour .......... 206 B2
Heatherbrae Gdns. N Bad ...... 53 F2
Heatherbrae La. Upt ............. 203 E3
Heatherdeane Rd. Southa ....... 79 D1
Heatherdene Rd. Fo Ca .......... 30 C1
Heatherdown Rd. W Moo ...... 139 D1
Heatherdown Way. W Moo .... 139 D1
Heatherfield. Buri ................... 65 E3
Heatherlands Rd. Rown .......... 78 C4
Heatherlea Rd. Bour ............. 208 B2
Heatherstone Ave. Hyt ......... 125 F1
Heatherton Mews. Ems ......... 136 C1
Heatherview. N Bad ................ 53 F3
Heathfield Ave. Fare ............. 130 B1
Heathfield Ave. Poole ........... 206 A4
Heathfield Cl. Ch Fo ............... 30 B1
Heathfield Cl. Southa ............ 104 A2
Heathfield Rd. Ch Fo .............. 30 B1
Heathfield Rd. Pet ................... 41 E2
Heathfield Rd. Ports ............. 157 E1
Heathfield Rd. Southa ........... 104 B2
Heathfield Rd. W Moo ........... 139 D1
Heathfield Rd. W Moo ........... 138 C1
Heathfield. Hyt ..................... 125 F1
Heathhouse La. He En .......... 105 E2
Heathlands Ave. Fern ........... 165 E1
Heathlands Cl. Ch Fo .............. 55 E4
Heathlands Cl. Ch Fo .............. 55 E4
Heathlands Rd. Ch Fo ............ 55 E4
Heathwood Ave. B on S ........ 211 F4
Heathwood Rd. Bour ............ 206 C4
Heathy Cl. B on S ................. 211 F4
Heaton Rd. Bour ................... 190 A1
Heaton Rd. Gos .................... 181 D4
Heavytree Rd. Poole ............. 205 D2
Hebrides Cl. Stubb ............... 154 A2
Heckfield Cl. Hav ................. 136 A3
Heckford Rd. Broa ................ 187 E3
Heckford Rd. Poole .............. 204 B2
Hector Cl. Wat ...................... 134 C1
Hedera Rd. Lo He ................. 128 C2
Hedge End Bsns Ctre. He En .. 81 D1
Hedge End Wlk. Hav ............ 136 A3
Hedgerley. B on S ................. 212 A4
Hedgerow Drive. Southa ......... 80 A1
Hedgerow Gdns. Ems ........... 136 C2
Heidelberg Rd. Ports ............ 182 C2
Heights App. Upt .................. 203 E4

Heights Rd. Upt .................... 203 E4
Heights The. Fare ................. 131 E1
Heights The. He En .............. 105 D3
Helena Rd. Ports ................... 182 C1
Helford Gdns. W End .............. 80 A1
Hellyer Rd. Ports .................. 183 D2
Helsby Cl. Fare ..................... 154 C4
Helsted Cl. Gos .................... 180 C2
Helston Dr. Ems ................... 136 C2
Helston Rd. Portc ................. 132 C1
Helvellyn Rd. Southa ............ 101 F4
Helyar Rd. Bour .................... 191 F1
Hemdean Gdns. W End ........... 80 B1
Hemlock Rd. Wat ................. 111 F2
Hemming Cl. Tot ................... 100 C3
Hempsted Rd. Cos ................ 133 D1
Hemsley Wk. Wat ................. 112 A2
Henbury Cl. Broa .................. 187 F3
Henbury Cl. Poole ................ 189 D1
Henbury Rise. Broa .............. 187 E3
Henbury View Rd. Broa ........ 187 E3
Henderson Rd. Ports ............ 183 E2
Hendford Gdns. Bour ........... 190 B1
Hendford Rd. Bour ............... 190 B1
Hengist Rd. Bour .................. 207 E2
Hengistbury Rd. B on S ........ 211 F4
Hengistbury Rd. Bour ........... 209 D2
Henley Gdns. Bour ............... 208 A4
Henley Gdns. Fare ................ 130 B2
Henley Rd. Ports .................. 182 C2
Henning's Park Rd. Poole ..... 204 C3
Henry Cl. Holb ..................... 150 A3
Henry Cl. Bish ....................... 56 B2
Henry Rd. Southa ................. 102 B4
Henry St. Gos ....................... 181 E2
Henry St. Southa .................. 102 C3
Henstead Rd. Southa ............ 102 C3
Hensting La. Co Com .............. 57 E4
Hensting La. Ows ................... 58 C1
Henty Rd. Southa .................. 102 A4
Henville Cl. Gos .................... 180 B4
Henville Rd. Bour ................. 207 E3
Henwood Down. Pet ............... 41 D2
Hepworth Cl. Southa ............ 104 B1
Herald Rd. He En .................... 81 D1
Herbert Ave. Poole ............... 205 E4
Herbert Rd. Bour .................. 206 A1
Herbert Rd. Gos ................... 180 C3
Herbert Rd. New M ............... 196 A2
Herbert Rd. Ports ................ 182 C1
Herbert Rd. Red ..................... 47 E3
Herbert St. Ports .................. 182 B4
Herbert Walker Ave. Southa . 102 B2
Herberton Rd. Bour .............. 208 B3
Hercules Ho. Hamw .............. 203 D2
Hercules St. Ports ................ 182 B4
Hereford Rd. Ports ............... 182 B2
Hereward Cl. Rom .................. 53 D4
Herm Rd. Poole .................... 189 E1
Hermitage Cl. Bi Wa ............. 83 D4
Hermitage Gdns. Wat ........... 134 C4
Hermitage Rd. Poole ............ 205 D3
Hern La. Fordi ........................ 94 A3
Herne Rd. Cos ...................... 157 F4
Herne Rd. Pet ......................... 41 D2
Heron Cl. Ports ..................... 183 D3
Heron Cl. Sway ..................... 172 A1
Heron Court Rd. Bour ........... 207 D4
Heron Dr. Wi Mi ................... 164 A4
Heron Quay. Herm ................ 161 D4
Heron Sq. Eastl ...................... 55 F1
Heron Way. Gos .................... 155 D2
Herons Cl. Stubb .................. 154 B2
Heronswood. Tot .................... 76 B1
Herrick Cl. Southa ................ 104 B2
Herriot Cl. Wat ..................... 112 A3
Herstone Cl. Poole ............... 188 C1
Hertford Cl. Fordi ................... 69 F2
Hertford Pl. Ports ................ 182 B4
Hertsfield. Lo He .................. 129 E2
Hesketh Cl. St Le .................. 140 A3
Hestan Cl. Christ .................. 192 B2
Hester Rd. Ports ................... 183 D2
Hestia Cl. Rom ....................... 53 E4
Heston Way. W Moo .............. 138 B2
Heston Wlk. Gos .................. 180 C2
Hewett Cl. Lo He .................. 153 F4
Hewett Rd. Lo He ................. 153 F4
Hewett Rd. Ports .................. 157 F1
Hewetts Rise. Lo He ............. 152 B4
Hewitt Cl. Gos ...................... 181 D4
Hewitt Rd. Hamw .................. 203 F2
Hewitt's Rd. Southa .............. 102 B3
Heyes Dr. Southa .................. 104 B2
Heysham Rd. Broa ................ 188 A2
Heysham Rd. Southa ............ 102 A4
Heyshott Rd. Ports ............... 182 C2
Heytesbury Rd. Bour ............ 208 B3
Heyward Rd. Ports ............... 182 C2
Heywood Gdns. Hav ............. 135 E3
Heywood Green. Southa ....... 104 C3
Hibberd Way. Bour ............... 190 B1
Hibbs Cl. Upt ....................... 203 E4
Hickory Cl. Upt ..................... 203 D4
Hickory Dr. Winch ................... 1 B2
Hickory Gdns. W End .............. 80 B2
High Cross La. Frox G ............ 18 B1
High Cross. Frox G ................ 18 C1
High Dr. Gos ........................ 155 E3

# High Firs Gdns. Rom

High Firs Gdns. Rom ............. 53 E4
High Firs Rd. Rom ................ 53 E4
High Firs Rd. Southa ............ 104 B3
High Howe Cl. Bour ............ 189 F2
High Howe Gdns. Bour ........ 189 F2
High Howe La. Bour ............ 189 F2
High Lawn Way. Hav .......... 135 F3
High Mead La. Fern ............ 165 D1
High Mead. Fare ................ 130 C2
High Mead. Fern ................ 165 D1
High Meadow. Southa .......... 104 B3
High Oaks Cl. Lo He ............ 129 D2
High Oaks Gdns. Bour ........ 189 F2
High Park Rd. Broa ............ 187 F2
High Rd. Southa .................. 79 E2
High Ridge Cres. New M ...... 196 B2
High St N. Poole ................ 204 B2
High St. Beaul .................. 148 C1
High St. Bi Wa .................... 83 E4
High St. Botl ...................... 106 A4
High St. Buri ...................... 65 E3
High St. Burs .................... 128 A4
High St. Christ .................. 209 D3
High St. Cos ...................... 157 F4
High St. Dame .................... 68 B3
High St. Down .................... 47 D4
High St. Drox ...................... 61 D1
High St. E Meo .................... 38 C1
High St. Eastl .................... 56 A1
High St. Ems .................... 160 C4
High St. Fare .................... 131 E1
High St. Fordi .................... 69 F1
High St. Gos .................... 181 E2
High St. Hambl .................... 86 B2
High St. Hamble ................ 128 A1
High St. Hyt ...................... 126 A3
High St. L on S .................. 179 F3
High St. Lo He .................. 153 F4
High St. Lym .................... 198 C2
High St. Lyn ...................... 121 F3
High St. M on S ................ 213 E2
High St. Meons .................... 61 E2
High St. Pet ........................ 40 C2
High St. Poole .................. 204 B1
High St. Ports .................. 182 A2
High St. Rin ...................... 140 C4
High St. Shed .................... 107 F4
High St. Sob ...................... 85 D2
High St. Southa ................ 103 D2
High St. Southw ................ 132 C3
High St. St Le .................. 139 F3
High St. Tot .................... 101 D4
High St. Twyf ...................... 32 A3
High St. W End .................... 80 B1
High St. Wi Mi .................. 163 D2
High St. Winch .................... 10 C4
High St. Woodg .................... 70 C4
High Town Hill. Rin ............ 141 F4
High Trees Dr. Winch ............ 1 C1
High Trees Wlk. Fern .......... 165 E4
High Trees. Wat ................ 134 C4
High View Way. Southa ...... 103 F4
High View. Portc ................ 132 B1
High Way. Broa .................. 187 F2
High Wlk. Fare .................. 130 C2
Highbank Ave. Wat ............ 134 B2
Highbury Cl. Fa Oa .............. 57 E1
Highbury Cl. New M ............ 196 A2
Highbury Gr. Cos ................ 158 A3
Highbury St. Ports ............ 182 A2
Highclere Ave. Hav ............ 135 F2
Highclere Rd. Southa .......... 78 B2
Highclere Way. Ch Fo .......... 55 D2
Highcliff Ave. Southa .......... 103 D4
Highcliffe Dr. Eastl .............. 56 A4
Highcliffe Rd. Christ .......... 210 B4
Highcliffe Rd. Gos ............ 180 C2
Highcliffe Rd. Winch ............ 11 D3
Highcroft La. Horn ............ 112 B4
Highcrown Mews. Southa ...... 79 D1
Highcrown St. Southa .......... 79 D1
Higher Blandford Rd. Broa . 187 F3
Higher Merley La. Broa ...... 187 F4
Highfield Ave. Fare ............ 154 C4
Highfield Ave. Lym ............ 198 B2
Highfield Ave. Rin ............ 141 D4
Highfield Ave. Twyf ............ 32 A3
Highfield Ave. Wat ............ 111 F1
Highfield Cl. Broa .............. 187 F3
Highfield Cl. Ch Fo .............. 55 F3
Highfield Cl. Southa .............. 79 D1
Highfield Cl. Sway .............. 172 A1
Highfield Cl. Wat .............. 111 F1
Highfield Cres. Southa .......... 79 D1
Highfield Dr. Rin .............. 141 D4
Highfield Gdns. Liss ............ 21 D2
Highfield Gdns. Sway ........ 172 A1
Highfield La. Red .................. 47 E3
Highfield La. Southa .............. 79 D1
Highfield Rd. Bour ............ 190 C1
Highfield Rd. Broa ............ 187 F3
Highfield Rd. Ch Fo .............. 55 F3
Highfield Rd. Gos .............. 180 C3
Highfield Rd. Lym ............ 198 B2
Highfield Rd. Pet .................. 40 C2
Highfield Rd. Ports ............ 182 B3
Highfield Rd. Rin .............. 141 D4
Highfield Rd. Southa ............ 79 D1
Highfield Rd. W Moo .......... 138 C2

Highfield. Lym .................. 198 B2
Highfield. Twyf .................... 32 A3
Highfields. Lo He .............. 128 C1
Highgate Rd. Ports ............ 158 A1
Highgrove Cl. Tot .............. 100 B3
Highgrove Rd. Ports .......... 183 D4
Highland Ave. Christ .......... 195 D1
Highland Cres. Bour .......... 190 B2
Highland Rd. Ems .............. 136 C1
Highland Rd. Poole ............ 205 D3
Highland Rd. Ports ............ 183 D1
Highland Rd. Wi Mi ............ 163 E3
Highland St. Ports ............ 183 D1
Highland Terr. Ports .......... 182 C2
Highland View Cl. Wi Mi .... 163 E3
Highlands Cl. Hyt .............. 126 A1
Highlands Cl. N Bad ............ 53 F3
Highlands Cres. Bour .......... 190 B2
Highlands Rd. B on S ........ 212 A4
Highlands Rd. Cos ............ 158 B4
Highlands Rd. Fare ............ 130 B2
Highlands Way. Hyt ............ 125 F1
Highlands Way. Whit ............ 24 A2
Highmoor Cl. Broa ............ 187 E3
Highmoor Cl. Poole ............ 205 E2
Highmoor Rd. Bour ............ 190 A1
Highmoor Rd. Broa ............ 187 E3
Highmoor Rd. Poole .......... 205 E2
Highmount Cl. Winch ............ 11 E4
Highnam Gdns. Lo He ........ 128 C2
Hightown Gdns. Rin .......... 141 E3
Hightown Rd. Rin .............. 141 D3
Hightrees Ave. Bour .......... 191 F1
Highview Cl. Christ ............ 192 C3
Highview Gdns. Poole ........ 205 E4
Highways Rd. Comp .............. 31 E3
Highwood Cl. Alderh ............ 92 B3
Highwood La. N Bad ............ 53 E4
Highwood Lawn. Hav .......... 135 E4
Highwood Rd. Brock .......... 172 C4
Highwood Rd. Gos ............ 180 B4
Highwood Rd. Poole .......... 205 F2
Higworth La. S Hay ............ 184 C3
Hilary Ave. Cos ................ 158 A4
Hilary Cl. Lyn .................. 122 A2
Hilary Rd. Broa ................ 188 B1
Hilda Gdns. Den ................ 111 D2
Hilda Rd. Poole ................ 205 F4
Hilden Way. Litt .................... 1 A3
Hilier Wlk. L on S .............. 179 F3
Hill Brow Cl. Hill B .............. 21 D1
Hill Brow Rd. Liss .............. 21 D1
Hill Cl. Bran .................... 194 A4
Hill Cl. Fa Oa .................... 57 E3
Hill Coppice Rd. Lo He ...... 129 E3
Hill Croft. Swanw .............. 129 F2
Hill Dr. Fare .................... 130 B2
Hill Farm Rd. Southa .......... 102 C3
Hill Head Rd. Stubb .......... 154 A1
Hill Houses La. Cher ............ 14 A3
Hill La. Bran .................... 194 A4
Hill La. Co Com .................. 31 F1
Hill La. Southa .................... 78 C1
Hill Park Rd. Fare .............. 130 B2
Hill Park Rd. Gos .............. 180 C3
Hill Pl. Burs .................... 128 A4
Hill Rd. Portc .................. 132 B1
Hill Rise. Twyf .................... 32 A3
Hill St. Ower ...................... 76 B3
Hill St. Poole .................. 204 B1
Hill Top Gdns. Horn .............. 88 B2
Hill View Rd. Brai ................ 28 B3
Hill View Rd. Fern ............ 165 E4
Hill View Rd. Mich .............. 27 E4
Hill View Rd. Portc ............ 132 B1
Hill View. E Meo .................. 38 B1
Hill Wlk. Fare .................. 130 B2
Hillary Cl. Fare ................ 130 C1
Hillary Rd. Christ .............. 209 F4
Hillborough Cres. Ports ...... 182 B2
Hillbourne Rd. Broa .......... 188 A1
Hillbrow Cl. Fare .............. 130 B2
Hillbrow Rd. Ro Ca ............ 113 D1
Hillbrow Rd. Bour ............ 208 A3
Hillbury Rd. Alderh .............. 93 D3
Hillcrest Ave. Ch Fo ............ 55 F3
Hillcrest Ave. Fern ............ 165 E4
Hillcrest Cl. Bour .............. 191 D2
Hillcrest Cl. N Bad .............. 53 F3
Hillcrest Dr. Ch Fo .............. 55 E3
Hillcrest Gdns. Shed ............ 83 E2
Hillcrest Rd. Bour .............. 191 D2
Hillcrest Rd. Broa .............. 187 E3
Hilldene Way. W End ............ 80 C1
Hillditch. Lym .................. 198 B3
Hilldown Rd. Southa ............ 79 D1
Hilldowns Ave. Ports .......... 157 E1
Hillgrove Rd. Southa ............ 79 F2
Hillier Way. Winch .................. 2 A1
Hillman Rd. Poole .............. 205 E3
Hillmead Gdns. Hav .......... 135 D1
Hillpound. Swan .................. 84 A2
Hillside Ave. Rom ................ 53 D4
Hillside Ave. Southa .............. 79 F1
Hillside Ave. Wat .............. 134 A1
Hillside Cl. Ch Fo .............. 55 E3
Hillside Cl. Horn .................. 88 B2
Hillside Cl. W Dean ................ 3 E1

Hillside Cl. Winch .................... 1 B1
Hillside Cres. Portc ............ 132 C1
Hillside Dr. Christ .............. 192 B2
Hillside Gdns. Broa ............ 187 E2
Hillside Ind Est. Horn ........ 112 B4
Hillside Mews. Broa .......... 187 E2
Hillside Rd. Broa .............. 187 E3
Hillside Rd. Lym ................ 198 B3
Hillside Rd. Poole .............. 189 F1
Hillside Rd. Ver ................ 114 C4
Hillside Rd. Winch .................. 1 B1
Hillside Rd. Woodl ............ 114 A3
Hillside Wlk. Woodl ............ 114 A3
Hillside. Curd .................. 106 C4
Hillsley Rd. Cos ................ 132 C1
Hillson Dr. Fare ................ 130 B2
Hillsons Rd. Botl .............. 106 B4
Hilltop Cl. Fern ................ 165 D4
Hilltop Cres. Wat .............. 134 B1
Hilltop Ct. Southa ............ 102 A3
Hilltop Dr. Southa ............ 104 B2
Hilltop Rd. Broa ................ 187 F3
Hilltop Rd. Fern ................ 165 D4
Hillview Rd. Bour .............. 190 B2
Hillview Rd. Hyt ................ 125 F2
Hillview. Wat .................... 112 B3
Hillway The. Ch Fo .............. 55 E4
Hillway The. Portc ............ 156 B4
Hillway. St Le .................. 139 F3
Hilly Cl. Ows ...................... 33 D2
Hillyfields. Nur .................... 77 E2
Hilsea Cres. Ports ............ 157 F3
Hiltingbury Ave. Hav .......... 136 A3
Hiltingbury Cl. Ch Fo .......... 30 B1
Hiltingbury Rd. Ch Fo .......... 30 B1
Hiltom Rd. Rin .................. 141 D4
Hilton Cl. Poole ................ 205 D3
Hilton Rd. Gos .................. 181 E2
Hilton Rd. He En .............. 105 E4
Hilton Rd. New M .............. 196 A2
Hinchcliffe Rd. Hamw ........ 203 F1
Hinchcliffe Rd. Hamw ........ 203 F1
Hinkler Rd. Southa ............ 104 C3
Hinton Cl. Hav .................. 135 E2
Hinton Cres. Southa .......... 104 C2
Hinton Hill. Cher .................. 14 C2
Hinton Rd. Bour ................ 206 C2
Hinton Wood Ave. Christ .... 194 C1
Hintonwood La. Christ ........ 194 C1
Hipley Rd. Hav .................. 136 A2
Hirst Rd. Hyt .................... 126 A2
Hive Gdns. Poole .............. 211 E3
Hives Way. Lym ................ 198 B3
Hoad's Hill. Wickh ............ 108 A1
Hoadlands. Pet .................... 41 D2
Hobart Dr. Hyt .................. 126 A2
Hobart Rd. New M .............. 195 F1
Hobb La. He En ................ 105 E3
Hobbs Park. St Le .............. 139 F2
Hobbs Pass. Gos .............. 181 F2
Hobbs Rd. Poole .............. 205 E4
Hobby Cl. Ports ................ 158 A2
Hobson Way. Holb ............ 150 B2
Hoburne Gdns. Christ ........ 194 B1
Hoburne La. Christ ............ 194 B1
Hockham Ct. Hav .............. 135 E4
Hockley Cl. Cos ................ 157 E4
Hocombe Dr. Ch Fo .............. 30 A1
Hocombe Park Cl. Ch Fo ...... 30 A1
Hocombe Rd. Ch Fo .............. 30 B1
Hocombe Wood Rd. Ch Fo .... 30 A1
Hodder Cl. N Bad ................ 55 D3
Hodges Cl. Hav ................ 136 A2
Hodges Cl. Poole .............. 204 C4
Hoe La. N Bad .................... 53 E2
Hoe Rd. Bi Wa .................... 83 F4
Hoe St. Sob .................... 109 F4
Hoe The. Gos .................. 155 F1
Hoeford Cl. Fare .............. 155 D3
Hogarth Cl. Pet .................. 41 D2
Hogarth Cl. Rom .................. 28 A1
Hogarth Cl. Southa ............ 104 B1
Hogue Ave. Bour .............. 190 B3
Holbeach Cl. Cos .............. 133 F1
Holbrook Rd. Fare ............ 155 D4
Holbrook Rd. Ports ............ 182 B3
Holbury Rd. Bour .............. 191 F2
Holbury Dro. Holb .............. 150 B2
Holbury La. E Tyth ................ 4 B2
Holbury La. Locke .................. 4 B2
Holcombe Rd. Upt .............. 203 D3
Holcot la. Ports ................ 158 B2
Holcroft Rd. Southa .......... 104 C3
Holdaway Cl. Ki Wo ................ 2 A4
Holden La. Meons ................ 34 C4
Holdenhurst Ave. Bour ...... 208 B4
Holdenhurst Cl. Horn ............ 88 B1
Holdenhurst Rd. Bour ........ 192 A2
Holdenhurst Rd. Bour ........ 207 E3
Hole La. Curd .................... 83 D1
Holes Cl. Hord .................. 196 C2
Holkham Cl. Southa .............. 77 F2
Hollam Cl. Fare ................ 154 A4
Hollam Cres. Fare ............ 154 A4
Hollam Dr. Fare ................ 154 A4
Hollam Rd. Ports .............. 183 D1
Holland Cl. Ch Fo ................ 55 D2
Holland Park. Lo He .......... 128 C2

Holland Pl. Gos ................ 155 E1
Holland Pl. Southa .............. 78 A1
Holland Rd. Ports ............ 182 C2
Holland Rd. Southa .......... 103 E1
Holland Rd. Tot .............. 100 B4
Holland Way. Broa ............ 187 F3
Hollands Cl. Litt .................... 1 A3
Hollands Wood Dr. New M . 196 A3
Hollies Cl. Sway .............. 172 A1
Hollingbourne Cl. Southa .. 103 E4
Hollman Dr. Rom .................. 52 B4
Hollow La. S Hay .............. 184 C2
Holloway Ave. Bour .......... 189 F3
Holly Cl. Hyt .................... 150 A4
Holly Cl. Lo He ................ 128 C2
Holly Cl. St Le .................. 139 E2
Holly Cl. Upt .................... 203 D4
Holly Dell. Southa .............. 78 C3
Holly Dr. Wat .................. 135 D3
Holly Gdns. Burt .............. 193 E1
Holly Gdns. M on S .......... 213 E3
Holly Gdns. W End ................ 80 B2
Holly Gr. Fare .................. 130 C2
Holly Gr. Ver .................... 114 C3
Holly Green Rise. Bour ...... 189 F2
Holly Hatch Rd. Tot .......... 100 C3
Holly Hedge La. Broa ........ 204 B4
Holly Hill Cl. Southa ............ 78 C3
Holly Hill La. Lo He .......... 128 B3
Holly Hill. Southa ................ 78 C3
Holly La. Christ ................ 195 E1
Holly La. Bold .................. 174 A1
Holly Oak Rd. Southa .......... 78 A2
Holly Rd. Ashu ................ 100 A1
Holly Rd. Black ................ 177 F4
Holly St. Gos .................. 181 E2
Hollybank Cl. Hyt .............. 126 A2
Hollybank Cl. Wat .............. 112 B3
Hollybank Cres. Hyt ............ 125 F2
Hollybank La. Ems ............ 136 C2
Hollybank Rd. Hyt ............ 125 F2
Hollybank. L on S .............. 179 F3
Hollybrook Ave. Southa ........ 78 B2
Hollybrook Cl. Southa .......... 78 A1
Hollybrook Gdns. Lo He ...... 129 D3
Hollybrook Rd. Southa .......... 78 B1
Hollywood Cl. N Bad ............ 53 F2
Hollywood La. Lym ............ 198 B3
Holm Cl. Rin .................... 117 E1
Holman Cl. Wat ................ 112 A1
Holmdale Rd. Gos ............ 180 C4
Holme Cl. Lym .................. 198 B1
Holme Rd. Christ .............. 211 D4
Holmes Cl. Net ................ 127 D3
Holmesland Dr. Botl .......... 105 F4
Holmesland La. Botl .......... 105 F4
Holmesland Wlk. Botl ........ 105 F4
Holmfield Ave. Bour .......... 208 B4
Holmfield Ave. Fare .......... 154 C4
Holmgrove. Lo He .............. 129 E2
Holmhurst Ave. Christ ........ 194 C1
Holmsley Cl. Lym .............. 198 A1
Holmsley Cl. Southa .......... 104 B4
Holmsley Pass. Bur .......... 170 B4
Holmsley Rd. Brock .......... 170 C1
Holmsley Rd. New M .......... 170 C1
Holmwood Garth. Rin ........ 141 E3
Holne Ct. Ports ................ 183 E2
Holnest Rd. Broa .............. 188 B1
Holst Way. Wat ................ 134 C3
Holt Cl. Wickh .................. 107 F2
Holt Cl. Southa ................ 126 C4
Holt Down. Pet .................. 41 D2
Holt Gdns. Ro Ca .............. 113 D2
Holt Rd. Poole ................ 205 F3
Holt Rd. Southa .............. 102 C3
Holt Rd. Ver .................... 138 B4
Holworth Cl. Bour ............ 189 F2
Holy Rood Pl. Southa ........ 103 D2
Holyborne Rd. Rom .............. 53 D4
Holybourne Rd. Hav .......... 135 F2
Holyrood Ave. Southa .......... 79 D1
Holyrood Cl. Wat .............. 135 D4
Holywell Cl. Broa .............. 188 B2
Holywell Rd. Shed .............. 84 B1
Home Farm Cl. Hyt ............ 126 A2
Home Farm La. Black ........ 177 F3
Home Farm Way. Ver ........ 114 C3
Home Mead. Den .............. 110 C2
Home Rd. Bour ................ 190 B3
Home Rule Rd. Lo He ........ 129 D2
Homefield Rd. Cos ............ 158 B4
Homefield Rd. Westb .......... 137 D2
Homefield. Rom .................. 28 A1
Homelands Estate. Christ .. 208 C3
Homer Cl. Gos .................. 180 A4
Homer Cl. Wat .................. 111 F1
Homeside Rd. Bour ............ 191 D1
Homewell. Hav ................ 135 F1
Homewood Cl. New M ........ 196 B2
Honey La. Bur .................. 142 C1
Honey La. Fare ................ 130 B3
Honeybourne Cres. Bour .. 209 D2
Honeysuckle Cl. Gos ........ 155 D2
Honeysuckle Cl. Winch ........ 10 C2
Honeysuckle Ct. Wat ........ 135 D3

Honeysuckle La. Broa ........ 187 F1
Honeysuckle Rd. Southa ...... 79 E2
Honeysuckle Way. Christ .. 210 A4
Honeywood Cl. Ports ........ 157 F2
Honeywood Cl. Tot .............. 76 B1
Honister Cl. Southa .......... 101 F4
Hood Cl. Bour .................. 190 A1
Hood Cl. Lo He ................ 129 D2
Hood Cres. Bour .............. 190 A1
Hood Rd. Southa .............. 104 C4
Hook Cl. Ch Fo .................... 30 A1
Hook Cres. Ch Fo ................ 30 A1
Hook La. Lo He ................ 153 D4
Hook Park Rd. Lo He ........ 152 C3
Hook Rd. Ampf .................... 29 F1
Hook Rd. Ch Fo .................... 29 F1
Hook Water Cl. Ch Fo .......... 30 A1
Hook Water Rd. Ch Fo ........ 30 A1
Hook's Farm Way. Hav ...... 135 E2
Hook's La. Hav ................ 135 E2
Hooke Cl. Poole ................ 189 D1
Hookpit Farm La. Ki Wo ........ 2 A4
Hookwood La. Ampf .............. 29 F1
Hop Cl. Upt .................... 203 D4
Hope Rd. W End .................... 80 C1
Hope St. Ports ................ 182 B3
Hopfield Cl. Wat .............. 134 C4
Hopfield Mews. Wat .......... 134 C4
Hopkins Cl. Bour .............. 192 A1
Horace Rd. Bour .............. 207 F2
Hordle La. Hord ................ 197 D1
Hordle Rd. Hav ................ 135 E2
Horlock Rd. Brock ............ 146 A1
Hornbeam Cl. He En .......... 105 E3
Hornbeam Rd. Hav .......... 136 A2
Hornbeam Way. Wi Mi ...... 163 F3
Hornby Cl. Lo He .............. 152 B4
Horndean Rd. Ems ............ 136 C2
Hornet Cl. Fare ................ 155 E2
Hornet Cl. Gos ................ 181 E2
Hornet Rd. Th Is .............. 161 D2
Horning Rd. Poole ............ 205 F3
Horns Drove. Rown ............ 77 F3
Horns Hill. Sob .................. 85 D1
Horsa Cl. Bour ................ 208 C2
Horsa Ct. Bour ................ 208 C2
Horsa Rd. Bour ................ 208 C2
Horsea La. Ports .............. 157 F2
Horsebridge Rd. Hav ........ 136 A2
Horsebridge Way. Rown ...... 77 F3
Horsecroft. Rom ................ 52 C4
Horsefair Ct. Rom ............ 52 C4
Horsefair The. Rom ............ 52 C4
Horseshoe Cl. Lo He ........ 129 E1
Horseshoe Cl. Wi Mi ........ 164 A3
Horseshoe Dr. Rom .............. 28 A1
Horseshoe Lodge. Lo He .. 128 C1
Horseshoe The. Poole ...... 216 B2
Horsham Ave. Bour .......... 190 B3
Horton Cl. Bour ................ 191 E2
Horton Rd. Gos ................ 155 E2
Horton Rd. St Le .............. 139 F3
Horton Rd. Ver ................ 114 A1
Horton Way. Bish ................ 56 C1
Horton Way. Ver .............. 114 B3
Hosier's La. Poole ............ 204 A1
Hosker Rd. Bour .............. 208 A3
Hospital La. Portc ............ 156 C3
Hospital Rd. Shed ............ 108 A4
Hotspur Cl. Hyt ................ 125 F3
Houchin St. Bi Wa .............. 83 E4
Houghton Cl. Hav ............ 136 A3
Houlton Rd. Poole ............ 204 C2
Hound Cl. Net .................. 127 E3
Hound Rd. Net .................. 127 E3
Hound Road Gdns. Net ...... 127 E3
Hound Way. Net ................ 127 E3
Hounds Way. Wi Mi .......... 164 A3
Houndwell Pl. Southa ........ 103 D2
Hounsdown Ave. Tot ........ 100 C3
Hounsdown Cl. Tot .......... 100 C3
Hounslow Cl. Hamw .......... 203 F1
House Farm Rd. Gos ........ 180 C2
Hoveton Gr. Ch Fo .............. 55 D4
Howard Cl. Bur ................ 143 D2
Howard Cl. Ch Fo ................ 55 E2
Howard Cl. Christ ............ 209 F3
Howard Cl. Fa Oa ................ 57 E1
Howard Cl. Southa .............. 79 F2
Howard Rd. Bour .............. 207 E4
Howard Rd. Ports ............ 157 F2
Howard Rd. Southa .......... 102 B3
Howard Rd. Ver ................ 114 C3
Howard's Gr. Southa ........ 102 B4
Howards Mead. Lym ........ 198 A1
Howe Cl. Christ ................ 209 F3
Howe Cl. New M .............. 195 F2
Howe La. Ver .................. 114 C3
Howe Rd. Gos .................. 180 B3
Howerts Cl. Lo He ............ 152 B4
Howeth Cl. Bour .............. 190 B1
Howeth Rd. Bour .............. 190 B2
Howlett Cl. Lym ................ 198 B2
Howton Cl. Bour .............. 190 B3
Howton Rd. Bour .............. 190 B3
Hoxley Rd. Bour .............. 190 B2
Hoyal Rd. Hamw .............. 203 E2
Hoylake Cl. Gos ................ 155 E1
Hoylake Rd. Cos .............. 134 B1

## Hoylecroft Cl. Fare

Hoylecroft Cl. Fare .............. 130 C2
Hubert Rd. Winch ................. 10 C2
Hudson Cl. Poole ................ 189 E1
Hudson Cl. Rin .................. 141 E4
Hudson Ct. Tot .................. 100 B3
Hudson Rd. Ports ............... 182 B2
Hugh's Cl. Black ................ 150 C1
Hulbert Rd. Hav ................. 135 D2
Hulbert Rd. Wat ................. 134 C4
Hull Cres. Bour ................. 189 F2
Hull Rd. Bour ................... 189 F2
Hull Way. Bour .................. 189 F2
Hulles Way. N Bad ................ 53 F2
Hulse Rd. Southa ................ 102 C4
Humber Cl. Stubb ................ 154 A2
Humber Gdns. Burs ............... 105 D1
Humber Rd. Fern ................. 166 A3
Hundred Acres Rd. Sob ........... 108 C3
Hundred Acres Rd. Wickh ......... 108 C3
Hundred La. Bold ................ 199 D4
Hundred The. Rom ................. 52 C4
Hundred The. Wat ................ 111 E1
Hungerfield Cl. Bran ............ 169 D1
Hungerford Hill. Fordi ........... 94 B3
Hungerford Rd. Bour ............. 191 E2
Hungerford. Burs ................ 128 A4
Hunt Ave. Net ................... 127 E3
Hunt Rd. Poole .................. 204 C3
Hunter Cl. Christ ............... 210 A4
Hunter Cl. Gos .................. 180 B4
Hunter Cl. Holb ................. 150 A3
Hunter Cl. Wi Mi ................ 164 B3
Hunter Rd. Ports ................ 183 D2
Hunter Rd. Th Is ................ 161 D2
Hunters Cl. Ver ................. 115 E3
Hunters Cres. Rom ................ 28 B1
Hunters Cres. Tot ............... 100 A3
Hunters Hill. Ashu .............. 100 B2
Hunters Lodge. Fare ............. 130 A1
Hunters Ride. Wat ............... 134 C3
Hunters Way. Bish ................ 57 D1
Huntfield Rd. Bour .............. 191 E1
Huntingdon Cl. Lo He ............ 129 E1
Huntingdon Cl. Tot ............... 76 C1
Huntingdon Dr. Oakl ............. 163 F1
Huntingdon Gdns. Christ ......... 193 D1
Huntley Cl. Cos ................. 133 D1
Huntly Rd. Bour ................. 206 B4
Huntly Way. Southa .............. 103 F4
Hunton Cl. Southa ................ 78 B2
Hunts La. Comp ................... 31 F4
Hunts Pond Rd. Lo He ............ 129 E2
Huntsbottom La. Liss ............. 21 D2
Huntvale Rd. Bour ............... 191 D2
Hurdle Way. Comp ................. 31 F4
Hurdles The. Christ ............. 208 C4
Hurdles The. Lo He .............. 129 E1
Hurlingham Gdns. Southa .......... 79 D3
Hurn Cl. St Le .................. 140 B3
Hurn Court La. Hurn ............. 191 F3
Hurn La. St Le .................. 140 B3
Hurn Rd. Christ ................. 192 B2
Hurn Rd. Hurn ................... 192 B2
Hurn Rd. St Le .................. 140 B2
Hurn Way. Christ ................ 192 B1
Hurricane Dr. Rown ............... 77 F3
Hursley Cl. Bour ................ 208 B4
Hursley Dr. Black ............... 177 F4
Hursley Rd. Ch Fo ................ 55 E4
Hursley Rd. Hav ................. 135 E3
Hurst Cl. Ch Fo .................. 55 D2
Hurst Cl. Christ ................ 195 E1
Hurst Cl. Stubb ................. 154 A1
Hurst Cl. Tot ................... 100 C4
Hurst Green Cl. Wat ............. 112 A1
Hurst Green. Gos ................ 155 D1
Hurst Hill. Poole ............... 216 B4
Hurst La. Co Com ................. 58 A4
Hurst La. Frox G ................. 18 A2
Hurst Rd. M on S ................ 213 F2
Hurst Rd. Rin ................... 117 D1
Hurstborne Pl. Southa ........... 126 C4
Hurstbourne Ave. Christ ......... 194 C1
Hurstbourne Cl. Hav ............. 135 E3
Hurstdene Rd. Bour .............. 191 E1
Hurstly La. Bold ................ 173 D2
Hurstville Dr. Wat .............. 134 C4
Hurstwood Ave. Southb ........... 137 F1
Hussar Ct. Wat .................. 111 E1
Hussey Cl. Winch .................. 2 A1
Hutwood Rd. Chilw ................ 79 D4
Huxley Cl. Lo He ................ 129 D1
Huxley Ct. Hyt .................. 125 E1
Hyacinth Cl. Broa ............... 187 F1
Hyde Abbey Rd. Winch ............. 11 D4
Hyde Church La. Winch ............. 2 A1
Hyde Church Path. Winch ........... 2 A1
Hyde Cl. Southa .................. 78 B1
Hyde Cl. Sway ................... 172 A1
Hyde Cl. Tot .................... 100 A4
Hyde Cl. Winch .................... 1 C1
Hyde Gate. Winch .................. 2 A1
Hyde La. Down .................... 46 B4
Hyde La. Fordi ................... 94 B3
Hyde Park Rd. Ports ............. 182 B3
Hyde Rd. Bour ................... 190 B3
Hyde St. Ports .................. 182 B2
Hyde St. Winch .................... 2 A1

Hyde The. New M ................. 195 F2
Hyden Farm La. Hambl ............. 87 E4
Hylton Rd. Pet ................... 40 C2
Hyman Way. Tot .................. 100 C4
Hynesbury Rd. Christ ............ 210 B4
Hythe By Pass. Hyt .............. 149 F4
Hythe Rd. Cos ................... 157 F4
Hythe Rd. March ................. 124 C4
Hythe Rd. Poole ................. 205 D4

Ibbertson Cl. Bour .............. 191 F1
Ibbertson Rd. Bour .............. 191 F1
Ibbertson Way. Bour ............. 191 F1
Ibbett Rd. Bour ................. 190 B2
Ibbotson Way. Tot ............... 100 B3
Ibsley Cl. Bour ................. 207 E3
Ibsley Dro. Ibs .................. 94 A1
Icarus Pl. Wat .................. 134 C1
Iddesleigh Rd. Bour ............. 207 D3
Idsworth Rd. Ports .............. 183 D4
Idsworth Rd. Wat ................ 112 A1
Iford Cl. Bour .................. 208 C3
Iford Gdns. Bour ................ 208 B4
Iford La. Bour .................. 208 C3
Ilex Cl. Ki Wo .................... 2 A4
Ilex Cres. Lo He ................ 128 C2
Ilex Wlk. S Hay ................. 185 E1
Imber Dr. Christ ................ 210 C4
Imber Rd. Winch .................. 11 E4
Imber Way. Southa ............... 104 B2
Imbre Ct. Poole ................. 216 C4
Imperial Ave. Southa ............ 102 A4
Imperial Rd. Southa ............. 103 D4
Imperial Way. Southa ............ 102 B3
Ingle Glen. Hyt ................. 126 A1
Ingle Green. Tot ................. 76 A1
Ingledene Cl. Gos ............... 181 D2
Ingledene Cl. Hav ............... 135 E1
Inglesham Way. Hamw ............. 203 F2
Ingleside Cl. Fare .............. 154 A4
Ingleton Rd. Southa .............. 77 E1
Inglewood Dr. New M ............. 196 A1
Inglis Rd. Ports ................ 182 C2
Ingoldfield La. Sob ............. 109 E4
Ingram Ct. Southa ............... 103 E4
Ingram Wlk. Wi Mi ............... 163 E2
Ingworth Rd. Poole .............. 206 A3
Inhams La. Den .................. 110 B3
Inhurst Ave. Wat ................ 135 D4
Inhurst Rd. Ports ............... 157 F1
Inkerman Rd. Southa ............. 103 E2
Inkpen Wlk. Hav ................. 135 E4
Inlands Rd. Southb .............. 161 F4
Inmans La. Pet ................... 41 D3
Insley Cres. Broa ............... 187 F3
International Way. Southa ....... 126 C4
Inveravon. Christ ............... 209 F2
Inverclyde Rd. Poole ............ 205 E2
Inverkip Cl. L on S ............. 179 F4
Inverleigh Rd. Bour ............. 208 B3
Inverness Ave. Fare ............. 130 C2
Inverness Rd. Gos ............... 181 D3
Inverness Rd. Poole ............. 216 C4
Inverness Rd. Ports ............. 182 C4
Inwood Rd. Liss .................. 21 D2
Ionic Cl. Ch Fo .................. 55 F4
Iping Ave. Hav .................. 135 F2
Ipley Way. Hyt .................. 126 A1
Ipswich Rd. Bour ................ 206 A2
Ireland Way. Wat ................ 134 C3
Iris Rd. Bour ................... 190 C1
Iris Rd. Southa .................. 79 D2
Iron Mill Cl. Fare .............. 130 B2
Ironbridge La. Ports ............ 183 E2
Ironmill La. Swanw .............. 130 A3
Irvine Cl. Fare ................. 131 D2
Irvine Way. Christ .............. 209 F4
Irving Rd. Bour ................. 208 B3
Irving Rd. Southa ................ 77 F1
Irwell Cl. N Bad ................. 55 D3
Isambard Brunel Rd. Ports ...... 182 B3
Isis Cl. Southa ................. 101 F4
Island Cl. N Hay ................ 160 A2
Island View Ave. Christ ......... 210 A3
Island View Cl. M on S .......... 213 F2
Island View Rd. B on S .......... 211 E4
Island View Terr. Ports ......... 157 E1
Island View Wlk. Portc .......... 132 B1
Islay Gdns. Cos ................. 133 F1
Itchen Ave. Bish ................. 56 C1
Itchen Cl. W Wel ................. 50 B2
Itchen Rd. Hav .................. 136 A3
Itchen Rd. Southa ............... 103 D1
Itchen View. Southa .............. 79 F2
Itchenor Rd. S Hay .............. 185 F1
Itchenside Cl. Southa ............ 79 F2
Itchin Cl. Tot .................. 100 B3
Ithica Cl. S Hay ................ 185 D2
Ivamy Pl. Bour .................. 189 F1
Ivanhoe Rd. Southa ............... 78 B1
Ivor Cl. Holb ................... 150 B2
Ivor Rd. Broa ................... 187 E2
Ivor Rd. Poole .................. 204 A1
Ivy Cl. St Le ................... 139 E2
Ivy Cl. Tot ...................... 76 C1
Ivy Ct. Wat ..................... 134 B2
Ivy Dene. Southa ................ 104 B2

Ivy La. Rin ..................... 117 D2
Ivy La. W End .................... 80 A1
Ivy La. W End .................... 80 B1
Ivy Orch. Clanf .................. 88 A3
Ivy Rd. Oakl .................... 188 B4
Ivy Rd. Southa .................. 103 E4
Ivyhouse La. Frox G .............. 18 C2
Iwerne Cl. Bour ................. 191 D2

Jackdaw Cl. Wat ................. 111 F2
Jackdaw Rise. Eastl .............. 55 E1
Jackman's Hill. Ows .............. 33 D3
Jackson Cl. Cos ................. 158 B3
Jackson Rd. Poole ............... 205 E3
Jacob's Gutter La. Tot .......... 101 D2
Jacob's St. Ports ............... 182 B3
Jacobean Cl. Christ ............. 195 D1
Jacobs Cl. Rom ................... 53 D4
Jacobs Cl. Rom ................... 53 D4
Jacobs Wlk. Tot ................. 100 C3
Jacomb Pl. Gos .................. 155 E1
Jacqueline Ave. Wat ............. 134 B2
Jacqueline Rd. Poole ............ 205 E4
Jamaica Pl. Gos ................. 181 E2
James Cl. Gos ................... 155 E2
James Cl. S Hay ................. 184 C2
James Copse Rd. Horn ............ 111 F3
James Grieve Ave. Lo He ......... 129 D1
James Rd. Gos ................... 155 E2
James Rd. Hav ................... 135 F1
James Rd. Poole ................. 206 A3
James St. Southa ................ 103 D2
Jameson Rd. Bour ................ 190 C1
Jameson Rd. Southa .............. 103 F2
Janaway Gdns. Southa ............ 103 E4
Janes Cl. Black ................. 177 F4
Janson Rd. Southa ............... 102 B4
Jarndyce Wlk. Ports ............. 182 B4
Jarvis Fields. Burs ............. 128 A4
Jasmine Cl. Lym ................. 198 C2
Jasmine Gr. Wat ................. 135 D3
Jasmine Rd. He En ............... 105 D4
Jasmine Wlk. Fare ............... 154 C4
Jasmond Rd. Cos ................. 157 F3
Jason Pl. Wat ................... 134 C1
Jason Way. Gos .................. 180 C4
Jaundrells Cl. New M ............ 196 B2
Java Dr. Swanw .................. 129 E4
Java Rd. Southa ................. 103 D1
Javelin Rd. Th Is ............... 161 D2
Jay Cl. Horn .................... 112 A4
Jay Cl. Stubb ................... 154 A2
Jay's Ct. Christ ................ 211 D4
Jealous La. Sway ................ 173 D1
Jefferson Ave. Bour ............. 207 E3
Jeffries Cl. Rown ................ 77 F3
Jellicoe Ave. Gos ............... 180 C2
Jellicoe Dr. Christ ............. 209 F3
Jenkins Gr. Botl ................ 106 A4
Jenkins Gr. Ports ............... 183 D4
Jenner Way. Rom .................. 53 E4
Jennings Rd. Poole .............. 205 E1
Jennings Rd. Tot ................ 101 D4
Jephcote Rd. Bour ............... 189 F2
Jermyns La. Abb .................. 28 B2
Jermyns La. Ampf ................. 28 B2
Jerome Ct. Southa ............... 104 B3
Jerram Cl. Gos .................. 180 C2
Jerrett's La. Nur ................ 77 E2
Jersey Cl. Poole ................ 189 E1
Jersey Cl. Southa ................ 77 F2
Jersey Cl. Stubb ................ 154 B1
Jersey Rd. Poole ................ 189 E1
Jersey Rd. Ports ................ 182 C4
Jervis Court La. Bi Wa ........... 84 A4
Jervis Court La. Swan ............ 84 A4
Jervis Dr. Gos .................. 181 D3
Jervis Rd. Ports ................ 157 E1
Jesmond Ave. Christ ............. 210 C4
Jesmond Gr. Lo He ............... 129 D1
Jessamine Rd. Southa ............. 78 A1
Jessica Ave. Ver ................ 114 B4
Jessica Cl. Wat ................. 112 A1
Jessie Rd. Gos .................. 181 D2
Jessie Rd. Hav .................. 135 E2
Jessie Rd. Ports ................ 182 C2
Jessop Cl. Bour ................. 190 C2
Jessop Cl. Hyt .................. 125 F3
Jessop Rd. Wi Mi ................ 164 A3
Jessop Wlk. Hyt ................. 125 F3
Jewell Rd. Bour ................. 192 A1
Jewry St. Winch .................. 11 D4
Jimmy Brown Ave. W Moo .......... 138 C3
Jinny La. Mich ................... 27 F3
Joanna Cl. Down .................. 46 B4
Jockey La. Bish .................. 56 C3
Jodrell Cl. Horn ................ 112 B4
John St. Southa ................. 103 D2
John's Rd. Southa ............... 103 D2
Johns Rd. Fare .................. 155 D4
Johnson St. Southa .............. 103 D2
Johnston Rd. Poole .............. 204 B4
Johnstone Rd. Christ ............ 209 F3
Jolliffe Ave. Poole ............. 204 B2
Jolliffe Rd. Poole .............. 204 B2
Jonathan Rd. Fare ............... 130 C1
Jonathon Cl. Lym ................ 198 C3
Jones La. Hyt ................... 126 A3

Jordans La. Bold ................ 199 D4
Jordans La. Sway ................ 172 B1
Joseph Nye Ct. Ports ............ 182 A3
Joseph St. Gos .................. 181 E2
Josian Wlk. Southa .............. 103 D3
Jowitt Dr. New M ................ 195 F1
Joyce Dickson Cl. Rin ........... 141 D3
Joys La. Bold ................... 199 F4
Joys Rd. W Moo .................. 138 C4
Jubilee Rd. Poole ............... 205 E3
Jubilee Ave. Portc .............. 132 C1
Jubilee Cl. Broa ................ 187 F4
Jubilee Cl. Eastl ................ 55 F1
Jubilee Cl. Fordi ................ 69 E1
Jubilee Cl. Rin ................. 141 E4
Jubilee Cres. Poole ............. 205 E3
Jubilee Ct. Fare ................ 155 D4
Jubilee Gdns. Bour .............. 190 B1
Jubilee Gdns. Southa ............ 104 A4
Jubilee Rd. Broa ................ 187 F4
Jubilee Rd. Fordi ................ 69 E1
Jubilee Rd. Gos ................. 181 D3
Jubilee Rd. Portc ............... 156 B4
Jubilee Rd. Ports ............... 182 C2
Jubilee Rd. Rom .................. 52 C4
Jubilee Rd. Wat ................. 111 F1
Jubilee Terr. Ports ............. 182 A2
Julia Cl. Christ ................ 210 C4
Julian Cl. Southa ................ 78 C3
Julian Rd. Southa ............... 104 A2
Julian's Rd. Rin ................ 163 D2
Julian's Rd. Wi Mi .............. 163 D2
Julie Ave. Fare ................. 130 C1
Juliet Ct. Wat .................. 135 D4
Julius Cl. Ch Fo ................. 55 F3
Julyan Ave. Poole ............... 206 A4
Jumar Cl. Lo He ................. 152 B4
Jumpers Ave. Christ ............. 208 C4
Jumpers Rd. Christ .............. 208 C4
Junction Rd. Bour ............... 206 C4
Junction Rd. Hamw ............... 203 E2
Junction Rd. Tot ................ 101 D4
Juniper Cl. Fern ................ 165 E4
Juniper Cl. Lym ................. 198 A1
Juniper Cl. N Bad ................ 53 F3
Juniper Cl. N Moo ............... 138 C4
Juniper Cl. Winch ................ 10 B3
Juniper Rd. Horn ................. 88 B1
Juniper Rd. Southa .............. 103 F4
Juniper Sq. Hav ................. 159 F4
Jupiter Cl. Southa ............... 77 F2
Jupiter Way. Broa ............... 187 F4
Jura Cl. Cos .................... 133 F1
Jurd Way. Burs .................. 104 C1
Justin Cl. Fare ................. 154 C4
Justin Gdns. Bour ............... 190 C2
Justinian Cl. Ch Fo ............. 55 F4
Jute Cl. Portc .................. 132 A1
Jutland Cl. Swanw ............... 129 E4

Kanes Hill. Southa .............. 104 C3
Kangaw Pl. Hamw ................. 203 E1
Karen Ave. Cos .................. 158 B3
Kassassin St. Ports ............. 183 D1
Kassel Cl. Wat .................. 135 D4
Katherine Chance Cl. Burt ....... 193 E2
Kathleen Rd. Southa ............. 104 A2
Katrina Gdns. S Hay ............. 185 D3
Katrine Cres. N Bad .............. 55 D3
Katterns Cl. Christ ............. 192 C1
Kayak Cl. Lo He ................. 128 C1
Kayleigh Cl. Tot ................ 100 B3
Kealy Rd. Gosp .................. 181 D3
Kearsney Ave. Ports ............. 157 F1
Keast Wlk. Gos .................. 155 E2
Keats Ave. M on S ............... 213 E3
Keats Ave. Portc ................ 132 C1
Keats Cl. Wat ................... 111 F2
Keats Cl. Winch .................. 10 B2
Keats Rd. Southa ................ 104 B3
Keble Cl. Ch Fo .................. 55 E2
Keble Rd. Ch Fo .................. 55 E2
Keble St. Winch .................. 10 B3
Keeble Gdns. Bour ............... 190 B3
Keeble Rd. Bour ................. 190 B3
Keel Cl. Ports .................. 158 B2
Keep The. Portc ................. 156 B4
Keepers La. Fern ................ 164 C3
Keepers Way. N Bad .............. 55 D3
Keepers Way. N Bad .............. 55 D3
Kefford Cl. Horn ................ 112 A3
Keighley Ave. Broa .............. 187 F1
Keith Cl. Gos ................... 181 D3
Keith Rd. Bour .................. 206 B4
Kelburn Cl. Ch Fo ................ 55 D4
Kellaway Rd. Poole .............. 204 C4
Kellett Rd. Southa .............. 102 C4
Kelly Cl. Poole ................. 204 C4
Kelly Rd. Wat ................... 134 C3
Kelmscott Gdns. Ch Fo ........... 30 A1
Kelsey Ave. Southb .............. 137 F1
Kelsey Cl. Liss .................. 21 D3
Kelsey Cl. Lo He ................ 129 D1
Kelsey Head. Ports .............. 157 D4
Kelvin Cl. Hyt .................. 126 A2
Kelvin Gr. Net .................. 127 E3
Kelvin Gr. Portc ................ 156 B4
Kelvin Rd. Eastl ................. 55 F1
Kemp Rd. Bour ................... 206 C4

Kempland La. Frox G .............. 17 E2
Kempton Pk. Wat ................. 112 A1
Kemshott Ct. Hav ................ 135 E3
Ken Berry Ct. Hav ............... 136 A3
Ken Rd. Bour .................... 208 C2
Kench The. S Hay ................ 183 F3
Kendal Ave. Ports ............... 158 A1
Kendal Ave. Southa .............. 101 E4
Kendal Cl. Ch Fo ................. 55 F4
Kendal Cl. Wat .................. 112 A2
Kenilworth Cl. L on S ........... 179 F4
Kenilworth Cl. New M ............ 196 A2
Kenilworth Dr. Eastl ............. 56 A3
Kenilworth Gdns. W End .......... 80 C1
Kenilworth Rd. Ports ............ 182 B1
Kenilworth Rd. Southa ........... 102 C3
Kenmore Cl. Tot ................. 100 C3
Kennard Ct. New M ............... 195 F2
Kennard Rd. New M ............... 195 F2
Kennart Rd. Broa ................ 204 A4
Kennedy Ave. Fare ............... 130 B2
Kennedy Cl. Wat ................. 134 C2
Kennedy Cres. Gos ............... 180 C1
Kennedy Rd. Southa ............... 77 F2
Kennel La. Litt .................. 1 B2
Kennet Cl. Gos .................. 181 D1
Kennet Cl. Rom ................... 53 E4
Kennet Cl. W End ................. 80 A2
Kennet Rd. Rom ................... 53 E4
Kennington La. Cadn .............. 99 D4
Kensington Park. M on S ......... 213 E2
Kensington Cl. Bish .............. 56 B3
Kensington Dr. Bour ............. 206 B2
Kensington Flds. Hyt ............ 125 E2
Kensington Rd. Gos .............. 181 E2
Kensington Rd. Ports ............ 157 F1
Kenson Gdns. Southa ............. 104 A2
Kent Gdns. Tot .................. 100 B3
Kent Gr. Portc .................. 156 B3
Kent La. Ibs ..................... 93 E1
Kent Rd. Ch Fo ................... 55 E2
Kent Rd. Gos .................... 155 D2
Kent Rd. Poole .................. 205 F3
Kent Rd. Ports .................. 182 B2
Kent Rd. Southa .................. 79 E1
Kent St. Ports .................. 182 A3
Kent St. Southa ................. 103 E3
Kentidge Rd. Wat ................ 134 B3
Kentish Rd. Southa .............. 102 B4
Kenwood Rd. Portc ............... 156 B3
Kenwyn Cl. W End ................. 80 A1
Kenya Rd. Portc ................. 156 A4
Kenyon Cl. Poole ................ 204 C4
Kenyon Rd. Poole ................ 204 C4
Kenyon Rd. Ports ................ 157 F1
Kepple Cl. Rin .................. 141 D4
Kerley Rd. Bour ................. 206 C1
Kern Cl. Southa .................. 77 F2
Kerrfield Mews. Winch ........... 10 B4
Kerrfield. Winch ................. 10 B4
Kerry Cl. Ch Fo .................. 55 E3
Kerry Cl. Lym ................... 198 C2
Kesteven Way. Southa ............ 104 A4
Kestrel Cl. Bi Wa ................ 83 D4
Kestrel Cl. Botl ................. 81 F1
Kestrel Cl. Clanf ................ 88 B2
Kestrel Cl. Fern ................ 165 D4
Kestrel Cl. March ............... 101 F1
Kestrel Cl. Southa ............... 78 A3
Kestrel Cl. Stubb ............... 154 A2
Kestrel Cl. Winch ................ 10 B2
Kestrel Cl. Rin ................. 141 D4
Kestrel Dr. Christ .............. 210 A3
Kestrel Pl. Cos ................. 158 C4
Kestrel Rd. Eastl ................ 55 F1
Kestrel Way. Alderh ............. 93 D3
Keswick Ave. Ports .............. 183 D4
Keswick Rd. Bour ................ 208 A2
Keswick Rd. New M ............... 196 A3
Keswick Rd. Southa .............. 103 E1
Keswick Way. Ver ................ 114 C3
Kettering Terr. Ports ........... 182 B4
Keverstone Ct. Bour ............. 207 E2
Kevlyn Cres. Burs ............... 104 C1
Kew La. Burs .................... 128 A4
Kewlake La. Cadn ................. 74 B1
Keydell Ave. Wat ................ 112 A3
Keydell Cl. Wat ................. 112 A3
Keyes Cl. Christ ................ 209 F3
Keyes Cl. Gos ................... 155 E2
Keyes Cl. Poole ................. 189 F1
Keyes Rd. Gos ................... 155 E2
Keyhaven Cl. Gos ................ 155 D1
Keyhaven Dr. Hav ................ 135 E3
Keyhaven Rd. M on S ............. 213 F2
Keynsham Rd. Southa ............. 104 A3
Keysworth Rd. Hamw .............. 203 E2
Khandala Gdns. Wat .............. 134 C2
Khartoum Rd. Southa .............. 79 D1
Khyber Rd. Poole ................ 205 D3
Kidmore La. Den ................. 110 C3
Kielder Cl. N Bad ................ 55 D4
Kielder Gr. Gos ................. 155 E1
Kilham La. Winch ................. 10 A3
Killarney Cl. Southa ............ 104 C3
Kilmarnock Rd. Bour ............. 190 C1
Kilmeston Cl. Hav ............... 135 F3
Kilmeston Rd. Cher ............... 14 B2

## Kilmeston Rd. Cher

## Kilmeston Rd. Kilm

Kilmeston Rd. Kilm .................. 14 B1
Kilmington Way. Christ .......... 210 C4
Kilmiston Dr. Portc ................ 132 B1
Kilmiston Rd. Ports ............... 182 C4
Kiln Acre. Fare ..................... 131 D2
Kiln Cl. Broa ......................... 187 E2
Kiln Cl. Hyt .......................... 125 F2
Kiln Hill. Sob ....................... 109 D4
Kiln La. Brai ........................... 28 B3
Kiln La. Buri .......................... 65 E3
Kiln La. Co Com ..................... 31 E1
Kiln La. Ott ............................ 31 E1
Kiln La. Red ........................... 47 F4
Kiln Rd. Ports ...................... 158 A1
Kilnside. Den ....................... 110 C2
Kilnyard Cl. Tot ..................... 76 B1
Kilpatrick Cl. Ports .............. 182 B4
Kilwich Way. Portc ............... 156 A3
Kimber Rd. Bour ................... 189 F2
Kimberley Cl. Christ ............. 208 C4
Kimberley Cl. Fa Oa ............... 57 E1
Kimberley Rd. Bour .............. 208 B3
Kimberley Rd. Poole ............ 205 D2
Kimberley Rd. Ports ............ 183 D1
Kimbers. Pet .......................... 40 C2
Kimbolton Rd. Ports ............ 183 D3
Kimbridge Cres. Hav ............ 136 A3
Kimbridge La. Mich ............... 27 D4
Kimmeridge Ave. Poole ........ 205 E4
Kimpton Cl. L on S .............. 179 F3
Kineton Rd. Southa ............... 78 C1
King Albert St. Ports ............ 182 B3
King Alfred Pl. Winch ............... 2 A1
King Alfred Terr. Winch ............ 2 A1
King Charles St. Ports .......... 182 A2
King Cl. St Le ....................... 139 F2
King Cup Ave. Lo He ............ 128 C2
King Edward Ave. Bour ......... 191 D1
King Edward Ave. Southa ..... 102 A4
King Edward Ct. Ports .......... 182 A2
King Edward's Cres. Ports .... 157 E1
King George Ave. Bour ......... 190 C1
King George Ave. Pet ............. 40 C2
King George Rd. Portc .......... 156 B4
King George's Ave. Southa ... 101 F4
King Henry 1 St. Ports .......... 182 A3
King John Ave. Bour ............. 189 E3
King John Ave. Portc ............ 156 A4
King La. Frox G ...................... 39 F4
King Richard 1 Rd. Ports ...... 182 A2
King Richard Dr. Bour ........... 189 E3
King St. Ems ......................... 161 D4
King St. Gos ......................... 181 E3
King St. Ports ....................... 182 B2
King St. Southa ..................... 103 D2
King St. Westb ..................... 137 D2
King St. Wi Mi ...................... 163 D2
King William St. Ports .......... 182 A3
King's Arms La. Rin .............. 140 C4
King's Arms Row. Rin ........... 140 C4
King's Ave. Christ ................. 208 C3
King's Cl. Ch Fo ..................... 55 E4
King's Copse Rd. Black ......... 177 E4
King's Croft La. Hav .............. 135 E1
King's La. Frox G .................... 18 B2
King's Park Dr. Bour ............. 207 F3
King's Park Rd. Bour ............ 207 F3
King's Park Rd. Southa ......... 103 D3
King's Rd. Bour .................... 207 D4
King's Rd. Ems ..................... 160 C4
King's Rd. Fare ..................... 131 D1
King's Rd. L on S .................. 179 F4
King's Rd. Ports ................... 182 A2
King's Saltern Rd. Lym ......... 199 D1
King's Terr. Ems ................... 160 C4
Kingcup Cl. Broa .................. 187 F1
Kingdom Cl. Lo He ............... 129 E3
Kingfisher Cl. Hamble ......... 128 A2
Kingfisher Cl. Ro Ca ............ 113 D1
Kingfisher Cl. W Moo ........... 138 C1
Kingfisher Copse. Lo He ....... 129 C2
Kingfisher Park. W Moo ........ 138 C3
Kingfisher Rd. Eastl ............... 55 F1
Kingfisher Way. Rin .............. 117 D1
Kingfishers The. Ver ............ 115 D3
Kingfishers. Christ ............... 209 D3
Kingfishers. Portc ................ 155 F4
Kings Ave. Hamble ............... 127 F2
Kings Ave. Poole .................. 205 E2
Kings Ave. Winch ................... 10 C3
Kings Cl. Lym ...................... 198 B2
Kings Cl. Lym ...................... 121 F3
Kings Cl. Ro Ca ................... 113 D1
Kings Cl. Twyf ....................... 32 A4
Kings Cl. W Moo ................... 138 C1
Kings Copse Rd. He En ........ 105 D1
Kings Cres. Lym ................... 198 B2
Kings Field. Burs ................. 105 D1
Kings Field. Burs ................. 105 D1
Kings Head Yd. Winch ........... 11 D4
Kings La. Chilc .................... 197 F4
Kings La. Sway .................... 197 F4
Kings Mede. Wat .................. 112 A3
Kings Rd. Ch Fo .................... 55 E3
Kings Rd. Gos ...................... 181 D3
Kings Rd. Lym ...................... 198 B2
Kings Rd. New M .................. 196 B2

Kings Rd. Pet ......................... 40 B2
Kings Rd. S Hay ................... 185 D3
Kings Rd. Winch ..................... 10 B3
Kings Ride. Black ................. 177 F4
Kings Somborne Rd. Brai ......... 7 E1
Kingsbere Ave. Bour ............ 190 A1
Kingsbere Gdns. Christ ........ 211 D4
Kingsbere Rd. Poole ............ 204 C3
Kingsbourne Rise. Southa .... 104 C3
Kingsbridge Rd. Poole ......... 205 E2
Kingsbury Rd. Southa .......... 103 D4
Kingsbury's La. Rin ............. 140 C4
Kingsclere Ave. Hav ............. 135 E3
Kingsclere Ave. Southa ........ 126 C4
Kingscote Rd. Cos ............... 132 C1
Kingscote Rd. Wat ............... 111 E2
Kingscroft Ct. Hav ............... 135 E1
Kingsdown Pl. Ports ............ 182 C3
Kingsdown Rd. Wat .............. 111 E1
Kingsdown Way. Southa ......... 80 A1
Kingsey Ave. Ems ................ 160 C4
Kingsfernsden La. Pet ........... 41 D3
Kingsfield. Lym .................... 199 D1
Kingsfield. Rin .................... 141 D4
Kingsfold Ave. Southa ........... 79 F2
Kingsford Cl. Red .................. 47 E3
Kingsgate Rd. Winch .............. 10 C3
Kingsgate St. Winch .............. 11 D3
Kingsland Cl. Cos ................ 133 E1
Kingsland Cres. Poole .......... 204 B1
Kingsland Sq. Southa ........... 103 D2
Kingsley Ave. Bour .............. 209 D2
Kingsley Cl. Bour ................ 209 D2
Kingsley Gdns. Tot ............... 100 A4
Kingsley Green. Hav ............ 135 E3
Kingsley Pl. Winch ................ 10 C3
Kingsley Rd. Gos ................. 180 C4
Kingsley Rd. Ports ............... 183 E2
Kingsley Rd. Southa ............ 102 A4
Kingsmead Ave. Stubb ........ 154 B1
Kingsmead. Sob ................... 108 B4
Kingsmill Cl. Gos ................ 180 C2
Kingsmill Rd. Poole ............ 204 C4
Kingston Cres. Ports ............ 182 B4
Kingston Gdns. Fare ............ 130 B2
Kingston Park. Lym .............. 198 B1
Kingston Rd. Gos ................. 180 C3
Kingston Rd. Poole .............. 204 B2
Kingston Rd. Ports ............... 182 C4
Kingston Rd. Southa ............ 102 B3
Kingston. Net ...................... 127 E4
Kingsway Cl. Christ ............. 192 C1
Kingsway The. Portc ............ 156 B4
Kingsway. Ch Fo .................... 55 F4
Kingsway. Fern ..................... 165 D4
Kingsway. N Hay ................... 160 A2
Kingsway. Southa ................ 103 D3
Kingswell Cl. Bour ............... 190 B1
Kingswell Gdns. Bour ........... 190 A1
Kingswell Gr. Bour .............. 190 A1
Kingswell Rd. Bour ............. 190 B1
Kingswell St. Ports .............. 182 B3
Kingswood. March ............... 102 A1
Kingsworthy Rd. Hav ........... 135 F2
Kinnell Cl. Ems ................... 160 C4
Kinross Cres. Cos ............... 158 A4
Kinross Rd. Bour ................ 206 C3
Kinross Rd. Tot ................... 100 C3
Kinsbourne Ave. Bour ......... 190 B1
Kinsbourne Cl. Southa ......... 104 C3
Kinsbourne Way. Southa ..... 104 C3
Kinson Gr. Bour .................. 190 B3
Kinson Park Rd. Bour .......... 190 B3
Kinson Rd. Bour .................. 190 B2
Kintyre Rd. Cos ................... 133 F1
Kinver Cl. Rom ...................... 28 A1
Kipling Rd. Eastl ................... 55 F2
Kipling Rd. Poole ................ 205 D3
Kipling Rd. Ports ................. 157 F2
Kirby Cl. Poole .................... 204 C3
Kirby Rd. Ports ................... 157 F1
Kirby Way. Bour .................. 208 B2
Kirkham Ave. Burt ............... 193 E2
Kirkstall Rd. Ports .............. 182 C1
Kirkway. Broa ...................... 188 A2
Kirtley Cl. Cos .................... 158 B3
Kirton Rd. Cos .................... 158 B4
Kitchener Cres. Broa ........... 188 A1
Kitchener Rd. Southa ............ 79 E1
Kitchers Cl. Sway ................ 172 A1
Kite Cl. Wat ......................... 111 F2
Kites Croft Cl. Lo He ............ 129 E1
Kitnocks Hill. Curd .............. 106 C4
Kitscroft Rd. Bour ............... 190 B3
Kitt's La. W Meo .................... 16 B1
Kittiwake Cl. Bour ............... 208 B3
Kittiwake Cl. Gos ................ 155 D1
Kitwalls La. M on S ............. 213 E3
Kitwood Green. Hav ............ 136 A3
Kivernell Rd. M on S ........... 213 E2
Kiwi Cl. Poole ..................... 204 C2
Knapp Cl. Christ .................. 209 D4
Knapp La. Ampf ..................... 29 E2
Knapp Mill Ave..Christ ......... 209 D4
Knapps Hard. W Meo ............ 37 D3
Knatchbull Cl. Rom ............... 52 C4
Knellers La. Ashu ............... 100 B4
Knight Cl. Winch ..................... 2 A1

Knighton Heath Cl. Bour ...... 189 F2
Knighton Heath Rd. Bour ..... 189 F2
Knighton La. Oakl ............... 189 E4
Knighton Park. B on S ......... 211 F4
Knighton Rd. Southa ........... 103 F2
Knights Bank Rd. Stubb ....... 153 F1
Knights Rd. Bour ................ 189 E3
Knightstone Grange. Hyt ..... 126 A1
Knightwood Ave. Hav .......... 136 A3
Knightwood Ave. Lyn .......... 121 F3
Knightwood Cl. Ashu ........... 100 A1
Knightwood Cl. Christ .......... 210 B4
Knightwood Cl. Lyn ............. 121 F3
Knightwood Rd. Ch Fo .......... 55 D3
Knightwood Rd. Hyt ............ 126 A2
Knightwood Rd. N Bad .......... 55 D3
Knobcrook Rd. Wi Mi ........... 163 D3
Knole Gdns. Bour ................ 207 E2
Knole Rd. Bour .................... 207 E2
Knoll Gdns. St Le ................ 139 F2
Knoll La. Broa ..................... 187 D4
Knowle Hill. Eastl ................. 56 A4
Knowle La. Fa Oa .................. 57 F1
Knowle Rd. Brock ............... 145 F1
Knowles Cl. Christ ............... 209 F4
Knowles Meadow. Hill B ........ 21 D1
Knowlton Gdns. Bour ........... 191 D2
Knowlton Rd. Broa .............. 188 C1
Knowsley Cres. Cos ............ 158 A4
Knowsley Rd. Cos ............... 157 F4
Knox Rd. Hav ...................... 135 E1
Knox Rd. Ports .................... 157 E1
Knutgrass Rd. Lo He ........... 128 C1
Knyght Cl. Rom ..................... 53 D3
Knyveton Rd. Bour .............. 207 E2
Kootenay Cl. Southa ............ 104 C4
Kooyong Cl. W Wel ............... 51 D1
Kynegils Rd. Winch ................. 1 C1
Kynon Cl. Gos ..................... 181 E4
Kyrchil La. Wi Mi ................ 163 F3
Kyrchil Way. Wi Mi ............. 163 F4
Kytes La. Durl ....................... 82 B3

Labrador Dr. Poole .............. 204 B1
Laburnum Ave. Cos ............. 158 B4
Laburnum Cl. Fern .............. 165 D3
Laburnum Cl. N Bad .............. 54 A3
Laburnum Cl. Ver ................ 115 E3
Laburnum Cres. Hyt ............ 150 A4
Laburnum Dr. Hord ............. 213 F4
Laburnum Gr. Eastl ............... 56 A2
Laburnum Gr. Ports ............ 157 F1
Laburnum Gr. S Hay ............ 185 D2
Laburnum Rd. Fare .............. 155 D3
Laburnum Rd. He En ............ 105 E3
Laburnum Rd. Southa ........... 79 E2
Laburnum Rd. Wat ............... 134 B3
Lacey Cres. Poole ............... 205 D3
Lackford Ave. Tot ............... 100 C3
Lacon Cl. Southa ................. 103 F4
Lacy Cl. Wi Mi .................... 163 E3
Lacy Dr. Wi Mi .................... 163 E3
Ladram Rd. Gos .................. 180 C2
Lady Betty's Dr. Lo He ......... 129 F3
Ladybridge Rd. Wat ............ 134 B2
Ladycross Rd. Hyt ............... 126 A1
Ladysmith Rd. Christ ........... 209 F4
Ladywood. Eastl .................... 55 F3
Lagado Cl. Poole ................ 216 B4
Lagland St. Poole ............... 204 B1
Lagoon Rd. Poole ............... 216 A4
Laidlaw Cl. Poole ............... 206 A4
Lake Ave. Hamw ................. 203 E1
Lake Cres. Hamw ............... 203 F2
Lake Dr. Hamw .................... 203 E1
Lake Farm Cl. He En ........... 105 E4
Lake Gr. New M ................... 196 A2
Lake Rd. Bour ..................... 190 B3
Lake Rd. Ch Fo ..................... 55 D4
Lake Rd. Curd ..................... 106 C4
Lake Rd. Hamw .................... 203 F1
Lake Rd. Ports .................... 182 B3
Lake Rd. Southa .................. 103 E1
Lake Rd. Ver ....................... 115 D3
Lakeland Gdns. March ......... 101 F1
Lakelands Dr. Southa .......... 102 A3
Lakeside Ave. Ports ............ 183 D4
Lakeside Ave. Rown .............. 77 F4
Lakeside Rd. Poole ............. 206 A1
Lakeside. Fare ..................... 130 C3
Lakeside. L on S .................. 179 F2
Lakeside. Rin ...................... 141 E3
Lakesmere Rd. Horn ............ 112 B3
Lakeview Dr. Rin ................. 141 E3
Lakewood Cl. Ch Fo .............. 55 E4
Lakewood Rd. Ashu ............ 100 B2
Lakewood Rd. Ch Fo ............. 30 C1
Lakewood Rd. Christ ........... 194 C1
Lambert Cl. Wat .................. 134 C3
Lambourn Cl. Fare .............. 154 B4
Lambourne Cl. Hyt .............. 125 F1
Lambourne Dr. Lo He .......... 129 D2
Lambourne Rd. W End ........... 80 A1
Lambs Cl. Broa ................... 188 B1
Lambsgreen La. Broa ........... 162 C1
Lammas Rd. Hyt .................. 126 A1
Lampeter Ave. Cos .............. 158 A4
Lancaster Cl. Broa .............. 187 F3

Lancaster Cl. Burs .............. 105 D1
Lancaster Cl. Christ ............ 210 B4
Lancaster Cl. L on S ............ 180 A2
Lancaster Cl. Portc ............. 132 A1
Lancaster Dr. Broa .............. 187 F3
Lancaster Dr. Ver ............... 114 C3
Lancaster Rd. Southa ............ 77 F2
Lancaster Way. Wat ............ 134 C3
Lander Cl. Poole ................. 204 B1
Landford Gdns. Bour .......... 191 E1
Landford Way. Bour ............ 191 E1
Landguard Rd. Ports ........... 183 D2
Landguard Rd. Southa ......... 102 B3
Landon Rd. Gos .................. 180 B4
Landport St. Ports .............. 182 A2
Landport St. Ports .............. 182 B3
Landport Terr. Ports ............ 182 A2
Landport View. Ports .......... 182 B3
Lands End Rd. Burs ............ 128 B4
Landsdowne St. Ports ......... 182 A2
Landseer Rd. Bour .............. 206 B2
Landseer Rd. Southa ........... 104 B2
Lane End Rd. Ems ............... 160 C4
Lane The. Bour .................... 207 E3
Lane The. Faw ..................... 151 D2
Lane The. Ports ................... 181 D1
Lane The. Ports ................... 182 C1
Lanes End. Stubb ................ 154 B1
Lanes The. New M ............... 196 A3
Lanesbridge Cl. Ne Ma .......... 99 F3
Langbar Cl. Southa ............. 103 F3
Langbrook Cl. Hav .............. 159 F4
Langdale Ave. Cos .............. 158 A4
Langdale Cl. Southa ............ 101 F4
Langdon Rd. Poole ............. 205 E2
Langdown Firs. Hyt ............ 126 A2
Langdown Lawn Cl. Hyt ...... 126 A1
Langdown Lawn. Hyt .......... 126 A2
Langdown Rd. Hyt .............. 126 A2
Langford La. Red .................. 47 F4
Langford Rd. Ports .............. 182 C4
Langham Cl. N Bad ............... 53 F2
Langhorn Rd. Southa ............ 79 E2
Langley Gdn. Fordi ............... 70 A2
Langley Green. Fordi ............ 70 A2
Langley Lodge Gdns. Black .. 177 F4
Langley Rd. Christ .............. 194 C1
Langley Rd. Poole ............... 205 F2
Langley Rd. Ports ............... 182 C4
Langley Rd. Southa ............. 102 A3
Langrish Cl. Hav ................. 136 A3
Langrish Rd. Southa ............. 78 A2
Langside Ave. Poole ........... 206 A4
Langstone Ave. Hav ............ 159 F4
Langstone High St. Hav ...... 159 F3
Langstone Rd. Hav ............. 159 F4
Langstone Rd. Ports ........... 183 D3
Langstone Wlk. Fare ........... 154 B4
Langstone Wlk. Gos ............ 155 D1
Langton Cl. B on S .............. 212 A4
Langton Cl. Winch ................. 1 C1
Langton Farm Gdns. Ports ... 182 C4
Langton Rd. Bi Wa ............... 83 E4
Langton Rd. Bour ............... 207 F3
Lanham La. Spar .................... 9 F4
Lanham La. Winch .................. 1 A1
Lankhills Rd. Winch ............... 2 A1
Lansdown Ave. Portc ........... 156 B3
Lansdowne Ave. Wat ........... 134 A1
Lansdowne Ave. Winch ......... 10 C3
Lansdowne Cl. Rom .............. 52 C4
Lansdowne Cres. Bour ........ 207 D2
Lansdowne Gdns. Bour ....... 207 D2
Lansdowne Gdns. Rom .......... 52 C4
Lansdowne Hill. Southa ....... 102 C2
Lansdowne Rd. Bour ........... 207 D3
Lansdowne Rd. Southa ........ 102 A4
Lansdowne The. Bour .......... 207 D2
Lantana Cl. Wat .................. 134 C3
Lapthorn Cl. Gos ................ 155 D2
Lapwing Cl. Gos .................. 181 D4
Lapwing Dr. Tot .................. 100 B4
Lapwing Gr. Portc ............... 155 F4
Lapwing Rd. Wi Mi ............. 164 A4
Lara Cl. Bour ...................... 191 E2
Larch Ave. Holb .................. 150 B3
Larch Cl. Broa .................... 187 F1
Larch Cl. Hord .................... 196 C2
Larch Cl. L on S .................. 180 A3
Larch Cl. St Le .................... 140 A2
Larch Rd. Southa .................. 78 A2
Larch Way. Fern .................. 165 E4
Larchdale Cl. Lo He ............ 152 B4
Larches Gdns. Fare ............. 130 B1
Larchfield Way. Wat ........... 112 B3
Larchwood Ave. Hav ........... 135 D2
Larchwood Rd. Tot ............. 100 B3
Larcombe Rd. Pet ................. 40 B1
Larg Dr. Winch ....................... 1 B2
Lark Hill Rise. Winch ............ 10 B2
Lark Rd. Christ .................... 210 A3
Lark Rd. Eastl ....................... 55 E1
Larkhill Rd. Ports ................ 157 F2
Larkhill Cl. New M .............. 196 A2
Larks Cl. Fern ..................... 165 D4
Larks Rise. Fern .................. 165 D4
Larksfield Ave. Bour ........... 191 E2
Larkshill Cl. New M ............ 196 A2
Larkspur Chase. Southa ...... 104 C3
Larkspur Cl. Lo He .............. 128 C1

Larkspur Dr. March ............. 124 C4
Larkspur Gdns. He En ......... 105 E3
Larkspur Gdns. Holb ........... 150 A2
Larkwhistle Wlk. Hav .......... 135 E4
Lascelles Rd. Bour .............. 208 A3
Laser Cl. Lo He .................... 128 C1
Lasham Green. Hav ............. 136 A3
Lasham Wlk. Fare ............... 154 B4
Latch Farm Ave. Christ ....... 209 D4
Latchmore Dr. Hyt .............. 125 E2
Latchmore Forest Gr. Wat ... 112 A2
Latchmore Gdns. Wat ......... 111 F2
Latelie Cl. Net ..................... 127 E3
Latham Cl. Fa Oa .................. 57 D1
Latham Cl. Southa ............... 102 A4
Latham Rd. Fa Oa ................. 57 D1
Latham Rd. Rom ................... 53 D4
Latimer Ct. Ports ................ 158 A2
Latimer Rd. Bour ................ 206 C4
Latimer St. Rom .................... 52 C4
Latimer St. Southa .............. 103 D2
Latimers Cl. Christ ............. 194 C1
Lauder Cl. Southb ............... 137 F1
Launcelyn Cl. N Bad ............. 53 F2
Launceston Dr. Eastl ............ 55 F3
Laundry La. M on S ............. 213 F2
Laundry Rd. Southa .............. 78 A1
Laurel Cl. Broa ................... 187 E3
Laurel Cl. Christ .................. 194 B1
Laurel Cl. Hord ................... 196 C2
Laurel Cl. Hyt ..................... 125 F2
Laurel Cl. Lo He .................. 129 D2
Laurel Cl. Southa ................ 103 E2
Laurel Cl. St Le ................... 139 F2
Laurel Dr. Broa ................... 188 B2
Laurel Gdns. Broa .............. 188 B2
Laurel Gdns. Lo He ............. 129 D2
Laurel La. St Le .................. 139 F2
Laurel Rd. Lo He ................. 129 D2
Laurel Rd. Wat .................... 112 B2
Laurels The. Fern ............... 165 E4
Lauriston Dr. Ch Fo .............. 30 A1
Laurus Cl. Wat .................... 135 D3
Laurus Wlk. L on S ............. 179 F3
Lavant Cl. Wat .................... 112 A1
Lavant St. Pet ....................... 40 C2
Lavender Cl. Ver ................. 115 E3
Lavender Rd. Hord .............. 196 C2
Lavender Rd. Wat ............... 135 D3
Lavender Way. Broa ............ 187 E2
Laverock Lea. Portc ............ 132 B1
Laverstoke Cl. Rown ............. 77 F3
Lavey's La. Swanw .............. 130 A3
Lavington Gdns. N Bad ......... 53 F2
Lavinia Rd. Gos .................. 181 D3
Lavinia Rd. Poole ............... 205 E4
Lawford Rd. Bour ............... 191 D2
Lawford Way. Tot ............... 100 C4
Lawn Cl. Gos ...................... 180 B4
Lawn Dr. Lo He ................... 129 D1
Lawn Rd. Eastl ...................... 56 A3
Lawn Rd. Lym ..................... 198 A2
Lawn Rd. M on S ................. 213 F2
Lawn Rd. Southa ................. 103 D4
Lawn St. Winch ..................... 11 D4
Lawns Cl. Wi Mi ................. 164 B3
Lawns Rd. Wi Mi ................ 164 A3
Lawns The. Christ ............... 211 D4
Lawnside Rd. Southa ........... 102 A4
Lawnswood Cl. Wat ............ 111 F1
Lawrence Ave. Wat ............. 111 F1
Lawrence Dr. Poole ............ 205 F1
Lawrence Gr. Southa ........... 103 F1
Lawrence La. Fordi ............... 94 A2
Lawrence Rd. Fare .............. 130 C1
Lawrence Rd. Ports ............ 182 C2
Lawrence Rd. Rin ............... 117 E1
Lawson Cl. Swanw .............. 128 B4
Lawson Rd. Poole ............... 205 D3
Lawson Rd. Ports ................ 182 C2
Laxton Cl. Lo He ................. 129 D2
Laxton Cl. Southa ............... 104 A1
Layard Dr. Wi Mi ................ 163 E1
Laymoor La. Fern ................ 164 B3
Layton Cl. Poole ................. 205 E3
Layton Rd. Gos .................. 155 E2
Layton Rd. Poole ................ 205 E3
Lazy Acre. Southb ............... 161 E4
Lea Cl. Black ...................... 177 F4
Lea The. Ver ....................... 115 D3
Lea Way. Bour .................... 189 F3
Leacock Cl. Swan .................. 84 A3
Leafy La. Lo He ................... 129 F3
Lealand Gr. Cos .................. 158 B4
Lealand Rd. Cos ................. 158 B4
Leamington Cres. L on S ..... 179 F3
Leamington Rd. Bour .......... 207 D4
Leander Cl. Eastl .................. 56 A3
Leaphill Rd. Bour ............... 208 A3
Lear Rd. Gos ....................... 181 D3
Learoyd Rd. Poole .............. 204 C4
Leaside Way. Southa ............. 79 E3
Leatherhead Gdns. He En ...... 81 E1
Leaway The. Portc .............. 156 B4
Lebanon Rd. Southa ............ 101 E4
Lechlade Gdns. Bour .......... 208 A4
Lechlade Gdns. Fare ........... 130 C2
Leckford Cl. Portc ............... 132 B1
Leckford Cl. Southa ............ 104 B4

## Leckford Cl. Southa

**Leckford Rd. Hav**

Leckford Rd. Hav ............ 136 A3
Ledbury Rd. Christ ............ 209 F3
Ledbury Rd. Cos ............ 133 E1
Lederle La. Gos ............ 155 E3
Ledgard Cl. Poole ............ 205 D2
Lee Church La. Rom ............ 76 C4
Lee Dro. Rom ............ 53 D1
Lee La. Nur ............ 77 D4
Lee Rd. Gos ............ 181 D3
Leedam Rd. Bour ............ 190 B2
Leelands. Lym ............ 198 B1
Leep La. Gos ............ 181 D1
Lees Cl. Christ ............ 192 B2
Lees La N. Gos ............ 181 D3
Lees La. Gos ............ 181 D3
Leesland Rd. Gos ............ 181 D3
Leeson Dr. Fern ............ 165 D4
Leeson Rd. Bour ............ 207 F4
Legg La. Wi Mi ............ 163 E2
Legion Cl. Hamw ............ 203 F1
Legion La. Ki Wo ............ 2 B4
Legion Rd. Hamw ............ 203 F1
Legion Rd. S Hay ............ 185 D2
Leicester Cl. Poole ............ 205 F2
Leicester Rd. Southa ............ 78 B1
Leicester Way. Winch ............ 2 B1
Leigh Gdns. Wi Mi ............ 163 E2
Leigh La. Wi Mi ............ 163 F3
Leigh Park. Lym ............ 198 B2
Leigh Rd. Ch Fo ............ 55 F2
Leigh Rd. Eastl ............ 55 F2
Leigh Rd. Fare ............ 131 D1
Leigh Rd. Hav ............ 135 F1
Leigh Rd. New M ............ 196 A2
Leigh Rd. Southa ............ 79 D1
Leigh Rd. Wi Mi ............ 163 E2
Leigham Vale Rd. Bour ............ 208 B2
Leighton Rd. Southa ............ 103 F2
Leisure The. Gos ............ 155 E2
Leith Ave. Portc ............ 132 B1
Lemon Rd. Southa ............ 102 A4
Lendorber Ave. Cos ............ 158 A4
Lennox Cl. Ch Fo ............ 55 F4
Lennox Cl. Gos ............ 181 E1
Lennox Cl. Southa ............ 77 F3
Lennox Rd N. Ports ............ 182 B1
Lennox Rd S. Ports ............ 182 B1
Lensyd Gdns. Wat ............ 111 F3
Lenthall Cl. Poole ............ 188 B1
Lentune Way. Lym ............ 198 B1
Leofric Ct. Ports ............ 183 E2
Leominster Rd. Cos ............ 133 D1
Leonard Rd. Gos ............ 181 E3
Leopold Dr. Bi Wa ............ 83 D4
Leopold St. Ports ............ 182 C1
Lepe Rd. Black ............ 178 A2
Lepe Rd. Exb ............ 179 A1
Lerryn Rd. Gos ............ 155 E1
Leslie Rd. Bour ............ 206 C4
Leslie Rd. Poole ............ 205 D2
Lester Ave. Hav ............ 135 E1
Lester Rd. Gos ............ 180 C3
Leven Ave. Bour ............ 206 B3
Leven Cl. Bour ............ 206 B2
Leven Cl. N Bad ............ 55 D4
Leventhorpe Ct. Gos ............ 181 E2
Leveson Cl. Gos ............ 180 C2
Levet's La. Poole ............ 204 A1
Leviathan Cl. Stubb ............ 154 B1
Lewens Cl. Wi Mi ............ 163 E2
Lewens La. Wi Mi ............ 163 E2
Lewesdon Dr. Broa ............ 187 F2
Lewin Cl. Co Com ............ 56 C4
Lewis Cl. Eastl ............ 56 A3
Lewis Cl. Hyt ............ 125 E1
Lewis Rd. Ems ............ 137 D2
Lewis Silkin Way. Southa ............ 78 A2
Lewry Cl. He En ............ 105 E4
Lexby Rd. Tot ............ 101 D3
Lexden Gdns. S Hay ............ 184 C2
Leybourne Ave. Bour ............ 190 B2
Leybourne Ave. Bour ............ 190 B3
Leybourne Ave. Southa ............ 104 A4
Leybourne Cl. Bour ............ 190 B3
Leydene Ave. Bour ............ 191 F1
Leydene Cl. Bour ............ 191 F1
Leyland Cl. Gos ............ 181 D2
Leyland Rd. Poole ............ 189 F1
Leyside. Christ ............ 209 F3
Leyton Rd. Southa ............ 103 E3
Liberty Cl. W Moo ............ 139 D3
Liberty Rd. Sob ............ 109 D4
Library Rd. Bour ............ 190 C1
Library Rd. Fern ............ 165 E3
Library Rd. Poole ............ 205 F3
Library Rd. Tot ............ 101 D4
Lichen Way. March ............ 101 F1
Lichfield Rd. Lo He ............ 129 E2
Lichfield Rd. Ports ............ 183 D3
Liddel Way. N Bad ............ 55 D3
Liddiard Gdns. Ports ............ 183 D1
Liddiards Way. Wat ............ 134 C2
Lightfoot Lawn. Ports ............ 183 E2
Lilac Cl. Rin ............ 141 D4
Lilac Rd. Southa ............ 79 D2
Lilliput Rd. Poole ............ 216 B4
Lily Ave. Wat ............ 134 A1
Limberline Rd. Ports ............ 158 A2
Limberline Spur. Ports ............ 158 A3

Lime Ave. Southa ............ 104 A3
Lime Cl. Hyt ............ 125 F1
Lime Cl. Southa ............ 104 A3
Lime Gdns. W End ............ 80 B2
Lime Gr. Cos ............ 133 D1
Lime Gr. Hord ............ 213 E4
Lime Gr. S Hay ............ 184 B2
Lime Kiln La. Holb ............ 150 A3
Lime St. Southa ............ 103 D2
Lime Wlk. Botl ............ 105 F4
Lime Wlk. Hyt ............ 125 F1
Limekiln La. Bi Wa ............ 59 F2
Limes Cl. Liss ............ 20 C2
Limes The. Gos ............ 155 E1
Limes The. Hav ............ 159 F4
Limes The. March ............ 102 A1
Limited Rd. Bour ............ 191 D1
Lin Brook Dr. Rin ............ 117 E1
Linacre Cres. Southa ............ 104 B3
Lince Gr. Burs ............ 127 F4
Lincoln Ave. Bour ............ 207 E3
Lincoln Ave. Christ ............ 192 C1
Lincoln Cl. Lo He ............ 129 E2
Lincoln Ct. Southa ............ 78 C1
Lincoln Rd. Poole ............ 205 E4
Lincoln Rd. Ports ............ 182 C3
Lincoln Rd. Wat ............ 112 A2
Lincolns Rise. Ott ............ 31 D1
Lind Cl. Cos ............ 134 C2
Lind Rd. Gos ............ 181 E1
Linda Gr. Wat ............ 111 F2
Linda Rd. Faw ............ 151 D2
Linden Cl. Fern ............ 165 E1
Linden Cl. Shed ............ 83 F2
Linden Dr. Liss ............ 20 C2
Linden Gdns. He En ............ 105 E3
Linden Gdns. Rin ............ 140 C4
Linden Gr. Ch Fo ............ 55 E4
Linden Gr. Gos ............ 181 D2
Linden Gr. S Hay ............ 185 D2
Linden Lea. Portc ............ 132 B1
Linden Rd. Bour ............ 191 D2
Linden Rd. Fern ............ 165 E1
Linden Rd. Poole ............ 205 E3
Linden Rd. Rom ............ 52 C4
Linden Rd. Southa ............ 78 A2
Linden Way. Hav ............ 135 F2
Linden Way. Lym ............ 198 B2
Linden Way. Wat ............ 112 B3
Linden Wlk. N Bad ............ 53 F3
Lindens Cl. Ems ............ 136 C1
Lindens The. Burt ............ 193 E2
Lindisfarne Cl. Cos ............ 158 A4
Lindley Ave. Ports ............ 183 D1
Lindsay Rd. Poole ............ 206 A2
Lindsay Rd. Southa ............ 104 B3
Lindway. Lo He ............ 129 D3
Lineside. Burt ............ 209 E4
Linford Cl. New M ............ 196 A2
Linford Cres. Southa ............ 78 B2
Linford Ct. Hav ............ 135 E4
Linford Rd. Rin ............ 117 E1
Ling Dale. Rown ............ 78 C4
Lingdale Rd. Poole ............ 189 D1
Lingdale Rd. Bour ............ 208 B3
Lingwood Ave. Christ ............ 209 F3
Lingwood Cl. Rown ............ 78 C4
Lingwood Wlk. Rown ............ 78 C4
Linhorns La. New M ............ 196 A3
Link Rd. Rin ............ 141 E4
Link Rd. Southa ............ 77 F2
Link Rise. Broa ............ 187 F3
Link The. Wat ............ 112 A1
Link Way. Stubb ............ 154 B1
Linkenholt Way. Hav ............ 135 E2
Links Cl. Ro Ca ............ 113 D1
Links Dr. Christ ............ 192 B1
Links La. Ro Ca ............ 113 D1
Links La. S Hay ............ 184 B2
Links Rd. Poole ............ 205 E1
Links Rd. Winch ............ 1 B1
Links The. Gos ............ 155 E1
Links View Ave. Poole ............ 205 F1
Linkside Ave. Bour ............ 207 F4
Linmead Dr. Bour ............ 190 A3
Linnet Cl. Pet ............ 41 E1
Linnet Cl. Rin ............ 141 E3
Linnet Cl. Wat ............ 111 F2
Linnet Ct. Gos ............ 180 C3
Linnet Sq. Eastl ............ 55 E1
Linnets The. Portc ............ 155 F4
Linnets The. Tot ............ 100 B4
Linnies La. Sway ............ 197 D4
Linthorpe Rd. Poole ............ 204 C2
Linwood Cl. Hyt ............ 126 A1
Linwood Rd. Bour ............ 207 D4
Lion St. Ports ............ 182 A3
Lion Terr. Ports ............ 182 A3
Lionheart Cl. Bour ............ 189 E3
Lionheart Way. Burs ............ 105 D1
Lions La. St Le ............ 139 E3
Lions Wood. St Le ............ 139 F2
Lisbon Rd. Southa ............ 102 B3
Lisle Cl. Lym ............ 198 B2
Lisle Cl. Winch ............ 10 A2
Lisle Court Rd. Bold ............ 199 E2
Lisle Ct. Winch ............ 10 C3
Lisle Way. Ems ............ 136 C2
Liss Rd. Ports ............ 182 C2

Litchfield Cres. Southa ............ 79 F1
Litchfield Rd. Southa ............ 79 F1
Litchfield Rd. Winch ............ 1 B2
Litchford Rd. New M ............ 196 B2
Little Abshot Rd. Lo He ............ 153 D4
Little Anglesey Rd. Gos ............ 181 D1
Little Arthur St. Ports ............ 182 C4
Little Ashton La. Bi Wa ............ 59 F2
Little Barrs Dr. New M ............ 196 A2
Little Bull La. Shed ............ 83 E1
Little Burn. Sway ............ 172 A1
Little Coburg St. Ports ............ 182 B3
Little Corner. Den ............ 111 D2
Little Croft Rd. Poole ............ 205 D3
Little Dene Copse. Lym ............ 198 A1
Little Dewlands. Ver ............ 114 B3
Little Dro. Woodg ............ 70 C4
Little Forest Rd. Bour ............ 206 C3
Little Gays. Stubb ............ 154 A1
Little George St. Ports ............ 182 C4
Little Green Orch. Gos ............ 181 D1
Little Green. Gos ............ 181 D1
Little Hambrook St. Ports ............ 182 A2
Little Kimble Wlk. He En ............ 105 E3
Little La. Gos ............ 181 D1
Little Lance's Hill. Southa ............ 103 F3
Little Lonnen. Wi Mi ............ 163 F4
Little Mead. Den ............ 111 D2
Little Minster St. Winch ............ 11 D4
Little Oak Rd. Southa ............ 78 C2
Little Park Cl. He En ............ 105 D3
Little Park Farm Rd. Lo He ............ 129 E3
Little Quob La. W End ............ 80 C1
Little Shore La. Bi Wa ............ 83 E4
Little Southsea St. Ports ............ 182 A2
Little Woodfalls Dr. Red ............ 47 E2
Littlecroft Ave. Bour ............ 191 D2
Littledown Ave. Bour ............ 207 F4
Littledown Dr. Bour ............ 207 F4
Littlegreen Ave. Hav ............ 136 A2
Littlemead Cl. Broa ............ 204 A4
Littlemeads. Rom ............ 52 B4
Littlemill La. Dame ............ 68 B3
Littlemoor Ave. Bour ............ 189 E2
Littlepark Ave. Hav ............ 135 D2
Littleton Gr. Hav ............ 135 F2
Littleton La. Litt ............ 1 A3
Littleton Rd. Litt ............ 1 A2
Littlewood Gdns. Lo He ............ 128 C2
Littlewood Gdns. W End ............ 80 B1
Liverpool Rd. Ports ............ 182 C3
Liverpool St. Southa ............ 103 D4
Livesay Gdns. Ports ............ 182 C3
Livingston Rd. Poole ............ 205 E3
Livingstone Ct. Gos ............ 180 B3
Livingstone Rd. Bour ............ 208 A3
Livingstone Rd. Christ ............ 209 E4
Livingstone Rd. Ports ............ 182 B2
Livingstone Rd. Southa ............ 103 D4
Livingstone Rd. Wi Mi ............ 163 F2
Llewellin Cl. Upt ............ 203 E4
Lloyd Ave. March ............ 101 F1
Loader Cl. Ki Wo ............ 2 B4
Loane Rd. Southa ............ 103 F2
Lobelia Cl. Wat ............ 135 D3
Lobelia Rd. Southa ............ 79 E3
Locarno Rd. Ports ............ 158 A1
Loch Rd. Poole ............ 205 F3
Lock App. Ports ............ 157 D4
Lock View. Ports ............ 157 D4
Locke Rd. He En ............ 105 E4
Lockerley Cl. Lym ............ 198 C1
Lockerley Cres. Southa ............ 77 F1
Lockerley Rd. Hav ............ 136 A2
Lockhams Rd. Curd ............ 106 C4
Locks Rd. Lo He ............ 129 D2
Locksheath Park Rd. Lo He . 129 D1
Locksheath Cl. Hav ............ 135 E3
Locksley Dr. Fern ............ 165 E2
Locksley Rd. Eastl ............ 55 F1
Locksway Rd. Ports ............ 183 E2
Lockswood Rd. Lo He ............ 128 C2
Lockyers Dr. Fern ............ 165 F3
Lode Hill. Down ............ 47 D4
Loders Cl. Broa ............ 188 B2
Lodge Ave. Cos ............ 158 A4
Lodge Cl. Poole ............ 205 F2
Lodge Dr. Hyt ............ 126 A1
Lodge Dro. Red ............ 47 E2
Lodge Gdns. Gos ............ 181 D2
Lodge Rd. Christ ............ 208 C4
Lodge Rd. Hav ............ 135 D1
Lodge Rd. Lo He ............ 129 D2
Lodge Rd. Lym ............ 198 A2
Lodge Rd. Southa ............ 103 D4
Lodge Vale. W Wel ............ 51 D1
Lodgebury Cl. Southb ............ 161 F4
Loewy Cres. Poole ............ 189 E1
Logan Cl. Southa ............ 77 F3
Lomax Cl. He En ............ 81 E1
Lombard Ave. Bour ............ 208 B3
Lombard St. Ports ............ 182 A2
Lombardy Cl. Gos ............ 155 F1
Lombardy Cl. Ver ............ 115 D3
Lombardy Rise. Wat ............ 134 C3
Lomer La. Ibs ............ 93 E2
Lomond Cl. Ports ............ 182 B4
Londesborough Rd. Ports ...... 182 C2
London Ave. Ports ............ 157 E1

London La. Sop ............ 166 C1
London Rd. Clanf ............ 88 B2
London Rd. Cos ............ 134 B2
London Rd. Hill B ............ 21 D1
London Rd. Horn ............ 88 B2
London Rd. Ki Wo ............ 2 A3
London Rd. Pet ............ 41 D3
London Rd. Ports ............ 157 F2
London Rd. Southa ............ 103 D3
London Rd. Steep ............ 41 E3
London Rd. Wat ............ 134 B2
Lone Barn La. Meons ............ 60 C4
Lone Pine Dr. Fern ............ 165 F2
Lone Pine Way. Fern ............ 165 F1
Lone Valley. Wat ............ 134 B2
Long Acre Ct. Ports ............ 182 C4
Long Beech Dr. Tot ............ 100 B3
Long Cl. Down ............ 46 C4
Long Copse La. Ems ............ 137 D2
Long Copse. Holb ............ 150 C2
Long Curtain Rd. Ports ............ 182 A1
Long Down. Pet ............ 41 D2
Long Dr. Gos ............ 155 E1
Long Dr. W End ............ 80 C1
Long La. Burs ............ 105 D1
Long La. Holb ............ 150 B3
Long La. March ............ 101 E1
Long La. Rin ............ 141 D2
Long La. Wi Mi ............ 163 F4
Long Lane Cl. Holb ............ 150 B2
Long Priors. W Meo ............ 37 D3
Long Rd. Bour ............ 190 B3
Long Rd. Sob ............ 85 E3
Long Water Dr. Gos ............ 181 E1
Long Wlk. It Ab ............ 2 C2
Longacre Dr. Fern ............ 165 E2
Longacre. Liss ............ 20 C2
Longacres. Lo He ............ 129 E2
Longbarrow Cl. Bour ............ 192 A1
Longbridge Cl. Tot ............ 76 B1
Longbridge Dr. Tot ............ 76 B1
Longbridge Park. Southa ............ 103 E2
Longclose Rd. He En ............ 105 E4
Longdean Cl. Cos ............ 133 D1
Longespee Rd. Oakl ............ 188 C4
Longfield Ave. Fare ............ 154 C4
Longfield Dr. Bour ............ 190 A3
Longfield Dr. Fern ............ 190 C4
Longfield Rd. Ems ............ 136 C2
Longfield Rd. Fa Oa ............ 57 E1
Longfield Rd. Hord ............ 197 D1
Longfield Rd. Winch ............ 11 E4
Longfleet Rd. Poole ............ 204 C2
Longlands Rd. Southb ............ 161 E4
Longleat Gdns. New M ............ 195 F2
Longleat Gdns. Southa ............ 78 A2
Longmead Ave. Bish ............ 56 B2
Longmead Gdns. Hav ............ 159 F4
Longmead Rd. Bur ............ 142 C2
Longmead Rd. Southa ............ 80 A1
Longmeadow Gdns. Hyt ............ 126 A2
Longmeadow La. Broa ............ 203 F4
Longmore Ave. Southa ............ 103 E1
Longmore Cres. Southa ............ 103 E1
Longmynd Dr. Fare ............ 154 B4
Longridge Rd. He En ............ 105 E3
Longs La. Stubb ............ 154 B2
Longs Wlk. Ports ............ 182 B4
Longshore Way. Ports ............ 183 E2
Longstaff Gdns. Fare ............ 130 C2
Longstock Cl. Southa ............ 127 D4
Longstock Cres. Tot ............ 100 C4
Longstock Rd. Hav ............ 136 A3
Longwood Ave. Wat ............ 112 A2
Longwood Dean La. Cher ...... 34 A3
Lonnen Rd. Wi Mi ............ 164 A4
Lonnen Wood Cl. Wi Mi ...... 164 A4
Lonsdale Ave. Cos ............ 158 A4
Lonsdale Ave. Portc ............ 156 B3
Lonsdale Rd. Bour ............ 206 C3
Loperwood La. Ne Ma ............ 76 A2
Loperwood La. Ower ............ 76 A2
Loperwood La. Tot ............ 76 A2
Loperwood. Ne Ma ............ 76 A1
Loraine Ave. Christ ............ 211 E4
Lord Cl. Poole ............ 204 C4
Lord Montgomery Way. Ports 182 A2
Lord Mountbatten Cl. Southa . 79 F2
Lord's Hill Centre E. Southa .... 77 F2
Lord's Hill Centre W. Southa .... 77 F2
Lord's Hill Way. Southa ............ 78 A3
Lordington Cl. Cos ............ 158 A4
Lords St. Ports ............ 182 B3
Lordswood Cl. Southa ............ 78 A2
Lordswood Gdns. Southa ...... 78 B2
Lordswood Rd. Southa ............ 78 B2
Lordswood. Co Com ............ 56 C4
Lorne Park Rd. Bour ............ 207 D2
Lorne Rd. Ports ............ 182 C2
Loughwood Cl. Eastl ............ 56 A3
Lovage Gdns. Tot ............ 100 B4
Lovage Way. Horn ............ 88 B1
Love La. M on S ............ 213 E3
Love La. Pet ............ 41 D2
Love La. Rom ............ 52 C4
Love La. Twyf ............ 32 A3
Love La. Woodg ............ 70 C4
Lovedean La. Horn ............ 111 F3

Lovedean La. Wat ............ 111 F3
Lovedon La. Ki Wo ............ 2 B4
Lovett Rd. Ports ............ 158 A2
Lovett Wlk. Winch ............ 1 B2
Lowcay Rd. Ports ............ 182 C1
Lowden Cl. Winch ............ 10 B2
Lower Alfred St. Southa ...... 103 D3
Lower Ashley Rd. New M ...... 196 B1
Lower Banister St. Southa .... 102 C3
Lower Bartons. Fordi ............ 69 F1
Lower Baybridge La. Ows ...... 33 E1
Lower Bellfield. Lo He ............ 153 F4
Lower Bere Wood. Wat ...... 134 C4
Lower Blandford Rd. Broa .... 188 A2
Lower Brook St. Winch ............ 11 D4
Lower Brookfield Rd. Ports .... 182 C3
Lower Brownhill Rd. Southa .... 77 E2
Lower Buckland Rd. Lym ...... 198 B3
Lower Canal Wlk. Southa ...... 103 D2
Lower Chase Rd. Shed ............ 83 F2
Lower Chase Rd. Swan ............ 83 F2
Lower Church Path. Ports .... 182 B3
Lower Church Rd. Lo He ...... 129 E2
Lower Common La. W Moo .. 139 D4
Lower Common Rd. W Wel .... 50 C2
Lower Crabbick La. Den ...... 110 A3
Lower Densome Wood. Woodg70 C4
Lower Derby Rd. Ports ............ 157 E1
Lower Drayton La. Cos ............ 158 A4
Lower Duncan Rd. Lo He ...... 129 D3
Lower Farlington Rd. Cos .... 158 C4
Lower Forbury Rd. Ports ...... 182 B2
Lower Golf Links Rd. Broa .... 188 A3
Lower Gr. Whits ............ 45 D1
Lower Grove Rd. Hav ............ 160 A4
Lower Heyshott. Pet ............ 41 D2
Lower La. Bi Wa ............ 83 E4
Lower Lamborough La. Cher .. 14 B2
Lower Mead End Rd. Sway .. 171 F1
Lower Mead. Pet ............ 41 D2
Lower Moors Rd. Co Com ...... 31 F1
Lower Mortimer Rd. Southa .. 103 E2
Lower Mullin's La. Hyt ............ 125 F2
Lower Northam Rd. He En .... 105 E4
Lower Pennington La. Lym .... 214 B4
Lower Quay Cl. Fare ............ 155 D4
Lower Quay Rd. Fare ............ 155 D4
Lower Quay. Fare ............ 155 D4
Lower Rd. Hav ............ 135 E2
Lower Sandy Down La. Bold . 173 E2
Lower Spinney. Lo He ............ 152 B4
Lower St Helens Rd. He En .. 105 E3
Lower St. Brai ............ 28 A4
Lower Stanmore La. Winch .... 10 C3
Lower Swanwick Rd. Swanw 128 B4
Lower Vicarage Rd. Southa .. 103 E2
Lower Wardown. Pet ............ 41 D2
Lower William St. Southa .... 103 E3
Lower Wingfield St. Ports .... 182 B3
Lower Woodside. Lym ............ 214 C4
Lower York St. Southa ............ 103 E3
Lowestoft Rd. Cos ............ 133 E1
Lowford Hill. Burs ............ 104 C1
Lowry Gdns. Southa ............ 104 B1
Lowther Gdns. Bour ............ 207 E3
Lowther Rd. Bour ............ 207 D3
Loxwood Rd. Horn ............ 111 F3
Luard Ct. Hav ............ 136 A1
Lucas Cl. Southa ............ 77 F3
Lucas Rd. Poole ............ 205 E3
Luccombe Pl. Southa ............ 78 B1
Luccombe Rd. Southa ............ 78 B1
Lucerne Ave. Bour ............ 208 B3
Lucerne Ave. Wat ............ 111 E1
Lucerne Gdns. He En ............ 105 D3
Lucerne Rd. M on S ............ 213 E2
Luckham Cl. Bour ............ 191 D1
Luckham Pl. Bour ............ 191 D1
Luckham Rd E. Bour ............ 191 D1
Luckham Rd. Bour ............ 191 D1
Lucknow St. Ports ............ 182 C3
Lucky La. Bold ............ 174 A1
Ludlow Rd. Cos ............ 133 E1
Ludlow Rd. Southa ............ 103 F2
Ludwell's La. Swan ............ 83 F1
Lugano Cl. Wat ............ 111 E1
Lulworth Ave. Hamw ............ 203 F1
Lulworth Cl. Ch Fo ............ 55 D2
Lulworth Cl. S Hay ............ 185 D3
Lulworth Cl. Southa ............ 77 F1
Lulworth Cres. Hamw ............ 203 F1
Lulworth Green. Southa ............ 77 F1
Lulworth Rd. L on S ............ 179 F3
Lumby Dr. Rin ............ 141 D4
Lumley Rd. Herm ............ 137 D1
Lumsden Ave. Southa ............ 102 B4
Lumsden Rd. Ports ............ 183 E2
Lundy Cl. Southa ............ 77 F3
Lundy Wlk. Stubb ............ 154 A2
Lunedale Rd. Hyt ............ 149 F4
Lupin Rd. Southa ............ 79 E3
Luther Rd. Bour ............ 206 C4
Lutman St. Ems ............ 136 C2
Luton Rd. Southa ............ 104 A2
Luzborough La. Rom ............ 53 E3
Lyburn Rd. Red ............ 48 C1
Lychgate Dr. Horn ............ 112 A4
Lychgate Green. Stubb ........ 154 B3

239

Lydford Rd. Bour May Cres. Holb

Lydford Rd. Bour 190 A1
Lydgate Cl. Southa 104 B2
Lydgate Cl. Southa 104 B2
Lydgate Green. Southa 104 B2
Lydgate Rd. Southa 104 B2
Lydgate The. M on S 213 D3
Lydgate. Tot 100 B4
Lydiard Cl. Eastl 56 A3
Lydlinch Cl. Fern 165 E1
Lydlynch Rd. Tot 100 C4
Lydney Cl. Cos 157 D4
Lydney Rd. Lo He 128 C2
Lydwell Cl. Bour 189 F3
Lyell Rd. Poole 205 E3
Lymbourn Rd. Hav 136 A1
Lyme Cl. Eastl 55 F3
Lyme Cres. Christ 210 C4
Lymefields. M on S 213 F3
Lymer La. Nur 77 E3
Lymington Rd. B on S 196 A1
Lymington Rd. Brock 146 A1
Lymington Rd. Christ 210 C4
Lymington Rd. M on S 213 F3
Lymore La. M on S 213 F3
Lymore La. M on S 214 A2
Lymore Valley. M on S 213 F3
Lynch Cl. Winch 1 C1
Lynch La. W Meo 37 E2
Lyndale Cl. M on S 213 F3
Lyndale Rd. Lo He 129 E2
Lynden Cl. Fare 154 A4
Lynden Gate. Southa 104 A2
Lyndhurst Cl. S Hay 185 D2
Lyndhurst Cl. Winch 1 B2
Lyndhurst Rd. Ashu 100 A1
Lyndhurst Rd. Bran 194 B1
Lyndhurst Rd. Bran 194 B3
Lyndhurst Rd. Brock 146 A1
Lyndhurst Rd. Bur 143 E3
Lyndhurst Rd. Burt 194 B3
Lyndhurst Rd. Cadn 98 C4
Lyndhurst Rd. Christ 194 B1
Lyndhurst Rd. Gos 181 D2
Lyndhurst Rd. Lan 49 E2
Lyndhurst Rd. Ports 157 F1
Lyndock Cl. Southa 103 F1
Lyndock Pl. Southa 103 F1
Lyndum Cl. Pet 40 C2
Lyne Pl. Wat 112 A3
Lyne's La. Rin 140 C4
Lynford Ave. Winch 1 C1
Lynford Way. Winch 1 C1
Lynn Cl. W End 80 A2
Lynn Rd. Ports 182 C4
Lynn Way. Ki Wo 2 B4
Lynric Cl. B on S 212 A4
Lynton Cres. Christ 192 B2
Lynton Gdns. Fare 130 C2
Lynton Gr. Ports 183 D4
Lynton Rd. He En 105 E4
Lynton Rd. Pet 40 C2
Lynwood Ave. Wat 111 E2
Lynwood Cl. Fern 165 E4
Lynwood Dr. Oakl 188 C4
Lynx Cl. Bish 56 C1
Lyon Ave. New M 196 A2
Lyon Rd. Poole 189 F1
Lyon St. Southa 103 D3
Lysander Cl. Christ 210 B4
Lysander Way. Wat 135 D4
Lysses Ct. Fare 131 E1
Lyster Rd. Fordi 70 A1
Lystra Rd. Bour 191 D2
Lytchett Dr. Broa 188 A2
Lytchett Way. Upt 203 D3
Lyteltane Rd. Lym 198 B1
Lytham Rd. Broa 188 A2
Lytham Rd. Southa 80 A1
Lythe La. Steep 40 A3
Lytton Rd. Bour 207 E3
Lytton Rd. Hyt 126 A1

Mabey Ave. Bour 190 B1
Mabey Cl. Gos 181 E1
Mablethorpe Rd. Cos 133 F1
Macandrew Rd. Poole 216 C4
Macarthur Cres. Southa 104 A4
Macaulay Ave. Portc 132 C1
Macaulay Rd. Broa 188 A2
Maclaren Rd. Bour 190 C2
Maclean Rd. Bour 189 F2
MacNacnaghten Rd. Southa 103 E4
Madden Cl. Gos 180 C2
Maddison St. Southa 102 C2
Maddoxford La. Botl 82 A1
Maddoxford Way. Botl 81 F1
Madeira Rd. Bour 207 D2
Madeira Rd. Poole 205 E3
Madeira Rd. Ports 157 F2
Madeline Cl. Poole 205 D4
Madeline Cres. Poole 205 D4
Madeline Rd. Pet 40 C2
Madison Ave. Bour 207 E3
Madison Cl. Gos 180 C4
Mafeking Rd. Ports 182 C2
Mag's Barrow. Fern 165 F1
Magazine La. March 102 A2
Magdala Rd. Cos 157 F4
Magdala Rd. S Hay 184 C2
Magdalen Hill. Winch 11 D4
Magdalen La. Christ 209 D3
Magdalen Rd. Ports 157 F2
Magdalene Way. Lo He 129 E1
Magennis Cl. Gos 180 B4
Magna Cl. Bour 189 F3
Magna Gdns. Bour 189 F3
Magna Rd. Bour 189 E4
Magna Rd. Oakl 189 E4
Magnolia Cl. Bour 209 D3
Magnolia Cl. Fare 154 C4
Magnolia Cl. Ver 115 E2
Magnolia Gr. Fa Oa 57 F1
Magnolia Rd. Southa 103 F3
Magnolia Way. Wat 112 B2
Magpie Cl. Bour 191 E2
Magpie Dr. Tot 100 B4
Magpie Gdns. Southa 104 B2
Magpie La. Eastl 55 F1
Magpie La. L on S 179 F4
Magpie Rd. Ro Ca 113 E3
Magpie Wlk. Wat 111 E2
Maiden La. Lym 198 C1
Maidford Gr. Ports 158 B2
Maidment Cl. Bour 189 F2
Maidstone Cres. Cos 133 F1
Main Quay. Hamw 204 A1
Main Rd. Co Com 32 A1
Main Rd. Faw 150 B3
Main Rd. Faw 150 B3
Main Rd. Herm 161 E4
Main Rd. Hyt 125 E3
Main Rd. Litt 1 A3
Main Rd. March 101 F1
Main Rd. Ows 33 D2
Main Rd. Southb 161 E4
Main Rd. Tot 100 C2
Mainstone. Rom 52 B3
Mainstream Ct. Bish 56 B2
Maisemore Gdns. Ems 160 B4
Maitland St. Ports 182 B4
Maizemore Wlk. L on S 179 F3
Majestic Rd. Nur 77 D2
Malan Cl. Poole 204 C4
Malcolm Cl. Ch Fo 30 C1
Malcolm Cl. Lo He 129 D2
Malcolm Rd. Ch Fo 30 C1
Malcomb Cl. Bour 209 D2
Malcroft Mews. March 102 A1
Maldon Cl. Bish 56 B2
Maldon Rd. Cos 157 E4
Maldon Rd. Southa 103 F2
Malibres Rd. Ch Fo 55 F4
Malin Cl. Southa 77 F2
Malin Cl. Stubb 154 A2
Malins Rd. Ports 182 B4
Mall The. Bur 143 D2
Mall The. Ports 157 E1
Mallard Cl. Bi Wa 83 D4
Mallard Cl. Bour 191 E1
Mallard Cl. Christ 210 A3
Mallard Cl. Hord 197 D2
Mallard Cl. Rom 52 C4
Mallard Gdns. Gos 155 D1
Mallard Rd. Bour 191 E1
Mallard Rd. Ports 183 D3
Mallard Rd. Ro Ca 113 D1
Mallard Rd. Wi Mi 164 A4
Mallards Rd. Burs 127 F4
Mallards The. Fare 131 D2
Mallards The. Hav 159 F4
Mallory Cl. Christ 209 F4
Mallory Cres. Fare 131 D2
Mallow Cl. Lo He 128 C1
Mallow Cl. Wat 134 C3
Mallow Rd. He En 105 D3
Mallows The. New M 196 B2
Malmesbury Cl. Fa Oa 57 E1
Malmesbury Gdns. Winch 1 B1
Malmesbury Park Pl. Bour 207 E3
Malmesbury Park Rd. Bour 207 D3
Malmesbury Pl. Southa 102 B4
Malmesbury Rd. Rom 52 C4
Malmesbury Rd. Southa 102 B4
Malmesbury Rd. St Le 139 F2
Maloren Way. W Moo 139 D1
Malory Cl. Southa 104 B3
Malt La. Bi Wa 83 E4
Malta Rd. Ports 182 C4
Malthouse Cl. It Ab 2 C2
Malthouse Cl. Rom 52 C4
Malthouse Gdns. March 101 F1
Malthouse La. Fare 131 D1
Malthouse Rd. Ports 182 B4
Malthouse. Poole 204 B1
Maltings The. Fare 131 E1
Malvern Ave. Fare 154 C4
Malvern Cl. Bi Wa 83 E4
Malvern Cl. Bour 191 D2
Malvern Dr. Hyt 125 E2
Malvern Gdns. He En 81 E1
Malvern Mews. Ems 136 C1
Malvern Rd. Bour 191 D1
Malvern Rd. Gos 180 C3
Malvern Rd. Hill B 21 D1
Malvern Rd. Ports 182 B1
Malvern Rd. Southa 78 B1
Malwood Ave. Southa 78 B2
Malwood Cl. Hav 136 A3
Malwood Gdns. Tot 100 B4
Malwood Rd W. Hyt 125 F2
Malwood Rd. Hyt 126 A2
Manchester Rd. Net 127 D3
Manchester Rd. Ports 182 C3
Manchester Rd. Sway 172 A2
Mancroft Ave. Stubb 154 B1
Mandale Cl. Bour 190 A2
Mandale Rd. Bour 189 F2
Mandela Way. Southa 102 C3
Manderley. M on S 213 F2
Manley Rd. Burs 104 C1
Manners Rd. Ports 182 C2
Manning Ave. Christ 194 B1
Manning's Heath Rd. Poole 189 D1
Manningford Cl. Winch 2 A2
Mannington Pl. Bour 206 C2
Mannington Way. W Moo 138 B1
Manns Cl. W End 80 B1
Mannyngham Way. Mich 27 E4
Manor Ave. Poole 189 E1
Manor Cl. Burs 104 C1
Manor Cl. Fern 165 F3
Manor Cl. Fordi 69 F1
Manor Cl. Hav 135 F1
Manor Cl. M on S 213 E3
Manor Cl. Tot 100 C3
Manor Cl. Wickh 108 A2
Manor Cl. Winch 11 D4
Manor Cres. Burs 104 C1
Manor Cres. Cos 158 A4
Manor Ct. Lo He 129 E2
Manor Ct. Rin 140 C4
Manor Ct. Ver 114 C3
Manor Farm Cl. Bish 56 C1
Manor Farm Cl. New M 195 F1
Manor Farm Gr. Bish 56 C1
Manor Farm La. Miche 6 C1
Manor Farm Rd. Bour 190 B4
Manor Farm Rd. Fordi 69 E1
Manor Farm Rd. Southa 79 E1
Manor Gdns. Rin 140 C4
Manor Gdns. Southb 137 E1
Manor House Ave. Southa 101 F3
Manor La. Ver 114 C3
Manor Lodge Rd. Ro Ca 113 D1
Manor Mews. Cos 158 B4
Manor Park Ave. Ports 183 D4
Manor Park. Poole 204 A3
Manor Rd N. Southa 103 F2
Manor Rd S. Southa 103 F2
Manor Rd. Bish 56 C1
Manor Rd. Bour 207 E2
Manor Rd. Chilw 54 B1
Manor Rd. Christ 209 D3
Manor Rd. Durl 82 B4
Manor Rd. Holb 150 B2
Manor Rd. Hyt 125 D2
Manor Rd. M on S 213 E3
Manor Rd. N Hay 184 C3
Manor Rd. New M 196 A2
Manor Rd. Ports 182 C4
Manor Rd. Rin 141 D4
Manor Rd. S Hay 184 C3
Manor Rd. Southb 137 E1
Manor Rd. Twyf 31 F3
Manor Rd. Ver 114 C3
Manor Terr. Burs 104 C1
Manor Way. L on S 179 F3
Manor Way. S Hay 185 D1
Manor Way. Southb 137 E1
Manor Way. Ver 114 C4
Mansbridge Rd. Eastl 56 A1
Mansbridge Rd. Southa 79 F2
Mansel Ct. Southa 77 F1
Mansel Rd E. Southa 77 F1
Mansel Rd W. Southa 77 E1
Mansell Cl. Hyt 125 F1
Mansell Rd. Rown 77 F4
Mansfield Ave. Poole 205 E2
Mansfield Cl. Fern 165 E1
Mansfield Cl. Poole 205 E2
Mansfield Rd. Bour 190 C1
Mansfield Rd. Gos 180 B4
Mansfield Rd. Poole 205 E2
Mansfield Rd. Rin 140 C4
Mansion Rd. Ports 182 C1
Mansion Rd. Southa 102 B3
Mansvid Ave. Cos 158 A4
Mantle Cl. Gos 180 B4
Manton Rd. Hamw 203 F2
Maple Cl. B on S 212 A4
Maple Cl. Christ 210 C4
Maple Cl. Ems 136 C1
Maple Cl. L on S 179 F3
Maple Cl. Rom 53 E3
Maple Cres. Clanf 88 B3
Maple Dr. Den 111 D2
Maple Dr. Fern 165 E4
Maple Dr. Ki Wo 2 A4
Maple Gdns. Tot 100 B3
Maple Rd. Bour 206 C4
Maple Rd. Hyt 150 A4
Maple Rd. Poole 204 B2
Maple Rd. Ports 182 B1
Maple Rd. Southa 103 F4
Maple Sq. Eastl 55 F1
Maples The. Eastl 55 E4
Mapleton Rd. He En 105 E3
Mapletree Ave. Wat 112 B2
Maplewood Cl. Tot 100 B3
Maplin Rd. Southa 77 E1
Mapperton Cl. Poole 189 D1
Marabout Cl. Christ 209 E4
Maralyn Ave. Wat 134 C3
Marathon Cl. Fa Oa 57 D1
Marbream Cl. Fordi 69 E1
Marchwood By Pass. Hyt 124 C4
Marchwood By Pass. March 124 C4
Marchwood By Pass. Tot 101 D2
Marchwood Rd. Bour 190 B2
Marchwood Rd. Hav 135 F3
Marchwood Rd. Southa 102 A3
Marchwood Rd. Tot 101 E2
Marcus Cl. Fa Oa 57 D1
Mardale Rd. Southa 101 E4
Mardale Wlk. Southa 101 E4
Marden Paddock. Brock 145 F1
Marden Way. Pet 41 D2
Mardon Cl. Southa 79 F3
Mare La. Twyf 32 C3
Margam Ave. Southa 103 F3
Margards La. Ver 114 C3
Margaret Cl. Wat 111 E1
Margarita Rd. Fare 130 C1
Margate Rd. Ports 182 B2
Margery's Ct. Ports 182 A3
Marian Cl. Broa 187 E2
Marian Rd. Broa 187 E2
Marianne Cl. Southa 101 F3
Marianne Rd. Poole 206 B4
Marianne Rd. Wi Mi 164 A4
Marie Ave. Down 46 B4
Marie Rd. Southa 104 B2
Marigold Cl. Fare 130 C1
Marina Cl. Bour 207 F2
Marina Cl. Ems 161 D4
Marina Dr. Poole 205 D1
Marina Gr. Portc 156 B3
Marina Gr. Ports 183 D4
Marina Keep. Ports 157 D3
Marina The. Bour 207 F2
Marina View. Christ 209 D3
Marine Ct. Ports 183 D1
Marine Dr E. B on S 212 A3
Marine Dr W. B on S 211 F4
Marine Dr. B on S 211 F4
Marine Par. Southa 103 D2
Marine Parade E. L on S 179 F3
Marine Parade W. L on S 179 E3
Marine Rd. Bour 208 B2
Marine Wlk. S Hay 185 E2
Mariner's Cl. Hamble 128 A2
Mariners Ct. Lym 198 C1
Mariners Mews. Hyt 126 A2
Mariners Way. Gos 181 E2
Mariners Way. Lo He 128 B1
Mariners Wlk. Ports 183 D3
Marion Rd. Ports 182 C1
Maritime Walk. Southa 103 D1
Maritime Way. Southa 103 D1
Marjoram Cres. Wat 112 A2
Mark Cl. Ports 157 F2
Mark Cl. Southa 102 A4
Mark Ct. Wat 134 C4
Mark's La. New M 196 A3
Mark's Rd. Stubb 154 C1
Markall Cl. Cher 14 B3
Market Cl. Poole 204 B1
Market La. Winch 11 D4
Market Par. Hav 135 F1
Market Pl. Fordi 69 F1
Market Pl. Rin 140 C4
Market Pl. Rom 52 C4
Market St. Eastl 56 A1
Market St. Poole 204 A1
Market St. Winch 11 D4
Market Way. Wi Mi 163 E2
Marketway. Ports 182 B3
Markham Ave. Bour 190 B4
Markham Cl. Bour 190 B3
Markham Rd. Bour 207 D4
Marks Rd. Bour 190 C2
Marks Tey Rd. Stubb 154 B3
Markway Cl. Ems 136 B1
Marlaxton Cl. Eastl 55 F3
Marlborough Cl. Wat 134 B3
Marlborough Ct. Hyt 125 F1
Marlborough Gr. Portc 156 B4
Marlborough Park. Hav 136 B2
Marlborough Pl. Wi Mi 163 E3
Marlborough Rd. Bour 206 B2
Marlborough Rd. Ch Fo 30 C1
Marlborough Rd. Gos 180 C3
Marlborough Rd. Poole 205 E2
Marlborough Rd. Southa 102 A4
Marldell Cl. Hav 136 A3
Marles Cl. Gos 180 B4
Marley Ave. New M 195 F2
Marley Cl. New M 195 F2
Marley Mount. Sway 171 F1
Marlhill Cl. Southa 79 F1
Marline Rd. Poole 205 E3
Marlott Rd. Poole 204 B3
Marlow Cl. Fare 130 C2
Marlow Dr. Christ 192 C2
Marlow Rd. Bi Wa 83 D4
Marlpit Dr. Christ 195 D1
Marlpit La. New M 196 A4
Marls Rd. He En 105 F3
Marmion Ave. Ports 182 B1
Marmion Green. Christ 209 F4
Marmion Rd. Ports 182 B1
Marne Rd. Southa 104 A4
Marnhull Rd. Poole 204 B2
Marpet Cl. Bour 189 F3
Marples Way. Hav 135 E1
Marquis Way. Bour 189 E3
Marram Cl. Lym 198 C3
Marryat Ct. Christ 211 D4
Marryat Rd. New M 195 F2
Marsden Rd. Cos 157 D4
Marsh Cl. Cos 158 B3
Marsh La. Brea 70 A4
Marsh La. Christ 192 C1
Marsh La. Faw 151 D2
Marsh La. Lym 198 C3
Marsh La. Southa 103 D2
Marsh La. Upt 203 D4
Marsh Par. Hyt 126 A2
Marsh The. Hyt 126 A2
Marshal Rd. Broa 188 A1
Marshall Rd. S Hay 185 E1
Marshfield. Wi Mi 163 F4
Marshlands Rd. Cos 158 B4
Marshwood Ave. Broa 188 C1
Marshwood Ave. Wat 135 D4
Marston Cl. New M 196 A3
Marston Gr. Christ 194 C1
Marston La. Ports 158 A2
Marston Rd. New M 196 A3
Marston Rd. Southa 104 C3
Martello Cl. Gos 180 B2
Martello Park. Poole 216 C4
Martello Rd S. Poole 216 C4
Martells Ct. Ports 182 A2
Martells The. B on S 212 A4
Martha St. Ports 182 B3
Martin Ave. Den 111 D2
Martin Ave. Stubb 154 B1
Martin Cl. Broa 203 F4
Martin Cl. L on S 179 F4
Martin Rd. Hav 136 A3
Martin Rd. Ports 183 D4
Martin Rd. Stubb 154 B1
Martin St. Bi Wa 83 D4
Martin's Rd. Brock 146 A1
Martindale Ave. Wi Mi 164 A3
Martingale Cl. Upt 203 E4
Martins Cl. Fern 165 F4
Martins Dr. Fern 165 F4
Martins Fields. Comp 10 B1
Martins Hill Cl. Burt 193 E1
Martins Hill La. Burt 193 E1
Martins The. Fa Oa 57 E1
Martins Way. Fern 165 F4
Martley Gdns. He En 81 E1
Marvic Ct. Hav 135 F3
Marvin Cl. He En 105 F4
Marvin Way. He En 105 E4
Marvin Way. Southa 104 B3
Marwell Cl. Bour 208 A4
Mary Mitchell Cl. Rin 140 C4
Mary Rose Cl. Fare 130 C2
Mary Rose St The. Ports 182 B3
Marybridge Cl. Tot 100 C3
Maryfield. Southa 103 D2
Maryland Cl. Southa 79 F2
Maryland Gdns. M on S 213 D2
Maryland Rd. Hamw 203 E2
Masefield Ave. Portc 132 C1
Masefield Cl. Eastl 55 F2
Masefield Cres. Wat 111 F2
Masefield Green. Southa 104 B3
Masseys La. E Bol 175 E4
Masten Cres. Gos 180 B4
Masterson Cl. Christ 209 E4
Matapan Rd. Ports 157 F2
Matchams La. Hurn 166 A2
Matchams La. St Le 166 A2
Matheson Rd. Southa 78 A3
Matley Gdns. Tot 100 A4
Matlock Rd. Fern 165 E2
Matthews Cl. Hav 135 E2
Matthews La. E Bol 175 E3
Maturin Cl. Lym 198 B2
Maundeville Cres. Christ 208 C4
Maundville Rd. Christ 208 C4
Maunsell Way. He En 81 E1
Maureen Cl. Poole 205 D4
Mauretania Rd. Nur 77 D2
Maurice Rd. Bour 207 E4
Maurice Rd. Ports 183 E2
Maury's La. W Wel 50 B2
Mavis Cres. Hav 135 F1
Mavis Rd. Bour 191 D1
Maxstoke Cl. Ports 182 B3
Maxwell Rd. Bour 207 D4
Maxwell Rd. Broa 187 F2
Maxwell Rd. Poole 216 C4
Maxwell Rd. Ports 183 D2
Maxwell Rd. Southa 104 A2
May Ave. Lym 198 B3
May Bush La. Sob 85 D1
May Cl. Holb 150 B2
May Copse. Holb 150 B2
May Cres. Holb 150 B2

May La. Bold

May La. Bold .......................... 174 A1
May Rd. Southa ..................... 102 B4
May Tree Cl. Winch .................. 10 B2
May's La. Stubb ..................... 154 B2
Maybray-King Way. Southa ...... 104 A4
Maybush Ct. Southa ................. 78 A1
Maybush Rd. Southa ................. 77 F1
Mayfair Ct. Botl ...................... 106 A4
Mayfair Gdns. Bour ................ 190 A2
Mayfair Gdns. Southa ............. 102 C4
Mayfield Ave. Poole ............... 205 F2
Mayfield Ave. Tot .................. 100 C4
Mayfield Cl. Fern ................... 165 E3
Mayfield Cl. Stubb ................. 154 B2
Mayfield Dr. Fern ................... 165 E3
Mayfield Rd. Bour .................. 191 D1
Mayfield Rd. Fordi ................... 69 E1
Mayfield Rd. Gos ................... 181 E2
Mayfield Rd. Ports ................. 157 F1
Mayfield Rd. Southa ................. 79 E2
Mayfield Way. Fern ................ 165 E3
Mayfield. L on S ..................... 179 F3
Mayford Rd. Poole ................. 206 A3
Mayhall Rd. Ports .................. 158 A1
Mayhill La. Drox ...................... 84 C4
Mayhill La. Swan .................... 84 C4
Maylands Ave. Ports .............. 183 D3
Maylands Rd. Hav .................. 135 D1
Mayles Cl. Wickh ................... 108 A2
Mayles La. Wickh ................... 107 F1
Mayles Rd. Ports ................... 183 D3
Maylings Farm Rd. Fare ......... 130 C2
Maylyn Rd. Upt ...................... 187 D1
Maynard Cl. Gos .................... 155 E2
Maynard Pl. Horn .................. 112 A4
Maynard Rd. Tot ................... 100 C4
Mayo Cl. Ports ...................... 182 B4
Maypole Villas. Ott .................. 56 A4
Mayridge. Lo He .................... 129 E2
Mays Firs. Woodg .................... 47 F1
Mays Gdns. Bour .................. 189 F2
Maytree Cl. Fa Oa ................... 57 E1
Maytree Cl. Lo He ................. 129 D2
Maytree Gdns. Wat ................ 111 F2
Maytree Rd. Ch Fo ................... 30 B1
Maytree Rd. Fare ................... 131 D1
Mayvale Cl. March .................. 101 F1
Mc William Rd. Bour .............. 191 D1
Mcintyre Rd. Hurn ................. 192 A4
Mckinley Rd. Bour ................. 206 B1
Mcwilliam Cl. Poole .............. 206 B4
Meacher Cl. Tot ..................... 100 C4
Mead Cl. Broa ....................... 188 A1
Mead Cl. Rom .......................... 53 D4
Mead Cres. Southa ................... 79 E2
Mead End Rd. Den .................. 111 D2
Mead End Rd. Sway ................ 171 F1
Mead. Ch Fo ............................ 55 E3
Mead. Lym ............................. 198 A1
Mead Rd. Winch ....................... 10 C2
Mead The. Gos ....................... 155 D2
Mead The. Hyt ....................... 125 F2
Mead The. Liss ........................ 20 C2
Mead Way. Fare ..................... 131 D2
Meadbrook Gdns. Ch Fo ........... 55 E3
Meadcroft Cl. Lo He ............... 152 B4
Meadend Cl. Hav ................... 136 A3
Meadow Ave. Fordi ................... 69 F1
Meadow Ave. Lo He ............... 129 D2
Meadow Cl. Bran ................... 194 A4
Meadow Cl. Bur ..................... 142 C1
Meadow Cl. Fern .................... 165 E1
Meadow Cl. Fordi ..................... 69 F1
Meadow Cl. N Bad .................... 54 A2
Meadow Cl. Rin ..................... 141 D4
Meadow Cl. Shed ..................... 83 F2
Meadow Cl. Sop ..................... 193 D4
Meadow Cl. Tot ..................... 100 C3
Meadow Cl. W End .................... 80 C1
Meadow Court Cl. Bour .......... 191 D2
Meadow Ct. Fordi ..................... 69 F1
Meadow Ct. Whit ..................... 24 B2
Meadow Edge. Wat ................ 134 A1
Meadow Farm La. Broa ........... 187 E4
Meadow Gdns. Shed ................ 83 F2
Meadow Gr. Ch Fo ................... 55 E2
Meadow Gr. Ver ..................... 115 D3
Meadow La. Burt .................... 193 E1
Meadow La. Hamble ............... 128 A1
Meadow La. Lym .................... 198 B1
Meadow Rd. New M ............... 196 A2
Meadow Rd. Rin ..................... 141 D4
Meadow Rise. Broa ................ 187 F3
Meadow Rise. Wat .................. 112 A4
Meadow St. Ports ................... 182 A2
Meadow The. Den ................... 110 C2
Meadow View Rd. Bour .......... 189 F2
Meadow Way. B on S .............. 212 A4
Meadow Way. Faw .................. 151 D2
Meadow Way. Rin ................... 141 D4
Meadow Way. Ver ................. 115 D3
Meadow Way. Winch ................. 10 B2

Meadow Wlk. Gos .................. 155 D3
Meadow Wlk. Liss ..................... 20 C2
Meadowbank Rd. Fare ........... 130 B1
Meadowbank. Upt ................. 203 E4
Meadowcroft Cl. Ott ................. 31 E2
Meadowhead Rd. Southa .......... 78 C2
Meadowland. Christ ............... 209 F3
Meadowland. Ki Wo .................... 2 A4
Meadowlands. Hav ................ 136 A1
Meadowlands. Lym ................ 198 B2
Meadowlands. Ro Ca .............. 113 E2
Meadowmead Ave. Southa ...... 102 A4
Meadows Cl. Upt .................... 203 E4
Meadows Dr. Upt .................... 203 E4
Meadows The. Fare ................... 88 B2
Meadows The. Fare ................ 131 E2
Meadows The. Lyn .................. 122 A2
Meadows The. Rom ................... 28 A1
Meadows The. Wat .................. 134 B4
Meadowside Cl. Southa ............ 79 F2
Meadowsweet Rd. Broa .......... 203 F4
Meadowsweet Way. Fa Oa ....... 81 E3
Meadowsweet. Wat ................ 112 A1
Meads The. N Bad ..................... 55 D3
Meads The. Rom ....................... 52 B4
Meadway The. Christ .............. 194 B1
Mears Rd. Fa Oa ....................... 57 E1
Meath Cl. S Hay ...................... 185 E1
Medina Cl. Ch Fo ...................... 55 F3
Medina Rd. Cos ...................... 157 F4
Medina Rd. Southa .................... 78 A1
Medina Way. Christ ................ 210 B3
Medlar Cl. Burt ...................... 193 E1
Medlar Cl. He En .................... 105 E3
Medstead Rd. Hav .................. 135 F2
Medwall Green. Southa .......... 104 B3
Medway Dr. N Bad ..................... 55 D4
Medway Rd. Fern .................... 166 A3
Meerut Rd. Brock ................... 145 F1
Meeting House La. Rin ........... 140 C4
Megan Rd. W End ..................... 80 B1
Megana Way. Brai ..................... 28 B3
Meggeson Ave. Southa ............. 80 A1
Melboure Rd. Christ ............... 192 C1
Melbourne Gdns. He En ......... 105 E3
Melbourne Pl. Ports ............... 182 B2
Melbourne Rd. Bour ............... 207 E3
Melbourne Rd. Christ ............. 192 C1
Melbourne Rd. He En .............. 105 E3
Melbourne St. Southa ............ 103 D2
Melbury Ave. Poole ............... 205 F4
Melbury Cl. Fern .................... 165 E2
Melbury Cl. Lym .................... 198 B2
Melchet Cl. Plai ........................ 25 D1
Melchet Rd. Southa ................ 104 B4
Melick Cl. March ................... 101 F1
Mellstock Rd. Poole .............. 204 B3
Melrose Cl. Ports .................. 183 D2
Melrose Ct. New M ................ 196 B2
Melrose Ct. Tot ........................ 76 B1
Melrose Gdns. Gos ................ 180 C4
Melrose Rd. Southa .................. 78 B1
Melverley Gdns. Wi Mi .......... 163 E3
Melville Cl. Southa ................... 78 B3
Melville Rd. Bour ................... 206 C4
Melville Rd. Gosp .................. 181 D4
Melville Rd. Ports .................. 183 E2
Mendip Cl. New M .................. 196 B1
Mendip Cl. Ver ...................... 114 C3
Mendip Gdns. Hyt .................. 125 E2
Mendip Rd. Southa ................ 101 F4
Mendip Rd. Ver ..................... 114 C3
Mendips Rd. Fare ................... 154 C4
Mengham Ave. S Hay ............. 185 D1
Mengham La. S Hay ............... 185 D2
Mengham Rd. S Hay .............. 185 D2
Menslands La. Sob ................ 109 F4
Mentone Rd. Poole ................ 205 D2
Menzies Cl. Southa .................. 77 F3
Meon Cl. Clanf ......................... 88 B2
Meon Cl. Gos ......................... 155 D1
Meon Cl. Pet ............................ 40 C2
Meon Cl. Rom ........................... 53 E4
Meon Cres. Ch Fo ..................... 55 E3
Meon Ct. Southa .................... 104 B4
Meon Rd. Bour ....................... 208 A4
Meon Rd. Ports ...................... 183 D3
Meon Rd. Rom ........................... 53 E4
Meonwara Cres. W Meo ........... 37 E3
Mercer Way. Rom ..................... 53 D4
Merchants Wlk. Southa .......... 102 C2
Merchistoun Rd. Horn ............ 112 A4
Mercury Cl. Southa ................... 77 F2
Mercury Gdns. Hamble .......... 128 A2
Mercury Pl. Wat ..................... 134 C1
Merdon Ave. Ch Fo ................... 55 E4
Merdon Cl. Ch Fo ..................... 55 E4
Meredith Gdns. Tot ................ 100 B3
Meredith Rd. Ports ................ 157 F2
Meredun Cl. Hurs ..................... 30 A4
Merepond La. E Meo ................. 17 D1
Merepond La. Frox G ................. 17 F2
Merganser Cl. Gos ................. 181 D4
Meriden Cl. Poole .................. 216 C4
Meriden Rd. Ports ................. 182 A2
Meridians The. Christ ............ 208 C3
Merino Way. W Moo ............... 138 C1
Merlewood Cl. Bour ............... 206 C2
Merley Dr. Christ ................... 211 D4

Merley La. Oakl ..................... 163 F1
Merley Park Rd. Broa ............ 187 F4
Merley Rd. Rd. Oakl .............. 163 E1
Merley Ways. Oakl ................ 163 E1
Merlin Cl. Bi Wa ...................... 83 D4
Merlin Cl. He En .................... 105 D4
Merlin Cl. Rin ........................ 141 E3
Merlin Dr. Ports .................... 158 A2
Merlin Gdns. Portc ................ 132 A1
Merlin Way. Christ ................ 210 A3
Mermaid Way. Southa ............ 103 D1
Merrick Way. N Bad ................. 55 D4
Merridale Rd. Southa ............ 103 F3
Merriefield Cl. Broa .............. 188 A3
Merriefield Dr. Broa .............. 188 A3
Merrieleas Cl. Ch Fo ................ 55 E4
Merrieleas Dr. Ch Fo ............... 55 E4
Merriemeade Cl. Hyt ............. 125 F1
Merriemeade Par. Hyt ........... 125 F1
Merrifield. Wi Mi .................. 163 F4
Merritown La. Hurn ............... 191 E4
Merrivale Ave. Bour .............. 208 C3
Merrivale Cl. Hyt ................... 125 F2
Merrivale Ct. Southb ............. 137 E1
Merrivale Rd. Ports ............... 157 F2
Merrow Ave. Poole ................ 206 A4
Merrow Cl. Portc .................. 156 A4
Merry Gdns. N Bad .................. 54 A3
Merryfield Ave. Hav .............. 135 E3
Merryfield Cl. Bran ............... 194 A4
Merryfield La. Bour ............... 190 B2
Merryfield Rd. Pet .................. 41 D2
Merryfield. Lo He .................. 129 E2
Merryoak Green. Southa ....... 103 F3
Merryoak Rd. Southa ............ 103 F3
Merrytree Cl. W Wel ................ 50 C2
Merryweather Estate. Rin ...... 141 E4
Mersea Gdns. Southa ............ 104 A2
Mersham Gdns. Southa .......... 104 A4
Merstone Rd. Gos .................. 155 E1
Merthyr Ave. Cos .................. 158 A4
Merton Ave. Portc ................ 156 B3
Merton Cl. Fordi ...................... 69 F2
Merton Cres. Portc ............... 156 B3
Merton Gr. Rin ...................... 140 C4
Merton Rd. Ports .................. 182 B1
Merton Rd. Southa .................. 79 D2
Meryl Rd. Ports .................... 183 E2
Mesh Pond. Down ..................... 46 B4
Mesh Rd. Miche ........................ 6 A1
Meteor Rd. Th Is .................... 161 D2
Methuen Cl. Bour .................. 207 E3
Methuen Rd. Bour ................. 207 D3
Methuen Rd. Broa ................. 188 A1
Methuen Rd. Ports ................ 183 D2
Methuen St. Southa ............... 103 D4
Metuchen Way. He En ........... 105 E2
Mews Ct. Ott ........................... 31 D2
Mews La. Winch ...................... 10 C4
Mews The. Black .................... 177 F4
Mews The. Rown ...................... 77 F3
Mewsey Ct. Hav .................... 135 E4
Mey Cl. Wat .......................... 135 D4
Meynell Cl. Eastl ..................... 55 F2
Meyrick Park Cres. Bour ....... 206 C3
Meyrick Rd. Bour .................. 207 D2
Meyrick Rd. Hav .................... 135 E1
Meyrick Rd. Ports ................. 157 E1
Michael Crook Cl. Hav ........... 135 E2
Michael's Way. Hyt ............... 125 F2
Michaels Way. Fa Oa ............... 57 E1
Michelgrove Rd. Bour ........... 207 F2
Michelmersh Rd. Rown ........... 77 F3
Michelmersh Green. Bour ...... 191 E1
Michigan Way. Tot ................ 100 B4
Mickleham Cl. Poole ............. 206 A4
Midanbury Cres. Southa .......... 79 F1
Midanbury La. Southa ........... 103 F4
Midanbury Wlk. Southa ......... 103 F4
Midas Cl. Wat ....................... 134 C2
Middle Brook St. Winch .......... 11 D4
Middle Common Rd. Lym ...... 198 A2
Middle Ct. Ports .................... 182 C4
Middle La. Rin ...................... 141 D4
Middle Mead. Fare ............... 154 A4
Middle Meadow. Liss .............. 21 D2
Middle Park Way. Hav ........... 135 E3
Middle Rd. Bour .................... 190 B3
Middle Rd. Lo He ................... 129 D3
Middle Rd. Lym ..................... 198 B2
Middle Rd. N Bad .................... 54 A2
Middle Rd. Poole .................. 204 C3
Middle Rd. Southa ................ 104 A2
Middle Rd. Sway ................... 172 A1
Middle Rd. Winch .................... 10 C4
Middle St. Ports .................... 182 B2
Middle St. Southa .................. 103 D4
Middlebere Cres. Hamw ........ 203 E2
Middlebridge St. Rom .............. 52 C3
Middlebrook. Bi Wa .................. 83 E4
Middlecroft La. Gos .............. 180 C3
Middlefield. W Wit ................ 186 C1
Middlehill Rd. Wi Mi ............. 164 A3
Middlesex Rd. Ports ............. 183 D2
Middleton Cl. Fare ................ 154 C4
Middleton Cl. Southa ............... 80 A1
Middleton Rd. Bour .............. 190 C1
Middleton Rd. Rin ................ 141 D4

Middleton Wlk. Fare ............. 154 C4
Midfield Cl. Fare ................... 154 C4
Midland Rd. Bour .................. 190 C1
Midlands Estate. W End .......... 80 B1
Midlington Hill. Drox .............. 85 D4
Midlington Rd. Drox ............... 85 D4
Midway Path. Poole .............. 216 B2
Midway Rd. Ports .................. 157 F3
Midway. Hyt ......................... 125 F2
Midways. Stubb .................... 154 B1
Midwood Ave. Bour .............. 191 F1
Milbeck Cl. Wat .................... 112 A2
Milborne Cres. Poole ........... 205 F4
Milbourne Rd. Fern ............... 165 E3
Milburn Close Rd. Poole ....... 206 A2
Milburn Rd. Bour .................. 206 A2
Milbury Cres. Southa ............ 104 A3
Mildmay St. Winch ................. 10 B3
Miles La. Whit ........................ 24 B3
Milestone Rd. Poole ............. 204 B3
Milford Cl. Hav ..................... 135 E2
Milford Cl. W Moo ................ 138 C1
Milford Cres. M on S ............ 213 F2
Milford Ct. Gos ..................... 180 B2
Milford Ct. M on S ............... 213 F2
Milford Ct. Ports .................. 183 D2
Milford Dr. Bour ................... 189 F3
Milford Gdns. Ch Fo ............... 55 F3
Milford Rd. B on S ................ 212 A4
Milford Rd. Lym .................... 198 A1
Milford Rd. Ports .................. 182 B3
Military Cl. Cos ..................... 134 B1
Military Rd. Fare .................. 131 E1
Military Rd. Gos .................... 181 E1
Military Rd. Gos .................... 202 A4
Military Rd. Ports ................. 157 F3
Milkwood Ct. Tot .................. 100 B4
Mill Cl. Den .......................... 111 D2
Mill Cl. Nur ............................ 77 E3
Mill Ct. Fordi .......................... 69 F1
Mill End. Dame ....................... 68 B2
Mill End. Herm ..................... 161 D4
Mill Hill Cl. Poole ................. 205 D2
Mill Hill. Botl ....................... 106 A3
Mill La. Bold ........................ 199 F3
Mill La. Brock ...................... 146 A1
Mill La. Bur .......................... 143 E2
Mill La. Burt ......................... 193 F1
Mill La. Christ ...................... 211 D4
Mill La. Crouch ...................... 22 B4
Mill La. Durl ........................... 82 B2
Mill La. Drox .......................... 61 E1
Mill La. Gos .......................... 181 D3
Mill La. Hav .......................... 135 E1
Mill La. Hav .......................... 159 F3
Mill La. Herm ....................... 137 D1
Mill La. Hum ......................... 192 A3
Mill La. Ki Wo .......................... 2 B3
Mill La. Lym .......................... 198 C2
Mill La. Min ............................ 98 C1
Mill La. Nur ............................ 76 C2
Mill La. Pet ............................. 41 D3
Mill La. Poole ...................... 205 D2
Mill La. Ports ........................ 182 B4
Mill La. Rom ........................... 52 B4
Mill La. Sh En ....................... 133 F2
Mill La. Southw ..................... 133 D4
Mill La. Steep ........................ 40 C4
Mill La. Westb ...................... 137 D1
Mill La. Wi Mi ....................... 163 E3
Mill La. Wickh ...................... 108 A3
Mill Pond Rd. Gos ................. 181 D3
Mill Pond The. Holb .............. 150 A3
Mill Quay. Herm .................... 161 D4
Mill Rd S. Bour ..................... 191 E1
Mill Rd. Bour ........................ 191 E2
Mill Rd. Bour ........................ 191 F2
Mill Rd. Christ ...................... 209 D4
Mill Rd. Den ......................... 111 D2
Mill Rd. Fare ........................ 155 D4
Mill Rd. Gos ......................... 181 D3
Mill Rd. Liss ........................... 21 D3
Mill Rd. Ports ....................... 157 E1
Mill Rd. Southa .................... 102 A4
Mill Rd. Tot .......................... 101 D4
Mill Rd. Wat ........................ 134 C3
Mill Rd. Westb ...................... 137 D2
Mill Rise. Mott .......................... 5 E1
Mill Rythe La. N Hay ............. 185 D4
Mill St. Broa ......................... 162 A1
Mill St. Eastl .......................... 56 A2
Mill St. Lo He ....................... 154 A4
Mill Way. Tot ....................... 100 C3
Millais Rd. Southa ................ 103 F2
Milland Rd. Winch .................. 11 D3
Millbank St. Southa .............. 103 E3
Millbridge Gdns. Southa ....... 104 A2
Millbrook Cl. Ch Fo ................ 55 D3
Millbrook Dr. Hav .................. 136 A3
Millbrook Point Rd. Southa ... 102 A3
Millbrook Rd E. Southa ......... 102 B3
Millbrook Rd W. Southa ........ 102 A3
Miller Cl. New M ................... 196 B2
Miller Dr. Fare ...................... 130 C1
Millers La. Hurst ...................... 9 F2
Millers La. Winch .................... 10 A2
Millers Way. Hyt ................... 125 F1
Millfield. Broa ...................... 204 A4

Millhams Cl. Bour ................. 190 D3
Millhams Dr. Bour ................ 190 A3
Millhams Rd. Bour ............... 190 A3
Millhams St N. Christ ........... 209 D3
Millhams St. Christ .............. 209 D3
Millstream Cl. Broa .............. 204 A4
Millstream Cl. Wi Mi ............ 163 E2
Millstream Rise. Rom ............. 52 B4
Millstream Trading Est. Rin ... 141 D3
Millyford Cl. B on S .............. 211 E4
Milne Cl. Hyt ........................ 125 E1
Milne Rd. Broa ..................... 188 A1
Milner Cl. Southa .................. 102 B4
Milner Pl. Winch .................... 10 C3
Milner Rd. Bour .................... 206 B1
Milnthorpe La. Winch ............. 10 C4
Milton Cl. Poole .................... 205 E2
Milton Gr. Lo He ................... 129 D1
Milton Gr. New M .................. 196 A1
Milton Mead. New M ............ 195 F1
Milton Par. Wat ..................... 111 F1
Milton Park Ave. Ports .......... 183 D2
Milton Rd. Bour .................... 207 D3
Milton Rd. Eastl ...................... 56 A3
Milton Rd. Poole ................... 205 E2
Milton Rd. Ports ................... 183 D3
Milton Rd. Southa ................ 102 C3
Milton Rd. Wat ..................... 111 F1
Milton Rd. Wi Mi .................. 163 E3
Milverton Cl. Christ .............. 194 C1
Milverton Cl. Tot .................. 101 D3
Milverton Rd. Tot ................. 101 D3
Milverton Rd. Winch ............. 10 C4
Milvil Rd. L on S ................... 179 F3
Mimosa Ave. Oakl ................ 188 C4
Mimosa Dr. Fa Oa ................... 57 F1
Mincingfield La. Durl .............. 82 B3
Minden Way. Winch ............... 10 B3
Minerva Cl. Wat .................... 134 C1
Minstead Ave. Southa ........... 104 B4
Minstead Cl. Winch .................. 1 B2
Minstead Rd. Bour ............... 190 B2
Minstead Rd. Ports .............. 183 D2
Minster La. Winch ................... 11 D3
Minster View. Wi Mi ............. 163 E3
Minster Way. Upt .................. 203 D4
Mint Rd. Liss .......................... 21 D3
Minter's Lepe. Wat ............... 134 C2
Mintern Cl. Bish ..................... 56 B3
Minterne Rd. Bour ............... 191 D1
Minterne Rd. Christ .............. 209 F3
Minterne Rd. Poole .............. 216 B4
Mirror Cl. Lo He ................... 128 C1
Mislingford Rd. Swan ............. 84 B2
Missenden Acres. He En ....... 105 E4
Mission La. Wat .................... 112 A2
Mission Rd. Broa .................. 188 A1
Misslebrook La. Chilw ............ 54 B2
Mitchell Cl. B on S ............... 212 A4
Mitchell Cl. Lo He ................ 129 E3
Mitchell Cl. Southa ............... 103 E2
Mitchell Dr. Fa Oa ................... 57 E2
Mitchell Point. Hamble .......... 127 F1
Mitchell Rd. Hav .................. 135 D2
Mitchell Rd. Poole ................ 204 C4
Mitchell Way. Ports .............. 158 A2
Mitchells Cl. Red ..................... 47 E3
Mitchells Cl. Rom ................... 52 C4
Mitre Copse. Bish ................... 56 C1
Moat Cl. Holb ....................... 150 A2
Moat Dr. Gos ........................ 180 B2
Moat Hill. Southa .................... 79 F2
Moat La. B on S .................... 211 F4
Moat Wlk. Gos ..................... 180 B2
Mockbeggar La. Ibs .............. 117 D4
Moffat Rd. Christ .................. 209 E4
Moggs Mead. Pet .................... 41 D2
Mole Hill. Wat ...................... 134 C3
Molesworth Rd. Gos ............. 181 E2
Molyneux Rd. New M ............ 196 B2
Momford Rd. Winch ............... 10 A2
Mon Cres. Southa ................. 104 B4
Monarch Cl. Lo He ................ 129 D1
Monarch Cl. Wat ................... 135 D4
Monarch Way. W End .............. 80 C1
Monastery Rd. Southa ........... 103 F4
Monckton Rd. Gos ................ 181 D1
Monckton Rd. Ports .............. 158 A1
Moneyfield Ave. Ports .......... 158 A1
Moneyfly Rd. Ver .................. 115 D3
Monk's Hill. Westb ................ 137 D3
Monks Brook Cl. Eastl ............ 55 F1
Monks Cl. W Moo .................. 166 A4
Monks Orch. Pet ..................... 40 C3
Monks Pl. Tot ....................... 100 B3
Monks Rd. Net ...................... 127 D3
Monks Rd. Winch ..................... 2 A1
Monks Way. Bour ................. 189 E3
Monks Way. Eastl .................. 55 F1
Monks Way. Southa ................. 79 F2
Monks Wlk. Hyt .................... 149 F4
Monks Wood Cl. Southa ......... 79 D3
Monks Wood. Pet ................... 40 C3
Monkshood Cl. Christ ........... 194 A1
Monkswell Green. Christ ....... 209 D3
Monkton Cl. Fern .................. 165 E3
Monkton Cres. Poole ............ 205 F4
Monkton La. Tot .................... 100 B3

Monkwood Cl. Hav .............. 135 E3
Monkworthy Dr. St Le ......... 139 F3
Monmouth Cl. N Bad ............. 55 D3
Monmouth Cl. Ver ................ 115 D2
Monmouth Ct. Rin ............... 140 C4
Monmouth Dr. Ver ............... 115 D2
Monmouth Rd. Ports ........... 157 E1
Monnow Gdns. W End ........... 80 A1
Monroe Cl. Gos ................. 180 C2
Monsal Ave. Fern ............... 165 E2
Montacute Way. Oakl ........... 188 C4
Montago Park. Christ ........... 211 D4
Montagu Rd. Christ ............. 211 D4
Montague Ave. Southa ......... 104 B2
Montague Cl. N Bad .............. 55 D3
Montague Cl. Southa ........... 104 B2
Montague Gdns. Pet ............. 41 E2
Montague Rd. Bish ............... 56 B2
Montague Rd. Bour ............. 208 A2
Montague Rd. Ports ............ 157 F1
Montana Ct. Wat ................ 135 D3
Monterey Dr. Hord .............. 196 C2
Montfort Cl. Rom ................. 53 E4
Montfort Rd. Rom ................ 53 E3
Montgomerie Rd. Ports ........ 182 B2
Montgomery Ave. Bour ......... 190 A2
Montgomery Ave. Tot ........... 100 B4
Montgomery Rd. Gos ........... 155 E2
Montgomery Rd. Hav ........... 136 A1
Montgomery Rd. Southa ........ 104 A4
Montgomery Way. Ch Fo ........ 55 D2
Montgomery Wlk. Wat .......... 134 B3
Montrose Ave. Portc ........... 132 C1
Montrose Dr. Bour .............. 190 A1
Montserrat Rd. L on S ......... 179 F3
Monument La. Bold .............. 199 D3
Monument La. Southw .......... 132 B2
Monument La. Wal .............. 137 F4
Monxton Green. Hav ............ 136 A3
Moody Rd. Stubb ............... 154 B1
Moody's Hill. W Dean ............. 3 E1
Mooncross Ave. Tot ............ 100 C2
Moonhills La. Beaul ............ 149 D1
Moonrakers Way. Christ ........ 194 C1
Moor La. Whit ..................... 48 B4
Moor Park. Wat ................. 112 A1
Moor Rd. Broa ................... 188 A3
Moor View Rd. Poole ........... 204 C4
Moorcroft Ave. Bour ........... 193 E1
Moordown Cl. Bour ............. 191 D2
Moore Ave. Bour ............... 190 A2
Moore Cl. New M ............... 195 F1
Moore Cres. Net ................ 127 E4
Moore Gdns. Gos ............... 180 C2
Moorfield Gr. Bour ............. 190 C1
Moorfields Rd. Poole ........... 216 C4
Moorgreen Rd. Hav ............. 136 A3
Moorgreen Rd. W End ........... 80 C1
Moorhead Ct. Southa .......... 103 E1
Moorhill Gdns. W End ........... 104 C4
Moorhill Rd. W End ............. 104 B4
Moorings The. Christ ........... 209 D3
Moorings Way. Ports ........... 183 E3
Moorland Ave. B on S .......... 211 F4
Moorland Cl. Lo He ............. 129 D2
Moorland Cres. Upt ............ 203 D4
Moorland Gate. Rin ............ 141 D3
Moorland Rd. Bour ............. 207 E2
Moorland Rd. Ports ............ 182 C3
Moorland Way. Upt ............. 203 D4
Moorlands Cl. Brock ........... 145 E1
Moorlands Cres. Southa ....... 104 A4
Moorlands Rd. Swan ............ 84 A4
Moorlands Rd. Ver .............. 114 C4
Moorlands Rd. W Moo .......... 138 C2
Moorlands Rise. W Moo ........ 138 C2
Moors Cl. Co Com ................ 31 F1
Moors Cl. Hurn ................. 192 A4
Moorside Cl. Bour .............. 190 A2
Moorside Rd. Bour ............. 190 A2
Moorside Rd. Broa .............. 187 E3
Moorside Rd. W Moo ........... 138 C1
Moorside Rd. Winch ............... 2 B1
Moortown Ave. Cos ............ 134 B1
Moortown La. Rin .............. 141 E2
Moorvale Rd. Bour ............. 191 D1
Moot Cl. Down .................... 47 D4
Moot Gdns. Down ................ 46 C3
Moot La. Down .................... 46 C3
Moot La. Red ...................... 46 C3
Mopley Cl. Black ............... 177 F4
Mopley. Black ................... 177 F4
Morant Cl. Rin .................. 117 D1
Morant Cl. Gosp ................ 181 E4
Moraunt Dr. Portc .............. 156 A3
Mordaunt Rd. Southa .......... 103 D4
Morden Ave. Fern .............. 165 E4
Morden Rd. Bour ............... 190 C1
Moreland Rd. Gos .............. 181 D3
Morelands Ct. Wat ............. 134 C2
Morelands Rd. Wat ............. 134 C2
Morestead Rd. Chilc ............. 11 F2
Morestead Rd. Ows .............. 11 F1
Morestead Rd. Ows .............. 58 C4
Morestead Rd. Winch ........... 11 E2
Moreton Rd. Bour .............. 191 D2
Morgan Rd. He En .............. 105 E3
Morgan Rd. Ports .............. 183 E2
Morgan's La. Pent ............... 42 A1

Morgans Dr. Stubb ............. 154 B3
Morgans Rise Rd. Red ........... 47 E4
Morgans Vale Rd. Red ........... 47 E3
Morland Rd. Southa .............. 78 B1
Morley Cl. Burt ................. 193 E2
Morley Cl. Southa .............. 103 F3
Morley Cres. Wat .............. 112 A2
Morley Dr. Bi Wa ................ 83 E4
Morley Rd. Bour ................ 208 A3
Morley Rd. Ports ............... 183 D1
Morningside Ave. Portc ........ 132 C1
Mornington Dr. Winch ............. 1 B1
Mornish Rd. Poole .............. 205 F1
Morpeth Ave. Tot ............... 100 C4
Morris Cl. Gos .................. 155 E2
Morris Rd. Southa .............. 102 C3
Morrison Ave. Poole ........... 205 F3
Morshead Cres. Fare ........... 131 D2
Mortimer Cl. Christ ............ 210 A3
Mortimer Cl. Ki Wo ................ 2 A3
Mortimer Cl. Net ............... 127 D3
Mortimer Cl. Tot .................. 76 B1
Mortimer Rd. Botl .............. 106 A3
Mortimer Rd. Bour ............. 191 D1
Mortimer Rd. Gos .............. 133 E1
Mortimer Rd. Southa ........... 103 E2
Mortimer Way. N Bad ............ 53 F2
Mortimers Dr. Fa Oa ............. 57 F3
Mortimers La. Fa Oa ............. 58 A2
Mortimers Lawn. Hav ........... 135 E4
Mortimore Rd. Gos ............. 180 C3
Mosdell Rd. Southb ............ 161 F4
Moss Cl. Liss ..................... 21 D2
Moss Dr. March ................. 101 F1
Moss Rd. Winch ................... 11 D4
Mossleigh Ave. Southa .......... 77 F3
Mossley Ave. Poole ............ 190 A1
Motcombe Rd. Poole ........... 206 A1
Mottisfont Cl. Southa .......... 102 A3
Mottisfont Rd. Eastl ............. 56 A2
Moulin Ave. Ports .............. 182 C1
Mound Cl. Gos .................. 181 D2
Mount Ave. New M ............. 196 A1
Mount Cl. New M ............... 196 A1
Mount Cl. Winch ................... 1 C2
Mount Dr. Ch Fo .................. 55 F2
Mount Dr. Fare ................. 154 A4
Mount Grace Dr. Poole ........ 216 B4
Mount House Cl. Hyt ........... 126 A3
Mount La. Locke .................. 25 F4
Mount Pleasant Dr. Bour ...... 191 F1
Mount Pleasant La. Lym ....... 198 A4
Mount Pleasant La. Rin ........ 141 D4
Mount Pleasant La. Sway ...... 198 A4
Mount Pleasant Rd. Gos ....... 181 D2
Mount Pleasant Rd. Southa ... 103 D3
Mount Pleasant. Ki Wo ........... 2 B3
Mount Rd. Bour ................. 190 A2
Mount Rd. Poole ................ 205 D3
Mount Temple. Rom .............. 53 D4
Mount The. Gos ................ 155 F1
Mount The. Rin ................. 141 E4
Mount The. Southa ............... 78 C2
Mount View Rd. Winch ........... 10 A2
Mount View. Eastl ................ 56 A2
Mountain Ash Cl. Southa ...... 104 B4
Mountbatten Cl. Christ ........ 210 A3
Mountbatten Cl. Gos ........... 155 E2
Mountbatten Cl. Winch ........... 1 C2
Mountbatten Dr. Fern .......... 165 E3
Mountbatten Dr. Wat ........... 134 B3
Mountbatten Gdns. Bour ...... 191 F1
Mountbatten Pl. Ki Wo ........... 2 B4
Mountbatten Rd. Bour ......... 206 A1
Mountbatten Rd. Eastl ........... 56 A3
Mountbatten Rd. Tot ........... 100 B4
Mountbatten Way. Rom .......... 52 C4
Mountbatten Way. Southa ..... 102 B3
Mountfield. Hyt ................. 125 F2
Mountjoy Cl. Oakl .............. 163 F1
Mountwood Rd. Southb ........ 137 E1
Mousehole La. Hyt ............. 126 A2
Mousehole La. Southa .......... 103 F4
Mousehole Rd. Portc ........... 132 C1
Mowbray Rd. Southa ........... 104 A2
Moxhams. Fordi ................... 69 F1
Mt Pleasant Dr. Bran .......... 169 E1
Mt Pleasant Rd. Poole ......... 204 B2
Muccleshell Cl. Hav ............ 136 A2
Muddyford Rd. Red ............... 47 E4
Mude Gdns. Christ ............. 210 A3
Mudeford Green Cl. Christ .... 209 F3
Mudeford La. Christ ........... 209 F3
Mudeford. Christ ............... 210 A3
Mulberry Ave. Cos ............. 158 A4
Mulberry Ave. Stubb ........... 154 B1
Mulberry Cl. Gos ............... 181 D2
Mulberry Gdns. Fordi ........... 93 F4
Mulberry Gr. Hord ............. 213 E4
Mulberry La. Cos ............... 158 A4
Mulberry Mews. Fordi ........... 93 F4
Mulberry Rd. March ............ 101 F1
Mulberry Wlk. Southa .......... 102 B4
Mullen Cl. Southa .............. 103 F2
Mullins Cl. Poole .............. 206 B4
Mumby Rd. Gos ................. 181 E3
Mundays Row. Horn .............. 88 B1
Munro Cres. Southa ............ 101 F4

Munster Rd. Poole ............. 205 E2
Munster Rd. Ports ............. 157 E1
Murefield Rd. Ports ........... 182 B3
Muriel Rd. Wat ................. 134 C4
Murley Rd. Bour ............... 207 D4
Murray Cl. Fare ................ 130 C1
Murray Cl. Southa ............. 104 C3
Murray Rd. Horn ............... 112 A3
Murrills Estate. Portc ......... 156 C4
Muscliffe La. Bour ............. 191 D2
Muscliffe Rd. Bour ............ 190 C1
Museum Rd. Ports ............. 182 A2
Mussett Cl. Tot ................ 100 C4
My Lords La. S Hay ............ 185 D2
Myers Cl. Swan .................. 84 A3
Myrtle Ave. Portc ............. 156 B4
Myrtle Ave. Tot ................ 100 B3
Myrtle Cl. Gos ................. 155 D2
Myrtle Cl. Hord ................ 196 C2
Myrtle Gr. Ports ............... 183 D4
Myrtle Rd. Bour ............... 207 E3
Myrtle Rd. Southa ............... 78 A2
Myvern Cl. Holb ................ 150 B2

Nada Rd. Christ ................ 194 B1
Nailsworth Rd. Cos ............ 133 D1
Nairn Rd. Bour ................. 206 C3
Nairn Rd. Poole ................ 216 C4
Naish Cl. Hav .................. 135 E4
Naish Dr. Gos .................. 156 A1
Naish Rd. B on S ............... 211 F4
Namu Rd. Bour ................. 190 C1
Nancy Rd. Ports ............... 182 C3
Nansen Ave. Poole ............. 204 B3
Napier Cres. Fare ............. 130 B1
Napier Rd. Hamw ............... 203 E2
Napier Rd. Horn ................ 112 B3
Napier Rd. Ports .............. 182 B1
Napier Rd. Southa ............. 104 C3
Narrow La. Rom .................. 52 C4
Narvik Rd. Ports ............... 157 E2
Naseby Cl. Cos ................. 133 D1
Naseby Rd. Bour ............... 191 D1
Nash Cl. Hyt ................... 125 E1
Nash Rd. Hyt ................... 125 E1
Nashe Cl. Fare ................. 130 B2
Nashe Way. Fare ............... 130 B2
Nasmith Cl. Gos ............... 180 B2
Nations Hill. Ki Wo ............... 2 B3
Navigator's Way. He En ....... 105 E4
Nea Cl. Christ .................. 210 B4
Nea Rd. Christ ................. 210 C4
Neath Way. N Bad ............... 55 D3
Needles Point. M on S ........ 213 E4
Neelands Gr. Portc ............ 156 C4
Neilson Cl. Ch Fo ............... 55 E4
Nelson Ave. Portc ............. 156 A4
Nelson Ave. Ports ............. 157 E1
Nelson Cl. Holb ................ 150 B2
Nelson Cl. New M .............. 195 F2
Nelson Cl. Rom .................. 52 C4
Nelson Cres. Horn ............. 112 B4
Nelson Ct. Fare ................ 154 C3
Nelson Ct. Hyt ................. 126 A1
Nelson Dr. Christ .............. 209 F3
Nelson La. Portc .............. 132 B1
Nelson Pl. Lym ................. 198 C2
Nelson Rd. Bish ................. 56 B2
Nelson Rd. Bour ............... 206 A2
Nelson Rd. Gos ................. 181 D2
Nelson Rd. Poole .............. 206 A2
Nelson Rd. Ports .............. 182 B4
Nelson Rd. Southa ............. 102 B3
Nelson Rd. Winch ................ 11 E3
Nepean Cl. Gos ................ 181 D1
Neptune Ct. Southa ............. 77 F2
Neptune Rd. Fare ............. 130 B1
Neptune Way. Southa .......... 103 D1
Nerissa Cl. Wat ................ 135 D4
Nerquis Cl. Rom ................. 53 D4
Nesbitt Cl. Gos ................ 155 D2
Nessus St. Ports ............... 182 B4
Netherfield Cl. Hav ........... 136 A1
Netherhall Gdns. Bour ........ 206 B2
Netherton Rd. Gos ............. 180 C4
Netherwood Pl. Wi Mi ......... 163 D3
Netley Cl. Ch Fo ................. 55 D2
Netley Cl. Poole ............... 205 D4
Netley Firs Cl. He En .......... 104 C3
Netley Firs Rd. He En .......... 105 D3
Netley Hill Estate. He En ..... 104 C2
Netley Lodge Cl. Net .......... 127 E3
Netley Rd. Lo He ............... 129 E1
Netley Rd. Ports ............... 182 B1
Netley Terr. Ports ............. 182 B1
Nettlecombe Ave. Ports ...... 182 C1
Nettlestone Rd. Ports ......... 183 D1
Nettlestone. Net .............. 127 E4
Nettleton Cl. Poole ........... 204 C4
Netton Cl. Crouch .............. 22 A4
Netton St. Crouch .............. 22 B4
Neva Rd. Southa ............... 103 F4
Nevil Shute Rd. Ports ......... 158 A2
Neville Ave. Portc ............. 156 B3
Neville Gdns. Ems ............. 136 C2
Neville Rd. Ports .............. 183 D4
New Borough Rd. Wi Mi ....... 163 E2
New Brighton Rd. Ems ........ 136 C1
New Cotts. Nur .................. 77 E1

New Cut. N Hay ................ 159 F2
New Down La. Cos ............. 134 A1
New Down La. Southw ........ 134 A1
New Forest Dr. Brock ......... 145 E1
New Harbour Rd. Hamw ...... 204 A1
New Harbour Rd W. Hamw .... 204 A1
New Inn Cotts. E Bol .......... 175 E3
New Inn La. Cadn ............... 99 D3
New Inn Rd. Cadn ............... 99 D4
New La. Hav ................... 136 A2
New La. M on S ................ 213 F2
New La. New M ................ 195 F3
New Merrifield. Wi Mi ......... 163 F4
New Orchard. Poole ........... 204 A1
New Par. Bour ................. 190 C2
New Par. Portc ................ 156 B4
New Park Rd. Bour ............ 208 B2
New Quay Rd. Hamw .......... 204 A1
New Rd E. Ports ............... 182 C4
New Rd. Ashu .................. 100 B1
New Rd. Black ................. 150 C1
New Rd. Bour .................. 190 C3
New Rd. Clanf ................... 88 B3
New Rd. Co Com ................. 31 F1
New Rd. Fa Oa .................. 57 D1
New Rd. Fare .................. 131 D1
New Rd. Faw ................... 150 B4
New Rd. Fern .................. 165 F2
New Rd. Hav ................... 135 F1
New Rd. Horn .................. 111 F3
New Rd. Hyt ................... 150 B4
New Rd. Ibs ................... 117 D4
New Rd. Lan .................... 49 F1
New Rd. Litt ..................... 1 A3
New Rd. Lo He ................. 152 C4
New Rd. M on S ................ 214 A2
New Rd. Meons .................. 61 E2
New Rd. Mich ................... 27 E4
New Rd. Net ................... 127 D3
New Rd. Poole ................. 205 E3
New Rd. Ports ................. 182 C4
New Rd. Rin ................... 141 D2
New Rd. Rockb .................. 44 C1
New Rd. Rom ................... 53 D4
New Rd. Southa ................ 103 D3
New Rd. Southb ................ 161 F4
New Rd. Swan .................. 84 A3
New Rd. Swanw ................ 128 C4
New Rd. Westb ................. 137 D2
New Rd. Woodl ................. 114 A3
New St. Lym ................... 198 C2
New St. Poole ................. 204 A1
New St. Rin ................... 141 D3
New Town. Portc ............... 156 B4
New Valley Rd. M on S ........ 213 E3
Newbarn La. Wal .............. 137 F4
Newbarn Rd. Hav .............. 135 E2
Newbolt Cl. Wat ............... 111 F2
Newbolt Rd. Portc ............ 132 C1
Newbridge Rd. Cadn ............ 75 D1
Newbridge Way. Lym .......... 198 B3
Newbridge. Net ................ 127 E3
Newbroke Rd. Gos ............. 180 C4
Newburgh St. Winch ............ 10 C4
Newbury Cl. Fa Oa .............. 57 D1
Newbury Dr. Bour ............. 190 B1
Newbury Rd. Southa ............ 78 B1
Newcliffe Gdns. He En ........ 105 D3
Newcombe Rd. Bour ........... 208 C3
Newcombe Rd. Southa ......... 102 C3
Newcombe Rd. W Moo ......... 138 B2
Newcome Rd. Ports ........... 182 C3
Newcomen Rd. Ports .......... 157 E1
Newcroft Gdns. Christ ......... 209 D4
Newenham Rd. Lym ............ 198 C1
Newfield Rd. Liss ............... 21 D3
Newfoundland Dr. Poole ...... 204 B1
Newgate La. Fare .............. 155 D2
Newgate La. Gos ............... 155 E3
Newgate La. Stubb ............ 155 D2
Newland Ave. Gos ............. 181 D2
Newlands Ave. Southa ......... 102 B4
Newlands Cl. Black ............ 150 C1
Newlands Copse. Black ........ 150 C1
Newlands La. Den .............. 134 A4
Newlands La. Southw .......... 134 A4
Newlands Rd. Bour ............ 208 A3
Newlands Rd. Christ ........... 209 F4
Newlands Rd. Faw ............. 150 C1
Newlands Rd. New M .......... 196 A1
Newlands Rd. Wat ............. 134 B3
Newlands Way. Broa ........... 187 E2
Newlease Rd. Wat ............. 134 C3
Newlyn Way. Poole ............ 205 F4
Newlyn Way. Ports ............ 157 D4
Newlyn Wlk. Rom ................ 28 A1
Newman St. Southa ............ 102 A4
Newman's La. W Moo .......... 138 B2
Newmans Cl. W Moo .......... 138 C3
Newmans Hill. Shed ............ 84 B1
Newmans Hill. Swan ............ 84 B1
Newmer Ct. Hav ............... 135 E3
Newmorton Rd. Bour .......... 191 D2
Newney Cl. Ports .............. 157 F2
Newport La. Brai ................ 28 B4
Newport Rd. Gos .............. 180 C3
Newstead Rd. Bour ............ 208 C2
Newton Cl. Stubb .............. 154 B3
Newton Cl. Whit ................. 24 A2

Newton La. Rom ................. 52 C3
Newton La. Whit ................. 24 A2
Newton Morrell. Poole ........ 205 E2
Newton Pl. L on S .............. 179 F4
Newton Rd. B on S ............ 212 A4
Newton Rd. Poole .............. 216 C4
Newton Rd. Southa .............. 79 F1
Newton Rd. Twyf ................ 32 A4
Newtown La. Broa .............. 187 E4
Newtown La. S Hay ............ 184 C2
Newtown La. Ver ............... 115 D3
Newtown Rd. Eastl .............. 56 A2
Newtown Rd. Lo He ............ 152 B4
Newtown Rd. Sh En .............. 26 A2
Newtown Rd. Southa ........... 104 A1
Newtown Rd. Ver ............... 115 D3
Nichol Rd. Ch Fo ................. 30 B1
Nicholas Cl. Christ ............ 195 D1
Nicholas Cres. Fare ........... 130 C1
Nicholas Gdns. Bour .......... 190 B1
Nicholas Rd. Black ............ 177 F4
Nicholl Pl. Gos ................ 155 E1
Nichols Rd. Southa ............ 103 D3
Nicholson Cl. Poole ........... 204 C4
Nicholson Way. Hav ........... 135 F2
Nicholson Wlk. Rown ........... 77 E3
Nickel Cl. Winch ................. 11 D4
Nickel St. Ports ............... 182 A2
Nickleby Gdns. Tot ............ 100 A4
Nickleby Rd. Clanf .............. 88 A3
Nightingale Ave. Eastl .......... 55 E1
Nightingale Cl. Gos ........... 180 C3
Nightingale Cl. Ro Ca ......... 113 D1
Nightingale Cl. Rom ............ 53 D4
Nightingale Cl. Ver ............ 115 D3
Nightingale Cl. W Wel ........... 50 B2
Nightingale Cres. Shed ........ 107 F4
Nightingale Dr. Tot ............ 100 B4
Nightingale Gr. Southa ....... 102 B4
Nightingale Mews. Net ........ 127 E3
Nightingale Park. Hav ......... 136 A1
Nightingale Rd. Burs .......... 127 F4
Nightingale Rd. Pet ............. 40 C1
Nightingale Rd. Ports ......... 182 A1
Nightingale Rd. Southa ....... 102 B4
Nightingale Wlk. Net .......... 127 E3
Nightjar Cl. Broa .............. 203 F4
Nile Rd. Southa ................. 79 D1
Nile St. Ems ................... 160 C4
Nimrod Dr. Gos ................ 180 B3
Nine Elms La. Fare ............ 131 F2
Ninian Cl. Fa Oa ................ 57 E1
Ninian Park Rd. Ports ......... 158 A1
Niton Cl. Gos .................. 155 E1
Noads Cl. Hyt .................. 125 F1
Noads Way. Hyt ................ 125 F1
Nobbs La. Ports ............... 182 A2
Nobes Ave. Gos ................ 155 E2
Nobes Cl. Gos .................. 155 E1
Noble Cl. Bour ................. 189 F1
Noble Rd. He En ............... 105 E3
Noel Cl. Brock ................. 146 A1
Noel Rd. Bour .................. 190 A1
Noel The. New M ............... 196 B2
Nook The. Eastl ................. 56 A3
Nook The. Gos ................. 155 F1
Noon Gdns. Ver ................ 115 D3
Noon Hill Dr. Ver .............. 115 D3
Noon Hill Rd. Ver .............. 115 D3
Norbury Cl. Ch Fo ............... 55 D4
Norbury Gdns. Hamble ........ 127 F1
Norcliffe Cl. Bour ............. 190 A2
Norcliffe Rd. Southa ........... 103 D4
Nordik Gdns. He En ........... 105 E3
Nore Farm Ave. Ems ........... 136 B1
Noreuil Rd. Pet .................. 40 B2
Norfolk Ave. Christ ........... 192 C1
Norfolk Cres. S Hay ........... 184 C1
Norfolk Rd. Gos ............... 180 C4
Norfolk Rd. Southa ............ 102 B4
Norfolk St. Ports .............. 182 B2
Norgett Way. Portc ............ 156 A4
Norham Ave. Southa ............ 78 B1
Norham Cl. Southa .............. 78 B1
Norland Rd. Ports ............. 182 C2
Norlands Dr. Ott ................. 31 E2
Norley Cl. Hav ................. 135 F3
Norleywood Rd. Bold .......... 199 F4
Norleywood. Christ ............ 210 C4
Norman Ave. Poole ............ 206 A3
Norman Cl. Portc .............. 156 B3
Norman Gdns. He En ........... 105 D3
Norman Gdns. Poole ........... 206 A3
Norman Rd. Black .............. 177 F4
Norman Rd. Gos ............... 181 D3
Norman Rd. Ports ............. 182 C2
Norman Rd. S Hay ............. 185 D1
Norman Rd. Southa ............ 102 B3
Norman Rd. Winch ............... 10 C3
Norman Way. Hav .............. 135 E1
Normandy Cl. Rown ............. 77 E3
Normandy Cl. Sway ............ 172 A1
Normandy Dr. Christ ........... 209 E4
Normandy Gdns. Gos .......... 180 C2
Normandy La. Lym ............. 198 C1
Normandy Rd. Ports ........... 157 F2
Normandy Way. Fordi ........... 69 F1
Normandy Way. Hamw ........ 203 E1

Normandy Way. March ........ 102 A1
Normanhurst Ave. Bour ...... 191 F1
Normanton Cl. Christ ......... 192 C1
Norris Cl. Rom ....................... 28 B1
Norris Cl. St Le ................... 139 F2
Norris Gdns. Hav ................ 160 A4
Norris Gdns. New M ........... 196 A1
Norris Hill. Southa ................ 79 F1
Norrish Rd. Poole .............. 205 E3
Norset Rd. Fare .................. 130 B1
North Ave. Bour .................. 190 B3
North Ave. Ports ................ 157 F3
North Bay. Th Is ................. 161 D2
North Cl. Gos ..................... 180 C2
North Cl. Hav ..................... 160 A4
North Cl. Lym .................... 198 C2
North Cl. Rom ...................... 28 B1
North Common La. Lan ........ 49 D3
North Common La. Sway ..... 197 F4
North Cres. S Hay .............. 185 D2
North Cross St. Gos ........... 181 E2
North Cross St. Ports ......... 182 B4
North Ct. Ports .................. 182 C4
North Dr. Litt ......................... 1 A3
North East Cl. Southa ........ 104 B3
North East Rd. Southa ....... 104 A2
North End Ave. Ports ......... 157 E1
North End Cl. Ch Fo ............. 55 E2
North End Gr. Ports ........... 157 E1
North End La. Ibs ................. 93 E2
North Front. Southa ........... 103 D3
North Greenlands. Lym ...... 198 B1
North Head. M on S ........... 213 D3
North Hill Cl. Winch ............... 1 C1
North Hill. Fare .................. 131 D2
North La. Beaul .................. 148 C3
North La. Buri ...................... 65 F3
North La. Clanf .................... 88 B4
North La. E Meo ................... 64 B1
North La. Red ...................... 73 E4
North La. W Tyth ................... 4 A4
North Lodge Rd. Poole ....... 205 F2
North Millers Dale. Ch Fo ... 55 D4
North Path. Gos ................. 180 B3
North Poulner Rd. Rin ........ 117 D1
North Rd. Bour ................... 207 F3
North Rd. Brock ................. 146 A1
North Rd. Horn ..................... 88 B1
North Rd. Hyt .................... 125 F1
North Rd. Ki Wo ..................... 2 A4
North Rd. Pet ...................... 40 C2
North Rd. Poole .................. 204 A1
North Rd. Poole .................. 205 D2
North Rd. Southa ............... 103 E4
North Shore Rd. S Hay ....... 184 B2
North St. Ems .................... 136 C1
North St. Gos .................... 181 E2
North St. Hav .................... 135 E1
North St. Lym .................... 198 B1
North St. Poole .................. 204 B1
North St. Ports .................. 182 B3
North St. Westb ................. 137 D2
North Town. Twyf ................ 32 A4
North Wallington. Fare ....... 131 E1
North Walls. Winch .............. 11 D4
North Way. Gos .................. 155 D2
North Way. Hav .................. 135 F1
North Way. Lo He .............. 129 F2
North Weirs. Brock ............ 145 E1
Northam Rd. Southa ........... 103 D3
Northam St. Ports .............. 182 B3
Northampton La. Black ....... 177 F4
Northarbour Rd. Cos .......... 157 E4
Northarbour Spur. Cos ....... 157 E4
Northbourne Ave. Bour ...... 190 B3
Northbourne Cl. Hyt .......... 126 A1
Northbourne Gdns. Bour .... 190 C3
Northbourne Pl. Bour ........ 190 B3
Northbrook Ave. Winch ........ 11 E4
Northbrook Cl. Ports .......... 182 B4
Northbrook Cl. Winch ........... 11 E4
Northbrook Rd. Broa .......... 188 A1
Northbrook Rd. Southa ...... 103 D3
Northcote Rd. Bour ............ 207 D2
Northcote Rd. Ports ........... 182 C2
Northcote Rd. Southa .......... 79 E1
Northcroft Rd. Gos ............ 180 C3
Northdene Rd. Ch Fo ........... 55 E3
Northend La. Drox ............... 61 D1
Northern Access Rd. Faw .... 151 E1
Northern Anchorage. Southa 103 E2
Northern Par. Ports ........... 157 F2
Northern Rd. Cos ............... 157 F4
Northerwood Ave. Lyn ....... 121 F3
Northerwood Cl. N Bad ........ 53 F2
Northey Rd. Bour ............... 208 C3
Northfield Ave. Fare ........... 154 C4
Northfield Cl. Bi Wa ............. 59 D1
Northfield Cl. Horn ............... 88 B1
Northfield Park. Portc ........ 132 A1
Northfield Rd. M on S ........ 213 F2
Northfield Rd. Rin .............. 117 D1
Northfield Rd. Southa .......... 79 F2
Northfields Farm La. Wickh . 108 A3
Northgate Ave. Ports ......... 182 C4
Northlands Cl. Tot ............. 100 B4
Northlands Dr. Winch ............ 2 A1
Northlands Gdns. Southa .... 102 C4
Northlands Rd. Eastl ........... 56 A2

Northlands Rd. Rom ............. 53 E3
Northlands Rd. Southa ....... 102 C4
Northlands Rd. Tot ............ 100 C4
Northleigh Cnr. Southa ........ 79 F3
Northleigh La. Wi Mi .......... 163 F3
Northmead Dr. Broa ........... 203 F4
Northmere Dr. Poole .......... 205 F4
Northmere Rd. Poole ......... 205 F4
Northmore Cl. Lo He .......... 129 D3
Northmore Rd. Lo He ......... 129 D3
Northney La. N Hay ............ 160 B2
Northney Rd. N Hay ........... 160 A2
Northolt Gdns. Southa ......... 78 A3
Northover La. Sway ........... 196 C4
Northover Rd. Lym ............. 198 A2
Northover Rd. Ports ........... 183 D4
Northumberland Rd. Ports .. 182 C3
Northumberland Rd. Southa 103 D3
Northways. Stubb .............. 154 B1
Northwood Cl. Southa .......... 79 D3
Northwood La. N Hay ......... 160 A1
Northwood Rd. Ports ......... 157 F3
Northwood Sq. Fare ........... 131 D1
Nortoft Rd. Bour ............... 207 D3
Norton Cl. Southa .............. 103 F2
Norton Cl. Southw ............. 132 C3
Norton Cl. Wat .................. 134 B4
Norton Dr. Fare ................ 131 D2
Norton Rd. Bour ................ 206 C4
Norton Rd. Southw ............ 132 C3
Norton Welch Cl. N Bad ....... 54 A2
Norway Rd. Ports .............. 158 A2
Norwich Ave W. Bour ......... 206 B2
Norwich Ave. Bour ............ 206 B2
Norwich Cl. Lo He ............. 128 C2
Norwich Pl. L on S ............ 179 F4
Norwich Rd. Bour .............. 206 C2
Norwich Rd. Cos ............... 133 E1
Norwich Rd. Southa ............ 79 F1
Norwood Pl. Bour .............. 208 A3
Nottingham Pl. L on S ........ 179 F4
Nouale La. Min .................. 141 E4
Novello Gdns. Wat ............. 134 C3
Noyce Dr. Fa Oa .................. 57 E1
Noyce Gdns. Bour .............. 192 A1
Nuffield Rd. Poole ............. 204 B4
Nugent Rd. Bour ............... 209 D2
Nunns Park. Whit ................ 24 A2
Nuns Rd. Winch .................... 2 A1
Nurse's Path. Twyf .............. 32 A3
Nursery Cl. Ems ............... 136 C2
Nursery Cl. Gos ................ 155 D2
Nursery Gdns. Ch Fo ........... 55 E2
Nursery Gdns. Rom ............. 53 D4
Nursery Gdns. Southa ....... 104 A3
Nursery Gdns. Wat ............ 112 A3
Nursery Gdns. Winch ........... 10 B4
Nursery Gr. He En .............. 105 E3
Nursery La. Stubb .............. 154 B1
Nursery Rd. Bour .............. 191 D2
Nursery Rd. Rin ................ 141 D3
Nursery Rd. Southa ............. 79 E1
Nursling Green. Bour ......... 191 E1
Nursling St. Nur .................. 77 E3
Nutash. Lo He ................... 129 E2
Nutbeem Rd. Eastl .............. 56 A1
Nutbourne Cl. Cos ............. 158 B4
Nutbourne Rd. S Hay ......... 185 F1
Nutburn Rd. N Bad .............. 54 A3
Nutfield Ct. Southa .............. 77 F2
Nutfield Pl. Ports ............... 182 B3
Nutfield Rd. Rown ................ 77 E3
Nuthatch Cl. Broa .............. 203 F4
Nuthatch Cl. Fern .............. 165 D4
Nuthatch Cl. Ro Ca ............ 113 D1
Nutley Cl. Bour ................. 189 F2
Nutley Rd. Hav .................. 135 E3
Nutley Way. Bour .............. 189 F2
Nutsey Ave. Tot .................. 76 B1
Nutsey Cl. Tot .................... 76 C1
Nutsey La. Tot ..................... 76 C1
Nutshalling Ave. Rown ......... 77 F3
Nutshalling Cl. Tot .............. 76 B1
Nutwick Rd. Hav ................ 136 A2
Nutwood Way. Tot ............... 76 C1
Nyewood Ave. Portc .......... 132 B1
Nyria Way. Gos ................. 181 E2

O'connell Rd. Eastl .............. 55 F1
Oak Ave. Christ ................. 208 B4
Oak Cl. Fern ..................... 165 F1
Oak Cl. Hyt ....................... 125 F1
Oak Cl. Lyn ...................... 121 F2
Oak Cl. Southa .................. 101 E4
Oak Cl. Uph ....................... 58 C3
Oak Cl. Wat ...................... 111 F1
Oak Coppice Cl. Fa Oa ......... 57 D1
Oak Dr. Fa Oa ..................... 57 E1
Oak Gdns. Hord ................. 213 E4
Oak Green Way. Southa ...... 104 A4
Oak La. Rin ...................... 141 D4
Oak Mews. Poole ............... 205 E3
Oak Rd. Alderh .................... 92 C3
Oak Rd. Bi Wa ..................... 83 F4
Oak Rd. Bour .................... 207 E3
Oak Rd. Burs .................... 127 F4
Oak Rd. Clanf ..................... 88 B3
Oak Rd. Fare ..................... 130 B1
Oak Rd. Hyt ...................... 125 F1

Oak Rd. New M .................. 196 B2
Oak Rd. Southa .................. 103 F1
Oak Rd. Upt ...................... 203 E3
Oak St. Gos ...................... 181 E2
Oak Tree Cl. Co Comm ......... 56 C4
Oak Tree Dr. Ems .............. 136 C2
Oak Tree Dr. Liss ................. 21 D2
Oak Tree Gdns. He En ........ 105 D3
Oak Tree Rd. Southa ............ 79 F1
Oak Tree Way. Eastl ............ 56 A3
Oak Vale. W End .................. 80 A2
Oakapple Gdns. Cos ........... 158 B4
Oakbank Rd. Bish ................ 56 B2
Oakbank Rd. Southa ........... 103 E2
Oakcroft La. Stubb ............ 154 B3
Oakdale Rd. Poole ............. 204 C3
Oakdene Cl. Wi Mi ............. 163 E3
Oakdene. Gos ................... 155 E1
Oakdene. Tot ..................... 100 B4
Oakdown Rd. Stubb ........... 154 B2
Oakenbrow. Hyt ................ 125 E2
Oakes The. Stubb .............. 154 A2
Oakfield Ct. Hav ............... 136 A3
Oakfield Rd. Cadn ............... 99 D4
Oakfield Rd. Poole ............. 204 B3
Oakfield Rd. Tot ................ 100 C4
Oakfields. Eastl ................... 56 A4
Oakford Ct. Bour ............... 191 E2
Oakgrove Gdns. Bish ........... 56 C1
Oakgrove Rd. Bish .............. 56 C1
Oakhill Cl. Burs ................. 105 D1
Oakhill Cl. Ch Fo ................. 55 F3
Oakhill. Burs ..................... 105 D1
Oakhurst Cl. Net ............... 127 E3
Oakhurst Cl. W Moo ........... 138 C1
Oakhurst Dr. Wat .............. 135 D4
Oakhurst Gdns. Wat .......... 134 A1
Oakhurst La. W Moo .......... 138 C1
Oakhurst Rd. Southa ............ 79 D2
Oakhurst Rd. W Moo .......... 138 C1
Oakhurst Way. Net ............ 127 E3
Oakland Dr. March .............. 101 F1
Oakland Wlk. Fern ............. 165 F1
Oaklands Ave. Tot ............. 100 C4
Oaklands Cl. Fordi ............... 69 F1
Oaklands Cl. Ver ............... 114 C3
Oaklands Gdns. Lo He ....... 129 E1
Oaklands Gr. Wat .............. 111 F2
Oaklands Rd. Hav .............. 136 A1
Oaklands Rd. Pet ................ 40 C2
Oaklands The. Ch Fo ............ 55 E2
Oaklands Way. Hyt ............ 125 E2
Oaklands Way. Lo He ......... 129 E1
Oaklands Way. Southa .......... 78 C2
Oaklands. Lym .................. 198 C1
Oaklea Cl. Wat .................. 134 A1
Oakleigh Cres. Tot ............ 100 C3
Oakleigh Dr. Red ................. 73 E4
Oakleigh Gdns. Rom ............ 53 D4
Oakleigh Way. Christ ......... 210 C4
Oakley Cl. Holb ................. 150 B2
Oakley Gdns. Upt ............. 203 D4
Oakley Hill. Oakl ................ 163 E1
Oakley La. Oakl ................. 163 F1
Oakley Rd. Hav ................. 135 E3
Oakley Rd. Mott .................... 5 F2
Oakley Rd. Oakl ................ 163 E1
Oakley Rd. Southa ............. 102 A4
Oakley Straight. Oakl ......... 163 F1
Oakmead Rd. Broa ............ 203 F4
Oakmeadow Cl. Ems ......... 137 D2
Oakmount Ave. Ch Fo .......... 55 E2
Oakmount Ave. Southa ........ 79 D1
Oakmount Ave. Tot ............ 100 C4
Oakmount Dr. Wat .............. 111 F1
Oakmount Rd. Ch Fo ........... 55 F3
Oakridge Rd. Southa .......... 101 E4
Oaks Coppice. Wat ............ 112 A3
Oaks Dr. St Le .................. 139 E2
Oaks The. Southa .............. 103 F3
Oaks The. Ver ................... 114 C4
Oakshott Dr. Hav .............. 136 A3
Oaktree Ct. M on S ............ 213 E2
Oakwood Ave. Hav ............ 135 D2
Oakwood Ave. New M ........ 196 B2
Oakwood Ave. Ott ............... 31 E2
Oakwood Cl. Bour .............. 191 D1
Oakwood Cl. Ch Fo .............. 30 B1
Oakwood Cl. Lo He ............ 152 B4
Oakwood Cl. Ott .................. 31 E2
Oakwood Cl. Rom ................ 28 B1
Oakwood Dr. Southa ............ 78 B3
Oakwood Rd. Bour ............. 191 D1
Oakwood Rd. Ch Fo ............. 55 E4
Oakwood Rd. Christ ........... 194 C1
Oakwood Rd. Ports ............ 157 F2
Oakwood Rd. S Hay ........... 184 C2
Oakwood Way. Hamble ....... 128 A2
Oasis Mews. Upt ............... 203 D4
Oates Rd. Bour .................. 190 C1
Oatfield Gdns. Tot ............... 76 B1
Oatlands Cl. Botl ................. 81 F1
Oatlands Rd. Botl ................ 81 F1
Oatlands. Rom .................... 52 C4
Oban Rd. Bour .................. 206 C4
Obelisk Rd. Southa ............ 103 F1
Ober Rd. Brock ................. 145 F1
Oberfield Rd. Brock ........... 145 E1

Oberland Ct. Lym .............. 198 B2
Oberon Cl. Wat .................. 135 D4
Occupation La. Lo He ......... 153 F4
Ocean Cl. Fare .................. 130 B1
Ocean Rd. Southa .............. 103 D1
Ocean Way. Southa ........... 103 D1
Ockendon Cres. Ports ........ 182 B2
Ocknell Gr. Hyt ................. 125 E2
Octavia Hill. Winch .............. 10 B3
Octavia Rd. Southa .............. 79 F2
Octavius Ct. Wat ............... 112 A1
Odell Cl. Fare .................... 130 C2
Odiham Cl. Ch Fo ................ 55 D2
Odiham Cl. Southa ............... 77 F2
Oelander Cl. Lo He ............ 129 D3
Oglander Rd. Winch ............... 2 A1
Ogle Rd. Southa ................ 102 C2
Okeford Rd. Broa ............... 188 B1
Okement Cl. W End .............. 80 A1
Old Barn Cl. Christ ............ 192 B1
Old Barn Cl. Rin ................ 141 E4
Old Barn Cres. Hambl .......... 86 B1
Old Barn Farm Rd. W Moo .. 139 D3
Old Barn Rd. Christ ........... 192 B1
Old Bound Rd. Upt ............. 203 E3
Old Brickyard Rd. Fordi ........ 69 D1
Old Bridge Cl. Burs ........... 128 A4
Old Bridge House Rd. Burs . 128 A4
Old Bridge Rd. Bour .......... 208 B4
Old Bridge Rd. Ports ......... 182 C1
Old Canal. Ports ................ 183 D2
Old Christchurch Rd. Hord .. 197 E1
Old Coastguard Rd. Poole .. 216 A2
Old Commercial Rd. Ports .. 182 B4
Old Common Gdns. Lo He .. 129 D2
Old Copse Rd. Hav ............ 136 A2
Old Cottage Cl. W Wel .......... 50 C2
Old Cracknore Cl. March .... 102 A1
Old Farm Cl. Rin ............... 117 E1
Old Farm Copse. W Wel ....... 50 C2
Old Farm Dr. Southa ............ 79 F2
Old Farm La. Stubb ............ 154 B1
Old Farm La. Westb ........... 137 E2
Old Farm Rd. Poole ........... 204 C3
Old Farm Way. Cos ........... 158 C4
Old Farm Wlk. Lym ............ 198 B2
Old Forge Cl. Alderh ............ 92 C3
Old Forge Rd. Fern ............ 164 C3
Old Garden Cl. Lo He ......... 129 E1
Old Gardens. Winch .............. 1 C1
Old Gosport Rd. Fare ......... 155 D4
Old Hillside Rd. Winch ........... 1 B1
Old Kennels Cl. Winch .......... 10 A2
Old Kennels La. Winch .......... 10 A2
Old Kiln Rd. Upt ................ 203 E4
Old Library Gdns. Hav ........ 135 F2
Old London Rd. Ports ......... 157 F2
Old Lyndhurst Rd. Cadn ....... 98 C4
Old Magazine Cl. March ...... 101 F1
Old Manor Cl. Wi Mi ........... 163 E2
Old Manor Way. Cos .......... 158 A4
Old Market Rd. Broa .......... 187 D4
Old Mill La. Hambl ............... 87 E2
Old Mill La. Steep ............... 41 D3
Old Mill Way. Southa ............ 78 A1
Old Milton Gn. B on S ........ 195 F1
Old Milton Rd. New M ........ 196 A1
Old Orchard. Poole ............ 204 B1
Old Orchards. Lym ............. 198 C1
Old Park Dr. Hav ............... 136 A2
Old Parsonage Ct. Ott .......... 31 E2
Old Pines Cl. Fern ............. 165 F2
Old Priory Cl. Hamble ........ 128 A1
Old Priory Rd. Bour ........... 208 C2
Old Rd. Gos ...................... 181 E2
Old Rd. Rom ....................... 53 D4
Old Rd. Southa .................. 103 D1
Old Rd. Wi Mi .................... 163 D3
Old Rectory Cl. Westb ........ 137 D2
Old Rectory Gdns. Ki Wo ....... 2 B3
Old Rectory Rd. Cos ........... 158 B4
Old Redbridge Rd. Southa ... 101 E4
Old Reservoir Rd. Cos ........ 158 B4
Old River. Den .................. 110 C2
Old Road The. Cos ............ 157 F3
Old Romsey Rd. Cadn .......... 98 C4
Old Salisbury La. Awb ......... 27 D1
Old School Cl. Net ............. 127 E4
Old School Gdns. W End ....... 80 C1
Old St. Stubb ................... 154 A2
Old Stacks Gdns. Rin ......... 141 E3
Old Star Pl. Ports .............. 182 A3
Old Station App. Winch ......... 11 D4
Old Swanwick La. Swanw ... 128 B4
Old Timbers. S Hay ............ 184 C1
Old Turnpike. Fare ............ 131 D2
Old Van Diemans Rd. Wat ... 134 B3
Old Vicarage Cl. Bour ........ 190 C3
Old Vicarage La. Sway ....... 197 E4
Old Vineries The. Fordi ......... 69 E1
Old Wareham Rd. Poole ..... 205 D4
Old Winchester Hill La. Plai .. 37 E1
Old Wymering La. Cos ........ 157 F4
Oldbarn Cl. Tot ................... 76 B1
Oldbury Ct. Southa .............. 77 E1
Oldbury Way. Fare ............ 154 B4
Oldgate Gdns. Ports .......... 157 F2
Olinda St. Ports ................ 182 C3
Olive Cres. Portc ............... 156 B3

Olive Rd. Southa .................. 78 A2
Oliver Rd. Lym .................. 198 B2
Oliver Rd. Ports ................ 183 D2
Oliver Rd. Southa ................ 79 E2
Oliver's Battery Cres. Winch .. 10 A2
Oliver's Battery Gdns. Winch 10 A2
Oliver's Battery Rd N. Winch . 10 A3
Oliver's Battery Rd S. Winch . 10 A2
Olivers Cl. Tot .................. 100 A4
Olivers Rd. Wi Mi .............. 164 A3
Olivers Way. Wi Mi ............ 164 A3
Olivia Cl. Wat ................... 112 A1
Olympic Way. Fa Oa ............ 57 D1
Omdurman Rd. Southa .......... 79 D1
Omega St. Ports ................ 182 B3
Onibury Cl. Southa ............... 80 A1
Onslow Gdns. Wi Mi ........... 163 E3
Onslow Rd. Ports ............... 182 B1
Onslow Rd. Southa ............. 103 D3
Ophir Gdns. Bour .............. 207 D3
Ophir Rd. Bour .................. 207 D3
Ophir Rd. Ports ................. 157 F2
Oracle Dr. Wat ................... 134 C2
Oratory Gdns. Poole .......... 216 C4
Orchard Ave. Bish ............... 56 C1
Orchard Ave. Poole ........... 204 C1
Orchard Cl. Broa ............... 187 E4
Orchard Cl. Christ ............. 209 D3
Orchard Cl. Co Com ............ 31 F1
Orchard Cl. Faw ................ 151 D2
Orchard Cl. Fern ............... 165 F3
Orchard Cl. Fordi ................ 69 F1
Orchard Cl. Gos ................ 156 A1
Orchard Cl. Horn ............... 112 B3
Orchard Cl. N Bad ............... 53 F3
Orchard Cl. Rin ................. 141 D4
Orchard Cl. Tot ................. 100 C3
Orchard Cl. Cadn ................ 98 C4
Orchard Ct. He En .............. 105 F4
Orchard Gdns. Fordi ............ 69 F1
Orchard Gr. New M ............ 196 A1
Orchard Gr. Portc .............. 156 A4
Orchard Gr. Wat ................ 187 E4
Orchard La. Broa ............... 187 E4
Orchard La. Herm .............. 161 D4
Orchard La. Rom ................. 52 C4
Orchard La. Southa ............ 103 D2
Orchard Mews. Christ ........ 209 D3
Orchard Pl. Southa ............ 103 D2
Orchard Rd. Fa Oa ............... 57 E1
Orchard Rd. Hav ............... 159 F4
Orchard Rd. Lo He ............. 128 C1
Orchard Rd. Ports ............. 182 C2
Orchard Rd. Red .................. 47 F4
Orchard Rd. S Hay ............ 185 D1
Orchard St. Bour ............... 206 C2
Orchard The. Bour ............. 189 E3
Orchard The. Bran ............. 194 B4
Orchard The. Chilw ............. 54 C1
Orchard The. Cos .............. 157 F4
Orchard The. Den .............. 110 C2
Orchard The. M on S .......... 213 E2
Orchard Way. Hyt .............. 125 F1
Orchardlea. Swan ................ 84 B2
Orchards Way. Southa .......... 79 D1
Orchards Way. W End ........... 80 B1
Orcheston Rd. Bour ........... 207 E3
Orchid Way. Christ ............ 209 E4
Ordnance Rd. Gos ............. 181 E2
Ordnance Rd. Southa ......... 103 D3
Ordnance Row. Ports ........ 182 A3
Oregon Cl. Southa .............. 104 A2
Orford Cl. Christ ............... 192 B2
Oriana Way. Nur .................. 77 D2
Oriel Dr. Lo He .................. 129 D1
Oriel Rd. Ports .................. 157 E1
Orient Dr. Winch ................... 1 B2
Oriental Terr. Southa ........... 77 F2
Orion Cl. Southa ................ 154 B1
Orion Cl. Stubb .................. 154 B1
Orkney Cl. Southa ............... 77 F2
Orkney Rd. Cos ................. 133 F1
Ormesby Dr. Ch Fo .............. 30 A1
Ormond Cl. Fa Oa ................ 57 D1
Ormonde Rd. Poole ............ 206 A1
Ormsby Rd. Ports .............. 182 B2
Orpen Rd. Southa .............. 104 B2
Orwell Cres. Lo He ............ 129 E1
Orwell Rd. Southa ............... 77 F1
Osborn Cres. Gos .............. 155 D2
Osborn Rd. Fare ................ 131 D1
Osborne Cl. Net ................ 127 E3
Osborne Cl. Wat ................ 135 D4
Osborne Dr. Ch Fo ............... 55 F3
Osborne Gdns. Fa Oa .......... 57 F1
Osborne Gdns. Southa ......... 79 E1
Osborne Rd S. Fare ........... 131 D1
Osborne Rd. Bour .............. 206 C4
Osborne Rd. L on S ............ 179 F3
Osborne Rd. Lo He ............ 152 B4
Osborne Rd. New M ........... 196 A1
Osborne Rd. Pet .................. 40 C2
Osborne Rd. Poole ............ 205 D2
Osborne Rd. Ports ............. 182 B1
Osborne Rd. Southa ........... 103 E4
Osborne Rd. Tot ................ 101 D2
Osborne Rd. Wi Mi ............ 163 E2
Osborne View Rd. Stubb .... 154 A1
Osier Cl. Ports .................. 157 E2

# Oslands La. Swanw

| | |
|---|---|
| Oslands La. Swanw | 128 B4 |
| Osprey Cl. Christ | 210 A3 |
| Osprey Cl. Cos | 158 C4 |
| Osprey Cl. March | 101 F1 |
| Osprey Cl. Southa | 78 A3 |
| Osprey Dr. S Hay | 185 D2 |
| Osprey Gdns. L on S | 179 F3 |
| Osprey Quay. Herm | 161 D4 |
| Ossemsley South Dr. New M | 195 F4 |
| Osterley Cl. He En | 105 F3 |
| Osterly Rd. Southa | 103 F3 |
| Oswald Cl. Bour | 190 C1 |
| Oswald Rd. Bour | 190 C1 |
| Othello Dr. Wat | 135 D4 |
| Otter Cl. Bish | 57 D1 |
| Otter Cl. Upt | 203 D3 |
| Otter Cl. Ver | 115 D3 |
| Otterbourne Cres. Hav | 135 E3 |
| Otterbourne Hill. Ott | 31 D1 |
| Otters Wlk. New M | 196 B3 |
| Ouse Cl. N Bad | 55 D4 |
| Outer Circle. Southa | 78 A2 |
| Outlands La. Curd | 106 B4 |
| Outram Rd. Ports | 182 B2 |
| Oval Gdns. Gos | 180 C2 |
| Oval Rd. Locke | 4 F1 |
| Oval The. Liss | 20 C2 |
| Over Links Dr. Poole | 205 E1 |
| Overbrook Way. N Bad | 53 F3 |
| Overbrook. Hyt | 125 F2 |
| Overbury Rd. Poole | 205 E2 |
| Overcliff Rise. Southa | 78 C2 |
| Overcombe Cl. Broa | 188 C1 |
| Overstrand Cres. M on S | 213 E2 |
| Overton Cres. Hav | 135 E3 |
| Overton Rd. Southb | 137 F1 |
| Oviat Cl. Tot | 100 A4 |
| Ovington Ave. Bour | 208 B4 |
| Ovington Gdns. Bour | 208 B4 |
| Ovington Rd. Eastl | 56 A1 |
| Owen Cl. Gos | 180 B4 |
| Owen Rd. Eastl | 55 F1 |
| Owen St. Ports | 183 D1 |
| Owen's Rd. Winch | 1 C1 |
| Owls Rd. Bour | 207 F2 |
| Owls Rd. Ver | 115 D3 |
| Owslebury Bottom. Ows | 33 D3 |
| Owslebury Gr. Hav | 135 F3 |
| Oxburgh Cl. Eastl | 55 F3 |
| Oxenwood Green. Hav | 135 E3 |
| Oxey Cl. B on S | 196 A1 |
| Oxford Ave. Bour | 208 B3 |
| Oxford Ave. Southa | 103 D3 |
| Oxford Cl. Fare | 131 D1 |
| Oxford La. Bour | 190 D3 |
| Oxford Rd. Bour | 207 D2 |
| Oxford Rd. Gos | 180 C3 |
| Oxford Rd. Ports | 182 C2 |
| Oxford Rd. Southa | 103 D4 |
| Oxford St. Southa | 103 D2 |
| Oxlease Cl. Rom | 28 A1 |
| Oxleys Cl. Fare | 154 A4 |
| Oyster Mews. Ports | 182 A2 |
| Oyster Quay. Ports | 157 D4 |
| Oyster St. Ports | 182 A2 |
| | |
| Packridge La. Rown | 53 F1 |
| Pacton Rd. Ems | 136 C2 |
| Padbury Cl. Ports | 157 F2 |
| Paddington Gr. Bour | 189 E2 |
| Paddington Rd. Ports | 157 F1 |
| Paddock Cl. Fern | 165 D3 |
| Paddock Cl. St Le | 139 F2 |
| Paddock End. Den | 110 C2 |
| Paddock Gdns. Lym | 198 B3 |
| Paddock Gr. Ver | 115 D3 |
| Paddock The. Eastl | 56 A3 |
| Paddock The. Fordi | 94 C3 |
| Paddock The. Gos | 181 D2 |
| Paddock The. Ki Wo | 2 B3 |
| Paddock The. Stubb | 154 B2 |
| Paddock The. Tot | 76 B1 |
| Paddock Wlk. Portc | 157 D4 |
| Paddocks Cl. Poole | 205 D4 |
| Paddocks The. Brock | 145 E4 |
| Paddocks The. Faw | 151 D2 |
| Padfield Cl. Bour | 208 C3 |
| Padget Rd. Bour | 117 E1 |
| Padnell Ave. Wat | 112 A1 |
| Padnell Pl. Wat | 112 A1 |
| Padnell Rd. Wat | 112 A1 |
| Padstow Pl. Fordi | 93 F4 |
| Padwell Rd. Southa | 103 D4 |
| Padwick Ave. Cos | 158 A4 |
| Paffard Cl. Gos | 180 B4 |
| Pages La. E Bol | 175 E3 |
| Paget Rd. Bour | 190 A2 |
| Paget Rd. Gos | 181 D1 |
| Paget St. Southa | 103 D2 |
| Pagham Cl. Herm | 161 D4 |
| Pagham Gdns. S Hay | 185 F1 |
| Paignton Ave. Ports | 183 D4 |
| Paignton Rd. Southa | 77 F1 |
| Pain's Rd. Ports | 182 B2 |
| Painswick Cl. Cos | 157 E4 |
| Painter Cl. Lo He | 128 C3 |
| Painter Cl. Ports | 158 A2 |
| Paisley Rd. Bour | 208 B3 |

| | |
|---|---|
| Palace La. Beaul | 149 D1 |
| Palfrey Rd. Bour | 190 B3 |
| Palk Rd. Hav | 135 E1 |
| Pallant Gdns. Fare | 131 E1 |
| Pallant The. Hav | 135 F1 |
| Pallet Cl. Co Comm | 56 C4 |
| Pallot Cl. Burs | 104 C1 |
| Palm Hall Cl. Winch | 11 E4 |
| Palm Rd. Southa | 78 A2 |
| Palmer Pl. New M | 196 A2 |
| Palmer Rd. Poole | 204 B3 |
| Palmer's Rd. Ems | 136 C1 |
| Palmers Cl. Fa Oa | 57 E1 |
| Palmerston Ave. Christ | 209 E3 |
| Palmerston Ave. Fare | 131 D1 |
| Palmerston Cl. Upt | 203 E4 |
| Palmerston Dr. Fare | 155 D4 |
| Palmerston Rd. Bour | 207 E3 |
| Palmerston Rd. Poole | 205 E2 |
| Palmerston Rd. Ports | 182 B1 |
| Palmerston Rd. S Hay | 185 D2 |
| Palmerston Rd. Southa | 103 D2 |
| Palmerston Rd. Upt | 203 E4 |
| Palmerston St. Rom | 52 C4 |
| Palmerston Way. Gos | 180 C1 |
| Palmyra Rd. Gos | 181 D4 |
| Pamplyn Cl. Lym | 198 B2 |
| Pan St. Ports | 182 B3 |
| Pangbourne Ave. Cos | 158 A4 |
| Pangbourne Cl. Southa | 104 A2 |
| Pannall Rd. Gosp | 181 D4 |
| Panorama Rd. Poole | 216 A2 |
| Pansy Rd. Southa | 79 D2 |
| Pantheon Rd. Ch Fo | 55 F4 |
| Pantiles The. Fordi | 69 E1 |
| Panton Cl. Ems | 136 C2 |
| Panwell Rd. Southa | 104 A4 |
| Parade Ct. Ports | 157 F3 |
| Parade The. Bour | 208 C2 |
| Parade The. Broa | 188 A1 |
| Paradise La. Bi Wa | 83 F3 |
| Paradise La. Ne Ma | 99 E3 |
| Paradise La. Portc | 131 F1 |
| Paradise La. Westb | 137 D2 |
| Paradise St. Poole | 204 A1 |
| Paradise St. Ports | 182 B3 |
| Parchment St. Winch | 11 D4 |
| Parchment The. Hav | 135 F1 |
| Pardoe Cl. He En | 105 E3 |
| Pardys Hill. Broa | 187 E4 |
| Parham Cl. New M | 195 F2 |
| Parham Dr. Eastl | 55 F2 |
| Parham Rd. Bour | 190 B1 |
| Parham Rd. Gos | 181 E3 |
| Parish Rd. Poole | 204 C2 |
| Park  View. Botl | 106 A4 |
| Park Ave. Bour | 190 B3 |
| Park Ave. Lym | 198 B2 |
| Park Ave. Wat | 134 B2 |
| Park Ave. Winch | 11 D4 |
| Park Cl. Brock | 146 A1 |
| Park Cl. Burt | 193 E2 |
| Park Cl. Gos | 180 C3 |
| Park Cl. Hyt | 126 A2 |
| Park Cl. M on S | 213 F2 |
| Park Cl. New M | 196 B3 |
| Park Cl. Winch | 2 A1 |
| Park Cres. Ems | 136 B1 |
| Park Ct. N Bad | 53 E3 |
| Park Dr. Ver | 114 C4 |
| Park Farm Ave. Fare | 130 B2 |
| Park Farm Cl. Fare | 130 B2 |
| Park Farm Rd. Wat | 134 B2 |
| Park Gdns. Christ | 209 F4 |
| Park Glen. Lo He | 129 E2 |
| Park Gr. Cos | 157 F4 |
| Park Hill Cl. Holb | 150 B4 |
| Park Homer Rd. Wi Mi | 163 F3 |
| Park House Farm Way. Hav | 135 E3 |
| Park La. Alderh | 92 C3 |
| Park La. Beaul | 200 A4 |
| Park La. Bour | 190 C2 |
| Park La. Cos | 158 A4 |
| Park La. Drox | 61 D1 |
| Park La. Fare | 131 D1 |
| Park La. Hav | 135 E2 |
| Park La. Holb | 150 A2 |
| Park La. Ki Wo | 2 B3 |
| Park La. M on S | 213 E2 |
| Park La. March | 101 E1 |
| Park La. Ott | 31 D1 |
| Park La. Ro Ca | 137 E4 |
| Park La. Stubb | 154 B2 |
| Park La. Swan | 60 B1 |
| Park La. Twyf | 32 A3 |
| Park La. Wi Mi | 163 E2 |
| Park Lane Rd. Poole | 204 C1 |
| Park Par. Hav | 135 F2 |
| Park Rd N. Hav | 135 F1 |
| Park Rd S. Hav | 135 F1 |
| Park Rd. B on S | 195 F1 |
| Park Rd. Bi Wa | 83 D4 |
| Park Rd. Bour | 207 D3 |
| Park Rd. Ch Fo | 55 E4 |
| Park Rd. Den | 110 C3 |
| Park Rd. Fordi | 69 F1 |
| Park Rd. Gos | 181 D2 |
| Park Rd. Lym | 198 B2 |

| | |
|---|---|
| Park Rd. M on S | 213 F2 |
| Park Rd. New M | 196 B3 |
| Park Rd. Poole | 204 C2 |
| Park Rd. Ports | 182 A3 |
| Park Rd. S Hay | 184 B2 |
| Park Rd. Southa | 102 B3 |
| Park Rd. Southb | 137 E1 |
| Park Rd. Wat | 134 B2 |
| Park Rd. Winch | 1 C1 |
| Park St. Gos | 181 D3 |
| Park St. Ports | 182 A2 |
| Park St. Southa | 102 A4 |
| Park The. B on S | 211 E4 |
| Park The. Drox | 61 D1 |
| Park View. He En | 105 D4 |
| Park Way. Fa Oa | 57 F1 |
| Park Way. Hav | 135 F1 |
| Park Way. W Moo | 138 C1 |
| Park Wlk. Fare | 130 B2 |
| Park Wlk. Southa | 103 D3 |
| Parker Cl. Gos | 156 A1 |
| Parker Gdns. Cos | 134 B1 |
| Parker Rd. Bour | 206 C4 |
| Parkland Cl. Ver | 115 E2 |
| Parkland Dr. B on S | 211 F4 |
| Parklands Ave. Wat | 112 A3 |
| Parklands Cl. Ch Fo | 55 E4 |
| Parklands Cl. Gos | 181 D3 |
| Parklands. Lo He | 129 D2 |
| Parklands. Southa | 79 F1 |
| Parkside Ave. Southa | 101 E4 |
| Parkside Gdns. Bour | 190 C1 |
| Parkside Rd. Poole | 205 E2 |
| Parkside. Christ | 194 B1 |
| Parkside. Hav | 135 E1 |
| Parkside. Rin | 141 D3 |
| Parkside. Tot | 100 C3 |
| Parkstone Ave. Poole | 205 E2 |
| Parkstone Ave. Ports | 182 C1 |
| Parkstone Hts. Poole | 205 D3 |
| Parkstone Rd. Poole | 204 C2 |
| Parkville Rd. Southa | 79 E2 |
| Parkwater Rd. Whit | 25 B1 |
| Parkway Dr. Bour | 207 F4 |
| Parkway Gdns. Ch Fo | 55 E4 |
| Parkway The. Gos | 155 D1 |
| Parkway The. Southa | 79 D3 |
| Parkway. Swanw | 129 F4 |
| Parkwood Cl. He En | 105 E4 |
| Parkwood La. Bour | 208 A3 |
| Parkwood Rd. Bour | 208 A2 |
| Parkwood Rd. Wi Mi | 163 E2 |
| Parley Cl. Fern | 165 F1 |
| Parley La. Hurn | 191 E4 |
| Parley Rd. Bour | 191 D1 |
| Parliament Pl. Winch | 10 B2 |
| Parmiter Dr. Wi Mi | 163 F2 |
| Parmiter Rd. Wi Mi | 163 F2 |
| Parmiter Way. Wi Mi | 163 F2 |
| Parnell Rd. Eastl | 55 F1 |
| Parr Rd. Cos | 157 E4 |
| Parr St. Poole | 205 D2 |
| Parry Rd. Southa | 104 B2 |
| Parsonage Barn La. Rin | 141 D4 |
| Parsonage Cl. Fordi | 69 F1 |
| Parsonage La. Durl | 82 A3 |
| Parsonage Park Dr. Fordi | 69 F1 |
| Parsonage Rd. Bour | 207 D2 |
| Parsonage Rd. Southa | 103 E3 |
| Parsons Cl. Ports | 157 F2 |
| Partridge  Dr. Poole | 205 E1 |
| Partridge Down. Winch | 10 A2 |
| Partridge Gdns. Wat | 111 E2 |
| Partridge Green. New M | 196 A3 |
| Partridge Rd. Brock | 172 C4 |
| Partridge Rd. Hyt | 125 F1 |
| Partridge Wlk. Poole | 205 D1 |
| Partry Cl. N Bad | 55 D4 |
| Pascoe Cl. Poole | 205 D2 |
| Passage La. Ne Ma | 128 A1 |
| Passfield Ave. Eastl | 55 F1 |
| Passfield Cl. Eastl | 55 F1 |
| Passfield Wlk. Hav | 136 A3 |
| Passford Hill. Bold | 198 B4 |
| Passingham Walk. Wat | 112 A2 |
| Pastures The. Cher | 14 B3 |
| Pastures The. Den | 110 C2 |
| Pastures The. Lo He | 129 E2 |
| Patchins Rd. Hamw | 203 D2 |
| Pathway Dr. Fare | 154 B4 |
| Patricia Cl. W End | 80 B1 |
| Patricia Dr. He En | 105 E4 |
| Patrick's Cl. Liss | 21 D2 |
| Patrick's Copse Rd. Liss | 21 D2 |
| Paulet Cl. Southa | 80 A1 |
| Paulet Pl. Winch | 10 C3 |
| Pauletts La. Ower | 76 A2 |
| Pauletts La. Tot | 76 A2 |
| Pauls La. Sway | 197 F4 |
| Paulsgrove Rd. Ports | 182 C4 |
| Paulson Cl. Ch Fo | 55 E4 |
| Pauncefoot Hill. Rom | 52 B3 |
| Pauncefote Rd. Bour | 208 A3 |
| Pauntley Rd. Christ | 209 F3 |
| Pavan Gdns. Bour | 190 B1 |
| Pavilion Rd. He En | 105 E4 |
| Paxton Cl. He En | 105 E3 |
| Paxton Rd. Fare | 155 D4 |
| Payne Cl. W Moo | 138 C3 |

| | |
|---|---|
| Payne's La. Fa Oa | 57 E1 |
| Payne's Rd. Southa | 102 B3 |
| Paynes Hay Rd. Brai | 28 B4 |
| Peace Cl. Bran | 194 A4 |
| Peach Rd. Southa | 78 A2 |
| Peacock Cl. Ports | 182 A2 |
| Peak Cl. Southa | 101 F4 |
| Peak Dr. Fare | 154 B4 |
| Peak La. Bi Wa | 59 D2 |
| Peak La. Fare | 154 B4 |
| Peak Rd. Clanf | 88 A3 |
| Peak The. Ro Ca | 113 E1 |
| Peake New Rd. Warnf | 61 F4 |
| Pealsham Gdns. Fordi | 69 F1 |
| Pear Tree Cl. Alderh | 92 C3 |
| Pear Tree Cl. Botl | 81 F1 |
| Pear Tree Cl. Bran | 194 A4 |
| Pear Tree Dr. Red | 73 E4 |
| Pearce Ave. Poole | 205 D1 |
| Pearce Ct. Gos | 181 E3 |
| Pearce Gdns. Poole | 205 D1 |
| Pearce Rd. Upt | 203 D3 |
| Pearl Gdns. Bour | 190 B2 |
| Pearl Rd. Bour | 190 B2 |
| Pearson Ave. Poole | 205 D3 |
| Pearson Gdns. Bour | 190 B3 |
| Peartree Ave. Southa | 103 F3 |
| Peartree Cl. Southa | 103 E2 |
| Peartree Cl. Stubb | 154 B2 |
| Peartree Cl. W Wel | 50 B2 |
| Peartree Ct. Lym | 198 C1 |
| Peartree Rd. Hyt | 125 F1 |
| Peartree Rd. Southa | 103 E2 |
| Pebble Ct. March | 101 F1 |
| Pebmarsh Rd. Cos | 157 E4 |
| Peckham Ave. New M | 196 A1 |
| Pedham Cl. Ports | 183 D2 |
| Pedlars Wlk. Rin | 140 C4 |
| Pedula Way. Bish | 56 C3 |
| Peel Cl. Poole | 205 E3 |
| Peel Cl. Rom | 28 B1 |
| Peel Rd. Gos | 181 E2 |
| Peel St. Southa | 103 E3 |
| Peewit Hill Cl. Burs | 105 D2 |
| Peewit Hill. Burs | 105 D2 |
| Pegasus Ave. Hord | 197 D1 |
| Pegasus Cl. Hamble | 127 F1 |
| Pegasus Cl. Southa | 77 F2 |
| Pelham Cl. Christ | 209 E3 |
| Pelham Rd. Gos | 181 D3 |
| Pelham Rd. Ports | 182 B2 |
| Pelican Cl. Fare | 130 B1 |
| Pelican Ct. Hurs | 30 A4 |
| Pelican Mead. Rin | 141 E3 |
| Pembers Cl. Fa Oa | 57 E1 |
| Pemberton Rd. Lyn | 122 A3 |
| Pembrey Cl. Southa | 78 A3 |
| Pembridge Rd. Fordi | 70 A1 |
| Pembroke Cl. Eastl | 55 F3 |
| Pembroke Cl. Ports | 182 A2 |
| Pembroke Cl. Rom | 52 C4 |
| Pembroke Ct. Tot | 101 D4 |
| Pembroke Cres. Stubb | 154 A1 |
| Pembroke Rd. Bour | 206 A1 |
| Pembroke Rd. Poole | 205 E4 |
| Pembroke Rd. Ports | 182 A2 |
| Pembroke Rd. Southa | 104 A2 |
| Pembury Rd. Hav | 160 A4 |
| Pembury Rd. Stubb | 154 B2 |
| Pemerton Rd. Winch | 1 B2 |
| Penarth Ave. Cos | 158 A4 |
| Pendennis Rd. Portc | 132 C1 |
| Pendle Cl. Southa | 101 F4 |
| Pendle Green. Locke | 4 C1 |
| Penelope Gdns. Burs | 104 C1 |
| Penfords Paddock. Bi Wa | 83 E4 |
| Pengelly Ave. Bour | 190 C3 |
| Penhale Gdns. Lo He | 129 D1 |
| Penhale Rd. Ports | 182 C3 |
| Penhale Way. Tot | 100 C3 |
| Penhurst Rd. Hav | 135 D1 |
| Peninsula Rd. Winch | 10 C4 |
| Penistone Cl. Southa | 104 A1 |
| Penjar Ave. Wat | 134 B2 |
| Penk Ridge. Cos | 158 B4 |
| Penn Cl. B on S | 195 F1 |
| Penn Ct. W Moo | 138 B1 |
| Penn Hill Ave. Poole | 205 F2 |
| Penn Way. Gos | 180 C2 |
| Pennant Hills. Hav | 135 D1 |
| Pennant Park. Fare | 131 E2 |
| Pennard Way. Ch Fo | 55 D2 |
| Pennerley Ct. Hav | 135 E4 |
| Pennine Gdns. Hyt | 125 E2 |
| Pennine Rd. Southa | 101 F4 |
| Pennine Way. Ch Fo | 55 E2 |
| Pennine Way. L on S | 180 A2 |
| Pennine Way. Ver | 114 C3 |
| Pennine Wlk. Fare | 154 C4 |
| Pennington Cl. Co Comm | 56 C4 |
| Pennington Cl. W Moo | 138 B1 |
| Pennington Cres. W Moo | 138 B1 |
| Pennington Oval. Lym | 198 A1 |
| Pennington Rd. W Moo | 138 B1 |
| Pennington Way. Fare | 130 B2 |
| Penns Rd. Pet | 40 C2 |
| Penny Hedge. B on S | 212 A4 |
| Penny La. Herm | 161 D4 |

| | |
|---|---|
| Penny Pl. Wat | 134 C2 |
| Penny St. Ports | 182 A2 |
| Penny's Cl. Fordi | 69 F2 |
| Penny's Cres. Fordi | 69 F2 |
| Penny's La. Fordi | 69 F2 |
| Penny's Wlk. Fern | 165 E3 |
| Penny-cress. Lo He | 128 C1 |
| Pennywell Gdns. New M | 196 B2 |
| Penrhyn Ave. Cos | 158 A4 |
| Penrhyn Cl. Eastl | 55 F3 |
| Penrith Cl. Ver | 114 C3 |
| Penrith Rd. Bour | 208 A2 |
| Penrose Cl. Ports | 157 E1 |
| Penrose Rd. Fern | 165 E3 |
| Penshurst Way. Eastl | 56 A3 |
| Pentagon The. Black | 151 D1 |
| Pentire Ave. Southa | 78 B1 |
| Pentire Way. Southa | 78 B1 |
| Pentland Cl. Hyt | 125 E2 |
| Pentland Rise. Portc | 132 B1 |
| Penton Rd. Twyf | 32 A4 |
| Pentons Hill. Fordi | 94 B3 |
| Pentridge Way. Tot | 100 C3 |
| Penwood Green. Hav | 136 A3 |
| Peper Harow. Wat | 112 A3 |
| Peppard Cl. Southa | 104 A4 |
| Pepys Ave. Southa | 104 B3 |
| Pepys Cl. Gos | 181 D1 |
| Pepys Cl. Ports | 182 C2 |
| Percival Rd. Ports | 182 C4 |
| Percy Cl. Hyt | 125 F3 |
| Percy Rd. Bour | 207 F2 |
| Percy Rd. Gos | 181 E2 |
| Percy Rd. Ports | 182 C2 |
| Percy Rd. Southa | 102 A4 |
| Peregrine Cl. Tot | 100 B3 |
| Peregrine Rd. Christ | 210 A3 |
| Peregrines The. Portc | 155 F4 |
| Pergin Cres. Broa | 204 A4 |
| Pergin Way. Broa | 204 A4 |
| Pern Dr. Botl | 106 A4 |
| Peronne Cl. Ports | 157 F3 |
| Peronne Rd. Ports | 157 F3 |
| Perran Rd. Southa | 77 E3 |
| Perry Gdns. Poole | 204 B1 |
| Perryfield Gdns. Bour | 208 A4 |
| Perrywood Cl. Holb | 150 B2 |
| Perrywood Gdns. Tot | 100 A4 |
| Perseus Pl. Wat | 134 C2 |
| Pershore Cl. Lo He | 129 D2 |
| Persley Rd. Bour | 190 C2 |
| Perth Cl. Christ | 192 C1 |
| Perth Rd. Gos | 155 E2 |
| Perth Rd. Ports | 183 D2 |
| Pervin Rd. Cos | 157 F4 |
| Peststead La. Sob | 85 E2 |
| Peterborough Rd. Cos | 133 F1 |
| Peterborough Rd. Southa | 103 D4 |
| Peterfields Rd. Chilc | 12 A3 |
| Peters Cl. Lo He | 128 C2 |
| Peters Rd. Lo He | 128 C2 |
| Peterscroft Ave. Ashu | 100 A1 |
| Petersfield La. Clanf | 88 B4 |
| Petersfield Pl. Bour | 208 A4 |
| Petersfield Rd. Bour | 208 A4 |
| Petersfield Rd. Buri | 65 E3 |
| Petersfield Rd. Cher | 14 B2 |
| Petersfield Rd. Hav | 135 F2 |
| Petersfield Rd. Winch | 11 E4 |
| Petersham Rd. Broa | 204 A4 |
| Petit Rd. Bour | 191 D2 |
| Petrel Wlk. Gos | 155 D1 |
| Petrie Rd. L on S | 179 F3 |
| Petticoat La. Red | 47 F4 |
| Pettinger Gdns. Southa | 103 E4 |
| Petty Cl. Rom | 53 D3 |
| Pettycot Cres. Gos | 155 D2 |
| Petworth Gdns. Eastl | 56 A3 |
| Petworth Gdns. Southa | 78 B3 |
| Petworth Rd. Ports | 183 D3 |
| Petwyn Cl. Fern | 166 A3 |
| Pevensey Cl. Southa | 77 E1 |
| Peverell Rd. Hamw | 203 D2 |
| Peverells Rd. Ch Fo | 55 F4 |
| Peverells Wood Ave. Ch Fo | 55 F4 |
| Peverells Wood Cl. Ch Fo | 55 F3 |
| Peveril Cl. St Le | 139 F3 |
| Peveril Rd. Southa | 103 F2 |
| Pewsey Pl. Southa | 78 B1 |
| Phelipps Rd. Broa | 187 F3 |
| Philip Rd. Wat | 134 C3 |
| Phillimore Rd. Southa | 79 E2 |
| Philpott Dr. March | 101 F1 |
| Phoenix Cl. Burs | 105 D1 |
| Phoenix Sq. Ports | 157 F2 |
| Phoenix Way. Gos | 155 E1 |
| Pickard Rd. Fern | 165 F3 |
| Pickering Cl. Broa | 188 A1 |
| Pickford Rd. Bour | 190 C1 |
| Picket Cl. Fordi | 69 F1 |
| Pier Rd. Ports | 182 A2 |
| Pier St. L on S | 179 F3 |
| Pig Shoot La. Hurn | 191 F3 |
| Pigeon House La. Southw | 133 E2 |
| Pikes Hill Ave. Lyn | 121 F3 |
| Pikes Hill. Lyn | 121 F3 |
| Pilands Wood Rd. Burs | 127 F4 |

Pilchards Ave. Fa Oa ............ 57 D2
Pilford Heath Rd. Wi Mi ... 164 A4
Pilgrim Cl. New M ........ 196 B2
Pilgrim Pl. Southa ......... 79 F2
Pilgrims Cl. Ch Fo ......... 55 D3
Pilgrims Cl. N Bad ......... 55 D3
Pilgrims Gate. Winch ....... 1 C1
Pilgrims Way. Broa ........ 204 A4
Pilgrims Way. Stubb ....... 154 A1
Pill Hill. Whit ........... 24 A2
Pilley Bailey. Bold ........ 174 A1
Pilley Hill. Bold .......... 173 F1
Pilley St. Bold ........... 174 A1
Pilning Cl. Fare .......... 154 B4
Pilot Hight Rd. Bour ....... 190 A2
Pilsdon Dr. Broa .......... 188 C2
Pimpern Cl. Broa .......... 188 C1
Pimpernel Cl. Lo He ....... 128 C1
Pine Ave. Bour ........... 208 B2
Pine Ave. Poole .......... 205 F4
Pine Cl. Ashu ............ 100 B2
Pine Cl. B on S .......... 211 F4
Pine Cl. Fern ............ 165 E4
Pine Cl. Hyt ............ 125 F1
Pine Cl. Lan ............ 49 E1
Pine Cl. N Bad ........... 53 F3
Pine Cl. Winch ........... 10 A2
Pine Cres. Christ ......... 210 C4
Pine Ct. Ems ............ 136 C2
Pine Dr E. Southa ......... 104 C4
Pine Dr. Clanf ........... 88 B3
Pine Dr. Poole ........... 205 F2
Pine Dr. Southa .......... 104 B4
Pine Dr. St Le ........... 139 F2
Pine Glen Ave. Fern ....... 165 E4
Pine Gr. Hav ............ 136 A1
Pine Manor Rd. St Le ...... 139 E3
Pine Rd. Alderh .......... 92 C3
Pine Rd. Bi Wa .......... 83 E4
Pine Rd. Bour ........... 207 D4
Pine Rd. Broa ........... 162 C1
Pine Rd. Ch Fo .......... 55 E4
Pine Rd. Rom ............ 53 E3
Pine Tree Gdns. Wat ....... 112 A1
Pine Tree Glen. Bour ...... 206 B2
Pine Trees Cl. Fare ....... 154 B4
Pine View Cl. Red ........ 47 E2
Pine View Cl. Upt ......... 203 E3
Pine View Cl. Ver ......... 114 B4
Pine View Rd. Ver ......... 114 B4
Pine Way. Rown ........... 78 C4
Pine Wlk. Liss ........... 21 D3
Pine Wlk. Lo He .......... 129 D3
Pine Wlk. Rown ........... 78 C4
Pine Wlk. Ver ........... 115 D3
Pinecliff Rd. Poole ....... 216 D4
Pinecliffe Ave. Bour ...... 208 B2
Pinecliffe Rd. B on S ..... 211 E4
Pinefield Rd. St Le ....... 79 F1
Pinegrove Rd. Southa ...... 103 F2
Pineholt Cl. St Le ........ 140 A3
Pinehurst Ave. Christ ..... 209 F3
Pinehurst Rd. Rown ........ 78 C4
Pinehurst Rd. W Moo ....... 138 C1
Pinelands Rd. Rown ........ 78 C4
Pines The. Portc ......... 132 A1
Pines The. Southa ........ 78 A2
Pinesprings Dr. Broa ...... 187 F1
Pinetops Cl. Lym ......... 198 A2
Pinetree Wlk. Broa ....... 203 F4
Pineview Cl. Burs ........ 105 D1
Pinewood Ave. Bour ....... 190 B3
Pinewood Ave. Hav ........ 135 D2
Pinewood Cl. Bour ........ 190 B3
Pinewood Cl. Christ ....... 195 D1
Pinewood Cl. Rom ......... 28 B1
Pinewood Cl. Stubb ....... 154 B2
Pinewood Cl. Upt ......... 203 D4
Pinewood Cres. Hyt ....... 126 A1
Pinewood Dr. Hyt ......... 126 A1
Pinewood Gdns. Fern ...... 165 E4
Pinewood Park. Southa .... 104 C3
Pinewood Rd . Upt ....... 203 D4
Pinewood Rd. Christ ...... 194 C1
Pinewood Rd. Fern ....... 165 E4
Pinewood Rd. Hord ....... 196 C2
Pinewood Rd. Poole ...... 206 A1
Pinewood Rd. St Le ...... 139 F2
Pinewood. Gos .......... 155 F1
Pinewood. Southa ....... 78 C3
Pink Rd. Ports ......... 182 C4
Pinkney La. Lyn ........ 121 F2
Pinks Hill. Fare ....... 131 E1
Pipers Ash. Rin ....... 141 E4
Pipers Cl. Tot ....... 100 B3
Pipers Dr. Christ ..... 210 A4
Pipers Mead. Clanf .... 88 A3
Pipers Wood Ind Park. Wat ... 134 B4
Piping Cl. Co Com ..... 56 C4
Piping Green. Co Com .. 56 C4
Piping Rd. Co Com ..... 56 C4
Pipit Cl. Gos ........ 181 D4
Pippin Cl. Christ .... 192 C1
Pirrie Cl. Southa .... 78 B1
Pit Hill La. Hambl ... 86 C1
Pitchponds Rd. Lo He . 152 B4
Pitcroft La. Buri .... 65 F3
Pitcroft Rd. Ports ... 157 E1
Pitmore Cl. Ott ...... 56 A4

Pitmore La. Sway ...... 172 B1
Pitmore Rd. Ott ...... 56 A4
Pitreavie Rd. Cos .... 157 F3
Pitt Rd. Southa ...... 102 B3
Pittmore Rd. Burt .... 193 E1
Pitts Deep La. Bold .. 200 B2
Pitts Pl. New M ...... 196 B1
Pitwines Cl. Poole ... 204 B1
Pitymoor La. Southw .. 133 D2
Place Cres. Wat ...... 134 C3
Place House Cl. Fare . 130 B1
Place La. Comp ....... 31 F4
Plaitford Gr. Hav .... 135 E3
Plaitford Wlk. Southa 77 F1
Plantaganet Cres. Bour 189 E3
Plantation Ct. Lym ... 198 B2
Plantation Dr. Christ 195 D1
Plantation Dr. March . 101 F1
Plantation Rd. Broa .. 188 B1
Plantation Rd. Hill B 21 D1
Plantation Rd. W Wel . 74 E4
Plantation. Hord ..... 213 F4
Plants Cl. W Wel ..... 51 D1
Plassey Cres. Bour ... 190 B3
Platform Rd. Southa .. 103 D1
Platoff Rd. Lym ...... 214 C4
Player Ct. Fordi ..... 69 F2
Players Cres. Tot .... 100 C3
Playfair Rd. Ports ... 182 B2
Playfields Dr. Poole . 205 F3
Pleasance Way. New M 195 F2
Pleasant La. Th Is ... 161 E1
Pleasant Rd. Ports ... 183 D2
Plecy Cl. Fern ....... 165 E1
Plemont Cl. Poole .... 189 F1
Pless Rd. M on S ..... 213 D3
Plough La. Bold ...... 85 E1
Plough Way. Winch .... 10 B2
Plover Cl. Southa .... 78 A3
Plover Cl. Stubb ..... 154 A1
Plover Dr. M on S .... 213 F2
Plover Rd. Tot ....... 100 B4
Plover Reach. Ports .. 183 D3
Plovers Down. Winch .. 10 A2
Plovers Rd. Horn ..... 112 A4
Plumer Rd. Broa ...... 188 A1
Plumley Wlk. Hav ..... 135 E4
Plumpton Gdns. Ports . 158 A2
Plumpton Gr. Wat ..... 112 A1
Plymouth Dr. Stubb ... 154 A2
Plymouth St. Ports ... 182 B2
Pococks La. Hawk ..... 19 F4
Poets Way. Winch ..... 10 B4
Pointout Cl. Southa .. 78 C2
Pointout Rd. Southa .. 78 C2
Poles La. Hurs ....... 30 B3
Poles La. Lym ........ 198 C1
Poles La. Ott ........ 31 D2
Police Station La. Drox 61 D1
Pollards Moor Rd. Cadn 75 D1
Pollesden Cl. Ch Fo .. 55 D4
Polygon The. Southa .. 102 C3
Pomona Cl. Fern ...... 165 E3
Pompey's La. Fern .... 165 D1
Pond Cl. March ....... 101 F1
Pond Cl. New M ....... 196 A2
Pond La. Clanf ....... 88 A3
Pond Piece. Den ...... 110 C2
Pond Rd. Lo He ....... 128 C3
Pondhead Cl. Holb .... 150 B2
Pondside La. Bi Wa ... 83 D4
Ponsonby Rd. Poole ... 205 F2
Pony Dr. Upt ......... 203 E4
Pook La. Fare ........ 131 E2
Pook La. Hav ......... 160 A4
Pooksgreen. March .... 101 E1
Poole Hill. Bour ..... 206 C2
Poole La. Bour ....... 190 A2
Poole La. Bour ....... 206 B2
Poole Rd. Poole ...... 206 B2
Poole Rd. Southa ..... 103 F2
Poole Rd. Upt ........ 203 E4
Poole Rd. Wi Mi ...... 163 E2
Popes Cl. Christ ..... 210 A4
Popes La. Uph ........ 58 D2
Popes Rd. Poole ...... 204 B3
Popham Ct. Hav ....... 135 E3
Poplar Cl. Christ .... 211 D4
Poplar Cl. Poole ..... 204 A1
Poplar Cl. Wi Mi ..... 163 E3
Poplar Cres. Rin ..... 141 D4
Poplar Dr. Fare ...... 154 C4
Poplar Dr. March ..... 101 E1
Poplar Gr. S Hay ..... 185 D2
Poplar La. Bran ...... 194 B4
Poplar Rd. New M ..... 196 B2
Poplar Rd. Southa .... 103 F3
Poplar Way. He En .... 105 E3
Poplar Way. N Bad .... 53 F3
Poplar Way. Rin ...... 141 D4
Poplars The. Shed .... 83 F2
Poppy Cl. Christ ..... 210 A4
Poppy Cl. Lo He ...... 128 C1
Poppy Rd. Southa ..... 79 E3
Porchester Pl. Bour .. 207 D3
Porchester Rd. Bour .. 207 D3
Porchester Rd. Southa 103 F2
Porlock Rd. Southa ... 77 E1
Port La. Hurs ........ 30 B4

Port La. Winch ....... 10 A1
Port Royal Rd. Ports . 182 B3
Port Way. Ports ...... 157 D4
Portal Rd. Bish ...... 56 B2
Portal Rd. Gos ....... 155 E2
Portal Rd. Southa .... 104 A2
Portal Rd. Tot ....... 100 B4
Portal Rd. Winch ..... 11 D3
Portarlington Cl. Bour 206 B1
Portarlington Rd. Bour 206 B1
Portchester La. Southw 132 B2
Portchester Rd. Portc 156 A4
Portchester Rd. Ports 182 C4
Portchester Rise. Eastl 56 A4
Portelet Cl. Poole ... 189 E1
Portelet Pl. He En ... 105 E3
Porter Rd. Broa ...... 204 A4
Porter's La. March ... 102 C2
Porters La. Wi Mi .... 164 B3
Portersbridge St. Rom 52 C4
Portesham Gdns. Bour . 191 D2
Portesham Way. Broa .. 188 C2
Porteus Cres. Ch Fo .. 55 F3
Portfield Cl. Christ . 209 D4
Portfield Rd. Christ . 209 D4
Portfield Rd. Ports .. 158 A2
Portland Dr. Gos ..... 180 B2
Portland Rd. Bour .... 207 D4
Portland Rd. Ports ... 182 B1
Portland Rd. Wat ..... 134 C4
Portland Sq. Liss .... 20 C2
Portland St. Fare .... 131 D1
Portland St. Ports ... 182 A3
Portland St. Southa .. 102 C2
Portland Terr. Southa 102 C2
Portman Cres. Bour ... 208 A2
Portman Rd. Bour ..... 207 F3
Portobello Gr. Portc . 132 C1
Portsdown Ave. Cos ... 158 B4
Portsdown Hill Rd. Cos 133 D1
Portsdown Hill Rd. Hav 135 D1
Portsdown Hill Rd. Portc 132 B1
Portsdown Rd. Portc .. 156 C4
Portsmouth Rd. Burs .. 105 D1
Portsmouth Rd. Co Com 57 E3
Portsmouth Rd. Cos ... 157 F4
Portsmouth Rd. Horn .. 112 A3
Portsmouth Rd. L on S 180 A2
Portsmouth Rd. Southa 104 B1
Portsmouth Rd. Wat ... 112 A3
Portsview Ave. Portc . 132 C1
Portsview Gdns. Portc 132 B1
Portswood Ave. Southa 103 D4
Portswood Dr. Bour ... 191 D2
Portswood Park. Southa 103 D4
Portswood Rd. Hav .... 135 E3
Portswood Rd. Ports .. 157 F3
Portswood Rd. Southa . 79 E1
Portview Rd. Southa .. 79 F1
Portway Cl. Southa ... 104 A4
Posbrook La. Lo He ... 153 F3
Posbrooke Rd. Ports .. 183 D2
Post Office La. Poole 204 B1
Post Office La. St Le 140 A3
Post Office Rd. Bour . 206 C2
Post Office Rd. Wat .. 134 B3
Postern Cl. Portc .... 156 B4
Potteries The. Fare .. 131 D2
Potterne Way. Ver .... 115 D2
Potters Ave. Fare .... 131 D2
Potters Heron Cl. Ampf 29 F2
Potters Heron La. Ampf 29 F2
Pottery Rd. Poole .... 205 E1
Pottery Rd. Poole .... 205 D1
Poulner Cl. Southa ... 104 A1
Poulner Ct. Hav ...... 135 E3
Poulner Hill. Rin .... 141 F4
Poulner Park. Rin .... 117 E1
Pound Cl. Gos ........ 180 B4
Pound Cl. Poole ...... 204 C3
Pound Cl. Rin ........ 141 D4
Pound Cotts. Meons ... 61 E3
Pound Gate Dr. Lo He . 153 E4
Pound La. Ampf ....... 29 D1
Pound La. Ashu ....... 100 C2
Pound La. Bour ....... 190 B3
Pound La. Bur ........ 142 C1
Pound La. Cadn ....... 75 E1
Pound La. Christ ..... 209 D3
Pound La. Dame ....... 68 A3
Pound La. Meons ...... 61 E3
Pound La. N Bad ...... 29 D1
Pound La. Plai ....... 50 B3
Pound La. Poole ...... 204 C3
Pound La. Sh En ...... 25 F1
Pound Lea. S Hay ..... 185 D3
Pound Rd. Burs ....... 104 C1
Pound Rd. Ki Wo ...... 2 B4
Pound Rd. Lym ........ 198 A1
Pound Rd. W Wit ...... 186 C1
Pound St. Southa ..... 104 A4
Pound Tree Rd. Southa 103 D2
Pounds Terr. Ports ... 182 A3
Powell Cres. Tot ..... 100 C3
Power Rd. Ports ...... 182 C3
Powerscourt Rd. B on S 211 F4
Powerscourt Rd. Ports 182 C4
Powis Cl. New M ...... 196 A2

Powlett Rd. Lym ...... 198 C2
Poynings Pl. Ports ... 182 A2
Precinct The. Wat .... 134 C4
Precosa Rd. He En .... 105 F3
Prelate Way. Lo He ... 129 E1
Premier Centre The. N Bad 53 E3
Preshaw Cl. Southa ... 78 B2
Preston Cl. Upt ...... 203 E4
Preston La. Burt ..... 193 E2
Preston Rd. Poole .... 204 B3
Preston Rd. Ports .... 182 C4
Preston Way. Christ .. 210 B4
Prestwood Cl. B on S 195 F1
Prestwood Rd. He En .. 105 E3
Pretoria Rd. He En ... 105 D3
Pretoria Rd. Ports ... 182 C2
Prickett Hill. Shed .. 107 F4
Pricketts Hill. Wickh 108 A3
Prideaux - Brune Ave. Gos 155 E2
Priest Croft Dr. Black 150 C1
Priest La. Sop ....... 193 D4
Priestlands Cl. Ne Ma 100 A3
Priestlands La. Lym .. 198 B2
Priestlands Pl. Lym .. 198 B2
Priestlands Rd. Lym .. 198 B2
Priestlands. Rom ..... 52 C4
Priestley Cl. Tot .... 100 B4
Priestley Rd. Bour ... 190 A1
Priestwood Cl. Southa 104 B4
Primate Rd. Lo He .... 129 E1
Primrose Cl. Gos ..... 155 D3
Primrose Cl. He En ... 105 E3
Primrose Ct. Wat ..... 135 D3
Primrose Gdns. Broa .. 187 F1
Primrose La. Ra ...... 21 E2
Primrose La. Red ..... 47 E3
Primrose Rd. Southa .. 79 D2
Primrose Way. Broa ... 187 F4
Primrose Way. Christ . 194 A1
Primrose Way. Christ . 210 B4
Primrose Way. Lo He .. 128 C1
Primrose Way. Rom .... 28 B1
Prince Albert Rd. Ports 183 D2
Prince Alfred St. Gos 181 D2
Prince George St. Ports 182 A3
Prince George's St. Hav 135 F1
Prince Of Wales Ave. Southa 102 A4
Prince Of Wales Cl. Wat 135 D4
Prince Of Wales Rd. Bour 206 B2
Prince Of Wales Rd. Gos 181 E2
Prince Rd. Rown ...... 77 F3
Prince William Ct. Bish 56 C1
Prince's Cl. Southa .. 103 E3
Prince's Pl. New M ... 196 B2
Prince's Rd. Ports ... 182 B4
Prince's Rd. Rom ..... 52 C4
Prince's St. Ports ... 182 B4
Prince's St. Southa .. 103 E3
Princes Cl. Bi Wa .... 83 D4
Princes Cl. Red ...... 47 F4
Princes Cres. Lyn .... 122 A3
Princes Dr. Wat ...... 112 A1
Princes Hill. Red .... 47 F4
Princes Pl. Winch .... 10 C3
Princes Rd. Fern ..... 165 E3
Princes Rd. Pet ...... 40 B2
Princes Rd. Southa ... 102 B3
Princess Ave. Christ . 209 D3
Princess Cl. W End ... 80 C1
Princess Gdns. Horn .. 112 B4
Princess Rd. Ashu .... 100 A1
Princess Rd. Bour .... 206 A2
Princess Rd. Poole ... 206 A2
Pringles Cl. Fern .... 165 F3
Pringles Dr. Fern .... 165 F3
Prinstead Cl. Winch .. 11 D3
Prinstead La. Southb . 161 E4
Prinsted Cres. Cos ... 158 B4
Priors Barton. Winch . 10 C3
Priors Cl. Christ .... 210 B4
Priors Cl. Southb .... 137 F1
Priors Dean Rd. Winch 1 B2
Priors Hill La. Net .. 127 F4
Priors Leaze La. Southb 137 F1
Priors Rd. Broa ...... 204 A4
Priors Way. Winch .... 10 A2
Priors Wlk. Wi Mi .... 163 D3
Priorsdean Ave. Ports 183 D3
Priorsdean Cres. Hav . 135 E2
Priory Ave. Southa ... 79 E1
Priory Cl. Bi Wa ..... 83 D4
Priory Cl. Christ .... 208 C4
Priory Cl. Southa .... 79 E1
Priory Cres. Ports ... 183 D2
Priory Gdns. Portc ... 156 B4
Priory Gdns. Wat ..... 111 F1
Priory Rd. Bour ...... 206 C1
Priory Rd. Eastl ..... 55 F1
Priory Rd. Fare ...... 130 B1
Priory Rd. Gosp ...... 181 D4
Priory Rd. Net ....... 127 D3
Priory Rd. Ports ..... 183 D1
Priory Rd. Southa .... 103 E4
Priory Rd. W Moo ..... 166 A4
Priory View Pl. Bour 191 D2
Priory View Rd. Bour 191 D2
Priory View Rd. Burt 193 E1
Privet Rd. Bour ...... 206 C4
Privett Pl. Gos ...... 180 C2

Privett Rd. Fare ..... 130 B1
Privett Rd. Frox G ... 18 C1
Privett Rd. Gos ...... 180 C2
Privett Rd. Wat ...... 134 B3
Prochurch Rd. Wat .... 112 A2
Proctor Cl. Southa ... 104 B3
Proctor Dr. N Bad .... 53 F2
Proctor La. Ports .... 182 C3
Promenade The. Ems ... 160 C4
Promenade The. Hyt ... 126 B3
Prospect La. Hav ..... 136 A3
Prospect Pl. Ch Fo ... 55 E3
Prospect Pl. Hyt ..... 126 A3
Prospect Rd. Ports ... 182 B4
Prosperous St. Poole 204 B1
Provene Cl. Shed ..... 83 F2
Provene Gdns. Shed ... 83 F2
Providence Hill. Burs 105 D1
Provost St. Fordi .... 69 F1
Pruetts La. Liss ..... 21 D4
Prunus Cl. Fern ...... 165 D4
Prunus Cl. Southa .... 78 B3
Prunus Dr. Fern ...... 165 D4
Pudbrooke Gdns. He En 105 D4
Pudding La. Ki Wo .... 2 A3
Puddletown Cres. Poole 188 C1
Puffin Cres. Stubb ... 154 A2
Puffin Gdns. Gos ..... 155 D2
Puffin Wlk. Wat ...... 111 E2
Pug's Hole. W Tyth ... 4 A3
Pulens La. Pet ....... 41 D2
Pump La. Gos ........ 155 E1
Pundle Green Estate. Cadn 99 D3
Punsholt La. W Meo ... 16 C3
Punsholt La. W Tis ... 16 C3
Purbeck Ave. Hamw .... 203 F1
Purbeck Cl. Upt ...... 203 D4
Purbeck Dr. Fare ..... 154 B4
Purbeck Dr. Ver ...... 114 C3
Purbeck Rd. B on S ... 211 E4
Purbeck Rd. Bour ..... 206 C1
Purbeck St. Ports .... 182 A3
Purbeck Wlk. Fare .... 154 B4
Purbrook Cl. Southa .. 78 B3
Purbrook Gdns. Wat ... 134 B3
Purbrook Heath Rd. Southw 134 A3
Purbrook Rd. Ports ... 182 C3
Purbrook Way. Hav .... 135 E2
Purcell Cl. Wat ...... 134 C3
Purcell Rd. Southa ... 104 B3
Purewell Cross Rd. Christ 209 E4
Purewell Mews. Hello 209 D3
Purewell. Christ ..... 209 E3
Purkess Cl. Ch Fo .... 55 E4
Purkiss Cl. Ne Ma .... 99 E3
Purley Way. Plai ..... 50 A2
Purrocks The. Pet .... 40 C3
Pussex La. Hurn ...... 192 A4
Putmans La. S Har .... 66 C4
Pycroft Cl. N Hay .... 160 B2
Pycroft Cl. Southa ... 104 A3
Pye Cl. Broa ........ 187 F4
Pye Cnr. Wi Mi ...... 163 D2
Pye St. Ports ....... 182 B3
Pylands La. Burs ..... 105 D2
Pyle Cl. Wat ........ 112 A2
Pylewell Rd. Hyt ..... 126 A2
Pyrford Cl. Gos ...... 180 C2
Pyrford Cl. Wat ...... 111 F1
Pytchley Cl. Stubb ... 154 A1

Quadrangle The. Eastl 56 A2
Quantock Rd. Southa .. 101 F4
Quantocks The. Hyt ... 125 D2
Quarely Rd. Hav ...... 135 E3
Quarry Cl. Wi Mi ..... 164 A4
Quarry Dr. Wi Mi ..... 164 A4
Quarry Rd. Wi Mi ..... 164 A4
Quarry Rd. Winch ..... 11 E4
Quartremaine Rd. Ports 158 A2
Quavey Rd. Red ....... 47 F3
Quay Haven. Swanw .... 128 B4
Quay Hill. Lym ....... 198 C2
Quay La. Gos ........ 156 A1
Quay La. Gos ........ 181 F2
Quay Rd. Christ ...... 209 D3
Quay Rd. Lym ......... 198 C2
Quay St. Fare ....... 131 E1
Quay St. Lym ........ 198 C2
Quay The. Hamble .... 128 A1
Quay The. Poole ..... 204 B1
Quayle Dr. Bour ..... 189 F3
Quayside Rd. Southa . 103 E4
Quebec Gdns. Burs ... 104 C1
Queen Anne Dr. Oakl . 188 C4
Queen Anne's Dr. Hav 135 E1
Queen Elizabeth Ave. Lym 198 B2
Queen Katherine Rd. Lym 198 C2
Queen Mary Ave. Bour 190 C1
Queen Mary Rd. Portc 156 B4
Queen St. Ems ....... 161 D4
Queen St. Lym ....... 198 B2
Queen St. Ports ..... 182 A3
Queen St. Twyf ...... 31 F3
Queen St. Woodg ..... 47 D1
Queen's Ave. Christ . 209 D3
Queen's Cl. Rom ..... 53 D4
Queen's Cres. Ports . 182 B2
Queen's Gr. Ports ... 182 B2

245

Queen's Par. Lyn

Rosedale Cl. Christ

Queen's Par. Lyn 121 F3
Queen's Park Ave. Bour 207 E4
Queen's Park Gdns. Bour 207 E4
Queen's Park Rd. Bour 207 E4
Queen's Park S Dr. Bour 207 E4
Queen's Park W Dr. Bour 207 E4
Queen's Pl. Ports 182 B2
Queen's Rd. Bour 206 B2
Queen's Rd. Broa 187 E3
Queen's Rd. Ch Fo 30 B1
Queen's Rd. Christ 209 F3
Queen's Rd. Fare 131 D1
Queen's Rd. Gos 181 E2
Queen's Rd. Lo He 152 B4
Queen's Rd. Poole 205 E2
Queen's Rd. Ports 182 C4
Queen's Rd. Southa 78 B1
Queen's Rd. Wat 111 F1
Queen's Rd. Winch 10 B4
Queen's Terr. Southa 103 D2
Queen's Way. Ports 182 B2
Queen's Way. Southa 103 D2
Queens Cl. Hyt 126 A2
Queens Cl. L on S 179 F3
Queens Cl. W Moo 138 B1
Queens Copse. Poole 206 A4
Queens Cres. Horn 112 B4
Queens Cres. Stubb 154 B2
Queens Ct. New M 196 B2
Queens Gdns. Bour 206 B2
Queens Gdns. Fordi 69 F1
Queens Gr. New M 196 B2
Queens Gr. Wat 134 B3
Queens Rd. Fern 165 E4
Queens Rd. L on S 179 F2
Queens Rd. Lyn 122 A3
Queens Rd. Pet 40 B2
Queens View. Net 127 D3
Queens Way. Rin 141 D4
Queensland Rd. Bour 208 A3
Queenstown Rd. Southa 102 B3
Queensway The. Portc 156 A4
Queensway. N Hay 160 A2
Queensway. New M 195 F2
Queenswood Ave. Bour 191 F1
Queenswood Dr. Fern 165 E4
Quilter Cl. Southa 104 B2
Quince La. Wi Mi 163 E3
Quinton Cl. Christ 210 C4
Quinton Cl. Ports 182 B2
Quintrell Ave. Portc 156 A4
Quob La. Eastl 80 C2
Quomp. Rin 141 D4

R L Stevenson Ave. Bour 206 A2
Racecourse View. Lyn 121 F3
Rachel Cl. Fa Oa 57 D1
Racton Ave. Cos 158 A4
Radcliffe Rd. Southa 103 D3
Radclyffe Rd. Fare 131 E1
Radipole Rd. Poole 189 D1
Radley Cl. He En 81 E1
Radnor St. Ports 182 B2
Radstock Rd. Southa 103 F2
Radway Cres. Southa 102 B4
Radway Rd. Southa 78 C1
Raebarn Cl. Cher 14 B3
Raeburn Dr. He En 105 E4
Raglan Cl. Ch Fo 55 D2
Raglan Gdns. Bour 190 A1
Raglan St. Ports 182 B3
Ragmore La. Frox G 18 C3
Rails La. S Hay 185 E1
Railway View Rd. Southa 103 E4
Railway View. Ports 182 B3
Rake Rd. Liss 21 D2
Raleigh Cl. Christ 209 F3
Raleigh Cl. New M 195 F2
Raleigh Cl. Rin 141 E4
Raleigh Rd. Poole 189 F1
Raley Rd. Lo He 129 D1
Ralph La. Rom 28 A1
Ralph Rd. Broa 187 F4
Ramalley La. Ch Fo 55 D4
Ramblers Way. Wat 112 B1
Ramley Rd. Lym 198 A2
Rampart Gdns. Ports 157 F3
Rampart Rd. Southa 103 E4
Rampart The. Lym 198 B3
Ramsay Pl. Gos 155 E1
Ramsay Rd. Ki Wo 2 B4
Ramsay Rd. S Hay 185 D2
Ramsdale Ave. Hav 135 E3
Ramsdean Rd. Langr 39 F1
Ramshill. Pet 41 D2
Rances Way. Winch 10 C3
Randall Cl. Tot 76 B1
Randall Rd. Ch Fo 30 B1
Randall's La. Bur 142 C3
Randalls Hill. Upt 187 D1
Randolph Rd. Bour 207 F2
Randolph Rd. Poole 205 E3
Randolph St. Southa 102 B4
Ranelagh Gdns. Southa 102 C4
Ranelagh Rd. Christ 210 C4
Ranelagh Rd. Hav 135 E1
Ranelagh Rd. Ports 157 E1
Range Gdns. Southa 104 A2
Range Gn. Ports 157 E2
Rannoch Cl. Fare 130 C2
Ransome Cl. Lo He 153 F4
Ranvilles La. Fare 154 A4
Rapson Cl. Cos 133 E1
Rareridge La. Bi Wa 83 F4
Ratcliffe Rd. He En 105 E4
Ratcliffe Rd. Hyt 125 F1
Ratley La. Awb 26 C2
Raven Rd. Southa 103 D3
Raven Sq. Eastl 55 E1
Raven Way. Christ 210 A3
Ravens Cl. Stubb 154 B1
Ravens Way. M on S 213 E2
Ravenscourt Rd. Bour 208 B3
Ravenscourt Rd. Lym 198 B1
Ravenscroft Cl. Burs 104 C1
Ravenscroft Way. Botl 81 F1
Ravenswood. Lo He 129 E2
Ravine Rd. Bour 208 A2
Ravine Rd. Poole 216 C4
Raymond Cl. Holb 150 B2
Raymond Cl. Ver 115 D3
Raymond Cl. W End 80 C2
Raymond Rd. Portc 132 C1
Raymond Rd. Southa 102 B4
Rayners Gdns. Southa 79 E2
Raynes Rd. Lon S 180 A2
Reading Room La. Curd 106 B4
Readon Cl. Pet 41 D2
Rebbeck Rd. Bour 208 A3
Recess The. Eastl 56 A3
Record Rd. Ems 136 C1
Recreation Rd. Poole 205 F3
Rectory Ave. Broa 162 B1
Rectory Cl. Gos 181 D1
Rectory Cl. Stubb 154 B2
Rectory Ct. Botl 105 F4
Rectory Hill. W Dean 3 E2
Rectory La. Brea 46 A1
Rectory La. Meons 61 E3
Rectory La. Mott 5 F1
Rectory La. Twyf 32 A3
Rectory Rd. Hav 159 F4
Rectory Rd. Poole 204 B3
Red Barn Ave. Portc 132 B1
Red Barn La. Fare 130 C2
Red Hill Cres. Southa 78 C2
Red Hill Way. Southa 78 C2
Red La. Broa 187 D4
Red La. Comp 31 F4
Red La. Ows 58 A3
Red La. W Tyth 4 A4
Red Leaves. Shed 83 F1
Red Lodge. Ch Fo 55 D2
Red Oaks Cl. Fern 165 D4
Redan Cl. Christ 210 C4
Redan The. Gos 181 E1
Redbreast Rd N. Bour 191 D2
Redbreast Rd. Bour 191 D2
Redbridge Causeway. Tot 101 D4
Redbridge Gr. Hav 135 E2
Redbridge Hill. Southa 77 F1
Redbridge La. Nur 77 E2
Redbridge Rd. Southa 101 E4
Redcar Ave. Ports 158 A1
Redcar St. Southa 102 A4
Redcliffe Cl. Burt 193 E2
Redcote Cl. Southa 104 A4
Redcotts La. Wi Mi 163 D3
Redcotts Rd. Wi Mi 163 D3
Redcroft La. Burs 105 D1
Redfords The. Tot 76 C1
Redhill Ave. Bour 190 C2
Redhill Cl. Bour 190 C2
Redhill Cl. Southa 78 C2
Redhill Cres. Bour 190 C2
Redhill Ct. Bour 191 D2
Redhill Dr. Bour 190 C2
Redhill Rd. Ro Ca 113 D1
Redhill. Southa 78 C2
Redhoave Rd. Broa 188 C1
Redhorn Cl. Hamw 203 E2
Redlands Dr. Southa 103 F3
Redlands Gr. Ports 183 E2
Redlands La. Ems 136 C2
Redlands La. Fare 154 C4
Redlands. Poole 205 F3
Redlynch Cl. Hav 136 A2
Redmans View. Ver 114 C3
Redmoor Cl. Southa 103 F3
Redrise Cl. Holb 150 B2
Redshank Cl. Broa 187 F1
Redshank Rd. Horn 112 A4
Redvers Cl. Lym 198 B1
Redvers Rd. Christ 209 F4
Redward Rd. Southa 77 F3
Redwing Ct. Ports 183 E3
Redwing Gdns. Tot 100 B4
Redwing Rd. Clanf 88 B2
Redwood Cl. Hyt 125 E2
Redwood Cl. Lym 198 B3
Redwood Cl. Rin 141 D4
Redwood Dr. Fern 165 E4
Redwood Dr. Portc 156 A4
Redwood Gdns. Tot 100 B4
Redwood Rd. Upt 203 D4
Redwood Way. Southa 79 D3
Reed Dr. March 101 F1
Reedmace Cl. Wat 135 D3
Reeds La. Liss 21 E3
Reeds La. Ra 21 E3
Reeds Pl. Gos 181 D3
Reeds Rd. Gosp 181 D4
Reeves Cl. W Wel 50 C2
Reeves Way. Burs 104 C1
Regal Cl. Cos 157 F4
Regency Ct. Hav 159 F4
Regency Gdns. Wat 134 B3
Regency Pl. Rin 141 D4
Regent Cl. Ott 31 E2
Regent Dr. Bour 207 F4
Regent Mews. Pet 40 B2
Regent Pl. Ports 182 A2
Regent Rd. Ch Fo 55 E3
Regent St. Ports 182 B4
Regent St. Southa 102 C2
Regent Way. Christ 209 D3
Regent's Gr. Southa 102 A4
Regent's Park Gdns. Southa 102 A4
Regent's Park Rd. Southa 102 A4
Reginald Rd. Ports 183 D2
Reid St. Christ 209 D4
Relay Rd. Wat 134 B4
Reliant Cl. Ch Fo 55 D3
Rempstone Rd. Oakl 188 B4
Renault Dr. Broa 188 A1
Renda Rd. Holb 150 B2
Renny Rd. Ports 182 C3
Renouf Cl. Lym 198 B2
Renown Cl. Ch Fo 55 D3
Renown Gdns. Wat 111 F3
Repton Cl. Gos 180 C2
Repton Gdns. He En 81 E1
Repton Gdns. He En 81 E1
Reservoir La. He En 105 D3
Reservoir La. Pet 40 C3
Rest-a-wyle Ave. S Hay 185 D3
Retreat Rd. Wi Mi 163 E2
Retreat The. Eastl 56 A2
Retreat The. Ports 182 B2
Retreat The. Tot 101 D3
Revenge Cl. Ports 183 E3
Rewlands Dr. Winch 1 B2
Reynolds Ct. Rom 53 D3
Reynolds Dale. Tot 100 B3
Reynolds Rd. Fa Oa 57 E1
Reynolds Rd. Southa 102 B4
Rhinefield Cl. Bish 56 C1
Rhinefield Cl. Brock 145 F1
Rhinefield Cl. Hav 135 E2
Rhinefield Rd. Brock 145 D1
Rhinefield Rd. Brock 170 C1
Rhiners Cl. Sway 172 A1
Rhyme Hall Mews. Faw 151 D2
Ribble Cl. Broa 188 A1
Ribble Cl. Ch Fo 55 E3
Ribble Ct. Southa 77 F1
Ricardo Cres. Christ 210 A3
Richard Cl. Upt 203 D4
Richard Gr. Gos 156 A1
Richards Cl. Lo He 129 D2
Richlans Rd. He En 105 E3
Richmond Cl. Ch Fo 30 B1
Richmond Cl. S Hay 184 C2
Richmond Cl. Tot 76 A1
Richmond Dr. S Hay 184 C2
Richmond Gdns. Bour 206 C2
Richmond Hill Dr. Bour 206 C2
Richmond Hill. Bour 206 C2
Richmond La. Rom 28 A1
Richmond Park Ave. Bour 207 E4
Richmond Park Cl. Bour 207 E3
Richmond Park Cres. Bour 207 E4
Richmond Park Rd. Bour 207 E4
Richmond Pl. Ports 182 A3
Richmond Rd. Gos 181 D2
Richmond Rd. L on S 179 F3
Richmond Rd. Poole 205 E2
Richmond Rd. Ports 182 B1
Richmond Rd. Southa 102 B3
Richmond Rd. Wi Mi 163 E2
Richmond Rise. Portc 132 B1
Richmond St. Southa 103 D2
Richmond Wood Rd. Bour 207 E4
Richville Rd. Southa 102 A4
Ridding Cl. Southa 78 B1
Riders La. Hav 135 F2
Ridge Cl. Clanf 88 B2
Ridge La. Rom 76 B4
Ridge La. Swanw 106 B2
Ridge The. Red 47 E3
Ridge Top La. Frox G 39 F3
Ridgefield Gdns. Christ 210 B4
Ridgemount Ave. Southa 78 C3
Ridgemount Gdns. Hamw 203 F2
Ridgeway Cl. Ch Fo 55 F3
Ridgeway Cl. Cos 132 C1
Ridgeway Cl. Fa Oa 57 E2
Ridgeway La. Lym 198 B1
Ridgeway The. Portc 131 F1
Ridgeway Wlk. Ch Fo 55 F3
Ridgeway. Broa 187 E4
Ridgeway. Broa 188 A2
Ridgeway. Fern 190 C4
Ridgeway. Winch 10 B3
Ridgewood Cl. Hyt 125 E2
Ridings The. Fa Oa 57 D1
Ridings The. Liss 21 D2
Ridings The. Ports 157 F2
Ridings The. Shed 83 F2
Ridley Cl. Holb 150 B2
Ridley Rd. Bour 206 C4
Ridout Cl. Bour 190 A1
Rigby Rd. Southa 103 D4
Riggs Gdns. Bour 189 F1
Rigler Rd. Hamw 204 A1
Rimington Gdns. Rom 28 A1
Rimington Rd. Wat 111 F2
Rimmer's Ct. Ports 181 F2
Ring The. Rown 78 C4
Ringbury. Lym 198 B3
Ringwood Dr. N Bad 53 F3
Ringwood Rd. Alderh 93 D3
Ringwood Rd. Bour 189 F2
Ringwood Rd. Bran 194 B3
Ringwood Rd. Bur 142 C3
Ringwood Rd. Christ 195 D1
Ringwood Rd. Fern 165 E2
Ringwood Rd. Fordi 94 B2
Ringwood Rd. Ne Ma 100 B4
Ringwood Rd. Poole 189 E1
Ringwood Rd. Poole 204 C3
Ringwood Rd. Ports 183 D2
Ringwood Rd. Sop 193 D4
Ringwood Rd. St Le 139 E1
Ringwood Rd. Tot 100 B4
Ringwood Rd. Ver 115 D3
Ringwood Rd. W Moo 138 C4
Ripley Gr. Ports 183 D4
Ripon Rd. Bour 191 D1
Ripplewood. March 102 A1
Ripstone Gdns. Southa 79 D2
Rise The. Brock 145 F1
Rise The. Wat 134 B1
Ritchie Ct. Southa 104 A2
Ritchie Pl. W Moo 138 B2
Ritchie Rd. Bour 190 A2
Rival Moor Rd. Pet 41 E1
River Cl. Wi Mi 163 E3
River Gdns. M on S 213 F2
River Green. Hamble 128 A1
River La. Fare 130 B3
River Mews. Bish 56 B2
River St. Ports 182 B2
River St. Westb 137 D2
River View Rd. Southa 79 E1
River Way. Christ 192 B1
River Wlk. Southa 79 F2
Riverdale Ave. Wat 135 D4
Riverdale Cl. Fordi 69 F1
Riverlea Rd. Christ 209 D3
Rivermead Cl. Rom 52 B4
Rivermead Gdns. Christ 192 C1
Riversdale Cl. Southa 126 C4
Riversdale Rd. Bour 209 D2
Riverside Ave. Bour 192 B1
Riverside Ave. Fare 131 E2
Riverside Cl. Cadn 99 E3
Riverside Cl. Liss 20 C2
Riverside Ct. Southa 103 E4
Riverside Gdns. Rom 52 C3
Riverside La. Bour 208 C3
Riverside Mews. Christ 209 E3
Riverside Park. Christ 209 D3
Riverside Rd. Bour 208 C3
Riverside Rd. W Moo 138 B1
Riverside Terr. Fare 131 E1
Riverside. Bish 56 B2
Riverside. Rin 140 C3
Riverview Terr. Swanw 128 B4
Riverview. Tot 100 C3
Road View. Ports 182 B4
Roads Hill. Horn 88 A1
Robert Cecil Ave. Southa 79 F2
Robert Whitworth Dr. Rom 52 C4
Roberts Cl. Hord 197 F1
Roberts Cl. Wickh 108 A2
Roberts La. Broa 204 A4
Roberts Rd. Bour 208 A3
Roberts Rd. Broa 188 A1
Roberts Rd. Gos 180 C3
Roberts Rd. Hyt 125 F2
Roberts Rd. Southa 102 C3
Roberts Rd. Tot 100 C3
Robin Gdns. Tot 100 B4
Robin Gdns. Wat 111 E2
Robin Sq. Eastl 55 E1
Robina Cl. Wat 135 D4
Robinia Grn. Southa 78 B3
Robins Cl. Stubb 154 B2
Robins Meadow. Lo He 129 E1
Robins Way. Christ 210 A3
Robinson Ct. Portc 132 B1
Robinson Rd. Stubb 154 A1
Robinson Way. Ports 158 B2
Robinswood Dr. Fern 165 E4
Rochester Rd. Bour 190 A2
Rochester Rd. Ports 182 C2
Rochester St. Southa 103 E3
Rochford Rd. Cos 157 E4
Rockall Cl. Southa 77 F3
Rockbourne Cl. Hav 135 E2
Rockbourne Gdns. B on S 211 E4
Rockbourne La. Dame 68 B4
Rockbourne La. Rockb 68 B4
Rockbourne Rd. Winch 1 B2
Rockford Cl. Bour 208 C2
Rockingham Way. Portc 156 A4
Rockleigh Dr. Tot 100 B3
Rockleigh Rd. Southa 78 B2
Rockley Rd. Hamw 203 F1
Rockram Cl. Cadn 99 D4
Rockram Gdns. Hyt 125 E2
Rockstone La. Southa 103 D4
Rockstone Pl. Southa 102 C3
Rockville Dr. Wat 134 C4
Rodbourne Cl. Hord 213 E4
Rodfield La. Ovin 13 E3
Rodney Cl. Gos 180 B3
Rodney Cl. Poole 206 A4
Rodney Ct. Southa 104 B2
Rodney Dr. Christ 209 F3
Rodney Rd. Ports 183 D3
Rodney Way. Horn 112 A3
Rodway. Wi Mi 163 E2
Rodwell Cl. Bour 190 B3
Roebuck Cl. Cos 157 F4
Roebuck Cl. New M 196 A2
Roeshot Cres. Christ 194 C1
Roeshot Hill. Christ 194 B1
Roewood Cl. Holb 150 B2
Roewood Rd. Holb 150 B2
Rogate Gdns. Portc 132 B1
Rogers Cl. Bish 56 C2
Rogers Cl. Gos 181 D3
Rogers Mead. N Hay 159 F2
Rogers Rd. Bish 56 C2
Roland Cl. Horn 112 A3
Rollestone Rd. Holb 150 B1
Rolls Dr. Bour 209 D2
Roman Cl. Ch Fo 55 F4
Roman Dr. Rown 78 C4
Roman Gdns. Hyt 125 E1
Roman Gr. Portc 156 B3
Roman Hts. Broa 187 F4
Roman Meadow. Down 46 C4
Roman Rd. Broa 187 F3
Roman Rd. Hav 136 B1
Roman Rd. Holb 150 A3
Roman Rd. Hyt 125 E1
Roman Rd. Hyt 149 F4
Roman Rd. Rown 78 C4
Roman Rd. Twyf 32 A3
Roman Way. Hav 135 E1
Roman Way. Hyt 125 E1
Roman Way. Pamp 162 B3
Roman's Rd. Winch 11 D3
Romford Rd. Lo He 152 B4
Romill Cl. W End 80 A2
Romney Cl. Bour 190 C2
Romney Rd. Bour 190 C2
Romsey Ave. Portc 156 A4
Romsey Ave. Ports 183 D3
Romsey Cl. Eastl 56 A2
Romsey Ind Est. Rom 52 C4
Romsey Rd. Cadn 75 E2
Romsey Rd. Eastl 56 A2
Romsey Rd. Horn 88 B1
Romsey Rd. Lyn 121 F3
Romsey Rd. Ower 75 E2
Romsey Rd. Rown 77 F2
Romsey Rd. Southa 77 F2
Romsey Rd. W Wel 51 D2
Romsey Rd. Whit 24 C2
Romsey Rd. Winch 10 B4
Rook Hill Rd. Christ 210 B3
Rookcliff Way. M on S 213 E2
Rookery Ave. Swanw 129 E4
Rookery La. Brea 45 F1
Rookery The. Herm 137 D1
Rookes Cl. Horn 112 A3
Rookes La. Lym 198 B1
Rookley. Net 127 E4
Rooks Down Rd. Winch 10 B3
Rooksbridge. Hyt 125 E2
Rooksbury Croft. Hav 136 A3
Rooksway Gr. Portc 155 F4
Rookwood Cl. Eastl 56 A3
Rookwood View. Den 110 C3
Roosevelt Cres. Bour 190 D3
Rope Hill. Bold 173 E1
Rope Wlk. Hamble 128 A1
Ropers La. Upt 203 E4
Ropley Cl. Southa 127 D4
Ropley Rd. Bour 208 B4
Ropley Rd. Hav 136 A3
Rosamund Ave. Oakl 163 F1
Roscrea Cl. Bour 209 D2
Roscrea Dr. Bour 209 D2
Rose Cl. He En 105 E4
Rose Cl. Hyt 126 A1
Rose Cres. Poole 204 C3
Rose Gdns. Bour 191 D2
Rose Hill. Wat 112 A3
Rose Rd. Southa 103 D4
Rose Rd. Tot 101 D3
Rosebank Cl. Rown 77 F3
Rosebay Ct. Wat 134 C3
Rosebay. Fa Oa 81 E3
Rosebery Ave. Cos 158 A4
Rosebery Ave. Hyt 126 A1
Rosebery Cres. Eastl 56 A3
Rosebery Rd. Bour 208 A3
Rosebud Ave. Bour 191 D1
Rosedale Ave. Rom 53 D4
Rosedale Cl. Christ 209 F3

## Rosedale Cl. Lo He

Rosedale Cl. Lo He .............. 153 F4
Rosehill Cl. Bran ................. 169 D1
Rosehill Dr. Bran ................. 169 D1
Roselands Cl. Fa Oa ............. 57 D2
Roselands Gdns. Southa ........ 79 D1
Roselands. W End ............... 104 B4
Roselands. Wat ................... 112 A3
Roseleigh Dr. Tot ................ 100 C3
Rosemary Gdns. He En ......... 105 E3
Rosemary La. Ports .............. 182 A3
Rosemary Rd. Poole ............. 205 E4
Rosemary Way. Wat ............. 112 A3
Rosemary Wlk. L on S .......... 179 F3
Rosemoor Gr. Ch Fo .............. 30 A1
Rosemount Rd. Bour ............ 206 A1
Rosendale Rd. Ch Fo ............. 55 E2
Rosery The. Gos .................. 181 D1
Rosetta Rd. Ports ................ 183 D2
Rosewall Rd. Southa .............. 77 F2
Rosewarne Ct. Winch .............. 2 A1
Rosewood Gdns. Clanf ........... 88 B3
Rosewood Gdns. March ......... 102 A1
Rosewood Gdns. New M ....... 195 F2
Rosewood. Gos ................... 155 F1
Rosina Cl. Wat ................... 135 D4
Roslin Gdns. Bour ................ 206 B4
Roslin Rd S. Bour ................ 206 C4
Roslin Rd. Bour .................. 206 C4
Rosoman Rd. Southa ............ 103 F2
Ross Gdns. Bour .................. 189 E3
Ross Gdns. Southa ................ 78 A1
Ross Glades. Bour ............... 206 C3
Ross Rd. Rin ...................... 117 E1
Ross Way. L on S ................ 179 F4
Rossan Ave. Lo He .............. 152 B4
Rossington Ave. Southa ........ 103 F4
Rossington Way. Southa ........ 103 F4
Rossiters La. Ne Ma .............. 99 F3
Rossley Cl. Christ ................ 194 C1
Rosslyn Cl. N Bad ................. 54 A2
Rossmore Rd. Poole ............. 205 E4
Rostrevor La. Ports ............. 182 C1
Rostron Cl. W End ................ 80 A1
Rosyth Rd. Southa ............... 103 F4
Rotary Cl. Wi Mi ................. 163 F4
Rotary Ct. Net .................... 127 D3
Rothbury Cl. Southa ............ 104 A2
Rothbury Cl. Tot ................... 76 B1
Rothbury Park. New M ......... 196 A1
Rother Cl. Pet ...................... 41 E2
Rother Cl. W End ................. 80 A1
Rother Dale. Southa ............ 104 C2
Rotherbank Farm La. Liss ....... 21 D3
Rothercombe La. Pet ............. 40 A2
Rotherfield Rd. Bour ............ 208 A2
Rotherfield Rd. Christ .......... 195 D1
Rotherwick Cl. Hav .............. 136 A3
Rothesay Dr. Christ ............. 210 C4
Rothesay Rd. Bour .............. 206 B3
Rothesay Rd. Gosp .............. 181 D4
Rothsbury Dr. N Bad ............. 55 D3
Rothville Pl. Ch Fo ............... 30 A1
Rothwell Cl. Cos ................. 133 D1
Rotterdam Dr. Christ ........... 209 E4
Roughdown La. Holb ............ 150 B1
Roumelia La. Bour .............. 207 F2
Round Hill. Fordi .................. 69 F1
Roundabouts The. Liss ........... 21 D3
Roundcopse. Hyt ................ 125 E2
Roundhaye Rd. Bour ............ 189 F3
Roundhill Cl. Southa .............. 80 A1
Roundhouse Dr. Tot ............ 100 A3
Roundhouse Meadow. Herm .. 161 D4
Roundway. Wat ................... 134 C4
Roundways. Bour ................ 189 F2
Routs Way. Rown .................. 77 F4
Row The. Red ....................... 47 E4
Row Wood La. Gos .............. 155 D1
Rowallan Ave. Gos .............. 180 B4
Rowan Ave. Wat ................. 112 A1
Rowan Cl. Christ ................. 210 B4
Rowan Cl. L on S ................ 179 F3
Rowan Cl. Rom .................... 53 E3
Rowan Cl. Southa ................. 78 A2
Rowan Cl. St Le .................. 139 E2
Rowan Cl. Swan ................... 84 A2
Rowan Cl. Sway .................. 172 A1
Rowan Cl. Tot .................... 100 B3
Rowan Ct. Ports ................. 182 C2
Rowan Dr. Broa ................... 187 F1
Rowan Dr. Christ ................ 210 B4
Rowan Dr. Ver .................... 115 D2
Rowan Gdns. He En ............. 105 E3
Rowan Rd. Hav ................... 136 A2
Rowan Tree Cl. Liss .............. 21 D2
Rowan Way. Fare ................ 154 B4
Rowans Park. Lym ............... 198 B2
Rowans The. March .............. 101 F1
Rowbarrow Cl. Broa ............ 188 C1
Rowborough Rd. Southa ....... 103 F4
Rowbury Rd. Hav ................ 135 E3
Rowdell Cl. Bour ................. 190 B3
Rowden Cl. W Wel ................ 50 C1
Rowe Asheway. Lo He .......... 128 C2
Rowena Rd. Bour ................ 208 C3
Rowes Alley. Ports .............. 181 F2
Rowes La. E Bol .................. 200 A4
Rowhay La. Ows ................... 58 B3
Rowhill Dr. Hyt .................. 125 E2

Rowin Cl. S Hay .................. 185 E1
Rowland Ave. Poole ............. 204 C3
Rowland Ct. Fare ................ 130 C1
Rowland Rd. Portc ............... 132 C1
Rowlands Castle Rd. Horn .... 112 C3
Rowlands Cl. Ch Fo ............... 55 D2
Rowlands Hill. Wi Mi ........... 163 E3
Rowlands Wlk. Southa ........... 80 A1
Rowley Cl. Botl .................. 105 F4
Rowley Dr. Botl .................. 105 F4
Rowlings Rd. Winch ................. 1 B2
Rowner Cl. Gos .................. 155 E1
Rowner La. Gos .................. 155 E1
Rowner Rd. Gos ................. 155 D1
Rowner Rd. Stubb ............... 155 D1
Rownhams Cl. Rown .............. 77 F3
Rownhams Ct. Southa ............ 77 F2
Rownhams La. Rown .............. 53 F1
Rownhams Rd N. Southa ........ 77 F3
Rownhams Rd. Bour ............ 191 E2
Rownhams Rd. Hav .............. 135 E3
Rownhams Rd. N Bad ............ 54 A2
Rownhams Rd. Southa ........... 77 F2
Rownhams Way. Rown ........... 77 F3
Royal Crescent Rd. Southa .... 103 D2
Royal Gdns. Ro Ca ............... 113 D1
Royal Oak Rd. Bour ............. 190 B3
Royal Way. Wat ................. 135 D4
Royden La. Bold .................. 173 E1
Royden Ave. Eastl ................. 56 A3
Royston Cl. Southa ................ 79 D1
Royston Dr. Wi Mi ............... 163 E3
Royston Pl. B on S .............. 212 A4
Rozel Ct. Southa ................... 77 F2
Rozelle Cl. Litt ...................... 1 A3
Rozelle Rd. Poole ................ 205 E2
Rubens Cl. New M ............... 196 A2
Ruby Rd. Southa ................. 104 A3
Rudd Lane. Mich .................. 27 F4
Rudgewick Cl. Portc ............ 156 A4
Rudmore Rd. Ports .............. 182 B4
Rudmore Sq. Ports .............. 182 B4
Ruffield Cl. Winch .................. 1 B1
Rufford Cl. Eastl ................... 56 A3
Rufford Gdns. Bour ............. 208 C3
Rufus Cl. Ch Fo ................... 55 F4
Rufus Cl. Rown ..................... 77 E3
Rufus Gdns. Tot ................. 100 B4
Rugby Rd. Broa .................. 188 A1
Rugby Rd. Ports ................. 182 C2
Rumbridge Gdns. Tot .......... 101 D4
Rumbridge St. Tot .............. 101 D3
Runnymede Ave. Bour ......... 189 F3
Runnymede. Fare ............... 130 B2
Runnymede. W End ............... 80 B1
Runton Rd. Poole ................ 205 F3
Runway The. Christ ............. 210 A4
Rushall La. Broa ................. 187 D3
Rushcombe Way. Broa ......... 187 F3
Rushes Rd. Pet .................... 40 C2
Rushes The. March .............. 101 F1
Rushford Warren. Christ ....... 209 F2
Rushington Ave. Tot ........... 100 C3
Rushington La. Tot .............. 100 C3
Rushmere La. Hambl ........... 110 C4
Rushmere Rd. Bour ............. 208 B4
Rushmere Wlk. Hav ............. 135 E3
Rushpole Ct. Hyt ................ 125 E2
Rushton Cres. Bour ............. 206 C3
Ruskin Ave. Bour ............... 191 D2
Ruskin Rd. Eastl .................. 56 A3
Ruskin Rd. Ports ................ 183 D3
Ruskin Way. Wat ................ 111 F2
Rusland Cl. Ch Fo ................. 55 D4
Russel Rd. Bour ................. 190 B3
Russell Cl. L on S ............... 179 F3
Russell Cotes Rd. Bour ........ 207 D1
Russell Dr. Christ ............... 209 E3
Russell Gdns. St Le ............. 140 A3
Russell Pl. Fare ................. 131 D1
Russell Pl. Southa ................ 79 D1
Russell Rd. Hav .................. 135 F2
Russell Rd. L on S .............. 179 F3
Russell Rd. Winch ................... 2 A1
Russell St. Gos ................... 181 D3
Russell St. Southa ............... 103 D2
Russell Way. Pet .................. 41 D1
Russet Cl. Fern .................. 165 E3
Russett Cl. Lym .................. 198 C1
Russett Cl. Swan .................. 84 A2
Rustan Cl. Fa Oa ................... 57 E1
Rustan Cl. He En ................ 105 D3
Rutland Rd. Bour ................ 207 D4
Rutland Rd. Christ .............. 192 C1
Rutland Way. W End .............. 80 A1
Ruxley Cl. Holb .................. 150 B2
Ryall Dr. Poole ................... 188 B1
Ryan Cl. Fern ..................... 165 E4
Ryan Gdns. Bour ................ 190 A3
Ryan Gdns. Fern ................. 165 E4
Rydal Cl. Christ .................. 192 B2
Rydal Rd. Gos .................... 181 D4
Ryde Pl. L on S ................... 180 A2
Ryde Terr. Southa ............... 103 D2
Rye Dale. Ashu .................. 100 B2
Rye Paddock La. Faw .......... 151 D2
Ryecroft Ave. Bour ............. 189 F3
Ryecroft. Lo He .................. 129 E1

Ryedown La. W Wel .............. 51 F2
Ryefield Cl. Pet ................... 41 E2
Rylandes Ct. Southa .............. 77 F2

Sabre Rd. Th Is .................. 161 D2
Sackville St. Ports .............. 182 B2
Saddle Cl. Wi Mi ................. 164 B3
Saddlers Cl. Eastl ................ 56 A3
Sadlers La. Hyt ................. 126 A1
Saffron Dr. Christ ............... 210 A4
Sage Cl. Wat ..................... 135 D3
Sages La. Frox G ................. 17 E3
Sailors La. Meons ................ 60 B4
St Agatha's Rd. Hamble ....... 128 A2
St Alban's Ave. Bour ........... 207 E4
St Alban's Cres. Bour .......... 207 D4
St Alban's Rd. Bour ............ 207 D4
St Alban's Rd. Hav .............. 136 A2
St Alban's Rd. Ports ........... 182 C2
St Alban's Rd. Southa ......... 103 D3
St Aldhelm's Cl. Poole ........ 205 F2
St Aldhelm's Rd. Poole ....... 205 F2
St Andrew Cl. Horn .............. 88 B1
St Andrew's Rd. Cos ........... 158 C4
St Andrew's Rd. Gos ........... 181 D2
St Andrew's Rd. Ports ......... 182 B2
St Andrew's Rd. S Hay ........ 185 D1
St Andrews Cl. Mich ............. 27 E3
St Andrews Cl. N Bad ........... 53 F3
St Andrews Green. Meons ...... 61 E3
St Andrews Park. Fa Oa ........ 81 E3
St Andrews Rd. Broa ........... 188 A3
St Andrews Rd. Southa ........ 103 D3
St Ann's Cres. Gos .............. 181 D3
St Ann's Rd. Horn ............... 112 B4
St Anne's Ave. Bour ............ 208 C3
St Anne's Gdns. Southa ....... 103 F1
St Anne's Gr. Fare .............. 154 C4
St Anne's Rd. Ports ............ 182 C2
St Anne's Rd. Southa .......... 103 F1
St Anne's Rd. Upt ............... 203 D4
St Annes Cl. Winch ............... 10 B2
St Annes Gdns. Lym ............ 198 B2
St Annes La. Shed .............. 107 F4
St Anthony's Rd. Bour ......... 206 C3
St Aubin's Ave. Southa ........ 104 A3
St Aubin's Park. S Hay ........ 184 B2
St Aubyns Cl. Poole ............ 204 A1
St Aubyns La. Rin ............... 117 F1
St Augustin's Rd. Bour ........ 206 C3
St Augustine Rd. Ports ........ 182 C2
St Augustines Gdns. Southa ... 79 E1
St Austell Cl. Bish ................ 56 C2
St Barbara Way. Ports ......... 157 F2
St Barbe Cl. Rom ................. 53 D3
St Bartholomew's Gdns. Ports 182 B2
St Birinus Rd. Red ................ 47 E3
St Blaize Rd. Rom ................ 53 E4
St Brelade Pl. Southa ............ 77 E2
St Brelades Ave. Poole ........ 189 E1
St Brelades. Poole .............. 205 E1
St Catherine St. Ports ......... 182 B1
St Catherine's Rd. Bour ....... 208 C2
St Catherine's Rd. S Hay ...... 184 B2
St Catherine's Rd. Southa ...... 79 F1
St Catherine's Rd. Winch ....... 11 D3
St Catherines Way. Christ .... 192 B2
St Catherines Rd. Eastl ......... 56 A3
St Catherines View. He En .... 105 D3
St Catherines Way. Portc ..... 131 F1
St Catherines. Wi Mi ........... 163 E2
St Chad's Ave. Ports ........... 157 F1
St Christopher Ave. Fare ...... 131 D2
St Christopher's Rd. Hav ...... 135 E2
St Christophers Cl. N Bad ...... 54 A2
St Christophers Gdns. Gos .... 155 E1
St Clair Rd. Poole ............... 216 C4
St Clares Ave. Hav ............. 135 E4
St Clement St. Winch ............ 11 D4
St Clement's Gdns. Bour ...... 207 E3
St Clement's Rd. Bour ......... 207 E3
St Clements Cl. Rom ............. 52 C4
St Clements La. Poole .......... 204 A1
St Clements Rd. Poole ......... 205 D4
St Colman's Ave. Cos .......... 158 A4
St Cross Rd. Winch ............... 10 C3
St Cuthberts Cl. Lo He ......... 129 D2
St Cuthberts La. Lo He ........ 129 D2
St David's Cl. Tot ................. 76 B1
St David's Rd. Clanf ............. 88 B3
St David's Rd. Ports ............ 182 B2
St David's Rd. Upt ............... 203 D4
St Davids Rd. Lo He ............ 128 C2
St Denys Rd. Southa ............. 79 E1
St Denys Wlk. Hav .............. 135 E3
St Edmund Cl. Lo He ........... 129 D1
St Edmund's Rd. Southa ...... 102 A4
St Edward's Rd. Gos ........... 181 D2
St Edward's Rd. Ports ......... 182 B2
St Edwards Rd. Net ............. 127 D4
St Elizabeth's Ave. Southa ... 104 A4
St Evox Cl. Southa ................ 77 F3
St Faith's Cl. Gos ............... 181 D3
St Faith's Rd. Ports ............ 182 B3
St Faith's Rd. Winch ............. 10 C3
St Francis Ave. Southa ........ 104 A4
St Francis Cl. Black ............. 177 F4
St Francis Pl. Hav .............. 135 F2
St Francis Rd. Black ............ 177 F4

St Francis Rd. Gos ............. 181 E1
St Gabriel's Rd. Southa ....... 104 A4
St George Cl. Burs .............. 104 C1
St George's Ave. Bour ......... 207 E4
St George's Ave. Hav .......... 136 A1
St George's Ave. Poole ........ 205 D4
St George's Bsns Ctr. Ports .. 182 A3
St George's Cl. Bour ........... 207 E4
St George's Cl. Christ ......... 210 B4
St George's Cres. Fordi ........ 69 F1
St George's Dr. Fern ........... 165 E2
St George's Rd. Cos ............ 157 F4
St George's Rd. Ports .......... 182 A2
St George's Rd. Ports .......... 183 D1
St George's Rd. S Hay ......... 184 B2
St George's Sq. Bi Wa ........... 83 E4
St George's St. Southa ........ 103 D2
St George's St. Winch ........... 11 D4
St George's Wlk. Wat .......... 134 C4
St Georges Cl. Bran ............ 194 A4
St Georges Rd. Fordi ............ 69 F1
St Georges Rd. Lo He .......... 128 C2
St Georges Sq. Ports .......... 182 A3
St Giles Way. Horn ............... 88 B1
St Helen's Cl. Ports ............ 182 C1
St Helen's Par. Ports .......... 182 C1
St Helen's Park Cres. Ports .. 182 C1
St Helen's Rd. Gos ............. 180 C2
St Helen's Rd. S Hay ........... 184 B2
St Helena Gdns. Southa ......... 79 F2
St Helena Way. Portc .......... 156 B4
St Helier Pl. Southa .............. 77 F2
St Helier Rd. Poole ............. 189 E1
St Hellen's Rd. Cos ............. 158 B4
St Hermans Rd. S Hay ......... 185 E1
St Hilda Ave. Horn ............... 88 B1
St Hubert Rd. Horn .............. 88 B1
St Ives End Rd. St Le ........... 140 A2
St Ives Gdns. Bour ............. 206 C3
St Ives Park. St Le .............. 140 A3
St Ives Wood. St Le ............ 140 A3
St James Cl. Clanf ............... 88 B2
St James Cl. Poole ............. 204 A1
St James Rd. Fern .............. 165 D3
St James Rd. Sway ............. 172 B1
St James Way. Portc .......... 156 B4
St James' La. Winch ............. 10 C4
St James Park. Meons .......... 61 E3
St James' Terr. Winch ........... 10 C4
St James's Cl. Southa ........... 78 B1
St James's Park Rd. Southa .... 78 B1
St James's Rd. Ports ........... 182 B2
St James's Rd. Southa ......... 102 B4
St James's Sq. Bour ............ 208 A3
St James's St. Ports ............ 182 A3
St John's Centre. He En ....... 105 E3
St John' S Rd. Southb .......... 137 E1
St John's Ave. Wat ............. 134 C2
St John's Cl. Gos ............... 181 D3
St John's Cl. Wi Mi ............. 163 E2
St John's Hill. Wi Mi ........... 163 E3
St John's Rd. Bour ............. 207 F2
St John's Rd. Christ ............ 209 D3
St John's Rd. Cos ............... 158 A4
St John's Rd. Eastl ............... 56 A2
St John's Rd. Hav ............... 135 E2
St John's Rd. He En ............ 105 D3
St John's Rd. Lo He ............ 129 D1
St John's Rd. Poole ............ 204 B2
St John's Rd. Winch ............. 11 D4
St John's St. Hyt ............... 126 A2
St John's St. Winch ............. 11 D4
St Johns Cl. Rown ................ 77 F3
St Johns Ct. March ............. 101 F1
St Johns Dr. March ............. 101 F1
St Johns Glebe. Rown ........... 77 F3
St Johns Rd. New M ............ 196 A4
St Johns Sq. Gos ............... 181 D3
St Joseph Cl. Lo He ............ 129 D2
St Just Cl. Fern .................. 165 E2
St Lawrence Cl. He En ........... 81 E1
St Lawrence Rd. Eastl ........... 56 A2
St Lawrence Rd. Southa ....... 103 D2
St Ledger's Pl. Bour ............ 207 E3
St Ledger's Rd. Bour .......... 207 E3
St Leonard's Ave. S Hay ...... 185 D2
St Leonard's Cl. Swanw ...... 129 F2
St Leonard's Rd. Bour ......... 207 D3
St Leonard's Rd. Winch ......... 11 E3
St Leonards Way. St Le ....... 139 E2
St Luke's Rd. Bour ............. 206 C4
St Luke's Rd. Gos .............. 181 D1
St Margaret's Ave. Christ .... 209 D3
St Margaret's Cl. Southa ...... 104 A4
St Margaret's Rd. Bish .......... 56 B1
St Margaret's Rd. Bour ........ 190 B1
St Margarets Cl. Wi Mi ........ 163 D3
St Margarets Hill. Wi Mi ...... 163 D3
St Margarets Rd. Lo He ....... 129 F1
St Margarets Rd. S Hay ....... 185 D2
St Mark's Cl. Gos ............... 181 D1
St Mark's Rd. Bour ............. 190 A2
St Mark's Rd. Gos .............. 181 D1
St Mark's Rd. Ports ............ 157 E1
St Marks Rd. Lym .............. 198 A2
St Martin Cl. Winch .............. 11 D4
St Martin's Cl. Southa ........... 77 F2

St Martins Rd. Upt .............. 203 D4
St Mary Gr. Hord ............... 197 D1
St Mary St. Winch ................ 10 B3
St Mary's Ave. Gos ............. 181 D1
St Mary's Cl. Ki Wo ............... 2 B3
St Mary's Cl. Red ................. 47 F2
St Mary's Pl. Southa ........... 103 D2
St Mary's Rd. Bour ............. 207 E3
St Mary's Rd. Fern ............. 165 E3
St Mary's Rd. Liss ................ 20 C2
St Mary's Rd. Net ............... 127 E3
St Mary's Rd. Poole ............ 204 C2
St Mary's Rd. Ports ............ 182 C3
St Mary's Rd. S Hay ........... 184 C2
St Mary's Rd. Southa .......... 103 D3
St Mary's Rd. Stubb ........... 154 B2
St Mary's St. Southa ........... 103 D2
St Marys Cl. Bran .............. 194 B4
St Matthews Cl. Southa ....... 103 D3
St Matthews Ct. Gos ........... 181 E3
St Matthews Rd. Winch .......... 1 B1
St Merrin's Cl. Bour ........... 190 B2
St Michael's Gdns. Winch ...... 10 C4
St Michael's Gr. Fare .......... 154 C4
St Michael's Pass. Winch ....... 11 D3
St Michael's Pl. Bour .......... 206 C2
St Michael's Rd. Bour ......... 206 C1
St Michael's Rd. Hav .......... 135 E2
St Michael's Rd. Ports ........ 182 A2
St Michael's Rd. Winch ........ 10 C3
St Michael's Sq. Southa ....... 102 C4
St Michael's St. Southa ....... 102 C2
St Michaels Cl. Ver ............. 114 C3
St Michaels Rd. Lo He ......... 129 D1
St Michaels Rd. Tot ............ 100 C4
St Michaels Rd. Ver ............ 114 C2
St Michaels Way. Horn .......... 88 B1
St Monica Rd. Southa .......... 104 A2
St Nicholas Ave. Gos .......... 180 B4
St Nicholas Rise. Ki Wo .......... 2 A3
St Nicholas St. Ports .......... 182 A2
St Nicholas' Rd. Hav ........... 135 E2
St Osmund's Rd. Poole ....... 205 E2
St Patrick's La. Liss ............. 21 E3
St Patrick's La. Ra ............... 21 E3
St Paul's Hill. Winch ............. 10 C4
St Paul's La. Bour .............. 207 D2
St Paul's Rd. Bour .............. 207 D2
St Paul's Rd. Lo He ............ 128 C3
St Paul's Rd. Ports ............. 182 A2
St Paul's Sq. Ports ............. 182 A2
St Peter St. Winch ............... 11 D4
St Peter's Ave. N Hay ......... 160 B1
St Peter's Gr. Ports ............ 182 B2
St Peter's Rd. Bour ............. 207 D2
St Peter's Rd. Pet ................ 40 C2
St Peter's Rd. Poole ........... 205 D2
St Peter's St. Bi Wa ............. 83 E4
St Peters Cl. Curd .............. 106 B4
St Peters Rd. N Hay ........... 160 B2
St Philip's Way. Southa ....... 104 A4
St Piran's Ave. Ports .......... 183 D4
St Roman's Ave. Ports ........ 182 C1
St Roman's Rd. Ports ......... 182 C1
St Sebastian Cres. Fare ...... 131 D2
St Simon Cl. Lo He ............. 129 D2
St Simon's Rd. Ports .......... 182 B1
St Stephen's Rd. Bour ........ 206 C2
St Stephen's Rd. Ports ....... 182 C4
St Stephen's Rd. Winch ......... 1 B1
St Stephen's Way. Bour ...... 206 C2
St Stephens La. Ver ........... 115 D4
St Swithin Cl. Bi Wa ............. 83 D4
St Swithun St. Winch ............ 11 D4
St Swithun's Cl. N Bad .......... 28 B1
St Swithun's Rd S. Bour ...... 207 D2
St Swithun's Rd. Bour ......... 207 D2
St Swithun's Rd. Ports ........ 157 F1
St Theresas Cl. Hav ........... 135 E2
St Thomas Ave. S Hay ........ 184 B2
St Thomas Park. Lym ......... 198 B2
St Thomas St. Winch ............ 11 D4
St Thomas's Cl. Bour .......... 190 C1
St Thomas's Rd. Gosp ........ 181 D4
St Thomas's St. Lym .......... 198 C2
St Thomas's St. Ports ......... 182 A2
St Tristan Cl. Lo He ............ 129 D2
St Ursula Gr. Ports ............ 182 B2
St Valerie Rd. Bour ............ 206 C3
St Valerie Rd. Gos ............. 181 D2
St Vigor Way. Co Com ......... 57 D4
St Vincent Cres. Horn ......... 112 A3
St Vincent Rd. Ports .......... 181 D3
St Vincent Rd. Ports .......... 182 B1
St Vincent St. Ports ........... 182 A2
St Winifred's Rd. Bour ........ 206 C3
St Winifred's Rd. Southa ....... 78 B1
Salcombe Ave. Ports .......... 158 A1
Salcombe Cl. Ch Fo .............. 55 D2
Salcombe Cres. Tot ............ 100 C3
Salcombe Rd. Southa .......... 102 B4
Salcombe Rd. Tot .............. 100 C3
Salcot Rd. Winch ................... 2 A1
Salem St. Southa ................. 78 B1
Salerno Dr. Gos ................. 180 C2
Salerno Pl. Hamw .............. 203 E1
Salerno Rd. Ports .............. 157 E2
Salerno Rd. Southa .............. 78 B2

# Salisbury Cl. Eastl

Salisbury Cl. Eastl ............ 56 A2
Salisbury Rd. Awb ............ 52 A3
Salisbury Rd. Bour .......... 207 F2
Salisbury Rd. Burt .......... 193 E2
Salisbury Rd. Cos ........... 158 A4
Salisbury Rd. Fordi .......... 70 A1
Salisbury Rd. Ower ........... 76 A2
Salisbury Rd. Poole ......... 205 E3
Salisbury Rd. Ports ......... 182 C1
Salisbury Rd. Rin ........... 140 C4
Salisbury Rd. Sop ........... 193 E2
Salisbury Rd. Southa ......... 79 D2
Salisbury Rd. Tot ............ 76 C1
Salisbury Rd. W Wel .......... 50 B2
Salisbury St. Fordi .......... 69 F1
Salisbury St. Southa ........ 102 C3
Salisbury Terr. L on S ...... 179 F3
Salmon Dr. Bish ............. 56 C1
Salt La. Meons .............. 34 C2
Salter Rd. Poole ............ 216 B2
Salterns Ave. Ports ......... 183 D3
Salterns Cl. S Hay .......... 185 E2
Salterns Estate. Fare ....... 155 D4
Salterns La. Burs ........... 128 A4
Salterns La. Fare ........... 155 D4
Salterns La. Faw ............ 151 D2
Salterns La. S Hay .......... 185 E2
Salterns Rd. Poole .......... 205 D2
Salterns Rd. Stubb .......... 179 D4
Salterns Way. Poole ......... 216 A4
Salters Acres. Winch ......... 1 B2
Salters La. Winch ............ 1 A1
Saltgrass La. M on S ........ 214 A2
Saltings Rd. Upt ............ 203 D3
Saltings The. Cos ........... 158 C4
Saltings The. Hav ........... 159 F3
Saltmarsh La. S Hay ......... 184 C3
Saltmarsh Rd. Southa ........ 103 D2
Salvia Cl. Wat .............. 135 D3
Salwey Rd. He En ............ 105 E3
Samber Cl. Lym .............. 198 B2
Samphire Cl. Lym ............ 198 C3
Samples Way. Poole .......... 204 C4
Samson Cl. Gos .............. 180 B4
Samson Rd. Hamw ............. 203 E1
Samuel Rd. Ports ............ 182 C3
San Diego Rd. Gos ........... 181 D3
Sancreed Rd. Poole .......... 205 F4
Sand Cl. W Wel ............... 50 C2
Sandbanks Rd. Poole ......... 205 D1
Sandbourne Rd. Bour ......... 206 B1
Sandbourne Rd. Poole ........ 204 B2
Sandcroft Cl. Gos ........... 180 C2
Sandecotes Rd. Poole ........ 205 E2
Sandell Ct. Southa ........... 79 D3
Sanderling Rd. Ports ........ 183 E3
Sanderlings The. S Hay ...... 185 D1
Sanderlings. Rin ............ 141 E3
Sandford Ave. Gos ........... 180 B2
Sandford Cl. Bour ........... 191 E2
Sandford Way. Broa .......... 187 F1
Sandhills Cl. Broa .......... 188 B1
Sandhurst Dr. W Moo ......... 139 D4
Sandhurst Rd. Southa ........ 102 C3
Sandilands Way. Hyt ......... 126 A1
Sandisplatt. Fare ........... 154 B4
Sandle Copse. Fordi .......... 69 D1
Sandleford Rd. Hav .......... 135 E4
Sandleheath Ind Est. Fordi ... 69 D1
Sandleheath Rd. Alderh ....... 92 C4
Sandlewood Cl. Clanf ......... 88 B3
Sandlewood Cl. Tot .......... 100 B4
Sandown Cl. Gos ............. 180 B2
Sandown Rd. Christ .......... 209 F3
Sandown Rd. Cos ............. 157 F4
Sandown Rd. Southa ........... 78 A1
Sandpiper Cl. Broa .......... 187 F1
Sandpiper Cl. Horn .......... 112 A4
Sandpiper Cl. March ......... 101 F1
Sandpiper Rd. Southa ......... 78 A3
Sandpipers. Cos ............. 158 C4
Sandpit La. Beaul ........... 200 B3
Sandpit La. Poole ........... 204 B2
Sandport Gr. Portc .......... 156 A4
Sandringham Cl. Bour ........ 191 D2
Sandringham Gdns. Bour ...... 191 D2
Sandringham La. Ports ....... 182 C3
Sandringham Rd. Fare ........ 154 B4
Sandringham Rd. Pet .......... 40 C2
Sandringham Rd. Poole ....... 205 E2
Sandringham Rd. Ports ....... 182 C3
Sandringham Rd. Southa ....... 79 F1
Sandy Beach Estate. S Hay .. 185 F1
Sandy Brow. Wat ............. 134 B2
Sandy Cl. Pet ............... 41 E2
Sandy Cl. Wi Mi ............. 164 A4
Sandy Down. Bold ............ 173 E2
Sandy La. Abb ............... 28 A2
Sandy La. Bish .............. 57 E1
Sandy La. Bour .............. 208 A3
Sandy La. Christ ............ 192 C1
Sandy La. Lo He ............. 153 F4
Sandy La. Lyn ............... 121 F3
Sandy La. N Bad ............. 54 A3
Sandy La. Pamp .............. 162 A3
Sandy La. Ra ................ 21 F2
Sandy La. Red ............... 47 F4
Sandy La. Shed .............. 83 E1
Sandy La. Shed .............. 107 E4

Sandy La. St Le ............. 140 A3
Sandy La. Upt ............... 203 D3
Sandy La. Ver ............... 115 D3
Sandy La. W Moo ............. 114 C1
Sandy La. Wi Mi ............. 164 A4
Sandy Mead Rd. Bour ......... 191 F1
Sandy Plot. Burt ............ 209 E4
Sandy Point Rd. S Hay ....... 185 F1
Sandy Way. Bour ............. 190 C2
Sandycroft. Lo He ........... 152 B4
Sandyfield Cres. Wat ........ 111 F2
Sandyhurst Cl. Broa ......... 188 B1
Sanross Cl. Stubb ........... 154 A1
Sapphire Ridge. Wat ......... 135 D4
Saracen Cl. Lym ............. 198 B1
Saracens Rd. Ch Fo ........... 55 F4
Sarah Cl. Bour .............. 208 A4
Sarah Sands Cl. Christ ...... 209 E4
Sark Rd. Poole .............. 205 E4
Sarnia Ct. Southa ........... 77 F2
Sarum Ave. W Moo ............ 138 C2
Sarum Rd. Ch Fo .............. 55 F3
Sarum Rd. Hurs ............... 9 F4
Sarum Rd. Winch ............. 10 A4
Sarum St. Poole ............. 204 A1
Sarum View. Winch ........... 10 A4
Sarum Wlk. Lym .............. 198 B3
Satchell La. Hamble ......... 128 A2
Saturn Cl. Southa ........... 77 F2
Saulfland Pl. Christ ........ 210 B4
Saulford Dr. Christ ......... 210 B4
Saunders La. Awb ............ 26 C3
Savage Cl. Gos .............. 180 B3
Savernake Cl. Gos ........... 155 E1
Savernake Cl. Rom ........... 28 A1
Saville Cl. Bish ............ 56 B3
Saville Cl. Gos ............. 180 C2
Saville Gdns. Fare .......... 131 D2
Sawyer Cl. Winch ............. 1 A1
Saxholm Cl. Southa .......... 78 C3
Saxholm Dale. Southa ........ 78 C3
Saxholm Way. Southa ......... 78 C3
Saxley Ct. Hav .............. 135 E3
Saxon Cl. Horn .............. 88 B2
Saxon Cl. Lo He ............. 128 C1
Saxon Cl. Portc ............. 132 A1
Saxon Gdns. He En ........... 105 D3
Saxon King Gdns. Bour ....... 209 D2
Saxon Meadow. Down ........... 47 D4
Saxon Pl. Lym ............... 198 B3
Saxon Rd. Black ............. 150 C1
Saxon Rd. Southa ............ 102 B3
Saxon Rd. Winch .............. 2 A1
Saxon Sq. Christ ............ 209 D3
Saxon Way. Alderh ........... 93 D3
Saxon Way. Rom .............. 53 D4
Saxonbury Rd. Bour .......... 208 C3
Saxonford Rd. Christ ........ 210 B4
Saxonhurst Cl. Bour ......... 190 C3
Saxonhurst Rd. Bour ......... 190 C2
Saxonhurst. Down ............ 47 D4
Sayers Rd. Bish ............. 56 C2
Scafell Ave. Fare ........... 154 B4
Scallows La. Plai ........... 50 C3
Scantabout Ave. Ch Fo ....... 55 F4
Scarf Rd. Poole ............. 204 C4
Scholars' Wlk. Cos .......... 158 B4
School Cl. Ch Fo ............ 55 D3
School Cl. N Bad ............ 55 D3
School Hill. Sob ............ 85 E3
School La. Bold ............. 198 C4
School La. Bour ............. 190 D3
School La. Bran ............. 169 F2
School La. Ch Fo ............ 55 D3
School La. Compt ............ 90 C1
School La. Den .............. 110 B3
School La. Ems .............. 160 C4
School La. Hamble ........... 128 A1
School La. Ki Wo ............. 2 A3
School La. Lym .............. 198 C2
School La. M on S ........... 213 F3
School La. Pet .............. 41 D3
School La. Red .............. 73 E4
School La. Rin .............. 141 D4
School La. Southb ........... 161 F4
School La. St Le ............ 140 A2
School La. W Moo ............ 138 C4
School La. Westb ............ 137 D3
School La. Wi Mi ............ 163 D3
School Rd. Bran ............. 169 E2
School Rd. Burs ............. 128 A4
School Rd. Faw .............. 151 D2
School Rd. Gos .............. 155 F1
School Rd. Hav .............. 135 F1
School Rd. Hyt .............. 126 A2
School Rd. Red ............... 48 A3
School Rd. Rom .............. 28 B1
School Rd. Tot .............. 101 D3
School Rd. Twyf ............. 31 F3
School Rd. W Wel ............ 50 C1
School Rd. Wickh ............ 108 A2
Schooner Way. Lo He ......... 128 C1
Schooner Way. Ports ......... 183 E3
Scimitars The. Stubb ........ 154 A2
Scivier's La. Uph ............ 58 B1
Scotland Cl. Fa Oa .......... 57 F1
Scott Cl. Poole ............. 189 F1
Scott Cl. Stubb ............. 154 B2
Scott Rd. Eastl .............. 55 F1

Scott Rd. Poole ............. 189 F1
Scott Rd. Ports ............. 158 A3
Scott Rd. Southa ............ 103 F1
Scott's Green. Christ ....... 209 F4
Scotter Rd. Bish ............ 56 B2
Scotter Rd. Bour ............ 208 A3
Scotter Sq. Bish ............ 56 B2
Scotts Cl. Co Com ........... 57 D4
Scotts Hill La. Christ ...... 209 E4
Scratchface La. Hav ......... 135 D1
Scratchface La. Wat ......... 134 C2
Scullards La. Southa ........ 102 C2
Sea Crest Rd. L on S ........ 179 F3
Sea Front. S Hay ............ 184 C2
Sea Grove Ave. S Hay ........ 185 D1
Sea Kings. Stubb ............ 154 A1
Sea La. Stubb ............... 179 E4
Sea Rd. B on S .............. 211 F4
Sea Rd. Bour ................ 207 F2
Sea Rd. Bour ................ 208 C2
Sea Rd. M on S .............. 213 F2
Sea Rd. Southa .............. 103 E2
Sea View Estate. Net ........ 127 D3
Sea View Rd. Cos ............ 134 B1
Sea View Rd. Poole .......... 205 D3
Sea View Rd. S Hay .......... 185 E2
Sea View Rd. Upt ............ 203 D4
Seabank Cl. Upt ............. 203 D4
Seabird Way. Fare ........... 155 D4
Seabourne Pl. Bour .......... 208 A3
Seabourne Rd. Bour .......... 208 A3
Seabreeze Way. M on S ....... 213 D3
Seacombe Green. Southa ...... 77 E1
Seacombe Rd. Poole .......... 216 A2
Seacroft Ave. B on S ........ 211 F4
Seafarers Wlk. S Hay ........ 185 F1
Seafield Cl. B on S ......... 211 F4
Seafield Dr. Bour ........... 208 C3
Seafield Park Rd. Stubb ..... 154 A1
Seafield Rd. B on S ......... 211 F4
Seafield Rd. Bour ........... 208 B2
Seafield Rd. Christ ......... 210 B4
Seafield Rd. Portc .......... 156 A4
Seafield Rd. Ports .......... 158 A1
Seafield Rd. Southa .......... 77 F2
Seafields. Ems .............. 160 C4
Seaford Cl. Burs ............ 104 C1
Seagarth Cl. Southa .......... 78 B2
Seagarth La. Southa .......... 78 B2
Seager's Ct. Ports .......... 181 F2
Seagrove Rd. Ports .......... 157 E1
Seagull La. Ems ............. 136 C1
Seagull Rd. Bour ............ 191 E1
Seagulls The. L on S ........ 180 A2
Seahorse Wlk. Gos ........... 181 E3
Seamans La. Min ............. 98 B2
Seamead. Stubb .............. 179 E4
Seamoor La. Bour ............ 206 A2
Seamoor Rd. Bour ............ 206 A2
Searles Hill. Twyf ........... 32 A3
Seaton Ave. Ports ........... 183 D4
Seaton Cl. Christ ........... 211 D4
Seaton Cl. Lym .............. 198 C3
Seaton Cl. Stubb ............ 154 B1
Seaton Cl. W End ............. 80 B1
Seaton Rd. Christ ........... 211 D4
Seatown Cl. Poole ........... 189 D1
Seaview Ave. Portc .......... 132 C1
Seaview Rd. B on S .......... 211 E4
Seaview Rd. Christ .......... 195 E1
Seaward Ave. B on S ......... 211 F4
Seaward Gdns. Southa ........ 103 F2
Seaward Rd. Hyt ............. 126 A2
Seaward Rd. Southa .......... 103 F2
Seaway Ave. Christ .......... 210 B4
Seaway Cres. Ports .......... 183 E2
Seaway Gr. Portc ............ 156 B3
Seaway Ave. M on S .......... 212 A4
Seawinds. M on S ............ 213 D3
Sebastian Gr. Wat ........... 135 D4
Second Ave. Cos ............. 157 F4
Second Ave. Cos ............. 158 C4
Second Ave. Ems ............. 136 A1
Second Ave. Southa .......... 101 E4
Second Ave. Southb .......... 161 E4
Second Marine Ave. B on S .. 212 A3
Sedbergh Rd. Southa .......... 77 E1
Sedgefield Cl. Portc ........ 156 C4
Sedgefield Cl. Tot .......... 100 B4
Sedgeley Gr. Gos ............ 181 D4
Sedgemead. Net .............. 127 D3
Sedgewick Cl. Gos ........... 180 B4
Sedgewick Cl. Bish .......... 56 B2
Sedgewick Rd. Southa ........ 104 B3
Sedgley Cl. Ports ........... 182 B2
Sedgley Rd. Bour ............ 206 C4
Segars La. Twyf .............. 31 F3
Segensworth Rd. Lo He ....... 129 F2
Selangor Ave. Ems ........... 136 B1
Selborne Ave. Hav ........... 135 E3
Selborne Ave. Southa ........ 104 B4
Selborne Rd. Tot ............ 100 B4
Selborne Wlk. Southa ........ 104 B4
Selbourne Dr. Eastl .......... 56 A2
Selbourne Gdns. Gos ......... 180 C2
Selbourne Rd. Hav ........... 135 F1
Selbourne Terr. Ports ....... 182 C3

Selby Cl. Broa .............. 188 A2
Seldon Cl. Winch ............ 10 A2
Seldown Br. Poole ........... 204 B1
Seldown La. Poole ........... 204 B2
Seldown Rd. Poole ........... 204 B2
Seldown. Poole .............. 204 B2
Self Rd. Poole .............. 204 A1
Selfridge Ave. Bour ......... 209 D2
Selhurst Way. Fa Oa .......... 57 E1
Seliot Cl. Poole ............ 204 B3
Selkirk Cl. Oakl ............ 163 F1
Sellwood Rd. Net ............ 127 E3
Sellwood Way. B on S ........ 211 E4
Selsdon Ave. Rom ............ 53 D4
Selsey Ave. Gos ............. 181 D4
Selsey Ave. Ports ........... 183 D1
Selsey Cl. S Hay ............ 185 F1
Selsey Cl. Southa ............ 77 F1
Selsmore Ave. S Hay ......... 185 E1
Selsmore Rd. S Hay .......... 185 D2
Selworth La. Sob ............ 85 D2
Selworthy Cl. Poole ......... 205 D1
Selwyn Gdns. Eastl ........... 56 A3
Sengana Cl. He En ........... 105 F3
Senlac Rd. Rom .............. 53 D4
Sennen Pl. Ports ............ 157 D4
Sentinel Cl. Wat ............ 112 A1
Sephton Cl. Gos ............. 180 B3
September Cl. W End .......... 80 B1
Serle Cl. Tot ............... 100 A4
Serle Gdns. Tot ............. 100 B3
Sermon Rd. Winch ............. 1 A1
Serpentine Rd. Fare ......... 131 D1
Serpentine Rd. Poole ........ 204 B2
Serpentine Rd. Ports ........ 182 B1
Serpentine Rd. Wat .......... 134 B2
Service Rd. Cos ............. 157 E4
Set Thorn Rd. Sway .......... 172 B1
Setley Gdns. Bour ........... 191 F2
Setters Cl. Co Comm ......... 56 C4
Settle Cl. Southa ........... 102 A4
Settlers Cl. Ports .......... 182 B3
Sevenoaks Dr. Bour .......... 208 A4
Sevenoaks Rd. Cos ........... 157 F4
Severn Cl. Cos .............. 133 D1
Severn Cl. Portc ............ 156 A4
Severn Rd. Fern ............. 166 A3
Severn Rd. Southa ........... 101 F4
Severn Rd. W End ............ 80 B1
Seward Ave. Bour ............ 208 B2
Seward Rise. Rom ............ 53 E4
Seymour Cl. Ch Fo ............ 55 F3
Seymour Cl. Ports ........... 182 B4
Seymour Cl. Southa ........... 78 B1
Seymour Cl. Tot ............. 76 B1
Seymour La. N Bad ........... 53 F2
Seymour Rd. Lo n S .......... 180 A2
Seymour Rd. Rin ............. 117 D1
Seymour Rd. Southa ........... 78 B2
Shackleton Rd. Gos .......... 180 B4
Shackleton Sq. Bran ......... 169 D1
Shadwell Rd. Ports .......... 157 F1
Shaftesbury Ave. Ch Fo ...... 55 E2
Shaftesbury Ave. Southa ...... 79 D1
Shaftesbury Ave. Wat ........ 134 C2
Shaftesbury Rd. Gos ......... 181 E2
Shaftesbury Rd. W Moo ....... 138 C1
Shaftesbury St. Fordi ........ 69 F1
Shaftsbury Rd. Bour ......... 207 E3
Shaftsbury Rd. Poole ........ 204 B2
Shaftsbury Rd. Ports ........ 182 B1
Shaggs Meadow. Lyn .......... 122 A3
Shakepear Rd. Ports ......... 182 C4
Shakespeare Ave. Southa ..... 103 D4
Shakespeare Dr. Tot ......... 76 B1
Shakespeare Gdns. Wat ....... 111 F2
Shakespeare Rd. Bour ........ 208 B4
Shakespeare Rd. Eastl ....... 56 A2
Shakespeare Rd. Wi Mi ....... 163 E3
Shalbourne Rd. Gos .......... 181 D4
Shalcombe. Net .............. 127 E4
Shalden Cl. Southa ........... 78 B2
Shaldon Rd. Hav ............. 136 A3
Shales Rd. Southa ........... 104 A4
Shallows The. Brea .......... 70 B4
Shamblehurst La N. He En ..... 81 E2
Shamblehurst La N. W End ..... 81 E2
Shamblehurst La S. He En ..... 81 E1
Shamrock Cl. Gos ............ 181 E2
Shamrock Rd. Southa ......... 103 E2
Shamrock Way. Hyt ........... 126 A3
Shanklin Cres. Southa ........ 78 B1
Shanklin Rd. Ports .......... 182 C2
Shanklin Rd. Southa .......... 78 B1
Shannon Cl. Fare ............ 130 B1
Shannon Rd. Stubb ........... 154 A2
Shannon Way. N Bad .......... 55 D3
Shapland Ave. Bour .......... 189 F3
Shappen Hill La. Bur ........ 142 C1
Shapton Cl. Holb ............ 150 A2
Shapwick Rd. Hamw ........... 204 A1
Shard Cl. Ver ............... 115 D3
Sharlands Cl. Broa .......... 188 A2
Sharon Rd. W End ............ 80 B1
Sharp Rd. Poole ............. 206 A4
Sharp's Rd. Hav ............. 136 A3
Sharpley Cl. Fordi ........... 69 F2
Sharpness Cl. Fare .......... 154 B4

Sharvells Rd. M on S ........ 213 E3
Shavard La. Meons ........... 61 E3
Shaves La. New M ............ 196 A3
Shaw Cl. Tot ................ 100 B4
Shaw Cl. W End .............. 80 A1
Shaw Rd. Rin ................ 117 E1
Shawfield Rd. Hav ........... 136 A1
Shawford Cl. Southa .......... 78 C2
Shawford Gdns. Bour ......... 191 E1
Shawford Gr. Hav ............ 135 E3
Shawford Rd. Bour ........... 191 E2
Shayer Rd. Southa ............ 78 B1
Shear Hill. Steep ............ 41 D3
Sheardley La. Sob ............ 29 D1
Shearer Rd. Ports ........... 182 C4
Shears Brook Cl. Bran ....... 169 D1
Shears Rd. Bish .............. 56 C2
Shearwater Cl. Gos .......... 155 D1
Shearwater Dr. Cos .......... 158 C4
Sheep Pond La. Drox ......... 61 D2
Sheep St. Pet ............... 40 C2
Sheepwash La. Den ........... 133 F4
Sheffield Cl. Bish ........... 56 B3
Sheffield Rd. Ports ......... 182 C3
Shelbourne Cl. Bour ......... 207 E3
Shelbourne Rd. Bour ......... 207 D3
Sheldrake Gdns. Hord ........ 197 D2
Sheldrake Gdns. Southa ....... 78 A3
Sheldrake Rd. Christ ........ 210 A3
Shelford Rd. Ports .......... 183 D3
Shell Ct. March ............. 101 F1
Shellcroft. Lo He ........... 152 B4
Shelley Ave. Portc .......... 132 C1
Shelley Cl. Christ .......... 210 B4
Shelley Cl. St Le ........... 139 F3
Shelley Cl. Winch ........... 10 B4
Shelley Gdns. Wat ........... 111 F2
Shelley Hill. Christ ........ 210 B4
Shelley La. Ower ............ 51 F1
Shelley Rd E. Bour .......... 207 F3
Shelley Rd. Bour ............ 207 E3
Shelley Rd. Eastl ........... 55 F1
Shelley Rd. Poole ........... 205 E3
Shelley Rd. Southa .......... 104 C3
Shelley Rd. Tot ............. 76 B1
Shelley Way. M on S ......... 213 E3
Shelton Rd. Bour ............ 208 B3
Shenstone Ct. New M ......... 196 A1
Shepards Cl. Fare ........... 154 B4
Shepherd Cl. Christ ......... 194 C1
Shepherds Cl. Cadn .......... 99 D3
Shepherds Cl. Winch ......... 10 A2
Shepherds Hey Rd. Tot ........ 76 A1
Shepherds La. Comp .......... 31 E3
Shepherds La. Ibs ........... 115 E4
Shepherds Purse Cl. Lo He .. 128 C1
Shepherds Rd. Cadn .......... 99 E3
Shepherds Way. Bour ......... 208 A4
Shepherds Way. Winch ........ 11 E4
Sheppards Field. Wi Mi ...... 163 D3
Sherborn Cres. Poole ........ 189 D1
Sherborne Ct. Eastl .......... 56 A3
Sherborne Dr. Fern .......... 165 E2
Sherborne Way. He En ........ 105 E3
Sherbrooke Cl. Ki Wo ......... 2 B4
Sherfield Ave. Hav .......... 136 A3
Sherfield Cl. Bour .......... 191 E1
Sherfield English La. Plai .. 50 B3
Sheridan Cl. Southa ......... 104 B3
Sheridan Gdns. Tot .......... 100 B4
Sheridan Cl. Winch .......... 10 B3
Sheringham Rd. Cos .......... 133 E1
Sheringham Rd. Poole ........ 205 F3
Sherley Green. Burs ......... 105 D1
Sherrin Cl. Poole ........... 204 B3
Sherringham Cl. Faw ......... 151 D2
Sherwin Wlk. Gos ............ 181 D2
Sherwood Ave. Fern .......... 165 E2
Sherwood Ave. He En ......... 105 E2
Sherwood Ave. Poole ......... 205 D2
Sherwood Cl. Liss ........... 21 D4
Sherwood Cl. Southa ......... 78 C2
Sherwood Dr. Ver ............ 115 D3
Sherwood Gdns. Lo He ........ 128 C2
Sherwood Rd. Ch Fo .......... 30 C1
Sherwood Rd. Gos ............ 181 D2
Sherwood Way. Black ......... 177 F4
Shetland Cl. Tot ............ 100 A4
Shillinglee. Wat ............ 134 C2
Shillingstone Dr. Bour ...... 191 D2
Shillito Rd. Poole .......... 205 F3
Shingle Bank Dr. M on S ..... 213 D2
Ship Leopard St. Ports ...... 182 A3
Shipcote La. Bi Wa .......... 59 E1
Shipley Rd. Twyf ............ 32 A4
Shipstal Ct. Hamw ........... 203 E2
Shipton Green. Hav .......... 135 E3
Shire Cl. Swanw ............. 129 D4
Shire Cl. Wat ............... 112 B1
Shires The. He En ........... 105 D3
Shirley Ave. Ports .......... 183 E2
Shirley Ave. Southa ......... 102 B4
Shirley Cl. Bran ............ 169 D1
Shirley Cl. W Moo ........... 138 C1
Shirley High St. Southa ..... 102 A4
Shirley Holms. Bold ......... 173 D1
Shirley Holms. Sway ......... 173 D1
Shirley Park Rd. Southa ..... 102 A4

# Shirley Park Rd. Southa

## Shirley Rd. Bour

Stacey Cl. Poole

Shirley Rd. Bour .................. 191 D1
Shirley Rd. Poole ................ 205 D3
Shirley Rd. Ports ................ 182 C1
Shirley Rd. Southa .............. 102 B4
Shoblands Way. Hyt ............ 126 A1
Shoe La. Uph ....................... 58 C3
Sholing Ct. Hav ................... 135 E3
Sholing Rd. Southa .............. 103 F2
Shoot Hill. Den ................... 109 E2
Shoot Hill. Southw .............. 109 E2
Shoot La. Gos ...................... 180 A4
Shoot La. Lon S ................... 180 A4
Shooters Hill Cl. Southa ....... 104 A2
Shop La. Southa ................... 104 C1
Shore Ave. Ports ................. 183 D3
Shore Ave. Upt .................... 203 E3
Shore Cl. M on S ................. 213 E2
Shore Cl. Upt ....................... 203 E3
Shore Cres. Bi Wa ................ 83 E4
Shore Gdns. Upt ................. 203 D3
Shore La. Bi Wa .................... 83 E4
Shore La. Upt ...................... 203 E3
Shore Rd. Hyt ..................... 126 A2
Shore Rd. Lo He ................... 128 B1
Shore Rd. Poole ................... 216 B3
Shorefield Terr. Liss .............. 20 C2
Shorefield Rd. M on S .......... 213 E3
Shorefield Rd. M on S .......... 213 D3
Shorefield Rd. March ........... 101 F1
Shorefield Way. M on S ........ 213 E3
Shorehaven. Portc ............... 156 C4
Shorewell. Net ................... 127 E4
Short Cl. Poole .................... 206 A4
Short Hill. Red ...................... 73 D4
Short Hill. Rom .................... 28 B1
Short Rd. Stubb ................... 154 A1
Shorts Cl. Burt .................... 193 E1
Shorts Rd. Fa Oa .................. 57 E1
Shotterfield Terr. Liss ........... 20 C2
Shotters Hill Cl. W End .......... 80 B1
Shotts La. Bold .................... 199 E2
Shottsford Rd. Poole ............ 204 B3
Shravenshill Cl. Tot .............. 76 B1
Shrubb's Ave. Lym ............... 198 C2
Shrubbery The. Gos ............. 180 C4
Shrubbs Hill Rd. Lyn ............ 121 F3
Shrubland Cl. Southa ........... 104 A4
Sibland Cl. Fare .................. 154 B4
Sidings The. Down ................ 47 D4
Sidings The. Net ................. 127 E3
Sidlesham Cl. S Hay ............. 185 F1
Sidmouth Ave. Ports ........... 183 D4
Silchester Cl. Bour .............. 206 C3
Silchester Rd. Ports ............ 183 D4
Silkin Gdns. Tot ................. 100 B3
Silkstead Ave. Hav .............. 135 F3
Sillen La. Mar ...................... 43 D2
Silver Birch Ave. Fare .......... 154 C4
Silver Birch Cl. Liss .............. 21 D2
Silver Birch Cl. Southa ......... 104 B2
Silver Bsns Park. Christ ........ 209 F4
Silver Hill. Winch .................. 11 D4
Silver St. Christ ................... 209 D3
Silver St. Lyn ..................... 121 E3
Silver St. Ports ................... 182 A2
Silver Way. Christ ................ 210 C4
Silverdale Cres. Alderh ......... 93 D3
Silverdale Cl. Bour .............. 187 F2
Silverdale Rd. Southa .......... 102 C4
Silverdale. B on S ............... 212 A4
Silverlock Cl. Ports ............. 182 B4
Silvers End. Hyt ................. 126 A1
Silvers Wood. Tot ................ 76 B1
Silverthorne Way. Wat ......... 134 B4
Silvertrees. Ems ................. 136 C1
Silvester Rd. Wat ............... 111 F1
Silwood Cl. Winch .................. 1 B1
Simmonds Green. S Hay ....... 185 E2
Simmonds Rd. Poole ............ 204 B3
Simmons Cl. He En ............... 105 E4
Simnel St. Southa ............... 102 C2
Simon Way. Southa ............. 104 C3
Simpson Cl. Portc ............... 156 B4
Simpson Rd. Ports .............. 157 E1
Sinah La. S Hay .................. 184 B2
Sinclair Rd. Southa ............... 78 A3
Singleton Dr. Bour .............. 190 B1
Sir George's Rd. Southa ....... 102 B3
Sirdar Rd. Southa ................. 79 E2
Siskin Cl. Bi Wa .................... 83 D4
Siskin Cl. Fern ................... 165 D4
Siskin Cl. Southa .................. 78 A3
Siskin Gr. Wat ................... 135 D3
Sissinghurst Rd. Portc ......... 156 A4
Siverdale Dr. Wat ............... 111 E2
Six Dials. Southa ................. 103 D3
Six Oaks Rd. N Bad .............. 54 A3
Sixth Ave. Cos ................... 157 F4
Sizer Way. Hyt ................... 125 D2
Skew Rd. Portc ................... 132 B1
Skinner St. Poole ................ 204 B1
Skintle Green. Co Comm ....... 56 C4
Skipper Way. L on S ............ 180 A3
Skipton Cl. Broa ................. 188 A1
Skipton Rd. Fa Oa ................ 55 E2
Sky End La. Hord ................ 197 D1
Slab La. Red ........................ 47 E3
Slab La. W Wel ..................... 50 C2
Slades Farm Rd. Bour .......... 190 B1

Slades Hill. Black ................ 150 C1
Sleepbrook Cl. Ver .............. 114 C3
Sleepers Delle Gdns. Winch .... 10 C3
Sleepers Hill Gdns. Winch ...... 10 B3
Sleepers' Hill Rd. Winch ........ 10 B3
Sleight La. Broa .................. 187 E4
Slepe Cres. Poole ............... 205 F4
Slindon Gdns. Hav .............. 135 F1
Slindon St. Ports ................ 182 B3
Slingsby Cl. Ports ............... 182 A2
Slinn Rd. Christ .................. 209 F4
Slip Way. Poole .................. 204 A1
Slipper Rd. Herm ................ 161 D4
Slipway The. Ports .............. 157 D4
Sloane Ave. Holb ................ 150 B2
Sloane Ct. Holb .................. 150 B2
Sloane Park. Shed ............... 107 E4
Sloe Tree Cl. Lo He .............. 129 E1
Slough La. Upt ................... 203 D3
Smallcuts Ave. Southb ......... 137 E1
Smeaton St. Ports .............. 157 E1
Smeeton Rd. L on S ............ 179 F3
Smith Cl. Black ................... 150 C1
Smith Gr. He En ................. 105 E3
Smith La. Th Is ................... 161 E1
Smith St. Gos ..................... 181 D3
Smith's Field. Rom ............... 28 A1
Smithfield Pl. Bour .............. 190 C1
Smiths La. Shed ................. 107 F4
Smithson Cl. Poole ............. 206 B4
Smithy La. New M ............... 195 F3
Smugglers La N. Christ ......... 194 C1
Smugglers La S. Christ ......... 210 C4
Smugglers La. Wi Mi ........... 163 F4
Smugglers Wood Rd. Christ .. 194 B1
Smythe Rd. Southa .............. 104 B2
Snailing La. Hawk ................. 20 B4
Snails La. Rin ..................... 117 D2
Snakemoor La. Durl .............. 81 F3
Snakemoor La. Fa Oa ........... 81 F3
Snape Cl. Gos ..................... 180 B4
Snapgragon Cl. Lo He .......... 128 C1
Snellgrove Cl. Tot ................. 76 B1
Snooks La. Bold .................. 199 D3
Snowdon Dr. Fare ............... 154 C4
Snowdon Rd. Bour .............. 206 B2
Snowdrop Gdns. Christ ........ 194 A1
Soake Rd. Den .................... 111 D2
Soalwood La. Frox G ............. 39 F4
Soberton Rd. Bour ............... 207 E3
Soberton Rd. Hav ............... 135 F2
Soldridge Cl. Hav ................ 136 A3
Solent Ave. Lym ................. 199 D2
Solent Ave. Southa .............. 104 C3
Solent Cl. Ch Fo .................. 55 F3
Solent Cl. Lym ................... 198 C2
Solent Dr. B on S ................ 212 A4
Solent Dr. Hyt .................... 125 F2
Solent Dr. Lo He ................. 152 B3
Solent Ind Est. He En ............ 81 D1
Solent Rd. B on S ............... 211 E4
Solent Rd. Bour .................. 209 D2
Solent Rd. Christ ................ 195 D1
Solent Rd. Cos ................... 158 B4
Solent Rd. Hav ................... 135 F1
Solent Rd. Hyt .................... 149 F4
Solent Rd. Southa .............. 102 C2
Solent Rd. Stubb ................ 154 A1
Solent View. Faw ................ 178 C4
Solent Village. Lo He ........... 129 F3
Solent Way. Gos ................. 180 C2
Solent Way. M on S ............. 213 F2
Solly Cl. Poole .................... 205 F4
Solomons La. Shed ............... 83 F1
Solona Cl. Ch Fo .................. 55 F4
Somborne Dr. Hav ............... 135 F3
Somerby Rd. Poole ............. 204 B3
Somerford Ave. Christ ......... 210 A4
Somerford Cl. Southa .......... 104 A3
Somerford Rd. Christ .......... 209 F4
Somerford Way. Christ ........ 209 F3
Somerley Rd. Bour ............. 207 D4
Somerley View. Rin ............. 141 D4
Somers Cl. Winch .................. 10 B3
Somers Rd N. Ports ............. 182 C3
Somers Rd. Ports ............... 182 B2
Somerset Ave. Southa ......... 104 B4
Somerset Cres. Ch Fo ........... 55 E2
Somerset Rd. Bour .............. 208 A3
Somerset Rd. Christ ............ 208 C4
Somerset Rd. Ports ............ 182 B1
Somerset Rd. Southa ............ 79 E1
Somerset Terr. Southa ......... 102 B3
Somerton Ave. Southa ......... 104 A4
Somerton Cl. New M ............ 196 B2
Somervell Cl. Gos ............... 181 D1
Somervell Dr. Fare ............. 131 D2
Somerville Pl. Ports ............ 157 E1
Somerville Rd. Bour ............ 206 B2
Somerville Rd. Ki Wo ............. 2 B4
Somerville Rd. Rin .............. 141 E4
Sonnet Way. Wat ................ 135 D4
Sonning Way. Bour ............. 191 D1
Soper's La. Christ ............... 209 D3
Sopers La. Broa .................. 188 A1
Sopwith Cl. Christ ............... 210 A3
Sopwith Cres. Oakl ............. 163 F1
Sorrel Cl. Rom ...................... 28 B1
Sorrel Cl. Wat .................... 135 D3

Sorrel Gdns. Broa ............... 187 F1
Sorrell Cl. Lo He ................. 128 C1
Sorrell Ct. Christ ................ 210 A4
Sorrell Way. Christ ............. 210 A4
South Ave. New M ............... 196 A1
South Ave. Ports ................ 157 F2
South Baddesley Rd. Bold .... 199 D2
South Bay. Th Is ................. 161 D2
South Cl. Gos ..................... 180 C1
South Cl. Hav ..................... 160 A4
South Cl. Rom ...................... 28 B1
South Cliff Rd. Bour ............ 206 C1
South Cross St. Gos ............ 181 E2
South Ct. Hamble ................ 127 F1
South Dr. Litt ........................ 1 A2
South East Cres. Southa ...... 104 A2
South East Rd. Southa ......... 104 A2
South End Cl. Hurs ................ 30 A4
South Front. Southa ............ 103 D2
South Grove. Lym ............... 198 C2
South Haven Cl. Hamw ......... 203 D2
South Hill. Alderh .................. 93 D3
South Hill. Drox .................... 85 D4
South Kinson Dr. Bour ......... 190 A2
South La. Clanf ..................... 88 A3
South La. Clanf ..................... 89 D2
South La. Down ..................... 46 C4
South La. Horn ..................... 89 D2
South La. Ows ...................... 65 E2
South La. Red ....................... 73 E4
South La. Southb ................ 137 F1
South La. Westb .................. 137 F2
South Lodge. Fare ............... 130 A1
South Mill Rd. Southa .......... 102 A4
South Millers Dale. Ch Fo ...... 55 D4
South Parr. Ports ................ 182 B1
South Park Rd. Poole ........... 206 A4
South Path. Gos ................. 180 B3
South Pl. Lon S ................... 180 A2
South Rd. Bour ................... 207 E3
South Rd. Broa ................... 187 F3
South Rd. Cos .................... 158 B4
South Rd. Horn ..................... 88 B1
South Rd. Ports .................. 182 C4
South Rd. S Hay ................. 184 C2
South Rd. Southa ............... 103 A4
South St. Eastl ..................... 80 A4
South St. Ems .................... 160 C4
South St. Gos ..................... 181 E2
South St. Hav ..................... 135 F1
South St. Hyt ..................... 126 A2
South St. Lo He ................. 153 F4
South St. Lym .................... 198 B1
South St. Ports .................. 182 A2
South Sway. Sway ............... 197 E4
South View Pl. Bour ............ 206 C1
South View Rd. Christ ......... 209 D3
South View Rd. Southa ........ 102 B4
South View Rd. Winch ........... 10 A2
South View. Winch ............... 10 C4
South Way. Lo He ............... 129 F2
South Weirs. Brock ............. 172 B4
South Western Cres. Poole ... 205 D1
Southampton Hill. Lo He ...... 129 F1
Southampton Rd. Cadn ......... 99 D4
Southampton Rd. Cos ......... 157 E4
Southampton Rd. Eastl .......... 56 A1
Southampton Rd. Fare ......... 131 D1
Southampton Rd. Fare ......... 154 A4
Southampton Rd. Fordi .......... 70 A1
Southampton Rd. Hyt .......... 125 F2
Southampton Rd. Lo He ....... 129 E2
Southampton Rd. Lym .......... 198 B2
Southampton Rd. Lyn .......... 122 A3
Southampton Rd. N Bad ........ 53 D3
Southampton Rd. Rin .......... 140 C4
Southampton Rd. Rom ........... 53 D3
Southampton St. Southa ...... 102 C3
Southbourne Ave. Cos ......... 158 A4
Southbourne Ave. Herm ...... 161 D4
Southbourne Ave. Holb ........ 150 B2
Southbourne Coast Rd. Bour 208 C2
Southbourne Gr. Bour ......... 208 B2
Southbourne Overcliff Dr. Bour 208 B2
Southbourne Rd. Bour ......... 208 B2
Southbourne Rd. Lym .......... 198 B2
Southbrook Cl. Hav ............. 159 F4
Southbrook Cl. Poole ........... 189 D1
Southbrook Rd. Hav ............ 159 F4
Southbrook Rd. Southa ........ 102 C3
Southcliff Rd. Southa ........... 103 D4
Southcliff. L on S ................ 179 F4
Southcliffe Rd. B on S .......... 211 E4
Southcliffe Rd. Christ .......... 210 B3
Southcote Rd. Bour ............. 207 E2
Southcroft Rd. Gos .............. 180 C3
Southdene Rd. Ch Fo ............ 55 D4
Southdown Rd. Comp ............ 31 E3
Southdown Rd. Cos ............. 158 A4
Southdown Rd. Horn ............. 88 A1
Southdown View. Wat .......... 111 E1
Southdown Way. W Moo ....... 138 C1
Southend La. Sob ................ 109 E4
Southern Ave. W Moo .......... 139 D1
Southern Gdns. Tot ............. 100 C4
Southern La. B on S ............ 211 F4
Southern Oaks. B on S ......... 195 F1
Southern Rd. Bour .............. 208 B2
Southern Rd. Lym ............... 198 B2

Southern Rd. Southa ........... 102 C2
Southern Rd. W End .............. 80 C1
Southernhay Rd. Ver ........... 115 D3
Southey Rd. Christ .............. 209 F4
Southfield La. Bur ............... 143 E1
Southfield Wlk. Hav ............ 135 E4
Southfield. Rin ................... 141 D3
Southfields Cl. Bi Wa ............ 83 E4
Southgate St. Winch .............. 10 C4
Southill Ave. Poole .............. 205 E3
Southill Gdns. Bour ............. 191 D1
Southill Rd. Bour ................ 191 D1
Southill Rd. Poole ............... 205 E4
Southlands Ave. Bour .......... 208 C2
Southlands Ave. Broa .......... 187 F3
Southlands. Cos .................. 158 A4
Southlands. Lym ................. 198 B1
Southlea Ave. Bour ............. 208 C2
Southleigh Gr. S Hay ........... 184 C2
Southleigh Rd. Hav ............. 136 B2
Southmead Rd. Fare ............ 130 C1
Southmoor La. Hav .............. 159 E4
Southsea Terr. Ports ........... 182 A2
Southview. Drox ................... 61 D1
Southville Rd. Bour ............. 208 A3
Southway. Gos ................... 155 E2
Southways. Stubb ............... 154 B1
Southwick Ave. Portc ........... 132 C1
Southwick Cl. Winch ............... 1 B2
Southwick Ct. Fare ............. 155 D3
Southwick Hill Rd. Cos ......... 133 F1
Southwick Pl. Bour .............. 208 B4
Southwick Rd. Bour ............. 208 B3
Southwick Rd. Cos .............. 133 E1
Southwick Rd. Den .............. 110 C2
Southwick Rd. Southw ......... 108 B2
Southwick Rd. Wickh ........... 108 B2
Southwood Ave. Bour .......... 208 B2
Southwood Ave. Christ ........ 195 D1
Southwood Cl. Christ .......... 195 D1
Southwood Cl. Fern ............ 165 E3
Southwood Gdns. Lo He ...... 128 C2
Southwood Rd. Ports .......... 157 F2
Southwood Rd. S Hay .......... 185 E1
Sovereign Cl. Bour .............. 207 F4
Sovereign Cl. Ports ............ 183 E3
Sovereign Cr. Bour .............. 208 A4
Sovereign Dr. He En ............ 105 E3
Sovereign Dr. Ports ............ 183 E3
Sovereign La. Wat .............. 134 C2
Sovereign Way. Eastl ............ 55 F3
Sowden Cl. He En ............... 105 D4
Sowley La. Beaul ................. 200 B3
Spa Rd. Southa .................. 102 C2
Spain The. Pet ..................... 40 C2
Spalding Rd. Southa ............ 104 C3
Spaniard's La. N Bad ............. 53 D2
Spaniard's La. Rom ............... 53 D2
Sparkford Cl. Bour .............. 208 A4
Sparkford Cl. Winch .............. 10 C3
Sparkford Rd. Winch ............. 10 C4
Sparrow Cl. Wat ................. 111 F2
Sparrow Ct. L on S .............. 179 F4
Sparrow Gr. Ott .................... 31 E2
Sparrow Sq. Eastl ................. 55 E1
Sparsholt Cl. Wat ............... 135 D3
Sparsholt Rd. Hurs ................. 9 E2
Sparsholt Rd. Southa ........... 126 C4
Spartan Cl. Stubb ............... 154 B3
Spartina Dr. Lym ................ 198 C1
Spear Rd. Southa ................ 103 D4
Specks La. Ports ................. 183 D3
Speedwell Cl. Ch Fo .............. 55 D3
Speedwell Cl. Lo He ............ 128 C1
Speedwell Dr. Christ ........... 210 A4
Speggs Wlk. He En .............. 105 E3
Speltham Hill. Hambl ............. 86 B1
Spencer Cl. S Hay ............... 185 D2
Spencer Ct. Stubb ............... 154 C1
Spencer Dr. L on S .............. 179 F3
Spencer Gdns. Wat ............. 111 F2
Spencer Rd. Bour ............... 207 E2
Spencer Rd. Eastl ................. 55 F1
Spencer Rd. Ems ................ 136 C2
Spencer Rd. New M ............. 196 A1
Spencer Rd. Poole .............. 216 C4
Spencer Rd. Ports .............. 182 C1
Spencer Rd. Southa ............ 104 B3
Spenlow Cl. Ports ............... 182 B4
Spenser Cl. Lo He ............... 152 B4
Spetisbury Cl. Bour ............ 191 D2
Spicer La. Bour .................. 189 F3
Spicer St. Ports ................. 182 B3
Spicer's Hill. Tot ................ 100 C3
Spicer's Way. Tot ............... 100 C3
Spinacre. B on S ................ 212 A4
Spindle Cl. Hav .................. 136 B2
Spindle Warren. Hav ........... 136 B2
Spindlewood Cl. B on S ........ 196 A1
Spindlewood Cl. Southa ........ 79 D3
Spindlewood Way. March .... 124 C4
Spinnaker Cl. S Hay ............ 184 C2
Spinnaker View. Cos .......... 135 D1
Spinners Cl. W Moo ............ 138 C1
Spinney Cl. St Le ................ 139 E2
Spinney Cl. Wat .................. 111 F2
Spinney Dale. Hyt ............... 126 A1
Spinney Gdns. Hyt .............. 126 A1
Spinney The. Comp ............... 31 E3
Spinney The. Den ................ 110 C2

Spinney The. Fa Oa ............... 57 D1
Spinney The. Gos ............... 155 E1
Spinney The. Portc ............. 131 F1
Spinney The. Southa ............ 78 C3
Spinney The. St Le .............. 139 F3
Spinney The. Tot .................. 76 B1
Spinney The. Wat ............... 112 A3
Spinney Way. New M ........... 196 A3
Spinney Wlk. Southa ............ 79 F2
Spinneys La. Fern ............... 165 E3
Spitfire Way. Hamble ........... 127 F1
Spithead Ave. Gos .............. 181 E1
Spittlefields. Rin ................ 141 D4
Spouts La. Plai ..................... 50 B3
Spring Cl. Fa Oa ................... 57 E1
Spring Cl. Southa ............... 103 F2
Spring Cres. Southa ............ 103 D4
Spring Ct. Poole ................. 205 E3
Spring Garden La. Gos ........ 181 E3
Spring Gdns. Ems .............. 161 D4
Spring Gdns. N Bad .............. 54 A3
Spring Gdns. Poole ............. 205 E3
Spring Gdns. Ports ............. 182 A3
Spring Gr. Burs .................. 105 D1
Spring House Cl. Co Com ....... 58 A1
Spring La. Bish .................... 56 B2
Spring La. Co Com ................ 31 F1
Spring La. New M ................ 196 B3
Spring La. Swan ................... 84 A3
Spring Pl. Rom ..................... 52 C4
Spring Rd. Bour .................. 207 E3
Spring Rd. Hyt .................... 126 A2
Spring Rd. Lo He ................ 128 C3
Spring Rd. Lym ................... 199 D2
Spring Rd. Southa ............... 103 F2
Spring Rd. Wat ................... 112 A2
Spring St. Ports .................. 182 B3
Spring The. Den .................. 110 C2
Spring Vale. Swan ................ 84 A2
Spring Vale. Wat ................ 112 A2
Springbank Rd. Bour ........... 207 F4
Springcroft. Gos ................ 155 D3
Springdale Ave. Broa .......... 187 F3
Springdale Gr. Broa ............ 187 F2
Springdale Rd. Broa ........... 187 F2
Springdale Rd. Bour ............ 209 D2
Springfield Ave. Christ ........ 192 B1
Springfield Ave. Holb .......... 150 B2
Springfield Cl. Co Com .......... 31 F1
Springfield Cl. Hav ............. 135 D1
Springfield Cl. Lym ............. 199 D2
Springfield Cl. Ver .............. 114 C3
Springfield Cres. Poole ........ 205 D2
Springfield Cres. Red ............ 47 E3
Springfield Dr. Tot .............. 100 C3
Springfield Gdns. New M ...... 196 B3
Springfield Gr. Holb ............ 150 B2
Springfield Rd. Poole .......... 205 D2
Springfield Rd. Ver ............. 114 C3
Springfield Way. Stubb ........ 154 B1
Springfields Cl. Co Com ......... 58 A1
Springford Cl. Southa ........... 78 A2
Springford Cres. Southa ........ 78 A2
Springford Gdns. Southa ....... 78 A2
Springford Rd. Southa ........... 78 A2
Springhill Rd. Ch Fo .............. 55 E3
Springles La. Swanw ........... 130 A3
Springvale Ave. Bour .......... 208 A4
Springvale Ave. Ki Wo ............ 2 A3
Springvale Rd. Ki Wo ............. 2 A4
Springwater Cl. Bour .......... 190 A2
Springwater Rd. Bour .......... 190 A2
Springwood Ave. Wat .......... 134 C3
Spruce Ave. Wat ................ 135 D4
Spruce Cl. Broa .................. 187 F1
Spruce Cl. Lo He ................ 152 B4
Spruce Dr. Southa .............. 104 C3
Spruce Wlk. L on S ............. 179 F3
Spur Cl. Wi Mi ................... 164 B3
Spur Hill Ave. Poole ............ 205 F2
Spur Rd. Cos ..................... 157 F4
Spur Rd. Poole ................... 205 F4
Spur Rd. Wat ..................... 134 C4
Spur The. Gos .................... 180 C1
Spurgeon Rd. Bour ............. 208 A3
Spurlings Rd. Fare .............. 131 E2
Square The. Bour ............... 206 B2
Square The. Faw ................ 151 D2
Square The. Gos ................ 181 E4
Square The. Hamble ........... 128 A1
Square The. Lo He .............. 153 F4
Square The. Lym ................ 198 A2
Square The. Pet ................... 40 C2
Square The. Sh En ................ 26 A2
Square The. Southb ............ 161 E4
Square The. Westb ............. 137 D2
Square The. Wi Mi .............. 163 D3
Square The. Wickh .............. 108 A2
Square The. Winch ............... 11 D4
Squarey Cl. Down ................. 46 C3
Squirrel Cl. Bish ................... 56 C1
Squirrel Dr. Southa ............. 104 A2
Squirrel Wlk. Ver ................ 114 C3
Squirrel's Cl. Christ ............ 192 B1
Squirrels Wlk. Hyt .............. 125 F1
Stable Cl. Lo He ................. 129 E1
Stacey Cl. Poole ................. 205 E4

Stacey Ct. Hav .................... 135 E4
Stacey Gdns. Bour ............... 191 F1
Staff Rd. Mich ....................... 27 D4
Staff Rd. Miche ....................... 6 A1
Stafford Rd. Bour ................ 207 D2
Stafford Rd. Pet ..................... 40 C3
Stafford Rd. Ports ............... 182 B2
Stafford Rd. Southa ............. 102 B3
Stag Cl. Bish .......................... 56 C1
Stag Cl. New M .................... 195 F2
Stag Gates. Black ............... 150 C1
Stagbrake Cl. Holb .............. 150 A2
Staghorn Rd. Horn .............. 112 B4
Stags La. Ows ....................... 33 D3
Stainer Cl. Southa ............... 104 B2
Stake's La. Uph ..................... 59 F4
Stakes Hill Rd. Wat ............. 134 C3
Stakes La. Uph ..................... 58 C2
Stakes Rd. Wat .................... 134 B2
Stalbridge Dr. Fern ............. 165 E2
Stalbridge Rd. Broa ............ 204 A4
Stalham Rd. Poole .............. 205 F3
Stallards La. Rin .................. 140 C4
Stamford Ave. S Hay ........... 184 C2
Stamford Rd. Bour .............. 208 B3
Stamford St. Ports .............. 182 C3
Stamford Way. Fa Oa ........... 57 E1
Stamshaw Rd. Ports ........... 157 E1
Stanbridge La. Awb ............... 27 D2
Stanbridge Rd. Hav ............. 136 A2
Standard Way. Fare ............ 131 F2
Standford St. Southa .......... 103 D2
Standing Hill. W Tyth ............. 3 F4
Stanfield Cl. Poole .............. 205 E4
Stanfield Rd. Bour .............. 206 C4
Stanfield Rd. Fern ............... 165 E3
Stanfield Rd. Poole ............. 205 E4
Stanford Cl. Cos ................. 157 E4
Stanford Ct. Southa ............ 104 B2
Stanford Hill. Lym .............. 198 B2
Stanford Rd. Lym ................ 198 B2
Stanford Rise. Sway ........... 172 A1
Stanhope Rd. Ports ............ 182 B3
Stanley Ave. Ports ............. 183 D4
Stanley Cl. Fare .................. 130 C1
Stanley Cl. Gos .................. 156 A1
Stanley Cl. Ver .................... 115 D3
Stanley Green Rd. Poole .... 204 B3
Stanley La. Ports ................ 182 B1
Stanley Rd. Bour ................ 207 E3
Stanley Rd. Christ ............... 211 D4
Stanley Rd. Ems ................. 161 D4
Stanley Rd. Holb ................. 150 B2
Stanley Rd. Lym .................. 199 D1
Stanley Rd. Poole ............... 204 B1
Stanley Rd. Ports ............... 157 E1
Stanley Rd. Southa ............... 79 E1
Stanley Rd. Tot ..................... 76 B1
Stanley St. Ports ................ 182 B1
Stanmore La. Winch .............. 10 B3
Stannington Cl. New M ....... 196 A1
Stannington Cres. Tot ......... 100 C4
Stannington Way. Tot .......... 100 C4
Stanpit. Christ ..................... 209 F3
Stansted Rd. Eastl ................. 55 F2
Stansted Cl. Ro Ca ............. 113 E1
Stansted Cres. Hav ............. 136 A3
Stansted Rd. Ports .............. 182 C2
Stanswood Rd. Black .......... 178 B3
Stanswood Rd. Faw ............ 178 C4
Stanswood Rd. Hav ............. 135 E3
Stanton Rd. Bour ................ 190 B1
Stanton Rd. Pet ..................... 40 C2
Stanton Rd. Southa ............. 102 A4
Stapehills Cres. Wi Mi ........ 164 B3
Stapehill Rd. Fern ............... 164 C2
Staple Ash La. Frox G ........... 39 E4
Staple Cl. Wat ..................... 111 E1
Staple Close La. Poole ....... 204 B3
Staple Gdns. Winch .............. 10 C4
Staplecross La. Burt ........... 209 F4
Stapleford Ave. Fern .......... 165 F3
Stapleford Cl. Rom ............... 28 A1
Stapleford La. Durl ............... 81 F3
Staplehurst Cl. Southa ....... 104 A1
Staplers Reach. Gos ........... 155 D1
Stapleton Rd. Ports ............ 183 D4
Staplewood La. Ashu .......... 124 B4
Staplewood La. March ........ 124 B4
Star La. Rin ......................... 140 C4
Stares Cl. Gos .................... 180 B4
Starina Gdns. Wat ............... 135 D4
Starling Sq. Eastl .................. 55 E1
Station App. Broa ................ 188 A2
Station App. Ports .............. 182 A3
Station Cl. Wickh ................ 108 A2
Station Hill. Burs ................ 128 A4
Station Hill. Curd ................ 106 B4
Station Hill. Eastl .................. 56 A2
Station Hill. Winch ................ 10 C4
Station La. Ch Fo .................. 55 E3
Station Rd N. Tot ................ 101 D4
Station Rd S. Tot ................ 101 D4
Station Rd. Alderh ................ 92 C3
Station Rd. Bi Wa .................. 83 E4
Station Rd. Bran .................. 194 C1
Station Rd. Bur ................... 170 B4
Station Rd. Burs .................. 128 A4
Station Rd. Christ ............... 209 D4

Station Rd. Cos ................... 158 B4
Station Rd. Fordi ................... 69 E1
Station Rd. Gos ................... 180 C4
Station Rd. Hamw ............... 204 A1
Station Rd. Liss ..................... 20 C2
Station Rd. Lo He ............... 129 D3
Station Rd. Net ................... 127 E3
Station Rd. New M .............. 196 A1
Station Rd. Nur ..................... 77 D3
Station Rd. Pet ..................... 40 C2
Station Rd. Poole ............... 205 D2
Station Rd. Portc ................ 156 B4
Station Rd. Ports ................ 183 D4
Station Rd. Rom .................... 52 C4
Station Rd. S Hay ................ 184 C2
Station Rd. Sob ..................... 85 E4
Station Rd. Southa .............. 101 E4
Station Rd. Southa .............. 103 F2
Station Rd. Sway ................. 172 A1
Station Rd. Ver ................... 114 C4
Station Rd. W Meo ................ 37 E2
Station Rd. W Moo .............. 138 B1
Station Rd. Wi Mi ................ 163 E2
Station Rd. Wickh ............... 108 A2
Station St. Lym ................... 198 C2
Station St. Ports ................. 182 B3
Station Terr. Wi Mi .............. 163 E2
Staunton Ave. S Hay .......... 184 B2
Staunton Rd. Hav ............... 135 F1
Staunton St. Ports .............. 182 B3
Stead Cl. S Hay ................... 185 D2
Stedman Rd. Bour .............. 208 A3
Steel St. Ports .................... 182 A2
Steele Cl. Ch Fo ................... 55 E2
Steels Dro. Woodg ............... 70 C4
Steels La. Dame .................... 68 B2
Steep Cl. Portc ................... 132 B1
Steepdene. Poole ............... 205 D2
Steeple Cl. Broa ................. 188 B2
Steeple Way. Lo He ............ 129 E2
Steepleton Rd. Broa ........... 188 B2
Steerforth Cl. Ports ............ 182 B4
Stein Rd. Southb ................ 137 E1
Stem La. New M .................. 195 F2
Stenbury Way. Net .............. 127 E4
Stenhurst Rd. Poole ........... 204 C3
Step Terr. Winch .................. 10 C4
Stephen Cl. Wat .................. 112 A1
Stephen Langton Dr. Bour ... 189 E3
Stephen Martin Gdns. Fordi .. 69 F1
Stephen Rd. Fare ................ 130 C1
Stephen's Wlk. Rin .............. 140 C4
Stephenson Cl. Gos ........... 181 D1
Stephenson Rd. Tot .............. 76 B1
Stephenson Way. He En ........ 81 E2
Steplake La. Sh En ................ 25 E1
Steplake Rd. Plai ................... 50 B4
Sterte Ave. Poole ............... 204 A2
Sterte Cl. Poole .................. 204 B2
Sterte Rd. Poole ................. 204 B2
Steuart Rd. Southa ............. 103 E4
Stevenson Cres. Poole ....... 205 F2
Stevenson Rd. Bour ............ 209 D2
Stevensons Cl. Wi Mi ......... 163 E2
Steventon Rd. Southa ......... 104 B4
Stewart Cl. Bour ................. 207 E3
Stewart Pl. Ports ................ 182 C4
Stewart Rd. Bour ................ 207 D3
Stewarts Green. Hambl ......... 86 B2
Stewarts Way. Fern ............ 165 F4
Stibbs Way. Bran ................ 169 E1
Stillmore Rd. Bour .............. 189 E2
Stinchar Dr. N Bad ............... 55 D3
Stinsford Cl. Bour ............... 191 D2
Stinsford La. Poole ............. 204 B4
Stinsford Rd. Broa .............. 188 B1
Stirling Ave. Wat ................. 134 C4
Stirling Cl. New M ............... 196 A2
Stirling Cl. Tot ...................... 77 D1
Stirling Cres. He En .............. 81 E1
Stirling Cres. Tot ................ 101 D4
Stirling Ct. Fare .................. 130 C2
Stirling Rd. Bour ................. 206 C4
Stirling St. Ports ................. 182 B4
Stirling Way. Christ ............. 210 A3
Stirling Wlk. Rom .................. 52 C4
Stirrup Cl. Upt .................... 203 E4
Stirrup Cl. Wi Mi ................. 164 B3
Stoborough Dr. Broa .......... 188 A1
Stock La. Lan ........................ 49 E3
Stock's La. Meons ................ 61 F3
Stockbridge Cl. Hav ............ 136 A3
Stockbridge Cl. Poole ......... 189 D1
Stockbridge Rd. Winch ........... 1 B1
Stocker Pl. Gos ................... 155 E1
Stockers Ave. Winch .............. 1 B1
Stockheath La. Hav ............. 135 F2
Stockheath Rd. Hav ............ 135 F2
Stockheath Way. Hav ......... 135 F2
Stockholm Dr. He En ........... 105 E3
Stockley Cl. Holb ................ 150 B2
Stockton Cl. He En .............. 105 E4
Stoddart Ave. Southa .......... 103 F3
Stodham La. Liss .................. 20 C1
Stoke Common Rd. Bish ....... 56 C3
Stoke Gdns. Gos ................. 181 E2
Stoke Hts. Fa Oa ................... 57 D2
Stoke Park Dr. Bish .............. 56 B2
Stoke Park Rd. Bish .............. 56 B2

Stoke Rd. Gos ..................... 181 E2
Stoke Rd. Southa ................... 78 A1
Stoke Rd. Winch ..................... 2 A2
Stoke Wood Cl. Fa Oa ........... 57 D1
Stoke Wood Rd. Bour ......... 206 C3
Stokes Ave. Poole .............. 204 B2
Stokes Bay Rd. Gos ............ 180 C1
Stokesay Cl. Hyt ................. 150 A4
Stone Gdns. Bour ............... 192 A1
Stone La. Wi Mi .................. 163 D3
Stone Sq. Hav ..................... 135 F2
Stone St. Ports ................... 182 A2
Stonechat Cl. Fern .............. 165 D4
Stonechat Cl. Pet .................. 41 E1
Stonechat Cl. Christ ............ 209 F4
Stonechat Dr. Tot ............... 100 B4
Stonechat Rd. Horn ............ 112 A4
Stonecrop Cl. Lo He ........... 128 C1
Stoneham Cemy Rd. Southa .. 79 F2
Stoneham Cl. Pet .................. 40 B2
Stoneham Cl. Southa ............ 79 E3
Stoneham Gdns. Burs ......... 104 C1
Stoneham La. Chilw .............. 79 E3
Stoneham La. Southa ............ 79 E3
Stoneham Park. Pet ............... 40 B2
Stoneham Way. Southa ......... 79 F3
Stonehills. Faw ................... 151 E2
Stoneleigh Ave. Hord .......... 196 C2
Stoneleigh Cl. Portc ........... 156 A4
Stoners Cl. Gos .................. 155 D2
Stoney La. Winch .................... 1 B1
Stony La S. Christ ............... 209 E3
Stony La. Burt ..................... 193 E1
Stonymoor Cl. Holb ............ 150 B2
Stopples La. Hord ............... 196 C2
Stour Cl. Pet ....................... 164 B2
Stour Cl. W End ..................... 80 A2
Stour Cl. W Wel ..................... 50 B2
Stour Rd. Bour .................... 207 E3
Stour Rd. Christ .................. 209 D3
Stour View Gdns. Pamp ...... 162 C1
Stour Way. Christ ................ 192 B1
Stourbank Rd. Christ .......... 209 D3
Stourcliffe Ave. Bour .......... 208 B2
Stourcroft Dr. Christ ........... 192 C1
Stourfield Rd. Bour ............. 208 A2
Stourpaine Rd. Broa ........... 188 B1
Stourvale Ave. Christ .......... 208 B4
Stourvale Gdns. Ch Fo ......... 55 E3
Stourvale Pl. Bour .............. 208 A3
Stourvale Rd. Bour ............. 208 B3
Stourwood Ave. Bour ......... 208 B2
Stourwood Rd. Bour ........... 208 B2
Stouts La. Bran ................... 169 D1
Stowe Rd. Ports .................. 183 D2
Stradbrook. Gos ................. 155 D1
Stragwyne Cl. N Bad ............. 53 F3
Straight Mile The. Ampf ........ 28 C1
Straight Mile The. N Bad ....... 28 C1
Strand St. Poole ................. 204 B1
Strand The. S Hay ............... 185 E1
Strand. Southa .................... 103 D2
Stratfield Dr. Ch Fo ............... 30 A1
Stratfield Park. Wat ............ 134 B4
Stratfield Pl. New M ............ 195 F2
Stratford Pl. Eastl .................. 56 A2
Stratford Rd. Lym ............... 198 B3
Stratford Rd. Wat ................ 135 D4
Strathmore Dr. Ver ............. 115 D3
Strathmore Rd. Bour .......... 191 D2
Strathmore Rd. Gos ........... 181 E2
Stratton Cl. Cos .................. 157 E4
Stratton Rd. Bour ............... 191 E2
Stratton Rd. Southa ............. 78 B1
Stratton Rd. Winch ............... 11 E4
Strawberry Fields. He En .... 105 D3
Strawberry Hill. Lo He ........ 128 C2
Streamleaze. Lo He ............ 129 E1
Street End. N Bad ................. 54 A3
Street The. Whit .................... 24 A2
Strete Mount. Christ ........... 209 F4
Stride Ave. Ports ................ 183 D3
Strides La. Rin .................... 140 C4
Strides Way. Tot ................. 100 A4
Strode Gdns. St Le ............. 140 A3
Strode Rd. Ports ................. 157 E1
Stroud Cl. Wi Mi ................. 164 A3
Stroud Gdns. Christ ........... 209 F3
Stroud Green La. Stubb ...... 154 B3
Stroud La. Christ ................ 209 F3
Stroud Park Ave. Christ ...... 209 F3
Strouden Ave. Bour ............ 207 D4
Strouden Ct. Hav ................ 135 E4
Strouden Rd. Bour ............. 191 D1
Stroudley La. Cos ............... 158 B3
Stroudley Way. He En ........... 81 E1
Stroudwood Rd. Fa Oa ......... 58 A2
Stroudwood Rd. Hav .......... 136 A2
Struan Cl. St Le .................. 139 F3
Struan Ct. St Le .................. 140 A3
Struan Dr. St Le ................. 140 A3
Struan Gdns. St Le ............. 139 F3
Stuart Cl. Stubb .................. 154 B1
Stuart Cl. Upt ..................... 203 D4
Stuart Cres. Winch ................ 10 C3
Stuart Rd. Christ ................. 211 D4
Stubbington Ave. Ports ....... 157 F1
Stubbington Green. Stubb ... 154 B2

Stubbington La. Stubb ......... 154 B1
Stubbington Way. Fa Oa ....... 57 E1
Stubbs Dro. He En .............. 105 E4
Stubbs Rd. Southa .............. 104 B1
Stuckton Rd. Fordi ................ 94 A4
Studland Cl. Southa .............. 77 E1
Studland Dr. M on S ........... 213 E3
Studland Rd. Bour .............. 206 B1
Studland Rd. L on S ............ 179 F3
Studland Rd. Southa ............. 77 E1
Studley Ave. Holb .............. 150 B2
Studley Cl. Christ ................ 211 E4
Studley Ct. B on S .............. 211 E4
Sturminster Rd. Bour .......... 191 D2
Styles The. Crouch ................ 22 B4
Sudbury Rd. Cos ................ 157 E4
Suetts La. Bi Wa ................... 83 F4
Suffolk Ave. Christ ............. 192 C1
Suffolk Ave. Southa ............ 102 B4
Suffolk Cl. Ch Fo .................. 55 E1
Suffolk Cl. Wi Mi ................ 164 B3
Suffolk Dr. Ch Fo .................. 55 E1
Suffolk Dr. Swanw ............. 129 E4
Suffolk Green. Ch Fo ............ 55 E1
Suffolk Rd S. Bour ............. 206 B2
Suffolk Rd. Bour ................ 206 B2
Suffolk Rd. Ports ............... 183 D2
Sullivan Rd. Southa ............ 104 B2
Sullivan Way. Wat .............. 134 C3
Sultan Rd. Ems ................... 136 C1
Sultan Rd. Ports ................ 182 B4
Sumar Cl. Stubb .................. 154 B3
Summer Field Cl. Wi Mi ...... 164 A2
Summer La. Exb .................. 177 D3
Summercroft Way. W Moo ... 138 C2
Summerfield Cl. Burt .......... 193 E1
Summerfield Gdns. Southa .... 79 E3
Summerfields. Bour ............ 207 F4
Summerfields. Lo He .......... 129 D1
Summerhill Rd. Wat ........... 112 A2
Summerlands Rd. Fa Oa ....... 57 E1
Summerlands Wlk. Hav ....... 136 A3
Summers Ave. Bour ........... 190 D3
Summers La. Burt ............... 193 F1
Summers St. Southa ........... 103 E3
Summertrees Ct. New M ..... 196 B2
Summit Way. Southa ............ 79 F1
Sumner Rd. Buri ................... 65 E3
Sun St. Ports ...................... 182 A3
Sunbeam Way. Gos ............ 181 D2
Sunbury Cl. Bour ................ 190 A3
Sunbury Ct. Fare ................ 130 C2
Sunderland Dr. Christ ......... 210 A4
Sunderton La. Clanf ............. 88 B3
Sundew Cl. New M .............. 196 B2
Sundew Rd. Broa ................ 187 F1
Sundridge Cl. Cos .............. 157 F4
Sunningdale Cl. Bish ............ 56 C1
Sunningdale Cl. Gos ........... 155 E1
Sunningdale Cres. Bour ...... 190 B2
Sunningdale Gdns. Southa .. 104 A4
Sunningdale Rd. Portc ........ 156 B4
Sunningdale Rd. Ports ........ 183 D4
Sunningdale. Hyt ................ 125 F2
Sunny Hill Rd. Poole ........... 205 E3
Sunny Way. Tot .................. 100 C4
Sunnybank Dr. Wi Mi .......... 164 A3
Sunnybank Rd. Wi Mi ......... 164 A3
Sunnybank Way. Wi Mi ....... 164 A3
Sunnydown Rd. Winch .......... 10 A2
Sunnyfield Rd. B on S ......... 212 A4
Sunnyheath. Hav ................ 135 F2
Sunnyhill Rd. Bour ............. 208 B3
Sunnylands Ave. Bour ........ 208 C2
Sunnymead Dr. Wat ............ 111 E1
Sunnymoor Rd. Bour .......... 190 A1
Sunnyside Rd. Poole ........... 205 E3
Sunnyside Wlk. Hav ............ 135 E4
Sunridge Cl. Poole ............. 206 A3
Sunset Ave. Tot .................. 100 C4
Sunset Rd. Tot .................... 100 C4
Sunvale Cl. Southa ............. 104 A2
Sunwood Rd. Hav ............... 135 E3
Surrey Cl. Christ ................. 192 C1
Surrey Cl. Tot ..................... 100 B3
Surrey Gdns. Bour .............. 206 B2
Surrey Rd S. Bour .............. 206 B2
Surrey Rd. Bour ................. 206 A2
Surrey Rd. Ch Fo .................. 55 E2
Surrey Rd. Poole ................ 206 A2
Surrey Rd. Southa .............. 103 E1
Surrey St. Ports ................. 182 B3
Sussex Cl. Bour .................. 191 D2
Sussex Gdns. Pet ................. 40 C1
Sussex Pl. Ports ................. 182 A3
Sussex Pl. Ports ................. 182 B3
Sussex Rd. Ch Fo .................. 55 E2
Sussex Rd. Pet ..................... 41 D1
Sussex Rd. Ports ................ 182 B3
Sussex Rd. Southa .............. 103 D2
Sussex St. Winch .................. 10 C4
Sussex Terr. Ports .............. 182 B2
Sutherland Ave. Broa ......... 187 F3
Sutherland Rd. Bour ............. 28 A1
Sutherland Cl. Ch Fo ............ 55 E1
Sutherland Rd. Ports .......... 182 C2
Sutherland Rd. Southa .......... 77 F3
Sutherlands Way. Ch Fo ........ 55 D4
Sutton Cl. Poole ................. 189 D1

Sutton Cl. Ports .................. 158 A2
Sutton Cl. Wat .................... 111 E2
Sutton Gdns. Winch ............. 11 D4
Sutton Pl. Brock .................. 146 A1
Sutton Rd. Bour .................. 191 D1
Sutton Rd. Tot ...................... 76 C1
Sutton Rd. Wat .................... 111 E2
Swale Dr. N Bad .................... 55 D4
Swallow Cl. Broa ................ 203 F4
Swallow Cl. Hav .................. 136 A1
Swallow Cl. Tot ................... 100 A3
Swallow Cl. L on S .............. 179 F4
Swallow Dr. M on S ............ 213 F2
Swallow Sq. Eastl .................. 55 E1
Swallow Way. Wi Mi ........... 164 A4
Swallow Wood. Fare ........... 131 D2
Swallows The. Clanf ............. 88 A3
Swan Cl. Ems ..................... 161 D4
Swan La. Winch .................... 10 C4
Swan Mead. Rin .................. 141 E3
Swan St. Pet ......................... 40 C2
Swanage Cl. Southa ........... 103 F2
Swanage Rd. L on S ............ 179 F3
Swancote. Portc ................. 155 F4
Swanley Cl. Eastl .................. 56 A3
Swanmore Ave. Southa ....... 104 B2
Swanmore Cl. Bour ............ 208 A4
Swanmore Cl. Winch .............. 1 B3
Swanmore Rd. Bour ........... 208 A4
Swanmore Rd. Drox .............. 84 C4
Swanmore Rd. Hav ............. 135 E4
Swanmore Rd. Swan ............ 84 A3
Swanmore Rd. Swan ............ 84 C4
Swansbury Dr. Bour ............ 192 A1
Swanton Gdns. Ch Fo ........... 55 D4
Swanwick La. Swanw .......... 128 C3
Swanwick Shore Rd. Swanw 128 B4
Swarraton Rd. Hav ............. 136 A2
Sway Gdns. Bour ................ 191 E1
Sway Rd. Brock ................... 172 C4
Sway Rd. Hord .................... 198 A3
Sway Rd. Lym ..................... 198 A3
Sway Rd. New M ................. 196 B3
Swaythling Rd. Hav ............ 135 E3
Sweetbriar Gdns. Wat ........ 134 C3
Sweyns Lease. E Bol .......... 175 E3
Swift Cl. Broa ..................... 203 F4
Swift Cl. Eastl ....................... 55 E1
Swift Cl. Horn ..................... 112 A4
Swift Cl. L on S ................... 179 F4
Swift Cl. Winch ..................... 10 B3
Swift Gdns. Southa ............. 103 E1
Swift Hollow. Southa .......... 103 E1
Swift Rd. Southa ................. 103 E1
Swift Rd. Th Is .................... 161 D2
Swinburn Gdns. Wat ........... 111 F2
Swincombe Rise. W End ....... 80 A1
Swiss Rd. Wat .................... 134 C4
Swivelton La. Fare .............. 132 A2
Sword Cl. Gos .................... 180 C1
Sword Sands Rd. Ports ....... 183 E4
Swordfish Dr. Christ ........... 210 A4
Sycamore Ave. Ch Fo ........... 30 B1
Sycamore Cl. Broa .............. 187 F1
Sycamore Cl. Christ ............ 208 B4
Sycamore Cl. Clanf .............. 88 B3
Sycamore Cl. Gos ............... 155 F1
Sycamore Cl. Lo He ............ 129 E1
Sycamore Cl. M on S .......... 213 E3
Sycamore Cl. N Bad .............. 53 F3
Sycamore Cl. Rom ................ 53 E3
Sycamore Cl. Wat ............... 111 F2
Sycamore Dr. Holb ............. 150 A3
Sycamore Dr. Ki Wo .............. 2 A4
Sycamore Dr. S Hay ........... 184 C2
Sycamore Rd. Bi Wa ............. 83 F4
Sycamore Rd. Hord ............ 196 C2
Sycamore Rd. Hyt ............... 125 F2
Sycamore Rd. Southa ........... 78 A1
Sycamore Wlk. Botl ............ 105 F4
Sydenham Terr. Ports ......... 182 C3
Sydling Cl. Poole ................ 189 D1
Sydmanton Cl. Rom .............. 53 D3
Sydmonton Ct. Hav ............ 136 A3
Sydney Ave. Hamble ........... 127 F2
Sydney Rd. Bish ................... 56 B2
Sydney Rd. Broa ................. 188 A2
Sydney Rd. Christ ............... 192 C1
Sydney Rd. Gos .................. 181 D2
Sydney Rd. Southa ............... 78 A1
Syers Cl. Liss ....................... 20 C2
Syers Rd. Liss ...................... 20 C2
Sylmor Gdns. Bour ............. 191 D1
Sylvan Ave. Southa ............ 104 B3
Sylvan Cl. Hord .................. 197 D1
Sylvan Cl. St Le .................. 139 E2
Sylvan Dr. N Bad .................. 53 F2
Sylvan La. Hamble .............. 128 A1
Sylvan Rd. Poole ................ 205 D3
Sylvan View. Wat ................ 134 C3
Sylvans The. Hyt ................ 125 E2
Sylvia Cres. Tot .................... 76 C1
Symes Rd. Hamw ............... 203 F2
Symes Rd. Rom .................... 53 D4
Symonds St. Winch .............. 11 D4
Sywell Cres. Ports .............. 158 B2

Tadburn Cl. Ch Fo ................. 55 E3
Tadburn Cl. Rom ................... 53 D4

Tadburn Rd. Rom ................ 53 D3
Tadden Wlk. Broa ............. 187 F1
Tadfield Cres. Rom ............. 53 D4
Tadfield Rd. Rom ............... 53 D4
Tagdell La. Horn .............. 111 F4
Tait Cl. Poole ................. 204 C4
Tait Pl. Gos .................. 155 E1
Talbot Ave. Bour .............. 206 C4
Talbot Cl. Hav ................ 135 E2
Talbot Cl. Southa .............. 78 C2
Talbot Dr. Christ ............. 194 C1
Talbot Dr. Poole .............. 206 A4
Talbot Hill Rd. Bour .......... 206 B4
Talbot Meadows. Poole ........ 206 A4
Talbot Mews. Bour ............ 190 A1
Talbot Rd. Bour ............... 206 C4
Talbot Rd. Hav ................ 135 E2
Talbot Rd. Hyt ................ 125 F1
Talbot Rd. Ports .............. 182 C2
Talbot Rise. Bour ............. 190 B1
Talland Rd. Lo He ............. 129 D1
Tamar Cl. Fern ................ 166 A3
Tamar Cl. Portc ............... 132 A1
Tamar Down. Wat .............. 135 D4
Tamar Gr. Hyt ................ 125 F2
Tamar. W End .................. 80 A1
Tamarisk Cl. Stubb ........... 154 B1
Tamarisk Cl. Wat ............. 135 D3
Tamarisk Gdns. Southa ........ 103 F4
Tamarisk Rd. He En ........... 105 D4
Tamella Rd. He En ............ 105 F3
Tammys Turn. Fare ............ 154 A4
Tamorisk Dr. Tot ............. 100 B3
Tamworth Rd. Bour ............ 207 F3
Tamworth Rd. Ports ........... 183 D3
Tan Howse Cl. Bour ........... 208 A4
Tanfield La. Wickh ........... 108 A2
Tanfield Park. Wickh ......... 108 A2
Tangier La. Bi Wa ............. 83 D4
Tangier Rd. Ports ............ 183 D4
Tanglewood. Fare ............. 131 D2
Tanglewood. March ............ 102 A1
Tangley Wlk. Hav ............. 136 A3
Tangmere Cl. Christ .......... 210 A3
Tangmere Dr. Southa ........... 78 A2
Tangyes Cl. Stubb ............ 154 B2
Tanhouse Cl. He En ........... 105 E3
Tanhouse La. He En ........... 105 E3
Tankerdale La. Steep .......... 41 E4
Tankerton Cl. Cos ............ 157 F4
Tankerville Rd. Southa ....... 103 E2
Tanner St. Winch .............. 11 D4
Tanner's Brook Way. Southa .. 101 F3
Tanner's La. Den ............. 111 D3
Tanner's Ridge. Wat .......... 134 C2
Tanneries Ind Est The. Hav .. 135 F1
Tanners La. Bold ............. 200 A2
Tanners La. Fare ............. 154 C3
Tanners La. W Wel ............. 51 E4
Tanners Rd. N Bad ............. 54 A2
Tanners The. Lo He ........... 129 E1
Tanslewood Cl. Wat ........... 134 B2
Tansy Cl. Wat ................ 135 D3
Tanyards The. Ch Fo ........... 30 A1
Taplin Dr. Broa .............. 105 E4
Taplings Cl. Winch ............. 1 B2
Taplings Rd. Winch ............. 1 B2
Taranto Rd. Southa ............ 78 B2
Tarbery Cres. Horn ........... 112 B4
Target Rd. Ports ............. 157 E1
Tarius Cl. Gos ............... 155 E2
Tarleton Rd. Cos ............. 133 D1
Tarn Dr. Broa ................ 203 F4
Tarn Rise. Horn ............... 88 B1
Tarrant Cl. Broa ............. 188 C1
Tarrant Gdns. Hav ............ 135 E2
Tarrant Rd. Bour ............. 191 D2
Tasman Cl. Southa ............ 103 D1
Taswell Rd. Ports ............ 182 B1
Tatchbury La. Ne Ma ........... 99 F4
Tate Rd. Southa .............. 101 E4
Tates Rd. Hyt ................ 126 A1
Tates Rd. Hyt ................ 126 A2
Tatnam Rd. Poole ............. 204 B2
Tattenham Rd. Brock .......... 172 C4
Tattershall Cres. Portc ...... 156 A4
Tatwin Cl. Southa ............ 104 B3
Tatwin Cres. Southa .......... 104 B3
Taunton Dr. Southa ........... 104 A4
Tavell's La. March ........... 101 F1
Tavells Cl. March ............ 101 F1
Taverner Cl. Poole ........... 204 B1
Taverners Cl. Southa ......... 104 B2
Tavistock Cl. Rom ............. 28 A1
Tavistock Gdns. Hav .......... 136 A1
Tavy Cl. N Bad ................ 55 D3
Taw Dr. N Bad ................. 55 D3
Tawny Owl Cl. Stubb .......... 154 A2
Taylor's Bldgs. Poole ........ 204 B1
Teachers Way. Holb ........... 150 A2
Teal Cl. Portc ............... 155 F4
Teal Cl. S Hay ............... 185 D2
Teal Cl. Tot ................. 100 B4
Teal Wlk. Gos ................ 155 D2
Teasel Way. W Moo ............ 138 C1
Teazle Cl. Fa ................. 41 E1
Tebourba Dr. Gos ............. 181 D2
Tebourba Way. Curd ........... 106 B4
Tebourba Way. Southa ......... 101 F4

Ted Kelly Ct. Ports .......... 182 A3
Tedder Cl. Bour .............. 190 A2
Tedder Gdns. Bour ............ 190 A2
Tedder Rd. Bour .............. 190 A2
Tedder Rd. Gos ............... 155 E2
Tedder Rd. Southa ............ 104 A4
Tedder Way. Tot .............. 100 B4
Teddington Rd. Ports ......... 183 D2
Tees Cl. N Bad ................ 55 D4
Tees Farm Rd. Co Comm ........ 56 C4
Tees Green. Co Comm .......... 56 C4
Teg Down Meads. Winch ......... 1 B1
Teg Down. Pet ................. 41 D2
Teglease Green. Hav .......... 135 E4
Teignmouth Rd. Gos ........... 180 C4
Teignmouth Rd. Ports ......... 183 D4
Telegraph Rd. W End ........... 80 C1
Telephone Rd. Ports .......... 182 C2
Telford Rd. Fern ............. 165 D4
Telford Rd. Ports ............ 157 F2
Teme Cres. Southa ............ 101 F4
Teme Rd. Southa .............. 101 F4
Tempest Ave. Wat ............. 135 D4
Templars Mede. Ch Fo .......... 55 D2
Templars Way. Chilw .......... 55 D2
Temple Gdns. Southa .......... 103 F1
Temple La. E Meon ............. 63 E4
Temple Rd. Liss ............... 21 D3
Temple Rd. Southa ............ 103 F1
Temple St. Ports ............. 182 B3
Templecombe Rd. Bish .......... 56 C1
Templemere. Fare ............. 154 A4
Templer Cl. Bour ............. 189 F1
Templeton Cl. Ports .......... 157 F2
Tenby Cl. Southa ............. 104 A4
Tenby Dr. Ch Fo ............... 55 D2
Tennyson Cl. Bi Wa ............ 83 F4
Tennyson Cl. Holb ............ 150 A3
Tennyson Cres. Wat ........... 111 E1
Tennyson Gdns. Fare .......... 131 D1
Tennyson Rd. Bour ............ 190 C1
Tennyson Rd. Eastl ............ 55 F1
Tennyson Rd. Poole ........... 205 D2
Tennyson Rd. Ports ........... 182 C4
Tennyson Rd. Tot .............. 76 B1
Tennyson Rd. Wi Mi ........... 163 E3
Tensing Cl. Fare ............. 131 D2
Tensing Rd. Christ ........... 209 F4
Tenterten Ave. Southa ........ 104 A1
Terence Ave. Broa ............ 188 B1
Terence Rd. Broa ............. 187 E3
Terminus Terr. Southa ........ 103 D2
Tern Cl. Bour ................ 208 B3
Tern Cl. Hyt ................. 126 A1
Tern Wlk. Gos ................ 155 D2
Terrace Rd. Bour ............. 206 C2
Terrace The. Dame ............. 68 B3
Terriate Cl. Ch Fo ............ 55 E4
Terrington Ave. Christ ....... 194 C1
Test La. Nur .................. 77 D1
Test La. Southa ............... 77 D1
Test Rd. Southa .............. 126 A4
Test Valley Bsns Centre. Nur . 77 E1
Testbourne Ave. Tot .......... 100 B4
Testbourne Cl. Tot ........... 100 B4
Testbourne Rd. Tot ........... 100 B3
Testcombe Rd. Gos ............ 181 D2
Testlands Ave. Nur ............ 77 E3
Testwood Ave. Tot ............. 76 C1
Testwood Cres. Tot ............ 76 B1
Testwood La. Tot ............. 101 D4
Testwood Pl. Tot ............. 101 D4
Testwood Rd. Hav ............. 135 E3
Testwood Rd. Southa .......... 102 A3
Tethering Dro. Woodg .......... 47 F2
Tetney Cl. Southa ............. 77 F2
Teviot Rd. N Bad .............. 55 D3
Tewkesbury Ave. Fare ......... 130 B2
Tewkesbury Ave. Gosp ......... 181 D4
Tewkesbury Cl. Cos ........... 157 E4
Texas Dr. Winch ............... 10 A2
Thackeray Rd. Southa ......... 103 D4
Thacking Green. Co Comm ...... 56 C4
Thames Alley. Poole .......... 204 A1
Thames Cl. Fern .............. 166 A3
Thames Cl. W End .............. 80 A2
Thames Dr. Fare .............. 130 B2
Thames Mews. Poole ........... 204 A1
Thames St. Poole ............. 204 A1
Thamesmead Cl. Gos ........... 180 C4
Theobald Rd. Hurn ............ 192 A4
Thetchers Cl. New M .......... 196 A3
Thetford Gdns. N Bad .......... 55 D4
Thetford Rd. Gos ............. 180 C4
Thetford Rd. Poole ........... 205 F3
Thicket The. Gos ............. 155 F1
Thicket The. Portc ........... 131 F1
Thicket The. Ports ........... 182 B2
Thicket The. Rom .............. 53 E3
Thicket The. Wat ............. 134 B2
Third Ave. Cos ............... 157 F4
Third Ave. Hav ............... 136 A1
Third Ave. Southa ............ 101 F3
Thirlmere Cl. Stubb .......... 154 B2
Thirlmere Rd. Southa .......... 77 F1
Thirlmere. Eastl .............. 55 F1
Thirlstane Firs. Ch Fo ........ 55 D2
Thistle Rd. He En ............ 105 D3

Thistlebarrow Rd. Bour ....... 207 F3
Thistledown. Wat ............. 112 A3
Thomas Cl. Tot ............... 100 B3
Thomas Lewis Way. Southa ..... 79 E1
Thomas Rd. N Bad .............. 54 A2
Thomas St. Ports ............. 182 B3
Thompson's La. Co Com ......... 57 F4
Thompsons La. Den ............. 55 B3
Thoresby Ct. New M ........... 195 F2
Thorn Cl. Eastl ............... 56 A3
Thorn Cl. Pet ................. 41 E1
Thorn Rd. Broa ............... 188 B2
Thornbrake Rd. Gos ........... 181 E2
Thornbury Ave. Black ......... 177 F4
Thornbury Ave. Southa ........ 102 C4
Thornbury Cl. Fare ........... 154 B4
Thornbury Hts. Ch Fo .......... 30 C1
Thornbury Rd. Bour ........... 209 D2
Thornbury Wood. Ch Fo ......... 30 C1
Thornby Ct. Ports ............ 158 A2
Thorncliffe Cl. Ports ........ 157 F2
Thorncombe Cl. Bour .......... 191 D2
Thorncombe Cl. Broa .......... 188 C1
Thorncroft Rd. Ports ......... 182 C3
Thorndike Cl. Southa .......... 78 A1
Thorndike Rd. Southa .......... 77 F1
Thorness Cl. Southa ........... 77 E1
Thorney Cl. Fare ............. 154 B4
Thorney Old Park. Th Is ...... 161 E1
Thorney Rd. Herm ............. 161 D3
Thorney Rd. Th Is ............ 161 D3
Thornfield Cl. Horn ........... 88 B1
Thornfield Dr. Christ ........ 194 C1
Thorngate Way. Gos ........... 181 E2
Thornham La. Th Is ........... 161 E3
Thornham Rd. New M ........... 196 B2
Thornhill Ave. Southa ........ 104 B3
Thornhill Cl. Black .......... 150 C1
Thornhill Park Rd. Southa .... 104 C4
Thornhill Rd. Black .......... 150 C1
Thornhill Rd. Southa .......... 78 C2
Thorni Ave. Fare ............. 130 B2
Thornleigh Rd. Southa ........ 103 F1
Thornley Rd. Bour ............ 190 B2
Thorns La. Beaul ............. 200 C3
Thornton Ave. Lo He .......... 128 B1
Thornton Cl. Wat ............. 134 A1
Thornton Rd. Gos ............. 181 D4
Thornycroft Ave. Southa ...... 103 E1
Thorold Rd. Ch Fo ............. 30 C1
Thorold Rd. Southa ............ 79 F1
Three Acre Dr. B on S ........ 211 F4
Three Acres. Den ............. 111 D2
Three Cross Rd. W Moo ........ 138 C3
Three Horse Shoes La. W Meo . 16 B1
Three Oaks. Southa ........... 104 C3
Three Tun Cl. Ports .......... 182 A3
Threefield La. Southa ........ 103 D2
Thresher Cl. Wat ............. 112 A1
Throop Cl. Bour .............. 192 A1
Throop Rd. Bour .............. 191 F2
Throopside Ave. Bour ......... 191 E2
Thrush Rd. Poole ............. 189 E1
Thrush Wlk. Wat .............. 111 E1
Thruxton Ct. Southa .......... 103 F3
Thruxton Rd. Hav ............. 135 E3
Thurbern Rd. Ports ........... 157 F1
Thurmell Cl. He En ........... 105 E2
Thurmell Wlk. He En .......... 105 E2
Thurmond Cres. Winch .......... 10 B3
Thurmond Rd. Winch ............ 10 B3
Thursby Rd. Christ ........... 194 C1
Thurston Cl. Ch Fo ............ 55 E4
Thwaite Rd. Poole ............ 206 A3
Tichborne Rd. Eastl ........... 80 A4
Tichborne Rd. Southa ......... 104 B4
Tichborne Way. Gos ........... 155 E1
Tickleford Dr. Southa ........ 104 A1
Tickner Cl. He En ............ 105 F3
Ticonderoga Gdns. Southa ..... 103 F1
Tidcombe Green. Hav .......... 135 E4
Tides Way. March ............. 101 F1
Tidworth Rd. Hav ............. 135 F2
Tiffany Cl. Hord ............. 196 C2
Tilbrook Rd. Southa .......... 102 A4
Tilburg Rd. Christ ........... 209 E4
Tilden Rd. Comp ............... 31 E3
Tilebarn La. Brock ........... 173 D3
Tilford Rd. Horn ............. 111 F3
Tillingbourn. Lo He .......... 129 E2
Tilmore Gdns. Pet ............. 40 C3
Tilmore Rd. Pet ............... 40 C3
Timberlane. Wat .............. 134 B2
Timberley La. Red ............. 48 A3
Timberly Cl. Holb ............ 150 B2
Timbers The. Fare ............ 130 B1
Timothy Cl. Bour ............. 190 B3
Timpson Rd. Ports ............ 182 C3
Timsbury Cres. Hav ........... 135 F1
Timsbury Dr. Southa ........... 77 F1
Timson Cl. Tot ............... 100 B3
Tincleton Gdns. Bour ......... 191 D2
Tindale Rd. Southa ............ 77 F1
Tinneys Cl. Red ............... 47 E2
Tintagel Cl. Southa ........... 78 B3
Tintern Cl. Cos .............. 133 D1
Tintern Gr. Southa ........... 102 C3
Tintern Rd. Gos .............. 181 D2
Tipner Green. Ports .......... 157 E2

Tipner La. Ports ............. 157 E2
Tipner Rd. Ports ............. 157 E1
Tiptoe Green. Hav ............ 136 A3
Tiptoe Rd. New M ............. 171 D1
Tiptree Cl. Eastl ............. 56 A3
Titchborne Cl. Hav ........... 135 E3
Titchfield Hill. Lo He ....... 154 A4
Titchfield Industries. Lo He . 154 A4
Titchfield La. Wickh ......... 107 E2
Titchfield Park Rd. Lo He .... 129 E2
Titchfield Rd. Fare .......... 154 A3
Tithe Barn. Lym .............. 198 C3
Tithe The. Den ............... 110 C2
Tithelands La. Bramd .......... 15 F2
Tithewood Cl. Ch Fo ........... 30 A1
Titus Gdns. Wat .............. 135 D4
Tivoli Cl. Ch Fo .............. 55 F4
Toby St. Ports ............... 182 B3
Todber Cl. Bour .............. 189 F2
Tokar St. Ports .............. 183 D1
Tokio Rd. Ports .............. 158 A1
Tollard Cl. Poole ............ 205 F4
Tollbar Way. He En ............ 81 D1
Tollerford Rd. Broa .......... 188 B1
Tollgate Rd. Swanw ........... 128 B4
Tollgate. Ch Fo ............... 55 E1
Tolpuddle Gdns. Bour ......... 191 D2
Tolstoi Rd. Poole ............ 205 D3
Toms La. Rin ................. 118 A4
Tonbridge St. Ports .......... 182 B1
Tonge Rd. Bour ............... 190 D3
Tonnant Cl. Stubb ............ 154 B1
Toogoods Way. Nur ............. 77 E3
Toothill Rd. Rown ............. 53 E1
Top La. Rin .................. 141 D4
Topaz Gr. Wat ................ 135 D4
Tor Cl. Cos .................. 134 C2
Tor Cl. Portc ................ 131 F1
Tor Way. Pet .................. 41 D2
Torbay Rd. Poole ............. 205 E2
Torberry Dr. Pet .............. 41 D1
Torch Cl. Fa Oa ............... 57 D1
Torcross Cl. Southa .......... 103 F1
Torfrida Ct. Ports ........... 183 E2
Tormead. Hyt ................. 125 F2
Tornay Gr. N Bad .............. 53 F2
Toronto Pl. Gos .............. 181 D3
Toronto Rd. Ports ............ 182 C4
Torquay Ave. Gos ............. 181 D4
Torquay Ave. Southa .......... 102 B4
Torre Cl. Eastl ............... 56 A3
Torridge Gdns. W End .......... 80 A2
Torrington Cl. Southa ........ 104 A2
Torrington Rd. Ports ......... 157 F2
Tortworth Cl. Fare ........... 154 B4
Torwood Gdns. Bish ............ 56 C1
Tosson Cl. Southa ............ 101 F4
Totland Cl. Southa ........... 101 F4
Totland Rd. Gos .............. 157 F4
Totland Rd. Gos .............. 155 E1
Totmel Rd. Poole ............. 189 D1
Totnes Cl. Eastl .............. 55 F3
Tottehale Cl. N Bad ........... 53 F2
Tottenham Rd. Ports .......... 182 C3
Totton By Pass. Tot .......... 101 D4
Totton Western By-pass. Tot . 100 B3
Totton Wlk. Hav .............. 135 E3
Tournerbury La. S Hay ........ 185 D2
Tourney Rd. Bour ............. 189 F3
Tovey Pl. Ki Wo ............... 2 B4
Tower Gdns. Southa ............ 78 C2
Tower La. Eastl ............... 56 B1
Tower La. Wi Mi .............. 163 E3
Tower Rd W. Poole ............ 206 A1
Tower Rd. Bour ............... 207 E3
Tower Rd. Poole .............. 206 A1
Tower Rd. Ports .............. 182 C2
Tower Rd. Winch ............... 10 C4
Tower St. Ems ................ 161 D4
Tower St. Ports .............. 181 F2
Tower St. Winch ............... 10 C4
Towers Farm. Broa ............ 187 E4
Towers Gdn. Hav .............. 159 F3
Towers Way. Broa ............. 187 E4
Town Hall Rd. Hav ............ 135 F1
Town La. Pet .................. 41 D3
Town Quay. March ............. 102 C1
Town Quay. Ports ............. 181 F2
Town St. Ports ............... 182 B3
Towngate Bridge. Poole ....... 204 B2
Townhill Way. Southa .......... 80 A1
Townhill Way. W End ........... 80 A1
Townsend Cl. Bour ............ 190 D3
Townsville Rd. Bour .......... 191 D1
Towpath Mead. Ports .......... 183 E2
Toynbee Cl. Eastl ............. 56 A2
Toynbee Rd. Eastl ............. 56 A2
Tozer Cl. Bour ............... 189 F1
Trafalgar Cl. Ch Fo ........... 55 D3
Trafalgar Ct. Christ ......... 209 F3
Trafalgar Cl. Fare ........... 154 C4
Trafalgar Pl. Ports .......... 182 C3
Trafalgar Rd. Bour ........... 206 C4
Trafalgar Rd. Southa ......... 102 B3
Trafalgar Sq. Gos ............ 181 D3
Trafalgar St. Winch ........... 10 C4
Trafalgar Way. Hyt ........... 126 A1
Trafford Rd. Fa Oa ............ 57 E1
Trampers La. Southw .......... 109 D1

Tranby Rd. Southa ............ 103 F2
Tranmere Cl. Lym ............. 198 C1
Tranmere Rd. Ports ........... 183 D2
Treadwheel Rd. Ro Ca ......... 113 D3
Treagore Rd. Tot .............. 76 B1
Trearnan Cl. Southa .......... 101 F4
Treble Cl. Winch .............. 10 A2
Tredegar Rd. Ports ........... 183 D2
Tree Hamlets. Upt ............ 203 E3
Tree Side Way. Wat ........... 111 F1
Treeside Ave. Tot ............ 101 D4
Treeside Rd. Southa .......... 102 B4
Treeside. Christ ............. 194 B1
Trefoil Cl. Wat .............. 135 D4
Tregaron Ave. Cos ............ 158 A4
Tregonwell Rd. Bour .......... 206 C1
Treloar Rd. S Hay ............ 185 F1
Treloyhan Cl. Ch Fo ........... 55 E2
Tremona Cl. Southa ............ 78 A1
Tremona Rd. Southa ............ 78 A1
Trenley Cl. Holb ............. 150 B2
Trent Cl. Southa .............. 79 F1
Trent Rd. Southa .............. 79 F1
Trent Way. Fern .............. 166 A3
Trent Way. L on S ............ 179 F3
Trent Way. W End .............. 80 B1
Trentham Ave. Bour ........... 208 A4
Trentham Cl. Bour ............ 208 A4
Tresillian Cl. Christ ........ 195 D1
Tresillian Gdns. W End ........ 80 A1
Tresillian Way. Christ ....... 195 D1
Trevis Rd. Ports ............. 183 E2
Trevone Cl. Tot .............. 100 C3
Trevor Rd. Ports ............. 182 C2
Trevose Cl. Ch Fo ............. 55 E2
Trevose Cl. Gos .............. 155 E1
Trevose Cres. Ch Fo ........... 55 E3
Trevose Way. Lo He ........... 129 D1
Triangle Gdns. Nur ............ 77 E2
Triangle La. Lo He ........... 153 F3
Triangle The. Bour ........... 206 C2
Triangle The. Upt ............ 203 D4
Triangle The. Whit ............ 24 A2
Tribe Rd. Gos ................ 181 D3
Tricketts La. Fern ........... 165 F3
Trigon Rd. Poole ............. 204 B4
Trimm's Dro. Woodg ............ 70 C4
Trinidad Cres. Poole ......... 205 E4
Trinity Cl. Gos .............. 181 F2
Trinity Cl. Tot ............... 76 C1
Trinity Gdns. Fare ........... 131 D1
Trinity Green. Gos ........... 181 F2
Trinity Rd. Bour ............. 207 D2
Trinity Rd. Southa ........... 103 D3
Trinity St. Fare ............. 131 D1
Tristan Cl. Faw .............. 171 F4
Triton Centre The. N Bad ...... 53 E3
Triumph Cl. Fare ............. 130 B1
Troak Cl. Christ ............. 209 F4
Trojan Way. Wat .............. 134 C2
Troon Cres. Cos .............. 134 B1
Troon Rd. Broa ............... 188 A3
Trosnant Rd. Hav ............. 135 F1
Trotters La. Wi Mi ........... 164 A3
Trotts La. March ............. 101 E1
Trotts La. Tot ............... 101 E2
Trowbridge Cl. Rown ........... 77 F3
Truman Rd. Bour .............. 190 D3
Truro Rd. Portc .............. 132 C1
Truro Rise. Bish .............. 56 C2
Truscott Ave. Bour ........... 207 D4
Trussell Cl. Winch ............. 1 B2
Trussell Cres. Winch ........... 1 B2
Tuckers La. Hamw ............. 203 F1
Tucks Cl. Bran ............... 194 A4
Tuckton Cl. Bour ............. 208 B2
Tuckton Rd. Bour ............. 208 C2
Tudor Ave. Ems ............... 136 C2
Tudor Cl. Alderh .............. 93 D3
Tudor Cl. Gos ................ 180 B4
Tudor Cl. Portc .............. 132 A1
Tudor Cl. Tot ................ 100 B4
Tudor Cres. Ports ............ 157 F3
Tudor Ct. Fare ............... 154 C4
Tudor Ct. Poole .............. 204 C3
Tudor Gdns. He En ............ 105 D3
Tudor Meadows. He En ......... 105 D3
Tudor Rd. Broa ............... 188 A2
Tudor Way. Ki Wo ............... 2 A4
Tudor Wood Cl. Southa ......... 78 C2
Tukes Ave. Gos ............... 155 D2
Tulip Rd. Southa .............. 79 E2
Tumulus Cl. Southa ........... 104 C2
Tunstall Rd. Southa .......... 104 C2
Tuppenny La. Herm ............ 161 D4
Turbary Ct. Wat .............. 111 F3
Turbary Park Ave. Bour ....... 190 A1
Turbary Rd. Fern ............. 165 F3
Turbury Cl. Poole ............ 205 E4
Turbury Rd. Poole ............ 205 E4
Turk's La. Poole ............. 205 D1
Turlin Rd. Hamw .............. 203 D2
Turner Ave. Gos .............. 155 E1
Turner Cres. Southa .......... 104 A1
Turner Rd. Ports ............. 182 B4
Turners Farm Cres. Hord ...... 197 D1
Turnpike Way. He En .......... 105 D4
Turnstone Gdns. Southa ........ 78 A3

Turnworth Cl. Broa .............. 188 B2
Turtle Cl. Stubb .................. 154 A2
Tuscan Wlk. Ch Fo ............... 55 F3
Tuscany Way. Wat .............. 135 D4
Tussocks The. March ........... 101 F1
Tutland Rd. N Bad ............... 53 F2
Tutt's La. W Wel .................. 50 C2
Tweed Cl. N Bad .................. 55 D4
Tweed La. Bold ................... 198 B4
Tweedale Rd. Bour ............. 191 E2
Twemlow Ave. Poole ........... 204 C2
Twiggs End Cl. Lo He .......... 128 C2
Twiggs La. March ............... 124 C4
Twiggs Lane End. Ashu ....... 124 B3
Twin Oaks Cl. Broa ............. 188 A2
Twyford Ave. Ports ............. 157 E1
Twyford Ave. Southa ............ 78 B1
Twyford Cl. Bour ................ 191 E1
Twyford Dr. L on S ............. 179 F3
Twyford Rd. Eastl ................ 56 A3
Twyford Way. Poole ............ 189 D1
Twynham Ave. Christ .......... 209 D4
Twynham Cl. Down ............... 46 C3
Twynham Cl. Bour .............. 208 C2
Twynhams Hill. Shed ........... 108 A4
Tylers Cl. Lym ................... 198 B3
Tyleshades The. Rom ............ 53 D3
Tyne Cl. N Bad ................... 55 D3
Tynedale Cl. Gos ................ 180 C4
Tyneham Ave. Poole ............ 205 E4
Tyrells La. Bur .................. 142 C2
Tyrrel Lawn. Hav ............... 135 E4
Tyrrel Rd. Ch Fo ................. 55 E4
Tyrrell Gdns. Bour ............. 192 A1
Tyrrells Ct. Bran ................ 169 D1
Tyseley Rd. Ports ............... 182 B2
Tytherley Green. Bour ......... 191 E1
Tytherley Green. Hav .......... 136 A3
Tytherley Rd. Southa ........... 104 B4

Uddens Dr. Wi Mi ............... 164 B4
Ullswater Ave. W End .......... 80 A1
Ullswater Rd. Oakl ............. 163 E4
Ullswater Rd. Southa ............ 77 F1
Ullswater. Eastl ................. 56 A1
Undercliff Dr. Bour ............ 207 E1
Undercliff Gdns. Southa ........ 78 C2
Undercliff Rd. Bour ............ 207 F2
Underdown Ave. Wat ........... 134 B1
Undershore Rd. Bold ........... 199 D2
Undershore Rd. Lym ........... 198 C3
Undershore. Lym ............... 198 C3
Underwood Cl. Broa ............ 188 A1
Underwood Ct. Southa ........... 78 C2
Underwood Rd. Bish ............. 56 C2
Underwood Rd. Southa ........... 78 C2
Unicorn Rd. Ports .............. 182 A3
Union La. Drox ................... 61 D1
Union Pl. Ports .................. 182 B3
Union Rd. Hav ................... 135 F1
Union Rd. Southa ............... 103 E3
Union St. Fare ................... 131 E1
Union St. Ports .................. 182 A3
Union St. Winch .................. 11 D4
University Cres. Southa ........ 79 D2
University Parkway. Chilw ..... 54 B1
University Rd. Southa ........... 79 D2
Upham St. Uph .................... 58 B3
Uplands Ave. B on S ............ 212 A4
Uplands Cl. W Moo ............. 166 A4
Uplands Cres. Fare ............. 131 D1
Uplands Rd. Bour ............... 191 E1
Uplands Rd. Cos ................. 158 B4
Uplands Rd. Den ................. 110 B3
Uplands Rd. Ro Ca .............. 113 E1
Uplands Rd. W Moo ............ 139 D1
Uplands Rd. Winch ................ 1 C2
Uplands Way. Southa ............ 79 D2
Upper Arundel St. Ports ....... 182 B3
Upper Banister St. Southa ..... 102 C3
Upper Bere Wood. Wat ........ 134 C4
Upper Brook Dr. Lo He ........ 128 C1
Upper Brook St. Winch .......... 11 D4
Upper Brownhill Rd. Southa .... 77 F2
Upper Bugle St. Southa ........ 102 C2
Upper Church Rd. Shed ........ 107 F4
Upper Common Rd. Lym ....... 197 F2
Upper Crabbick La. Den ....... 110 B3
Upper Crescent Rd. N Bad ..... 53 F3
Upper Deacon Rd. Southa ..... 104 B3
Upper Golf Links Rd. Broa .... 188 A3
Upper Gordon Rd. Christ ...... 195 D1
Upper Heyshott. Pet ............. 41 D2
Upper High St. Winch ........... 10 C4
Upper Hinton Rd. Bour ........ 206 C2
Upper House Ct. Wickh ........ 108 A2
Upper Market St. Eastl .......... 56 A2
Upper Mead Cl. Fa Oa .......... 57 E1
Upper Moors Rd. Co Comm .... 56 C4
Upper Mullins La. Hyt .......... 125 F2
Upper New Rd. W End .......... 80 B1
Upper Northam Cl. He En ...... 105 D3
Upper Northam Dr. He En ..... 104 C3
Upper Northam Rd. He En ..... 105 D3
Upper Norwich Rd. Bour ...... 206 C2
Upper Old St. Stubb ............ 154 A2
Upper Piece. Den ................ 111 D2
Upper Rd. Poole ................. 205 E3
Upper Shaftesbury Ave. Southa 79 D1

Upper Spinney. Lo He .......... 152 B4
Upper St Helens Rd. He En .. 105 D3
Upper St Michael's Gr. Fare . 154 C4
Upper Terrace Rd. Bour ....... 206 C2
Upper Toothill Rd. Rown ....... 77 F4
Upper Wardown. Pet ............ 41 D2
Upper Weston La. Southa ..... 104 A1
Upper Wharf. Fare .............. 155 E4
Uppleby Rd. Poole .............. 205 E3
Upton Cl. Hav ................... 135 E4
Upton Cl. Upt ................... 203 D4
Upton Cres. Rown ................ 77 E4
Upton Ct. Upt ................... 203 E4
Upton Grey Cl. Winch ............. 1 B2
Upton Heath Estate. Upt ....... 203 E4
Upton La. Nur .................... 77 E3
Upton Rd. Broa .................. 204 A4
Upton Rd. Poole ................. 203 F4
Upton Way. Broa ................ 187 F2
Upwey Ave. Hamw .............. 203 F2
Utrecht Ct. Christ ............... 209 E4

Vaggs La. Hord .................. 196 C3
Vaggs La. New M ................ 196 C3
Vale Dr. Southa .................. 79 F1
Vale Gr. Gos ..................... 181 D4
Vale Rd. Bour .................... 207 E2
Vale Rd. Poole ................... 205 F2
Vale Rd. Red ...................... 47 E3
Vale Rd. Winch .................... 11 E3
Vale The. Horn .................... 88 B1
Vale The. Hyt .................... 125 F2
Vale The. Ports .................. 182 B1
Valencia Cl. Christ ............. 192 B2
Valentine Ave. Southa ......... 104 B2
Valentine Cl. Fare .............. 130 B1
Valentine Ct. Southa ........... 104 B2
Valentine Ct. Wat ............... 135 D4
Valerian Cl. Fa Oa ............... 81 E3
Valerian Rd. He En ............. 105 E3
Valetta Park. Ems .............. 160 C4
Valetta Rd. Th Is ............... 161 E1
Valette Rd. Bour ................ 191 D2
Valiant Rd. Th Is ............... 161 E1
Valiant Way. Christ ............ 210 A4
Valley Cl. Black ................. 150 C1
Valley Cl. Christ ................ 192 C2
Valley Cl. Co Com ............... 56 C4
Valley Cl. Red ..................... 47 E3
Valley Cl. Wat ................... 134 B2
Valley La. Bran .................. 169 F2
Valley Park Dr. Clanf ........... 88 B2
Valley Rd. Bour ................. 191 F2
Valley Rd. Ch Fo ................. 55 E4
Valley Rd. Litt ..................... 1 A3
Valley Rd. Tot ................... 100 C3
Valley Rise. Lo He .............. 128 C2
Valley The. Winch ................ 10 B3
Valley View. Poole ............. 206 A4
Valleydene. Hyt ................. 125 F1
Vallis Cl. Poole .................. 204 B1
Valsheba Dr. Stubb ............. 154 A1
Vanburgh Way. Ch Fo ........... 30 A1
Vanguard Rd. Bour ............. 191 F1
Vanguard Rd. Poole ............ 204 B1
Vanguard Rd. Southa ........... 104 A4
Vanstone Rd. Gos .............. 180 B4
Vardy Cl. Southa ............... 104 B2
Varna Rd. Southa ............... 102 B3
Varsity Rd. Th Is ............... 161 E1
Vaudrey Cl. Southa .............. 78 B1
Vaughan Cl. Southa ............ 104 C3
Vaughan Rd. Hyt ............... 125 E2
Vauxhall Way. Pet ............... 40 C2
Vecta Cl. Christ ................. 210 B3
Vectis Rd. B on S ............... 211 E4
Vectis Rd. Gos .................. 180 C2
Vectis Way. Cos ................. 157 F4
Velder Ave. Ports .............. 183 D3
Vellan Ct. Southa ................ 77 E1
Velmore Rd. Ch Fo ............... 55 D3
Velsheda Ct. Hyt ................ 126 A3
Venator Pl. Wi Mi .............. 163 E3
Venice Cl. Wat ................... 135 D4
Venning Ave. Bour ............. 189 F3
Ventnor Ct. Southa .............. 79 E3
Ventnor Rd. Gos ................ 155 D2
Ventnor Rd. Ports .............. 182 C2
Ventnor Way. Portc ............ 131 F1
Ventura Pl. Broa ................ 203 E3
Venture Rd. Chilw ................ 54 B1
Verbena Cres. Wat .............. 112 A2
Verbena Way. He En ........... 105 E3
Verdon Ave. Hamble ........... 127 F2
Verger Cl. Lo He ................ 129 E2
Verity Cres. Poole .............. 189 D1
Vermont Cl. Southa .............. 78 C2
Vernalls Cl. Bour ............... 190 B3
Vernalls Gdns. Bour ........... 190 B3
Verne Rd. Ver ................... 115 D3
Verney Cl. Bour ................. 190 A2
Verney Rd. Bour ................ 190 A2
Vernham Rd. Winch ............... 1 C1
Verno La. Christ ................ 194 B1
Vernon Ave. Ports .............. 183 D3
Vernon Cl. Gos .................. 181 D3
Vernon Hill. Bi Wa ............... 59 E1
Vernon Mews. Ports ........... 183 D3
Vernon Rd. Gos ................. 181 D3

Vernon Rd. Ports ............... 158 A1
Vernon Wlk. Southa ............ 102 C3
Verona Ave. Bour .............. 208 B3
Verona Rd. Ch Fo ................ 55 F3
Verulam Pl. Bour ............... 206 C2
Verulam Rd. Poole ............. 204 C2
Verulam Rd. Southa ............ 103 D4
Verwood Cres. Bour ........... 209 D2
Verwood Rd. Hav ............... 136 A3
Verwood Rd. Ibs ................ 116 A1
Verwood Rd. St Le ............. 116 A1
Verwood Rd. St Le ............. 140 B4
Verwood Rd. Ver ............... 114 A4
Verwood Rd. W Moo ........... 114 C1
Verwood Rd. Woodl ............ 114 A4
Veryan. Fare ..................... 130 C1
Vespasian Rd. Southa ......... 103 E4
Vespasian Way. Ch Fo .......... 55 F4
Vesta Way. Ch Fo ................ 55 F4
Vetch Cl. Christ ................. 210 B4
Vian Cl. Gos ..................... 155 E2
Vian Pl. Ki Wo ..................... 2 B4
Vian Rd. Wat .................... 134 C3
Vicarage Dr. He En ............. 105 D3
Vicarage Gdns. Hord ........... 197 D1
Vicarage La. Cadn ................ 75 D1
Vicarage La. Curd .............. 106 B4
Vicarage La. Hambl .............. 86 B2
Vicarage La. Hord .............. 197 D1
Vicarage La. Stubb ............. 154 B2
Vicarage La. Swan ............... 84 B3
Vicarage Park. Red .............. 47 E3
Vicarage Rd. Bour .............. 190 C1
Vicarage Rd. March ............ 101 F1
Vicarage Rd. Poole ............. 204 B3
Vicarage Rd. Red ................. 48 A3
Vicarage Rd. Ver ............... 114 C3
Vicarage Way. Burt ............ 193 E1
Vice La. Bramsh ................. 74 A2
Viceroy Rd. Southa ............ 104 A2
Vickers Cl. Bour ................ 192 A1
Vickery Way. Christ ........... 209 E4
Victena Rd. Fa Oa ............... 57 E1
Victor Rd. Ports ................ 182 C4
Victor Rd. Th Is ................. 161 E1
Victor St. Southa ................. 78 A1
Victoria Ave. Bour ............. 190 C1
Victoria Ave. S Hay ............ 184 C2
Victoria Ave. Wat .............. 134 A2
Victoria Cl. Broa ............... 187 E3
Victoria Cres. Poole ........... 205 E3
Victoria Gdns. Fern ............ 165 E3
Victoria Gdns. Fordi ............ 69 E1
Victoria Glade. Net ............ 127 E3
Victoria Gr. Ports .............. 182 B2
Victoria Park Rd. Bour ........ 190 C1
Victoria Pl. Bour ............... 207 E3
Victoria Pl. Gos ................. 181 D2
Victoria Pl. Wi Mi .............. 163 D3
Victoria Rd N. Ports ........... 182 B2
Victoria Rd S. Ports ............ 182 B1
Victoria Rd. Bi Wa ............... 83 D4
Victoria Rd. Bour ............... 207 E3
Victoria Rd. Christ ............. 209 F3
Victoria Rd. Eastl ................ 56 A3
Victoria Rd. Ems ............... 136 C1
Victoria Rd. Fern ............... 165 E3
Victoria Rd. Fordi ................ 69 E1
Victoria Rd. M on S ............ 213 E2
Victoria Rd. N Hay .............. 159 F1
Victoria Rd. Net ................ 127 D3
Victoria Rd. Poole .............. 205 E3
Victoria Rd. Southa ............ 103 E1
Victoria Rd. Wat ............... 134 C4
Victoria Rd. Wi Mi ............. 163 D3
Victoria Rd. Winch ................ 1 C1
Victoria Sq. L on S ............. 179 F3
Victoria St. Gos' ............... 181 E3
Victoria St. Ports .............. 182 B4
Victoria St. Southa ............. 103 E3
Victory Cl. Ch Fo ................ 55 D3
Victory Cl. W Moo .............. 139 D3
Victory Cres. Southa ........... 102 A3
Victory Gn. Ports ............... 157 E1
Victory Rd. Ports ............... 182 A3
Victory Rd. Southa ............. 102 A3
Victory Rd. Stubb .............. 154 B1
Victory Sq. Southa ............. 102 A3
Victory Way. Rown .............. 77 F4
Viewside Cl. Broa .............. 187 E3
Viking Cl. Black ................. 177 F4
Viking Cl. Bour .................. 209 D2
Viking Cl. Southa ................ 77 F2
Viking Cl. Stubb ................ 154 A2
Viking Way. Bour ............... 209 D2
Viking Way. Christ ............. 210 A3
Viking Way. Horn ................ 88 B2
Vikings The. Rom ................ 53 D4
Villa Gdns. Wat ................. 134 C4
Village Rd. Gos ................. 180 C1
Village St. Pet .................... 41 D3
Villette Cl. Christ .............. 193 D1
Villiers Rd. Hyt ................. 149 F4
Villiers Rd. Ports .............. 182 B1
Villiers Rd. Southa ............. 102 B4
Vimoutiers Ct. Fordi ............ 69 F1
Vince Cl. Bour ................... 190 D3
Vincent Ave. Southa ............. 78 B1
Vincent Cl. New M .............. 196 A1

Vincent Gr. Portc ............... 156 B4
Vincent Rd. New M ............. 196 A1
Vincent St. Southa ............. 102 B4
Vincent's Gr. Southa ........... 102 A4
Vincent's Wlk. Southa ......... 103 D2
Vine Bank. Southa .............. 104 A4
Vine Cl. Bour .................... 208 A4
Vine Cl. Lo He ................... 128 B2
Vine Coppice. Wat ............. 134 C2
Vine Farm Cl. Poole ........... 206 B4
Vine Farm Rd. Poole ........... 206 A4
Vine Gdns. Southa ............... 77 F2
Vine Hill. Pamp ................. 162 C3
Vine Rd. Southa .................. 78 A2
Vinegar Hill. M on S ........... 213 E3
Vineries Cl. Wi Mi .............. 163 F3
Vineries The. Wi Mi ............ 163 F3
Vinery Gdns. Southa ............ 78 B1
Vinery Rd. Southa ............... 78 B1
Vinery The. New M ............. 196 A1
Vineside. Gos ................... 155 F1
Viney Ave. Rom .................. 53 D4
Viney Rd. Lym ................... 198 C1
Vineyard Cl. Southa ............ 103 E2
Vineyards The. N Bad ........... 54 A2
Vinnells La. W Meo ............. 37 E3
Vinneys Cl. Burt ................ 193 E1
Vinson Rd. Liss ................... 21 D2
Violet Cl. Stubb ................. 154 A1
Violet Farm Cl. Broa .......... 187 E4
Violet La. New M ............... 196 A2
Violet Rd. Southa ................ 79 D2
Virginia Cl. Poole .............. 205 E4
Virginia Park Rd. Gos ......... 180 C3
Viscount Ct. Bour .............. 189 E3
Viscount Dr. Christ ............ 210 A3
Viscount Wlk. Bour ............ 189 E3
Vita Rd. Ports ................... 157 F2
Vivash Rd. Ports ............... 182 C3
Vixen Cl. Stubb ................. 154 A1
Vixen Wlk. New M .............. 196 A3
Vulcan Cl. Southa .............. 101 F3
Vulcan Rd. Southa ............. 101 F3
Vulcan Rd. Th Is ............... 161 E1
Vulcan Way. Christ ............ 210 A4

Wad The. W Wit ................. 186 C1
Wade Court Rd. Hav ........... 160 A4
Wade La. Hav ................... 160 A4
Wadham Rd. Ports ............. 157 E1
Wadhurst Gdns. Southa ....... 127 D4
Wadhurst Rd. He En ........... 105 E3
Wagtail Way. Portc ............ 155 F4
Wainscot Rd. Ports ............ 183 D1
Wainsford Cl. Lym ............. 198 A1
Wainsford Rd. Hord ........... 197 F1
Wainsford Rd. Hord ........... 213 F4
Wainsford Rd. Lym ............ 197 F1
Wainwright Cl. Cos ............ 158 B3
Wait End Rd. Wat .............. 134 C3
Wake Lawn. Ports .............. 183 E2
Wakefield Ave. Bour .......... 190 C3
Wakefield Ave. Fare ........... 130 C2
Wakefield Ct. Southa ........... 80 A1
Wakefield Rd. Southa ........... 80 A1
Wakefords Way. Hav ........... 136 C4
Wakely Gdns. Bour ............ 190 A3
Wakely Rd. Bour ............... 190 D3
Walberton Ave. Cos ........... 158 A4
Walcheren Pl. Hamw .......... 203 E2
Walcott Ave. Christ ........... 192 C1
Walden Gdns. Horn ............ 112 A4
Walden Rd. Ports .............. 157 E1
Walditch Gdns. Broa .......... 188 C1
Waldren Cl. Poole .............. 204 C1
Wales St. Winch .................. 11 D4
Walford Cl. Wi Mi .............. 163 E3
Walford Rd. Cos ................ 133 E1
Walhampton Hill. Lym ......... 198 C3
Walker Gdns. He En ............ 81 E1
Walker Pl. Gos .................. 155 E1
Walker Rd. Ports ............... 157 E1
Walker's Lane S. Black ........ 177 F4
Walkers Cl. Fa Oa ............... 57 E1
Walkers La N. Black ........... 150 C1
Walkford La. New M ........... 195 E2
Walkford Rd. Christ ........... 195 E1
Walkford Way. Christ ......... 195 D1
Walkwood Ave. Bour .......... 208 A4
Wallace Rd. Broa ............... 188 A2
Wallace Rd. Ports .............. 182 C4
Wallace Rd. Southa ............ 103 F1
Wallington Ct. Fare ............ 154 C3
Wallington Dr. Ch Fo ........... 55 D4
Wallington Hill. Fare .......... 131 E1
Wallington Rd. Ports ........... 157 F1
Wallington Shore Rd. Fare ... 131 E1
Wallington Way. Fare .......... 131 E1
Wallis Gdns. Wat ............... 111 F1
Wallis Rd. Bour ................. 190 A1
Wallis Rd. Wat ................... 111 F1
Walliscott Rd. Bour ........... 190 A1
Wallisdean Ave. Fare .......... 154 C4
Wallisdean Rd. Ports .......... 183 D4
Wallisdown Rd. Bour .......... 190 A1
Wallisdown Rd. Poole ......... 206 B4
Wallrock Wlk. Ems ............ 136 C2
Walmer Cl. Eastl ................. 56 A4
Walmer Rd. Ports .............. 182 C3

Walnut Ave. Southa ............. 79 F3
Walnut Cl. Ch Fo ................. 30 B1
Walnut Cl. Southa ................ 77 F1
Walnut Dr. Stubb ............... 154 A1
Walnut Gr. Southa ............... 77 F1
Walnut Tree Cl. S Hay ........ 184 C2
Walnut Tree Dr. Westb ....... 137 F2
Walpole Rd. Bour .............. 207 F3
Walpole Rd. Gos ............... 181 E2
Walpole Rd. Winch .............. 10 B3
Walpole Terr. Gos ............. 181 D2
Walsall Rd. Ports .............. 183 D3
Walsford Rd. Bour ............. 206 B3
Walsingham Cl. Cos ........... 133 E1
Walsingham Dene. Bour ...... 207 F4
Walsingham Gdns. Southa ..... 79 F2
Waltham Cl. Drox ................ 61 D1
Waltham Cl. Portc .............. 132 B1
Waltham Cres. Southa .......... 78 B2
Waltham Rd. Bour .............. 208 A3
Waltham St. Ports .............. 182 A2
Walton Cl. Gos .................. 181 D2
Walton Ct. Fare ................. 130 B2
Walton Pl. Winch ................ 10 B3
Walton Rd. Bour ................ 190 B1
Walton Rd. Cos ................. 158 A3
Walton Rd. Gos ................. 181 D2
Walton Rd. Poole ............... 205 D3
Walton Rd. Southa ............. 104 B2
Waltons Ave. Holb ............. 150 B2
Wandesford Pl. Gos ........... 156 A1
Wangfield La. Curd .............. 82 B1
Wansbeck Cl. N Bad ............ 55 D3
Wanstead Cl. Rin ............... 117 D1
Warbler Cl. Southa .............. 78 A3
Warbler Cl. Upt ................. 203 D4
Warblington Ave. Hav ......... 136 A1
Warblington Cl. Ch Fo .......... 55 D2
Warblington Rd. Ems .......... 160 C4
Warblington St. Ports ......... 182 A2
Warborne La. Bold ............. 199 D4
Warbrook Ct. Southa .......... 104 C2
Warburton Cl. Southa ......... 104 C2
Warburton Rd. Poole .......... 204 C4
Warburton Rd. Southa ........ 104 C2
Warburton Way. Clanf .......... 88 B2
Ward Cres. Ems ................ 137 D2
Ward Rd. Ports ................. 183 D1
Warden Cl. W End ............... 80 B1
Wardens Cl. S Hay ............. 184 C3
Wardle Rd. Co Com ............. 56 B4
Wareham Rd. Broa ............. 187 E2
Wareham Rd. Upt .............. 187 E2
Warfield Ave. Wat .............. 134 C4
Warfield Cres. Wat ............. 134 C4
Warland Way. Broa ............ 187 F4
Warlock Cl. Southa ............ 104 B2
Warmwell Cl. Bour ............ 191 D2
Warmwell Cl. Poole ........... 188 C1
Warnes La. Bur ................. 142 C1
Warnford Cl. Gos .............. 180 C2
Warnford Cres. Hav ........... 135 E3
Warnford Rd. Bour ............ 208 B4
Warren Ave. Ch Fo .............. 55 F3
Warren Ave. Christ ............ 209 F3
Warren Ave. Ports ............. 183 D3
Warren Ave. Southa ............. 78 A1
Warren Cl. Ch Fo ................ 55 F3
Warren Cl. S Hay ............... 184 B2
Warren Cl. Southa ............... 78 A1
Warren Cl. St Le ............... 140 B3
Warren Cres. Southa ............ 78 A1
Warren Dr. St Le ............... 140 B3
Warren Edge Cl. Bour ......... 208 C2
Warren Edge Rd. Bour ........ 208 C2
Warren Gdns. Rom .............. 28 A1
Warren La. Beaul .............. 201 F4
Warren La. Cole .................. 19 E3
Warren La. Frox G ............... 19 D2
Warren La. Ows ................... 33 F4
Warren La. St Le ............... 140 B3
Warren Pl. Tot .................... 76 B1
Warren Rd. Bour ............... 206 A1
Warren Rd. Liss .................. 21 D4
Warren Rd. Poole .............. 205 E2
Warren Rd. Winch ................ 11 E4
Warren The. Holb .............. 150 A3
Warren Wlk. Fern .............. 165 D4
Warrior Bsns Ctr The. Cos ... 158 C4
Warrior Cl. Eastl ................. 55 D2
Warrys Cl. Hyt .................. 150 A4
Warsash Cl. Hav ............... 135 F3
Warsash Gr. Gos ............... 155 D1
Warsash Rd. Lo He ............ 129 D1
Warton Cl. E Bol ............... 175 E3
Warwick Ave. New M .......... 196 A2
Warwick Cl. Ch Fo .............. 55 D2
Warwick Cl. Lon S ............. 180 A2
Warwick Cl. Winch ................ 2 A1
Warwick Cres. Burs ........... 127 F4
Warwick Cres. Ports .......... 182 B2
Warwick Pl. Bour .............. 208 A3
Warwick Pl. W Wel .............. 50 C2
Warwick Rd. Bour ............. 208 A3
Warwick Rd. Poole ............ 205 E2
Warwick Rd. Southa ............ 78 B1
Warwick Rd. Tot ............... 100 C4
Wasdale Cl. Horn ................ 88 B1
Washbrook Rd. Cos ............ 133 E1
Washington Ave. Bour ........ 207 E3

Washington Rd. Ems ............ 136 C1
Washington Rd. Ports ............ 182 B4
Watcombe Rd. Bour ............ 208 B3
Water Cl. Winch ............ 11 D4
Water La. Bour ............ 208 B4
Water La. Hyt ............ 125 F1
Water La. Tot ............ 100 C4
Water La. Winch ............ 11 D4
Water Tower Rd. Broa ............ 188 B2
Water's Edge. He En ............ 105 D3
Waterbeech Dr. He En ............ 105 E4
Waterberry Dr. Wat ............ 111 E1
Waterditch Rd. Bran ............ 194 A2
Waterditch Rd. Burt ............ 194 A2
Waterford Cl. Lym ............ 198 C2
Waterford Cl. Poole ............ 205 D1
Waterford Cl. Christ ............ 211 D4
Waterford Pl. Christ ............ 211 D4
Waterford Rd. Christ ............ 211 D4
Waterford Rd. New M ............ 196 B2
Waterhouse La. Southa ............ 102 A4
Waterhouse Way. Southa ............ 102 A4
Waterlock Gdns. Ports ............ 183 E2
Waterloo Cl. Wat ............ 111 E2
Waterloo Ind Est. He En ............ 81 D1
Waterloo Rd. Bour ............ 206 C4
Waterloo Rd. Broa ............ 187 D3
Waterloo Rd. Broa ............ 204 B4
Waterloo Rd. Gos ............ 181 E1
Waterloo Rd. Hav ............ 135 F1
Waterloo Rd. Lym ............ 198 C2
Waterloo Rd. Southa ............ 102 B3
Waterloo St. Ports ............ 182 B2
Waterloo Terr. Southa ............ 102 C3
Watermans La. Hyt ............ 125 F1
Watermead Rd. Cos ............ 158 C4
Watermead. Christ ............ 209 D3
Watermill Rd. Christ ............ 209 D4
Waters Edge Gdns. Ems ............ 160 C4
Waters Green Ct. Brock ............ 146 A1
Waters The. Fare ............ 130 C3
Watersedge Rd. Portc ............ 157 D4
Watership Dr. Rin ............ 141 E3
Waterside Cl. Rin ............ 117 D1
Waterside Gdns. Fare ............ 131 E1
Waterside La. Portc ............ 156 C3
Waterside Rd. Rom ............ 28 A1
Waterside Sq. Hyt ............ 125 F3
Waterside. Christ ............ 209 F2
Waterside. Hyt ............ 126 A3
Waterworks Rd. Cos ............ 158 B4
Waterworks Rd. Ott ............ 31 E2
Waterworks Rd. Pet ............ 41 D3
Watery La. Christ ............ 210 A4
Watery La. Upt ............ 203 D4
Watkin Rd. Bour ............ 207 F2
Watkin Rd. He En ............ 81 E1
Watley La. Twyf ............ 32 A3
Watson Wlk. Tot ............ 100 B4
Watton Cl. Bour ............ 192 A1
Watton La. Meons ............ 61 F1
Watton Rd. Holb ............ 150 B2
Watts Rd. He En ............ 105 E4
Watts Rd. Ports ............ 182 B4
Wavell Ave. Broa ............ 188 A1
Wavell Rd. Bour ............ 190 A2
Wavell Rd. Gos ............ 155 E2
Wavell Rd. Southa ............ 104 A4
Wavell Way. Winch ............ 10 B3
Wavendon Ave. B on S ............ 211 F4
Waveney Green. Southa ............ 77 F1
Waveny Cl. L on S ............ 179 F3
Waverley Ave. Net ............ 127 E3
Waverley Cl. Fordi ............ 69 F2
Waverley Cl. Rom ............ 28 A1
Waverley Cres. Poole ............ 204 B3
Waverley Rd. Net ............ 127 E3
Waverley Rd. Ports ............ 182 C1
Waverley Path. Gos ............ 180 C2
Waverley Rd. Bour ............ 207 D2
Waverley Rd. Cos ............ 158 B4
Waverley Rd. Fordi ............ 69 F2
Waverley Rd. New M ............ 196 A1
Waverley Rd. Ports ............ 182 C1
Waverley Rd. Southa ............ 102 B3
Wayfarer Cl. Le He ............ 128 C1
Wayfarer Cl. Ports ............ 183 E3
Wayground Rd. Broa ............ 162 C1
Wayman Rd. Broa ............ 187 F3
Wayne Rd. Poole ............ 205 D3
Waynflete Cl. Bi Wa ............ 83 E4
Waynflete Cl. Winch ............ 10 B3
Wayside Cl. M on S ............ 213 E3
Wayside Rd. Bour ............ 208 C2
Wayside Rd. St Le ............ 166 C4
Wayte St. Cos ............ 157 F4
Weald Cl. Lo He ............ 129 D2
Weardale Rd. Ch Fo ............ 55 E2
Weavers Cl. W Moo ............ 138 C1
Weavers Green. Hav ............ 136 B2
Weavers Pl. Ch Fo ............ 55 D4
Weavills Rd. Bish ............ 57 D1
Web Cl. Eastl ............ 56 A2
Webb Cl. S Hay ............ 185 D1
Webb La. S Hay ............ 185 D1
Webb Rd. Portc ............ 156 B3
Webb's Way. Bour ............ 189 F1
Webbs Cl. St Le ............ 139 E3
Webbs Way. St Le ............ 139 F3

Webburn Gdns. W End ............ 80 A2
Webster Rd. Bour ............ 191 D2
Webster Rd. Winch ............ 1 A1
Wedgewood Cl. Holb ............ 150 B2
Wedgewood Cl. Stubb ............ 154 B1
Wedgewood Way. Wat ............ 111 F1
Wedgwood Dr. Poole ............ 205 D1
Wedgwood Gdns. Bran ............ 169 E1
Wedmore Cl. Winch ............ 10 A2
Weeke Manor Cl. Winch ............ 1 B1
Weevil La. Gos ............ 181 E3
Welbeck Ave. Southa ............ 79 D1
Welch Rd. Gos ............ 181 D4
Welch Rd. Ports ............ 182 C1
Welch Way. Southa ............ 77 F3
Welchwood Cl. Wat ............ 111 F3
Weldon Ave. Bour ............ 189 F3
Well Cl. New M ............ 195 F1
Well Copse Cl. Horn ............ 88 B1
Well Hill. Hambl ............ 110 B4
Well House Cl. Whits ............ 45 D2
Well House La. Ki Wo ............ 1 C3
Well La. Hamble ............ 128 A1
Well La. Poole ............ 204 B2
Well La. Swan ............ 84 A4
Well Meadow. Hav ............ 135 F3
Welland Gdns. W End ............ 80 A1
Welland Green. Southa ............ 101 F4
Welland Rd. Wi Mi ............ 163 E2
Wellands Rd. Lyn ............ 122 A3
Wellbrook Gdns. Ch Fo ............ 55 D4
Wellers Cl. Tot ............ 100 A4
Welles Rd. Ch Fo ............ 55 E3
Wellesley Ave. Christ ............ 210 B4
Wellesley Cl. Wat ............ 134 C4
Wellesley Ave. Christ ............ 210 B4
Wellington Ave. Southa ............ 104 A4
Wellington Cl. Horn ............ 112 B3
Wellington Cl. New M ............ 196 A2
Wellington Gr. Portc ............ 156 B4
Wellington Pl. Cadn ............ 98 C4
Wellington Rd. Bour ............ 207 D3
Wellington Rd. Poole ............ 205 E2
Wellington Rd. Southa ............ 79 F1
Wellington St. Ports ............ 182 B2
Wellington Way. Wat ............ 134 C4
Wellow Cl. Hav ............ 135 E2
Wellow Cl. Southa ............ 104 B4
Wellow Dro. Plai ............ 50 C4
Wellow Gdns. Lo He ............ 129 E1
Wellow Wood Rd. Plai ............ 50 B4
Wellowbrook Cl. N Bad ............ 55 D3
Wells Pl. Eastl ............ 56 A1
Wellsmoor. Lo He ............ 129 E2
Wellswood Gdns. Ro Ca ............ 113 E2
Wellsworth La. Ro Ca ............ 113 E2
Wembley Gr. Cos ............ 158 A3
Wembley Way. Fa Oa ............ 57 E1
Wendover Cl. B on S ............ 195 F1
Wendover Rd. Hav ............ 135 F1
Wentwood Gdns. New M ............ 196 B1
Wentworth Ave. Bour ............ 208 A2
Wentworth Cl. Bour ............ 208 A2
Wentworth Dr. Broa ............ 188 A3
Wentworth Dr. Horn ............ 112 A4
Wentworth Gdns. Holb ............ 150 B2
Wentworth Gdns. Southa ............ 104 A1
Wentworth Gr. Holb ............ 150 B2
Wescott Way. Bour ............ 189 F2
Wesley Cl. Southa ............ 104 B2
Wesley Gr. Ports ............ 158 A2
Wesley Rd. Ki Wo ............ 2 B4
Wesley Rd. Wi Mi ............ 163 F3
Wessex Ave. New M ............ 196 A1
Wessex Cl. Black ............ 177 F4
Wessex Cl. Christ ............ 210 B4
Wessex Dr. Winch ............ 1 C1
Wessex Estate. Rin ............ 141 D4
Wessex Gdns. Portc ............ 156 A4
Wessex Gdns. Rom ............ 53 D4
Wessex La. Southa ............ 79 E2
Wessex Rd. Horn ............ 88 B2
Wessex Rd. Poole ............ 205 D2
Wessex Rd. Rin ............ 141 D4
Wessex Trade Centre. Poole 205 D4
Wessex Way. Bour ............ 207 E3
West Ave. W Moo ............ 138 C4
West Bargate. Southa ............ 102 C2
West Bay Rd. Southa ............ 102 B3
West Borough. Wi Mi ............ 163 D3
West Butts St. Poole ............ 204 A1
West Cl. Lym ............ 198 A1
West Cl. Ver ............ 114 B3
West Cliff Gdns. Bour ............ 206 C1
West Cliff Mews. Bour ............ 206 C1
West Cliff Rd. Bour ............ 206 B1
West Common. Black ............ 177 F4
West Ct. Ports ............ 182 C4
West Downs Cl. Fare ............ 131 D2
West Dr. Bish ............ 56 B2
West End Cl. Winch ............ 10 C4
West End Rd. He En ............ 104 C2
West Haye Rd. S Hay ............ 185 E1
West Hayes. Lym ............ 198 C2
West Hill Dr. Hyt ............ 125 F3
West Hill Dr. Winch ............ 10 C4
West Hill Park. Winch ............ 10 B4
West Hill Pl. Bour ............ 206 B2
West Hill Rd. Bour ............ 206 C1

West Hoe La. Bi Wa ............ 83 F4
West Horton La. Bish ............ 56 C1
West Howe Cl. Bour ............ 190 A2
West La. Hord ............ 197 F1
West La. N Bad ............ 53 F3
West La. N Hay ............ 184 C3
West La. S Hay ............ 184 C3
West Marlands Rd. Southa .. 102 C3
West Moors Rd. Fern ............ 165 E4
West Moors Rd. W Moo ............ 138 B3
West Moors Rd. W Moo ............ 138 C4
West Overcliff Dr. Bour ............ 206 B1
West Park La. Dame ............ 68 B3
West Park Rd. Southa ............ 102 C3
West Quay Rd. Poole ............ 204 A1
West Quay Rd. Southa ............ 102 C2
West Rd. Bour ............ 208 A2
West Rd. Bran ............ 194 A4
West Rd. Ems ............ 160 C4
West Rd. He En ............ 104 C3
West Rd. Hyt ............ 125 E1
West Rd. M on S ............ 213 D3
West Rd. Southa ............ 103 D1
West Rd. Southa ............ 103 F1
West Row. Wi Mi ............ 163 D2
West St. Ems ............ 160 C4
West St. Fare ............ 131 D1
West St. Fordi ............ 69 F1
West St. Hambl ............ 86 B1
West St. Hav ............ 135 F1
West St. Hyt ............ 125 F3
West St. Lo He ............ 153 F4
West St. Poole ............ 204 A1
West St. Portc ............ 156 B4
West St. Ports ............ 181 F2
West St. Rin ............ 140 C4
West St. Sob ............ 85 E3
West St. Southa ............ 102 C2
West St. Southw ............ 132 C3
West St. Wi Mi ............ 163 D3
West Station Terr. Bour ............ 206 B2
West View Rd. Christ ............ 209 F3
West View Rd. Poole ............ 204 B2
West Way Cl. Bour ............ 191 D1
West Way. Bour ............ 191 D1
West Way. Broa ............ 188 A2
West Way. Lo He ............ 129 F2
West Way. Lym ............ 198 B1
Westbeams Rd. Sway ............ 172 A1
Westborn Rd. Fare ............ 131 D1
Westbourne Ave. Ems ............ 137 D1
Westbourne Ave. Holb ............ 150 B2
Westbourne Cl. Bour ............ 206 B2
Westbourne Cl. Ems ............ 137 D1
Westbourne Cres. Southa ............ 79 D1
Westbourne Park Rd. Bour .. 206 A1
Westbourne Rd. Ems ............ 137 A2
Westbourne Rd. Ports ............ 182 C4
Westbourne Rd. Westb ............ 137 D2
Westbroke Gdns. Rom ............ 27 F1
Westbrook Cl. Lo He ............ 129 D3
Westbrook Gr. Wat ............ 134 B2
Westbrook Rd. Portc ............ 156 B3
Westbrook Way. Southa ............ 79 E2
Westbrooke Cl. Wat ............ 112 A3
Westbury Cl. B on S ............ 212 A4
Westbury Cl. Bran ............ 194 A4
Westbury Cl. Christ ............ 194 B1
Westbury Ct. Cos ............ 133 D1
Westbury Ct. He En ............ 105 E3
Westbury Rd. Fare ............ 131 D1
Westbury Rd. Rin ............ 141 D4
Westbury Rd. Southa ............ 101 F4
Westby Rd. Bour ............ 207 F2
Westcliff Cl. L on S ............ 179 F4
Westcliff Wlk. Hyt ............ 125 F3
Westcot Rd. Holb ............ 150 A2
Westcroft Par. New M ............ 196 A1
Westcroft Park. Broa ............ 188 B2
Westcroft Rd. Gos ............ 180 C3
Westdown Rd. Bour ............ 190 D3
Westend Rd. Southa ............ 104 A4
Westerham Cl. Cos ............ 157 F4
Westerham Rd. Bour ............ 206 A2
Westering. Rom ............ 53 E4
Westerley Cl. Lo He ............ 128 C1
Western Ave. B on S ............ 211 E4
Western Ave. Bour ............ 190 B2
Western Ave. Ems ............ 160 B4
Western Ave. Poole ............ 205 F1
Western Ave. Southa ............ 102 A3
Western Cl. Bour ............ 190 B3
Western District Cut. Southa . 102 B4
Western Espl. Southa ............ 102 C2
Western Par. Ems ............ 160 C4
Western Par. Ports ............ 182 A1
Western Rd. Ch Fo ............ 30 C1
Western Rd. Cos ............ 157 E4
Western Rd. Fare ............ 131 D1
Western Rd. Hav ............ 135 F1
Western Rd. Liss ............ 20 C2
Western Rd. Lym ............ 198 B2
Western Rd. Poole ............ 206 A1
Western Rd. Poole ............ 216 C4
Western Rd. W End ............ 80 C1
Western Rd. Winch ............ 10 C4
Western Terr. Ports ............ 157 E1
Western Way. Fare ............ 131 D1
Western Way. Gos ............ 180 C1

Westfield Ave. Fare ............ 154 C4
Westfield Ave. S Hay ............ 184 C2
Westfield Cl. Fa Oa ............ 81 E4
Westfield Cl. Hamble ............ 127 F1
Westfield Cl. Wi Mi ............ 163 D3
Westfield Cnr. Southa ............ 79 F2
Westfield Comm. Hamble .... 127 F1
Westfield Cres. Ch Fo ............ 55 E2
Westfield Dro. Beau ............ 34 C4
Westfield Gdns. Christ ............ 194 A1
Westfield Rd. Bour ............ 208 C2
Westfield Rd. Ch Fo ............ 55 E2
Westfield Rd. Gos ............ 181 D2
Westfield Rd. Lym ............ 199 D1
Westfield Rd. Ports ............ 183 D2
Westfield Rd. Southa ............ 102 A4
Westfield Rd. Tot ............ 100 C4
Westgate Park. Bour ............ 206 A2
Westgate St. Southa ............ 102 C2
Westgate. Stubb ............ 154 B1
Westham Cl. Broa ............ 188 C2
Westheath Rd. Broa ............ 188 A2
Westland Dr. Wat ............ 134 C2
Westland Gdns. Gos ............ 181 D2
Westlands Ct. Bran ............ 194 A4
Westlands Gr. Portc ............ 156 B4
Westley Cl. Winch ............ 1 B1
Westley Gr. Fare ............ 154 C4
Westmead Cl. S Hay ............ 184 C2
Westminster Gate. Winch ............ 10 A3
Westminster Gdns. Lo He .... 129 E2
Westminster Pl. Ports ............ 182 B4
Westminster Rd E. Poole .... 206 A1
Westminster Rd. M on S .... 213 D2
Westminster Rd. Poole ............ 206 A1
Westmorland Way. Ch Fo ............ 55 F3
Weston Ave. Ports ............ 183 D2
Weston Cl. Southa ............ 103 F1
Weston Cres. Southa ............ 104 B4
Weston Dr. Bour ............ 207 D2
Weston Grove Rd. Southa ............ 103 E1
Weston La. Buri ............ 65 E4
Weston La. Nur ............ 77 D2
Weston La. Southa ............ 103 F1
Weston Par. Southa ............ 126 C4
Weston Rd. Eastl ............ 56 A4
Weston Rd. Pet ............ 41 D2
Weston Rd. Wi Mi ............ 163 F4
Westons La. Poole ............ 204 B1
Westover La. St Le ............ 140 B3
Westover Rd. Bour ............ 206 C2
Westover Rd. M on S ............ 213 D2
Westover Rd. Ports ............ 183 D4
Westover Rd. Southa ............ 101 D4
Westridge Rd. Southa ............ 103 D4
Westrow Gdns. Southa ............ 102 C4
Westrow Rd. Southa ............ 102 C4
Westside View. Wat ............ 111 E1
Westview Rd. Spar ............ 1 A1
Westward Rd. He En ............ 105 E4
Westway. Cos ............ 158 C4
Westways. Stubb ............ 154 B1
Westwood Ave. Fern ............ 165 E3
Westwood Cl. Ems ............ 137 D1
Westwood Ct. Tot ............ 76 B1
Westwood Gdns. Ch Fo ............ 55 F4
Westwood Rd. Lyn ............ 121 F3
Westwood Rd. Net ............ 127 D4
Westwood Rd. Ports ............ 157 F2
Westwood Rd. Southa ............ 103 D4
Westwood View. Kilm ............ 14 C1
Wetherby Cl. Broa ............ 188 A1
Wetherby Cl. Tot ............ 100 B4
Wetherby Gdns. Tot ............ 100 B4
Weyhill Cl. Hav ............ 135 E3
Weyhill Cl. Portc ............ 132 B1
Weyman's Ave. Bour ............ 190 B3
Weymans Dr. Bour ............ 190 B3
Weymouth Ave. Gos ............ 180 C4
Weymouth Rd. Poole ............ 205 E3
Weymouth Rd. Ports ............ 157 E1
Whaddon Chase. Stubb ............ 154 A1
Whaddon Ct. Hav ............ 135 D3
Whaddon La. Co Com ............ 58 A4
Whaddon La. Ows ............ 33 D2
Whale Island Way. Ports ............ 157 E1
Whalesmead Cl. Bish ............ 56 C1
Whalesmead Rd. Bish ............ 56 C1
Wharf Cl. Poole ............ 205 F3
Wharf Hill. Winch ............ 11 D3
Wharf Rd. Ports ............ 182 B4
Wharf Rd. Southa ............ 103 E2
Wharfdale Rd. Bour ............ 206 B2
Wharfdale Rd. Poole ............ 205 F3
Wharncliffe Gdns. Christ ............ 211 D4
Wharncliffe Rd. Bour ............ 207 D2
Wharncliffe Rd. Christ ............ 211 D4
Wharncliffe Rd. Southa ............ 103 D2
Whartons Cl. Ashu ............ 100 B3
Whartons La. Ashu ............ 100 B2
Whatleigh Cl. Poole ............ 204 B1
Wheatcroft Dr. Southa ............ 80 A1
Wheatcroft Rd. L on S ............ 179 F3
Wheatear Dr. Pet ............ 41 E1
Wheatears Dr. W Wel ............ 50 C2
Wheatland Cl. Winch ............ 10 B3
Wheatlands Ave. S Hay ............ 185 F1
Wheatlands Cl. S Hay ............ 185 F1
Wheatlands. Lo He ............ 129 E2

Wheatley Green. Hav ............ 135 E2
Wheaton Rd. Bour ............ 208 A3
Wheatsheaf Ct. He En ............ 105 D3
Wheatsheaf Dr. Wat ............ 111 E2
Wheatstone Rd. Ports ............ 182 C2
Wheeler Cl. Gos ............ 181 D3
Wheelers La. Bour ............ 189 E3
Wheelers Wlk. Black ............ 177 F4
Whernside Cl. Southa ............ 101 F4
Whichers Gate Cl. Hav ............ 136 A4
Whichers Gate Cl. Ro Ca .... 136 A4
Whichers Gate Rd. Ro Ca .... 136 A4
Whitemoor La. Rom ............ 75 F2
Whimbrel Cl. Ports ............ 183 E3
Whinchat Cl. Fare ............ 130 B2
Whinchat Cl. Southa ............ 78 A3
Whincroft Cl. Fern ............ 165 F4
Whincroft Dr. Fern ............ 165 F4
Whinfield Rd. Hyt ............ 149 F4
Whinwhistle Rd. W Wel ............ 51 D1
Whippingham Cl. Cos ............ 157 E4
Whistler Cl. Southa ............ 104 B2
Whistler Rd. Southa ............ 104 B2
Whitaker Cres. Lym ............ 198 C2
Whitby Ave. Broa ............ 188 A1
Whitby Cl. Christ ............ 192 B2
Whitby Cres. Broa ............ 188 A1
Whitby Rd. M on S ............ 213 D2
Whitchurch Ave. Broa ............ 188 B2
Whitcombe Cl. Tot ............ 100 C4
Whitcombe Gdns. Ports ............ 182 C3
White Barn Cres. Hord ............ 197 D2
White Beam Rise. Clanf ............ 88 B3
White Cl. Poole ............ 205 D4
White Cloud Park. Ports ............ 182 C2
White Cloud Pl. Ports ............ 182 C2
White Dirt La. Horn ............ 88 B2
White Farm Cl. Bour ............ 206 B4
White Gates. Durl ............ 82 A3
White Hart La. Cadn ............ 98 C4
White Hart La. Portc ............ 156 B4
White Hart Rd. Fa Oa ............ 57 E1
White Hart Rd. Gos ............ 181 D2
White Hart Rd. Ports ............ 182 A2
White Heather Ct. Hyt ............ 126 A3
White Horse Dr. Poole ............ 204 B3
White Horse La. Den ............ 111 D3
White Horses. B on S ............ 211 F4
White House Gdns. Pet ............ 40 C3
White House Gdns. Southa .. 102 A3
White Knights. B on S ............ 211 F4
White Ladies Cl. Hav ............ 136 A1
White Lion Wlk. Gos ............ 181 E3
White Lodge Gdns. Fare ............ 130 C2
White Rd. Bish ............ 56 B2
White Swan Rd. Ports ............ 182 A3
White Way. Meons ............ 61 D4
White's Rd. Southa ............ 104 A3
Whitebeam Cl. Fare ............ 154 C4
Whitebeam Cl. Wat ............ 112 B3
Whitebeam Rd. He En ............ 105 E3
Whitebeam Way. N Bad ............ 54 A3
Whitebeam Way. Ver ............ 115 D3
Whitechimney Row. Westb .... 137 D2
Whitecliff Cres. Poole ............ 205 D1
Whitecliff Rd. Poole ............ 204 C1
Whitecliffe Ave. Ports ............ 183 D4
Whitecross Cl. Broa ............ 188 C2
Whitecross Gdns. Ports ............ 157 F2
Whitefield Rd. Holb ............ 150 B3
Whitefield Rd. New M ............ 196 A1
Whitefield Rd. Poole ............ 205 D1
Whitehall. Christ ............ 209 D3
Whitehaven. Horn ............ 112 B3
Whitehayes Cl. Burt ............ 193 E1
Whitehayes Rd. Burt ............ 193 E1
Whitehorn Dr. Red ............ 73 E4
Whitehorn Rd. S Hay ............ 185 D2
Whitehouse Rd. Oakl ............ 163 E1
Whitelands. Bran ............ 169 E2
Whitelaw Rd. Southa ............ 102 A4
Whiteleaf La. Meons ............ 86 B4
Whitelegg Way. Bour ............ 190 C3
Whiteley La. Lo He ............ 129 F3
Whiteley La. Swanw ............ 106 B1
Whiteley Way. Lo He ............ 129 E3
Whitemoor Rd. Brock ............ 145 E1
Whitenap Cl. Rom ............ 53 D3
Whitenap La. Rom ............ 53 E3
Whiteoak Wlk. Hav ............ 136 A3
Whites Hill. Ows ............ 33 D2
Whites La. Faw ............ 151 D2
Whiteshoot Hill. Red ............ 47 F3
Whiteshoot Rd. Red ............ 47 F2
Whiteshute La. Winch ............ 10 C3
Whitestone Cl. Southa ............ 101 F4
Whitewater Rise. Hyt ............ 125 F1
Whiteways. Wi Mi ............ 163 F3
Whitfield Park. St Le ............ 140 B3
Whitle Cl. Westb ............ 137 D3
Whitley Way. New M ............ 196 A3
Whitsbury Cl. Bour ............ 191 E1
Whitsbury Rd. Fordi ............ 69 F2
Whitsbury Rd. Has ............ 136 A3
Whitstable Rd. Cos ............ 157 F4
Whittington Cl. Hyt ............ 125 F2
Whittle Ave. Lo He ............ 129 E3
Whittle Rd. Fern ............ 164 C4
Whittles Way. Poole ............ 204 A1

## Whitwell Rd. Ports

Whitwell Rd. Ports .............. 182 C1
Whitwell. Net ...................... 127 E4
Whitworth Cl. Gos ............... 181 D2
Whitworth Cres. Southa ...... 103 E4
Whitworth Rd. Gos .............. 181 D3
Whitworth Rd. Ports ........... 182 C4
Whitworth Rd. Southa ......... 103 E4
Whyte Cl. Holb ................... 150 A2
Whyteways. Eastl ............... 56 A2
Wick Cl. New M .................. 195 F1
Wick Dr. New M .................. 195 F1
Wick Farm. Bour ................ 209 D3
Wick La. Bour ..................... 209 D3
Wick La. Christ ................... 209 D3
Wick La. Down ..................... 46 A4
Wicket Rd. Bour .................. 190 B3
Wicket The. Hyt .................. 125 F1
Wickfield Ave. Christ ........... 209 D3
Wickfield Cl. Christ ............. 209 D3
Wickham Dr. Broa ............... 187 E2
Wickham Rd. Bour ............... 208 A3
Wickham Rd. Drox ................. 85 D3
Wickham Rd. Fare ............... 131 D3
Wickham St. Ports ............... 182 A3
Wicklea Rd. Bour ................ 209 D2
Wicklow Dr. N Bad ................ 55 D3
Wickmeads Rd. Bour ........... 209 D3
Wickor Cl. Ems ................... 137 D1
Wickor Way. Ems ................ 137 D1
Wicor Mill La. Portc ............ 156 A4
Widbury Rd. Lym ................ 198 B1
Widden Cl. Sway ................. 172 A1
Widdicombe Ave. Poole ...... 205 F1
Wide La. Southa .................... 79 F3
Wide Lane Cl. Brock ........... 145 F1
Widecombe Dr. Hyt ............. 125 F2
Widgeon Cl. Gos ................. 181 D4
Widgeon Cl. Southa .............. 78 A3
Widgeon Ct. Portc ............... 155 F4
Widlers La. Uph ..................... 58 C3
Widley Court Dr. Cos .......... 158 A4
Widley Ct. Fare .................... 155 D3
Widley Gdns. Wat ............... 134 B2
Widley Rd. Cos ................... 158 A4
Widley Rd. Ports ................. 157 E1
Widley Wlk. Southa ............. 133 F2
Widworthy Dr. Broa ............ 187 F3
Wield Cl. Hav ...................... 135 E2
Wigan Cres. Hav ................. 135 D1
Wight Wlk. Fern .................. 165 F1
Wilberforce Cl. Winch ........... 10 B3
Wilberforce Rd. Gos ........... 181 E1
Wilberforce Rd. Ports ......... 182 B2
Wilby La. Ports ................... 158 B2
Wild Ridings. Fare .............. 154 B4
Wild Rose Cres. Lo He ........ 128 C1
Wildburn Cl. Tot .................... 76 B1
Wilde Cl. Tot ...................... 100 B4
Wildern Cl. Lo He ............... 128 C2
Wildern La. He En ............... 105 E4
Wilderness Hts. W End .......... 80 B1
Wilderton Rd W. Poole ........ 206 A2
Wilderton Rd. Poole ........... 205 F2
Wildfell Cl. Christ ............... 193 D1
Wildmoor Wlk. Hav ............. 136 A3
Wildown Gdns. Bour ........... 209 D2
Wildown Rd. Bour ............... 209 D2
Wilfred Rd. Bour ................. 207 F2
Wilkins Cl. Clanf ................... 88 A3
Wilkins Way. Poole ............. 204 A1
Wilkinson Dr. Bour .............. 192 A1
Willersley Cl. Cos ............... 133 E1
Willett Cl. Broa .................. 162 C1
Willett Rd. Oakl .................. 163 E1
William Cl. Christ ................ 195 D1
William Cl. Stubb ................ 154 B1
William Rd. Bour ................. 207 F4
William Rd. Lym .................. 198 C3
William St. Southa .............. 103 E3
Williams Cl. Gos ................. 180 B4
Williams Cl. Holb ................ 150 B2
Williams Rd. Ports .............. 158 A2
Willis Ave. N Bad .................. 54 A2
Willis Rd. Gos .................... 181 E2
Willis Rd. Ports ................... 182 B3
Willis Rd. Southa .................. 79 E3
Willis Way. Poole ............... 204 A3
Willis Waye. Ki Wo ................ 2 B3
Willow Ave. Fordi .................. 69 F1
Willow Cl. Hav .................... 136 A1
Willow Cl. He En ................. 105 E3
Willow Cl. St Le .................. 139 E2
Willow Cl. Uph .................... 203 E3
Willow Cl. W End ................... 80 C2
Willow Cl. Southa .................. 78 A2
Willow Dr. Christ ................. 209 D3
Willow Dr. March ................ 124 C4
Willow Dr. Rin .................... 141 D3
Willow Dr. Wi Mi ................. 164 B3
Willow Gdns. N Bad .............. 53 F3
Willow Gdns. Westb ............ 137 D2
Willow Gr. Fa Oa ................... 57 E1
Willow Herb Cl. Lo He ......... 128 C1
Willow La. Bran .................. 169 E2
Willow Mead. Bour .............. 191 E2
Willow Park. Poole .............. 205 D2
Willow Pl. Christ ................. 209 E3
Willow Rd. Gos ................... 181 D3
Willow Rd. Bi Wa .................. 83 F4

Willow Rd. Liss ..................... 21 D2
Willow Tree Ave. Wat .......... 112 A1
Willow Tree Gdns. Fare ....... 154 C4
Willow Tree Rise. Bour ........ 190 A2
Willow Tree Wlk. Southa ..... 104 A2
Willow Way. Christ .............. 209 D3
Willow Way. Fern ................ 165 E4
Willowdale Cl. Pet ................. 40 A2
Willowdene Cl. Hav ............. 135 D2
Willowdene Cl. New M ........ 196 B2
Willows The. B on S ............ 212 A4
Willows The. Den ................ 110 C2
Wills Cl. Broa .................... 187 E2
Wills Rd. Poole ................... 205 F2
Wills Way. Rom .................... 53 D3
Willwood Cl. Broa ............... 188 C2
Wilmer Rd. Eastl ................... 56 A1
Wilmington Cl. Southa .......... 79 F2
Wilmot Cl. Bish .................... 56 C3
Wilmott Cl. Gos .................. 180 C3
Wilmott La. Gos .................. 180 C3
Wilmur Cres. Poole ............. 204 C3
Wilson Gr. Ports ................. 182 C2
Wilson Rd. Bour ................. 207 F3
Wilson Rd. Poole ................ 205 E2
Wilson Rd. Ports ................ 157 E1
Wilson St. Southa ............... 103 E3
Wilton Ave. Southa ............. 102 C3
Wilton Cl. Christ ................. 192 B1
Wilton Cl. Gos .................... 180 C2
Wilton Cres. Southa .............. 78 B1
Wilton Dr. Wat .................... 112 A3
Wilton Gdns. New M ........... 195 F2
Wilton Gdns. Southa ............. 78 B1
Wilton Pl. Ports .................. 182 B1
Wilton Rd. Bour .................. 207 F3
Wilton Rd. Southa ................. 78 B1
Wilton Terr. Ports ............... 182 B1
Wiltshire Gdns. Bran ........... 193 F4
Wiltshire Rd. Bran .............. 193 F4
Wiltshire Rd. Ch Fo .............. 55 E2
Wiltshire St. Ports .............. 182 A2
Wilverley Ave. Bour ............ 191 F1
Wilverley Ave. Hav ............. 136 A2
Wilverley Cl. Lym ............... 198 A1
Wilverley Pl. Black .............. 150 C1
Wilverley Rd. Brock ............ 145 F1
Wilverley Rd. Christ ............ 210 A4
Wimbledon Park Rd. Ports ... 182 B1
Wimborne Rd E. Fern .......... 165 E3
Wimborne Rd W. Fern ......... 164 B3
Wimborne Rd W. Wi Mi ....... 164 B3
Wimborne Rd. Bour ............. 190 B3
Wimborne Rd. Bour ............. 206 C3
Wimborne Rd. Broa ............. 162 C1
Wimborne Rd. Poole ........... 204 B3
Wimborne Rd. Ports ............ 183 D2
Wimborne Rd. Wi Mi ........... 163 D3
Wimborne Rd. Wi Mi ........... 163 F3
Wimpole St. Ports ............... 182 B3
Wimpson Gdns. Southa ......... 77 F1
Wimpson La. Southa ............ 101 F4
Wincanton Way. Wat ........... 112 A1
Winchcombe Rd. Cos ........... 133 D1
Winchester By Pass. Comp .... 10 C1
Winchester By Pass. Twyf ..... 10 C1
Winchester By Pass. Winch ... 11 D2
Winchester Cl. Net ............. 127 D3
Winchester Hill. Rom ............ 53 D4
Winchester Rd. Bi Wa ........... 83 D4
Winchester Rd. Botl .............. 81 F2
Winchester Rd. Ch Fo ............ 55 F4
Winchester Rd. Durl .............. 81 F2
Winchester Rd. Fa Oa ............ 81 F2
Winchester Rd. Langr ............ 39 F2
Winchester Rd. N Bad .......... 53 F2
Winchester Rd. New M ......... 196 B2
Winchester Rd. Ows .............. 58 B2
Winchester Rd. Pet ............... 39 F2
Winchester Rd. Ports .......... 182 C4
Winchester Rd. Rom .............. 28 B1
Winchester Rd. Rom .............. 52 C4
Winchester Rd. Shed ............. 83 F1
Winchester Rd. Southa .......... 78 B1
Winchester Rd. Uph .............. 58 B2
Winchester St. Botl ............. 106 A4
Winchester St. Southa ......... 102 C3
Winchester Way. Tot ........... 100 B4
Winchfield Cl. Southa .......... 104 A1
Winchfield Cres. Hav ........... 135 E2
Wincombe Cl. Fern .............. 165 E2
Windbury Rd. Southa ............ 77 F1
Windermere Ave. Southa ....... 77 F1
Windermere Ave. Stubb ....... 154 B2
Windermere Gdns. Tot ......... 100 C4
Windermere Rd. Bour .......... 207 D4
Windermere Rd. Ports ......... 157 F2
Windermere Rd. W End ......... 80 A1
Windgreen Estate. Broa ....... 187 F4
Windham Mews. Bour .......... 207 E3
Windham Rd. Bour .............. 207 E3
Windhill Field. Den ............. 111 D2
Windmill Cl. Clanf ................ 88 B3
Windmill Cl. M on S ............ 213 E2
Windmill Copse. Hyt ........... 125 F1
Windmill La. Burs ............... 105 D1
Windmill La. St Le .............. 140 B2

Windmill La. St Le .............. 140 B2
Windover Cl. Southa ........... 104 B3
Windrush Gdns. Wat ........... 134 B4
Windrush Rd. Southa .......... 101 F4
Windrush Way. Hyt ............. 126 A2
Windsor Cl. Hord ................ 196 C2
Windsor Cl. St Le ............... 139 F2
Windsor Gate. Eastl ............. 56 A3
Windsor Rd. Bour ............... 207 F2
Windsor Rd. Christ .............. 208 C4
Windsor Rd. Cos ................ 157 F4
Windsor Rd. Gos ................ 181 D2
Windsor Rd. Pet ................... 40 C2
Windsor Rd. Poole .............. 205 D2
Windsor Rd. Portc .............. 156 B3
Windsor Way. Alderh ............ 93 D3
Winfield Way. Ems .............. 136 C2
Winfrith Cres. Poole ........... 205 F4
Winfrith Way. Nur ................. 77 E3
Wingate Dr. Southa ............ 104 A3
Wingate Rd. Gos ................ 155 F1
Wingate Rd. Tot ................. 100 B4
Wingfield Ave. Christ .......... 194 B1
Wingfield Ave. Poole ........... 204 B3
Wingfield St. Ports ............. 182 B4
Wingrove Rd. Ashu ............. 100 B2
Winifred Cl. Fa Oa ................ 57 E2
Winifred Rd. Poole .............. 204 C3
Winifred Rd. Wat ................ 134 C4
Winkfield Row. Wat ............. 112 A3
Winkle St. Southa ............... 103 D1
Winkton Cl. Burt ................. 193 E2
Winkton Cl. Hav ................. 135 E2
Winn Rd. Southa ................... 79 D1
Winnall Cl. Winch ................... 2 B1
Winnall Manor Rd. Winch ...... 11 E4
Winnall Valley Rd. Winch ...... 11 E4
Winnards Close. Fern .......... 165 F1
Winnards Park. Lo He ......... 128 B2
Winnham Dr. Portc .............. 132 A1
Winnington Cl. Fare ............ 130 B2
Winnington. Fare ............... 130 B2
Winscombe Ave. Wat .......... 112 A1
Winsford Ave. Bish ............... 57 D1
Winsford Cl. Bish ................. 57 D1
Winsford Cl. Christ .............. 194 B1
Winslade Rd. Hav ............... 135 E3
Winslade Rd. Winch ................ 1 B2
Winsley Ave. Bour .............. 208 B2
Winsor Cl. S Hay ................ 185 E1
Winsor La. Cadn ................... 99 D4
Winsor La. Ne Ma ................. 99 E4
Winsor Rd. Cadn .................. 75 E1
Winsor Rd. Tot ................... 101 D3
Winsor Rd. Wat ................... 111 E1
Winspit Cl. Hamw ............... 203 F2
Winstanley Rd. Ports .......... 157 E1
Winston Ave. Poole ............. 206 A3
Winston Churchill Ave. Ports 182 B2
Winston Cl. Eastl .................. 56 A2
Winston Cl. S Hay ............... 184 C2
Winston Cl. Poole ............... 206 A3
Winston Rd. Bour ............... 191 D2
Winston Way. Rin ............... 141 D4
Winstone Cres. N Bad .......... 54 A2
Winter Rd. Ports ................ 183 D2
Winterbourne Cl. Poole ....... 204 B3
Winterbourne Rd. Cos ......... 132 C1
Winterbourne Rd. Poole ...... 204 B3
Winterbourne Rd. Rom ......... 28 A1
Winterhayes Cl. Broa .......... 188 C2
Winterhill Rd. Cos .............. 157 E4
Winters Cl. Holb ................. 150 B2
Winters Hill. Bi Wa ............... 82 C4
Winters Hill. Co Com ............ 58 C1
Winters Hill. Durl ................. 82 C4
Winters Rd. Shed ................. 84 A1
Winterslow Dr. Hav ............ 135 F3
Winton Cl. Lym ................... 198 C2
Winton Rd. Pet .................... 40 C2
Winton Rd. Ports ................ 157 F1
Winton St. Southa .............. 103 D3
Winton Way. New M ............ 196 A3
Wisborough Rd. Ports ......... 182 C1
Wish Pl. Ports .................... 182 C2
Wishart Gdns. Bour ............ 191 D3
Wisteria Dr. Ver .................. 115 E2
Witchampton Cl. Hav .......... 136 A3
Witchampton Rd. Broa ........ 187 F1
Witham Cl. N Bad .................. 55 D3
Withedwood Ave. Southa ..... 102 B4
Witherbed La. Lo He ........... 129 F3
Withermoor Rd. Bour .......... 206 C4
Withers La. E Bol ................ 175 E4
Withies Rd. Gos .................. 180 B4
Withingham Rd. Poole ......... 205 F2
Withington Cl. Cos .............. 133 D1
Witley Rd. Horn .................. 111 F3
Witt Rd. Fa Oa ...................... 57 E1
Wittensford La. Cadn ............ 98 B4
Wittering Rd. S Hay ............ 185 F1
Wittering Rd. Southa ............ 78 A2
Witts Hill. Southa .................. 79 F1
Woburn Cl. Eastl .................. 56 A3
Woburn Rd. Southa ............... 78 B3
Wode Cl. Horn ...................... 88 B2
Wodehouse Rd. Southa ....... 103 F3
Woking Rd. Poole ................ 205 E2
Wolfe Cl. Christ .................. 209 E4

Wolfe Cl. Winch .................... 10 B3
Wollaston Rd. Bour ............. 208 C2
Wollaton Cres. Fern ............ 165 E2
Wollaton Rd. Fern ............... 165 E2
Wollstonecraft Rd. Bour ...... 207 F2
Wolseley Rd. Poole ............. 205 E3
Wolseley Rd. Southa ........... 102 B4
Wolsey Way. M on S ........... 213 E3
Wolterton Rd. Poole ........... 206 A3
Wolverley Ct. Southa ............ 78 B2
Wolverton Rd. Bour ............ 207 F3
Wolverton Rd. Hav ............. 135 F3
Wolverton Rd. Southa ......... 103 D3
Wonston Rd. Southa ............. 78 A2
Wood Cl. Southa ................. 104 B2
Wood Glade Cl. March ......... 101 F1
Wood La. Bour .................... 189 F3
Wood La. Bramd ................... 15 F3
Wood La. M on S ................ 213 E2
Wood Lark Gdns. Pet ............ 41 E2
Wood Lawn Cl. B on S ......... 211 F4
Wood Lodge. Tot ................. 76 A1
Wood Rd. Ashu ................... 100 A1
Wood View. Wi Mi .............. 164 A4
Woodacre Gdns. Fern ......... 165 F2
Woodberry La. Ro Ca .......... 136 C4
Woodbourne Cl. Liss ............ 21 D2
Woodbourne La. Fare .......... 130 B1
Woodbury Ave. Bour ........... 191 F1
Woodbury Ave. Hav ............ 159 F4
Woodbury Ave. Pet ............... 40 C3
Woodbury Cl. Christ ............ 192 C2
Woodcock La. Hord ............. 197 D2
Woodcocks Cres. Bour ........ 208 A4
Woodcot Cres. Hav ............. 136 A3
Woodcote Dr. Upt ............... 203 D3
Woodcote La. Stubb ........... 155 D2
Woodcote Rd. Southa ........... 79 E2
Woodcroft La. Wat .............. 111 F3
Woodend Rd. Bour .............. 206 C4
Woodend Rd. Burs .............. 127 F4
Woodend Rd. Rin ............... 141 F3
Wooderson Cl. Fa Oa ............ 57 D2
Woodfield Ave. Cos ............ 134 C1
Woodfield Dr. Winch ............. 10 A3
Woodfield Gdns. Christ ....... 194 B1
Woodfield Rd. Bour ............. 190 D3
Woodford Cl. Rin ................ 141 E4
Woodford Rd. Bour ............. 207 E3
Woodgason La. N Hay .......... 160 B1
Woodgreen Ave. Hav .......... 135 E2
Woodgreen Dr. Bour ........... 189 E2
Woodgreen Rd. Winch ............ 1 B2
Woodgreen Wlk. Tot ............ 76 A1
Woodhall Way. Fare ............ 130 C2
Woodhay Wlk. Hav .............. 136 A3
Woodhayes Ave. Christ ....... 194 C1
Woodhouse La. Bold ........... 174 A1
Woodhouse La. He En ......... 105 F4
Woodhouse La. Ro Ca ......... 113 E2
Woodington Cl. Hav ............ 136 A3
Woodington Rd. W Wel .......... 51 E3
Woodland Ave. Bour ........... 208 A2
Woodland Cl. Southa ........... 104 B4
Woodland Cl. W Wel .............. 51 D1
Woodland Mews. W End ........ 80 B1
Woodland St. Ports ............. 182 C3
Woodland View. Horn .......... 111 F3
Woodland Way. Christ ......... 210 B4
Woodland Way. M on S ........ 213 E2
Woodland Wlk. Fern ............ 165 F4
Woodlands Ave. Ems ........... 136 C2
Woodlands Ave. Hamw ........ 203 F2
Woodlands Cl. Bran ............ 194 A4
Woodlands Cl. Ch Fo ............ 30 B1
Woodlands Cl. Hyt .............. 125 F1
Woodlands Cl. Lo He ........... 128 C3
Woodlands Cres. Hamw ....... 203 F2
Woodlands Ct. Hyt .............. 125 F1
Woodlands Dr. Net .............. 127 E3
Woodlands Drove. Ashu ......... 99 F2
Woodlands Gdns. Rom .......... 28 A1
Woodlands Gr. Wat ............. 134 B3
Woodlands La. Liss ............... 21 D2
Woodlands La. S Hay .......... 184 C3
Woodlands Rd. Ashu ............. 99 F2
Woodlands Rd. B on S ........ 211 F4
Woodlands Rd. Brock ......... 172 C4
Woodlands Rd. Ne Ma .......... 99 F2
Woodlands The. Ki Wo ........... 2 B3
Woodlands Way. Hav ........... 135 F2
Woodlands Way. N Bad .......... 53 F2
Woodlands Way. New M ....... 196 A3
Woodlands Way. Southa ...... 102 C4
Woodlands Way. St Le ......... 139 F2
Woodlands. Fare ................ 131 E1
Woodlane Cl. Bramd ............. 15 E3
Woodlea Cl. Winch ................. 1 C1
Woodlea Gdns. W End ........... 80 C1
Woodlea Way. Ampf ............. 31 F1
Woodleaze Cl. Broa ............. 188 A3
Woodley Cl. Rom .................. 28 B1
Woodley Gdns. Lym ............ 198 B3
Woodley La. Rom .................. 28 A1
Woodley Rd. Gos ................ 181 E2
Woodley Rd. Southa ............ 103 E4
Woodley Way. Rom ............... 28 B1
Woodlinken Cl. Ver ............. 115 D3
Woodlinken Dr. Ver ............ 115 D3

Woodlinken Way. Ver .......... 115 E2
Woodmancote La. Westb ...... 137 F2
Woodmancote Rd. Ports ...... 183 D2
Woodmill La. Southa ............. 79 F1
Woodpath. Ports ................. 182 B2
Woodpecker Cl. Hav ............ 136 A1
Woodpecker Cl. Ver ............ 114 C3
Woodpecker Copse. Lo He ... 129 D2
Woodpecker Dr. Broa .......... 203 F4
Woodpecker Dr. March ........ 101 F1
Woodpecker Dr. Winch ........... 1 B1
Woodpecker Way. Eastl ......... 55 E1
Woodroffe Wlk. Ems ........... 136 C2
Woods View Rd. Bour .......... 206 B4
Woodsedge. Wat ................ 135 D3
Woodside Ave. Eastl ............. 55 F2
Woodside Ave. Lym ............ 198 C1
Woodside Cl. Fern ............... 165 F3
Woodside Cl. Lym ............... 198 C1
Woodside Cl. March ............ 101 F1
Woodside Cres. Chilw ........... 54 C1
Woodside Gdns. Ashu .......... 100 B2
Woodside Rd. Bour ............. 208 A2
Woodside Rd. Eastl ............... 55 F2
Woodside Rd. Fern .............. 165 F3
Woodside Rd. N Bad ............. 53 F2
Woodside Rd. Poole ............ 205 D2
Woodside Rd. Southa .......... 103 D4
Woodside Rd. W Moo ........... 138 B2
Woodside Way. He En .......... 105 D3
Woodside. Chilw ................... 54 C1
Woodside. Gos ................... 155 D3
Woodstock Ave. Hav ........... 112 A3
Woodstock Cl. Fare ............. 130 C1
Woodstock Cl. He En ........... 105 E3
Woodstock Cl. Poole ........... 205 D1
Woodstock Dr. Southa ........... 79 D1
Woodstock La. Rin .............. 141 D3
Woodstock Rd. Burt ............ 193 E1
Woodstock Rd. Gos ............. 181 E2
Woodstock Rd. Hav ............. 135 E1
Woodstock Rd. Poole ........... 205 D1
Woodthorpe Gdns. Lo He .... 129 D2
Woodvale Gdns. New M ....... 196 B2
Woodvale. Fare .................. 130 B1
Woodview Cl. Southa ............ 79 D3
Woodville Ave. Fare ............ 151 D2
Woodville Dr. Ports ............ 182 A2
Woodville Rd. Hav .............. 135 D1
Woodward Cl. Gos .............. 180 C2
Woofferton Rd. Cos ............ 133 D1
Wool Rd. Poole .................. 205 D4
Woolfield La. Frox G .............. 18 A2
Woolford Cl. Winch ............... 10 B3
Woolmer La. Rin ................. 117 D1
Woolmer St. Ems ............... 136 C2
Woolner Ave. Cos ............... 158 A4
Woolner Ave. Pet .................. 40 C2
Woolsbridge Rd. St Le ......... 139 F3
Woolslope Cl. W Moo .......... 138 C1
Woolslope Gdns. W Moo ...... 138 C1
Woolslope Rd. W Moo ......... 138 C1
Woolston Rd. Hav ............... 135 E3
Woolston Rd. Net ................ 127 E4
Woolven Cl. Poole .............. 205 D3
Woolwich Cl. Burs .............. 104 C1
Wootton Farm Rd. Brock ..... 170 C1
Wootton Gdns. Bour ........... 207 D2
Wootton Mount. Bour ......... 207 D2
Wootton Rd. Lon S .............. 180 A2
Wootton Rd. New M ............ 196 B4
Wootton Rough. New M ....... 196 A4
Wootton St. Cos ................. 157 F4
Wootton. Net ..................... 127 E4
Worbarrow Gdns. Poole ...... 205 E4
Worcester Pl. Lym .............. 198 C1
Worcester Pl. Southa .......... 104 A1
Wordsworth Ave. Bour ........ 191 F1
Wordsworth Ave. Portc ....... 132 C1
Wordsworth Cl. Bi Wa .......... 83 F4
Wordsworth Cl. Winch .......... 10 B4
Wordsworth Rd. Southa ........ 78 B1
Worgret Rd. Poole .............. 204 B4
Workhouse La. E Meo ........... 38 B1
Worldham Rd. Hav .............. 136 A3
Worrell Dr. Poole ............... 205 E4
Worsley Rd. Ports .............. 182 B2
Worsley St. Ports ............... 183 D1
Worthing Ave. Gos ............. 180 C4
Worthing Rd. Ports ............. 182 B1
Worthington Cres. Poole ..... 205 D2
Worthy La. Winch .................. 1 C1
Worthy Rd. New M .............. 196 A2
Worthy Rd. Winch .................. 2 A1
Wortley Rd. Christ .............. 211 D4
Wraysbury Park Dr. Ems ...... 136 C2
Wren Cl. Christ ................... 210 A3
Wren Cl. Rin ...................... 141 E3
Wren Cl. Winch .................... 10 B3
Wren Cres. Poole ................ 206 A3
Wren Gdns. Alderh ................ 93 D3
Wren Rd. Eastl ..................... 55 F1
Wrenway. Portc .................. 155 F4
Wrexham Gr. Horn ................ 88 A1
Wright's Hill. Southa ........... 104 A1
Wroxham Rd. Poole ............ 205 F3

## Wroxham Rd. Poole

## Wryneck Cl. Southa

Wryneck Cl. Southa ............... 78 A3
Wuthering Heights. Winch ....... 10 C3
Wyatts Cl. Broa .................... 187 E3
Wyatts La. Broa .................... 187 E3
Wyborn Cl. S Hay ................. 185 D1
Wych La. Gos ....................... 155 D2
Wychwood Cl. Bour .............. 206 C2
Wychwood Dr. Black ............ 177 F4
Wychwood Dr. Bour .............. 206 C2
Wychwood Gr. Ch Fo ............. 55 F4
Wycliffe Rd. Bour ................. 206 C4
Wycliffe Rd. Southa ............... 80 A1
Wycote Rd. Gos .................... 155 D2
Wyeford Cl. Hav ................... 136 A3
Wyelands Ave. Fern .............. 164 B3
Wykehams Ave. Ports ........... 157 F1
Wykeham Cl. Net .................. 127 D3
Wykeham Cl. Poole................ 204 C4
Wykeham Cl. Southa ............... 78 C2
Wykeham Field. Wickh .......... 108 A2
Wykeham Pl. Lym ................. 198 C2
Wykeham Pl. Winch ................ 10 B3
Wykeham Rd. Net .................. 127 D3
Wykeham Rd. Ports ............... 157 F1
Wyld Green La. Liss ............... 21 D3
Wylds La. Buri ....................... 65 E4

Wyllie Rd. Ports ................... 157 F2
Wylye Cl. W End .................... 80 A2
Wymering La. Cos ................. 133 F1
Wymering Manor Cl. Cos ...... 157 E4
Wymering Rd. Ports .............. 182 C4
Wyncombe Rd. Bour ............. 208 A3
Wyndcliffe Rd. Ports ............. 182 C2
Wyndham Cl. Christ .............. 195 D1
Wyndham Cl. Wat ................. 112 A2
Wyndham Mews. Ports .......... 182 A2
Wyndham Pl. Southa ............. 102 C3
Wyndham Rd. Christ .............. 195 D1
Wyndham Rd. Poole .............. 205 D2
Wynford Rd. Bour ................. 191 D2
Wynford Rd. Poole ................ 205 E2
Wynne Cl. Broa ..................... 187 F2
Wynter Cl. Bour .................... 207 F4
Wynter Rd. Southa ................ 104 A4
Wynton Way. Fare ................. 130 B2
Wynyards Gap. N Bad ............ 53 F2
Wyre Cl. N Bad ...................... 55 D3
Wyvern Cl. Ch Fo ................... 55 E3
Wyvern Cl. Poole .................. 205 E4

Yaldhurst La. Lym ................ 198 A2
Yapton St. Ports ................... 182 B3

Yarborough Rd. Ports ........... 182 B2
Yardlea Cl. Ro Ca ................. 113 D1
Yardley Cl. Ports .................. 158 B2
Yardley Rd. He En ................ 105 E3
Yarmouth Cl. Poole .............. 206 A3
Yarmouth Gdns. Southa ......... 78 A1
Yarmouth Rd. Poole .............. 205 F3
Yarrell Mead. Lym ................ 198 A2
Yarrells Cl. Upt .................... 203 E3
Yarrells Dr. Upt .................... 203 D4
Yarrells La. Upt .................... 203 E3
Yarrow Cl. Christ .................. 210 A4
Yarrow Rd. Poole .................. 205 D4
Yarrow Way. Lo He ............... 128 C1
Yateley Cl. Hav .................... 135 E3
Yaverland. Net ..................... 127 E3
Yeatminster Rd. Poole .......... 188 C1
Yelverton Ave. Hyt ............... 150 A4
Yelverton Rd. Bour .............. 206 C2
Yeo Ct. Ports ....................... 183 E2
Yeomans Ind Park. Bour ...... 191 F1
Yeomans Rd. Bour ............... 191 F2
Yeomans Way. Bour ............ 191 F1
Yeomans Way. Tot ............... 100 C4
Yeovil Chase. Southa ........... 104 A4
Yeovilton Cl. Hord ............... 197 F1

Yew La. New M .................... 196 B2
Yew Rd. Southa .................... 104 A4
Yew Tree Ave. Wat ............... 112 A1
Yew Tree Cl. Fa Oa ................ 57 E2
Yew Tree Cl. He En .............. 105 D3
Yew Tree Cl. Wi Mi .............. 163 E3
Yew Tree Ct. Fordi ................. 93 F4
Yew Tree Dr. Swanw ............ 129 E4
Yew Tree Gdns. Den ............ 110 C2
Yew Tree Pl. Liss .................. 21 D2
Yew Tree Rd. N Hay ............. 185 D4
Yews The. Horn .................... 112 B4
Yewside. Gos ....................... 155 F1
Yewtree La. Nur .................... 77 D2
Yoells Cr. Wat ...................... 111 F3
Yoells La. Wat ...................... 111 F3
Yokesford Hill. Abb ............... 27 F2
Yonge Cl. Eastl ..................... 56 A2
York Ave. New M ................. 196 A2
York Bldgs. Southa .............. 103 D2
York Cl. Broa ........................ 188 A1
York Cl. Christ ..................... 208 C4
York Cl. Pet ........................... 40 B2
York Cl. Southa .................... 103 E3
York Cl. Tot .......................... 101 D4
York Cres. L on S ................. 180 A2

York Dro. Red ....................... 73 E4
York Dro. Southa .................. 104 A4
York Gdns. Portc .................. 156 C3
York Pl. Bour ....................... 208 A3
York Pl. Ports ....................... 182 A3
York Rd. Bour ...................... 207 D2
York Rd. Broa ....................... 188 A1
York Rd. Eastl ....................... 80 A4
York Rd. Net ........................ 127 D3
York Rd. Southa .................. 102 B4
Yorke St. Ports ..................... 182 B2
Yorke Way. Hamble .............. 127 F2
Yorkwood. Liss ...................... 20 C2
Youngs Rd. Bour .................. 190 D3
Yves Mews. Ports ................. 182 B1

Zamek Cl. Bour .................... 190 D3
Zetland Rd. Cos ................... 158 B4
Zetland Rd. Gos ................... 181 D3
Zeus La. Wat ........................ 134 C2
Zinnia Cl. Bour .................... 190 C1

## Zinnia Cl. Bour

# Ordnance Survey

# STREET ATLASES

**The Ordnance Survey Street Atlases provide unique and definitive mapping of entire counties**

## Street Atlases available

- **Berkshire**
- **Bristol and Avon**
- **Buckinghamshire**
- **Cardiff, Swansea and Glamorgan**
- **Cheshire**
- **Derbyshire**
- **Durham**
- **Edinburgh**
- **East Essex**
- **West Essex**
- **Glasgow**
- **Greater Manchester**
- **North Hampshire**
- **South Hampshire**
- **Hertfordshire**
- **East Kent**
- **West Kent**
- **Lancashire**
- **Merseyside**
- **Nottinghamshire**
- **Oxfordshire**
- **Staffordshire**
- **Surrey**
- **East Sussex**
- **West Sussex**
- **Tyne and Wear**
- **Warwickshire**
- **South Yorkshire**
- **West Yorkshire**

*The Street Atlases are revised and updated on a regular basis and new titles are added to the series. Each title is available in three formats and as from 1996 the atlases are being produced in colour. All the atlases contain Ordnance Survey mapping.*

*The series is available from all good bookshops or by mail order direct from the publisher. However, the order form on the following pages may not reflect the complete range of titles available so it is advisable to check by telephone before placing your order. Payment can be made in the following ways:*

**By phone** *Phone your order through on our special Credit Card Hotline on* **01733 371999** *(Fax: 01733 370585). Speak to our customer service team during office hours (9am to 5pm) or leave a message on the answering machine, quoting your full credit card number plus expiry date and your full name and address.*

**By post** *Simply fill out the order form (you may photocopy it) and send it to:* **Reed Books Direct, 43 Stapledon Road, Orton Southgate, Peterborough PE2 6TD.**

# STREET ATLASES ORDER FORM

## NEW COLOUR EDITIONS

|  | HARDBACK | SPIRAL | POCKET | £ Total |
|---|---|---|---|---|
|  | Quantity @ £10.99 each | Quantity @ £8.99 each | Quantity @ £4.99 each | £ Total |
| **BERKSHIRE** | ☐ 0 540 06170 0 | ☐ 0 540 06172 7 | ☐ 0 540 06173 5 | ➤ |
|  | Quantity @ £10.99 each | Quantity @ £8.99 each | Quantity @ £3.99 each | £ Total |
| **MERSEYSIDE** | ☐ 0 540 06480 7 | ☐ 0 540 06481 5 | ☐ 0 540 06482 3 | ➤ |
|  | Quantity @ £12.99 each | Quantity @ £8.99 each | Quantity @ £4.99 each | £ Total |
| **SURREY** | ☐ 0 540 06435 1 | ☐ 0 540 06436 X | ☐ 0 540 06438 6 | ➤ |
|  | Quantity @ £12.99 each | Quantity @ £9.99 each | Quantity @ £4.99 each | £ Total |
| **DURHAM** | ☐ 0 540 06365 7 | ☐ 0 540 06366 5 | ☐ 0 540 06367 3 | ➤ |
| **GREATER MANCHESTER** | ☐ 0 540 06485 8 | ☐ 0 540 06486 6 | ☐ 0 540 06487 4 | ➤ |
| **HERTFORDSHIRE** | ☐ 0 540 06174 3 | ☐ 0 540 06175 1 | ☐ 0 540 06176 X | ➤ |
| **TYNE AND WEAR** | ☐ 0 540 06370 3 | ☐ 0 540 06371 1 | ☐ 0 540 06372 X | ➤ |
| **SOUTH YORKSHIRE** | ☐ 0 540 06330 4 | ☐ 0 540 06331 2 | ☐ 0 540 06332 0 | ➤ |
| **WEST YORKSHIRE** | ☐ 0 540 06329 0 | ☐ 0 540 06327 4 | ☐ 0 540 06328 2 | ➤ |
|  | Quantity @ £14.99 each | Quantity @ £9.99 each | Quantity @ £4.99 each | £ Total |
| **LANCASHIRE** | ☐ 0 540 06440 8 | ☐ 0 540 06441 6 | ☐ 0 540 06443 2 | ➤ |

## BLACK AND WHITE EDITIONS

|  | HARDBACK | SOFTBACK | POCKET | £ Total |
|---|---|---|---|---|
|  | Quantity @ £12.99 each | Quantity @ £9.99 each | Quantity @ £4.99 each | £ Total |
| **BRISTOL AND AVON** | ☐ 0 540 06140 9 | ☐ 0 540 06141 7 | ☐ 0 540 06142 5 | ➤ |
| **CARDIFF** | ☐ 0 540 06186 7 | ☐ 0 540 06187 5 | ☐ 0 540 06207 3 | ➤ |
| **CHESHIRE** | ☐ 0 540 06143 3 | ☐ 0 540 06144 1 | ☐ 0 540 06145 X | ➤ |
| **DERBYSHIRE** | ☐ 0 540 06137 9 | ☐ 0 540 06138 7 | ☐ 0 540 06139 5 | ➤ |
| **EDINBURGH** | ☐ 0 540 06180 8 | ☐ 0 540 06181 6 | ☐ 0 540 06182 4 | ➤ |
| **GLASGOW** | ☐ 0 540 06183 2 | ☐ 0 540 06184 0 | ☐ 0 540 06185 9 | ➤ |
| **STAFFORDSHIRE** | ☐ 0 540 06134 4 | ☐ 0 540 06135 2 | ☐ 0 540 06136 0 | ➤ |

 # STREET ATLASES ORDER FORM

## BLACK AND WHITE EDITIONS

| | HARDBACK Quantity @ £12.99 each | SOFTBACK Quantity @ £8.99 each | POCKET Quantity @ £4.99 each | £ Total |
|---|---|---|---|---|
| **EAST ESSEX** | 0 540 05848 3 | 0 540 05866 1 | 0 540 05850 5 | ➤ |
| **WEST ESSEX** | 0 540 05849 1 | 0 540 05867 X | 0 540 05851 3 | ➤ |
| **NORTH HAMPSHIRE** | 0 540 05852 1 | 0 540 05853 X | 0 540 05854 8 | ➤ |
| **EAST KENT** | 0 540 06026 7 | 0 540 06027 5 | 0 540 06028 3 | ➤ |
| **NOTTINGHAMSHIRE** | 0 540 05858 0 | 0 540 05859 9 | 0 540 05860 2 | ➤ |
| **OXFORDSHIRE** | 0 540 05986 2 | 0 540 05987 0 | 0 540 05988 9 | ➤ |
| **EAST SUSSEX** | 0 540 05875 0 | 0 540 05874 2 | 0 540 05873 4 | ➤ |
| | Quantity @ £12.99 each | Quantity @ £9.99 each | Quantity @ £4.99 each | £ Total |
| **BUCKINGHAMSHIRE** | 0 540 05989 7 | 0 540 05990 0 | 0 540 05991 9 | ➤ |
| **SOUTH HAMPSHIRE** | 0 540 05855 6 | 0 540 05856 4 | 0 540 05857 2 | ➤ |
| **WEST KENT** | 0 540 06029 1 | 0 540 06031 3 | 0 540 06030 5 | ➤ |
| **WEST SUSSEX** | 0 540 05876 9 | 0 540 05877 7 | 0 540 05878 5 | ➤ |

## BLACK AND WHITE EDITIONS

| | HARDBACK Quantity @ £10.99 each | SOFTBACK Quantity @ £8.99 each | POCKET Quantity @ £4.99 each | £ Total |
|---|---|---|---|---|
| **WARWICKSHIRE** | 0 540 05642 1 | — | — | ➤ |

Name..........................................................................

Address......................................................................

.................................................................................

.................................................................Postcode

◆ Free postage and packing

◆ All available titles will normally be dispatched within 5 working days of receipt of order but please allow up to 28 days for delivery

☐ Please tick this box if you do not wish your name to be used by other carefully selected organisations that may wish to send you information about other products and services

Registered Office: Michelin House, 81 Fulham Road, London SW3 6RB.
Registered in England number: 1974080

I enclose a cheque / postal order, for a **total** of ☐

made payable to *Reed Book Services*, or please debit my

☐ Access   ☐ American Express   ☐ Visa

account by ☐

Account no ☐☐☐☐ ☐☐☐☐ ☐☐☐☐ ☐☐☐☐
Expiry date ☐☐ ☐☐

Signature.....................................................................

Post to:
Reed Books Direct, 43 Stapledon Road, Orton Southgate, Peterborough PE2 6TD